Praise for
PETER LAWFORD:
The Man Who Kept the Secrets

"The charming, suave and debonair actor who was probably best-known for being married to JFK's sister Pat and keeping the confidences of the President and Marilyn Monroe, managed to keep his biggest secret—*himself*—from the public, until now. Your heart will break as Spada takes you through this courtesan of Camelot's tragic life."

—*Showbiz*

"Lively and gripping ... Spada ... does heavy research and strong fact-packaging."

—*Kirkus Reviews*

"Telling [Lawford's] life story in incredible, disturbing detail, Spada evokes the world of MGM-contract players in 1940s Hollywood; the Camelot of the Kennedy years ... the horror of life after the President's assassination; and twenty years of descent into hell. It not only makes a brutal, fascinating story but offers glimpses into some events that still obsess us."

—*Cosmopolitan*

PETER
LAWFORD

The Man Who Kept the Secrets

JAMES SPADA

BANTAM BOOKS
NEW YORK · TORONTO · LONDON · SYDNEY · AUCKLAND

PETER LAWFORD: THE MAN WHO KEPT THE SECRETS
A Bantam Book

PUBLISHING HISTORY
Bantam hardcover edition published July 1991
Bantam paperback edition/August 1992

Cover photos left to right: photo with Lana Turner © Pictorial Parade;
photo with Frank Sinatra © Leo Borr; photo with Elizabeth Taylor ©
Culver Pictures; photo with Marilyn Monroe © UPI/Bettmann; photo
with John F. Kennedy © Shooting Star; photo at funeral © UPI/Bett-
mann; photo with Ava Gardner © Culver Pictures; photo with the "Rat
Pack" © Don Pack; photo at Sydney's wedding © Brian Quigley.

ISBN 0-553-29714-7

Published simultaneously in the United States and Canada

CONTENTS

PETER
LAWFORD

PROLOGUE

AUGUST 1962

"Say good-bye to the President."
> —Marilyn Monroe to Peter Lawford,
> August 4, 1962

SATURDAY, AUGUST 4, 1962, had been so hot in Los Angeles that by one in the morning the temperature still hovered in the upper seventies. At 1342 North Laurel Avenue, a quiet palm-tree-lined street in West Hollywood, private investigator Fred Otash, sleeping fitfully in the heat, awakened to the insistent jangle of his telephone. A man used to late-night summonings, Otash snapped alert and picked up the receiver. "Fred," the voice on the line said, "this is Peter Lawford. I have a big problem. I need to come and see you."

"What is it, Peter?" Otash asked.

"I can't talk now. I'll be over in a few minutes."

Otash mumbled his assent, got out of bed, and put on his robe. Uneasy, he telephoned an associate and asked him to come over so that someone else would be present when Lawford got there. He put on a pot of coffee and waited for the actor's arrival.

Peter Lawford and Fred Otash had had a long, if sporadic, relationship. As a vice cop in the Los Angeles Police Department, Otash had first met Lawford in the late 1940s when the handsome Englishman was one of MGM's biggest stars. That meeting had been at Otash's insistence—he wanted to give Peter a warning. "I told him to cool it," Otash later recalled. "Every time we busted a bunch of hookers, his name was always in their trick books. Every hooker in LA had him down as a fifty-dollar trick."

Otash had then left the police department and gone into private practice as an investigator. He had become

3

known as the "PI to the stars," handling, among others, Sheilah Graham, Rock Hudson's wife Phyllis Gates, Frank Sinatra, and Marilyn Monroe. One of his regular clients was *Confidential* magazine, a leering, sensationalistic monthly that often got the goods on celebrities.

In 1954, Peter Lawford had married Patricia Kennedy, the daughter of Joseph P. Kennedy, the former American ambassador to Great Britain, and sister of Massachusetts senator John F. Kennedy. This had put Lawford in a vulnerable position. *Confidential* had damaged or destroyed the careers of dozens of stars with exposés of their sexual peccadilloes, drinking, or drug use. The magazine, Peter had learned, knew about his frequent forays to brothels, and he was worried. A scandal could destroy his marriage and career, and might seriously tarnish the fast-rising political star of his brother-in-law, already being touted as a prospect for higher office.

So Peter had gone to see Otash. "Fred," he told him, "I know *Confidential* has got something coming out on me. Now that I'm married to Pat Kennedy, I really can't afford this horseshit."

Otash had helped Lawford out of that scrape and gotten the story killed. In 1959, Lawford had called on the investigator again, this time to lend him electronic eavesdropping equipment so that Lawford could bug his own telephone. Peter hadn't said why he wanted to do this, but Otash knew the Lawfords were having marital problems and he assumed that Peter suspected Pat was cheating on him.

Fred Otash was a man for hire, one with few personal loyalties. Before long he had helped bug the Lawford house again, but not for Peter. This time it was for a variety of parties who had wanted to develop a "derogatory profile" of Jack Kennedy in anticipation of his nomination for president by the Democrats in 1960.

In 1962, Peter Lawford was the brother-in-law of the President and the attorney general of the United States, two men with enemies ranging from their political adversaries to the corrupt Teamsters to mob members whom Attorney General Robert Kennedy had targeted for investigation. All of these factions, according to Otash, were expressing great interest in what the wiretaps in Lawford's home would reveal.

As Otash and other of the Hollywood cognoscenti knew, both Jack and Bobby Kennedy had been sexually involved with Marilyn Monroe, the world's reigning movie sex goddess, and their trysts—sometimes at Lawford's Santa Monica beach house—were of particular interest to Otash's clients. The situation was explosive. A scandal involving the sex lives of these two Catholic family men could topple the Kennedy administration, and there were many who would welcome the fall.

Now, in the early morning hours of August 5, when Otash opened his door to Lawford, he was struck by the fact that the actor was "half crocked or half doped." At the very least, he looked a nervous wreck—"squirming like a worm in a frying pan," as Otash's associate later described him.

"Marilyn's dead" were Lawford's first words. As Otash recalled it: "He told me that Bobby Kennedy had broken off the affair with Marilyn and that she was hysterical and calling the White House and the Justice Department and Hyannis Port, insisting that Bobby get in touch with her. And that the Department of Justice had called Bobby in San Francisco and told him, 'You'd better get your ass down to LA because she's out of control.'"

Lawford told Otash he was terrified that an investigation of Marilyn's death would reveal her affairs with the Kennedy brothers. He had already been to her house to "clean up," and had removed what incriminating evidence he could find. But he was afraid he'd missed things. He wanted Otash to return to the scene and finish the job.

"Me?" Otash responded. "You gotta be fucking nuts! If I went within four miles of that place—I mean, I'm too well-known. I want no part of it."

But Otash did send over his associate—the same man who had installed surveillance wires in Marilyn's house several months earlier. "He knew the place very well," Otash said. "He finished the job that Lawford started, and he found things that Lawford had left behind."

MARILYN MONROE'S death sent shock waves around the world. Editorial-page writers raged against the heartless exploitation by the Hollywood star factories. Millions were saddened by the descriptions they read of the private Marilyn: her crippling lack of self-esteem that stemmed from a loveless childhood and uncertain parentage, her sexual molestation as a child, her frequent affairs as an adult that had brought her little fulfillment. It was reported that she could be charming, giving, and thoughtful one minute, vicious and hurtful the next. She had abused alcohol and drugs to the impairment of her health; her death was a result of that abuse. And she took a great many provocative secrets about equally famous people with her to the grave.

No one could have anticipated that twenty-two years later the same description, in every particular, would apply as well to Peter Lawford.

PART ONE

THE DARK SIDE OF GENTILITY

"Peter was an awful accident."
—Lady Lawford

"Peter wasn't brought up, he was dragged up."
—Peter's cousin Valentine Lawford

ONE

FRIDAY MORNING, September 7, 1923, dawned blustery in London, the first chill of autumn sweeping through after a warm late-summer rainstorm. Inside the gracious row house at 17 Artillery Mansions in Victoria Street, May Aylen, the wife of Ernest Vaughan Aylen, a major in the Royal Army Medical Corps, lay in her oak-paneled third-floor bedroom and waited to become a mother. When she felt the first of a series of sharp labor pains, she summoned Miss Hemming, the squat, earnest Royal Red Cross nurse she had retained to help her with the delivery.

The labor, excruciatingly painful, lasted for hours, complicated by May's slim hips and the fact that this was the nearly forty-year-old woman's first pregnancy. She bore the pain as long as she could, but when Miss Hemming left the room to summon the doctor, May reached under her pillow, pulled out her husband's service revolver, and put the cold steel barrel into her mouth. Just as she was about to press the trigger, Miss Hemming raced back into the room and snatched the gun away from her.

"Such agony!" May later said of the labor, but it was nothing compared to her suffering during the delivery itself, which didn't come until the late afternoon. The baby was large—nine and a half pounds—and in the breech position inside May's womb. For nearly twenty minutes the doctor struggled to pull the infant—a boy—through May's cervix, trying not to injure him, tugging at his feet as carefully as possible. When the child's head was finally freed the doctor saw that the umbilical cord was wrapped around his neck and had almost choked him. The baby was listless, his left arm apparently paralyzed, his color poor. Out of earshot of Mrs. Aylen, the doctor told Miss Hemming, "He'll be dead before midnight."

"I wasn't going to let that baby die," Miss Hemming said years later. While his exhausted mother slept, the nurse labored over him most of the night, massaged his limp arm, rubbed and patted him, splashed him with brandy to get his circulation going. As dawn broke the next morning, the child revived, and he cried lustily as Miss Hemming handed him, bundled in a blue blanket, to his mother.

May Aylen was not overjoyed at the birth of her son. "I can't stand babies!" she said years later. "They run at both ends; they smell of sour milk and urine." For the sixteen years of her marriage, she had refused Major Aylen's pleas that she give him a child.

When May finally did allow herself to conceive early in December 1922, it was not because she longed for the rewards of motherhood; nor was it so that she could make her husband's fondest wish come true. No, this baby had been planned with an altogether less altruistic goal in mind.

Ernest Aylen was not present when his wife gave birth, because he knew the baby was not his child. The boy's father was Aylen's fifty-seven-year-old commanding officer, Lieutenant General Sir Sydney Lawford. As May had hoped, the birth of her baby—she named him Peter—eventually resulted in her marriage to Sir Sydney. At that point, May, an inveterate social climber, realized a lifelong dream, a goal so important to her that she had allowed herself to become pregnant despite the dangers for a woman her age and her abhorrence of children. As Sydney Lawford's wife, she was immediately elevated from merely Mrs. Ernest Aylen to *Lady Lawford*. And she reveled in what she called "this handle" for the rest of her life.

PETER LAWFORD, in a moment of rare public candor, described his mother as "a dreadful snob." May was unquestionably that, and hers was the worst kind of snobbery: it stemmed from delusions of superiority rather than from the real thing. Throughout her long life she invented details of her background, large and small, designed to improve her stature in the eyes of all she met.

May Aylen was to her core a product of the society and the era into which she had been born. George Orwell called England "the most class-ridden country under the sun," and in the Victorian nineteenth century this was more true than it had ever been or would ever be again. By the early 1900s, nearly ninety percent of the capital value bequeathed to heirs in Britain belonged to less than four percent of the population.

The sharp distinctions between the upper and lower classes were vividly apparent on London's streets. Dapper gentlemen in bowler hats and black silk capes brandished gold-and-ivory walking sticks to shoo away maimed beggars; ladies dressed in layers of satin, taffeta, and tulle, resplendent with diamonds and rubies, alighted from carriages and deftly sidestepped homeless mothers surrounded by half-naked children caked with the soot and grime showered on London every day by the belching smokestacks of the Industrial Revolution.

A subtler but only slightly less rigid distinction existed within the privileged classes themselves. Money itself did not bring prestige; that could be won only through the acquisition of a title or a landed estate. As British historian John Stevenson has put it, "gentility [was] an attribute of status rather than income for which some families paid by a constant struggle to preserve appearances." Stevenson quotes a woman brought up at the same time as Lady Lawford: "I remember girls at school judging each other's wealth by the number of maids each had. And sometimes, I suspect, inventing an extra one to impress their friends."

It was into this milieu that Peter Lawford's mother was born on Sunday, November 4, 1883, the forty-sixth year of Queen Victoria's reign. The delivery, as was common practice then and long afterward, took place in her parents' bedroom in the family's eighteen-room country house at 33 Coley Mile, Reading, outside of London. Named May Somerville Bunny, she was the daughter of Frank William Bunny, a lieutenant in the 66th Regiment of Queen Victoria's army (later, a colonel), and the former Caroline Stanley

Todd. Her father's side of the family had a history of military distinction dating back to 1100, when they first migrated from France to England. Their surname was properly pronounced "Bon-nay," and May grew testy in later years whenever it was mispronounced "as if I were one of those Hugh Hefner *Playboy* rabbits!"

Frank Bunny had inherited a sizable estate from his father, the distinguished general Arthur Courtney Bunny, who had served forty-one years in India. It was more than enough to keep his family—which eventually included a son, Brice, and three daughters, Kathleen, Gretta, and May—comfortably well off. They lived in London in a spacious four-story house in a fashionable area, and their country house shared its dozens of acres with a carriage house, stables, and enormous manicured gardens abrim with flowers. Both residences were staffed with several household servants and personal maids, a governess, a butler, a cook, a gardener, and a "knife boy" whose job it was to clean knives, black boots, bring in coal, and chop wood for the fireplaces.

May, the youngest daughter, was a pretty, dark-haired girl with coal-black eyes, and from an early age she exhibited a feisty temperament that frequently got her into trouble. On one occasion when she was four, May went out in search of the family cat. Fourteen hours later she returned to a frantic mother and an angry father. When she was asked where she had been, she exclaimed, "That bloody cat ran away!" She was promptly spanked for swearing, and sent directly to bed.

On its surface, May's childhood seems to have been close to idyllic. She was educated at an exclusive finishing school run by Queen Victoria's daughter Princess Helena. She had her own horses as a girl, expensive ball gowns as a young woman. At eight, she lived in Ceylon with her family, and she remembered it vividly: "What a beautiful cinnamon garden there was! It was at least forty acres of wonderfully scented blossoms among which there were religious statues and a particularly lovely Buddhist temple."

Frank Bunny's wealth made his life comfortable, but it was his family's military accomplishments that put him among the highest echelons of English society. Next to the aristocracy, no one was more accepted into royal circles in the Victorian and Edwardian eras than military heroes. As such, Frank Bunny was in a position to befriend Queen Victoria's son and heir to the throne, Prince Edward, and—when May was eight—to have his three daughters presented at court to Princess Alexandra, Edward's wife. With a single ostrich feather in their hats to signify that they were unmarried (married women wore three feathers), their billowy satin skirts rustling, the Bunny girls curtsied slowly and gracefully, just as their mother had rehearsed them, and paid homage to their future sovereign's wife. Wide-eyed at the opulence around her—the gentlemen of the palace household were in full court dress, the yeomen of the guard in scarlet and gold—the nervous young May could manage only a mumbled pleasantry as she shook Alexandra's hand. Then the princess spoke, and May had several of her illusions shattered: "Never have I heard such an awful voice. It was worse than a peahen!"

Like the prickly voice beneath Alexandra's fluid elegance, the harsher aspects of Victorian attitudes and taboos lay just below the surface of May Bunny's girlhood. In the upper classes of Victorian society, the primary care of children was delegated to governesses, with whom the first meaningful bonding took place. Parental visits to the nursery were confined to bedtime visits for a good-night kiss. On rare occasions, children were "presented" to their parents, dressed and groomed, while their governess made her report on their behavior. Until she was fourteen, May Bunny ate her meals with the maid or her governess.

Youngsters were not to speak unless spoken to; many Victorian fathers refused to converse with their children until they were capable of carrying on an "intelligent" conversation. Winston Churchill—born nine years before May Bunny—recalled a conversation with his father when he was a teenager after which Lord Randolph said to his son, "I have talked to you more in this holiday than my father talked to me in his whole life."

When Caroline and Frank did spend time with the children, it was to teach them athletic skills so as to instill in them strength of character. At the age of five, May was practicing high jumps on her mother's horse when the animal reared up and threw her. Slammed to the ground but not seriously injured, the terrified child began to wail. Caroline slapped her daughter hard across the backside, mocked her tears, and immediately put her back on the horse to try the jump again.

Such methods may have been harsh, but the English saw their end results—perseverance and fearlessness—as admirable traits in a child. And Caroline set herself up as an example. May recalled an afternoon when her mother rode her horse into the stable after a gallop with both her collarbones broken in a fall. When her children rushed to help her off the horse, she shooed them away. "Pshaw," she said as she dismounted, "what are collarbones for if not to break?"

Caroline and Frank reserved their harshest treatment for their son, Brice. He followed his father into a military career, and during one of Britain's skirmishes in India in 1907, was shot in both arms. He remained shell-shocked and hospitalized for eighteen months. Never once did any member of the family visit him. When he died without leaving the hospital, his mother said only, "He gave his life for his country. Is there a better death?"

Then there were the sexual repressions and taboos of Victorian England, which were brought home to the young May Bunny when she was sixteen. Fascinated by the glamorous photographs of actress Lillie Langtry that she had seen in the newspapers and magazines, May begged her mother to take her to see Langtry's latest play, *The Degenerates*.

The sensation of the 1899 season, the piece was about an abandoned society woman. Caroline wanted to see it, but she was wary of bringing May to so adult a drama. The girl pleaded, threw temper tantrums, wheedled and cajoled until she got her way. Caroline was less rigid in these matters than her husband; she reasoned that at sixteen May was probably old enough, and she certainly understood her daughter's desire to see Lillie Langtry. But under no circumstances, Caroline told her daughter, were they to let Father know. Within a fortnight, mother and daughter took a carriage into London for a matinee performance at the Prince of Wales Theatre.

Lillie Langtry, the mistress of Prince Edward, had completely charmed London a decade before when she had been introduced into society. "How can words convey the vitality, the glow, the amazing charm, that made this fascinating woman the center of any group that she entered?" asked Daisy, Countess of Warwick, who would replace Langtry in Edward's affections.

Langtry had as strong an effect on the impressionable young May as she sat in the theater that afternoon. As she rode home with her mother in their carriage May couldn't stop chattering. "I want to be just like Lillie Langtry!" she proclaimed.

"Oh pshaw," replied Caroline. "Forget such absurd notions."

At dinnertime May was still bubbling. Old enough now to eat with her parents, she dressed prettily in an embroidered blue dress with a blue sash, and a blue satin ribbon in her hair. She later said: "As a well-mannered young lady, I waited to be addressed, although I was brimming over with excitement. Finally my father said, 'And you, dear, what did you do today?'"

Forgetting her pact with her mother, May told him, then burst forth with her desire to follow in Lillie Langtry's footsteps. "She is so thrilling and beautiful, Father! Can I please give up some of my lacrosse and tennis and take dramatic lessons?"

There was, May said, a "dead cold silence." Caroline began to sniffle into her handkerchief and asked to be excused from the table. "No!" Frank replied. "I want to talk to you." He then ordered May to go up to her room: "I want you to memorize every Bible verse about Jezebel, young lady, and then come back down at ten P.M. and recite them!"

When Spencer, the butler, brought May's dinner upstairs, he said to her, "Blimey, girl, you really have torn it this time! The colonel is going to bite your head off!" After May finished her ten o'clock Bible recital, her father lectured her about the wickedness of the theater: "All the women on the stage are Jezebels!" he bellowed.

"Oh, Father," May protested. "Do you think that about Mrs. Langtry? She's so beautiful."

"She's the worst of them all," Frank responded, doubly offended that Lillie, the daughter of an elder in the Church of England, had chosen to lead such a sinful life.

In spite of her father's admonitions, May's fascination with the theater never waned. She was a vivacious young girl, verbally clever, who adored the dramatic and clearly possessed an actress's temperament. But it was unthinkable that her father would ever allow her to pursue a stage career. She was crushed, but never was there any question in her mind that she would obey her father.

When May turned eighteen in 1901, the same year Queen Victoria died and Prince Edward ascended to the throne, her parents began to search for a suitable husband for her—in order, they said, "to take her mind off such foolish ideas." But May's unpreparedness for marriage cannot be overstated. A Victorian girl had little chance to acquire the most rudimentary knowledge of sex, much less a healthy attitude toward sexuality. She was separated from boys at school from the age of ten; at no time was there any discussion of sex, or even of intimate hygiene, with an adult. Modesty was valued in a young woman above all else, and it was assiduously preserved, especially in matters of dress: at a ball, a maiden might carry half a dozen layers of clothing around the dance floor.

When she reached "marriageable age"—usually eighteen—the Victorian girl, naive and woefully ignorant, was expected to marry and "fulfill her wifely duties"—which she most often assumed meant cooking and taking care of the house. For May, the realities of sex would come as a terrible shock; after her marriage, she said, she would lie awake at night thinking up excuses "to keep from having to endure that horrible, messy, unsanitary thing that all husbands expect from their wives."

O N E O F T H E potential husbands mentioned to May was Lord Berry, an elderly millionaire confined to a wheelchair. Frank's rationale for this match was that Berry's money would serve his daughter well; his infirmity wouldn't matter because, as May claimed he told her, "you aren't very sexy."

May protested and the notion was dropped, but before long a far more attractive prospect appeared: Henry Ashley Cooper, a handsome thirty-four-year-old captain in Britain's India Army, known to his friends as Harry. The son of the late William Marsh Cooper, who had served as Queen

Victoria's consul to China, Harry was a neighbor and friend of the Bunnys' and was of a class and profession well suited to win Frank and Caroline's approval as a son-in-law.

Harry Cooper, born in China, had been educated in British schools there, and then in the English public school system. He had attended a military academy and been commissioned an officer in Her Royal Highness's army in 1885, at the age of eighteen. Two years later he was appointed to the India Army, and in 1902 made captain. At that point he was granted one-year leave out of India, during which he courted and wed May Bunny.

All the Bunny girls married high-ranking officers of the British army. Cooper was a bachelor who cut a dashing figure in his uniform, and May was attracted to him—not least of all because he flattered her. "He told me I was pretty. Nobody else ever did."

May Bunny at eighteen wasn't exceptionally pretty, but the men who were attracted to her rarely noticed that. Her vibrant inky eyes and raven hair drew attention away from her too-sharp nose, and so did her petite figure. It was her vivacity, though, her intelligence, her wit, her outspokenness and sense of fun that her suitors found most appealing. She loved to dance, and when the party was her own, she was, in the words of a friend, "a gay little bird of a hostess."

Many men found her exciting to be around, and she responded to their attentions with a coy flirtatiousness that fascinated them even further. Harry Cooper was no exception. After a few months of courtship, Cooper asked May to marry him. She wasn't in love with him, but she liked him and thought he was nice looking. She accepted his proposal—mainly because her parents expected it of her.

After a two-month engagement, during which Cooper didn't so much as kiss his fiancée, Harry and May were married, on July 1, 1902, at their families' parish church, St. Peter's in Ealing. They had a fine wedding, May recalled, "with white horses, white ostrich feathers in my hair, and a mile-long train."

The reception was a gay affair at which May drank champagne for the first time, got a little tipsy, and danced merrily for hours with her husband and most of the other

men. Afterward, Cooper brought his bride back to his home
at 13 The Grove in Ealing and asked her what she would
like to do for the rest of the evening. "Go dancing," she
replied. Cooper said he thought she must be tired. "Why
don't you go upstairs and get undressed?"

Trembling, vaguely fearful of what was to come, May
climbed the stairs to Harry's bedroom and got herself ready
for sleep by donning a dainty blue nightdress and nightcap.
Cooper followed a few minutes later, climbed into bed next
to his bride and kissed her. "He kissed me *on the lips!*"
May recalled. "It was the first time for me. Then he started
some other shenanigans!" She jumped out of bed, awash
with tears, and ran downstairs.

For the remainder of the night, the new Mrs. Cooper
sat in an overstuffed wing-backed chair and sobbed; she
didn't stop even after Harry placed a Bible next to her,
opened to a passage about a wife's duty to submit to
her husband. When dawn broke May went home to her
parents.

Later, she blamed them for her horrible wedding night.
"They should have prepared me for what was to happen. . . .
I just assumed God sent [babies] somehow." The Bunnys
tried to explain to their inconsolable daughter that what
Harry wanted was "a natural part of marriage." An aunt
and the family doctor were also called in to help put May's
mind at ease.

Unconvinced, but once again eager to please her parents,
May returned to her husband's home, where Cooper promised
to help her "learn the art of love." She learned it—but, she
professed, she never did like it. "It was so messy. It was the
only part of marriage I couldn't stand." May agreed to "submit" to her husband barely once a month.

Harry Cooper returned to India about six months after
the wedding, having had sexual relations with his wife only
a handful of times—during each of which she had lain stiffly
still "while he mauled me over."

Cooper rejoined his regiment a disturbed and unfulfilled man. He was devastated by his wife's frigidity and
brooded about his own responsibility for it. When further
visits home saw no improvement in May's responsiveness,
he sought sexual satisfaction elsewhere—but this brought
him little except guilt.

Increasingly troubled, Cooper threw himself into the
military career at which he excelled: he made major in August 1903, and by the end of 1904 he was third in command
of the 62nd Punjabis in India. Before long, Cooper started
to receive puzzling reports: his wife had become involved
in amateur theatricals, had been seen dancing and flirting
with other men. She was gaining a reputation, Harry was
told, as a "fast" young lady.

The reports were exaggerated: there was nothing sexual
in May's flirtatiousness. Only twenty-one, she enjoyed the
attentions of men and loved to arouse jealousy in other
young ladies. It was little more than a girlish game, but
Harry Cooper couldn't know that, and the gossip ate away
at him. Brooding night after night alone in his bedroom, he
convinced himself that he was being cuckolded by a woman
who made his most basic human needs seem dirty and
loathsome.

It was all too much for him. On Thursday evening,
January 5, 1905, Harry Cooper stood alone in his office,
cocked the trigger of his revolver, put the barrel to his temple, and fired a bullet through his brain.

TWO DAYS later, May received a telegram in London
from Lieutenant Colonel R. M. Rainey-Robinson, commandant of the 62nd Punjabis, informing her of Harry's suicide.
No reason for his action was mentioned.

May felt less sorrow over her husband's death than
shock and shame at the manner of it. The Victorians loathed
and feared suicide, and many ancient superstitions about it
still lingered in an Edwardian society on the verge of a more
modern age. It had been only a few generations in England
since suicides were routinely buried with a stake through
their hearts under a crossroads, where it was hoped the
traffic would keep their tortured souls from rising and wan-
dering about.

A soldier's suicide brought dishonor to his regiment
and to his family; Cooper's obituaries in both the local Indian newspaper and the London papers omitted the cause
of death. But friends and neighbors of the Coopers and
Bunnys knew the truth, and May felt disgraced. She declined
to travel to Bengal for Harry's funeral, and within a few
days she moved back into her father's house.

Frank Bunny treated his daughter no differently as young widow than he had when she was a child. He continued to dictate her behavior and wouldn't allow her to read in her room after ten o'clock or leave the house unescorted. "I was virtually held captive," May said.

She mourned Harry Cooper for a very short time; soon after his death she once again became involved in amateur theatricals, danced at balls, and flirted with handsome young men. She had liked her first taste of champagne, and every so often she'd drink too much of it. Frank was appalled at his daughter's unwidowlike behavior and tried to keep her in line. But May was now "used to freedom," as she put it, and she bridled at her father's restrictions. The only way for her to be free of his "tyrannical orders," she knew, was to find another husband.

It didn't take long for a prospect to appear: Ernest Vaughan Aylen, a twenty-nine-year-old captain in the Royal Army Medical Corps. May found the trim, pleasant Aylen "good-looking, clever, and quite bright." The attraction was mutual.

Later May would inflate Aylen's stature and describe him as "a fine doctor in Harley Street" who had paid the equivalent of sixty thousand dollars for his exclusive practice. Aylen, however, had gone directly from his hospital internship into the army and never had a Harley Street practice. May would claim that Aylen showered her with gifts—diamonds, horses, ball gowns—but he had no independent means, and such extravagances would not have been possible with his moderate army pay.

The Aylen family was upset when Ernest became engaged to May—especially his father, Sam Aylen. The elder Aylen, a puritan, was disturbed by the fact that May's husband had just committed suicide. That was reason enough, in Aylen's view, to consider May unsuitable as a wife for his son.

There was another reason for the Aylens' opposition. According to Ernest Aylen's niece Katharine Eden, "My mother always used to say that May had some Indian blood in her. I don't know if it was true, but her people had been in India for generations—and she *was* a bit *dusky,* you know? It affected the family's opinion of her, believe me."

Ernest refused to back down. He liked "exciting" women, he said, and he found May fascinating. Ernest's father remained skeptical, but he did attend his son's wedding to May on Thursday, November 1, 1906, at St. Jude's Church in Portsea. The bride was three days shy of her twenty-third birthday.

May later expressed amazement at how well she and Aylen got on in the beginning of their marriage—"except for one thing." May hadn't learned to appreciate sex any more than she had as a virgin bride, and Captain Aylen found himself, like Harry Cooper, a very frustrated husband. At most, his wife would agree to sex once a month; to avoid having to "submit" more often, she would slip down to the kitchen and rub uncooked meat on her nightdress, then tell Aylen that it was "that time of month."

As she had with Cooper, when May did have sexual relations with Aylen, she would "grit my teeth and clench my hands." Finally Aylen bellowed at her, "You're like sleeping with a wet umbrella! All you can say is 'Don't!' and 'Hurry up!' I'd rather be in bed with a dead policeman!"

But Ernest Aylen was a more sanguine man than Harry Cooper, and he was able to live at first with his wife's aversion to sex, ever hopeful that things might improve. "She was the love of his life," Katharine Eden said. "She was an exciting sort of woman."

That, in fact, was what kept the marriage intact. Now that May was a twice-married young matron, she had come into her own as a person. She was a woman Aylen could talk to as he would a man, a woman who challenged him, both intellectually and by temperament, as a man would. Aylen found her stimulating company, especially in an era when most women, even after marriage, were submissive and servile. Sex aside, May was a perfect wife for Ernest Aylen.

She tried to be a good mate in other ways as well. She worked hard to win over his relatives, and had some success. Shortly after the wedding, the couple visited Ernest's parents, staying at a hotel nearby at "great expense," according to Ernest's mother, who wrote to a friend after the visit to tell of her sorrow that some family members had shunned May and Ernest: "Mr. Good, nor Daisy and Kate did not call on them. Of course I did not expect them to, and never should have asked them to."

The elder Mrs. Aylen was pleased, though, that "all our old friends did so, and I thought it very kind of them, and it made things more comfortable for us." May, she found, "makes Ernest a very good wife. . . . She is most economical, makes anything do."

THOSE TALENTS would be put to good use during the dark days of World War I. Ernest Aylen, who had made major the year before, was captured by the Turks after the Siege of Kut in 1915, and languished in a prisoner-of-war camp for over a year, where he read Rudyard Kipling ("the only thing that kept me sane") and kept a diary in which he wrote of his love for May. As a doctor, he cared for his malnourished and sickly compatriots and tried, against all odds, to improve the conditions in which they found themselves.

Major Aylen's service in Kut won him the Distinguished Service Order, Britain's second-highest military honor. When he was released from prison in exchange for Turkish prisoners and sent home on discharge, he looked, according to his niece, like "an absolute skeleton. They had been practically starved to death. He brought a biscuit that they'd given him to eat and you had to soak it in water for an hour before you could even bite into it."

May was aghast at her husband's condition, and she nursed him for over a year until his health and weight were restored. As part of his recuperation, they went to visit his sister Winifred Aylen Good, Katharine Eden's mother. As Mrs. Eden recalled, "My father was a country parson, and Uncle Ernest and Aunt May came to stay with us at the rectory in Northamptonshire. Aunt May could be a bit extravagant. But she always looked *very* smart. I remember she wore Russian boots, which had just come into fashion, and a sort of Russian hat when she went to church. The villagers were absolutely astonished by her—they'd never seen anything like it before."

The neighborhood children were taken with this stylish woman, too. "She was very sweet to us, and great fun," said Mrs. Eden. "We loved her. But she didn't like children. She put up with us because we were just there today and gone tomorrow. Uncle Ernest always begged her to have children with him, but she refused. It was the great sadness of his life."

On November 11, 1918, an armistice was signed between Britain and Germany that formally ended "the war to end all wars." With his country again at peace, Major Aylen was appointed to Britain's India Army, where he would serve as a medical corpsman and specialize in dermatology. He and May left London for New Delhi. On the train en route, while eating dinner with Ernest, May noticed a "dark-skinned hand" reach through the curtains that separated them from the next compartment. She grabbed her fork and stabbed the hand until it was pinned to the wooden sill beneath the curtain. May went to summon an attendant, but by the time they returned, the intruder was gone. Her husband, May admitted, "was not pleased at my action."

Railway journeys back and forth through India became commonplace for the Aylens. Compartments were long and spacious, each with a large attached bathroom and four electric fans that could be turned in any direction. The fans were godsends, May said, because railway travel in India "is not pleasant in summer." The temperature inside the cars sometimes reached 120 degrees; it could be brought down to 100 degrees by training all four fans on a 160-pound block of ice that sat in a huge tin tub in the middle of the compartment.

May's sojourn in India between 1918 and 1920, despite what she called its "hot monotony," provided her with the most gracious life she had enjoyed since girlhood. Along with the other officers of the British raj, Major Aylen and his wife lived as virtual royalty, surrounded by white-turbaned, dark-skinned servants who took care of their every need. May loved the obsequious natives, who bowed and scraped before her, called her "memsahib"—the master's wife—and carried her aloft in a palanquin so she wouldn't strain herself walking in the heat. In India, May Aylen was in her element.

But her marriage was crumbling. As the years passed, May's abhorrence of sex didn't lessen; Aylen told his wife that if call-house girls deserved the finest champagne, she wouldn't get a crust of bread. When May contracted malaria shortly after their arrival in India, the one redeeming aspect of the illness, she later said, was that it offered her an excuse to avoid sex with her husband.

Ernest and May spent more and more time apart, with

May usually out dancing at the weekly servicemen's socials. "To keep the soldiers out of trouble with the local women," May said, "the officers' wives used to put on little sketches and concerts in the barracks every Saturday night."

One afternoon, the Aylens' chauffeur came to May with his resignation. Eager to keep him, May offered him more money, but he refused it—that wasn't why he was leaving. "I am freezing to death every night waiting for your husband," he told her. While May was out, the major would have the chauffeur drive him to a lady's house and would keep him waiting in the cold until three or four o'clock in the morning. (In the northern regions of India, the winters can be as cold as the summers are hot.) May told the man to stay on and raised his salary. She also gave him two wool blankets and—almost every night—a thermos of hot coffee to keep him warm while he waited for Aylen to complete his missions.

Stories of May's nights out filtered back to her husband—stories of her flirtatiousness and her drinking, stories that suggested she was being publicly unfaithful. According to Katharine Eden, May "was always going off with other men. She had lots of—I don't know if they were lovers, but boyfriends."

As before, it is unlikely that May's relationships with other men were anything but platonic, but Ernest Aylen couldn't know that, and May had acquired quite a reputation. One of Aylen's fellow officers later described her as "the joy of the regiment," and Aylen's suspicion that his wife might be cheating on him while she refused him sexual favors threatened to undo him, just as it had Harry Cooper. Life in the Aylen household grew very tense. May drank to calm her nerves; and her strong will and contentious temperament, which Aylen had found attractive at first, turned ugly when she was drunk. Recriminations flew; Aylen called her a "whore"; May screamed back that he was "sleeping with every black nigger in India." Finally, according to May, Aylen tried to kill her by giving her oleander tablets—which can cause insanity or death—as treatment for an illness. Their butler recognized the pills and snatched them away from her.

Always high-strung—she had often thrown temper tantrums during the marriage—May soon collapsed with a nervous breakdown. Her doctor ordered her to Bombay to rest, and it was there that she decided to leave Ernest and return to London. When Aylen came to see her, he discovered her railway tickets and confronted her. Her admission that she was leaving sent him into a rage, and he tried to push her out a second-story window. May fought back furiously. "I kicked him in the you-know-where and fled," she said.

Finally, the Aylens agreed to live apart, and in early 1920 May returned to London to regain her emotional equilibrium. Just before she left India, May met Ernest's new commanding officer, Lieutenant General Sir Sydney Lawford, a knighted World War I hero. Lawford was, at fifty-four, seventeen years May's senior, and married. He was also handsome, mustachioed, and dapper, called "Swanky Syd" by his men. At their initial meeting, both he and May felt a strong attraction.

Sir Sydney's marriage was an unhappy one, and over the next three years he discreetly saw May whenever he was in London. He was a debonair, imposing figure, regal in his much-decorated uniform, beloved by his men for his courage and his compassion for them, respected by royalty and statesmen alike. He was wealthy, with large landholdings throughout England. Most impressive of all to May was his title. Sir Sydney's wife was properly addressed as Lady Lawford, and she was accorded all the respect due the name.

Early in December 1922, Sir Sydney asked his sister Ethel, the Honourable Mrs. Lubbock, to invite May to a weekend at her country estate, where he was also a guest. May and the general spent most of Saturday together, strolling through the garden, bundled up against the windy damp. They sought warmth in a small chapel on the edge of the grounds and remained there talking for two hours.

As the sun began to set, they joined the other guests for conversation and a cocktail before dinner. Mrs. Lubbock's supper was a long, leisurely affair with five sumptuous courses accompanied by both red and white wines. There was a dessert wine, followed by an after-dinner drink and more conversation.

By eleven, May was feeling quite tipsy and excused herself for the evening. Sir Sydney did the same, engaging her in conversation once again as they ascended the huge winding staircase to the bedrooms. When May reached the door to her room, she realized that the general hadn't continued down the hall but was standing right behind her. She opened her door and without a word let Lawford follow her inside. "My lips trembled and my fingers turned to ice," May remembered. But she allowed Sir Sydney to make love to her. Two months later May Aylen, thirty-nine years barren, discovered she was pregnant with Sydney Lawford's child.

TWO

WHENEVER SOLDIERS who had fought for Britain in World War I gathered at a local pub to down a few pints and reminisce, someone would recount the amazing story of Brigadier General Sydney Lawford's heroism in the first Battle of Ypres, in which the British suffered severe losses as they tried to halt further German advances into France.

As General Lawford led his men in a charge against German trenches, his horse's head was blown off by shrapnel. The animal continued to run for nearly a minute, while its rider stayed on horseback until what remained of the beast collapsed and nearly crushed him. Lawford immediately got up, jumped on another mount—"as if nothing had happened," one of his lieutenants related—and continued the charge.

Lawford's bravery was only one reason for the respect and affection his men felt for him. His aide-de-camp, Sir Jocelyn Lucas, wrote warmly of his recollections of the general during the Battle of Ypres. "When nearly every officer in the brigade had been killed or wounded, he personally led a successful charge against the German trenches, armed only with his cane. On the retreat from Ghent and Ypres, he stayed up all night fighting to get a train to save the wounded from certain capture by the enemy. He succeeded. Immaculate in appearance and jaunty in carriage, he was a great sportsman and a fine horseman. He will be remembered, with affection and admiration, by all who served under him."

SYDNEY LAWFORD was born on November 16, 1865, at Tunbridge Wells in the county of Kent, and christened Sydney Turing Barlow Lawford. Also born in England that year were Rudyard Kipling, who would write about an India Sydney Lawford came to know well, and the future King George V, who became Lawford's friend.

Lawford was born into the rarefied world of landed gentry, the finest schools, the most exclusive men's clubs. His wealth had originated with his grandfather Samuel Lawford II, a Kent banker. Samuel's sixth son, Thomas Acland Lawford, had married Janet Turing Bruce and settled in Kinellan, Wimbledon Common, where in turn had four sons—Archibald, Herbert, Sydney, and Ernest—and three daughters, Jessie, Evelyn, and Ethel.

The Lawfords were far wealthier than the Bunnys. They traveled in more exclusive circles, playing host to the top echelons of the aristocracy and royalty. Whereas the Bunny girls married military men, several of the Lawfords married titles. Sydney embarked on a military career with a strong assist from his uncle Edward, a general, and after his graduation from Wellington College, passed the series of rigorous examinations required for acceptance into The Royal Military College at Sandhurst. He was admitted in 1883 as a cavalry cadet.

Life at Sandhurst was a microcosm of the privileged world of the British upper classes. Young, eager Sydney Lawford caught his first glimpse of the college's stately buildings as he rode in a carriage with other wide-eyed cadets past thick rows of birch, pine, and larch trees. The campus, set on a sprawling plain, included two lakes, shooting ranges, and parade grounds. It had been, since 1812, the premier military school in Britain; students left the institution as certified "officers and gentlemen."

Handsome, dark haired, well built, six feet tall, Lawford looked resplendent in his cadet uniform of gold lace, pantaloons, and pillbox cap. He owned his mount and had a batman who served as his valet, blacked his boots, cleaned his rifle, maintained his uniform, and emptied his slop bucket in the morning.

Sydney and the other cadets scrambled out of bed every daybreak to the sound of reveille, and by nine o'clock were in formation for parade maneuvers, followed by gymnastics, horsemanship, and practice skirmishes. At four o'clock, they sat for high tea served on sterling silver platters; then they studied for two hours before dinner. In the evenings, mirroring their fathers' men's club rituals, the cadets would retire to dens where they read, discussed military strategy or the politics of the day, and played billiards and whist.

A military education in mid-1880s England was a purely theoretical exercise. Britain had enjoyed an unprecedented period of peace since its last war with France had ended in 1814, interrupted only by the Crimean War of 1854–1856 and the Indian Mutiny of 1856–1857. This sustained tranquility frustrated patriotic young men trained for warfare. Winston Churchill, who entered Sandhurst ten years after Sydney Lawford, once said of his military schooling that it was "a pity that it all had to be make-believe, and that the age of wars between civilized nations had come to an end forever.... Fancy being nineteen in 1793 with more than twenty years of war against Napoleon in front of one!"

It was a view shared by Sydney Lawford. He was a young man learning skills that he might never be able to use. An ambitious soldier, he knew that it was valor in battle, not schoolboy exercises, that would distinguish him and elevate him to the rank of colonel or general.

After he graduated from Sandhurst with honors in 1885, at the age of twenty, he joined the Royal Regiment of Fusiliers. His army life was a replica of his school days: maneuvers, practices, maintenance of a superb readiness for combat—and a seemingly futile wait for a war, any war, to call him to battle.

That would come, but first Sydney Lawford took a wife. In 1893, the nearly twenty-eight-year-old lieutenant married Lilian Maud Cass, a clerk's daughter and spinster six years his senior. The marriage took place on September 30 in St. Paul's Church, Knightsbridge.

Little is known about Sydney Lawford's marriage to Lilian Cass. In all his published biographical material, including his listing in *Burke's Peerage* and his official Royal Fusiliers biography, no mention is made of her. What can be reconstructed is that they had no children and lived most of the time at their country estate, Bath House, in Hounslow, Heston—and that, seven years after their marriage, on November 26, 1900, Lilian died at Bath House of carcinoma of the lung. Sydney later omitted Lilian from his biographical sketches because of the stigma the Victorians attached to multiple marriages.

Lawford had little time to grieve. A few weeks after Lilian's death, fifteen years after his graduation from Sandhurst, Lieutenant Lawford was summoned to war. The British were fighting the Boers in South Africa, and he was called up to accompany General Horatio Kitchener into battle.

The Boer War, prompted by Britain's desire to gain governmental control over the Dutch Boers who had settled in the Transvaal region of South Africa—and the gold and diamonds that had recently been discovered there—lasted two years. The British won, but most observers considered their conduct of the war unbecoming and the cause unjust. The Crown, however, looked upon its victory as further proof of Britain's world dominance and the righteousness of its imperial designs.

However questionable the context, Sydney Lawford proved himself in battle as he had so longed to do. His repeated acts of valor won him the Queen's Medal with three clasps and a promotion to colonel. In 1907, with Britain once again at peace, Lawford became the assistant commandant of the School of Mounted Infantry; he was named its commandant in 1912.

By early 1914, rumors of a European war were sweeping the world. Britain and the continental powers all increased their military expenditures during the spring, and after the assassination of Archduke Francis Ferdinand of Austria, war seemed inevitable.

Sydney Lawford, by this time commander of the Essex Infantry Brigade, would certainly be called upon to serve, despite his age—he was approaching his forty-ninth birthday. While he waited, he decided to get married again. He had been a widower for fourteen years, and he was a lonely man.

For several months he had discreetly courted Muriel Williams Watt, the beautiful thirty-four-year-old wife of Walter Oswald Watt. Fourteen years Sydney's junior, Muriel was the daughter, from his first marriage, of Sir Hartley Williams, the present husband of Sydney's sister Jessie. Muriel obtained a divorce from Walter Watt late in

1913, and on May 20, 1914, she and Sydney were married at the Register Office in London. The Lawfords enjoyed a three-month honeymoon, during which Muriel sat for the American painter John Singer Sargent. When Britain declared war on Germany on August 4, Sydney was made a brigadier general and named to command the 22nd Infantry Brigade, 7th Division. He was put in command of the 41st Division in 1915.

It was in this, the Great War, that Lawford truly distinguished himself. Seven times he was dispatched to lead men into battle in various parts of the world, and stories of his bravery became commonplace. The tale of his ride atop the headless horse was always guaranteed to astonish.

Lawford's service to his country in World War I won him the French and Belgian Croix de Guerre and the Russian Order of St. Vladimir. At the end of the hostilities in 1918, he was promoted to the rank of major general and knighted for his valor by his friend King George V, who had ascended to the throne on the death of his father, King Edward, in 1910. Thenceforth, Sydney Lawford would be known as Sir Sydney Lawford—and his wife properly addressed as Lady Lawford.

Sydney and Muriel, as May and Ernest Aylen had before them, repaired to India not long after the war ended. There, Sir Sydney was promoted again, to lieutenant general, and he was appointed the general officer commanding for the Lahore District. Shortly thereafter, Major Ernest Aylen was named his deputy assistant director of medical services.

MAY LATER claimed that she didn't purposefully become pregnant to ensnare Sir Sydney into marriage and gain the title Lady Lawford. About her discovery that she was two and a half months pregnant, she said: "Oh, God! Even too late for an abortion. . . . Peter was an awful accident!"

But there are strong indications to the contrary. According to Katharine Eden, "The great sadness for Uncle Ernest was that he was very anxious to have a child and she refused, all the years of their marriage. She must have known what precautions to take because she never had a child before. But she wanted very much to be Lady Lawford. She was a social climber, and to have that title was supremely important to her."

When May told her husband that she was pregnant by his commanding officer, Aylen was, as Katharine Eden understates, "very upset." Still, May implored him to remain married to her until the baby was born in order to give the child legitimacy. Shattered, but a gentleman to the core, Aylen agreed.

Once the baby was born in September 1923 the painful reality of May and Sydney's adultery could no longer be avoided. A month after the delivery, the child's birth certificate was registered in the county of London. Major Ernest Vaughan Aylen was listed as his father, and his full name was given as Peter Sydney Ernest Aylen. (May at least gave the general top billing!)

The next day, October 9, 1923, Aylen sued May for divorce, charging her with adultery and naming Sir Sydney as corespondent. On November 2, Muriel Lawford sued Sir Sydney for divorce on the same grounds. Less than a year later, both divorces were final.*

At that point, details of the divorces became a part of the public record, and it was then that May's worst fears were realized. "There it was, splashed across the center pages of one of the tabloid newspapers," Katharine Eden recalled. "Pictures of Uncle Ernest, awful pictures just after he'd come out of prison, and a picture of Aunt May in a fancy dress. It was a tremendous scandal because Sir Sydney Lawford was a very famous war hero and it just wasn't done for a senior officer to seduce a junior officer's wife."

In matters of sexual mores, the England of May and Sir Sydney's generation and social strata had raised hypocrisy to the level of art. It was less important to be faultless than to appear so, and discretion was admired, even rewarded. But once a scandal surfaced, once adultery was charged in court, the participants became social pariahs. A divorce ruined a

---

*May's marriage to Aylen was eventually annulled. A proud man, he let family and friends believe that Peter was indeed his son, and several times during the boy's childhood May and Peter met for lunch with Ernest so that Aylen could see him. Aylen retired from the army a lieutenant colonel, and he never remarried. On October 12, 1947, at the age of seventy, he learned that he had cancer of the larynx. He returned from his doctor's office to his rooms at the Three Crowns Hotel at Angmering-on-Sea, Sussex, removed a cache of barbiturates from a dresser drawer, fed a handful to his dog, and then ingested a lethal dose himself.

man's career, destroyed a woman's reputation. Even the in-nocent parties in divorce cases were routinely shunned, no longer received at court or invited to "proper" receptions.

Thus was May Aylen's dream of a new life among the highest level of society washed away by the purple ink of London's scandal sheets. Sir Sydney was forced to retire from His Majesty's army. He and May were certain to be ostracized by all the best Londoners, their son branded a bastard. May couldn't bear the thought of it.

There was only one thing to do. On September 11, 1924, a week after their respective divorces were final, May—nearly forty-one but listing her age as thirty-nine—and Sir Sydney—soon to be fifty-nine—were married in a civil ceremony at London's Caxton Hall. Immediately after-ward, they bundled up one-year-old Peter and sailed across the English Channel to France.

THEY SETTLED into a large suite of rooms in an exclu-sive residence hotel in Deauville, an elegant watering place just across the Channel in northern France. They hired a married French couple who served as valet and maid, and a German governess for Peter.

May was devastated by the vilification she had suffered in London, and she sought solace in alcohol more than she ever had before. Sir Sydney, who never drank to excess, stayed clear of his wife when she was drunk and let the episodes pass. There was no help to be had for alcoholism in this era or for long thereafter; it was a family secret to be kept at all costs. It was easier to live with May's problem than it might have been because long periods passed when she wouldn't touch a drop. But then something might set her off and she would drink herself into a stupor.

Peter's care had been left to nurse Hemming for the first year of his life, and after that almost exclusively to his governesses. Miss Hemming had strapped Peter's good right arm down occasionally to force him to use his underdevel-oped left one, and as a result he grew up ambidextrous.

May avoided the more unappetizing aspects of infant care; she refused to hold her son until he was bathed, tal-cumed, and perfumed. "I never wanted Peter," she said, and she made the general promise that there would be no more babies. Because Sir Sydney was so much older, May said, he "did not bother me much," and the couple never had sex after Peter reached age three.

If May Lawford had to have a child, she would have preferred a daughter—and she often treated Peter as though he *were* a girl. By the time he was three, he was a beautiful child with brilliant blue eyes and thick eyelashes. It was a lingering Victorian practice to dress male toddlers in girls' clothes, and May followed the custom publicly until Peter was four or five. She then continued it privately until he was eleven. May later claimed that Peter "used to fancy himself a girl" and enjoyed wearing female clothing. If so, the seed had been planted by May herself.

Peter was raised to respect his parents, but there wasn't an excess of love in the Lawford household. The little boy never ran to his father for a kiss, never threw his arms around him, never climbed on his shoulders for a piggyback ride. Peter felt great affection for his father—"I adored him"—but he showed it in the only way he could: he saluted the general.

May hired a succession of governesses and tutors to mold Peter into a perfect little boy who would not embarrass her in front of the society people she had begun to court in France. She carefully interviewed Peter's prospective guardians to screen out those whose manner or diction did not meet her standards and who, she suspected, would not be diligent in teaching Peter the points of etiquette that, she said, "are the hallmark of a cultured gentleman." Among the infractions Peter was punished for over the years were licking his fingers, failing to take off his hat indoors, eating between meals, interrupting someone else's conversation, and going through a door ahead of a woman. (May dismissed one governess who allowed Peter to do this, and then made him write "Ladies First" fifty times.)

As Peter grew older, his life became very regimented. May's dietary rules were strict; she was an early proponent of "health foods," and Ernest Aylen's specialization in dermatology had taught her what foods to avoid for clear skin and general good health. Peter was fed "plenty of vegetables and fruit," May said, and "only one hundred percent whole wheat bread." He was allowed meat just three times a week and was forbidden to eat pastry, sweets, or canned food of any kind. When he was a little older, May did allow him white wine with lunch and dinner, in keeping with the continental custom.

Taught that "cleanliness is next to godliness," Peter bathed in the morning and the evening and gargled twice daily (and after every swim in a pool or the sea) with a mixture of salted water, bicarbonate of soda, and a mild disinfectant. He also had to wash his hands with disinfectant before each meal. Peter never suffered from the normal childhood illnesses, May said, because of this regimen.

With clothes that were handmade by King George V's tailor, Peter was, by five, a perfect Little Lord Fauntleroy. Sailing with his parents aboard the ship *Bremen,* Peter walked up to the queen of Spain, bowed low, and asked her, "Would Her Majesty deign to dance with me?" Charmed, the queen consented.

Carefully, Lady Lawford was re-creating her life and her family for maximum social stature. During Peter's childhood, the Lawfords traveled extensively, first throughout Europe and then around the world. Everywhere they went, May corrected people who called her Mrs. Lawford: "It's *Lady* Lawford." She never corrected anyone who called her Lady May—a form of address she would have been entitled to only if she had been born to a father who held a title by heredity—because that mistake elevated her standing. After May's marriage to Sir Sydney, Peter was referred to only as Peter Lawford, although Aylen remained his legal surname.

Late each fall, as winter's cold enveloped northern France, the Lawfords left Deauville and traveled south to the warmer climes of the Riviera, where they rented villas in Monte Carlo, Nice, Cannes, and Menton. With his first five years spent mainly in France, Peter's native language was French. Both his parents spoke it fluently; May, in fact, called him "Pierrot" for most of his childhood. Later, it was a struggle for him to master English.

The little boy also grappled with loneliness. He had no brothers or sisters to play with, and his family's nomadic life-style made it difficult for him to make or keep friends. His personality didn't help the problem. Surrounded almost exclusively by adults, and well aware of his mother's obsession with etiquette, Peter was quite unlike other children his age.

May remembers sailing from the Bahamas to Australia

when Peter was six, accompanied this time by a French maid for May, Peter's tutor, and Sir Sydney's manservant. May had taken advantage of a half fare for Peter that required him to eat with the other children aboard ship rather than with his parents. When the time came for his first meal, Peter donned a suit and silk stockings up to his knee breeches. Proud of his outfit, he twirled three times for his mother's inspection, then was off to the children's dining room.

In a matter of minutes, he returned. He refused, he announced, to eat with the other children because of their appalling manners. They were playing with their food and talking with their mouths full, he said: "I'd rather not eat than have dinner with those little barbarians." Pleased by her son's good taste, May arranged to pay full fare for Peter, and he joined his parents at the captain's table. May later said, "The captain was both annoyed and amazed at Peter's proper manners."

Young Peter's attitude was not one to endear him to potential playmates, but he had an artistic bent and could spend hours by himself drawing finely detailed pen and crayon renderings of the ships he sailed on and the sights he had seen (the Arc de Triomphe was his favorite). He composed rhymes and performed little skits in front of no one in his parents' stateroom.

To Sir Sydney's disappointment, the boy expressed no interest at all in the military; he had announced at age three that he wanted to be an actor and a dancer. Even at four, Peter had been aware that he was a general's son, and one day he had asked his parents and the servants to gather around to hear a recitation: "There was a boy/Who was born to fight war/But he wanted to become an Actor/Because he didn't believe in wars."

Insulated, withdrawn, young Peter was shunned by most children his age, and he sought closeness wherever he could find it. While his family was staying in Monte Carlo, Peter's parakeet died. He was devastated, and he gently buried the bird under a tree on the grounds of the villa the Lawfords had rented. Thirty years later, he astonished his manager during a trip to Monaco when he showed him exactly where he had put the bird in its final resting place.

The Lawfords spent a good deal of time in Monte Carlo, principally because Sir Sydney had developed a taste for gambling, which was illegal in France and Italy but was practiced amid pomp and elegance in Monaco. He liked nothing more than to play golf during the day and roulette in the evening in the vast Belle Epoque game room with its ornate crystal chandeliers that dropped sixty feet into the room. After one particularly successful turn at the tables he handed May a diamond bracelet he had just won; another time he collected twelve thousand dollars on one spin of the wheel.

Peter was fascinated by the casino and its patrons, all dressed in formal evening clothes, especially since as a child he wasn't allowed in. "I used to stand outside," he recalled, "and the glimpses I caught as the doors opened and closed made it all seem so exciting, gay, and glamorous."

The boy's travels—the Lawfords made three trips around the world before he was fifteen—gave him a priceless education in the diversity of cultures and in languages (he could speak French, English, Spanish, and some German). He was quick-witted and intelligent, but his formal education was spotty. He never attended school; rather he was taught the rudiments of writing, reading, and mathematics first by his governesses and then by a tutor who sometimes traveled with the family. He longed for knowledge; at six, in Deauville, having just learned English, he met a boy his age who could speak French, English, Italian, and Spanish. Dejected, he went to his parents and asked to be taught Spanish and Italian.

May long maintained that Peter's education was superior to any he could have received at an institution. "I do not send him to school," she said, "because I do not think any school I have heard of pays enough attention to languages or religion—I once heard an Oxford don get the worst of an argument with a Paris porter."

But May was deluding herself, and Peter knew it. Because he never went to school, he said later, he always felt inferior. At seven, he couldn't read as well as other children, and his skills remained so poor that he finally tried to teach himself. He kept a dictionary by his nightstand and studied two new words every evening before going to sleep.

When Peter was about ten, May decided that he was

"quite unfitted for any career except art," so she ordered his tutor to cut mathematics and Latin from his lessons and substitute dramatics. These and other gaps in his education made Peter feel inadequate for the rest of his life.

His mother, Peter later said, was "cotillionesque, easily swayed by other people." She believed in astrology and reincarnation, and wrote of seeing UFOs in the skies and ghosts in her bedroom. For a time, she embraced a series of religions, among them Christian Science and Zen Buddhism. "Naturally, I was dragged along," Peter said—and, impressionable as he was, he became fanatically religious.

When May sent him to a Christian Scientist practitioner to be cured of hay fever, he returned after the sixth visit carrying a bouquet of flowers. Aghast, May braced herself for a night spent listening to Peter's sneezes. "Oh no," he told her. "We've trodden on the devil and no more hay fever." He then recited a Scientific Statement of Being and buried his face in the flowers. He was, May professed, never again troubled by allergies.

Somewhat later, Peter refused to play with a little girl aboard ship because she was wearing denim slacks. "She's an abomination unto the Lord!" he cried. "It says so plainly in the twenty-second chapter of Deuteronomy!"

PETER LAWFORD'S unconventional upbringing, under any circumstances, would have created a number of personality confusions in a young boy. The added element of his mother's emotional instability left him with virtually no defenses. As he grew older, May drank more and more heavily, and he could never be sure what kind of day it would be or at what point during a bout of drinking his mother's personality would change. The woman careered between smothering attention and chilly indifference to him. In her cups, effusive, she would coddle him, dress him as a girl, and play with him as though he were a doll; at other times she ignored him and foisted him off on the servants, often for months at a time.

Peter learned at an early age not to anger his mother, and his life revolved around keeping her happy and calm. After May passed out on her bed during a particularly bad drinking binge when Peter was seven, he frantically searched for a way to help her. Finally, he soaked the edges of her pillow with her favorite eau de cologne in the hope that that would please her. Then he stood by her bed for two hours softly telling her all the children's stories he knew—just to make her feel better.

Sometimes May was indifferent to Peter for so long that the only way he could get her attention was to misbehave. May "believed in the hairbrush," as she put it, and Peter began to enjoy this form of motherly heed so much that he would engage in all kinds of contrived mischief to achieve it. Once, he pasted the pages of a spelling book together and waited for her to summon him. When she did, the usual scene was played out. "We had a little talk," May later said, "at the end of which he frankly admitted he had done wrong. Then, without too many protestations, he bent over my knee and I applied the corrective treatment where it would do the most good. . . . I still insist, and Peter agrees, that the spankings did more than anything else to fit him for his present role."

When Peter was five, and living with his parents in a Paris hotel, he surprised a burglar clambering into his bedroom window: "I saw a man with a sharp, evil face, carrying a weighted stick." He cried out, and May ran into his room with Sir Sydney's revolver. When she saw the man she shot him, and he fell backward out the window. "I was perfectly justified in killing him," May said. "No charges were filed against me."

Peter was so shocked and frightened, he later said, that he could no longer sleep if he was alone. He shared the same bed with his parents until he was eleven—a practice that may have been more a result of his need for parental closeness than his terror at a burglar.

Not long after Peter's seventh birthday, May discovered him smoking the cigarette butts and drinking the alcohol left behind by her guests after a party. She watched him down glass after glass. "I waited for him to get tipsy or something," she said. "He must have an iron digestive tract! It didn't faze him."

May wasn't much bothered by this until one of the servants told her that the behavior was frequent and he feared that "Master Peter is becoming an alcoholic." Rather than take the hairbrush to him this time, May waited until her next gathering and instructed the servants to put emetic tablets in all the glasses that still contained alcohol after the party ended. Before long, she heard Peter become violently ill. "Such terrible heaving!" she recalled. It broke him of the habit.

BEGINNING IN 1928, May set out to reestablish her reputation in the British Isles. Her chief weapon in the battle was a series of dispatches she wrote for London newspapers from various cities throughout Europe, which became very popular.

Bylined "Noted traveler and writer Lady Lawford," the columns, published chiefly in the *Evening News* and *Daily Express,* offered May's impressions of the various countries she'd lived in and visited, and gave advice to women about health, the proper use of perfume, interior decorating, how to find a good flat in London, and how to keep one's figure after forty. She described the latest Paris fashions in one column; in another she declared that "the best scrambled eggs I ever tasted were made at a picnic in the hills of India by a young subaltern over a fire of sticks under three stones."

May's writing was always interesting, sometimes vivid. In a column about her sojourn in Peshawar, Pakistan, she described invading Afghan tribesmen: "They have faces like a bit of hewn rock and eyes like a hungry panther; their long restless fingers are forever caressing the triggers of their rifles."

Several of her dispatches concerned Peter. One was entitled "My Son Teaches Me: Our Children Are True Mirrors of Ourselves" and told of seven-year-old Peter's admonishment of her when she spoke ill of a friend after an argument. "Mummy," he said to her. "You didn't really mean that she was a horrid woman, did you? Because you must love her."

"Why?" May bristled, still indignant.

"Well, you called her 'my enemy,' and you know you've got to love your enemies."

"That remark," May wrote, "gave me food for thought and took a great deal of the resentment and sting out of my real or imagined wrongs."

The columns stood May in good stead when the Lawfords were forced, after six years abroad, to return to London in 1930 because of the worldwide depression precipitated by the international stock market crashes of October 1929. Sir Sydney's investment income suffered badly. He wasn't wiped out, but the family had to economize; they could no longer afford to travel or rent lavish villas in France and Monaco. They moved back into their London flat and commuted to their country home in Toddington, both of which Sir Sydney owned outright.

May worried about their reception in London, but six years had passed since the publicity of their divorces; other, fresher scandals occupied London society. Few remembered the details of the Lawford-Aylen imbroglio, and fewer cared. The Lawfords, although still shunned by the prissier members of society, were welcomed back by most, especially those who had become fans of May's columns.

In fact, it wasn't long before May's outspokenness and strongly conservative political views won her a position in the United Empire Party, a fringe group headed by Lords Beaverbrook and Rothermere, Britain's two most powerful newspaper barons. She was again in her element, cheered by crowds as she expressed her opinions, able to hold her own among the members of the old-boy network of British politicians—and match them pint for pint. May delivered fiery speeches warning against the dissolution of the British Empire, and she reveled in the attention. She was, she bragged, followed and admired by thousands.

Audiences loved her outrageous retorts to hecklers; once, after an Irish woman asked her why she was wearing a Paris hat instead of one made in England, she shot back, "Because such a goose as you can't make them as good!"

But May's latest enthusiasm kept her away from her family so much that Peter's tutor saw a need to reproach her. "What about the general?" he asked her. "He never sees you in the mornings, you occasionally lunch with him, and in the evenings you see him mainly at dinners and parties attended by large numbers."

Nothing was said about Peter, who saw his mother now even less than Sir Sydney did. He continued to live in his own little fantasy world, shutting himself in his room for hours with a Gramophone to practice dance steps and imitate Charlie Chaplin.

Despite Peter's antiwar recitation when he was four, Sir Sydney still harbored hope deep in his military soul that his son would straighten up and follow him through Wellington and Sandhurst and into the Royal Fusiliers. But he abandoned the notion by the time Peter was seven, when it became even clearer that the boy's aptitudes were far from regimental. Peter later recalled that his father was not one of those who demanded, "Follow in my footsteps, boy!"—because Sydney could see that any attempt to force his son to do so would be futile.

Which isn't to say that the general was pleased by Peter's theatrical interests. His attitude toward show business was not far removed from Frank Bunny's (the general and May's father, it should be remembered, were of the same generation). According to May, Sir Sydney's reaction to the first hint that Peter wanted to be a performer was bilious: "My son a common jester with a cap and bells, dancing and prancing around in front of people!"

May, of course, was far more enthusiastic about it. Her girlhood ambitions, the theatricals she had done, gave her a deep empathy for her son's fascination with the theater. Although she would never admit it to Sir Sydney, she harbored her own hopes that Peter might have an acting career. She knew that with the worldwide popularity of Jackie Coogan, child actors were much in demand. Peter—a handsome, photogenic, self-possessed boy enthralled by performing—might easily win film work and contribute to the family's finances.

It was one of May's Empire Party associates who opened the door for Peter to make his professional acting debut. Sir Thomas Paulson owned a major interest in Elstree, a film production complex in Borehamwood, north of London. One of the centers of the fledgling British film industry, Elstree was owned by British International Films and had several movies in production at all times.

In January 1931, Peter visited his mother at the Empire Party offices in London. Aware of Sir Thomas's ties to Elstree, Peter wrangled his way into Paulson's office and sat in front of his desk. After a few pleasantries, Paulson asked him, "Have you decided what regiment you're going into when you grow up?"

Peter replied, "None, sir. I'm not going to be a soldier. I'm going to be an actor."

"Good Lord, son!" Paulson gasped. "Don't ever say such a thing in front of your father, for God's sake."

Peter ignored the comment and said, "I hear, sir, that you have an interest in Elstree."

"Why yes," Paulson replied, amused. "I have a few shares."

"I wonder, sir, if you could give me a letter to the studio manager—so I can find out if I'm an actor or not."

"You mean you want to visit Elstree, son? Well, I think that can be arranged. I'll give them an order to show you through. How about tomorrow?"

The next morning May and Peter boarded a train to Borehamwood. He could barely sit still as he stared out of the railway coach and watched scenes of the English countryside slip past the windows like frames of a movie. His mind wandered, and he imagined himself up on a giant silver screen, the light and shadow that flickered past his mind's eye more real to him than the lonely reality of his life.

THREE

PETER'S EYES nearly popped out of his head as he and May were escorted around Elstree. Called "the British Hollywood," the studio was only a few years old and was completely equipped for sound production. "Lady Lawford and Master Peter" toured prop rooms with Roman columns and Louis XIV chaises longues, costume rooms with World War I soldiers' uniforms and Victorian bustles. In the makeup rooms they watched actors apply their greasepaint, and Peter was intoxicated. "I'll never forget the smell," he said.

Then he set foot on his first soundstage. Peter's stare widened at the sight of arc lights, scaffolding, sound booms, cameras. After a few moments he and his mother were told to be as quiet as possible—a scene was about to be shot. The production was one of the first British talkies, *Poor Old Bill,* starring the portly low comedian Leslie Fuller, and Peter watched with rapt attention as the director, Monty Banks, orchestrated a scene in which a small boy puts his father's clothes on his dog.

It was not going well. The dog was doing fine, but the young actor playing the boy repeatedly botched his lines. "It's no good!" the mercurial Banks cried over and over. "Do it again!" He was ready to walk off the set when he spotted Peter standing next to his mother on the sidelines. The right age, angelically pretty, Peter seemed the answer to the director's prayers. "That's the type of boy I want!" Banks exclaimed, pointing at Peter. "Come here!"

May brought Peter over to Banks, who spoke with him for a few minutes. He then asked May if he could audition the boy in his office that afternoon. She agreed, and Banks shut down production for the rest of the day.

After a lunch at which the excited Peter barely touched his food, he and May were escorted into Banks's office. As May sat in a corner chair, Peter stood in front of the director's desk and asked, "Would you like me to recite in English, Spanish, or French?" May thought to herself, *Poor man, he's really in for it.*

Peter recited a bit of child's nonsense called "Tony Goes to War," then danced and did imitations for the director—who was very pleased. "Wonderful, perfect, he's in," Banks told May. "Let's sign the contracts."

May wasn't prepared for such abrupt success. "Now, wait just a minute," she stammered. "I'll have to talk to his father." Banks handed the telephone to May and she, with some trepidation, dialed Sir Sydney.

The general was not pleased. "Are you insane, my dear?" he asked May. "I think you'd better come home." May told Banks that she would have to discuss the matter with her husband and would let him know the next day. All the way home, Peter pleaded with May to convince his father to let him take the job. "He must let me do it!" Peter cried over and over. "He must!"

At home, things did not go well. The general refused to allow Peter to accept Banks's offer, despite hours of pleading by May and Peter's tearful refusal to eat dinner that evening. But the next morning, as Peter's hunger strike continued through breakfast, Sir Sydney softened. May convinced him that this would be only a one-time event, and that in fact Peter's appearance in a film might "get such nonsense out of his system." With the caveat "Just this one picture," the general agreed.

May signed a contract for Peter, who was paid ten pounds a day for what amounted to five days' work. He, of course, cared nothing about the money. What he loved was the atmosphere of the soundstage, the frenetic activity, the warmth of the lights, the glamorous actors and costumes and sets. He felt immediately at home on a movie set, and he took to acting as though it were encoded in his genes. He remembered his lines perfectly and performed the scene with the dog with a naturalism that thrilled Banks. The director got what he wanted in just two takes.

The best part of it all for Peter was that while he was acting he was the center of attention, not just an occasional addendum to the world in which his mother was the vortex. It gave him an exhilarating feeling of freedom—and for the first time, a real sense of self-esteem.

That self-esteem was heightened by the publication of a major profile of him in the London *Sunday Dispatch* on April 26, 1931. Jackie Coogan's worldwide success had created an inordinate interest in fledgling child actors, and the article, titled "Wise Little English Film Star," dubbed Peter "Britain's Jackie Coogan." The unnamed author of the piece described Peter as "the stuff that stars are made of" and quoted him on his opposition to a military career: "It would be very nice to be like Daddy, but it would take too long to be a general. I could become a film star at once. I would rather a profession where I can start at the top." Then he added, "Besides, think of being in that war." The writer then editorialized, "So a rational attitude towards the stupidity of war has succeeded the child's hero-worshipping 'What did you do in the war, Daddy?' "

The profile went on to describe Peter as "quite unselfconscious and at the same time quite unspoilt by his success. He can dance with a savage vigour and rhythm which would not be out of place in Harlem, and he has even picked up tap-dancing. He can already play the ukelele with technical efficiency."

It was heady stuff for such a small boy—and so too were his admiring reviews once *Poor Old Bill* was released. But when Peter saw himself on-screen for the first time, he squirmed with embarrassment. "I really thought I looked like a bloody fool," he said. Still, the acting bug had bitten him, and he nagged at his parents to let him do another role.

They refused, because by now there was mounting hostility toward the idea from both sides of his family. Peter's quotes in the *Sunday Dispatch* had angered May's father, now in his early seventies, who telephoned her and bellowed, "Do you think nothing of putting your only child into hell?" And Sydney's sister Ethel, a widowed millionairess, threatened to disinherit Peter, to whom she had planned to leave her entire estate, unless he "got over this nonsense once and for all!"*

That didn't seem likely. Peter's vague, childish dreams of acting were cemented by the joy he felt at appearing in *Poor Old Bill;* he talked constantly about making more films and pleaded with his parents to allow it. May managed to convince Sir Sydney to let Peter do one more film, *A Gentleman of Paris,* before they returned to France in 1932. There, Peter appeared in several films during the next twelve months, but his fledgling career didn't have any more of a chance in France than it had in Britain: in 1933, Peter was once again uprooted.

Sir Sydney's financial picture had improved through a moderate inheritance, and he decided that the family should travel—as much to get Peter away from soundstages as to fulfill his own desire to see more of the world. Over the next five years, the Lawford family would not live in any one region of the earth for more than nine months at a time.

AS HIS cousin Valentine Lawford has said, "Peter wasn't brought up, he was dragged up." During his adolescence, he traveled with his parents to India, Australia, Tasmania, Tahiti, Colombia, Brazil, Hawaii, Spain, Portugal, Ceylon, Bermuda, Panama, Cuba, Nassau, and the United States.

Peter remembered this nomadic existence fondly. "I loved it and it never occurred to me that it might be an odd way of growing up." In India, he rode elephants and haggled with merchants in the bazaars of Bombay. In Ceylon, the family stayed at the opulent Grand Oriental Hotel and May showed him the cinnamon gardens and Buddhist temples that had captivated her as a girl.

The boy's most vivid memories of this period were of Tahiti, where the family settled for six months in 1933, living in a thatched hut on the Blue Lagoon. "It is a beautiful spot," Peter recalled. "I'll never forget the coal-black sand glistening in the sunlight. We had a place right on the ocean. The water was so clear you could see the coral underneath.

---

*Because Peter later returned to acting, he never did receive an inheritance from Ethel, and Frank Bunny, who died in 1940, omitted May from his will for the same reason.

I lived in shorts, had my own canoe, and swam from dawn to dusk. It was a boy's paradise."

He was thrilled with Hawaii as well. In October 1934, the Lawfords sailed into Los Angeles harbor aboard the Italian liner *California* and spent a week in LA before embarking again for Hawaii. They remained in Honolulu for nine months, living in the sumptuous Royal Hawaiian Hotel, the "Pink Palace" on the still-pristine, uncrowded sands of Waikiki Beach. One evocative photograph shows Peter sitting at a table beneath a huge umbrella, with Diamond Head behind him in the distance. Dressed entirely in white, two-tone oxfords on his feet, his hair slicked back, he calls to mind a boy F. Scott Fitzgerald.

Hawaii enchanted Peter, and he returned there again and again throughout his life. It was in Waikiki that he first learned to surf, a sport that was to obsess him as a young man. He learned the hard way: "The surfboards tip up if you're not careful, and one day mine tipped, hit me over the head and knocked me out." He was saved from drowning by a companion.

The Lawfords were in Nassau, the Bahamas, in December 1936 when the newly crowned King Edward VIII abdicated his throne in order to marry the American divorcée Wallis Warfield Simpson. Lady Lawford saved until her death a one-sheet bulletin from the *Nassau Guardian* that announced the abdication, and she—like many other Britons—never forgave Mrs. Simpson for stealing her sovereign. For years she referred to the woman who became the Duchess of Windsor as "that whore" and added gleefully, "She was a prostitute. One officer who had slept with her said that she was quite good, but not *that* good!"

The family's travels kept them on shipboard almost as much as on land. At sea they lived in palatial staterooms, often given to them gratis by captains who were friends of the general or by the shipping line, since their arrivals usually made news in the local papers and provided free publicity for the ocean liner.

Sir Sydney and May ate at the captain's table and dressed in tuxedoes and ball gowns for elegant receptions. Sometimes, May and Peter performed skits for the amusement of the other passengers. On a return trip from Australia in 1937, Peter learned of a father-and-son talent contest.

When Sir Sydney refused to participate, an undaunted Peter persuaded May to allow him to masquerade as a girl and enter the mother-and-daughter contest with her. They donned Tahitian grass skirts and coconuts from their luggage trunks, performed as Lady Lawford and her little girl, and won the contest. Then Peter grandly announced that he was really a boy, and was nevertheless allowed to keep the first prize. (What that was remains unrecorded—as does Sir Sydney's reaction to all this.)

His family's travels did nothing to dilute Peter's dreams of getting back into the movies. The day after they arrived in Tahiti, May noticed a movie crew on the sand about three quarters of a mile from their hut. As she walked closer along the beach, she saw cameras, lights, reflectors, and microphones. When she got close enough to recognize faces, sure enough, there was Peter, bustling happily amid the confusion, delighted to do anything the crew needed him to do.

Peter took every opportunity to *see* movies as well. Everywhere the family traveled, he went to the pictures as often as possible, sometimes three or four times a week, sometimes in a primitive hut with a generator to run the projector. He would sit, completely absorbed in the fantasy world that flickered to life in front of him, fascinated by the performers, the sets, the costumes. But he couldn't enjoy the films completely; watching movies only reminded him that he wanted to be appearing in them himself. Still, he went back again and again because, he said, he hoped he might somehow see himself up on the screen.

WHEN PETER was around nine, he began to receive a new kind of attention that had nothing to do with acting, one that both excited and frightened him. He was an eye-catching lad, his brown hair thick and wavy, his blue eyes captivating. Fair, smooth skinned, and slim, he had a sweet, sad shyness about him that charmed many of the adults he encountered and drew some of them to him in sexual arousal.

The first such advance, according to May, occurred when the famed British war correspondent Ward Price encountered Peter in a deserted hotel hallway, pulled the boy close, and tried to kiss him. Peter resisted and went back to his parents' room to complain: "He thinks I'm something

I'm not." Lady Lawford wasn't too concerned. She said of Price, "Even though he did run on two currents—AC and DC—I couldn't help but like him."

Soon thereafter, Peter was molested by a friend of the family, a man he had come to know as his "uncle." Peter was never comfortable talking about the incident; all he would say later was that a pillow had been pushed over his face to silence him and that the experience traumatized him.

He had more ambivalent feelings about his first sexual encounter with a woman, when he was ten. While staying in the south of France, Peter's beautiful thirty-five-year-old German governess took him on a picnic. After their lunch, as they sat in the cool shade of a sprawling tree surrounded by wildflowers fluttering in a soft breeze, the woman pulled Peter toward her and put his head in her lap.

Deeply contented, Peter began to drift into sleep when he was roused by the woman's hand under his shirt. She rubbed his stomach, then worked her way down into his shorts and began gently to caress his penis. Peter recalled that the sensation was highly pleasurable—"and for some reason, most natural."

The governess then asked Peter to kiss and suckle her breasts. He began clumsily and she stopped him. *"Douce-ment,"* she told him. "Gently." He resumed in a dreamy slow motion. After a few moments, the woman became aroused and held Peter's head against her bosom, more insistent now. He didn't realize it at the time, but he later surmised that the woman soon reached orgasm, because she suddenly lifted herself up, turned Peter on his back and started "eating me alive." The woman fellated Peter to climax—his first.

He later said that this experience had not been an isolated one, that several of his nannies had taken sexual advantage of him around this age. He found himself deeply confused by the experiences, his emotions a jumble of pleasure, guilt, and fear.

Sexual relations with a governess—or any mother substitute—can be as disturbing to a child as incest, and Peter transferred his deeply conflicted feelings about them to his mother. Speaking of his parents years later, Peter said, "I adored him and loathed her, from a very early age."

It wasn't as simple as that. Peter's third wife, Deborah

Gould, remembers him telling her about these early sexual experiences: "Peter said that he resented his mother leaving him with these women who took advantage of him. But he really didn't know what to think about it at that age. He loved his mother and hated her at the same time."

FOUR

ON A COOL cloudy day in the early spring of 1937, Peter romped among the huge spreading magnolia trees that dotted the lush grounds of an exclusive French spa hotel at Aix-les-Bains. Several times a year when they were in Europe, May and Sir Sydney checked into the spa for rest and rejuvenation. They ate health foods, drank mineral water, dropped some excess weight, and cleansed their bodies of the toxins that red meat and too much alcohol had left in their systems. Their stay was usually about six weeks—or, as Peter later said, however long it took "to clean the liver."

Peter loved the spa's grounds, where he could cavort freely, bicycle through tree-lined paths, swim in natural spring waters, and play tennis on grass courts. He had developed a passion for the sport at around ten, and now that he was thirteen he displayed real talent for it—talent he had inherited, Sir Sydney proudly insisted, from his uncle Herbert, who was the third Wimbledon champion in 1879.

On the first Sunday after his arrival, Peter spent the morning on the courts and then joined a group of children about his age as they played under a magnolia tree that stood at the top of a grassy sloping hill. It was the favorite tree of the resident kids, because they could climb it, jump off its low-hanging limbs, and roll all the way down the hill.

Bored after an hour of this, he ran back to the Lawfords' bungalow. It was around three-thirty. May was shopping, and Sir Sydney was playing golf. Peter scrambled up the steps to the entrance, a large multipaned French door, and grabbed the handle, expecting it to be unlocked as usual. But a maid had latched the door, and when it didn't open Peter slammed into it. His right arm smashed through one of the panes and he instinctively pulled it back out. "That's when the damage was done," he said.

A jagged shard of glass sliced through his upper arm, slit muscles and tendons, and severed an artery. As blood gushed from his arm in a pulsing stream, spreading a deep scarlet stain over his tennis whites, his first thought was, *I'm going to get the devil for this.* He decided to bandage the wound himself so his parents wouldn't learn what had happened to him. He bolted to the bathroom and grabbed some gauze from the medicine cabinet, but even as he wrapped it around his arm he realized, *This ain't gonna handle it.*

The bandage slowed the bleeding but didn't stop it, and by now Peter felt queasy. He knew he needed help. He ran fifty yards through the gardens to the hotel lobby and stood before the concierge's desk. The man looked down at him. "What's this? Blood all over my carpet?"

Peter mumbled an apology just as his legs gave way. He fell to the floor and the concierge realized the boy was seriously hurt. He put a pillow under Peter's head and yelled for a doctor. As Peter lay on the floor, he could see the five landings of the hotel's open staircase rising above him to the top floor. At the fifth level, a white-haired man leaned over the railing to see what the commotion was.

When the man saw Peter prostrate on the floor in the middle of a spreading stain of scarlet, he yelled down, *"Je suis médecin!"* ("I'm a doctor!") and bounded down the stairs. The elderly retired physician tore off his tie to make a tourniquet, wrapped it around Peter's arm and asked for some ice. He then told the concierge to call for the hotel bus to take Peter to a clinic about a mile away.

By this time someone had summoned Sir Sydney, and when he saw his son he exclaimed, "Good God! What did you do?" Peter, who had lost nearly two pints of blood, weakly explained what happened. Then he asked, "I'll still be able to play tennis, won't I, Father?"

Lady Lawford stepped through the gates of the hotel

complex just as the bus carrying Peter and Sir Sydney passed by. The driver stopped and Sir Sydney got out to tell May what happened. When she climbed into the bus she said, "Couldn't you have done this another day, Peter? You knew I was dining out tonight." It was exactly the right thing for him to hear, Peter later said. "If she had carried on over me I wouldn't have been able to take it. Sometimes the stiff upper lip business really does work."

At the clinic, the doctor confronted a deep, long gash in Peter's arm. He picked up a metal instrument and was able to pull back the muscle far enough to see bone. "What am I to do with this?" he asked his nurse. Peter, falling into shock, was wheeled into an anteroom as the doctor told his parents that there was no way he could save Peter's arm. Gangrene was sure to set in, he said, and the only alternative was to amputate at the shoulder.

May was appalled. Peter heard her tell the physician that she would not give him permission to cut her son's arm off. "Do the best you can," she cried. "At least try!" Peter later said, "I will always remember her for this. She was good in this kind of situation."

When the man continued to insist on amputation, May pulled herself up to her full height, looked him squarely in the eye and said, *"Va te faire foutre, monsieur le docteur!"* ("Fuck off, doctor!") The Lawfords then called in a surgeon who told them he thought he could save Peter's arm, and they gave him permission to operate. As Peter slid in and out of consciousness, the doctor painstakingly labored over the wound, applying thirty-seven tiny stitches to the layers of muscle, tendon, and skin. "He did a damn good job," Peter said years later.

The Lawfords were warned that gangrene was still a danger; there was nothing they could do but wait. During the night, a nurse brought stone hot water bottles to Peter's bed to warm him. She wrapped them in towels and placed them around his ankles and lower legs. Peter was unconscious and did not feel the burning stone next to his skin when one of the towels fell away from a bottle. He awoke with third-degree burns on his ankles and feet.

May berated the nursing staff the next day and summoned Miss Hemming—"a *competent* nurse!"—from London. The blisters on Peter's feet took several days to drain. "The funny thing," he recalled, "was that my feet were killing me but I had no pain whatsoever in my arm. All my nerves had been severed so I didn't feel a thing."

Within a few days, the danger of gangrene had passed, but it was clear that Peter would never again have full use of his arm. He spent a week in the hospital, then six weeks back at the hotel in bed with his arm in a sling. As the nerves healed, Peter remembered, he started to feel the pain. Like a dull headache at first, then like a stabbing migraine. After the stitches were removed, the pain was sometimes unbearable.

Once the wound had healed, the arm remained limp. Peter couldn't use his hand, which had curled into a half fist like a claw. He tried again and again to open it, but the effort was too painful. Afraid that the arm would atrophy, May brought him back to the doctor who had performed the surgery. As the man examined Peter he took hold of the arm and twisted it slightly to test its responsiveness. The stab of pain that shot through Peter made him throw up all over the doctor's shoes.

The physician told Peter and his parents that the nerves leading to the lower arm and hand were damaged irreparably—Peter would never again have sensation in his arm and hand or enjoy full use of either. He gave Peter a tennis ball to squeeze to prevent his muscles from withering and told him to try to use the arm and hand in other ways as much as he could.

That he had been ambidextrous proved good luck for Peter, but he did have to relearn everything he'd done with his right hand before the accident—writing, playing tennis, eating—and painstakingly become a total southpaw at the age of thirteen.

The injury left Peter's psyche nearly as scarred as his shredded arm. He feared that he was now "a gimp" and would be an object of ridicule—or worse, of pity. He worried that he might never work in films or play tennis again. He fell into a depression; some days he was so deeply enclosed he wouldn't respond when spoken to.

There was no counseling in 1937 to help Peter cope with this disaster and his reactions to it. His parents, he said, "didn't know from psychiatrists," nor did they attempt to sit down and talk things out with him at any length themselves. Sir Sydney did give his son a few words of solace. The general reminded Peter that there were people in much worse straits than his and told him he was extremely lucky that his arm didn't need to be amputated. "That did help me," Peter recalled.

May, on the other hand, "didn't take the time or trouble to find out what was going on [with me]," Peter said. She did urge him to use his hand whenever possible and prodded him to play the ukelele in front of guests—insensitive to the fact that he couldn't play it as well as he had before the accident and felt ashamed. Sometimes he couldn't control his fingers at all and they'd become entangled in the strings, but still May continued to insist that he play.

Peter began to keep his hand in his pocket almost all the time, and he came to dread shaking hands, something one can do with most people only with one's right hand. He was afraid, he said, that those he greeted would think, *What is that? He's not whole.*

BY EARLY May, Peter's wound had completely healed and his continual squeezing of the tennis ball had restored some of his muscle strength. But he still had a great deal of pain in his upper arm and shoulder, made worse by the cool damp weather at Aix-les-Bains. His doctor recommended that the family move to a warmer climate and suggested either Florida or Southern California.

May wanted to go to Los Angeles, and Sir Sydney agreed—he had found the area pleasant when the family visited it on their way to Hawaii in 1934. May and Peter were thrilled. Now that it seemed he would regain at least some use of his arm, his dreams of acting had freshened in his mind, and May, more solidly behind his ambitions than ever, knew that if he lived near Hollywood there would be ample opportunity for another movie role. It was the era of the child star; Shirley Temple and Mickey Rooney were among the biggest box-office attractions in the world. So too was Freddie Bartholomew, a British boy one year younger than Peter who had created a sensation in MGM's film version of Charles Dickens's *David Copperfield*. MGM specialized in filming British classics (Bartholomew had starred as well in *Little Lord Fauntleroy, Captains Courageous,* and *Kidnapped*), and May was sure they would need an English lad of her son's qualifications for future projects.

The third week of May, the Lawfords boarded the liner *Bremen* from a dock in Le Havre and crossed the Atlantic to New York. From there they would take another ship down the Atlantic coast of the United States, through the Panama Canal, and up the Pacific coast to Los Angeles. They remained in New York for a few days before boarding the ocean liner to Los Angeles, and Peter begged his parents to take him to Radio City Music Hall to see the latest Fred Astaire and Ginger Rogers musical, *Shall We Dance?* As they walked along Fifty-seventh Street, with Peter in a suit with short pants and white socks, a group of about ten "street urchins" (as Peter later called them) threw a rock at him and yelled, "Hey, white socks!"

Instinctively, Peter picked the rock up and threw it back. The youths threw several more objects at the Lawfords, and things nearly got out of hand before his parents pulled Peter away. "It was ten to one," Peter said. "They would have eaten me alive." When they got back to their hotel, Sir Sydney said to Peter, "Good work," proud that his son had defended himself. Then he told May that Peter was too old to wear shorts and white socks. He never had to again.

On June 2, the Lawfords embarked from a dock on the Hudson River for the voyage to Los Angeles. Aboard ship, they met pretty, eighteen-year-old Louise Barker, who had just completed her freshman year at Radcliffe and was traveling to the West Coast with her mother. Louise retained vivid memories of Peter Lawford: "I was enjoying the company of the ship's young purser, Charles Stuart, and Peter was definitely cramping my style because he kept following me around like a puppy dog. He had a crush on me, I guess, and it seemed that whenever Charlie and I were looking for a little privacy (respectable as it was!) Peter was always around. Our main conversation with him was to tell him to walk aft until he heard a big splash!"

Louise remembered Peter as "a good-looking boy, but pale and thin, with a very fragile manner about him. He was very shy, and seemed sad and lonesome. I felt sorry for him, but I didn't have much time for anyone else because I was so preoccupied with Charlie Stuart."

Distracted though she was, Louise could readily discern the relationship between Peter and his mother. "She didn't let him have any independence. She never seemed to take her eyes off him. She dominated him so thoroughly that he was afraid to call his soul his own. She was just smothering him."

To the other passengers aboard the ship, the Lawford family group presented a curious tableau. As Louise recalled, "We didn't know what to make of them. Here was this frail little boy, who seemed much younger than fourteen, dressed in blue blazers and gray flannel pants and looking like he'd just got out of Groton or Middlesex, and these two older people who looked more like his grandparents than his parents. We all thought they *were* his grandparents at first."

Louise's mother was skeptical of the Lawfords' aristocratic airs, because of May's constant talk about Peter's becoming the next Freddie Bartholomew. "My mother had the feeling that nobody with a legitimate title would be pushing her child to Hollywood. But she liked the Lawfords, and she said that if they were phony they were putting on a great act because they spoke so well and were so well mannered."

Louise never saw Peter Lawford again, although her mother and May kept in touch through letters. Years later she still felt guilty about the short shrift she gave Peter during their passage together. "He wanted companionship more than anything else," she said. "I felt very sorry for him."

WHEN PETER and his parents arrived in Los Angeles, they stayed at the Ambassador Hotel for several weeks before settling into a flat in the Coronet Apartments on the Sunset Strip. May wasted not a day before she telephoned every agent in Hollywood, explaining that her son had been called "the Jackie Coogan of Britain" and was now available for films in the States. Most of the agents were unresponsive. One who agreed to see Peter was Ruth Collier, a woman who had met Lady Lawford in London.

The Lawfords took their son to Ruth's office. After introductions were exchanged, May told Peter to play his ukelele for Mrs. Collier. Peter took the instrument out of its black case and began to strum, but his gnarled fingers became entangled in the strings and he stopped, his face burning with embarrassment.

Despite his poor musical performance, Collier thought

Peter had potential and she made inquiries on his behalf at the studios, without immediate success. Several months later, however, she learned that MGM planned a film entitled *Lord Jeff*, about an orphaned British boy disguised as an aristocrat by a gang of thieves as part of a robbery. The boy is caught and sent to Dr. Barnardo's, a home for wayward youths, to prepare him for service in the British Merchant Marine.

The film's director, Sam Wood, had already cast Freddie Bartholomew as Lord Jeff and Mickey Rooney as an antagonist who becomes a friend. But he still needed a group of boys behind the two stars to play lesser roles as their classmates. Wood hired Peter on the spot. Peter remembered thinking, *Mickey Rooney—wow!*

Although Peter's part was a small one (he had only a few lines and received seventh billing), the MGM publicity department immediately took him under its wing. They made much of his tender age (twelve, according to one press release), his war-hero father, his English pedigree (his parents were usually called Lord and Lady Lawford), his flawless manners, and his world travels.

Peter *was* a colorful young man, and profiles began to appear long before the release of the film. On Christmas Eve, he was brought to a party at the Beverly Hills home of Louella Parsons, the formidable Queen of Gossip with the power to make or break movie stars. She was holding court that holiday eve and made a lasting impression on Peter. "I was terribly frightened," he said years later.

He was intimidated too by the enormity of the MGM studios. The sprawling production facilities in Culver City dwarfed anything he'd known in England or France, and so did the giant studio's reputation. Louis B. Mayer's personal fiefdom, MGM was the most successful manufacturer of movies in the world; its oft-quoted boast was that its roster contained "more stars than there are in heaven." With contract players like Greta Garbo, John Barrymore, Norma Shearer, Clark Gable, Joan Crawford, Jean Harlow, Judy Garland, Mickey Rooney, Jeanette MacDonald, Nelson Eddy, and Spencer Tracy, its claim wasn't just braggadocio. And its profits, more than those of the other eight major film companies combined, made it a behemoth, the most desirable employer for any aspiring actor, director, writer, or craftsman. Metro, everyone knew, could afford the most impressive talent in the business.

Peter was as starry-eyed and starstruck as any young newcomer to Hollywood had ever been. He asked every actor he met for an autographed photo and carefully pasted the pictures in a scrapbook that he kept among his valuables for the rest of his life.

When the *Lord Jeff* shoot began in February 1938, Peter's nervousness was eased by Sam Wood, who had directed Jackie Coogan in his first starring film, *Peck's Bad Boy,* in 1921 and knew how to soothe the fears of juvenile actors. He was also helped by Mickey Rooney, who at seventeen was the number-four box-office star in America. (He reached the number-one position the following year.) Rooney coached Peter with his few lines and taught him how to act natural as part of a scene's background. The two became inseparable friends, and Peter was soon emulating the high-spirited, mischievous Rooney.

May, checking on Peter once after midnight, peered in his bedroom and found him gone, the window wide open. She telephoned Mickey's mother, and when she checked, Mickey wasn't in his room either. The next morning both showed up on the set on schedule; that night Peter got a stern reprimand from May and a lecture about showing more responsibility now that he was making an MGM picture.

Toward the end of filming, Freddie and Mickey brought Peter to one of the Sunday brunches Louis B. Mayer often gave for his actors at his sprawling, hacienda-style mansion on the beach in Santa Monica. If one was invited, one had to attend; the gatherings featured a groaning board of bagels and lox, herring in sour cream, and other Jewish noshes. There might be a few songs or a skit, and often an unreleased MGM picture was screened.

Peter stayed in the background, too frightened to introduce himself to the MGM paterfamilias, but he did meet fifteen-year-old Judy Garland, who would remain one of his closest friends, and twelve-year-old Jane Withers, on whom he developed a crush. (When he and Jane went on a chaperoned "date," Peter couldn't take his eyes off Jane's gun-toting bodyguard.)

Peter was exhilarated to meet these young actors who

were doing what he had yearned to do for so long, and he knew that he belonged with them, that he wanted to stay in Hollywood the rest of his life. As he looked out the windows of the Mayer house at the Pacific Ocean waves crashing against the shore just a few yards away, the thought crossed his mind that this was exactly the kind of house he'd like to live in someday.

LORD JEFF was released to uniformly good notices in June 1938 and earned MGM a tidy profit of $360,000. Peter was mentioned in several reviews as part of a strong supporting cast, and he should have moved on to additional roles, but that didn't happen. There was no work for a British boy in any film in the months after Lord Jeff wrapped. Ruth Collier was able to find some radio work for him, but within weeks catastrophe struck: Peter's voice started to change. Its pitch would alter alarmingly at the most inopportune times, often in the middle of a line of dialogue; sometimes he sounded most like Alfalfa in the Our Gang comedies. Acting assignments were out of the question until Peter's voice settled down again. Crushed, Peter realized that his budding "stardom" would have to be put on hold.

One of the reasons May was so eager to push Peter into movies was that the Lawfords were once again in financial difficulties. Sir Sydney had invested a good deal of his money in several highly questionable business ventures (one was to use sugar beets in the construction of houses), and now he could no longer afford to keep his family in Hollywood unless Peter brought in some money. Since he couldn't, the general decided to take his family back to England.

They had booked their transatlantic passage on the Rex when May and Sydney got very bad news in a letter from a friend in London: Freddie Bartholomew, in a magazine interview, had spoken of the 1924 scandal surrounding Peter's parents. The article strongly implied that Peter was illegitimate. May had thought this unpleasantness long behind her, and she was shattered. She had been treated as nobility, she had been accorded respect. Peter seemed destined, within a few years at the most, for a bright career in movies. Now, if the family returned to London, everything threatened to fall apart.

Depressed and angry, May had a few drinks and canceled their booking without telling Sir Sydney. When he found out, he confronted a drunken May and she grew furious. Sydney tried to convince her as soothingly as possible that her reaction was too extreme, that they didn't have the money to stay in America, but she would not be swayed. Sobbing, frantic, she screamed at him that she couldn't bear the thought of hearing snickers behind her back. "I hate England! I hate all those awful snobs! Go back yourself if you want to! I'll never set foot in England again!"

Peter would lie in his bed and "listen to them fighting, night after night." He heard things that confused and puzzled him. He thought they were talking about him sometimes, but he couldn't be sure. He knew that if his mother had been drinking, the row could last all night, and he would hear the angry words until suddenly there was silence. He would sleep fitfully and arise the next morning to find his mother passed out in her wing-backed chair. After a week of such arguments, Sir Sydney finally gave in—they would stay in America. What won him over to May's side was when she told him—sober, when Peter was out of the house—that she never wanted their son to find out that there was any question about his parentage.

If they were to stay in the United States, there was little recourse for the family but to spend the summer on Long Island, where they could save money by staying with a relative of Sir Sydney's. They moved to Manhasset, and it was there that Peter Lawford, for the first time, lived among average American teenagers for an extended period. He found it very difficult.

Muriel O'Brien was a perky, athletic seventeen-year-old who lived across the street from the Lawfords in Manhasset. A year later, she would be an ice-skating star at the 1939 New York World's Fair, and she conducted a jitterbug dance school for the neighborhood kids. For thirty-five cents they could come and spend the whole afternoon in Muriel's class. Soon after his arrival in Manhasset, Peter became one of her pupils.

Harry McNaughton, an actor who had inscribed a photograph of himself to Peter in Hollywood, was a friend of the O'Briens', and he told Muriel that Peter was poised for a career at MGM. Muriel, however, was unimpressed with his talents. She told her mother, "This kid's never going to make it. He has no rhythm, he can't sing, he's off key, he can't dance. He's just never going to make it—I don't care what MGM does with that guy."

But Peter worked hard for Muriel and improved under her tutelage. "He would do anything I wanted," she recalled, "because he had a case for me, although I didn't know that at the time." Years later, after Peter became a star, he told a reporter that his first love was an ice-skater on Long Island. Muriel hadn't realized he felt that strongly about her. "When I read that I thought, 'You *loved* me?' "

If Harry McNaughton and Muriel's parents had had their way, she would have become Mrs. Peter Lawford. "They had me set up for a relationship with Peter before I even met him," Muriel said. "Harry would talk as if Peter was close to the king of England. Everyone was impressed with that. My family were social climbers *extraordinaires,* and they wanted to see me marry Peter and become part of British royalty. They wanted me to be Mrs. Lord Fauntleroy or something." Muriel could not have been less interested. "It wasn't my thing. I was a jitterbugger, and I liked that kind of guy, not some English idiot. That's the way I thought in those days."

So did the other teenagers in Manhasset, who mocked Peter's manners, his accent, his impeccable grammar. "Peter tried to be one of the guys," Muriel recalled, "but he was teased terribly, and he was very sensitive about that."

The fall of 1938 hardened into winter and New York's weather turned icy, so May and Sydney decided to move to the warmth of the exclusive enclave of Palm Beach, Florida, one of the winter playgrounds of the wealthy. A friend of Sir Sydney's offered them his sprawling villa for the season, complete with servants and a chauffeur, at no cost. As Muriel O'Brien later put it, "They didn't have much money, but you know how royalty always gets put up and never pays for anything? It was like that with the Lawfords."

Palm Beach was a spot the Lawfords could never have afforded without the largesse of their friends—and the more socially conscious of their acquaintances, who hoped to become their friends. The winter "season" at Palm Beach consisted largely of debutantes' coming-out balls, holiday balls, and balls-just-for-the-sake-of-balls. Invitations were voraciously sought to the best parties; one's inclusion on a select guest list could make one's social status—and exclusion could spell disaster.

Sir Sydney and Lady Lawford joined the ranks of desirable invitees immediately upon their arrival. Ambitious hostesses loved to stress their titles as they introduced them to the other guests, because their presence elevated the proceedings. During their first year in this rarefied atmosphere, the Lawfords made the acquaintance of some of America's most monied families—the Mellons, the Fords, the Vanderbilts. But they didn't have the chance, that season, to meet the most talked-about local clan of all. The Kennedys had begun to winter in Palm Beach the year before, but in 1938 they were three thousand miles away in London, where their patriarch, Joseph P. Kennedy, was serving as America's ambassador to the Court of St. James's.

FIVE

EVER SINCE her arrival in the United States a year
earlier, May had kept herself abreast of events in England through letters from friends and relatives and
with subscriptions to London newspapers and magazines.
Now, as she sat under a huge striped umbrella on the ve-
randa of her friend's elegant Palm Beach home, the Atlantic
Ocean glistening before her, her temper became as hot as
the Florida air. She had received a letter from her sister,
and what Gretta was telling her about America's new ambassador to Great Britain was the catalyst for her lifelong hatred
of Joseph P. Kennedy and his family.

One of the great American success stories of the age,
Joe Kennedy had attained everything but what he craved
most: political power and social position. The son of poor
Irish-Catholic immigrants, he had amassed a huge fortune
through businesses that ranged from bootlegging to movies
(acquiring, in the process, one of Hollywood's legendary
stars, Gloria Swanson, as a mistress). Now, thanks to a hundred-thousand-dollar contribution to Franklin D. Roosevelt's successful campaign for the presidency in 1932, a four-
year stint as the first chairman of the Securities and Exchange Commission, and some hard lobbying on his part,
Joe Kennedy had won the appointment he hoped would
finally assure his arrival at the very top: the ambassadorship
to Great Britain.

Now he would dine with King George VI; his advice

would be sought by politicians on both sides of Parliament; his invitations to the homes of dukes and earls would be envied; his daughters would be presented at court during the most lavish social events in the world. It was the most prestigious position in the diplomatic sphere, and no Irish-American had ever held such a lofty post in England. How better for Joe Kennedy to thumb his nose at the Boston Brahmins who had looked down on him and his family than to have their counterparts—in many cases their relatives—in Britain paying him homage?

In March 1938 Joe Kennedy arrived in England, followed shortly thereafter by his wife and seven of his nine children (the two eldest, Joe Junior and Jack, stayed behind to finish their college terms). Immediately, the Kennedy clan took London by storm. They moved into the six-story, thirty-six-room embassy mansion at 14 Prince's Gate in fashionable Knightsbridge, which had been donated by J. P. Morgan as the American ambassador's residence. The rooms were decorated in the French grand style; the great reception hall was a duplicate of the hall at the Palace of Versailles; the Pine Room—Mrs. Kennedy's personal reception area—boasted rare English and French tapestries on the walls. An enormous marble staircase led from the reception quarters to the ambassador's study.

Joe Kennedy's introduction to England was a happy one. He was viewed by most Britons as "refreshingly blunt" and "typically American," his country's "Nine-Child Envoy." His eldest daughter, Kathleen, became the darling of English society; fourteen-year-old Patricia was dubbed "an Irish beauty." Photos of the children appeared in the newspapers almost daily: Teddy taking a picture of the changing of the guard while holding his camera upside down; Kathleen riding a bicycle through the streets of London; thirteen-year-old Bobby speaking shyly with twelve-year-old Princess Elizabeth.

But the honeymoon didn't last long. Kennedy's earthiness soon came to be considered gaucherie by the likes of Lady Lawford, who was infuriated by what she learned of the Kennedys' behavior. "Those barefoot Irish peasants!" she huffed when she read accounts of a Joe Kennedy faux pas with the queen. Tradition dictated that the new ambassador approach the queen, take her proffered left hand and lead her into a waltz once around the ballroom. Kennedy had told her, "Wrong hand!" and shaken her right hand, then spun her into a spirited polka. The queen had smiled valiantly through a few whirls before she snapped, "That is sufficient!" and returned to her throne.

Worse was to come. What finally destroyed Kennedy's ambassadorship and caused him to leave England in disgrace was his unshakable commitment to appeasing Adolf Hitler, on the grounds that Britain would be unable to win a war with Germany. That position seemed vindicated when Prime Minister Neville Chamberlain returned from his Munich conference with Hitler with a nonaggression pact. "It is peace in our time," Chamberlain declared as he waved the agreement above his head before a cheering crowd. But the Nazi conquests proceeded. Hitler's armies invaded Czechoslovakia in March 1939 and prepared to attack Poland.

Aghast at the thought of a war in Europe and of American involvement in it—a possibility that posed a threat to the lives of his beloved sons Joe and Jack—Joe Kennedy continued, in the face of mounting evidence of the Nazi threat, to support appeasement. He would, he said, "sell ten Polands down the river in order to save the life of one British soldier."

In March 1939, Chamberlain announced that if Germany invaded Poland, Britain would go to war against the Nazis. On September 1, Hitler's tanks stormed across the Polish border. The world waited to see if Britain would keep its pledge. When Secretary of State Cordell Hull asked Joe Kennedy that question, he replied, "No." But Kennedy was no longer privy to inside information. On September 3, Neville Chamberlain, telling friends that everything he had devoted his life to was in ruins, declared war on Germany. Joe called President Roosevelt and cried, "It's the end of everything!"

By July 1940 the Nazis had begun a devastating air war against London and nearby areas, killing fourteen thousand civilians in the first three months. The English held up under the blitz, stubbornly refusing to allow the Germans to destroy their resolve. Few fled London for safer terrain—not even the royal family, who remained in Buckingham Palace as an example to the British people.

But Joe Kennedy left. He had sent his wife and children

home shortly after the declaration of war, and within a month of the first attack, he rented a seventy-room country mansion, spending more and more time there as the bombings increased. Criticism of Kennedy mushroomed. He was accused of using strong-arm tactics to gain scarce shipping space for his liquor cargo on transatlantic transport, and of having made a hundred-thousand-dollar profit by selling Czech securities on the London exchange in anticipation of the German invasion. He was denounced as a coward on the floor of Parliament, and Winston Churchill, the new prime minister, urged Roosevelt to recall Kennedy. As England's valiant struggle rallied more and more Americans to the British cause, Roosevelt saw no recourse but to do so. In November, he accepted Joe Kennedy's resignation.

After he returned home, Joe told associates that Britain had better get used to living under German rule, and he said publicly that "democracy is finished in England." His obstinate defeatism made him the object of British ridicule for years, and it left May Lawford with a bitter hatred for him and his family that she carried the rest of her life: "The fire of hell," she spat, "isn't too hot for old Kennedy!"

THE LAWFORDS had been told in August 1939 that the villa they lived in would soon no longer be available to them, and they were looking for alternate accommodations when word came that Sir Sydney's bank accounts back home had been frozen. Because of the war, no sterling was allowed to leave England; the only way the Lawfords could have access to what little money they still had would be to return to London.

Sir Sydney strongly wanted to do so. A military man to his marrow, he longed to be in some way a part of Britain's war effort, despite his approaching seventy-fourth birthday. May refused. She was still loath to face the whispers and disapproving glances she was sure awaited her because Freddie Bartholomew had cast doubt upon Peter's paternity. And she didn't want to endanger her family—especially the son who, clearly, was the best hope for her to retain anything like the grand style of living to which she was accustomed.

May, as usual, got her way. The Lawfords remained in Palm Beach, but were unable to convince anyone else to put them up or lend them a house, and they had no luck borrowing money. According to Louise Barker, May wrote to Louise's mother, a casual acquaintance, to ask for a loan, which Mrs. Barker was unable to make. May did manage to borrow a few hundred dollars, and the Lawfords moved to a lesser section of Palm Beach's considerably poorer neighbor, West Palm Beach. Their new home was a small, shabbily furnished Spanish-style bungalow near a railroad track on Avenida Hermosa that they rented for forty dollars a month. It was drafty and in need of repair. The plumbing leaked, the heating system was temperamental, and every few hours the walls would rattle with the deafening rumble of a passing freight train.

It was the first time he had experienced "the other side of the tracks," Peter said, and it was a shock for the whole family. May reacted to her reduced circumstances more emotionally than she had to anything since her nervous breakdown twenty years earlier. She was, she said, in a "terrible condition." She would drink too much and burst into tears at the slightest provocation. Her hands shook so badly she dropped teacups; if one of them broke, "I would just go all to pieces."

When she wasn't crying in her bedroom she was "crabby and irritable"—especially so because, for the first time in her life, she had no servants and had to do household chores herself. It was a major problem for her. As a child, she hadn't been allowed in the kitchen; Victorian ladies of a certain station were not expected to toil over a stove. Thus, at fifty-six, May Lawford had no idea of how to cook.

Her first attempt to light the oven almost ended in tragedy when gas fumes ignited, spewing out a fireball that seared off her eyebrows and some of her hair. She was hospitalized with second-degree burns. When she came home she decided to try again, and made a chicken. It was an unforgettable meal, Peter later said. "I think she boiled it. It was like rubber. You could have bounced it from the floor to the ceiling. But we ate it. Most of her other dishes were pretty bleak, but we ate those, too. We didn't have much choice."

May's culinary skills improved, but the family's financial situation didn't. Peter had just turned sixteen and hadn't been tutored for several years. He should have enrolled in Palm Beach High School, but he was the only possible breadwinner, and he instead went to work pumping gas at a filling station in West Palm Beach. Friends who had looked on the Lawfords as "some kind of royalty" were appalled. "When I heard he was peddling gas," Muriel O'Brien recalled, "I almost had a stroke. I felt very badly for him. He was very embarrassed, I'm sure."

He was, but on another level working brought him satisfaction. To hold down a job was a way for Peter to make a first tentative step toward independence from May, a start toward becoming more than a mama's boy. At the same time, ironically, it was a way to please his mother and win her approbation, something he craved as much as he craved freedom from her clutches. She made it clear to him that the family's financial welfare was now his responsibility, and he took it very seriously. As he had all through his childhood, Peter would do everything it took to keep his mother happy, calm, and on firm emotional footing.

Peter's stint as a gas jockey didn't last long; it soon led to a much better position parking cars at Carl Brukenfeld's lot behind Worth Avenue, the fashionable shopping center of Palm Beach. Peter didn't have a driver's license, but he had known how to drive since the age of eight, when his father had taught him as he sat on the general's lap behind the wheel. Brukenfeld found Peter polite, energetic, and able to take initiative, and after just a few weeks asked him to manage the lot and supervise two other boys his own age. They parked cars and occasionally washed them as well; Peter collected the monthly rents from the customers who worked in the area and parked there every weekday. His pay was twenty-five dollars a week plus tips. Peter later said, "I felt lucky to get it."

The tips were very good, because many of Brukenfeld's clients were among Palm Beach's wealthiest residents. The biggest tipper, the "heavy cat," as the boys called him, was Joe Kennedy, who regularly handed them a quarter when he claimed his car. (The standard gratuity was ten cents.)

But Peter's initial meetings with Joe Kennedy weren't all pleasant. Peter's fellow workers were both black, and when business was slow the three of them would sit under a tree at the side of the unpaved lot to cool off, eat ham and tomato sandwiches, and play penny ante poker.

The Kennedy patriarch wasn't pleased when he saw Peter fraternizing with his co-workers. He complained to Brukenfeld, "It doesn't look good to see the niggers sitting under the tree with the white boy." Brukenfeld held no prejudices but realized that in a southern city a reaction like Mr. Kennedy's wouldn't be an isolated one. Embarrassed, he told Peter it wasn't a good idea for all three of them to take their lunch break at the same time. "But we jump up when a car comes in," Peter replied, puzzled. Finally Brukenfeld told him the truth, that his friendliness with "the Negro boys" was hurting business. "I didn't understand," Peter later said—but he did as he was told.

It was Peter's first taste of racism. He harbored no prejudices himself; his world travels had exposed him to dozens of races, different skin colors, and exotic cultures. Although May was racist and anti-Semitic, she gave Peter free rein in his choice of playmates, "providing they had clean noses and no spots." In Nassau, Peter's friends were exclusively black. He learned at an early age to judge people by who they were and not by their religion or nationality or skin color.

Ironically, Peter suffered discrimination himself in Palm Beach, simply because he wasn't like most of the other kids. Muriel O'Brien's picture of him as "some kind of English idiot, the Earl of Clownsville" wasn't an isolated opinion. Connie Savage, a girl about his age whom he befriended in West Palm Beach, recalled that Peter didn't have many close friends. "The Palm Beachers aren't the easiest people to get friendly with," she said, "especially if you're a little different."

The local girls adored Peter, who seemed to grow better looking by the day, but his shyness kept him from getting close to most of them. The boys resented him, according to Connie, "because he had this British demeanor and he was an aristocrat." They taunted him, sniggered behind his back about his bum arm. They hid his motor scooter and waited until he had walked home to give it back to him.

Peter tried to fit in; he played tennis and gave rides to the other kids on his scooter, which his relative in New York had sent him. Tennis was a struggle. He had not been able to master using his left hand to serve, and his face flushed with embarrassment whenever he delivered a weak, inaccurate lob or lost a game to an inexperienced player.

But he had a piece of luck: one of the professionals who tutored the wealthy kids asked him if he was related to Herbert Lawford. When Peter said, "Yes, he's my uncle," the pros started treating him like a celebrity—Herbert Lawford, originator of the "Lawford stroke," was one of their idols. From then on the instructors gave Peter free lessons, working with him every day to teach him how to compensate for his handicap.

The first time he played really well, he ran all the way home and called out to his parents from the front yard. When May and Sir Sydney came out on the porch, Peter threw a ball in the air with his right hand and delivered a sizzling serve that sent the ball crashing through the living room window. Sir Sydney only laughed, delighted by his son's progress. "Break every window in the house if you like," he cried. "Good boy!"

In September 1940 Peter turned seventeen, and May realized that he was past the point of aspiring to be the next Freddie Bartholomew. Seventeen is an awkward age for an actor—too old to play adorable little boys and not old enough to be a leading man. Peter, although handsome, was thin, gangly, and uncoordinated. May would have to wait for her son to become the dashing movie star she was sure he was destined to be. Peter himself clearly felt that he was in a holding pattern in Palm Beach. He joined a small theater workshop to practice his craft until he could get back to Hollywood. And for the first time, he risked ridicule by telling one of his Palm Beach friends about his dreams of stardom.

Connie Savage never forgot the day Peter invited her to the house on Avenida Hermosa. As they sat alone in his living room, he showed her his scrapbook and told her that he had been in *Lord Jeff* and had done some movie work in England.

"Let me tell you what I'm going to do," he said. "I'm going to go to Hollywood and become a star."

"Peter!" Connie exclaimed. "How could you do that? Who do you know out there?"

"I know three people," he replied. "I know Mickey Rooney, Freddie Bartholomew, and Jane Withers."

Connie was awestruck. "It seemed like an impossible dream or something to me, but Peter said it like there was no question about it. 'I'm going to go to Hollywood and become a star,' he told me. Just like that."

ON DECEMBER 7, 1941, three months to the day after Peter's eighteenth birthday, Japanese bombers attacked the American naval base at Pearl Harbor, Hawaii. Within twenty-four hours, America was at war, and any able-bodied male between the ages of eighteen and thirty-five who didn't volunteer was soon drafted. In Hollywood, many of the leading male stars volunteered for service, either in Britain or in the United States—and there were few young actors available to take their places. Lucille Ryman was head of talent at MGM when America entered the war, and her orders were to "sign up any man who was six feet tall and 4-F. If we signed someone who had no talent, we just used him for background."

Peter heard about the shortage of men in Hollywood and recognized a golden opportunity. His arm disqualified him from military service, he was over six feet tall, he was extremely good-looking, and he had talent. Now there was no way, he thought, that he wouldn't make it big in Hollywood, just as he had bragged to Connie Savage that he would.

But how was he to get there? His income from the parking lot barely kept him and his parents in food and lodging. When he told the Palm Beach socialite Mary Sanford that he was going to Hollywood, she asked him how much money he had. "Ten dollars," he replied. "You're going to Hollywood with ten dollars?" she asked incredulously. "I have enough money," Peter insisted, "and I have a lot of friends out there if I need money in California." Mary offered to give him a few dollars, but he refused it.

Then he got a lucky break. One of the girls he played tennis with, Gloria Butler, told him that she and her mother were planning to drive to California but couldn't find a chauffeur willing to take them that far. "How about me?" Peter asked.

"You're joking!" Gloria responded.

"Certainly not," he replied. "I want to move to California anyway. Once we get out there you can hire someone to drive you back."

Mrs. Butler would have preferred a round-trip driver,

but she liked the idea of making the trip west with someone she and her daughter knew. She said Peter would be fine. Now he'd have to run the idea by May.

She was all for it and told Peter that she and Sir Sydney would follow in a few weeks—it was time to get Peter back to Hollywood and on track toward a movie career. Sir Sydney, seventy-six, was reluctant to uproot himself yet again, and even less excited by the fact that he and May would have to drive themselves across country. But he knew that in Hollywood, Peter could make a great deal more money, even in bit parts, than he could doing anything else in Palm Beach.

The day after Christmas, Peter and the Butlers embarked on their journey, which Peter recalled as "interminable." The threesome stopped at every conceivable landmark or point of interest along the way, and by the time they reached the Petrified Forest, Peter said, "we looked like we belonged there." Finally they arrived in Santa Barbara, where they checked into the Biltmore Hotel for a two-week stay, during which Peter and Gloria swam, played tennis, and sunbathed. It was his first taste in more than two years of the kind of life Peter had been used to, and he had to admit he missed it.

Back in Palm Beach, May was able to borrow a few hundred dollars and buy a questionably reliable 1929 jalopy for thirty-seven dollars. She loaded it up with as many of the family's possessions as she could fit in the trunk and backseat, made sure that Sir Sydney was as comfortable as possible in the passenger seat, and started out on a trek to California that took them through northern Florida, Alabama, Mississippi, Louisiana, Texas, New Mexico, and Arizona.

It was the most disheartening journey they had ever experienced—worse even than the time they had taken a tramp steamer to Tahiti in an effort to save money and the ship's refrigeration had gone bad, forcing them to live on rice and potatoes for almost a month. Every day they drove through dusty small towns; every night they stopped at a dingy motel. The food appalled them both; May thought that if she had to eat grits and gravy one more time she would surely die.

At last, they drove through the gates of the Biltmore in

Santa Barbara, their car sputtering and misfiring, and met up with their son. That night they stayed at an inexpensive but pleasant motel, and the next morning at dawn they began the trip down the coast to Los Angeles, all three excited by what lay ahead of them, all three marveling at the beauty of the California coastline, all three sensing that Los Angeles was where they would spend the rest of their lives.

PART TWO

A THOROUGHBRED IN THE MGM STABLE

"If Metro signed you, you were put into that machine—wrapped in cotton wool, looked after, looked over, looked under."
—Peter Lawford

SIX

WHEN THE Lawfords arrived in the Los Angeles area in the middle of January 1942 they realized they wouldn't be able to afford the cost of hotel rooms in Hollywood. Instead, they took up temporary residence in the low-priced Mission Bell Motel on Ventura Boulevard in the San Fernando Valley north of Los Angeles, then a sparsely developed area of citrus groves, horse ranches, and chicken farms. The motel was at the foot of a road that led to a sprawling property owned by Mickey Rooney, who was now the number-one box-office star in the world. Peter was so embarrassed by his family's financial straits that when he saw Rooney drive by one day in a gleaming new sports car he ducked behind a eucalyptus tree so that Mickey wouldn't see him.

The money May had borrowed for the trip west wouldn't last much longer, and Peter had to find work quickly. Ruth Collier had retired, so May made calls to some of the influential people whose paths they had crossed in 1938. She learned that Sue Carol, a former actress and now Mrs. Alan Ladd, had recently opened a talent agency and had decided to specialize in "impressive young people" and build a stable of promising young players.

Peter was nothing if not that, and Carol took him on. She knew that British actors would soon be very much in demand in Hollywood because the movie industry planned to produce a spate of war propaganda films. Americans and British would be fighting side by side in Europe against

Hitler and Mussolini, and there would be plenty of roles fo
young Englishmen in Hollywood's versions of the war. O
the back of Peter's first photo composite, Carol wrote prom
inently, "British."

May knew that Peter needed to be closer to the cente
of the action if he were to be available at a moment's notic
for auditions. (The bus trip from the valley to Hollywoo
took two hours.) She found a small apartment on Benecia
Avenue in the Rancho Park area that rented for forty dollar
a month and was just a few minutes' walk from the Twenti
eth Century-Fox studios and a couple of miles from MGM

The Los Angeles the Lawfords settled into early in 1942
was a city full of contradictions, unlike any other major
metropolitan area the family had ever lived in. Because of
the movie industry's situation in and around it, Los Angeles
had become world famous, but it was far from being world
class. Culturally, as Marlon Brando put it a decade later, it
was a "boneyard." There was no opera company, no ballet
company, no major art museum. Geographically, it was
spread out so loosely that Dorothy Parker called it "seventy-
two suburbs in search of a city."

Los Angeles, in fact, was largely a company town in
1942, like any other except that the companies happened to
be movie studios and defense plants. Within Hollywood,
community life was shaped by the studios' business. There
was little nightlife, except on the weekends; a good many
of LA's denizens were in bed by ten o'clock in order to get
up at four-thirty or five A.M. and head for the studio.
Makeup and wardrobe people would have to be there by
six o'clock to make the stars ready to face the cameras by
eight; executives would have to be there even earlier to
make phone calls to the money men in New York as soon
as they began their day on the East Coast.

The Lawfords loved living in Southern California. The
hot, dry weather was soothing to May's and Sir Sydney's
arthritis and Peter's still-healing arm, and Peter was thrilled
to have beaches within a half hour's drive. He marveled at
the climate: he had never before lived in an area so near an
ocean that wasn't oppressively humid.

May adored the scent of night-blooming jasmine and
citrus blossoms that wafted through her windows in the evenings, and she appreciated the fact that in this desert climate

even the hottest days were followed by relatively cool evenings. All three Lawfords were certain they'd moved to paradise.

Their own small part of that paradise, however, left a lot to be desired. They possessed not a stick of furniture, and the apartment on Benecia Avenue was unfurnished. Peter took on the challenge of decorating it as cheaply as possible. He found a store with a bargain basement in downtown LA, where he bought a mahogany dining room set for forty-nine dollars, a brown-chintz-covered living room suite for thirty dollars, and a lamp with an onyx base for three dollars.

Sue Carol, in the meantime, had less luck finding Peter parts. She sent him on a few auditions without success: Hollywood's rash of war-movie productions hadn't started yet. There were a few being filmed, but those had already been cast. Peter was finally forced to admit to Sue that he needed to find a job—*any* job—or his family's financial situation would become desperate. She told him that the Village Theater in Westwood, owned by MGM's parent company, Loew's Inc., had an opening for an usher. Peter went for an interview and was hired on the spot for fifteen dollars a week.

Five days a week he hopped on the westbound trolley on Santa Monica Boulevard and then transferred to the northbound one on Westwood Boulevard to the theater, where he donned his gray striped pants and white gloves and showed people to their seats to see a movie.

And every day he telephoned Sue Carol to ask if any acting jobs had appeared on the horizon. To his deepening discouragement, the answer was always no. With his youthful impatience, he didn't reflect on the fact that he'd been in Hollywood less than two months and that many screen hopefuls seek employment for years. He was wildly eager to *do something*—and he was mortified to be ushering when he should be making movies. When MGM held a preview of Mickey Rooney's latest film at the Village, Peter once again avoided Mickey, hiding his face as the movie's star was led down the aisle to his seat.

Then, after Peter had worked at the Village a few weeks, he got a call from Sue Carol at the start of a busy Saturday: "MGM is looking for a British boy your age for

Mrs. Miniver!" Peter asked a co-worker to cover for him hopped on a trolley down Westwood to Washington Boulevard, and sprinted the four blocks to the imposing Metro front gate.

Within minutes, he was on the *Miniver* set, where one of the picture's climactic scenes, in an air force base, was being filmed. The movie starred Greer Garson and Walter Pidgeon and revolved around an upper-crust London family's courage and sacrifice in the face of Hitler's blitz. In the scene being filmed that day, Mrs. Miniver (Garson), her son (Richard Ney), and his fiancée (Teresa Wright) had driven onto the base when an air raid siren begins to wail.

Director William Wyler needed a fresh-faced young man to play a flier who runs past Mrs. Miniver's car in response to the sirens and yells just one line. The assistant director handed Peter and three other boys a side of dialogue to read. Wyler listened to all four and then pointed at Peter. "He's good." The AD dismissed the other boys and told Peter, "Okay, run up to wardrobe and get your flying suit."

"Now?" Peter asked, dumbstruck.

"Not tomorrow! We're making a picture!"

Peter had thought he'd have to wait a week to hear if he'd been hired and another week to do the scene. But his bit had been a last-minute addition to the script, and Wyler wanted it in the can *today*. Dazed, Peter got into his RAF uniform and helmet, listened carefully as the AD explained the scene to him, and waited for Wyler to call, "Action!" When he did, Peter ran across the set and yelled into Greer Garson's car, "The Jerries are over London in the hundreds. Looks like a big show!"

Before six that evening, Peter was back at the Village Theater, filling in for the girl who'd covered for him that afternoon and regaling his young co-workers with stories of his day on an MGM soundstage. His appearance in *Mrs. Miniver* lasts only a few seconds, and he's unrecognizable unless one knows where to look for him. But it was a start, and Peter was thrilled.

Mrs. Miniver was the biggest hit of 1942. It netted Metro a profit of nearly five million dollars, a staggering sum for the period, and won seven Oscars, including best picture and best actress. Its success had as much to do with the patriotism sweeping America as with the film's quality, and before long a tidal wave of war movies burst forth, with Peter playing bit parts in many of them: Universal's *Eagle Squadron;* Republic–British Lion's *The Purple V, Someone to Remember,* and *The London Blackout Murders;* and Twentieth Century-Fox's *The Immortal Sergeant.*

Peter's ten-dollar per diem income as a day player on these pictures, although sporadic, was a welcome addition to the family's meager finances. It wasn't enough, though, when he was fired from his ushering job after he was caught sneaking friends into the theater. Happily, Sue Carol called within a few days to tell him that he'd been offered a six-week assignment as an extra in another flyboy picture, *Thunder Birds,* a Twentieth Century-Fox film with Gene Tierney. He'd have to go to Phoenix, he was told, and because it was a location shoot he'd be paid a hundred dollars a week. Peter was ecstatic. In six weeks he'd have a bankroll it would have taken him five months of ushering to save.

He went to Phoenix in May and had worked on *Thunder Birds* for two weeks when a telegram came from Sue Carol: "MGM over a barrel. Can't find English boy for major role in 'Yank at Eton' with Bartholomew and Rooney. Picture starts next week. Director will see you if you can come to LA. Can you get off the picture? Please advise."

Peter's head swam as he put the yellow piece of paper in his pocket. *A major role!* But he might not be able to get out of his *Thunder Birds* contract, and even if he did, there was no guarantee he'd get the part in *A Yank at Eton.* Then he'd be back where he was before, broke and unemployed. He couldn't sleep that night as he weighed his options and agonized over what was best to do. Whatever his decision, he vowed, he'd make it without any consultations with his mother.

He decided the gamble was worth it. He approached the assistant director and told him about his dilemma. The man knew that the opportunity that had presented itself to Peter was extraordinary. "Sure," he said, "go ahead. What's another extra more or less? I'll get you a release."

Peter returned to Los Angeles on a day coach, feeling as hot as the Arizona desert: he'd caught the flu and had a 103-degree fever. Sue Carol met him at Union Station in downtown Los Angeles and drove him the ten miles to

MGM, where his audition was scheduled for that afternoon. On the way, he made Sue stop at a gas station so he could vomit. All the time his worst worry was that the film's director, Norman Taurog, would shake his hand, wonder what was wrong with his arm, and decide not to cast him.

Much to Peter's relief, that didn't happen. Taurog told him the part was a boys' school bully and asked him to be prepared to read for him in an hour. Peter studied the sides of dialogue and thought about all the encounters with bullies he'd had in his life. Then, weak and dizzy, he read for Taurog. When he was finished, the director said, "You've got the part. We start on Monday."

Sick and feverish, still Peter was ecstatic. He remembered later that he thought to himself, *This is it. My first real part. Now I'm a star.* It certainly was a leap up from day work. His part was the third lead and paid him two hundred dollars a week for six weeks, a substantial sum compared to the Lawfords' income over the last four years. May celebrated by preparing a steak dinner for the family, and all through the meal she wavered between waxing grandiose about Peter's future and warning him not to blow this chance. Then she put Peter to bed for three days so he'd be healthy for the first day's shooting.

A Yank at Eton was developed to capitalize on the 1938 success of *A Yank at Oxford,* which had starred Robert Taylor. The story concerns an American high-school football player (Mickey Rooney) who enrolls at Eton after his mother marries an Englishman and proceeds to trample on British tradition and get himself in trouble. Along the way he battles Ronnie Kenvil (Peter), a snobby, conniving upperclassman determined to keep him out of the school steeplechase competition. Kenvil sets the American up to be blamed for a barroom brawl, but at the last minute the Yank proves himself innocent and is allowed to run the race—in which he bests Kenvil.

The film was shot on the MGM lot and on location in Connecticut, and it afforded Peter his first taste of everyday life at Metro as a featured player. He arrived at the studio at seven A.M. and went straight to makeup, where he was given a light pancake base and a dusting of powder to make his skin less reflective. Then the wardrobe women outfitted him in his uncomfortable Eton schoolboy uniform: a formal black suit, high-collared starched white shirt, and black tie.

He reported to the set at eight A.M. and then, more days than not, experienced the bane of all movie actors: the interminable waiting. He waited while scenes were set up. He waited while lights and camera angles were adjusted. He waited while the director conferred with the producer and the producer conferred with the star. He waited while takes were reshot for one reason or another. For only a small fraction of his day did he do what he was hired to do: act.

After a morning's shoot on *A Yank at Eton,* Peter, Mickey, Freddie, and the others would lunch at the fabled MGM commissary. The studio's patriarch, Louis B. Mayer, ordered that it be, like everything else at MGM, the best of its kind. Its decor was created by Cedric Gibbons, who designed the Oscar statuette and won the second Academy Award ever given for set decoration. Green and chromium, the enormous room had a seating capacity of 225 and served lunch to twelve hundred people every day. Mickey Rooney usually sat with Judy Garland and MGM's other young musical stars at a table set aside for the Music Department, and that's where Peter ate his lunch during *A Yank at Eton* filming. He was awestruck at the number of stars he had long admired who were on the lot at the time and whom he would see in the commissary from time to time: Spencer Tracy and Katharine Hepburn, beginning *Keeper of the Flame;* Joan Crawford filming *Reunion in France;* Hedy Lamarr shooting *White Cargo;* Lana Turner making *Slightly Dangerous;* and Robert Taylor working on *Stand by for Action.*

To Peter's joy, there were also dozens of beautiful young women just starting out at MGM for him to gawk at, among them Ava Gardner, Kathryn Grayson, Esther Williams, Donna Reed, Marilyn Maxwell, Gloria De Haven, June Lockhart, and Cyd Charisse. It was enough to distract a young man from his lunch. What Peter was too excited to notice at first was that most of these dazzlers were checking him out thoroughly as well.

After a month of studio work, the cast and crew of *A Yank at Eton* moved to Connecticut for location work. Peter found the month and a half he spent there very pleasurable. There were fewer restrictions on him three thousand miles away from May and the studio heads, and although Mickey Rooney had just married Ava Gardner, while alone on location with his buddies he acted like a bachelor. Mickey, Freddie, and Peter spent most scene breaks playing poker and most evenings barhopping.

Still, for all the camaraderie on the set of *A Yank at Eton,* Peter took his job seriously. He worked hard, and his efforts show: he's very good in the picture. As the *Daily Variety* reviewer put it, Peter "ably enacts" the rather thankless Kenvil role, second only to Rooney's in length and impact. He more than holds his own in his exchanges with the veteran scene-stealer, and it is fascinating now to watch him as an eighteen-year-old lad on the cusp of manhood. He looks handsome and adult in a jacket, tie, and camel-hair topcoat, but in the film's climactic sequence, in which Peter runs the steeplechase wearing shorts and tank top, his youth is betrayed by his stick-thin, gangly body, all arms and legs.

When *A Yank at Eton* was released in October to huge box-office grosses and good reviews for Peter, he and Sue Carol were convinced that he would immediately be cast in other important roles and then be signed to an MGM contract. It didn't happen. There were still a limited number of major roles for British boys his age, so it was back to extra bits, to day work in a number of movies for various studios.

Over the next year, Peter worked for Universal, Twentieth Century-Fox, RKO, Columbia, and Republic–British Lion, but it was Metro-Goldwyn-Mayer that most fascinated him. The studio was the Tiffany of Hollywood, and if Peter was impressed with that, May was positively adamant that it was at MGM that Peter ought to be. She continually telephoned Sue Carol to badger her about getting Peter a contract with the studio, and each time Carol patiently explained that she was doing the best she could.

Metro did put Peter in several major productions, among them *Random Harvest* (with Greer Garson again), which was an enormous hit, and *Above Suspicion,* Joan Crawford's last MGM film after eighteen years with the studio. But he was still a mere extra. He began to fear that *A Yank at Eton* had been a fluke and that his one big acting opportunity had been wasted. Then, in a twist that could happen only in Hollywood, a brief, uncredited, nonspeaking role in his next picture finally won Peter entree into the gilded circle of MGM contract players.

Peter was hired as an extra on George Sidney's unusual war drama, *Pilot #5,* starring Franchot Tone, Gene Kelly,

Marsha Hunt, and Van Johnson. Tone played a flier chosen for a suicide mission against the Japanese in Java. The story is told in flashbacks and it ends as he embarks on his final mission. Sidney decided at the last minute that he wanted the film to end more emotionally than with just a shot of Tone's plane taking off. Noticing Peter, a beautiful boy barely out of childhood incongruously dressed in the vestments of war, the director saw his ending. He shot Peter in tight close-up, his angelic face etched with concern as his eyes follow the plane's liftoff toward his fellow flier's certain death. The young airman senses that he is watching his own future as well.

George Sidney's wife, Lillian Burns, was the head drama coach at MGM, and she remembers vividly the impact Peter's close-up had on all who saw the film. "Peter's face was just magical," she says. "He had tremendous charisma in that scene. The look on his face, in that one shot, caused him to be put under contract to MGM."

An MGM contract! Peter was beside himself when he signed the document on June 7, 1943. He was still a teenager, and he could scarcely believe its terms: a one-year agreement with an option for a second year, it paid him one hundred dollars a week with a guarantee of forty weeks' work a year and an increase to two hundred dollars a week if it was renewed. (It was a good contract; by contrast, Janet Leigh's starting salary in 1947 was fifty dollars a week with three-month renewal options.)

The other terms were all in MGM's favor, and it was clear that Peter Lawford was now the property of Metro-Goldwyn-Mayer. He could not do stage or radio work, or act for any other studio, without MGM's permission, but MGM could lend him out to anyone else whenever it so chose without additional compensation to him. Should his appearance or his voice change in any substantial way, or should he become unable to work, or should he refuse to perform in any picture for any reason, he could be summarily suspended without pay. In fact, the contract could be terminated at any time, for any reason, at MGM's whim.

His private life was no longer his own; another clause informed him that if he committed "any act or thing that would tend to bring him into public hatred, contempt, scorn or ridicule or tend to shock, insult or offend the community," he could be suspended or terminated. Even his name was on tenuous footing. Not only could the studio change it, they could change it as often as they liked: "We may advertise and/or publicize him under his true name, or under any fictitious, assumed, professional or stage name or names we may select from time to time."

But Peter paid no heed to the fine print. He was ecstatic to be an MGM contract player, guaranteed four thousand dollars a year, with the vast resources of the finest studio in the world at his disposal. He would receive acting lessons, dancing lessons, singing lessons. He would be taught to fence, taught to feign a fistfight, taught to use the lights and the cameras to his advantage.

To Peter's thinking, Metro was by far the best studio he could have signed with, and not just because it was the most prestigious and had the most facilities to help him become a success. Far more important, MGM was the perfect studio for Peter Lawford's temperament. It was a fiefdom in which Louis B. Mayer's serfs did whatever he demanded, and in return had all of their needs completely taken care of. Peter had grown up with maids, butlers, tailors, and valets; at MGM he had them all once again.

For most of his life—lonely as it had been—Peter had been swathed in a cocoon of creature comforts. At MGM, he would enter another cocoon, one that sat on two hundred acres in Culver City and employed three thousand men and women to manufacture America's dreams out of papiermâché, makeup, paint, and tinsel. Now, in June 1943, many of these people, among the most talented artisans of their kind in the world, would begin to make their studio's newest contract player's dream a reality: they would turn Peter Lawford into a movie star.

A FEW WEEKS after Peter signed his contract, he and his parents were taken to meet Louis B. Mayer. Sitting in the waiting room outside Mayer's baronial office, Peter thought about the power the mogul now held over his life and trembled like the Tin Man waiting to see the Wizard of Oz.

Mayer had risen from a scrap dealer to a theater owner to a film distributor by the age of thirty, when he made a fortune by obtaining distribution rights to D. W. Griffith's *The Birth of a Nation* in 1915. He then went into film production, and in 1924 he merged his Louis B. Mayer Productions with Metro Pictures and Goldwyn Pictures to form MGM.

What Mayer created was a virtual movie factory. There were stables of actors, directors, producers, and writers, all of whom were paid weekly salaries and had to be available at any time for any project.

On its surface this structure seems incompatible with artistic accomplishment, but Mayer was able to produce some of the greatest films of the thirties and forties by this method. The reason was money. MGM was the only studio to show a profit during the early years of the Great Depression, when Paramount, Twentieth Century-Fox, and RKO went bankrupt. In 1937 its net profits were over fourteen million dollars, a success level the studio maintained for almost a decade afterward. Thus it had the money to create lavishly produced "event" movies with the finest talent available. Metro was able to pay such high salaries (some of its writers, directors, and stars were being paid five thousand dollars per week in the 1930s) that the studio—even at its dehumanizing assembly-line worst—could attract just about any talent it wanted.

An emotionally complex man, Louis B. Mayer was a thick-skinned, hard-driving businessman who could summarily suspend a wayward employee, but who also took such a personal interest in all of his contractees that they might have been his children. Robert Taylor remembered Mayer as "kind, understanding, fatherly, and protective, always there when I had problems." But the screenwriter and wit Herman Mankiewicz said of Mayer, "He had the memory of an elephant and the hide of an elephant. The only difference is that elephants are vegetarians and Mayer's diet was his fellow man."

On that warm June day in 1943, all the nineteen-year-old Peter Lawford knew was that he was about to meet the most powerful man in Hollywood, a man in whose hands his future rested. Mayer's environment certainly reflected his position. Just as MGM's artisans and technicians built wondrous worlds for the movies, so had they created Mayer's office as a monument to his power. It was so large that Sam Goldwyn quipped, "You need an automobile to reach the desk." Furnished entirely in white—the walls, the carpet, the enormous round desk, the grand piano—it was designed to inspire awe of the man who sat behind the desk. And it did.

The man himself was disconcertingly short, but one forgot that when confronted by his intense black eyes, which instantly sized up all who entered his domain. Now, he was appraising his newest contract player and his parents, and he liked what he saw. Mayer had been a poor Russian Jewish immigrant, and he was fascinated by the trappings of wealth and nobility. The Lawfords, of course, had nothing but the trappings, but Mayer didn't know that. He heard the clipped accents and May's liberal use of French phrases; he saw Sir Sydney's regal bearing; he was told of the general's valor in war and his knighting by King George. It was impressive stuff, and Mayer was duly impressed. He called May "the thoroughbred mare" and later told her—during an argument—that she was the only person in the world from whom he would take such verbal abuse.

Now, however, all was pleasantries. Mayer startled Peter when he characterized his employment at MGM as an act of patriotism and told him that despite his 4-F classification, Peter could help the war effort by doing the best work he could in the war dramas in which the studio planned to cast him. Peter assured Mayer that he would do his best for MGM and world peace, and finally he and his parents were ushered out of Mayer's office.

He was scheduled for his first full day of employment the following Monday. For a week, he listened as May harangued him with her lists of dos and don'ts: Play by the rules. Do what the studio tells you. Don't make trouble. Work hard. Don't jeopardize this opportunity. Get along. Don't let me and your father down. Don't disgrace the family. And above all, Peter, *make sure you do whatever you have to do to become a star.*

Peter Lawford was perfect fodder for the MGM personality manufacturers. He was pleasant, agreeable, and malleable: all the things May told him he must be to become a success. And Metro was primed to mold him. That first Monday on the lot, he was taken to Howard Strickling, MGM's chief of publicity, who listened to his life story and knew instinctively that it was good copy. Was there anything, Strickling asked him, anything at all, that he was holding back? Anything that might prove, well, embarrassing if the press got hold of it? "If you tell me now, Peter, I can make sure that anything like that stays out of the press. Or if we can't keep it out of the press, I can make sure it's revealed in the most positive light possible. I don't want any surprises when I open my morning paper."

Peter wasn't exactly sure what Strickling was talking about. He knew nothing about his questionable paternity, so that issue was never raised. He did tell Strickling that his family was very low on money, that their funds had been frozen in England because of the war. "That's nothing to be ashamed of," Strickling told him. "We'll play up the sacrifice for the war effort angle. By the way, why aren't you in the service?" Peter told him about his arm injury, and Strickling instructed him to bring that up in every interview. "We don't want people wondering why you're not fighting this war."

Confident there weren't any skeletons in the Lawford family closet, Strickling assigned one of his thirty-five minions to take Peter around to the various studio departments for his introduction to the MGM star-making machine.

The first stop on Peter's rounds was the wardrobe department, where he was outfitted for his first studio portrait session. The wardrobe woman took one look at him and knew he'd be easy to fit. He had by now filled out into a perfectly proportioned young male—he was over six feet tall, with broad shoulders and slim hips—and clothes would hang well on him. She took his measurements (fifteen-and-a-half-inch neck, thirty-five-inch sleeve, twenty-nine-long pant, thirty-eight-regular jacket), created a file on him for future reference, and dressed him in a light tweed, double-breasted brown suit with a subtle plaid pattern, a light blue shirt, and a dark maroon tie with a tiny brown print.

Now he was ready to be photographed. In Clarence Sinclair Bull's studio, some of the world's most glamorous people had been made to seem even more beautiful. Some needed to have their hairlines changed with electrolysis, their teeth fixed, their noses bobbed, or their hair dyed. One of Bull's staff photographers looked Peter over approvingly from top to bottom—there was very little that would have to be done with this young man. His hair was thick and lustrous, his hairline perfect. His eyebrows were bushy but they didn't meet over the top of his nose as some heavy brows did—no need to trim them. His teeth were straight and white, his smile engaging. "What about my nose?" Peter asked self-consciously. "It's a little big, isn't it?"

The photographer assured Peter that his nose was no problem, and told him that his flawless skin reflected light beautifully. (May's strict dietary rules had paid some dividends.) It was obvious that Peter's face was made for the camera. He posed with delight for a series of portraits, acting for the still camera as he might for the motion picture— now thoughtful, now happy, now sullen, now boyish. When the photographer saw the results of one of the "looks" he had tried on Peter—his hair severely slicked down, his expression pouty—he quickly rejected it, and the surviving portrait shows why: he looked much better with his wavy hair left natural and his engaging smile allowed to shine.

After a quick lunch at the commissary, Peter was whisked away to meet Lillian Burns, MGM's drama coach, who usually coached actors only for specific roles, but who often made herself available on Friday afternoons to anyone who wanted her to critique a scene they had prepared. Miss Burns—as everyone on the lot called her—was favorably impressed with Peter. "Peter was talented," she recalled. "He had a real personality, and ability. He was charming and likable. But he was also the most insecure of the many young people that I've known—he had almost an inferiority complex."

Miss Burns didn't feel that Peter needed her help very much. "I don't think you can teach acting. You can teach the fundamentals—voice, diction, speech, body movement— the technical things. But Peter didn't really need that. He had good diction, a good voice. What Peter needed was self-development; he needed help in becoming his own man."

With its extraordinary policy of producing one picture per week, MGM had plenty of movies in which to place a neophyte contract player. They put Peter to work immediately as a last-minute extra in *Girl Crazy*, but they viewed him as valuable chiefly for productions requiring Brits, and there weren't any of those on the lot at that time.

And so, after appearing in just one MGM picture as an extra since he'd signed his contract, Peter was lent out to other studios. It was a common—and lucrative—practice:

if Metro didn't have enough work for one of its players, his services would be provided to another studio, usually at considerably more per week than MGM was paying him. The studio, of course, pocketed the difference. Over the next few months, Peter worked at Columbia in *Sahara,* starring Humphrey Bogart; at Universal on *Flesh and Fantasy,* with Barbara Stanwyck and Edward G. Robinson; and at Twentieth Century-Fox in *Paris After Dark,* with George Sanders.

Finally, in September, Metro went into production with exactly the kind of film they had hired Peter Lawford for. On his twentieth birthday he was added to the cast of a prestige war picture, *The White Cliffs of Dover,* featuring Irene Dunne, one of Hollywood's top stars, and Alan Marshal. Peter grew excited as he read the script. The role was an important one, his biggest and most challenging since *A Yank at Eton:* he would play John Ashwood II, the adult son of an American woman and an English nobleman killed in World War I. Young Ashwood is now fighting in World War II and his mother fears she will lose her son to this war as she did her husband to the earlier conflict.

Peter found working with Irene Dunne a rewarding experience. Forty-three and the veteran of such classics as *Cimarron, Magnificent Obsession,* and *Show Boat,* Dunne took a liking to the young Englishman playing her son. She later recalled him as "a dear, dear sweet person," and—as he freely admitted—she helped his performance tremendously. "Miss Dunne would take me to the rushes each evening," he told an interviewer in 1945. "She'd have me watch a scene I'd worked in. Then she'd point out my mistakes. . . . Afternoons, while we were working in the picture, she'd rehearse with me. She was so patient and kind. No young actor has ever been helped so much by a star."

In the film's final scene, Ashwood, wounded in battle, lies in a hospital as his mother, a nurse, comforts him. The scene, Peter knew, would require a good deal of dramatic skill, and he did turn to Lillian Burns for help before the filming began. The coaching he received from both Dunne and Burns paid dividends; Peter is very touching as the dying soldier.

When *The White Cliffs of Dover* was released in May 1944, it met with tremendous critical acclaim and netted

MGM a healthy profit of $1.7 million. More important to Peter, he got the kind of notices young actors dream about. The Los Angeles *Examiner* critic's comments were typical: "The news of the picture is an English newcomer, Peter Lawford, who heads straight for the top in his role as the son grown to manhood. Peter is a different and interesting personality who possesses all the qualities that contribute to eventual stardom."

He kept the clipping in his wallet and walked on air for a week after it was published. But he was brought rudely back down to earth when he went to see the film at a local theater. He was surrounded, he recalled, by a group of noisy children. "Just as I was dying on screen I heard the sound of popcorn rattling out of bags. Then a voice behind me called out, 'He's not so hot.'"

SEVEN

ON JUNE 7, 1944, Peter's contract was picked up for another year, and his salary was raised to two hundred dollars per week. This translates to nearly a thousand dollars a week in 1991 dollars, and for the Lawfords, who just three years earlier had been living on twenty-five dollars a week and tips, it was real affluence. To celebrate, Peter bought a 1940 Mercury convertible four-door sedan, blue with red leather interior, and began the systematic purchase of a sparkling new wardrobe. The Lawfords moved a few blocks, to a much nicer but still "tiny" house on Comstock Avenue.

There were no other major expenditures. May didn't trust the money to keep coming, and she didn't want to risk their future security. Most of Peter's salary went into a savings account, and the Lawfords continued to live almost as frugally as they had for the past five years. They were still without servants, and each member of the family had specific chores to do around the house. May usually prepared supper, but Peter often cooked breakfast. He also mopped floors and made the beds. Sir Sydney, seventy-eight now, was spared anything heavier than dusting and helping to dry the dishes.

Peter's life at this point was a study in dichotomy. On the one hand he was a young man who still lived with his parents, hadn't cut his mother's apron strings, and was responsible for household chores. On the other, he was a rising young star beginning to make an impact in the glamour capital of the world. He had quickly become a staple at Hollywood's swell night spots—such as the Mocambo, the Trocadero, and Ciro's—where he was never refused a drink although he wasn't yet twenty-one.

Hollywood's nightlife was confined to the weekends, but what weekends they were! The biggest movie stars in the world partied to the hilt, their merrymaking as much business as pleasure. It was important for stars—both fledgling and veteran—to be seen by fans and photographed for movie magazines. Couples the studio wanted to promote as romantic pairs would dance cheek to cheek at Ciro's; a long-married celebrity who wanted to scotch separation rumors might dine with his wife by candlelight at "the Troc."

The clubs provided romantic intrigue galore, and gossip columnists got their scoops flitting from table to table. Ex-husbands rubbed shoulders with ex-wives and their new spouses; spurned lovers did a slow burn as they watched the object of their recent affection whirl around the dance floor with a sexy new paramour.

Lana Turner was one of the most regular—and glamorous—of the Mocambo revelers. Steve Crane, her second husband, considered the Mocambo "the perfect setting for a young man on the make," and it certainly was that for Peter. There and in the other clubs, he charmed some of the most beautiful women in the world: Rhonda Fleming, Anne Baxter, Betty Grable, Judy Garland, Ava Gardner, and Marilyn Maxwell, among others. Witty, a marvelous dancer, his English manners and accent impressive to everyone, Peter soon became one of the most sought after dates in Hollywood. The things about him that had alienated the teenagers of Manhasset and Palm Beach were precisely what entranced the show biz set.

Hollywood adored the British. Like Louis B. Mayer, most of the actors, producers, writers, and directors had come from humble beginnings, and they fawned over anyone who seemed to possess the breeding and background they pretended to. The British community in Hollywood was assiduously courted, because their presence lent an aura of genuine sophistication and elegance to any function—just as Sir Sydney and Lady Lawford's had to Palm Beach parties.

The British had mastered it all centuries earlier—the courtliness, the regal carriage, the precise speech patterns, the fastidious dress, the showy dinner parties. Hollywood was nothing if not a community in love with artifice and the trappings of "class," and the surest signs of success were the purchase of a grand house, the hiring of a butler and a governess for the children, and the purchase of a Rolls-Royce. Then, a lavish party—to show everyone that the host and hostess were "to the manor born."

Peter Lawford *was* to the manor born, and although his family was now relatively poor, he had what no amount of money could ever buy: genuine breeding. More than it had anywhere else in the world, Peter's upbringing served him well in Hollywood.

PETER PURSUED still another life, one that many of his friends believe reflected his true personality: the life-style of the California beach scene. The beaches along the coast west of Los Angeles were uncrowded and pristine in 1942, dotted with small refreshment stands and a few umbrellas, and were the favorite spots of an athletic, sun-worshipping group of youngsters who glowed with vitality and golden tans.

Most of the boys at the beach either were too young to serve in the armed forces or were 4-F, and they put the war out of their minds except during the occasional blackout or when news of an injured or killed friend or relative intruded into their idyll. They had carved out a separate peace on the white sand along the warm and shimmering California coast, trying to hold on to the innocence of their youth as long as possible, playing volleyball, surfing, frolicking in the water by day, drinking beer and romancing girls on the sand at night.

As soon as he arrived in Hollywood, Peter sought out the friendship of these habitués of Malibu and State and Venice beaches who were having fun in the sun twenty years before the Beach Boys and *Gidget* and the surfing craze swept the country. They were attractive young people, down-to-earth and unpretentious. The friends Peter made "doing the beach scene" remained his friends for the rest of his life.

One of them was Peter Sabiston, now a Hollywood agent, who noticed Peter watching his volleyball team play at Santa Monica Beach. Peter approached Sabiston, introduced himself, and asked how he could get into the game. "I didn't know who he was," Sabiston recalled. "I told him that you had to put your name on a list. The guys who won would stay on the court and be challenged by the guys on the list. We played two-man teams, so you had to have a partner. We got him into the game that day. It's not as easy as it looks, but he was reasonably proficient at it. Peter was a very good athlete. He was able to overcome the handicap of his bad arm because he had natural ability."

Peter loved the informality of the beach; after a week of wearing makeup and the clothing of a Victorian gentleman, for instance, he liked nothing better than to throw on jeans and a sweatshirt and head for the beach. The movie magazines, of course, were quick to pick up on the "elegant Brit as beach boy" angle with Peter, and they ran innumerable photo essays about him and his friends at the shore.

Peter and Sabiston were part of a regular beach group that included Roy Marcher, whose family was prominent in the fine costume jewelry business; Joe Naar, a compact, pugnacious UCLA football player and boxer; handsome Charlie Dunne from USC and his sprightly wife, Molly, a movie extra who swam in Esther Williams's pictures; and Dick Livingston, a friend of Charlie's from USC. The beach was a major part of all their lives, Molly Dunne recalled. "That's all we did was go to the beach. We'd go to bed early so we could get up early and make sure we got the right spot on the sand, and so they could get their names on the waiting list for volleyball."

Peter sometimes slept on the beach so that he could wake up early enough to get in a few hours of surfing before he had to be at the studio. The boards in those days were enormous—about nine feet long—heavy and clunky. Built like a ship's hull, they were more like paddleboards, were hollow, and had a drain. The first time a surfer used a smaller, more compact board—dubbed a "potato chip"—it caused a sensation.

Dick Livingston met Peter as he drove past the Comstock Avenue house in 1944. "I had a blue 1940 Mercury coupe with red leather interior," Livingston recalled, "and I saw this man—boy, really—washing his car, and it was Peter. He had the same car as mine in the same colors. So I stopped and said, 'God, your car is terrific!' He said, 'Mine is just like yours except mine is a four-door!' " They became fast friends. "Peter was such a regular guy. Not

'Hollywood' at all. The whole time I knew him, most of his friends weren't movie people. He associated with us mostly."

But Peter had fine-tuned a rare ability to compartmentalize his life, and he developed friendships with fellow actors as readily as with beach boys. In Hollywood, he was virtually inseparable from three fellow MGM actors: Van Johnson, a twenty-eight-year-old boy-next-door type Metro was grooming for stardom; Keenan Wynn, also twenty-eight, the son of vaudeville star Ed Wynn and a talented character actor; and the charismatic, emotionally unstable thirty-year-old leading man Robert Walker.

All three men loved motorcycles and zoomed around the Hollywood Hills at night on their machines. Peter rode his bike, an Enfield, to the studio every morning—until MGM put a stop to that. Robert Walker had had a minor accident on his motorcycle a few weeks earlier, and the studio wasn't going to take any more chances. "You have a future with us," an executive told Peter, "and we don't think it's an advantage for you to break your neck."

Metro's warning didn't stop Peter from riding after hours, but a near-tragedy did. In March 1945 Keenan Wynn had a smashup with a car at Sunset and Hilgard in Westwood. He fractured his skull, sprained his back, and broke his jaw in five places. "That's all, brother," Peter said—and sold his Enfield.

Keenan and his wife, the former actress Evie Lynn Abbott, were friendly with most of the biggest stars in Hollywood, and Peter was eager to meet them. "We were always giving parties," Evie remembered. "I gave one in particular that Peter wanted to come to, and I told him, 'I can't have you, Peter, because this party is for people we've known a lot longer than we've known you. It's not your group.' "

Peter begged Evie to invite him. "Oh, please, I'll do anything. I'll hide behind the curtains. Just let me be there." Finally Evie agreed, but she told him, "You had better stay behind the curtains." She made him do it, too—kiddingly. "Then of course he came out and started saying hello to people. We used to laugh about that a lot. And from then on our friendship really grew. He was a very funny fellow, had a great sense of humor, and he was a very open and honest guy. We liked him immediately."

The closeness of Peter's friendship with Van, Keenan,

and Evie caused rumors around Hollywood. The more cynical gossips wondered aloud if Peter wasn't involved in a sexual *ménage à quatre*. When Evie divorced Keenan in 1947 and four hours later married Van, the jokesters had a field day. For weeks, the most popular question in Hollywood was, "Who's going to get custody of Peter?"

According to Evie Johnson, the rumors that Peter was sexually involved with Van and Keenan were untrue—but, she said, "Peter and I had an affair, in the late forties. It wasn't an *affair,* just a quick thing one night on the beach. We had a few mint juleps or something and I got very relaxed, and the next thing I knew, *pow!*"

Peter's relationships with women were usually as partitioned as the rest of his life. He dated many of the college girls and beach bunnies he met at the shore, girls who were thrilled to be with a budding movie star. And he dated beautiful actresses, of whom *he* was frequently in awe. "Everybody had a crush on him," said Molly Dunne. "He was taking out every girl in town."

It was hardly surprising. Peter Lawford at twenty-one was one of the most attractive and charming young men to be found in Hollywood since Errol Flynn had become a star in 1935—and his success with women would soon be almost as legendary as Flynn's. Few could resist his boyishly open face, dazzling smile, and tight physique, or his endearing English accent, impeccable manners, and quick wit.

Molly Dunne was Peter's closest female confidante at this time. She first met him in 1943 and remained a lifelong friend. Married to Peter's best beach buddy, Charlie Dunne, Molly was strictly a friend to Peter at first. "Everybody thought that Peter and I had an affair while I was married to Charlie, but we didn't. Later, when I got divorced, Peter and I did have a thing, and no one knew about it."

Almost from the beginning, Molly was privy to Peter's sex life. Most of his relationships were sexual, she knew, but he never took any of the girls home because of his parents. "They'd go someplace else—to her house, usually. Or sometimes they'd just stay in his car. He used to keep a bottle of Cepacol in the backseat. I remember the first time I asked him, 'What is this for?' and he gave me one of those know-it-all looks and said, 'Oh, you're so dumb.'

"He was into oral sex. He could and did do the other,

but he preferred oral sex. That's what the Cepacol was for, because most girls of my generation thought oral sex was dirty. I flatly refused to do it when we were together. That's what ended our physical relationship. And a lot of other girls wouldn't do it either."

PETER COULDN'T find Lana Turner, and he was frantic. For eight months, since early 1944, they had been involved in an affair, and every morning she picked him up in her jeep so they could ride together to the studio. This morning she had not shown up, and when Peter called her house, she wasn't there. He waited an hour, then hopped in his own car and sped to the studio. He barely made the first setup.

Lana wasn't at the studio either, and nobody knew where she was. Peter was beside himself with worry, because by this time he was deeply in love with her. They had met at Keenan and Evie Wynn's. "God, she was a beautiful woman!" Peter said years later. "She was already a heavyweight among stars, but her own weight was distributed perfectly."

She *was* one of the loveliest women ever to grace a movie screen, and she affected men the way Peter affected women. She had, since her arrival in Hollywood in 1937, dated just about every eligible bachelor in town, including Victor Mature, Robert Stack, Howard Hughes, Frank Sinatra, Buddy Rich, and Tony Martin. In 1940, at nineteen, she had eloped with the bandleader Artie Shaw. Less than four months later, she filed for divorce and underwent an abortion.

Two years later, Lana eloped again—this time with a businessman, Steve Crane. They divorced six months later, then remarried in March 1943 with Lana six months pregnant with his child. Less than a year after their daughter, Cheryl, was born, they were divorced again. It was at this point that Lana met Peter Lawford. She was twenty-four and a very big star, a full-fledged leading lady opposite the likes of Spencer Tracy (*Dr. Jekyll and Mr. Hyde*) and Clark Gable (*Somewhere I'll Find You*).

Peter, not yet twenty-one, was at first intimidated by Turner's attraction to him. "But I soon found out," he said, "that she was not one of those stars who won't mix with lesser beings. She never gave me any of that movie star bull. I was a man and she was a woman, and we really hit it off."

For the first eight months, they were inseparable. They took drives in Lana's light-blue 1939 Lincoln Continental out to Malibu, "where it was deserted and private," Peter recalled. They talked, laughed, made love on the sand as the sun set behind the Pacific Ocean. Weekends, they made the rounds of nightclubs and parties, ensuring that their names were in the columns and their pictures in the newspapers.

After their nights on the town, they'd go back to Turner's. "We couldn't go to my place," Peter recalled, "because my mother would eat alive any girl that even called there, acting like they were all out to get their hands on her precious son."

Lana was precisely the kind of girl Peter most responded to: one equally at home with sophistication and outdoorsy athleticism. "Lana has been publicized as a tremendous glamour girl," Peter said at the time. "Few people realize that she really has very simple tastes. She loves to go to the beach, she plays tennis, she rides beautifully. She is one of those amazing girls who does well everything she tries." Another thing he liked about her, he said, was that she was the kind of woman "you can call up and say, 'Come and help me bury Dad—I just shot him,' and she would be there without question."

Before long the sight of Peter's car parked in front of Turner's house had become a Beverly Hills fixture, and one day Keenan Wynn and the young actor Jackie Cooper decided to play a joke on Peter. When they noticed his car in Lana's driveway at one A.M. they let the air out of all four tires. "It was just a stupid, mean, terrible thing to do," Cooper now admits. "He had to call a service station, and she was screaming at him."

Peter wanted to marry Lana Turner, but kid stuff like the trick with his tires caused her to reconsider the romance. Then she disappeared on him, and he heard nothing from her for three days. He called every friend of hers he knew—no one could say where she was. He didn't want to raise the alarm with the studio, but by the fourth day he was ready to do something desperate. Then, out of the blue, she called him. Peter was shaking, but he kept his cool. "Hi, baby, how are you?" he said to her. "Where ya been?"

"I took a trip. I'm in Boston."

"Boston?" Peter tried to keep his voice even. "When will you be coming back?"

"I don't know. Whenever the studio wants me back." Then there was a long pause and Lana said, "Oh, by the way, Peter, it's over between us."

"What?"

"It's over, Peter."

He felt his stomach lurch, but still he maintained his composure. "Oh" was all he said. "Is there someone else, then?"

"Yes. Gene Krupa."

Peter later told Milton Ebbins, who would become his personal manager and closest friend, that Lana Turner broke his heart. "She went to Boston with Gene Krupa and dropped Peter cold!" Ebbins recalled. "He said to me, 'Milt, she hung me out on a tree and I couldn't come down for a *year*.'"

Lana Turner's affair with Krupa didn't last long, and when she returned to Hollywood she began a publicized romance with Turhan Bey, a dapper Turk who had appeared in *Ali Baba and the Forty Thieves*. Privately, Peter took out his anger at Lana on Bey. He referred to him snidely as "Turban" Bey, and when he found a publicity still of Bud Abbott in Arab robes in the just-released picture *Lost in a Harem*, he recaptioned it "Turban Bey's father, Oi Bey."

Peter's breakup with Lana Turner changed the way he treated women. "After that," recalled Milton Ebbins, "he started to just drop women when he was finished with them. He could be cruel, heartless. It was Lana who taught him that."

EIGHT

MAY LAWFORD wasn't the least bit pleased by her son's carefree ways off the movie set. She disapproved of his long weekends playing volleyball and surfing, and she was upset by his late nights spent wining and dining Lana Turner. May was indeed, as Peter had put it, terrified of losing her "precious son"—not only to a woman, but to his career as well. As she saw it, what she had so long pushed her son to achieve had driven a wedge between them, and she tried everything she could to insinuate herself into his career. He actively discouraged her efforts at every turn—and so did everyone else at Metro whenever she tried to meddle.

Lillian Burns was one of her targets. Whenever they saw each other, May told her, "You must come to tea" or "I'll come and have tea with you." Lillian was afraid May wanted to give her advice on how to coach Peter, and she demurred. "I told her, 'I really don't have time for it.' And I didn't. She always wanted me to know that she was *Lady* Lawford. I was not impressed."

When May learned that Elizabeth Taylor's mother, Sara, received a weekly paycheck from MGM, she went to Louis B. Mayer. "She thought she should be put under contract and be on the payroll," Lillian recalled. Mayer turned May down and pointed out that because Elizabeth was still a child, her mother's presence on the set was important for her welfare. Just the opposite was true of Peter.

May couldn't control Peter's career, so she tried to control his personal life. She was cold and rude to any young ladies he dared befriend. Molly Dunne once phoned Peter before she had met May and said, "Hello, Mrs. Lawford, may I speak to Peter?"

May replied, in her stiffest English manner, "Mrs. Dunne, it is *Lady* Lawford. Peter is not here. I will put you on the list." Then she abruptly hung up.

If Peter dated a girl more than a few times, May would give her the cold shoulder when he brought her to the house, and after she left May would harangue Peter about all her bad qualities. Peter, according to one girlfriend, soon learned the value of reverse psychology: after three dates and much vitriol from May, he told her he didn't like the girl at all. "We figured the best way to get May to lay off me was for her to think Peter wasn't interested," the woman recalled.

May resented all of Peter's close friends, not only the women, and she could be just as rude to his male pals. When Peter introduced Joe Naar to May, he told her, "This is my friend Joe Naar. He's in television." May said to Naar, "Would you mind taking a look at my set?"

Naar despised her: "She was the worst person I ever met. She knew I was Jewish, and she didn't like that. She made anti-Semitic remarks—not in front of me, but to Peter. She was racist, the kind of person who is quick to label people—gays, Jews, you name it. She was a bad human being."

Sometimes May's superior airs were laughable. Dick Livingston came to the Lawford house one afternoon with a friend. The Lawfords had a spinet piano in the hall, and Dick's companion sat down and started to play it. After a few moments, Lady Lawford walked over and said, "Please, I don't mean to insult you, but that's a very special piano and we only let very special people play it. Would you mind stopping?" The man at the keyboard was André Previn.

May's self-righteousness often brought her to heights of hypocrisy; when she learned that Evie Wynn planned to divorce Keenan, she stopped speaking to her. Peter's friends took their revenge by tormenting her. They would telephone and say, "Hi, Mrs. Lawford! Is Peter there?" Then the conversation would progress like this:

"It's Lady Lawford."

"Oh, okay, Mrs. Lawford. May I speak to Peter?"

"It's *Lady* Lawford!"

"Oh, yeah, sure. Well, thanks, Mrs. Lawford." Then they would hang up.

May's rudeness to Peter's friends and lovers had the opposite effect from the one she intended: it pushed him farther away from her. He now avoided her at all costs, hated to go home, and barely spoke to her when he was home. Her fear of losing him grew stronger, worsened by her increasingly frequent drinking bouts. When her mind was clouded by alcohol, May's paranoia knew no bounds; she alternated between self-pitying despair and anger.

Anger won out. Late one night, boozy, maudlin, May made up her mind to punish her son for the way he had hurt her, to hit back at him for abandoning her. What she did next to Peter made every indignity she had ever subjected him to pale in comparison.

IT WAS AT THE height of Peter's affair with Lana Turner that May telephoned Louis B. Mayer and asked to see him. Mayer had learned to avoid May whenever possible and asked if they couldn't discuss whatever was on her mind over the phone. "No, Mr. Mayer," she replied. "This is a highly important matter and I must see you *in person* as soon as possible."

Mayer agreed to see May the next day, and when she and the general sat down in front of the studio head's huge circular desk she did all the talking. Dispensing with pleasantries, she came immediately to the point. "Mr. Mayer, there is no use to beat about the bush. I'm concerned that my son is a homosexual."

More than May realized, her remark touched a sore spot with L. B. Mayer. The mogul was vociferously homophobic, suspicious of any unmarried actor who didn't "chase skirt." He was prudish about all sexuality and woefully ignorant about same-sex attractions. But while May's suspicions about Peter disturbed Mayer, they didn't surprise him. There were a number of actors on the lot he knew to be homosexual or bisexual; the studio routinely sent them on arranged dates, even into arranged marriages, to keep their sexual preferences secret. If someone got into trouble with the vice squad—Lucille Ryman, head of talent at MGM, recalled being awakened in the middle of the night because a famous actor had been caught *in flagrante delicto* with an eight-year-old boy—the studio was right there to hush things up and keep a lucrative career from being destroyed.

As in Victorian England, appearances were much more important than reality in the Hollywood of the forties. Studios demanded that their stars adhere to the morality clauses in their contracts, but if they didn't, their transgressions could be covered up with payoffs to newsmen and even to police officials. If a star's peccadilloes couldn't be kept from the public, his or her career was usually over, without so much as a helping hand from the studio.

Double standards were rampant. William Randolph Hearst destroyed any number of promising careers with the sensationalistic coverage his newspapers gave to Hollywood scandals, yet he expected everyone to turn a blind eye to his affair with Marion Davies, the mistress he tried valiantly to turn into a movie star. Harry Cohn, the head of Columbia Pictures, and Darryl Zanuck, head of Twentieth Century-Fox, were among the most vocal moralizers and most notorious womanizers in Hollywood, often demanding sexual favors from the very women they expected to convey virginal public images. Even Louis B. Mayer wasn't able to resist the temptations of the flesh when his wife, Margaret, took ill; he had several extramarital affairs.

Homosexuality, however, was truly taboo. If an actor was caught in a lewd act with another man, the studio would attempt to cover it up only if he were a big enough or promising enough star. Then he would usually be forced to enter into a sham marriage to preserve appearances. Sometimes, there was a cynical exchange program between a studio and the press. In the late 1950s, when reporters wanted to reveal Rock Hudson's homosexuality, Universal Studios convinced them to lay off Hudson by offering up another handsome young gay actor; the revelations about him effectively ended his career.

The intimations May Lawford was making about her son were thus very serious ones. Mayer listened to May's suspicions and replied, "What makes you think that, Lady Lawford?"

"Because of some of the actors he's been hanging out with. He's constantly with them. And I know that several of them are homosexual."

"What would you like me to do?"

"There must be something you can do! Can't you find
out if he is or not? Send him to the Menninger Clinic and
have his glands tested. Then you'll have your answer—yes
or no!"

Mayer assured May that he would call Peter in and
have a talk with him. The next day, Peter sat in front of
Mayer, nervous and puzzled by the summons. He and L.B.
had had a touchy relationship ever since the last time Mayer
had called him into his office, to dress Peter down for ignoring Mrs. Mayer in the commissary. "But Mr. Mayer," Peter
had protested. "I've never met your wife and I didn't know
who she was." Mayer wasn't placated—any employee of his,
he reasoned, should take the time to learn who his wife was.

At this next confrontation, Mayer was too embarrassed
to be direct. For the first few minutes, Peter had no idea
what he was talking about.

"We know about your problem, Peter," Mayer stammered. "It's okay. We can help cure you."

"Cure me of what, Mr. Mayer?"

Mayer remained oblique. "We have other young men
on the lot who have your problem, Peter, and we've been
giving them hormone shots to help them—extract of mon-
key glands, I think it is. We can do that for you, too—and
we can fix you up with some beautiful women, and—"

Suddenly, Peter understood. His face burned with
anger but he remained as controlled and polite as possible.
"Mr. Mayer, if you're suggesting that I'm a homosexual,
you're very much mistaken. I've been seeing Lana Turner
for months. How could I be homosexual?"

Mayer wasn't convinced. "I think you should take the
injections, Peter. We have several actors on the lot who are
taking them and they seem to be working—"

Now Peter let his voice rise. "Mr. Mayer, I'm telling
you I don't need any hormone shots. Call Lana Turner and
ask her if you want to. If you insist on this, I'll go to work
for another studio. Good day." He rose and walked out of
the office.

The strength of Peter's indignation impressed Mayer
favorably, and his intuition told him that Peter was being
truthful. Still, he did call Lana. When she told the boss
that Peter was a perfectly good lover, Mayer relented. He
apologized to Peter, but refused to tell him who or what
had stirred his concern.

A year later, Peter found out. Although May always maintained that Mayer had asked to see her, and not the other way around, Peter knew better. He was appalled, and he never forgave her. He couldn't believe that his mother would jeopardize his career at MGM—and the family's live-lihood—just to get back at him for some real or imagined injustice. After this incident, Peter's feelings against May hardened. Molly Dunne soon realized that "Peter *hated* his mother. He really intensely disliked her."

"She was a dreadful woman," recalled the producer Arthur Julian, another of Peter's friends. "She combined all the worst elements of Jewish mothers and Italian mothers, and all the classic bad mothers were in her."

Peter continued to live with May and Sir Sydney for the next eight years—unusual for a single, sexually active young film actor with a good income, but particularly so for a man who (he later admitted) "loathed" his mother. The reason Peter remained at home was his concern for Sir Sydney, who turned seventy-nine in November 1944.

Peter was disturbed by the general's dependence on May, principally because he felt she didn't treat him well. She was a youthful, sprightly sixty-one, and her attitude toward her husband, in Peter's view, was one of "having to put up with that old man," as though she resented the fact that taking care of him tied her to the house and restricted her socially. Whenever May treated Sir Sydney in anything less than the patient, respectful, and loving way Peter thought she should, he fumed at her and agonized for his father.

He tried to convince the general to move with him into another house—without May. Sir Sydney refused. However badly May treated him, she was his wife and his caregiver. And Sydney knew that no matter how much Peter loved him, no matter how concerned he was, he would never be able to give him the time and attention that May did, even if resentfully.

The situation gnawed at Peter. Jean MacDonald, a girl-friend, remembered him "sitting in my house teary-eyed be-cause of his mother's unkindness to Sir Sydney. He said he wished things were better at home for his father, wished that he lived in a happier house. He felt that in his old age Sir Sydney was a captive of Lady Lawford and governed by her whims. It weighed on him pretty heavily, but there was only so much he could do."

*   *   *

THAT WAS especially true in 1944 and 1945 because MGM kept Peter very busy. He played a juicy role as Lord Thornley, a young man enmeshed in an affair with an older woman in *Mrs. Parkington,* an immensely popular reteaming of Greer Garson and Walter Pidgeon, but his part was close to eliminated in the cutting room. "I could have fallen through my seat at the preview," he said.

He fared better as Anthony de Canterville in the comedy *The Canterville Ghost,* with Robert Young, Charles Laughton, and the precocious moppet Margaret O'Brien, but the picture was a flop. Late in 1944, MGM assigned Peter his most important picture since *The White Cliffs of Dover:* a lavish screen adaptation of Oscar Wilde's brilliant, epigrammatic Victorian morality tale *The Picture of Dorian Gray.*

The studio had paid $849.87 for the screen rights to the book, a modern classic since its publication in June 1890. As Wilde described Dorian—a destructive hedonist whose youthful beauty is "a form of genius"—Peter would have been perfect for the title role. But the producers opted instead to give Dorian an otherworldly quality and cast screen newcomer Hurd Hatfield in the part. Among a distinguished group of actors that included George Sanders and Angela Lansbury, Peter was given a part written into the script by the director, Albert Lewin—that of a young suitor to Donna Reed.

Dorian Gray was a difficult shoot, especially for Hatfield, who was in just about every scene and spent five months working on the film, a very long time in those days. The intensity of his role caused him to blow up at Peter one afternoon. "Peter was always happy-go-lucky, joking on the set," Hatfield later recalled. "I came out of a very rigorous theater training, and Peter just didn't seem serious enough about the work to me. He was always on the telephone, making dates or whatever."

Finally, Hatfield got short with him. "Peter!" he shouted. "Get off the phone, for God's sake! We're starting a scene and it's very difficult unless we all pull together." Peter shaped up after that, but when Hatfield later asked him out to lunch, Peter declined. Thereafter, said Hatfield, "he treated me like I was a leper."

The Picture of Dorian Gray was released on March 1, 1945, more than a year after it began production. MGM, worried about its commercial appeal, tried to sell it as a thriller, and its ad copy screamed: "Behind his fascinating face lived the soul of a killer!" In fact, the picture turned out to be first-rate, with a daring enough script for the time (although the novel's homoerotic undertones were suppressed), lavish production values, and strong performances. Peter's role as the young suitor is decidedly secondary, but he plays it perfectly—and he looks so handsome in the film that Hatfield suffers in comparison.

The reviews were mostly glowing, and the picture received three Academy Award nominations (Harry Stradling's moody cinematography won). But the studio's concerns about its box-office potential were well founded. American audiences did not respond to it, and while it did better overseas (particularly in Britain), it lost money.

Dorian Gray was very nearly the start of still another Lawford acting career: Sir Sydney's. When the general visited Peter on the set one day, Albert Lewin spotted him and told him he'd be perfect to play a minor character in a party scene. Would he be interested? The general harrumphed a few times, but said he might be. That night, Peter was touched by his father's admission that he had hesitated because he was afraid he would offend his son. "I thought you might not like it," he said. "Sort of like barging in on your territory."

Peter replied that he thought it was a wonderful idea, and the general spent two days filming his part. At a preview of the film in Pasadena, Peter and his parents waited to catch sight of Sir Sydney. "We sat on the edge of our seats so we'd be sure not to miss him," Peter recalled. "It was great excitement. But we never did see him. The sequence he was in had been cut, and nobody thought to tell him. Poor thing, he was crushed."

Sir Sydney did appear in small roles in several films after that, among them *The Amazing Mr. Nordill, The Suspect,* and *Kitty.* "He's very puffed up about the whole thing," Peter gleefully told a reporter. "He even has an agent. He spends his days sitting by the telephone waiting for a call from the studio."

ON MAY 7, 1945, Germany surrendered under the relentless onslaught of British, American, and Russian troops, and the European war was over. On August 15, the conflict that had killed fifty million people ended when Japan unconditionally surrendered after atomic bombs were dropped on Hiroshima and Nagasaki. Two weeks later, Peter, Keenan and Evie Wynn, Kay Thompson, and Chill Wills put on a variety show for returning fliers at a Santa Ana, California, air force base. The hour-long show featured Kay singing "On the Atchison, Topeka and Santa Fe"; Keenan as a country boy trying to direct draftee Peter to mythical Floogle Street for his army physical; Chill Wills demonstrating the "super-deluxe, aromatic, acrobatic potato peeler" that denudes defenseless spuds until they're "naked as Gypsy Rose Lee"; Peter and Keenan as politicians who rifle each other's pockets as they pass on the street; and the whole company in a finale—"M-O-T-H-E-R spells 'Sergeant' because he's been more than a mother to me."

The guys loved it, the performers had a good time, and Peter felt a real sense of accomplishment in entertaining men who had been through the horrors of hell defending their country.

"LASSIE WAS a vicious bastard!" Peter said years after he made his next picture, *Son of Lassie,* a wartime saga set in England with the canine superstar. "You want to know how we did those scenes [of affection between man and dog]? I had raw meat stuck under my arms and under my shirt and rubbed on my face and stuck up my clyde, and that animal was eating me alive! What you saw on the screen, what you thought was the true love of a dog for his master, wasn't that at all . . . no, it was sheer animal hunger!"

When Peter first found out that MGM had assigned him to the picture, however, he was thrilled. The studio was giving him an extraordinary opportunity: for the first time, he would be the top-billed star of a motion picture, the actor on whose shoulders the film rested. It was a prospect that both excited and frightened him; he began to suffer from back pain, a problem he would frequently have in the future when under stress.

The box-office appeal of *Son of Lassie* was virtually guaranteed. Producer Sam Marx had scored a huge hit in 1943 with *Lassie Come Home,* the heartwarming story of the beautiful collie's struggle to be reunited with her owner, the young Roddy McDowall. Eleven-year-old Elizabeth Taylor, in her second movie, played a moppet who sets the animal free.

For the sequel, Peter's first Technicolor production, he and June Lockhart were cast to play the adult versions of Roddy and Elizabeth.* Pal, a male dog who was called "the only star who could play a bitch better than Bette Davis," played the dual roles of Lassie and her pup, Laddie.

Peter played Joe Carraclough, a strapping young man strongly attached to Laddie, an adorable if none-too-bright animal. When Joe leaves home for RAF training, his girlfriend (Lockhart) promises to take care of Laddie, but the dog runs forty miles to follow Joe. After battles with Nazi soldiers and raging rapids, man and dog are reunited, Joe returns to his girl, Laddie rejoins his mother, and everyone lives happily ever after.

Location filming took place at Patricia Bay, near Vancouver, British Columbia, in August and September 1944. Peter did his own swimming in the treacherous, thirty-two-degree waters of the Columbia River, a task made more difficult by his limited use of his right arm. He pointedly did not ask for a double to swim for him, however, because he never wanted his bosses to feel he wouldn't be up to the physical demands of whatever role they wanted him to play. He knew that such an attitude could severely limit his career.

Peter found himself amused during filming by the star treatment accorded his canine costar. While he went without a dressing room, he said, "Lassie was checked into a two-bedroom suite, accompanied by a whole retinue—sort of like a small Frank Sinatra unit."

The amusement turned to anger, however, when he realized that the studio provided Lassie with safety measures not accorded him. Shooting the scenes in the rapids, Peter noticed that Pal had been securely tethered to shore with rope to make sure he didn't drown, while Peter was left to his own devices. Neither was Peter pleased to learn that Pal

---

*Lockhart, of course, went on to play the mother on the 1950s TV show *Lassie*.

had been insured for a million dollars. "I had the suspicion that if I was insured at all, it was for a substantially smaller amount."

There was no love lost between actor and dog; Peter nicknamed the film "Son of a Bitch." Even while doing publicity for the picture, he expressed reservations about working with an animal: "As an actor you haven't a dog's chance when you act with a dog. You can be acting for all you're worth, sure you have audience attention. Then the dog wags its tail, or tosses a soulful glance, and the spectators whoop and coo. The human actor might as well not be there."

Moviegoers, of course, knew nothing of the antipathy between Peter and Pal. They went to see *Son of Lassie* in droves, and even the critics approved. The film became one of the top-grossing movies of 1945, netting MGM a $1.5 million profit. Peter's performance drew the highest critical praise of his career—he played the role with "boyish charm and simplicity," summed up one reviewer. But Lady Lawford was unimpressed: her only comment to Peter was, "I couldn't tell you apart—both with that long shaggy hair. He's prettier in Technicolor, anyway."

The public responded strongly to Peter's first full-length movie role. Shortly after *Son of Lassie* was released in June, his fan mail, which had amounted to dozens of letters a week, jumped to hundreds, and movie magazines started to pay attention to him. He won a *Modern Screen* readers' poll as the most popular actor in Hollywood (and was awarded "a handsome engraved Gruen watch"). It was a remarkable feat considering the competition, and a sure indication that young female moviegoers, at least, had sat up and taken notice of him.

NINE

ANOTHER STRONG sign of Peter's new box-office appeal came when Twentieth Century-Fox asked MGM to lend them his services for Ernst Lubitsch's movie version of a bestselling novel, *Cluny Brown*. The director of Garbo's *Ninotchka,* among other classics, Lubitsch's "touch" was golden in Hollywood, and *Cluny Brown* was a top Fox title about a Czech author who falls in love with a plumber's niece. With Peter offered third lead after Charles Boyer and Jennifer Jones, and with the studio receiving a thousand dollars per week for his services (they pocketed seven hundred fifty dollars of it), Metro realized that they had a potential major star in Peter Lawford.

Fortuitously, Peter's contract came up for renegotiation just as the Fox loan-out request came in. He had agreed to one six-month extension at two hundred fifty dollars per week in June, but it was now time for MGM to decide whether or not to make a real commitment to him. There was little debate. Even though the war was over and established stars and newcomers alike were again in abundance, Peter had proved himself more than just a draft-proof substitute. He was developing into an audience favorite, and MGM wanted to keep him.

On December 5, 1945, Peter, at twenty-two, signed a seven-year contract beginning at five hundred dollars per week, with six yearly renewal options. Again, forty weeks of work a year were guaranteed. The first time Peter's option was picked up, his salary would be increased by two hundred dollars, the next two times it would rise by three hundred dollars, and the last two by two hundred fifty dollars. If the studio exercised each of the options, by the end of the contract's seven-year term Peter would be earning two thousand dollars per week. He was also given a ten-thousand-dollar signing bonus.

It was a star's contract, and Peter was well on his way to proving himself worthy of it. *Cluny Brown* was released in June 1946, to good reviews and strong box office. The *Variety* critic praised Peter: "He shades his comedy with feeling." Four days after the film's premiere, another Peter Lawford film opened across America. *Two Sisters from Boston* was a lavishly produced light musical in which Peter played the love object of the sisters, June Allyson and Kathryn Grayson. Lauritz Melchior, the Danish heldentenor, performed light-opera duets with Grayson, and vaudeville veteran Jimmy Durante weighed in with "G'wan Home, Your Mudder's Callin'." Reviews for the film and for Peter were excellent, and box-office receipts were solid.

During the filming, Peter found himself quite taken with June Allyson, whom he had met in passing on the lot a few times but had never gotten to know. One of MGM's fastest-rising ingenues in the girl-next-door mold, she had captured the hearts of fans across the country with her marriage to Dick Powell. (In the early forties, she had dated Joe Kennedy's son Jack during one of what he called his "hunting expeditions" for girls in Hollywood. "I didn't know his father was an ambassador and I certainly didn't know I was being pursued by a future president of the United States," Allyson later wrote. "We laughed a lot. He reminded me of Peter Lawford—both had the same charm and fun-loving ways.")

Peter worked his own magic on June early in the *Two Sisters* shoot, and he was a bit surprised when she responded to his advances, because her "perfect marriage" to Powell had been tremendously publicized. According to Jackie Cooper, "Peter was crazy about June Allyson. He really loved her." June was attractive to him, Peter explained, because she was "helpless, completely" and acted "as a spur to the protective and resourceful male in me. She's a little China doll, June is. She's sweet, she's nice, she's intelligent."

The couple occasionally stole chances to be together at Cooper's house. "Peter used to bring a number of famous married ladies over to my house," Cooper recalled, "so they could keep company there. A little kissing and hugging, that was all. Peter felt very comfortable at my place, and I never embarrassed him about it.

"Just so it would look good," Jackie continued, "June Allyson would have her husband pick her up every so often—so that it would seem like she was just visiting me and my wife."

Whenever June and Dick had a party, Peter would be invited—but June insisted he bring a girl with him as a decoy. "Peter used to tell me how hard it was for him," Cooper recalled, "to go to June's parties and be there with her but not be able to touch her or hold her hand or talk to her the way he wanted to. Yeah, he was just crazy about her."

As discreet as Peter and June were, rumors about their romance did crop up, and soon blind items were appearing in the gossip columns: "Metro executives are worried about two up-and-coming stars who are seeing a lot of each other while her husband is out of town." Peter's bosses forbade him to make a trip to New York because June was going to be there at the same time. "This thing is out of hand," Peter said they told him, "and it will explode and hurt you both if you are seen in New York at the same time."

In her autobiography, June would say only that she "was often over at Peter Lawford's house. I never was as close to him as I was Van [Johnson]. But I grew very fond of him in a mildly romantic way. We had a lot of fun. I loved his devil-may-care attitude, and his British accent fascinated me."

In any event, the romance was over before it had a chance to "explode" into the public eye as MGM had feared it might, and it ended with ill feelings on both sides. According to Peter's later manager, Milton Ebbins, "Peter *hated* June Allyson. He used to say the most uncomplimentary things about her."

WITH THE virtually simultaneous release of *Cluny Brown* and *Two Sisters from Boston,* Peter was a "hot item" in the summer of 1946. In the latter film, a box-office hit, Peter was presented for the first time as a romantic leading man, a situation just about guaranteed to turn a good-looking young actor into a bobby-sox idol—and that's exactly what happened. He appeared on his first two movie magazine covers that summer, and *Photoplay* ran articles on him in seven of the year's twelve issues. His fan mail rose to over a thousand letters a week, surpassing that of Van Johnson, at the time considered the most popular teen idol on the MGM lot.

With all this attention focused on him, Peter's fans sought him out as never before. His phone number had been listed, but the number of fans' calls became so great that May found herself on the telephone most of the day. Peter changed the number, and the telephone company agreed that it would be unpublished. The first day the new number was installed, the Lawford phone rang off the hook. Peter called information, asked for his own number, and was given it without hesitation. "That's one hell of a confidential number!" Peter shouted at the startled operator.

He was usually left unbothered at the beach, but one day as he waded into the surf he noticed a young girl following him. He went out a little farther; so did she. Finally both of them were up to their necks, and the girl held her arms aloft. When she got closer to him, Peter saw that she was carrying an autograph book. He watched her approach him, struggling to keep her head above water, and laughed out loud when she asked, "Do you have a pencil?"

Peter Lawford was now a movie star—and he was expected to act like one. With his signing bonus, he bought a new car, an enormous Chrysler convertible, maroon with wine-red leather interior and yards of richly grained wood. He spoke so proudly of it to columnist Dorothy Kilgallen during an interview that she wrote, "For a moment I expected him to whip out his wallet and show me a picture of it lying on a white fur rug."

His most lavish expenditure was for something no movie star could be without: a home of his own. The studio kept reminding Peter that it wouldn't do for one of MGM's top attractions to live in a tiny rental, and after a few weeks' search Peter found a place he loved: a two-bedroom ranch-style home at 11571 Sunset Boulevard in West Los Angeles, near Barrington Avenue. The white, red-shuttered home offered a separate "apartment" for Peter (on the opposite side of the house from his parents' bedroom), comprising a bedroom, bath, and den. There was a large flagstone porch in the front and a small garden where Sir Sydney could grow his beloved mignonette flowers. All three of the Lawfords fell in love with the house, and Peter agreed to buy it.

MGM's parent company, Loew's Inc., offered Peter a mortgage on the house—a common practice, according to Jackie Cooper. "That was a trap that Mr. Mayer was very careful to see that everyone got into—they'd say, 'We don't want you to live in anything less than a lovely home befitting a star. We'll take care of the mortgage and you'll owe us.'

"People were tickled to death that they could get a great house and appear very successful. The money they owed the studio kept piling up, and then they'd have to stay another year if the studio wanted them. If the studio didn't want them, they took the house away."

But Peter wasn't thinking in those terms in August 1946—he was indeed "tickled" to sign a forty-five-thousand-dollar deed of trust with Loew's Inc. at four percent interest (the going rate; no bargains here) in order to purchase the house.

The payments on the mortgage were $162.50 a week for four years and two hundred dollars a week for the next four years, all to be deducted from Peter's weekly paycheck. Thus, in the last five months of 1946, Peter's salary was reduced by more than thirty percent by his mortgage payments. In 1947, when his salary rose to seven hundred dollars per week, the payments were more manageable.

Peter was excited about the new house—the first he had ever owned—and he immediately set out to decorate it. He hadn't been able to exercise his creativity through any channel but acting since his childhood stabs at drawing; now, he worked delightedly as a decorator, and exhibited a talent for it.

In the ultramodern living room, Peter accented gray carpeting and walls with a maroon leather sofa and recliners. Lady Lawford wasn't too happy with Peter's choices (the gray, she complained, belonged in a mortuary), and she insisted on putting out things she'd had shipped from England after the war: autographed pictures of the king and queen of Belgium, the duke of Windsor and the king and queen of Sweden in ornate frames; small Oriental objets d'art; and antique wooden pieces. This compromise between two distinct tastes left the Lawfords with an extremely eclectic environment.

Peter's den, however, was entirely his own. His bookshelves contained an actor's handbook by Stanislavski. His record collection was predominantly jazz. On the walls were photographs of surfers and military aircraft, and an autographed portrait of Frank Sinatra. There was also a preview reaction card mailed to MGM after a showing of *Son of Lassie*. It read: "Peter Lawford wonderful. Nuts to Van Johnson."

DURING PETER'S rise in Hollywood, he became friends with much bigger stars than his own position in the motion picture industry would have suggested. He attended so many parties in the midforties—and threw so few of his own—that he gained a reputation as "America's guest." Rocky Cooper, for one, didn't mind. The wife of Gary Cooper, she had met Peter in 1944 at Keenan and Evie Wynn's house in Brentwood, which was directly across the street from the Coopers'. Rocky and Gary took to Peter immediately. "Everybody was into tennis," Rocky recalled, "and whenever he would visit we'd be playing. He played very well. So that was an entree for him right there. And those were the days that Gary and I would do a lot of entertaining, and gosh knows you couldn't find a more attractive 'extra man' than Peter. He'd come and be beautiful and play tennis."

Rocky Cooper became a lifelong friend of Peter's—so close in fact that rumors began of a romance. Peter did speak glowingly of Rocky in an interview in which he chose her as Hollywood's most exciting woman. "One of the things that is exciting to me is adaptability," he said, "and a woman who has it will always intrigue me. Such a woman is Rocky Cooper. . . . Rocky is the out-of-doors, athletic type by day, and a sophisticated, smartly gowned, well-informed woman by night."

Rocky Cooper's athleticism, in fact, led her to become part of Peter's beach scene, a world he usually kept separate from his Hollywood life. "Those were the glory years," she recalled. "The days at the beach. It was really a Rat Pack down there. That's where, I swear to God, Sinatra picked up the lingo. They set out those boards all day waiting for a wave. Some people we'd call 'onshore'—they were chicken and wouldn't go into the water because some of the waves were really big, big, big. They were all *beautiful* people. Gary used to say, 'God, they are the best-looking guys I've ever seen in my life. Better even than cowboys.'"

Just as Peter had brought some of his movie star friends into the beach scene, he now tried to include the beach gang in his Hollywood social whirl—particularly pretty girls he'd met at the beach and wanted to woo. To his disappointment, the young women almost invariably acted differently on a date than they had at surfside.

"As free and uninhibited and natural as Nature herself when on the beach," Peter told a magazine reporter, "no sooner does [his date] step into my car than she is metamorphosed into a lethal cutie-pie, posturing, posing, batting her eyelashes, giggling, and also making—although she is an Amazon on the sand and in the sea—like Little Red Riding Hood at the mercy of the Big Bad Wolf! . . . Arrive at Chasen's or Romanoff's for dinner, and the first thing cutie-pie does is order a double Scotch! When you ask her—as nervous, by this time, as she is—'Are you sure you can take it?' she brushes you off with a knowing smile. Fifteen minutes later she turns green on you and spends the rest of the evening in the powder room!"

Peter stopped taking beach girls to the clubs, but he didn't stop going—he just went with more sophisticated people. He had developed a taste for jazz, and he loved to bring his movie star friends to see the latest singers on the Sunset Strip. Rocky Cooper recalled that "Peter taught both Gary and me a heck of a lot about music. Jazz and blues. He'd take us to see people like Eddie Heywood and Lena Horne, at one of the first gigs she did at the Mocambo on Sunset. She was really new on the scene, and Peter insisted that we go with him to see her."

It was on the club beat that Peter earned his reputation as a man who never met a check he couldn't avoid. Rocky

Cooper remembered that "Peter would always ask us to do the town with him—but guess who paid?" Peter's beach friends, though, saw another side of him. As Molly Dunne recalled, "People said Peter was cheap, but with us he was more than generous. He always picked up the tab, because he knew we couldn't afford it. When he went out with people richer than himself, he'd let them handle it. Otherwise, he'd pay for everybody."

TEN

ARLY IN December 1946, Peter was mingling with the celebrants at a Hollywood Christmas party. He chatted with the other guests for about an hour, but none of the young ladies there caught his fancy. Then Rita Hayworth arrived. For the rest of the evening he couldn't take his eyes off the sultry redhead who was, at twenty-eight, a veteran of forty films, a World War II pinup girl, and the recent sensation of *Gilda* with her torrid song and dance number "Put the Blame on Mame."

Sparks flew that night between Lawford and Hayworth, who had been separated from Orson Welles for over a year. But Rita needed to be circumspect—she had come to the party with someone else. Jackie Cooper recalled what transpired: "At one point in the party Rita surprised me by handing me a note. She said, 'That's my phone number. Tell Peter to call me. I'll be home tonight around twelve.' So I gave the note to Peter and evidently he was expecting it.

"My wife and I got him on the phone the next morning and he gave us a blow-by-blow description of their night together. He was naughty that way, just terrible. A lot of times just to get laughs he'd exaggerate, tell wild stories so he wouldn't seem like someone who was just kissing and telling. You never knew if he was telling the truth."

Rita Hayworth once said of herself, "Men go to bed with Gilda, but they wake up with me." Peter was no exception. He told friends that Rita was "the worst lay in the

world. She was always drunk and she never stopped eating."
After they'd have sex, he said, Hayworth would go into the
kitchen, sit down in front of the refrigerator, open the door,
and devour everything on the shelves.

The Hayworth-Lawford affair was short-lived, but Peter
had better luck with another sex goddess, Ava Gardner, the
North Carolina belle with green almond-shaped eyes and
inviting lips who had been voted the most beautiful woman
in the world. Peter first met her on the set of *Pilot #5*
early in 1943 and took her out shortly afterward when she
separated from her first husband, Mickey Rooney. She was
lithe and lean rather than voluptuous, traits that appealed
to Peter, but she exuded a lush sensuality that could drive
a man crazy. Still, the first time she went out with Peter, in
June 1944, Ava had to compete for his undivided attention.

He had driven to her house in his new Mercury convertible, and as they sat on the couch Ava was disconcerted
by Peter's half-witted answers to her questions—he was
quite obviously distracted. At one point he jumped up and
looked out the front door, then returned with more ab-
stracted snippets of conversation. The second time he did
this, Ava asked him, "Is there something out there I ought
to know about?"

"It's my new car," Peter replied. "I just wanted to
make sure she was all right."

"She's doing better than I am," Ava grumbled.

Despite this inauspicious start, the two saw each other
off and on for several years, particularly after Ava's second
marriage, to Lana Turner's ex-husband Artie Shaw, foundered. She and Peter danced at Ciro's, went to baseball
games, and shared an interest in books and music. "You
can really talk to Ava," Peter said. "She has an insatiable
thirst for knowledge."

She also had an insatiable hunger for men. "She was
sexually uninhibited, wild, all kinds of goodies and quick,"
Phil Silvers's wife, Jo-Carroll, has said. "You couldn't get
ahold of her. She was gone and off with somebody else
before you knew where you were."

Peter would soon learn the truth of this observation.
On New Year's Eve in 1946, he spent a romantic evening
with Ava. They went to a party together, embraced and
kissed each other as the clock struck twelve, and then went
back to her place for a romp. For the first time, Peter sensed

that their casual relationship was starting to get more serious.

As he prepared to leave at about three in the morning, however, his illusion was shattered. The young crooner Mel Tormé appeared at the door, and as Peter said his good-nights to Ava, Tormé settled down on the couch. Mel and Ava spent the rest of New Year's Day on a romantic drive up the coast, and Tormé's affair with Ava began.

Peter's fling with Ava Gardner was over, but it would come back to haunt him because of his friendship with her future husband—the most volatile, emotional, jealous, and violent man he was ever to meet in his life: Frank Sinatra. Their paths first crossed in 1945, when Peter attended an-other of Louis B. Mayer's command-performance gatherings at his Santa Monica beach house, this one, according to Peter, a "ferociously boring" dinner party for fifty in honor of Henry Ford II and his wife. Boring it may have been, but Peter and Sinatra hit it off famously. Sinatra had just signed a contract with MGM after three years of phenome-nal success as a singer, during which he had become the highest-paid—and most swooned over—concert performer in the country.

Peter's date for this Mayer soirée was Marilyn Maxwell, the sexy blond perennial starlet he was seeing at the time. Maxwell knew Sinatra, and she introduced him to Peter. All three sat together at dinner and found that they shared a wry outlook on the proceedings and "the ever-present ass kissers, sycophants, court jesters, and a plethora of terminal egos," as Peter put it. They laughed a lot under their breaths at what they saw going on around them.

Peter had been curious to meet this singing sensation who seemed to have "a built-in, smoldering, quiet mys-tique," but he wasn't prepared to be so beguiled by him. He found Sinatra in an expansive mood, brimful of marvel-ous tales, and with a brittle sense of humor very close to Peter's own. Most surprising was that Sinatra seemed mod-est, completely unaffected by his great success. Peter and Frank became fast friends. They "did the clubs" together, played poker, met religiously every week to watch *The Fri-day Night Fights* on television. For the next seven years, Peter carried in his wallet a membership card from the "Sigh Guy Frank Sinatra Fan Club."

In the fall of 1946, Peter received word that he had

been cast in Sinatra's third MGM picture, *It Happened in Brooklyn,* a musical romance with Kathryn Grayson and Jimmy Durante that was little more than an excuse to string together some terrific Sammy Cahn–Jule Styne musical numbers: Sinatra and Grayson were to duet on "Time After Time," and Durante and Sinatra would perform a rousing number in a music store, "The Song's Gotta Come from the Heart."

There were no plans at first to have Peter sing or dance in *It Happened in Brooklyn.* He had never done either on film, but he had sung reasonably well and danced the jitterbug excellently at so many Hollywood parties that *Brooklyn* director Richard Whorf decided at the last minute to give Peter a number called " 'Tain't Right to Love You Like I Do."

Sing in a movie starring Frank Sinatra? Peter wasn't sure he wanted to try, but Whorf was insistent. Nervous, he practiced the song for hours, took advice from Sinatra, and performed it flawlessly in one take. As it turned out, the number practically stole the show. Not because of Peter's singing—which was only adequate—but because of the furious jitterbug he let loose with in the middle of the song. An exciting bit of business, it showed Peter's trim, long-legged physique off to great advantage and took audiences completely by surprise. They loved it. As columnist Sheilah Graham noted, "When the girls who squeal young men into fame saw and heard Peter's number at a sneak preview, they screamed. For a few minutes they even forgot Frankie Boy and carried on fit to kill for Mr. Lawford. Now he's a star."

Female moviegoers weren't the only ones who were impressed. MGM executives, after gauging the preview audience's reaction, increased Peter's billing in the film's ads from sixty percent of the title type size to one hundred percent. When the picture was released in March 1947, critics agreed that Peter was terrific. Jack D. Grant of *The Hollywood Reporter* wrote, "Peter Lawford, who has built up a swoon-following to rival Sinatra's, is a sensation as the English kid." The *Los Angeles Times* added, "His jive number is a show stopper." The film, however, was a disappointment at the box office. Modestly budgeted, it took in only thirty-eight dollars more domestically than it cost to make, and after the expenses of advertising and promotion were added, lost $138,000.

In June, Peter's second film of 1947 opened. *My Brother Talks to Horses* was an amusing but slight comedy, directed by Fred Zinnemann, that cast Peter as second fiddle to nine-year-old Jackie "Butch" Jenkins, a popular child star of the day who would retire three films later when he developed a stutter. The story had Butch as a boy able to converse with horses, and Peter as his older brother who uses Butch's talent to win bets at the racetrack. The movie was promoted as "the most novel comedy ever filmed" and was well reviewed as a "small picture," but it fared abysmally at the box office, losing Metro nearly a million dollars.

IF PETER was anxious about singing one song and dancing a brief jitterbug in *It Happened in Brooklyn,* he was positively terrified by his next assignment: to star with June Allyson in a remake of Metro's 1930 production *Good News,* a college musical originally presented on Broadway with a score by DeSylva, Brown, and Henderson that included "The Varsity Drag," "Lucky in Love," and "The Best Things in Life Are Free."

This version of *Good News* was to be the latest production from MGM's prestigious Freed Unit, headed by the studio's resident musical genius, Arthur Freed. A lyricist turned producer, Freed's credits included many of the finest musical films ever made in Hollywood, from *The Wizard of Oz* to *Babes in Arms, Cabin in the Sky, Girl Crazy, Meet Me in St. Louis, Ziegfeld Follies,* and *Till the Clouds Roll By.*

Freed had been given virtual carte blanche, both artistically and financially. He attracted the finest musical talents in the country to MGM, and by the midforties the Freed Unit was as much a family as it was a well-oiled movie production machine. Freed surrounded himself with sophisticated New York talents like musical supervisor Roger Edens, writers Leonard Gershe, Kay Thompson, Betty Comden, and Adolph Green, and directors Vincente Minnelli, Charles Walters, and Busby Berkeley. And he had, of course, the crème de la crème of performers at his disposal—Judy Garland, the star of fifteen of his first twenty-four films, Mickey Rooney, Gene Kelly, Frank Sinatra, Fred Astaire, Kathryn Grayson, Howard Keel, and Ann Miller, among others.

Peter was nervous about being in this kind of company, and so intimidated by the reputation of the Freed Unit that he doubted he'd be able to pull off what the producer expected of him. Not only would he have to carry a musical motion picture by singing and dancing in half a dozen elaborate numbers, but he was to play Tommy Marlowe, an all-American college football hero—a part originally planned for either Van Johnson or Mickey Rooney!

Moments after he received notification of the assignment, Peter telephoned Betty Comden and Adolph Green, who had been hired by Freed and the film's director Charles Walters to write the screenplay and some new songs. "You've got to get me out of this picture!" he screamed into the phone. "I'll make an absolute ass of myself!"

As the writing partners listened patiently on the other end of the line, Peter rattled off the reasons why he couldn't possibly play the part. "I'm English. I have a British accent. I'm *not* your all-American 'Joe College.' I've never played football in my life!" He took a deep breath and concluded, "I'm stupefied."

Comden and Green just giggled at Peter's frantic state. "Of course you can do it," they told him. "You were fine in *It Happened in Brooklyn*. You'll be fine in this picture too. You'll just have to work on your American accent, that's all. It's all part of acting. It'll be a good experience for you."

Still, Peter later said, "I wasn't at all sure it would be good news for me." But if he refused to do the film, MGM would put him on suspension, as they had Gloria De Haven when she refused one of the film's lesser roles, and that was something he couldn't afford. He reported for work on February 11, 1947—his nerves raw, his back muscles in spasm—for the most challenging assignment of his career.

Peter worked harder on *Good News* than he had on anything before it. He took singing and dancing lessons daily both before and during the shoot, worked on his musical numbers with the film's associate producer, Roger Edens, who had long been Judy Garland's musical supervisor, and studied with a vocal coach to perfect an "American accent." Peter's days of goofing off and making telephone calls on the set were behind him. For *Good News*, he frequently worked from seven in the morning until nine at night, virtually nonstop.

The plot of *Good News* was formulaic: Tait College's football hero can play in the big game only if he passes astronomy, his weakest subject. He's tutored by Connie (June Allyson), a bookish girl who's mad for him. He pursues a gorgeous coed (Joan McCracken), who pays attention to him only because she thinks he's a millionaire. He passes, wins the game, gets the right girl, and all live happily ever after.

Comden and Green wanted to write a song for the tutoring scene, but thought to themselves, *astronomy?* They decided to change Tommy Marlowe's weakness to French, and they and Roger Edens developed a wonderful piece of special material, "The French Lesson," in which Connie teaches Tommy the rudiments of the language.

Peter coached June in French for hours so that she would sound reasonable teaching him the same thing on-screen. "My French accent was atrocious—his was superb," June later wrote. Finally Peter told her, "This is the most ridiculous part I've ever had or hope to have."

Tommy, as played by Peter, picks the language up in absurdly short order, responding to Connie's cues with a flawless accent. Later in the film, Peter sings the entire second verse of "The Best Things in Life Are Free" in beautiful French. It's all very silly, but no one seemed to mind—because the numbers, and Peter and June's performances of them, were charming.

Peter's singing presented more of a problem. During a preview of the film, an audience "reactograph" was prepared to monitor scene by scene whether the audience liked or disliked what they were seeing. At the point when Peter began to sing his first solo number, the graph registered the strongest negative reaction, and it improved only after four other singers joined him. But once audiences grew accustomed to the fact that Peter wasn't really a singer and was, as one critic later pointed out, "sensibly talking his lyrics rather than singing them," few seemed to mind that he wasn't going to threaten Frank Sinatra or Bing Crosby.

Despite Peter's efforts to Americanize his speech, Tommy Marlowe's "A"s were suspiciously long every now and then. "When I'd slip," Peter recalled, "Chuck Walters would nudge me and urge, 'Cut the Back Bay stuff.' "

Peter found it a strain to work with June Allyson after the breakup of their romance. His stand-in, Ken DuMain, recalled that Peter took some petty snipes at her. "You know," he told Ken, "June is considerably older than we are, although she doesn't profess to be." (Allyson was thirty, Peter and DuMain both twenty-three.) But the filming went along uneventfully, and the two stars were completely professional in their deportment.

Good News was released in December 1947, and it was an immediate hit, netting more than two and a half million dollars domestically. *Collier's* chose it as "picture of the month" and "musical of the year." It was, the magazine said, "a youthful, tuneful, joyous shot in the arm in the form of the gayest, fastest-paced film ever brightened by Technicolor's magic.... The cast couldn't be improved upon. June Allyson gives an acting, singing, and dancing performance which makes us remember how she first caught the public eye. Peter Lawford ... fulfills his promise as the most personable romantic lead on the screen."

Peter is delightful in *Good News*. He's believable as Tommy Marlowe, and his dancing is so vigorous, athletic, and exciting in numbers like "Be a Ladies' Man" and "Varsity Drag" that the viewer is willing to forgive him a few flat and raspy musical stretches. Muriel O'Brien, the young woman who had tried to teach Peter to sing and dance back in Manhasset before she gave up in despair, was amazed by his performance. "I kept watching him singing and dancing and thought, *Oh my God!* They really had a splendid school at MGM and it showed. Anybody who could teach that boy to sing and dance in time has got to be a genius!"

PETER'S CAREER was at its peak as 1948 unfolded, and he was a man who seemed to have it all. He was "impossibly handsome," had a great physique, was world famous, was making nine hundred dollars a week, and had women throwing themselves at his feet. But he was also a man haunted by demons, not the least of which was his sexuality.

His mother had handed down to Peter an unfortunate Victorian legacy: the conviction that sex was dirty, something to be got over with as quickly as possible. Peter had a strong sex drive, but he rarely enjoyed the act in any truly romantic sense. To him, it was purely a physical release, something to satisfy his baser animal needs. And because Peter was such a sensitive man, his painful rejection by Lana Turner made it difficult for him to give of himself emotionally again.

Both of these elements had combined by 1948 to make Peter Lawford—to all appearances one of the world's most desirable men—an unsatisfactory sex partner. "Peter was not the best lover in the world," Molly Dunne recalled, "because he was not a tender, loving type when he was involved with his sex. He mostly just wanted oral sex. He didn't have an impotence problem—he could and did have intercourse—but he preferred oral sex."

This created a problem for Peter, because most of the women he took out refused to perform fellatio on him. And they were sorely disappointed in him as a lover; his partners soon lost their romantic visions of languid lovemaking with Peter Lawford. "His relationships didn't last very long," Molly Dunne recalled.

To achieve the kind of sexual release he desired, Peter began a furtive activity that he kept secret from even his closest friends, but that the FBI discovered during an investigation of "white slave traffic" in Los Angeles. According to the FBI file on Peter, "on December 17, 1946, [he] had contacted [a] well-known call-house madam in an effort to talk to one [of her] call-girls. [She] was not in at the time and Lawford requested that she call him at the Mocambo Night Club. On another occasion, information was developed that a call-house girl . . . was 'reportedly a frequent trick for movie actor Peter Lawford.' Another Los Angeles prostitute reportedly 'bragged' that she knew the movie star, Peter Lawford, and on several occasions [our informant] had overheard her attempting to reach Lawford by phone."

Peter's pursuit of prostitutes brought him perilously close to scandal a number of times. Fred Otash was then a member of the Los Angeles Police Department assigned to the administrative vice squad downtown, and one day he gave Peter some advice. "Look, asshole," he told him, "knock it off, okay? Your name is in every goddamn trick book of every whore we ever busted. They've got you down as a fifty-dollar trick. You'd better cool it or you're gonna get in trouble."

He never did cool it, but he was discreet enough to avoid being busted on a morals charge or having his name make the papers when the girls were rounded up. Peter was so discreet, in fact, that he was able to keep this side of his life secret even from his closest male friends.

But despite his active sex life with women of all descriptions, from movie stars to beach bunnies to hookers, rumors that he also enjoyed the sexual company of men followed Peter most of his life. There are numerous reports of his involvements with men, and Lady Lawford supplied several of them. In her autobiography, she claimed that Peter had lived with a gay man to whom he gave a great deal of money, and she mentioned another affair Peter supposedly had had with a young actor.

There are stories from others as well. Actor Sal Mineo, in an interview published after his death, named Peter as one of his Hollywood affairs. Prince Franz Hohenlohe, a good friend of Lady Lawford's, tells of a dinner he shared with Van Johnson in Johnson's chalet at Vevey, Switzerland. "Van got to talking about Peter, and he told me more or less explicitly that Peter had had an affair with Keenan Wynn."

Wayne Parks was a young beach boy who used to hang out at Will Rogers State Beach in the early fifties. "Some days," Parks recalled, "I'd use the john on the beach and I'd see Peter in there. He'd loiter for hours, sitting on the toilet playing with himself. It was a notorious john for that sort of thing. I didn't even want to go in there unless I had to go desperately. I'm sure Peter got picked up by guys in there."

Peter Dye, who as the husband of Marjorie Post lived next door to Peter in Santa Monica years later, says that a number of people described Peter to him, crudely, as "the screaming faggot of State Beach."

Richard Fielden, now a Lutheran Sunday-school teacher in Palm Beach, recalled an incident in Santa Monica in the late 1950s. "I was with my wife—this was before we got married. We were down by the beach, close to the Lawford house. I was lugging the beach umbrella and everything else and I really wasn't watching where I was walking. I guess we were trespassing on Lawford's property at one point and I practically tripped over Peter Lawford and [another young actor] lying on the beach with their arms around each other. When they saw us it was too late to disengage. My wife couldn't believe her eyes. I recognized both of them instantly. They giggled and were very embarrassed that they were discovered."

Don Pack, a photographer for the Santa Monica *Evening Outlook* in the early 1960s, heard from gay friends that

Peter had "attended a couple of all-boy parties in Hawaii in the midsixties," and says that Peter made an awkward, abortive pass at him around the same time.

And yet, Peter's closest friends and associates all say that they never saw the slightest hint that he was anything but completely heterosexual. No one knew Peter better than Milton Ebbins, his personal manager and best friend, and while Ebbins thinks Peter may have fought homosexuality all his life, "I never saw him make an overt move in over thirty years. We slept in the same bed one night in Spain when the hotel had only one bed for the two of us. Don't think I didn't sleep with one eye open. But he never showed that side, *ever*."

Joe Naar saw no sign that Peter might have been sexually interested in men either: "If Peter didn't want to get laid, he'd get a girl to suck his cock. Every night of his life. That doesn't sound like a homosexual to me. I'd be with a girl, and the next thing I knew she'd be with him."

There can be no question that Peter Lawford was turned on by women. Still, there is enough evidence to conclude that he occasionally sought out homosexual liaisons, and it isn't surprising that he was able to keep them secret from his friends, just as he did his brothel visits. Surely he would have made every effort to keep his friends from finding out something that might have caused some of them to spurn his friendship.

Ironically, it wasn't indiscretions with men that started the rumors about Peter's sexuality in Hollywood. Questions were being asked about him long before May went to L. B. Mayer with her own suspicions. The rumors started—and persisted—mainly because of Peter's demeanor. As Fred Otash put it, "People from England have that effete air about them; they have kind of a feminine way of talking and acting."

Leonard Gershe, the writer and composer with the Freed Unit who befriended Peter, had another observation. "There were rumors about a lot of actors. They were young, good-looking, single. A lot of women who couldn't get to bed with Peter, rather than accept that he wasn't attracted to them, would start saying, 'Well, he's obviously gay. Why else wouldn't he want me?' I've *heard* women say that."

Sometimes, it was Peter himself who caused tongues to

wag about him, and eventually this got him called into Mayer's office yet again—after he and Peter Sabiston returned from an East Coast publicity junket in the late forties. "We were doing five or six shows a day," Sabiston says, "and you get punchy after a while. Peter could do a pretty convincing gay guy act, and so could I. We did that sometimes when we got back to our hotel room, just for laughs. In every city we went, there was always an MGM executive who would hook up with us. One of these guys heard us fooling around like that and he made a complaint to Mayer. Mayer called us into his office when we got back to LA and wanted to know if there was any credence to this. We assured him there wasn't, that it was only a lark."

ELEVEN

AFTER THE success of *Good News,* MGM handed Peter a lemon of a role in an Esther Williams aquatic extravaganza called *On an Island With You*—that of a Navy lieutenant who kidnaps his favorite movie star (Williams) and flies her to a desert island to show his love for her. Peter knew he was playing second fiddle to Williams's swimming sequences, which were always the raison d'être of her movies ("Wet, she's a star," said Fanny Brice), and he grew to dislike her and the film. His scenes are curiously flat; he seems, for the first time, to have walked through a picture.

When the film was released in June 1948 most critics dismissed it as "cute" and "predictable." Still, it did bang-up business at the box office and earned a profit of $816,000. *The Hollywood Reporter* was kindest to Peter: "Lawford has the appeal to make his starry-eyed character convincing."

Peter's next movie experience was far more enjoyable for him, and the results were classic. *Easter Parade* was MGM's top Freed Unit production of the year, a lavish showcase for a score of Irving Berlin tunes. It was scheduled to be directed by Vincente Minnelli and star his wife, Judy Garland, with Gene Kelly. Peter was assigned the third lead, and Ann Miller and Jules Munshin rounded out the cast.

The production got off to a rocky start in December 1947. Judy Garland had just been released from a sanato-

rium where she had been treated for emotional disturbances
and drug dependency. Her doctors thought it risky for her
to be directed by her husband, with whom she was having
marital problems, and Minnelli was taken off the picture.
Crushed, he sought psychiatric help, but within a few weeks
he had turned his attention to a new project. At home, he
and Judy never discussed his removal from *Easter Parade*.

Garland's fragile emotional state weighed heavily on
Peter during filming. The two had had a brief affair in the
early forties, and he had remained very close to her. "She
was one of the most honest people I've ever known," Peter
later said. "She was marvelous fun, with a brittle, delicate
humor. I'd have her sing for me—I've never heard 'Somewhere Over the Rainbow' without feeling a pang and a
bang."

But there was the other side of Judy, the troubled,
emotionally floundering side. Peter often drove her to her
psychiatric sessions, and he always got an earful on the way
there and back: "She unleashed on me the torrents of emotion that built up in her relationships with the studio and
the men in her life. She grew up with a mother thing and
every man tried to be her father. I really went all the way
'round the mulberry bush with her."

Judy Garland's life at MGM was a paradigm of the
downside of movie stardom. Viewed by millions as a wonderfully talented, carefree young girl reveling in the plea-
sures of stardom, Garland was in fact one of the first and
worst victims of the studio system. Her seemingly effortless
performances were achieved at great personal sacrifice. She
worked eighteen-hour days on some of the gargantuan musicals she and Mickey Rooney were expected to carry on their
diminutive shoulders, always at such a fever pitch that when
she was allowed to rest she couldn't sleep.

MGM executives, thinking they had a new panacea at
their disposal, gave Garland sleeping pills to help her rest,
even if only for a few hours between scenes. When the
cameras were ready for her again, she was given amphetamines to help her get back up to top form. It was a vicious
cycle, and it turned the teenager into a drug addict.

Metro treated its younger contract players like children,
then became hostile when they acted like children. Many of
the young people who grew up at MGM suffered arrested

emotional development, while others rebelled against the studio's strictures as they would a parent's. Some felt the world owed them a living, and entered real life woefully unprepared to face its everyday demands. Elizabeth Taylor didn't learn how to write a check until after her second marriage ended.

Peter wasn't affected by the system as badly as Judy Garland was, but it did leave him with absolutely no business sense and a constant need for a strong steadying influence in his life. He said years later that in the forties, *he* was the steadying influence for other actors, such as Judy and Robert Walker: "It's funny, Judy and Bob were both very disturbed people and they were my best friends. They always would seek me out. I was probably the level-headed one."

WITH MINNELLI out of *Easter Parade,* making the movie was a positive experience for Garland despite her emotional problems. Arthur Freed chose Charles Walters, who had done so well with *Good News,* his first directing job, to take over *Easter Parade,* much to Walters's astonishment and delight.

Although she liked Walters, his inexperience made Garland skeptical. "Look, buster," she told him, "you're in the big time now. You're not doing a little college musical here. This is a big picture, an 'A' picture, and I ain't no June Allyson. Don't get cute with me—none of that batting of the eyelids bit or fluffing the hair routine for me, buddy! I'm Judy Garland and you just watch it!"

After a few days' work, she relaxed. She knew she was in good hands; Walters was no Minnelli, but he was very talented. Then, just as she and Peter became convinced that everything would go swimmingly, Gene Kelly broke his ankle and had to bow out of the production. This could have been a disaster, but the cinematic gods were smiling on *Easter Parade:* Fred Astaire agreed to come out of a brief retirement to play opposite Garland. She and Peter were ecstatic. Their film was now an even more important, more noteworthy movie than before. Filming proceeded from this point on without incident; by all accounts it was a very happy production.

The Frances Goodrich–Albert Hackett script, extensively doctored by Sidney Sheldon, was again little more than a framework for the Berlin music. But it all makes for great fun; in Technicolor, the sets and costumes were ravishing, the performers all in top form, the songs matchless. The best among them: "Easter Parade," "It Only Happens When I Dance with You," "I Love a Piano," "A Couple of Swells," and "Steppin' Out with My Baby."

Peter gives a strong, well-shaded, likable performance in *Easter Parade.* He sings one song, a duet with Garland, "A Fella with an Umbrella," which he delivers with verve even if he occasionally fails to land squarely on a note.

Easter Parade was a huge hit, and it received virtually unanimous raves. It became MGM's highest-grossing musical of the year, taking in over $6.8 million at the box office—almost two and a half times its production cost—for a net profit of $864,000. Once again, Peter had been a major part of a highly successful motion picture for MGM, and no one could say he wasn't earning his nine-hundred-dollar-a-week salary.

AS 1949 APPROACHED, Peter's career had been on a steady ascension for six years, and his popularity was stronger than ever. In a few months his salary would rise to twelve hundred dollars a week—an income which, if it wasn't close to the highest in Hollywood, was nonetheless enormous: the average *annual* salary in America in 1949 was $1,320.

Peter Lawford seemed to all the world a man without worries. The usually astute and skeptical Dorothy Kilgallen waxed expansive about how happy and well adjusted a lad he was: "His existence on this planet is unwrinkled and unblemished, every step on the upgrade, every day on the upbeat.... If you are delighted by swains who see their psychiatrist twice a day, he is not for you."

In truth, however, Peter was a troubled young man. Not only did he have ongoing worries about Sir Sydney's welfare, and guilt about the dark side of his sexuality, but he harbored deep-seated demons as well, neuroses that persistently nagged at him and that he only vaguely understood. In a moment of remarkable public candor around this time, he told reporter Herb Howe that "I have frightening depressions. I have great days, then one like death. At one o'clock I may be on top of the world in the sun, then the thing

starts rolling in and by six, I am ready for the hemlock.
Why? I have everything. More than a man of twenty-five
should have."

Years after it happened, Peter told his friend Dick
Sargent, the actor, about a terrifying experience he had had
while surfing. He was straddling a wave when suddenly a
tremendous fear washed over him. The outdoors itself terrified him—the sky, the sea, the beach. He had fallen off his
surfboard, swum blindly to shore, and driven frantically
home, where he had locked himself in his room. He could
not muster the courage to come out until the following
morning.

Peter didn't understand these disturbing episodes, and
he didn't like to talk about them. His closest friends, those
who knew him for forty years and more, agree on one thing:
he never poured out his heart to them, never revealed his
innermost feelings, and certainly never told them what his
demons were. He *had* them, they all agree, but he never
would tell anyone what they were—if he himself completely
knew.

They stemmed, as most do, from his childhood. Only
he and Lady Lawford knew exactly what went on between
them behind closed doors; but one needn't have the imagination of a novelist to envision the scarring effect May's
personality had on her sensitive, impressionable, affection-
starved son.

Every now and then Peter would act so inexplicably
that his friends could only shake their heads and wonder.
By all accounts he adored his father, but a strange incident
between Peter and Milton Ebbins casts doubt even on his
childhood relationship with Sir Sydney.

Ebbins had gone to Los Angeles International Airport
to pick Peter up. He drove up in his car, a beautiful Jaguar
Mark IX that looked like a Rolls-Royce, and Peter would
not get into it. "He simply refused," Ebbins recalled. "He
took a taxi home. I said, 'Peter, what is your problem with
my car? It's a beautiful car! Why won't you ride in it with
me?' "

Quietly, Peter explained himself. "My father had a Rolls-
Royce. I was brought up with it. I hated that car with a
passion. Your car reminds me of that car and I will not ride
in it." What could have happened in his father's Rolls-Royce

that would make Peter refuse, twenty years later, to ride in
a car that resembled it? "He never explained it to me any
further than that," Ebbins said. "We talked three times a
day. He told me everything. But he never told me what his
demons were."

Peter might have sought psychiatric help, but he didn't
believe in it. He saw how little two hospitalizations had
helped Judy Garland, and he told an interviewer that he
had never been analyzed: "I've known people who have
been and they end up more confused than ever. It's better
to leave certain things alone."

AS PETER worked on his next picture, he got caught up
in another romantic imbroglio—this one with a twist. *Julia
Misbehaves* reunited him with Greer Garson and Walter
Pidgeon and was MGM's attempt to lighten up Garson's
image with a mildly slapstick romantic comedy. Peter didn't
have much to do in the film, but he recalled it fondly as
the production that brought him together with Elizabeth
Taylor, the ingenue of the story. Had she and her mother
had their way, she might also have become the first Mrs.
Peter Lawford.

Taylor turned sixteen during filming, on February 27,
1948. She was still a child, but she was a child quickly
budding into womanhood, and she craved romance. The
minute she saw Peter Lawford, she melted. "Peter to me
was the last word in sophistication," she later said, "and he
was so terribly handsome." She fell hard, and that caused
her great embarrassment one day on the set.

"The whole company knew I had a crush on him," she
later explained. "In the scene where he had to kiss me I
was supposed to say, 'Oh, Ritchie, what are we going to
do?' After the kiss I looked at him and said, 'Oh, Peter,
what am I going to do?' And the whole company fell down
laughing."

For his part, Peter couldn't help but be stirred by this
exquisite creature. "She was incredible," he said. "You just
couldn't believe it. . . . The nose was perfect, the eyes, everything. I'd be awfully dumb if I said I wasn't attracted to her
sexually."

Young Elizabeth wasn't shy, either. "She was coming
on strong," Peter recalled, "batting those beautiful eyes and

ʌying things like, 'You love the beach and I love the beach,
ɔ why don't we go together one day?' "

Sara Taylor, the actress's strongly ambitious mother,
ɛncouraged the budding romance. She was very impressed
ʏ Sir Sidney's and Lady Lawford's apparently lofty social
ɭation, and she told MGM executives that there should be
ɲ announcement of an engagement between Peter and her
ɑughter.

Lucille Ryman, head of talent at MGM, knew that Eliz-
ʙeth was very eager to get married. "Liz was chasing after
ʏerybody and trying to find a husband," she said. "When
ɑne Powell announced that she was getting married, Liz
ɽame running into my office and stomped her foot and said,
Miss Ryman, you've got to stop that marriage!' I said,
Why?' She said, 'Because I'm the queen of this lot and I
ɲave to get married first!' "

But the fervor of Taylor *mère et fille* put Peter off, and
ɲe asked to talk with Lillian Burns about it. "He was fright-
ɛned to death," Miss Burns says, "because she was sixteen
ʏears old, and he was afraid of any involvement. He really
ɽared about Elizabeth as a friend, and he was aware that at
ɬhat age she was really just in love with the idea of love."

If Peter had his own reservations about an affair with
Taylor, the MGM brass made sure he was aware of theirs.
"The word around the studio," he recalled, "was that any-
ʙody who touched the girl would be banished forever. They
didn't want anything to befoul their investment. The joke
was that anyone who took her virginity would be in violation
of the Pure Food and Drug Act."

Peter did take her on a date to the beach—"against my
better judgment," he said. "In a bathing suit she was stunning. But it was an innocuous day. Because no matter how
beautiful she was, I had to stay on ice. I saw nothing but
trouble in getting involved. I had the feeling we were being
constantly watched."

Peter didn't want to "foul up her head," so he told
Elizabeth as gently as possible that there was no hope of
the relationship going any further. Devastated, she took to
her bed and refused to leave it. Sara begged Peter to come
and speak to her, but he felt that would only make the
situation worse. After a few more days of this, he finally
agreed and went up to her room, where they had a long

talk. Peter never said what he told her, but he apparentl soothed her feelings enough so that, as he put it, "she g over it. It resolved itself without any bad things comin down."

Julia Misbehaves was a moderate hit, but a barrage negative criticism greeted Greer Garson's zany new person Bosley Crowther in *The New York Times* called the fil "grotesque" and decried "the awkward spectacle of Gree Garson being a card—or, if you'll excuse the expressio sowing another wild oat."

What happy memories Garson took away from *Jul Misbehaves* she attributed to Peter: "One day Pete men tioned that he was off the next day and was going to shoo skeet with some man from Texas who was in Hollywoo for a visit. He planned to bring him to lunch in the commis sary at MGM and then take him on a tour of the studio Would it be okay to bring him over to our set? I said, 'O course.'

"It was better than okay, as the visitor was none othe than E. E. 'Buddy' Fogelson."

Garson married Fogelson shortly thereafter and re mained his wife until his death nearly forty years later. Al their life together, she said, "Buddy and I always felt a ver special affection for our cupid."

BY 1949, Peter had not only his two distinct social lives among the beach scene and the Hollywood crowd, but a third as well. He now mingled with New York, Palm Beach, and London society. He had befriended the Henry Fords, hobnobbed with millionaires Ned McLean and Bob Neal (heir to the Maxwell House coffee fortune), and dated the highly publicized socialites Elizabeth Firestone and Melissa Weston.

The novelist Dominick Dunne, who befriended Peter about this time, recalled that Melissa was "*the* most daz zlingly beautiful girl in New York society. Bar none. She and Peter had a hot romance." It didn't last very long, however, and Peter soon turned his attentions to one of Melissa's best friends: Sharman Douglas, the blond, twenty year-old daughter of the then American ambassador to the Court of St. James's, Lewis Douglas.

Sharman Douglas had taken London by storm when

r father was named ambassador in 1947. Then eighteen,
etty, and vivacious, she was the "deb of the year." She
came best buddies with seventeen-year-old Princess Mar-
ret, whom she nicknamed "Magget," and frequently slept
er at Windsor Castle. She was the star attraction at what
e called "gay balls," constantly surrounded by "devas-
ting swains" eager for her attentions. She was linked ro-
antically to a marquess (Blandford) and an earl
Westmoreland). More than a few times she and Margaret
ompeted for the same young men.

But it wasn't until the spring of 1949, when she met
eter Lawford in New York, that Sharman Douglas fell in
ve. Peter found himself beguiled in return. He told Gladys
Hall, the journalist, that he liked Miss Douglas because she
as "young and fresh and witty and gay, and reflects the
ollege girl. I'm partial to college girls. Sharman loves the
each." She also, Peter said, fulfilled one of his chief re-
uirements in a girl—she was adaptable. "Sharman has ac-
limated herself to any place or situation she's been put in—
nd these have been more than varied, in view of her fami-
/'s social and political position."

One of the original jet-setters, Sharman Douglas flitted
onstantly from London to Paris to New York to Los
Angeles. Then, to recover from the rigors of all this travel,
he'd alight at her family's cattle ranch in Arizona—where,
ot coincidentally, Peter could easily make a quick jaunt
rom Los Angeles and spend time with her. During one
memorable visit he arrived at the Douglas ranch late one
afternoon, flew back to Los Angeles the following morning,
bought Sharman a diamond-studded bracelet, and then re-
urned immediately to give it to her.

Most of their courtship, however, was conducted via
long-distance telephone calls and letters between Los
Angeles and the ambassador's residence at 14 Prince's Gate
in London (which the Kennedys had overrun in 1938). The
pair talked by telephone almost every night, and Sharman
sometimes wrote Peter twice a day or more. When the letters didn't rhapsodize about how much she loved Peter and
missed him, they were chatty and gossipy, filling him in on
every detail of her daily activities—all-day shopping sprees,
jazz-club parties, canasta games with friends, high tea with
the queen and Princess Margaret at Buckingham Palace.

Her activities with the princess when the queen wasn'
present, Sharman admitted, weren't always so sedate. On
week her usually quiet night out at the movies with "Ma
get" became "hysterical" and wound up at twelve-thirty A.M
with the two of them racing up and down the halls of Buck
ingham Palace and creating "chaos." They spent the better
part of the next day in the princess's bedroom, gossiping

Sharman became impatient with the continual grillin
about Peter to which Margaret subjected her. She kidde
him in a letter that she had told the princess about h
"twitch" and other appealing characteristics. As a result, sh
averred, Margaret had decided that Peter wasn't all he wa
cracked up to be. And that was fine with her, Sharma
concluded, because "I know that girl"—and Sharma
wanted to keep Peter all to herself.

Sharman wasn't aware of the reason behind Margaret
intense interest: Peter had dated the princess before he me
Sharman. As Milton Ebbins recalled, "Princess Margare
was crazy about Peter. He could have continued it, but h
didn't. He was too young, he didn't want to get involved
He was a movie star, he didn't want to be married to
princess. He knew what it was going to entail. So he didn'
pursue it."

In January 1950, Sharman paid a visit to Peter in Lo
Angeles, a trip that excited a good deal of press attention
The *Los Angeles Times* ran a story bannered "Peter Law
ford's Parents to Fete Sharman Douglas" and reported tha
"Sir Sydney and Lady Lawford today will give a cocktai
party honoring the international dazzler."

The soirée was not, in fact, in honor of Sharman, bu
rather a celebration of a one-year contract May had jus
signed with MGM as an actress and a consultant on al
things British.* Sharman attended as Peter's guest, although
May wasn't any more fond of Sharman than she had been
of any of Peter's other girlfriends. "That Sharman Douglas
threw herself at Peter," she later said. "I never cared for
her."

---

*May appeared in two MGM movies, *Mr. Peabody and the Mermaid* (1948) and
Hong Kong (1952), which featured Ronald Reagan.

Although they constantly denied romance rumors, Peter and Sharman made little effort to hide their feelings for each other, even in public. They dined at Ciro's seven nights in a row. One night they nibbled at the same sandwich, all the while gazing into each other's eyes. By the time the sandwich was gone, observers related, their lips had come together in a kiss.

In March, they met in New York, where they made the rounds of nightclubs. After Sharman returned to London, she wrote Peter of a dinner out with Van and Evie Johnson. She hadn't wanted to go, she said, but she missed Peter so badly that the Johnsons provided her with her only link to "my little private wonderful world."

In April Peter flew to London, which prompted further headlines ("Peter Lawford Flying Over to His Charmin' Sharman") and speculation that they would soon wed. The engagement rumors were fueled by a report in London's *Daily Mail:* "Actor Peter Lawford, who has already proposed several times to Sharman Douglas, will propose again this week. . . . Peter has told friends, 'Sharman is the nicest girl I've ever met.' Who invited him to London? Sharman's parents."

Peter didn't pop the question, but he and Sharman did spend two romantic weeks together. After he left she wrote him that she would never forget the "heavenly memories" he had given her. A few weeks later, they decided to become engaged, and her parents gladly gave their blessing. Ecstatic, Sharman told her friends and Princess Margaret, who, according to Milton Ebbins, promised to throw them "the biggest party anyone had ever seen. Sharman was walking on air."

Fortunately the betrothal was never officially announced, because four days later Peter saw Sharman in New York and backed out. Not just out of the engagement, but out of the romance as well. As fond as he was of her, he told her, he wasn't in love. Sharman was devastated and told him that she didn't believe him. He had, she said, broken the romance out of fear and out of lack of confidence in his own judgment.

She may have been correct. Several of Peter's closest friends made no secret of their feeling that she wasn't "right" for him, and it is likely that he allowed their view to become his own. "I think I talked him out of that engagement," Molly Dunne recalled, "because I knew that it wasn't going to be right for him at all. I liked Sharman and she did try to be one of us, but it wasn't easy.

"She invited us once to her family's ranch in Arizona. I didn't go, but Peter Sabiston and Peter went. Peter got bored. He called me and said, 'You've got to come here.' So I flew out. And you know, Sharman Douglas was the kind of a gal who'd come out in the morning and have her hair in curlers and be wearing a tatty old slip, and I said to Peter, 'Peter, you're not marrying this girl. That's it, you're just *not*!' Peter Sabiston and I kept teasing him about her and finally he went, 'Oooh, I think you're right.' "

One might have thought that Peter would have appreciated Sharman's lack of vanity, especially since he was confronted with so much artifice in Hollywood. But he was very particular about the women he dated. He liked them to look their best at all times, to be tanned, to be slim, to be athletic. He had overlooked those shortcomings in Sharman, but after Molly's comments he began to look at her more closely.

It took Sharman Douglas a long time to get over Peter Lawford. Immediately after the breakup she wrote him a letter, by turns plucky and desolate, saying that she would always love him because he was "fine and thoroughly nice." She would measure all her future relationships, she admitted, against her romance with Peter, who had made her realize exactly what it was she wanted from "love and life."

AT THE SAME TIME Peter had first entranced Sharman Douglas, early in 1949, he was working his special magic on millions of other girls in movie theaters across America with his most appealing performance since *Good News*. MGM had considered no one else to play Laurie, the lonely young man who lives across the street from the March girls, in the studio's sumptuous Technicolor version of Louisa May Alcott's *Little Women*.

Producer-director Mervyn LeRoy, who had produced *The Wizard of Oz,* spared no expense to re-create the nostalgic world of the March family in Civil War America. June Allyson was cast as the high-spirited tomboy Jo (a role Katharine Hepburn had made her own in RKO's black-and-white 1933 version), Janet Leigh as level-headed Meg, Elizabeth

Taylor as vain, silly Amy, and Margaret O'Brien as earnest, doomed little Beth. Leon Ames played their father, and Mary Astor their mother, Marmee.

Spirits were buoyant on the set. All four of the girls—even June Allyson, who, as Peter might have pointed out, was playing a teenager at thirty-two—giggled a lot, often to the distraction of Mary Astor, who wasn't amused. The respected Oscar-winning veteran of over seventy films later wrote: "The girls all giggled and chattered and made a game of every scene. Taylor was engaged, and in love, and talking on the telephone most of the time (which is fine normally, but not when the production clock is ticking away the company's money). June Allyson chewed gum constantly and irritatingly, and Maggie O'Brien looked at me as though she were planning something very unpleasant.

"In the scene where Jo got her hair cut, Peter Lawford was supposed to arrive at the house and say, 'What have you done?! You look like a porcupine!' Except that for some reason the pronunciation of porcupine eluded him. It came out 'porkypine.' It took an entire afternoon [for Peter to get it right], and everyone, even Mervyn LeRoy, was doubled up with laughter. . . . My sense of humor, my sense of fun, had deserted me long ago. And it just wasn't all *that* funny."

Most reviews of *Little Women* were positive, although some critics compared it unfavorably to the Hepburn version. Ironically, whereas Hepburn's version was praised for restoring "old-fashioned family values" to movies, this version was criticized for doing the same. One reviewer wrote, "The story of the genteel Marches is a long, sentimental one, not exactly geared to our streamlined age. [It is a] souvenir of granny's day." Moviegoers didn't seem to mind. *Little Women* was an "event film," and its box-office receipts pleased exhibitors mightily. Some credit for that was given to Peter's appealing presence, which reportedly prompted young girls to see the picture two and three times. Peter Lawford's career had taken another leap forward.

IN EACH of his prior ten movies, Peter had played light, charming roles, parts he later derisively called "those 'Tennis, anyone?' bits." He wasn't being asked to play "real people," he complained, "the kind who if you cut them with a knife, you could believe would bleed." He wanted more challenges as an actor and let it be known that he would "give anything to do a remake of *Night Must Fall,* which Bob Montgomery did so brilliantly."

His next picture wasn't in that league, but *The Red Danube* was a serious-minded melodrama with a first-rate cast that gave him a complex character to play. Its story, taken from the novel *Vespers in Vienna,* by Bruce Marshall, concerned a British colonel (Walter Pidgeon) and his junior officer Major John "Twingo" McPhinnister (Peter), whose job it is to repatriate Russian citizens in post–World War II Vienna. McPhinnister falls in love with a beautiful ballet dancer (Janet Leigh), who turns out to be a Russian citizen so terrified of being returned to her native land that ultimately she kills herself.

Peter was worried about whether he was up to the emotional demands of playing McPhinnister, and he sought help from Lillian Burns, whose husband, George Sidney, was directing the film. Lillian was able to help Peter call up the proper emotions by tapping her own feelings about the Holocaust. But Janet Leigh noticed that Peter wasn't comfortable with strong emotionalism, and she recalled an incident that sheds some light on his limitations as an actor. "During the scene when I jump out the window, I got very emotional. It was a very difficult scene for me. I was really very overwrought—I had burst into tears and I couldn't turn it off after the cameras stopped rolling.

"Peter said, 'Now, Janet, what's that all about?' It was like he was saying, 'Just do it and forget it. This is only a movie.' But I couldn't turn it off that quickly. I guess it was his British inwardness, that reserve, where you don't show your emotions that readily. Maybe he didn't feel as comfortable in a dramatic situation as other people. He was more comfortable playing the sophisticate or playboy."

The Red Danube was a box-office dud when it was released in December 1949 (it lost almost a million dollars), and its reviews, positive and negative, were usually based on the critic's opinion of its anticommunist message. To bolster the film's poor box-office receipts, MGM sent Peter, Walter Pidgeon, and Janet Leigh on a ten-city promotional tour. Sometimes all three went to a city together, sometimes they split up. They made appearances at supermarkets, gave interviews to local newspapers, attended luncheons with reporters, and sometimes, at theaters that still had vaudeville stages, put on a show before the movie started.

Peter brought Peter Sabiston and Joe Naar along. His main job, Naar recalled, "was to get pretty girls together and have a party." Sometimes, Naar and Sabiston took part in the improvised stage shows, during which they trotted out the routines they had often done at Hollywood parties. As Peter gave thoughtful, serious answers to a reporter's questions in front of a theater full of fans, Sabiston would stand up and begin to heckle him: "Pardon me—is that your nose or are you eating a banana?" Nervous laughter would erupt as Peter ignored the jibe.

Then Naar would call out, "There's a train leaving in ten minutes, we'd like you to be under it." Audiences would catch on that Sabiston and Naar were plants when Peter would turn and shoot back, "If you don't behave, I'll have the manager take you out," and Naar would reply, "Sorry, I don't go out with managers."

There was a bit of the college fraternity boy in Peter, something Joe Naar and Peter Sabiston liked and helped draw out. Together, they could act like adolescents—whether it was Peter and Sabiston mimicking feminine gay mannerisms or the three of them tormenting unsuspecting people on the phone. "There used to be a man named Chipp in the Chicago phone book," Peter recalled. "We'd call him up and say, 'Hello, is this Mr. Chipp?' He'd say yes it was, and then we'd say, 'Well, good-bye, Mr. Chipp!'"

Sophomoric to be sure, but these were innocent high jinks that Janet Leigh looked back on with nostalgia. "We had a great time," she said. "Those days were a lot of fun."

TWELVE

FOR YEARS after he left MGM, Peter told stories about the ways the studio could find to waste money. One of his favorites concerned a spider web: "In the late forties, MGM built an enormous cobweb about twenty-five feet across on Lot 2 that they were going to use for a picture. Well, they had a twenty-four-hour guard sitting there next to it to ensure that no one either walked or drove through it. Finally, after about a year, Eddie Mannix, who was then number three in the Metro hierarchy, came down to Lot 2 and noticed it. So he asked around about it, and it finally turned out that the picture that the huge cobweb was to be used for had been canceled almost a year before!"

It was because of extravagances like this, among other reasons, that MGM's seemingly perfect financial health took a sharp turn for the worse as America entered the decade Peter called "the dreary fifties." At what should have been the apex of his career, he and many other top stars were caught in the middle of immense changes in the studio system that had molded their careers and controlled their lives over the prior decade.

It wasn't only waste but changing audience tastes that threatened to destroy the spun-sugar castle that Mayer had created in Culver City. The world had been through a devastating six-year war, during which MGM's lighthearted musicals had helped the women on the homefront cope with their loneliness and fear. But now their husbands and sons

150

and brothers were back. The nightmare these men had shared had changed them forever, and movies like *Good News* and *Little Women* seemed to them like so much silly fluff.

There had been a steady decline in the box-office receipts of MGM's patented musicals since 1945, and in July 1948 Loew's Inc. chairman Nick Schenck brought in a new head of production, Dore Schary, a forty-three-year-old writer-producer who had been production chief at RKO since 1945. Schary's charge was to produce harder-edged films, streamline MGM's overall operations, cut production costs—and, presumably, clear away some cobwebs.

Schary's films were successful, and L. B. Mayer's paeans to old-fashioned values were less and less so. Clearly out of step with the times, Mayer was forced out as head of the studio in June 1951—to his lasting embitterment. But to replace Mayer was to put a Band-Aid on a hemorrhaging wound. The studio system was by now outmoded and had been abandoned by the other majors years before MGM saw the light. Since MGM's practice of the system had been the most all-encompassing, its transition was the most protracted and debilitating.

All the worst flaws of the studio system were present at MGM, along with its best advantages. Great talents were discovered and signed, but often for the wrong reasons. Young singers were brought on the lot to scare a recalcitrant Judy Garland back into line; young dancers were signed just to keep Fred Astaire and Gene Kelly looking over their shoulders. Sometimes, these young players made names for themselves; more often the studio didn't know what to do with them and their careers foundered.

Peter Lawford's tenure at MGM is one of the best examples of how a Metro contract could both elevate and sabotage a performer's career. Peter's association with the studio put him in some of the best, most expensive, most popular films produced in the United States in the 1940s. With few exceptions, however, his roles were secondary and demanded little more of him than that he look handsome and act charming.

Peter was undeniably talented, and he showed promise when forced to stretch himself. But MGM had so many extraordinarily gifted performers that someone with relatively modest abilities, like Peter, was expendable. "Most of the time [I spent] sunbathing in my backyard," he said. "Every now and then the postman would throw a new script through the front door which I'd be obliged to do whether I wanted to or not."

Please Believe Me, Peter's one 1950 release, and *Royal Wedding,* his one 1951 release, pointed up his dilemma at MGM. In the former, a pleasant enough little comedy starring Deborah Kerr, Peter is fourth-billed behind Kerr, Robert Walker, and Mark Stevens (his lowest billing since *Two Sisters from Boston*); he plays a millionaire competing for the romantic favors of Kerr with the two other men. Although Peter is thoroughly engaging in the film and displays the lightest comic touch of the quartet (the Los Angeles *Examiner* said he "gives up camera posing to turn in a top-notch performance") his assignment as the least important element of an ensemble was a definite comedown after *Little Women* and *The Red Danube.*

Royal Wedding was a much better movie, but it presented another kind of problem for Peter. A lavish Freed Unit musical, it starred Fred Astaire and Jane Powell as a brother-and-sister dance team in London during Princess Elizabeth's November 1947 wedding to Prince Philip. Peter played a young lord with whom Jane falls in love, and Sarah Churchill, the daughter of Sir Winston, enacted a chorus girl who captures Fred's heart. The film boasted a series of remarkable production numbers, including the musical question "How Could You Believe Me When I Said I Love You When You Know I've Been a Liar All My Life?" and Astaire's now legendary dance routine up a room's walls and across its ceiling.

It was all quite wonderful, but unfortunately for Peter, he had very little to do. His one musical number—"Every Night at Seven," a duet with Jane Powell—was cut, and he was left with surprisingly little screen time. As he had in *On an Island With You,* Peter gives a lackluster performance, again because of his disappointment with his assignment. By casting him in *Please Believe Me* and *Royal Wedding,* MGM had made it plain that it no longer had any idea what to do with Peter Lawford.

At another studio with lesser talent resources, Peter might have been given the chance to follow up on a first-rate star turn like *Good News;* at MGM he never got another role that approached it. He might also have had the opportunity to stretch himself as an actor outside musicals—in something like *Night Must Fall*—as he continually expressed a desire to do. But another negative by-product of MGM's rigid system was that its actors were pigeonholed, typecast. A young English lord? Peter Lawford. A wide-eyed ingenue? June Allyson. Rarely were contract players given a role that went even slightly against type.

Why didn't Peter fight for the better, the more dramatic roles he professed to covet? Part of the reason has to be his insecurity about his ability to pull them off. His position in the MGM hierarchy of talent wasn't lost on him; the more closely he observed the company he was in, the more he realized that his own talents were modest at best.

Lillian Burns considered Peter "the most insecure of the many young people I have known." His lack of self-confidence was a legacy from his mother, who taught him that he wasn't good enough to demand more, wasn't strong enough to survive without her. There would be no compliments from May after one of Peter's performances; she didn't, she said, want "his head to swell." And she constantly reminded him of the family's financial misfortunes, of how much she and his father depended on his weekly paycheck. He was to toe the line, do as Mr. Mayer said. "As quickly as all this came, Peter, it can be taken away just as quickly," she would tell him.

While a part of Peter wanted to rebel, wanted to be rid of May's suffocating presence, another piece of him felt great guilt over his ambivalent feelings toward his mother. That and his concern for Sir Sydney's welfare kept Peter in line. May knew exactly what she was doing.

AT THE END of October 1950, Peter *was* handed a strong dramatic opportunity—by Twentieth Century-Fox. MGM lent the rival studio Peter's services to play a crook who swindles a rancher and romances his daughter in the drama *Kangaroo*, set in the outback of Australia and costarring Richard Boone and Maureen O'Hara, a major Fox star. Set to direct was Lewis Milestone, a highly respected two-time Oscar winner who had created such fine films as *All Quiet on the Western Front*, *The Front Page*, and *Of Mice and Men*.

The cast and crew set off for Sydney via Hawaii, where

they enjoyed a six-day stopover in Honolulu. It was Peter's first visit to the islands since his boyhood, and he was determined to make the most of it. He and Richard Boone played beach bums, grew beards, and drew crowds as they played volleyball or surfed the Waikiki waves. Boone wasn't used to the gawkers. "Everywhere we go we get mobbed by teenagers," he told a reporter. "Of course, they're after Peter, and I get the backwash. I don't care so much for being hugged, kissed, petted, and squeezed by hundreds of screaming youngsters."

Peter kept an eye out for available local girls, and he soon met raven-haired, earthy Jean MacDonald, a twenty-year-old Finch College alumna and a society reporter for the *Honolulu Star-Bulletin*. Jean remembered the period with great fondness. "We went out and danced the hula, went body surfing and board surfing, played volleyball, sunbathed on the beach. We had so much fun." Soon, a romance blossomed. "There was a little something between me and Peter," Jean recalled. "It just sort of came out of that daytime friendship."

Characteristically, Peter found Jean's combination of finishing-school poise and "great gal" earthiness very appealing. On his last night in Honolulu, the two of them drank "a few too many fogcutters" and Jean had difficulty walking in her high heels. Peter nicknamed her "Waddle," and he loved the fact that she laughed as much about it as he did.

Peter didn't want to leave this appealing girl, and he urged her to follow him to Australia. "I can get you a job working on the picture," he told her. "Please come." She wasn't at all sure she could, but she told Peter she'd try, and the two said their good-byes. No sooner did Peter arrive in Sydney than he began a telegram campaign to persuade Jean to follow him there. On November 1 he and Boone cabled her, "Stop ignoring us. Are you crazy? Get your passport lover. Clyde and Homer."

Peter found Jean very much on his mind in Australia, even though there was no dearth of attractive women Down Under. On November 22, he wrote to Robert Walker that he had been in Australia for three weeks and had been "drunk and disorderly" for only nineteen days: "I'm getting better, don't you think?" He told Walker that the girls in Australia were in keeping with their particular tastes and that Walker would "go crazy" there.

Jean, however, was foremost in his mind. She was intrigued by Peter's offer to join him, but she was "scared to death" of flying off to so remote a country to see a man she barely knew. Her mind was made up, however, when Lewis Milestone's wife, Kendall—at Peter's urging—asked Jean to join her on a tour of the Orient. The trip was to begin with a few weeks in Australia, and in the middle of December, Jean arrived in Sydney.

"I got to the Hotel Australia," she recalled, "and there must have been fifty bouquets of flowers in my room— Peter and Richard had taken them out of all the rooms and restaurants in the hotel—and there was a big banner that said 'Welcome Waddle.' That night we were in a restaurant and the orchestra stopped playing and the orchestra leader said he had an announcement: 'Welcome Waddle.' It was fantastic. It was like I was in a fairyland."

Jean got to know Peter much better in Sydney and, later, when the *Kangaroo* company moved to Port Augusta. When Peter wasn't filming, the couple went to movies, played charades, surfed, rode horseback, and took riverboat trips. Jean felt her attraction to Peter turning into love. "He had tremendous charm and a kind of brotherly-fatherly touch that was nearly irresistible," she said. "My mother and father were divorced when I was young, and strangely enough Peter had a very fatherly image—a very kind, gentle manner. It wasn't that it wasn't a sexual romance, but it was a very gentle, big-brother kind of relationship."

The *Kangaroo* shoot was a difficult one. The Australian desert was in the grip of a drought that was integral to the plot, and temperatures ranged between 100 and 126 degrees during the day. Peter lost twelve pounds, thought he would go crazy from the flies that constantly buzzed around, and was shocked to discover that his hair had begun to fall out. No cause, except perhaps the heat and stress, was ever found for the phenomenon, which happily ceased once Peter returned to Hollywood.

Milestone expected to have to film the movie's climactic scene—a downpour that finally breaks the drought—on a set back in Hollywood, and it was with tongues firmly in cheeks that the cast and crew attended a native rain dance one Saturday night. The next morning at four-thirty, Peter and the rest of the company were roused from their beds by the production manager. "Get out of bed!" the frantic man shouted. "Get dressed, get ready to shoot! *It's raining!*" Half asleep, everyone rushed to the set and worked for five hours in the drenching downpour.

Kangaroo wrapped on February 15, 1951, and met with mixed critical reaction when it opened just three months later. Most critics panned its story while praising its breathtaking cinematography and locations, and agreed with Maureen O'Hara that she and Peter had been badly miscast.

From Australia, Peter returned with Jean MacDonald to Honolulu, where he tried to convince her that she could advance her writing career more readily in Los Angeles. She knew Peter wanted to be close to her, and the prospect didn't displease her, but she was hesitant. "I still didn't know Peter that well," she says, "and I was timid about leaving Honolulu." For several months, she remained indecisive.

AS PETER waited for Jean MacDonald to make up her mind about coming to LA, he made an insubstantial comedy with Janet Leigh, *Just This Once,* and began an affair with Dorothy Dandridge, the singer and actress. "He was very smitten with her," Molly Dunne recalled, "and she was very taken with him. We used to go see her when she was performing at the Mocambo. Then we went to Vegas when she was there."

It was Peter's first romantic involvement with a black woman, and it gave him his first taste of racial prejudice since his days as a parking attendant for Carl Brukenfeld. It was an era in America when black entertainers could perform on the stage of a nightclub, but after the show weren't allowed to sit in the club with friends and have a drink; an era when the legendary Billie Holiday sang in a hotel lounge but had to take the freight elevator from floor to floor.

Peter's lack of bigotry didn't extend to fighting the system and risking negative reaction. In some areas of the country, a white man risked physical violence for dating a black woman. Rocky Cooper recalled "playing the beard" when Peter and Dorothy visited her and Gary on a film location in a redneck area: "I had to sit in the front seat with Peter while he drove through town, and poor Dorothy had to crouch down in the backseat, out of sight."

Even in Hollywood, where the atmosphere was far less threatening, Peter wasn't willing to risk the negative publicity the affair might cause. Peter Sabiston felt that "Peter didn't have the courage to take Dorothy Dandridge to parties. He'd have me pick her up and I'd walk into the party with her; then she'd hook up with Peter. I remember once I took her to a party for him at Charlie Feldman's house. He was a big agent and everybody was there. When we walked in every man in the room started paying attention to her—Richard Burton, William Holden, David Niven, all of them. She was a gorgeous woman and a very nice person."

The affair faced too many obstacles to last, Peter and Dorothy both realized, and they ended it amicably. But by then another problem in Peter's romantic life had turned up, one he hadn't remotely anticipated. Sharman Douglas had moved to Los Angeles and was staying in an apartment owned by Elizabeth Firestone that was only a few blocks from Peter's house. She professed a desire simply to be friends with Peter, a declaration he found suspect, especially since she tended to show up at just about every function he attended. Before long she was a member of his most intimate circle of friends.

Sharman's presence caused a number of unpleasant scenes, one of them between Peter and Peter Sabiston. At a dinner party at Lewis and Kendall Milestone's, Peter was taken aback to see Sabiston arrive with Sharman on his arm. Glaring at his friend, Peter reached into his pocket, pulled out a few dollars, stood up, and handed the money to Sabiston. "What's this for?" Sabiston asked. "Go out and buy yourself some good taste and manners and come back and try again," Peter replied. The remainder of the evening was, to put it mildly, strained.

Several months later, Jean MacDonald finally made up her mind to join Peter in Hollywood. As soon as she arrived, she discovered that Sharman Douglas was someone with whom she would have to deal. "It was a shock because I didn't know that much about her relationship with Peter," Jean recalled, "and I learned that it had really been a big thing."

Sharman went to great lengths to show Jean that she harbored no hard feelings. She threw a party in Jean's honor with a Polynesian theme, complete with beachboys strumming guitars, pineapples, and coconuts. The elaborate gesture managed mostly to make Jean feel more uncomfortable, and Peter complained to friends that he wished Sharman would just leave him alone. "I'm reserving judgment on her 'Let's be friends and buddies' attitude," he told Jean, "until she really proves it. I fell for that one before!"

Jean was a houseguest of the Milestones' when she first arrived. Then she got her own apartment, and she and Peter grew closer. "Peter used to drive a Jeep, and I drove a Jeep, and we'd both go to work at MGM with surfboards tied to the roofs." They double-dated with Frank Sinatra and Ava Gardner, who were not yet married, but whose relationship was already tempestuous. "Ava would read something about Frank and another woman in a movie magazine and she'd go off," Jean recalled. "And he was the same way. They had a great romance, but neither of them had the self-confidence to handle it. Peter and I would go out on dates with them and we would always wind up with the check because they'd get into a terrible fight and storm out in the middle of dinner."

It wasn't long before Peter and Jean's romance made the newspapers and magazines. In an August 1951 interview, Peter said, "Jean is my steady. We have a sort of unofficial understanding. After all, I wouldn't be going with her for almost a year just to pass the time away." The reporter asked Jean if she planned to marry Peter Lawford. "I have no engagement ring as yet, and the question of marriage hasn't been broached." Before the year was out, it would be.

IN AUGUST 1951 Peter was aboard the *Queen Mary,* sailing to England to film his next movie, and he was miserable. The entire trip, he later told Jean MacDonald, had been a disaster. His steward had taken a "violent dislike" to him the very first day and refused to speak to him for the duration. In the middle of the Atlantic, a storm had blown up and buffeted the ship for thirty-six straight hours—leaving all the passengers, Peter said, "looking like death at Southampton."

Things didn't improve much on English soil. Peter arrived in London with "a monster cold" at one-thirty in the morning, only to learn that his room wasn't ready. The hotel put him in a dubiously furnished "hole on the eighth floor," as he put it, where he slept restlessly and tried to shake off both his cold and his loneliness. He was so desperate for company, he said, "I set traps for anyone who came in . . . whether they were waiter, valet, or busboy."

Just when he thought nothing more could happen to add to his misery, Peter's back went out and he had to remain in bed for two days. It was a sure indication that he was unhappy about the picture he was in England to do: a grade-B potboiler called *The Hour of Thirteen* that co-starred English newcomer Dawn Addams and cast Peter as a suave jewel thief unjustly sought as a murderer.

Peter telephoned Jean almost every day, telling her that in all his twenty-seven years he had never felt as lonely as he had his first few weeks in London and that being without her was "the most terrible emotional experience I think I have been through." His first three nights there, he told her, he had cried himself to sleep. He admitted that he felt quite lost without her—an unpleasant sensation that aroused a good deal of jealousy in him. When he read in a gossip column that Jean had gone to a Hollywood function with a young actor named Clay Randolph, he asked her testily, "What do you call him? 'Randykins' or 'My little Clay-pigeonface'?"

He assured her of his own fidelity to her, insisting that he had "not been naughty once" since leaving Los Angeles. He sensed that she didn't believe him, "but as God is my judge it's true."

Often, Peter regaled Jean with gossip. He told her that Elizabeth Taylor and the English actor Michael Wilding were "having a *torrid* affair!" and suggested that Jean cook dinner for Taylor when she returned to Los Angeles because Wilding would be unable to accompany her and she'd be lonely and unhappy. He asked Jean to treat her well because "she is a very confused little girl and a nice friend wouldn't do her any harm."

A few days after Peter's arrival in London, Sharman Douglas turned up in town. Peter was angry at what he considered Sharman's continual meddling in his romance with Jean. When he heard that Sharman had told a friend that Jean had said she and Peter would soon be married, he confronted Sharman because he knew it wasn't like Jean to do that. Sharman, he told Jean, "pulled a quick switch" and said that she had not heard this directly from Jean but rather from someone very close to Jean. When Peter asked her who that someone was, Sharman told him she didn't want to betray a secret. "It sounded like a complete cock-and-bull story to me," Peter told Jean, "so I let it drop. Do you believe that girl? She never gives up!"

After several months, Peter felt guilty about his treatment of Sharman, and he asked her out to dinner and a movie. He was pleased, he told Jean, that Sharman hadn't tried to get "possessive or 'for old times sake'-sy once. I think maybe she is finally getting over it and is settling down to the fact that I am in love with you. I hope so!"

During one conversation, Jean complained to Peter about his mother's cold and discourteous treatment of her while he was away. May was distressed by the apparent seriousness of Peter's relationship with Jean, and she had begun to write him what he called "subtly nasty" letters "full of anti-marriage propaganda." He assured Jean that he was composing a reply to May that he would have to wrap in asbestos because that was the only way it would get through the mail.

He had expected a sharp answer, and he got it. "She naturally took the stand of the downtrodden, long-suffering martyr," he told Jean. In the meantime he had found out about his mother's checkered background. He had picked up "some very interesting information," he said, that proved his mother was "not quite the 'saint' she sets herself up to be." He added that his new knowledge "really gives me an ace in the hole!"* He pleaded with Jean not to let the problems she was having with May upset her: "I'll handle it when I get home. I swear I think my mother is losing her mind."

Clearly, Peter had had it with May. He stopped corresponding with her and decided to move out of the house on

---

*When Peter found out, upon his first employment at MGM in 1938, that his real surname was Aylen, May told him that a legal technicality had forced her to give him the name of her previous husband. Fifteen and naive, Peter believed her. In London in 1951, Peter learned of the Aylen-Lawford divorce scandals— and of his "illegitimacy."

Sunset when he returned to Los Angeles, despite his concern for Sir Sydney. He asked Jean to look for a place for him quickly so that he could move as soon as he got back.

The Hour of Thirteen was an MGM throwaway. It wound up $424,000 in the red, and the only thing Peter liked about it was the way he looked. He praised the talents of cinematographer Guy Green: "He even managed to make my nose look halfway human, which is a fantastic feat in itself!"

Peter arrived home just in time for Christmas of 1951. He and Jean spent a romantic holiday together, and it wasn't too much later that he asked her to marry him. "We were going to a movie one night with Joe Naar," Jean recalled, "and Peter told Joe that he had proposed to me earlier in the day. Joe fell on the floor in the middle of the theater lobby."

Jean accepted the proposal, and she and her friends started to plan the wedding. But once again, when Peter was confronted with the reality of marriage instead of its romantic fantasy, he began to back away. "Once he had said it and a few people knew about it," Jean said, "he just kept putting it off. It was kind of like what happened with Sharman, except that this time it just wore itself down naturally. My mother was saying, 'You've gotta get married,' and Peter kept going back and forth. We'd break up over it and get back together and then Peter would waffle again and I'd say, 'Okay then, we won't get married.' You can only do that for a certain period of time, and then things wear out. That's what happened to us. Our relationship just kind of wound down."

Peter and Jean remained friends for the next twenty-five years, and although there were bumpy stretches later in their relationship, Jean kept only fond memories of her first few years as a friend of Peter Lawford's. "He was a wonderful man, an innately kind and good person," she said. "He was warm, gracious, and sensitive. Those were the things that attracted me to him."

THIRTEEN

MARILYN MONROE and her best girlfriend, Jeanne Carmen, couldn't figure Peter Lawford out. Both of them had dated him, and both of them had had the same disappointing experience. "Marilyn and I used to talk about Peter," Jeanne said, "and we'd say, 'What is it with him? Do you think he's gay?' We were the sexiest things on two feet, and Peter wasn't making plays for us."

Peter met Marilyn in his agent's office in 1951. She was, he said, such an "alarmingly pretty" girl that "it really made me sit up." The twenty-five-year-old Monroe, a voluptuous, sexy-but-innocent blonde with a feathery voice, was born Norma Jeane Baker to a mentally unstable mother. The identity of her father was never firmly established; her birth certificate lists her mother's husband at the time, Edward Mortensen, but it was more likely C. Stanley Gifford, a co-worker of her mother's at Consolidated Film Industries, where she worked as a film cutter.

Abandoned by Mortensen when she told him she was pregnant, Norma Jeane's mother, Gladys, struggled for several years to provide for her baby, but she suffered a nervous breakdown and was institutionalized. (Gladys's mother had died in an institution, and her maternal grandfather had committed suicide.) The sensitive, quiet little girl was shuttled from foster home to foster home, living with families that took her in only because the government paid them to do so.

She grew up confused and psychologically battered.

One family insisted she read the Bible constantly and harangued her about the evils of sex and drink; another gave her empty liquor bottles as playthings. At eight she was raped by a man who lived in the boardinghouse run by her foster parents. When she attempted to tell them what had happened, the woman slapped her and told her not to tell lies. Shortly afterward, she began to stutter.

By sixteen, she had developed into a curvaceous beauty who turned the heads of boys at school, and she loved the attention. She married the young man next door, primarily to avoid being returned to an orphanage when her foster family could no longer keep her. But there were deep scars within her psyche; she had a nearly pathological need for the attention and adoration of as many people as possible, to make her feel, if only for a time, like a worthwhile person.

She went into modeling and, when she achieved a measure of success at it, divorced her husband and went into the movies. By 1951 she had worked steadily in Hollywood for four years and appeared in over a dozen films, but she was only now on the verge of the phenomenal success that would propel her to the top of the entertainment world and put her every public move on the front pages.

Peter and Marilyn dated a few times that spring of 1951, both alone and in foursomes. She was taken with him and puzzled by his lack of sexual interest in her. A close friend of Marilyn's, Robert Slatzer, recalled her telling him that "when she had a date with Peter, he was more interested in having a girl as a showpiece than in doing anything with her. It was always just a hug and a kiss good-night."

Jeanne Carmen, herself an attractive, buxom blonde, had no clue as to why Peter didn't respond to her or Marilyn the way most men did. "Neither of us really cared all that much about sleeping with Peter, but we tended to be surprised when men didn't want to sleep with *us*. We would wonder, 'What's wrong with me?' Or, more often, 'What's wrong with *him*?' "

In a 1951 interview Peter said, "There are many girls with long blond hair and sexy figures whom men consider beautiful. But I don't. To me a girl with a well-groomed look, not the flamboyant type, but a quiet beauty who radiates health and vitality is the greatest beauty of them all. I go for the typical college type, not movie sirens."

Peter was initially attracted to Marilyn because at that time in her life she did have a wholesome, down-to-earth side. She loved the beach, worked out with weights to firm up her figure, and had an abundance of girlish high spirits. But the more he got to know and like her, the less interested he was in her sexually. Many aspects of the private Norma Jeane appealed to him: he loved her subtle, skewed sense of humor, her vulnerability, her tentative intelligence. But he was put off by the Marilyn Monroe persona she adopted publicly, the brassy blonde in skin-tight dresses and plunging décolletage. It was precisely this dynamic between innocence and wantonness that made Marilyn so fascinating to the public, but the wanton side left Peter cold.

He was put off, too, by what he saw as Marilyn's lack of hygiene. Joe Naar recalled picking Marilyn up along with Peter and Joe's date, the actress Barbara Darrow. "Peter went into her apartment and her dog had done something on the carpet and she didn't seem to care. He was so disgusted he said to me, '*You* take her out.' So we switched dates. He knew Barbara because I'd dated her before, so he took Barbara home and I took Marilyn home."

Peter later said that he had stepped in the dog's mess, and Marilyn poked her head out of the bathroom door and chirped, "Oh dear, he's done it again!" The dog, Peter added, "turned out to be the smallest chihuahua I've ever seen. Heaven knows how it had produced such a pile!"

Peter did date Marilyn a number of times afterward, but the evenings never extended beyond "a hug and a kiss good-night." On one occasion Peter would never forget, he went to pick Marilyn up and found two burly bodyguards standing on either side of her front door. They asked him what he wanted. "I have a date with Miss Monroe," he told them warily.

"She's not going out," one of the men growled.

"But I have a date with her!" Peter replied, indignant.

"Forget it. She's staying here tonight."

Peter sensed he had better leave, but he called Marilyn the minute he got home. "What the hell's going on?" he asked her. "It's Howard Hughes," Marilyn replied in a whisper. "I went out with him and he's so jealous that he won't let me out of the house at night. I'm a prisoner in my own home." Luckily for Marilyn's freedom, the eccentric billionaire's attentions were soon diverted to other pretty starlets.

MARILYN AND Peter remained casual friends throughout the fifties, but it wasn't until the end of the decade that their relationship grew much closer. In the years between, Marilyn's career at Twentieth Century-Fox took off like a Roman candle, while Peter's fizzled at MGM. Now, instead of making "B+" movies with "A" costars like Deborah Kerr and Janet Leigh, he was making "B−" movies with "B" costars like Dawn Addams and Jane Greer. In 1952 it was *You for Me,* a slight, TV-ish situation comedy with Greer directed by Don Weis in which Peter played a rakish millionaire. The picture was well reviewed as "light, escapist fare," and Peter was delightfully boyish in it, but it lost money and served mainly to bolster Peter's growing reputation as a Metro has-been.

Perhaps fittingly, Peter's last film at MGM was his most ignominious. *Rogue's March* cast him as a member of the Royal Midland Fusiliers who is sent to India (much like Sir Sydney) to put down uprisings against the British along the Afghanistan border. It was, in the sarcastic words of John Douglas Eames, "an Eastern. No cowboys, but lots of Indians."

Showing emotion on film was still something that did not come easily to Peter, even in his forty-fourth motion picture role. The film's director, Allen Davis, recalled that when Peter was required to cry for the camera—for the first time in his career—he couldn't do it. "In a hopefully moving scene, the big set piece of the movie, he was to be drummed out of his regiment, stripped of rank, regimental insignia, buttons, et cetera. He could not give me the ashamed, silent but heartbroken tears I wanted. So we had to use a spray with onion juice in it to get the tearful effect."

Rogue's March did not turn out well; MGM executives had so little regard for the film that they never released it in New York. It did have a short run in Los Angeles and elsewhere around the country, where it lost $247,000 at the box office despite a total budget of only $659,000.

Peter was now in the final year of his contract, and

Metro was paying him two thousand dollars a week to appear in third-rate productions. Clearly, something would have to give. In December, when his contract was up for renewal, the word came down from Nick Schenck, head of Loew's Inc., that Peter Lawford's employment at MGM would be allowed to lapse.

The studio's financial problems had worsened in the early fifties, when television was making deep inroads into the American entertainment audience. When families could stay at home and watch—for free—Milton Berle or *I Love Lucy* or first-rate live drama, it took more than flimsy comedies or sluggish melodramas to get them to leave the house and pay for cinema admission. More than ever, movies had to be "events" to score big at the box office, and theaters needed superstar names on their marquees. The films that Peter Lawford made after *Little Women,* with the exception of *Royal Wedding,* were the hardest hit by the drop in movie attendance: entertainment not much better (and in some cases, worse) than what most people could now get at home on television.

MGM's profits in 1952 were its lowest in twenty years, and Loew's Inc. cut costs by dropping the contracts of many of their highest-paid players. Peter wasn't alone. Some of their brightest lights were let go—Greer Garson, Esther Williams, George Murphy, Clark Gable, Van Johnson, Deborah Kerr, Kathryn Grayson, Lionel Barrymore, and June Allyson, among others. (In some cases, the break was cruel. The day June Allyson left, a studio executive accompanied her to make sure she didn't steal anything. "He had a long inventory sheet of things in my dressing room that were studio property," the actress recalled. "He told me he just couldn't do that to me, so I took the sheet myself and went around checking things off—all the ashtrays and the pictures off the walls.")

With his employment at MGM ended, Peter saw the chance to get away from second-rate pictures. He had heard about the huge amounts of money actors could make by producing their own movies and television shows, and he was intrigued. Television executives, he was told, were eager to use established names in their shows, and many stars could pretty much write their own tickets. Peter promised himself he'd look into it.

*   *   *

ON SUNDAY, February 15, 1953, eighty-seven-year-old
Sir Sydney awoke and complained of abdominal pain. Lady
Lawford called the general's doctor, who, she claimed, in-
formed her between drunken hiccups that Sir Sydney suf-
fered from a double hernia and should be operated on.
"Absolutely not," May replied. "Do you want him to die?
He probably wouldn't even survive the anesthetic. If he
must die, he will die in peace."

May shooed the doctor away and walked Sir Sydney
out to his mignonette garden, where they sat and talked.
The general told her, May said, that she had been a good
wife to him: "You've always gone beyond the call of duty."
He then asked her to make sure that Peter took care of
their cat, a stray he had found in an alley eight years before.
Then Sir Sydney Lawford nodded off, seemingly to sleep.
He was dead.

Peter had gone to Hawaii to visit Jean MacDonald and
other friends, and May telephoned him there with the news.
She later claimed that Peter told her he didn't want to cut
his vacation short for his father's funeral and she should
"keep him on ice" until he returned the following Friday.
She further claimed that when Peter arrived in Los Angeles
he joked about his father's death and went out night-
clubbing after his funeral.

May hoped to show with these anecdotes that Peter was
unmoved by his father's death, that he disliked Sir Sydney as
much as he disliked her. But the opposite was true. Jean
MacDonald was with Peter when he got the news, and she
saw him react "with shock and sadness" to his father's
death: "One of Peter's strengths was his great pride in his
father. That gave quality and meaning to his life; it was a
strong side of his personal character. He felt tremendous
loss at Sir Sydney's death."

Peter *was* reluctant to come home for the funeral, but
only because he wasn't sure he could bear the emotional
ordeal of burying his father, and he dreaded having to cope
with his mother at the same time. Milton Ebbins, who had
just become his manager, told him, "You've *gotta* come
back."

"I don't think I can handle it, Milt," Peter replied.
Finally, however, he did agree to return. As he said to Ebbins, "It will look bad if I don't, won't it?"

If there was any flippancy on Peter's part once he did get back, it was clearly directed at May; she chose to interpret it as callousness toward his father's death. There can be no doubt that Peter was deeply affected by Sir Sydney's passing. Molly Dunne recalled, "I went with Peter to the mortuary to help pick out his father's coffin. He was devastated by Sir Sydney's death. You couldn't mention his name for months afterward that Peter wouldn't well up with tears."

Lieutenant General Sir Sydney Turing Barlow Lawford was laid to rest on February 21, 1953, in a service conducted by the Canadian Legion of the British Empire Service League at Inglewood Park Cemetery on the outskirts of Los Angeles. Peter, Lady Lawford, and nearly fifty others watched as his casket, draped with Britain's Union Jack, was lowered into the ground amid the sounds of a lone bagpipe. The British consul-general in Los Angeles, Sir Robert Haddow, eulogized the general: "Sir Sydney was the embodiment of a soldier and a gentleman. Here his body lies among his comrades in the Canadian Legion plot, but his spirit has been promoted to a fellowship with God."

IN THE SPACE of a few short months, Peter's life had fundamentally altered, and his mind was awhirl with mixed emotions. He was pleased to be free of the MGM shackles, but the cessation of his weekly two-thousand-dollar paycheck was less pleasant. He had saved a hefty nest egg, but he was loath to dip into it any more than he had to. It was for this reason that Peter continued to live in the Sunset Boulevard house with his mother for more than a year after Sir Sydney's death, although he had considered moving out so often in the past. He knew that to set either himself or May up in a separate residence would be a drain on his finances that he couldn't afford.

When Peter's contract was dropped, Loew's Inc. demanded immediate payment of the balance on his mortgage with them, which was $18,573.28. He took out a new mortgage for that amount, with monthly payments of $250, less than one-third of the eight hundred dollars MGM had been deducting from his paycheck each month.

Peter sold the house fourteen months later for eighty-five thousand dollars, netting a smart profit of forty thousand dollars in seven years' time. He set May up in a small apartment in Westwood, and she was heartbroken at having to leave the Sunset house. The day she moved, she pried the address plaque off the clapboard to keep as a souvenir. "I was so happy here," she said to a friend. "Why do I have to leave?"

FOURTEEN

SHORTLY AFTER his release by MGM, Peter met Milton Ebbins, a pleasantly full-faced native of Springfield, Massachusetts, in his late twenties. Ebbins had been the road manager of Count Basie's band for several years and then turned to personal management, handling Basie, Billy Eckstine, and others. Ebbins knew Joe Naar, who had just become a television agent, and Joe introduced him to Peter. Joe knew that Peter needed career guidance now that he was no longer with MGM, and in the course of the conversation he piped up, "Why don't you hire Milt? You're floundering. You gotta get somebody to help you."

Peter took Ebbins to lunch and asked him, "Do you think you can do something for me?" When Ebbins replied that he did, Peter agreed to sign on with him. "I didn't get paid anything for the longest time," Ebbins remembered. "But I didn't care at that point about getting paid. I didn't think I was going to be with him very long anyway, because Peter was a very strange guy."

Ebbins was wrong about the longevity of the relationship—he remained Peter's most intimate associate for most of the next thirty-two years, involved in every aspect of his career and most aspects of his personal life. When Peter went on location, he and Ebbins traveled together and shared hotel suites. If Peter was too tired to drive all the way home, he'd crash at his manager's place. If the two didn't see each other during the day, they would talk on the phone half a dozen times. Ebbins was Peter's best friend, his confidant, his adviser, his champion, his protector, his conscience. If ever a man was all things to another man, it was Milt Ebbins to Peter Lawford.

IN THE SPRING of 1953, the director George Cukor signed Peter to appear in his new picture *It Should Happen to You,* a comedy written by Garson Kanin about Gladys Glover, an unsuccessful New York model who purchases a billboard, plasters her name over it, and becomes an immediate celebrity. Judy Holliday was cast as Gladys, Peter as an advertising executive who woos her in order to wrest away the coveted billboard space, and Jack Lemmon, a newcomer to the screen, as a documentary filmmaker who loves Gladys for herself.

The film put Peter in top-notch company. Holliday had won the 1950 best actress Oscar playing the not-as-dumb-as-she-seems blonde Billie Dawn in *Born Yesterday,* also written by Kanin and directed by Cukor, who had been one of the most highly respected talents in Hollywood for twenty years. Peter was pleased with the opportunity to work with an artist of Cukor's caliber, and he was thrilled to be able to choose a project rather than be assigned to one. He told a reporter on the set, "As a free agent, an actor has to be on his toes. . . . His next assignment will be the result of the merits of the performance he gave in the last one. And since the actor has taken the part because he believes in it, he is likely to give a punchier show."

It Should Happen to You was a big improvement over the films Peter had done his last few years at MGM, but the role wasn't. The picture belonged to Judy Holliday, and Jack Lemmon's character was flashier and more interesting than Peter's. Lunching in Hollywood with Peter the first day of rehearsals, Lemmon said to him, "It's a marvelous script, isn't it? The parts are so good."

"Yours is," Peter replied.

"He said it with a smile," Lemmon said, "but it *was* a better part . . . and there was more of it. It had a little more depth than Peter's part."

Lemmon recalled that Peter was gracious and helpful to him. "And I think it was out of his good nature, period, not because he felt, 'Oh, I'll help this kid because he's get-

ting his feet wet and he doesn't know.' I think it was just
his nature. He was a hell of a nice guy."

Not long into the shooting of interiors in Hollywood,
Peter and Judy Holliday began an affair. She was a pretty,
perky blonde with a cute figure, and Peter liked her
sprightly personality, unaffected manner, and wry humor.
Judy was married and having domestic problems; she wasn't
separated from her husband, but she allowed Peter to believe that she was. She had been under tremendous strain for
a long time, besieged by a lengthy court case, her mother's
breakdown, a difficult pregnancy, a blacklisting for alleged
Communist ties, a large weight gain, and then dieting to
restore her figure. She needed a diversion, needed reassurance that she was still a desirable woman. She welcomed
Peter's attentions, and it wasn't long before she found herself head over heels in love with him.

In June, the company was given a week off before everyone had to report to New York for location work. Peter
and Judy decided to take a train across country, and Peter
asked Milton Ebbins to accompany them. As the train glided
through small towns and wheat fields, Peter and Judy played
poker, challenged each other with word games, and practiced their scenes together. Judy hung on Peter's every word
as he described his childhood travels and regaled her with
stories of his father's heroism, and Ebbins realized for the
first time just how much in love Judy was: "Her eyes would
bulge out every time she looked at him."

Exterior filming in New York went smoothly in spite
of a heat wave that left everyone exhausted by noon and
led Judy to take a cold bath between takes with her makeup
and hat still on. Peter got along well with George Cukor,
who seemed relieved that Peter was giving him just what he
wanted without prodding. After the first week of filming,
Cukor made an overture to get closer to Peter. The director
telephoned him at his hotel room Friday night and invited
him to dinner the following evening aboard the boat Cukor
was living on during the shoot.

"Who else is going to be there, George?" Peter asked.

"Just you and I, Peter. We'll have a little dinner, then
we'll go sailing up the East River. It'll be very nice."

Politely, Peter lied to Cukor that he already had a dinner engagement he couldn't break, and refused the offer.
When he hung up he turned to Ebbins, who had heard

Peter's end of the conversation. "I knew that was going to happen," Peter said. "If I go over there, he'll be all over me like a tent." Despite Peter's turndown of Cukor's subtle pass, things remained cordial between the two men and there were apparently no hard feelings.

Ebbins shared a two-bedroom suite with Peter at the Madison Hotel for the two-week shoot, and it was there that he saw signs of strain in Peter during filming. One morning about seven he heard Peter stirring in the living room. He got up, but didn't want Peter to know he was awake because he wanted to get some more sleep. He opened the door just a crack and saw Peter drinking from a bottle of Tanqueray gin: "It was like he was drinking soda—*gulp, gulp, gulp*. Then he put some drops on his tongue to disguise the smell of the alcohol and rushed out of the suite. He didn't even put the gin bottle back."

The company returned to Hollywood to complete principal photography, and the production wrapped in late July. Peter and Judy continued their affair, and Judy suggested they put together a nightclub act. When Peter seemed intrigued, she arranged a meeting for them with Betty Comden and Adolph Green and sent out feelers to the Sands Hotel in Las Vegas about a November opening. But Peter soon lost interest, and he showed even less enthusiasm for Judy's idea that they appear together in regional theater.

On August 13, Louella Parsons wondered in print why Judy still appeared to be keeping company with Peter when filming on *It Should Happen to You* had ended weeks earlier. She had spoken with Judy the day before and quoted her denial that she was having an affair with Peter: "If you ever saw my husband, you would know how nice he is and that I am really in love with him." Parsons quoted herself as replying, "Okay, Judy, any girl who talks as sincerely as you do must mean it."

By this time, however, Peter had tired of Judy Holliday. According to Milt Ebbins, it had never been a serious romance for Peter, but rather a conquest, and after the Parsons item appeared, Peter felt it was time to end the affair. To do so, he simply stopped speaking to Judy. She couldn't figure out what she had done wrong. Hurt and confused, she telephoned Ebbins. "What happened, Milt? Ask him what happened."

"Peter just wouldn't talk to her," Ebbins recalled. "I

couldn't understand it. He had been intimate with this woman, it was a full-blown affair, and he just dumped her. He avoided her like you wouldn't believe. He and I went to the Latin Quarter one night and Judy found out about it. She got somebody to take her there, and she met us in the lobby as we were leaving. *Peter walked right by her!* I stopped and she said to me, 'What is this, Milt? What did I do?' "

Ebbins met up with Peter on the sidewalk in front of the club and refused to get in the cab with him. "You son of a bitch!" he shouted. "How could you treat the woman that way?"

"What did you stop and talk to her for?" Peter shot back.

"Because I'm a gentleman, which you're not!"

While the cabdriver waited, Peter explained himself. "Listen, Milt, these things, when they're over they have to be over. The only way to do it is to make the break. It's much kinder that way in the long run." Ebbins replied that Peter had acted badly and no amount of rationalization would change that. "Peter didn't know how to handle the breaking off of relationships," he recalled. "Normally, he was a gentleman, but when it came to ending affairs, it was like he was Dr. Jekyll turned into Mr. Hyde."

PETER WOULD soon see the demonic side of a man who had remained one of his closest friends, Frank Sinatra, whose talent, cool, and magnetic personality he idolized. Sinatra, after a career slump, was back on top with his starkly dramatic performance as Maggio in *From Here To Eternity,* and there was talk of a best supporting actor Oscar nomination. But his private life wasn't going as well. Late in 1951 he had married Ava Gardner, by all accounts the love of his life, but in October 1953 Ava announced that the volatile union was over and unsalvageable. After one of the couple's frequent fights during the marriage, Frank had pretended to shoot himself while talking to Ava on the phone, sending her into a frenzy; after another, he took an overdose of sleeping pills. Frank was devastated by the divorce, "torching like mad" for Ava, as a friend put it.

Peter found himself pulled into this maelstrom after he and Milt Ebbins ran into Ava having lunch with her business manager at Frascati's, in Beverly Hills. When they stopped to say hello, Ava explained that she was in the middle of a business meeting, and invited them to join her at The Luau restaurant for drinks later that afternoon.

Peter was afraid to go. As he took his seat at Frascati's, he whispered to Ebbins, "Jesus, Milt, what about Frank? I'm gonna get in trouble!"

"What trouble could you get in?" Ebbins asked him. "You're gonna have a drink with her, that's all. I'll be with you. What's the big deal?" The two of them met up with Ava and her sister Bea at The Luau, laughed, caught up, reminisced a little, and then left after forty-five minutes.

An hour later, Ebbins got a call at home—from one of Louella Parsons's legmen. "Hey, Milt," he said, "I hear Peter had a date with Ava Gardner."

"Yeah, he did," Ebbins replied.

"Well, what do you think's gonna happen?"

"What do you mean, what's gonna happen? They just had a few drinks, that's all!"

The next day, the Parsons column reported the "date" and hinted that Peter and Ava were rekindling their earlier romance. That night, at two in the morning, Frank Sinatra called Peter. "Do you want your legs broken, you fucking asshole?" Sinatra screamed at him. "Well, you're going to get them broken if I ever hear you're out with Ava again. So help me, I'll kill you!"

Without allowing Peter a word of explanation, Sinatra slammed down the phone. "I was panicked," Peter said. "I mean really scared. Frank's a violent guy and he's good friends with too many guys who'd rather kill you than say hello." He telephoned Ebbins for advice, and Milt decided to call Jimmy Van Heusen, with whom he knew Sinatra was staying in New York.

When Ebbins got Van Heusen on the phone, the songwriter told him in exasperation that Sinatra was driving him to distraction. "This goddamn son of a bitch, he's gone crazy! And that fucking Englishman of yours—he's got a monocle up his ass. Will you talk to Frank, Milt, *please,* because he's driving me nuts!"

Sinatra agreed to speak to Ebbins. "Frank," Milt began, his tone of voice as reasonable and soothing as he could make it, "Peter didn't have a date with Ava. I was there. It was no date. We had a drink at The Luau, that's all. Her sister was there, too. There was nothing to it, Frank."

"Are you sure?" Sinatra sputtered.

"I was *there*, Frank. Peter has no intention of seeing Ava. He'll never see her again."

Frank seemed placated. Still, he refused to speak to Peter Lawford for the next five years.

PETER TURNED thirty in September 1953, and as far as he was concerned the birthday was a watershed for him. Ever since he had first arrived in Hollywood, he had told interviewers that he didn't plan to get married until he was thirty.

He had flirted with the idea of marriage to Lana Turner, only to have his hopes dashed. He had proposed to Sharman Douglas and Jean MacDonald, but in the first case got cold feet and in the second allowed the engagement to end through sheer inertia. He wasn't ready.

Now he was. And that was the main reason he had cut Judy Holliday out of his life so abruptly. What he saw as Sharman Douglas's attempts to interfere in his relationship with Jean MacDonald had infuriated him, and he didn't want to risk a repeat with Judy Holliday—especially since he had now met the woman he wanted to make his wife.

PART THREE

AMONG THE KENNEDYS

"He ruled the roost. She looked up to him, did everything he said. Boy, did *that* change!"

—Milton Ebbins, on the early years of Peter's marriage to Pat Kennedy

PART THREE

1 AMONG THE KENNEDYS

FIFTEEN

IT WAS ALMOST as though he'd planned it. Peter had insisted for ten years that he wouldn't marry before he was thirty, and his oft-repeated litany of appealing female characteristics could have been tailor-made to describe Patricia Kennedy. As early as 1944, he had told a reporter who asked him what he looked for in a girl, "I'd want her to be attractive and have something on the ball mentally. I'd want her to be all things at all times—serious when the occasion arises and very gay and mad at other times. I'd want a girl who likes everything; who is a gracious hostess inside her own home and who also fits into any occasion, a dance at a night club, swimming at the beach, or talking about world affairs!"

The sixth of Joe Kennedy's nine children, Pat was born on May 6, 1924. Her father, in New York on business, didn't see her until she was three months old. (When he stepped off the train in Boston, his other five children, ages nine to three, ran up to him yelling, "Daddy, Daddy, we have a new baby!")

Of all the Kennedy girls, Patricia was—in the words of Pearl S. Buck—"the most attractive, the least dominating, the most yielding and gentle." As she grew to adulthood, she wasn't conventionally beautiful (the Kennedy looks sat much better on men than on women), but she was tall and slender and had a vivacity and intelligence that drew men to her. She was educated at the finest convent schools and graduated from Rosemont College, a private women's liberal arts school in Pennsylvania.

The Kennedys were all film fans, and none more so than Patricia. Joe installed a movie theater in their Hyannis Port compound and was usually able, with his Hollywood contacts, to show the latest pictures before their release to the public. Throughout her girlhood, Pat had collected the autographs of all the celebrities to whom her father introduced her. One of her favorite stars was Peter Lawford; her friends recall that when she saw him in *Good News* she murmured, "Isn't he divine?"

Few observers wondered what it was Pat saw in Peter, but some suspected that his interest in her centered on the Kennedy family's extraordinary wealth. He had often told his friends that he wanted his wife to be a woman of some importance and high social standing; implicit in that desire was that she be rich. The Kennedys, of course, had long been among America's most monied families; Joe's net worth was estimated at between one hundred million and four hundred million dollars, and the trust funds he had set up for his children had made them extremely wealthy as well. By her thirtieth birthday, in 1954, Pat Kennedy would have a personal fortune of ten million dollars.

But Peter wasn't interested in Pat Kennedy because of her money; he might have married any number of girls for that. His friends have no doubt that Peter genuinely fell in love with her, because she was precisely the kind of girl he was looking for. "Pat's a tremendous person," Peter said. "She has a terrific mind. A great sense of loyalty. She's so honest—there's no pretense about her at all. And she has such a wonderful outlook on everything."

By the 1950s, the Kennedys were accumulating political power as well as money and social status. Jack Kennedy was elected to the U.S. Senate from Massachusetts in 1952 at the age of thirty-five, and was being touted as a possible Democratic vice-presidential candidate in 1956. His younger brother Robert had made a name for himself as assistant chief counsel to Senator Joseph McCarthy's Subcommittee on Investigations and would soon be named by Senate Democrats as their minority counsel.

Despite his mother's vociferous aversion to the Kennedys, Peter had retained fond memories of Joe, the "heavy cat" as he had called him in Palm Beach, and he had taken an instant liking to Jack when he met him at the Gary Coopers' early in 1944: "I thought he was rather an extraordinary fellow," Peter said. Jack, it seemed, had been equally impressed by the young British actor—intrigued by his international background, his easygoing style, and especially his magnetic appeal to the opposite sex. They had stayed in touch and saw each other occasionally when they were in Palm Beach, but Peter had been too embarrassed to tell Jack that he had parked Joe Kennedy's car as a teenager. When Peter read about the death of Jack's younger sister Kathleen in a plane crash over France in 1948, he sent off a note of condolence to the family, just as he had done after the death of Jack's older brother Joe in a fighter plane explosion in August 1944.

In 1949, during one of his trips to London, Peter met Pat Kennedy at a party. The starstruck woman was thrilled to meet Peter Lawford, but he—involved with Sharman Douglas—was little more than pleased to meet Jack Kennedy's sister. Later that year, Pat came to Hollywood to work as a production assistant on Kate Smith's radio program; she did the same for Father Peyton's *Family Rosary Crusade,* the show that coined the phrase "the family that prays together stays together." Peter and Pat ran into each other again at the NBC studios, and he asked her if she'd like to join him for a party that night. She agreed, but they went their separate ways before the evening was over.

It wasn't until 1952, when Peter and Pat saw each other again—at the Republican National Convention in Chicago—that anything resembling a spark flew between the movie star and the heiress. It was probably the least likely spot on earth for John F. Kennedy's sister to get to know her future husband; she was there as "an enemy observer." Peter, apolitical, attended the GOP bash only because he was a houseguest of Henry Ford's. "He was going to the convention," Peter said later, "and I went along."

A staunch Republican, Ford knew the Kennedys from Palm Beach and liked them despite their politics. He and Peter sat with Pat and her sisters Jean and Eunice to watch the convention, and Peter was much amused by Pat's repeated outbursts: "*Oh!* Those Republicans! Who are they kidding!" she'd grumble during every speech. To play devil's advocate, Peter argued with her, reciting complaints he'd heard Henry Ford and his other Republican friends make about the Democrats. Pat fired back volleys of countercomplaints, and the arguments frequently became "terrible," Peter said, "but always friendly." He was more than willing to give in to Miss Kennedy because of his merely passing interest in the American political system; Peter wasn't a citizen and couldn't vote.

Still, he found Pat's political passion stimulating, and he was surprisingly drawn to her. At a dinner party on the closing night of the convention, he saw Pat's more sophisticated side and enjoyed her knowledgeable and enthusiastic discussion of her experiences in radio. But once again, they lost contact with each other. He returned to Hollywood and she to Massachusetts, where her brother Jack, then a congressman, was running for the Senate. The Kennedy women held a series of homey teas, during which they discussed Jack's boyhood and his World War II heroism and occasionally touched on an issue or two. When Jack won the election handily, the "Kennedy teas" were given much credit.

In November 1953, Peter encountered Pat again, this time walking down Madison Avenue in New York. Working in television now, again for a Catholic family show, Pat had taken an apartment on East Fifty-fifth Street and was shopping for groceries—in a mink coat. This time, Peter asked her out on an official date. "I had always felt drawn to her," Peter said. "I admired her complete honesty. She was one of the *purest* people I'd ever met."

The couple went to dinner twice in the next week, and they found themselves more and more intrigued and attracted. When Pat mentioned that she would be spending the Christmas holidays with her family in Palm Beach, Peter said that he too planned to be there, to visit Henry Ford. "Neither of us likes to fly alone," Peter said, "so we decided to fly to Florida together."

On the flight, Pat and Peter spent more time focused on each other than they ever had before, and Peter later told Jean MacDonald that it had been a revelation to him. "Peter kept talking about this wonderful person and how exciting it all was," Jean recalled. "He was just caught up by her intelligence, her intellect, her personality. He was attracted to her strength."

And he was touched by her vulnerability. As the plane

flew over Tampa, a fierce electrical storm came up, "the roughest" he'd ever been through, Peter recalled. He was frightened, but Pat was terrified, visions of her brother Joe's and sister Kathleen's deaths flashing in her mind. "We were clutching each other," Peter later said—and the experience brought them still closer together.

During the ten days they spent in Palm Beach, Peter and Pat were virtually inseparable. They dined out almost every night, played tennis, met each other's friends. Peter showed Pat the modest house on Avenida Hermosa he'd lived in—"that was a nice Democratic touch," he said. They laughed when he drove past Carl Brukenfeld's parking lot and told her that her father had been his biggest tipper thirteen years earlier.

Peter finally got a proper introduction to old Joe at the Kennedys' palatial hacienda-style mansion at 1095 Ocean Boulevard on the beachfront. The meeting was brief but memorable—not least from a sartorial perspective. Peter recalled that he wore white pants, a blue blazer, and bright red socks: "Mr. Kennedy couldn't seem to take his eyes off the socks."

Kennedy *père* found Peter polite and pleasant enough, and was amused by the hubbub his presence aroused among Pat's sisters and the female house staff. But once Peter left, Joe was wary in his response to Pat's imploring queries about his reaction to her latest beau. "He seems like a nice young man" was all the cautious patriarch would allow. In any case he knew that his daughter would soon embark on a trip around the world during which she planned to be reunited in Tokyo with Frank Conniff, a correspondent with the International News Service, who had been her most serious suitor for several years. Pat's plan, according to a Kennedy friend, was to "talk him into coming back and marrying her."

Pat's blossoming feelings for Peter complicated matters, but she was unsure of the actor's intentions and proceeded with her travel plans. She and Peter shared another airplane trip, this time from Palm Beach to Los Angeles, where Pat planned to stay for a few days before hopping a shuttle to San Francisco for her flight to the Far East.

On Pat's last night in LA, Peter took her to Frascati's and in the course of a romantic candlelight dinner told her, "I'm crazy about you. I'd like to marry you eventually."

"How about April?" Pat replied.

Hearing that, Peter drew back and stammered that he didn't really want to make definite plans right now. Amused at his discomfort, Pat then told him why she was going to Tokyo, and hinted that if he made his intentions more concrete, she *might* cancel her plans. Peter didn't do that, and the evening ended on a strained note. Pat left the next morning for San Francisco.

Overnight, Peter realized he had made a mistake. If Pat and Frank Conniff decided to marry, he would lose her forever. Whether she had consciously used reverse psychology or not, Pat had succeeded in making Peter want something he wasn't sure he could have. As Joe Naar had earlier told a reporter, "As soon as a girl pursues Peter, he loses interest. Any girl who gets him is going to have to give him a hard time."

Peter telephoned Pat at her hotel first thing in the morning, but he was too late: she had already checked out. Frantic to head her off, he booked the next flight to San Francisco, but by the time he got there Pat's plane had departed. He waited what seemed an eternity until he could reach her at her Tokyo hotel.

"Okay, Pat," he yelled over a scratchy connection. "Please come home. April it will be."

Pat laughed. "I accept your eloquent proposal of marriage," she told him—and took the next flight back.

The couple spent a few days together in Los Angeles when Pat returned, and then flew to New York so that Peter could formally ask Joe Kennedy for his daughter's hand. The ambassador, who could keep his nine children in line simply by giving them "one of Daddy's looks," was "bristling," Peter recalled. The first thing Kennedy said as the intimidated Peter entered his study was, "If there's anything I'd hate more for a son-in-law than an actor, it's a *British* actor!"

Then he recited Peter's bank balance. "I'd been thoroughly checked out," Peter said. "I could understand it. There were droves of fortune hunters sniffing around Pat. She was as rich as she was attractive." But Joe Kennedy didn't have much to worry about on that score; Peter had saved enough of his MGM income—nearly a hundred thousand dollars—to make it clear that he didn't need Pat Kennedy's money to live comfortably.

What Peter never knew was just *how* thoroughly Joe Kennedy proceeded to check him out after this second meeting. Joe gave the couple tentative approval of their marriage plans but insisted they keep them secret for several weeks— enough time for him to find out if there was anything in Peter Lawford's past or personality that made him unsuitable as a husband for Pat.

Kennedy first telephoned some of his old friends in the movie business, and he was disturbed by what he heard: Peter's circle of friends at MGM had included several homosexuals, and there had been persistent rumors that Peter himself was bisexual. Joe decided to call Louis B. Mayer, whom he assumed would know the truth. Mayer, who had been convinced by Peter's denials in his office years before, told Kennedy that the rumors were no more than that.

Still, Joe took no chances. His next call was to FBI director J. Edgar Hoover, who agreed to supply Kennedy with any information he possessed that related to Peter Lawford. Hoover ordered his staff to review the files, and the following day he received a three-page summary of FBI materials pertinent to Peter, which he passed on to Joe Kennedy.

The document is headed, "Peter Lawford, also known as Peter Ernest Sydney Lawford, Peter Aylen, Peter Sydney Ernest Aylen." It describes Peter as having been fingerprinted under Alien Registration in 1940, gives his 1941 Palm Beach address, and lists his occupation as "parking lot attendant at Peruvian and Coconut, Palm Beach, Florida. Previous employment in 1940 was at Metro-Goldwyn-Mayer, Hollywood."

The file continues with a notation that "on October 10, 1947, the Los Angeles Office forwarded a letter which Peter Lawford had received from George Pepper, Executive Director of the Arts, Sciences and Professions Council of the Progressive Citizens of America. Lawford turned this letter over to the Bureau, writing on the communication 'Oh so Red' and decorating the outside of the envelope with a hammer and sickle—and the words 'And how!' with an arrow pointing to the return address of George Pepper."

The document's lengthiest section contains information obtained about Peter during the FBI's "investigation of White Slave activities in Los Angeles, California." Kennedy read that the inquiry had discovered that Peter frequented prostitutes employed by a "well-known call house madam" and that another young hooker "was a frequent trick of movie actor Peter Lawford."

Such information would have turned most fathers against a prospective son-in-law, but not Joe Kennedy. To his way of thinking, the report cast Peter in a favorable light. Long a lusty, amoral man, Kennedy viewed prodigious sexual activity—even the extramarital kind—as normal for any red-blooded American male. The report set his mind at ease about Peter's sexual preferences, and the accusation against Pepper proved to Kennedy that Peter was, like him, a dedicated anticommunist.

The patriarch decided that the "British actor" would in fact make a perfectly fine husband for his daughter, and Peter soon cleared another major hurdle as well: Rose Kennedy. The formidable matriarch had at first balked at the marriage because of Peter's Episcopal religious background. But when she realized that Pat and Peter would not be easily dissuaded, and when she reflected on the terrible sorrow she had felt at her alienation from her daughter Kathleen over the same issue,* her opposition softened. Peter's promise to allow his children to be raised as Catholics, and to take instruction in the religion himself, cinched it. Rose gave Pat and Peter her blessing.

Joe Kennedy asked the family lawyer to prepare a prenuptial agreement "three miles long," Peter said. The document was meant to assure that Peter's and Pat's assets would remain separate, but when it came time for Peter to sign the papers, Joe pulled them away and handed them back to his attorney. "We won't be needing these," he said. "Apparently," Peter later mused, "I had passed the test."

NOW, PETER had to get Pat an engagement ring—but the Kennedys swore him to secrecy until they made the official announcement. He called his beach friend Roy

---

*In 1944, Kathleen had married William Cavendish, the marquess of Hartington and a British Protestant. Rose had never forgiven her, and their relationship had been badly strained for the rest of Kathleen's life—a fact that Rose deeply regretted after her daughter's death.

Marcher, whose family was in the jewelry business, and asked him to help him buy an engagement ring "for a friend."

"I said, 'Sure,'" Marcher recalled, "and asked him what size it should be, what does the guy want, all of that. He went into this whole routine, had all the information, and I said, 'A friend of yours, huh? Peter, this is me, don't give me that "friend of yours" crap.'" But Peter was too afraid of offending the Kennedys to admit the truth, even to a friend as close as Marcher, so he decided instead to wait until the announcement was made before buying the ring.

Despite Peter's efforts to keep the engagement secret, items popped up in gossip columns by early February, and Louella Parsons broke the story several days before the announcement was scheduled to be made. The Kennedys still didn't want Peter to confirm the story until then, a situation that caused him some embarrassment. On February 12, he was cornered by a reporter who asked him if the rumors were true. He replied, "There definitely is no romance between Patricia Kennedy and myself. I love my freedom. I'm not adverse to the idea of getting married, but not for a long time."

The comments were incorporated by most newspapers into their stories the next day reporting the Kennedy family's announcement of the engagement. Confronted about his lack of candor, Peter sheepishly explained himself. "I had promised the Kennedys not to say anything to anybody. I guess I was just nervous, and I had said all those things so many times about preferring freedom to marriage that it was easy to repeat them."

The betrothal made headlines across the country; May Lawford's scrapbook of the wedding contains hundreds of newspaper clippings of the news. Some papers ran pictures of Jean Kennedy instead of Pat (oddly, this happened most frequently in Massachusetts), and some of the pictures of Pat had been taken while she was in England at the age of fourteen, which made Peter seem like a cradle robber.

It Should Happen to You had opened less than a month earlier and was doing excellent business, which made the story even more newsworthy. The New York society columnist Cholly Knickerbocker called the Kennedy-Lawford engagement "one of the great romances of the year—a romance that has been serialized on the front pages of the world." For weeks, newspapers feuded about which columnist had broken the story first, then published rumors that the engagement had been either postponed or called off. Much was made of May Lawford's huffy comment that "we would have preferred Peter to choose a bride from court circles." Reporters and photographers followed the couple as they strolled through Central Park, and gleefully reported Peter's discomfort when his former fling Rita Hayworth and her husband Dick Haymes crossed their path. On March 5, reports came out of Florida of Peter and Pat "padding around" the Palm Beach Country Club holding hands, she in pigtails and pedal pushers, he in dungarees.

At this point Peter still hadn't given Pat a ring, but his friend Bob Neal, the Maxwell House heir, came to the rescue. He told Peter that he had bought an eight-carat diamond from Van Cleef & Arpels and given it to a nurse. When they broke up he took it off her finger and put it in a bank vault. It had cost Neal over twenty-two thousand dollars, but he would let Peter have it for thirteen thousand. Peter bought the ring, and as Milton Ebbins recalled, "He was making payments to Bob for a *year!*"

AS WAS TRUE so often in the past, the one glitch in Peter's happiness was his mother. Peter insisted that May give some gracious comments about Pat to the press to counter her "court circles" remark; she did so, but they were typically self-serving: "I used to pray—as mothers do pray—that Peter would find the right girl," she purred. "I didn't care whether she had money, or worked in a bank, or whether she was a gardener's daughter. Just so she was a decent, God-fearing girl. But, if I could have made her with my own hands, I couldn't have made anybody who'd suit Peter better."

Still, the Kennedys knew of May's low opinion of them, knew that she referred to them as "barefoot Irish peasants," called Pat "a bitch," and complained that Peter had been "trapped" into the marriage. She snipped that she always knew Peter would marry beneath himself "and now, God help him, he has." Once when Pat came to the Lawford house to visit Peter, she brought with her Francis Cardinal

McIntyre. Why did Pat need a chaperone, May wondered: "Do you think Peter will rape you?"

It was an inauspicious start to the in-law relationship. May decided to throw an engagement party for "my friends" in honor of Peter and Pat, but by the time it was held, Pat had had her fill of Lady Lawford. She arrived two hours late for the gathering, dressed in sports clothes. According to May, her future daughter-in-law claimed illness and insisted that Peter leave with her immediately. They then went out to dinner. "That *bitch*!" May exclaimed.

May succeeded equally well in alienating Pat's parents. She was invited to dine with Joe Kennedy and then, separately, with Rose; she complained that this was improper etiquette and was annoyed that their secretaries had called with the invitations instead of the Kennedys themselves. At his luncheon with May, Joe reiterated in jest his horror at his daughter's marrying a British actor. May took great offense. "I didn't like old Kennedy's appearance, his background, his manners, or his speech," she said. She stood up, called Kennedy "an old fogey,"* told him she wanted nothing more to do with him, and stormed out of the restaurant.

For the rest of her life, May complained about her treatment by the Kennedys. Her friend Prince Franz Hohenlohe recalled that May "started saying all these horrible things. That they didn't really want her at the wedding, that they were ashamed of her, that they hated her, that Peter tried to eliminate her from the guest list."

An impartial observer might conclude, however, that the Kennedys (and Peter) showed great magnanimity toward May in view of her treatment of them. She, needless to say, didn't see it that way. Her every slight by the Kennedys, prompted by her sarcastic contempt of them, was further proof to her that she was correct in that contempt. It was a vicious cycle that only worsened as the years went by.

But there was little time for Peter to worry about his mother. The wedding was barely two months away, and Peter told all of his beach buddies that they were expected

---

*At sixty-four, Joe Kennedy was six years younger than May.

to be at St. Thomas More's Church in Manhattan on April 24 to lend him moral support on the most important day of his life.

PETER GREW edgy as his wedding date approached, and by the week of the ceremony he was a wreck. He had asked Milton Ebbins to be his best man, but Milt was having some health problems and couldn't attend. Peter turned to Bob Neal, who headed up a "beach delegation" that included Molly Dunne, Peter Sabiston, Joe Naar, and Dick Livingston. The Kennedys flew Peter's friends into New York on April 21 and put them up at the Plaza Hotel. (All except Molly, who chose instead to stay with Jean Kennedy.)

Peter's anxiety mushroomed when Neal didn't show up until an hour and a half before the four P.M. ceremony after some bacchanalian revelry the night before. "We got into separate cars," Neal recalled, "and went to the church. Peter gave me the ring and said, 'Now look, don't fuck this up. When they ask for the ring, that means you're supposed to bring it up to the altar. Now really, *don't fuck this up!*'"

As it turned out, Peter was himself a few minutes late. Inside the beautiful church on East Eighty-ninth Street between Fifth and Madison avenues, Pat stood with her father next to the baptismal font and waited along with the 250 guests for her intended to arrive.* She looked resplendent in a gown described by a reporter as "simple yet magnificent." Designed by Hattie Carnegie with pearl-white satin, it had a portrait neckline, tight-fitting bodice, and three-quarter-length sleeves. Her skirt was form fitting in front, its fullness flowing to the back to form a modified train. A single strand of pearls and a bouquet of orchids offset a voluminous tulle veil that cascaded from a small satin cap down her back to the floor.

Ushers were Pat's brothers Jack, Bob, and Teddy, their close friend LeMoyne Billings, and Peter Sabiston. Eunice Shriver, pregnant, did not attend, and Jean Kennedy was her sister's only bridesmaid. She wore a Christian Dior silk

---

*The Kennedys were not allowed to use St. Patrick's Cathedral, as they had the previous year for Eunice's wedding to R. Sargent Shriver, because Peter wasn't Catholic.

taffeta dress covered with pink-and-blue hydrangeas and a large blue picture hat trimmed in purple velvet ribbon. "Quite incorrect," Lady Lawford sniffed. "A true lady never covers her face from cameras. . . . *I* wore a small off-the-face chapeau just like the queen wears."

Peter, for reasons known only to himself, didn't invite any of his Hollywood friends to the wedding (with the exception of Jackie Cooper, who didn't attend because "I didn't think Peter belonged in that Kennedy milieu"), and the only movie stars there, Greer Garson and Marion Davies, were friends of the Kennedys. Among the other guests were Prince Christian of Hanover; Hugh and Nina Auchincloss; Prince Franz Hohenlohe and his mother, Princess Stephanie; Justice William O. Douglas; Bernard Baruch; Melissa Weston Bigelow; Prince Mahmoud Pahlevi, younger brother of the Shah of Iran; Igor Cassini; Madame Louis Arpels; Lawrence Spivak; and Mr. and Mrs. Morton Downey, Sr. "The people I brought to the wedding," Lady Lawford stressed, "were the only titled people there."

After a few minutes' wait for the tardy Peter, a great roar from the street signaled to everyone in the church that he had arrived. Three thousand people had gathered outside, filling the entire block from stoop to stoop and avenue to avenue, most of them "screaming women and uninhibited bobbysoxers," as one reporter put it, who had come to catch a glimpse of Peter. They didn't get much of a chance; the groom-to-be sprinted from the limousine into the church without so much as a sideward glance after a flying wedge of policemen cleared a path for him. There was such bedlam after he disappeared from sight that "fifty housewives"—as the press described them—were able to sneak in and watch the nuptials from the rear of the church.

The ceremony, performed by former Notre Dame president the Reverend John J. Cavanaugh, was not a high mass (again because Peter wasn't Catholic) and it lasted less than ten minutes. Cavanaugh spoke of the couple's obligation to "have faith in each other" and to "surrender individuality" for the sake of marriage, and when he called for the ring, Peter glanced anxiously at Bob Neal. "I concentrated on what I had to do and I produced the ring without incident," Bob recalled. "Peter looked at me and smiled with a mixture of surprise and appreciation."

Pat pronounced her vows calmly and forthrightly, but observers could barely hear Peter, who appeared "very nervous." The press made much of the fact that after Cavanaugh pronounced them man and wife, Peter "forgot" to kiss his bride. But May later said he never intended to kiss her because "he knew it would be in poor taste."

When Peter and Pat appeared in the doorway of the church, squinting into the brilliant sun, the crowd roared and surged toward them. This time, Peter's fans would not be denied a close look. The couple struggled to get into their limousine as the mob closed in; they were so badly jostled Pat almost lost her cap and veil. Once they got into the car the pandemonium grew worse as reporters and photographers grappled with fans for a good vantage point from which to peer through the car's windows.

As flashbulbs popped and fans screamed Peter's name and cried, "Isn't he *gorgeous*?!" the limo started to rock back and forth as hundreds of bodies pushed against it on either side. Peter and Pat grew frightened as minute after interminable minute passed with the car unable to move. It took nearly a half hour for twenty-three policemen to clear a path so that the chauffeur could make his way down Eighty-ninth Street to Fifth Avenue and deliver the Lawfords to the Plaza Hotel, where another large but more dignified crowd waited to greet them and the other celebrities as they filed into the hotel for the wedding reception.

First the wedding party gathered in Joe Kennedy's suite, joined by Peter's fellow in-laws Jacqueline and Ethel Kennedy and Sargent Shriver. "Everybody kissed each other and sipped champagne," Bob Neal recalled, "and then we went down to the ballroom, which was beautifully decorated."

The Plaza's Grand Ballroom *was* a lovely sight—each table covered entirely in pink, with candles and centerpieces holding pink snapdragons, tulips, and delphiniums. A hedge of white hydrangeas ran the full length of the wedding party's table, which held candelabra at each end. A similar hedge, of pink hydrangeas, led to a stage where Emil Coleman's orchestra played.

The newlyweds and their parents stood for half an hour in a receiving line to welcome the three hundred guests. Then Peter took his bride's hand and walked her to the center of the dance floor, where they whirled to the strains of "Stranger in Paradise." Joe Kennedy then danced with his daughter, while Peter led first Rose Kennedy and then his mother across the floor.

As was traditional at Kennedy weddings, each member of the wedding party made a toast to the bride and groom. All were touching and tasteful, and Peter Sabiston was the last to rise. "Now, I had about nine dollars to my name," Sabiston recalled, "and that included the value of my car and the money I had in my pocket. And here I am staying at the Plaza and hobnobbing with all these multimillionaires. I raised my glass and said, 'Captain, please bring me the check for this party.' Well, I thought Peter and the Kennedys would fall on their faces laughing, because they knew how poor I was. All except Joe Kennedy—he didn't think it was funny at all."

After the toasts were completed, the three Kennedy brothers stood on the dais behind the bride and groom and sang to them, their Irish tenor voices lilting lyrics written especially for Peter and Pat by Sammy Cahn. Then the guests ate, drank, and danced away the remainder of the evening.

Years later, May claimed that Jack Kennedy got very drunk the night of the wedding and, despite being on crutches because of an injury, insisted on dancing with her. She refused, she said, and told him, "This is a wedding. You're going to turn it into your funeral."

According to Molly Dunne, this was nonsense. "I didn't see Jack on crutches, and I didn't notice him drinking too much. *She* was obnoxious, and she was shunted off to the side. There was a dinner the night before the wedding and it was just Peter and Pat, Peter Sabiston and myself, and Joe and Rose. Nobody wanted her around at all." (Photographs of the wedding show Jack and May dancing quite normally, crutches nowhere in sight.)

After the reception, Peter invited Bob Neal, Peter Sabiston, and Molly Dunne back to his suite. He got out of his tuxedo and felt comfortable enough with Molly to walk around the room in his undershorts, sipping champagne. "There was a knock on the door," Molly recalled, "and here were all the Kennedy men—including Joe the father. Peter became totally unglued. He was terrified of the Kenne-

dys. He was so embarrassed to be in his undershorts that
he grabbed a towel to wrap around his waist. So now I'm
feeling like an idiot—he doesn't cover up for *me* but he
does for the Kennedy men!"

Toward the early morning hours of Sunday, Peter and
Pat were finally able to steal a few hours alone as man and
wife. They ensconced themselves in the bridal suite at the
Plaza for the day and then left for a two-week honeymoon
in Hawaii, with an overnight stop in Chicago en route. Their
plane arrived in Honolulu at six forty-five Tuesday evening
and they were greeted by Jean MacDonald, her mother, and
Jean's friends Rab and Alice Guild. A large crowd of well-
wishers stood behind a fence that separated the airstrip from
the terminal, and the Lawfords walked along it shaking
hands—"just like a politician and his wife," one observer
noted. Pat was heaped with leis—six in all—and photos
show her smiling broadly above a mass of flowers.

"We were astonished," Jean MacDonald recalled, "because the first thing Pat said after 'Hello' was 'The Hawaii
state legislature session opens tomorrow. How do I get
there?' And my mother said, 'Huh?' Here Pat was on her
honeymoon and her first thought was politics."

The Guilds found Pat "happy and warm" most of the
time, but thought that she could also be "a little aloof."
Alice recalled that she was "reserved. I don't know that she
would have chosen any of us as friends, but because we
were a given, she accepted us."

Peter was pretty much on his own the first few days of
the trip, while Pat attended the legislature sessions ("It was
a pretty unconventional honeymoon," one of Peter's friends
observed), but afterward he and Pat went sailing, swam in
the crystal-clear azure waters of Waikiki, and played tennis.
Pat tried her hand at surfing the big waves along Oahu's
northern shore, but she didn't much like it; she had more
fun playing golf. (If she and Peter couldn't agree on a recreation, they went their separate ways. This puzzled Peter's
friends, but the couple in question didn't seem to give it a
second thought.) On May 6, Peter threw his bride a surprise
birthday party in a teahouse, to which he invited all his
friends. "Pat was wonderful that night," Alice Guild recalled. "She was funny and fun and I realized I liked her."

That weekend, Peter and Pat planned to spend time in

the mountains of Oahu, and Peter asked to borrow Rab Guild's car for the trip. "I had a red Oldsmobile convertible that was the love of my life and I lent it to Peter," Rab recalled. "Afterward, we were headed up to visit them and it was very difficult to get to where they were staying, so Peter said he'd come down to Waipahu and pick us up. Well, we waited and waited and finally they showed up about an hour and a half late. He said, 'I'm sorry we're late, but I wrecked your car.' I said, 'Ha ha ha.' He said, 'No, really, I wrecked your car.'

"So he drove us up the mountain and showed me where he'd lost the brakes on a twenty percent downward grade and laid the car into a ditch. Here was my beautiful convertible lying on its side. I was heartbroken, and all Peter could say was, 'You're lucky I didn't get killed.' "

Toward the end of the honeymoon, Jean MacDonald, her husband, Bob Anderson, and the Guilds took Peter and Pat to a movie. They arrived late, after the film had begun. When it was over, some members of the audience filing out of the theater recognized the Lawfords. A few stopped to congratulate them on their marriage, and that's when they learned that they had missed a newsreel about the wedding that had preceded the film.

Rab approached the manager and asked him to run the newsreel again, and he agreed. The lights went down as the six of them sat alone in the theater, all anticipation. When the newsreel started, a blazing white headline flashed across the black screen: "Pat Kennedy Marries Actor."

"Peter was crushed," Rab Guild recalled. "He was just *crushed*. They hadn't even used his *name*."

SIXTEEN

FROM THE OUTSET, the Lawfords were an unconventional couple. Neither Pat nor Peter had ever been hidebound about the way to live, she because of her wealth and he because of his decade in the Hollywood community, where, as Liza Minnelli has said, "We don't live like other people."

As they had at times on their honeymoon, Peter and Pat acted independently of each other far more than most newlyweds. Soon after the wedding, she began a marriage-long practice of taking trips without Peter, and he spoke to the reporter Maxine Arnold early in 1955 about the very "laid back" quality of his marriage.

"We have a wonderful, easy relationship," he said. "This thing about henpecked people—of having to account for every hour—I believe this has been fostered a lot by gag men. You know, the where-were-you-last-night routine. I call Pat when I'm working, as a matter of courtesy, but she wouldn't say anything if I didn't call her. And if I should call now and say, 'I'm not coming home for dinner,' she wouldn't say a word. I wouldn't have to say why—or where I was going."

When Peter's friends learned that he and Pat had separate bedrooms, some of them worried that the Lawfords were a little *too* unlike traditional newlyweds. Peter pooh-poohed their concerns, pointing out that he and Pat were both thirty and more set in their ways than a lot of young marrieds. He assured his friends that he and his wife's mutual independence would be no problem whatsoever in their marriage.

But Pat's wealth hovered over the Lawfords like an enormous carnivorous bird, always threatening to peck away at Peter's self-esteem. He was sensitive to whispers that he'd married Pat for her money, and he knew that he would have to steer very carefully to keep the marriage on an even keel. A reporter said to him, "If your wife has fourteen million, or whatever she happens to have, why should you take a desk job just to prove you can earn your own way?" In agreement, Peter offered this anecdote:

"I know a woman who was so rich she had her own DC-3. The works. She married a man without any money. One day he told her that he couldn't stand living on her money any longer, that they would have to live in keeping with his salary. They got divorced. She went and married some other cat, and he's a swinger, and he said, 'Okay, baby, it's your money, let's go!' She was delighted, and the marriage has been a great success."

Peter went to neither of the extremes illustrated by his little parable. He insisted on holding up his end of the monetary bargain to the best of his financial ability, but he never denied Pat the right to give the two of them the life she wanted. The Lawfords agreed that she would pay for their travel, any parties they gave, the food and utility bills, and most of the servants; Peter would pay for the gardener, the maid, and the mortgage.

The first two years of the marriage, the Lawfords rented houses on the beach in Malibu, because when Joe Kennedy offered to buy them a house as a wedding present, Peter refused. He wanted to purchase their residence himself, in order to have a major financial responsibility in the marriage and thus keep things on something approaching an equal footing.

Although Joe Kennedy had torn up the prenuptial agreement keeping Peter and Pat's assets separate, Peter never did know exactly how much Pat was worth, and he was never made privy to any of the details of his wife's finances. Each year at tax time, he was given a blank 1040 form to sign and handed it over to Pat's accountants with his financial information for the year. He never saw the return again. When Milton Ebbins complained about this to Peter's business manager, Bob Schiller, he was told, "What are you worrying about? Peter gets a big refund every year."

One year a copy of the return was sent to Peter in error. Curious, he looked it over and discovered that Pat had paid $286,000 in taxes for the previous year. The tax had been levied solely on her interest income.

IF PETER were to have any hope of holding his own financially in a marriage to Pat Kennedy, he would have to get back to work. The success of *It Should Happen to You* had been credited mostly to Judy Holliday and Jack Lemmon, and to Peter's deep chagrin, he received no further movie offers, despite his enhanced renown as the groom of the year. He finally had to admit that it looked as though his movie career was over.

Peter had no interest in theater work, so his only alternative was television. He had mixed feelings about the medium. It was clearly a cultural phenomenon; the number of sets in America had mushroomed from an estimated ten thousand in 1946 to more than fourteen million in 1953. In just a few years, television had altered the world's notion of what constituted a night of entertainment. No longer did Americans have to leave their homes and pay admission to a theater to see their favorite performers. Shows like Milton Berle's variety hour, Sid Caesar's *Your Show of Shows,* George Burns and Gracie Allen's sitcom, Jackie Gleason's *The Honeymooners,* and, most spectacularly, Lucille Ball's *I Love Lucy* kept people happy within the womb of their own living rooms every night.

A movie might attract hundreds of thousands of people to the box office, but a single television show might be watched by ten million. So many people tuned into the episode of *I Love Lucy* in which Lucy and Ricky's baby was born, New York City officials reported, that during the commercials water pressure in the city dropped to dangerously low levels.

But most people in the Hollywood community looked down their noses at television as second-rate, a poor stepchild of theater and the movies. Few stars with strong movie careers considered doing television; those who did were often mocked as "washed up in Hollywood." Specials—then called "spectaculars"—were rarely anything but showcases for musical performers.

Drama anthologies such as *Ford Theatre, G.E. Theatre,* and *Schlitz Playhouse of Stars* did carry a certain amount of prestige, and Peter appeared on all three in 1953 and 1954, in five separate teleplays. But series television remained problematic for many actors concerned about their public images. Peter dragged his heels for a long time before he decided to star in and produce a situation comedy. What made up his mind—as it did many another actor in the same quandary—was the money.

"I tried to get Peter to commit to it but he wouldn't do it," Milt Ebbins recalled. "He was gun-shy. He never could make a decision. Peter and Pat and I had a meeting and she said to him, 'This sounds good, Peter, why don't you do it?' He hemmed and hawed. Pat said, 'You're gonna get paid, aren't you?' I said, 'Sure he is—five thousand dollars a week.' Pat said, '*What!* Peter, you *have* to do this!' So he did it. She was the one who made him do it."

Peter had read through two dozen scripts when he came to *Dear Phoebe.* He saw that it was about a male advice-to-the-lovelorn columnist (or, as the British call them, an agony aunt) and put it unread at the bottom of the stack. But most of the other scripts called for him to play a British spy, he said, "in a trench coat with fog swirling around my head." When Alex Gottlieb, the writer-producer of *Dear Phoebe,* insisted that Peter read the script or send it back, he read it—and discovered that *Dear Phoebe* had some real comic possibilities. "Then I got excited."

Phoebe also gave Peter the opportunity to own a piece of a production and potentially earn a great deal more than his weekly salary. He and Pat each put up $12,500 for a combined one-half share of the series; Alex Gottlieb was to put up $25,000 for the other half. When Gottlieb found a network, NBC, and the network found a sponsor, Campbell's Soup, Peter went to work filming the pilot.

The comedy in *Dear Phoebe* stemmed from the employment of Bill Hastings, a former college professor, to write an advice column under the byline "Phoebe Goodheart" for a Los Angeles newspaper. To further challenge sexual stereotypes and add grist to the battle-of-the-sexes mill, Hastings's love interest, Mickey Riley, is one of the paper's sportswriters. Gottlieb hired Marcia Henderson, a Universal International Studios starlet who'd made a hit in 1950 as Wendy in the Broadway production of *Peter Pan,* to play Mickey. Peter's friend Don Weis was set to direct.

The plots usually involved jealousy—romantic or professional—on either Bill's or Mickey's part: Bill gets an exclusive interview with one of the victims of a kissing bandit—Mickey is unhappy. Mickey befriends an athlete she writes about—Bill is unhappy. Bill gets psychiatric help from a shapely blond doctor—Mickey is unhappy.

Although silly in the way only a TV sitcom can be, *Dear Phoebe* appealed to Peter, the producers, and NBC executives not only because the scripts were bright and funny, but also because they were more sophisticated than most of the fare flooding the airwaves. As *TV Guide* put it, ever since the debut of *I Love Lucy* in 1951, "the medium has been overwhelmed with situation comedies based on American family life as it is rarely, if ever, lived. It has remained for a former MGM glamour boy, British-born Peter Lawford, to take the play away from his elders with a role once dear to the heart of the American movie-goer but in recent years as hard to find as a kind word in Hollywood—the romantic young man with an infinite capacity for getting in and out of more-or-less adult trouble. . . . It could be that in *Dear Phoebe* NBC has come up with the new show of the year."

Optimism suffused the set of *Dear Phoebe* as production began. Despite the fact that the schedule called for the filming of two episodes a week, spirits were high—and the only problems were caused by Peter's sense of mischief. As a producer for the first time, he apparently felt unconstrained about behaving himself, and the *Dear Phoebe* set sometimes resembled a college dormitory. The show's assistant director, Paul Wurtzel, remembered that "for some reason everybody had a water pistol. You always tried to get the other guy with the water pistol—even while they were filming scenes. Someone would be doing a close-up and Peter would squirt him and water would be running down his face. Lots of takes got ruined. The production guys were going crazy—they were trying to make this thing cheap. It just got out of hand. The electricians started doing it, and everybody wanted to get the biggest pistol that would shoot the farthest. The wardrobes were getting soaked. This went on for weeks."

It got so that the crew members were throwing buckets of water at each other, and finally a lens and a light globe were shattered, prompting studio executives to issue a simple directive: "All right, that's it." But the gags didn't stop, they simply became more sedate. The show's sponsor was Campbell's Soup, and the crew filmed the commercials at the same time as the shows. For one ad spot, Campbell's executives came on the set and built a huge display, stacking fifty cans of Campbell's vegetable soup in a pyramid. The next morning—the day the spot was to be filmed—Peter arrived before anyone else, stealthily pulled out the center can, and replaced it with one of Heinz soup. The Campbell's people never caught on.

Pat, who was thrilled to be involved in television production again, even if only peripherally, spent a lot of time watching from the sidelines and had a couple of walk-on bits in the show. Her brother Jack, who was fascinated by the inner workings of show business, visited several times and asked questions incessantly. The cast and crew liked Pat, and on her first visit to the set they gave her a wedding present—a money clip. "We were always kidding Peter about how much money the Kennedys had," Wurtzel recalled. When Pat opened the box, she didn't know what it was. When she was told she went around to everybody on the set and said, "Okay, put some money in it"—and they did. *She's a good sport,* Wurtzel thought.

So was Peter, especially about the demands of television and its lack of coddling. "This is TV, it isn't Metro" was Wurtzel's favorite phrase. When Peter would ask, with perhaps a little more British clip in his voice than called for, "What scene is this, my good man?" the reply might easily be, "The scene where you go down on your head." Peter would reply with exaggerated dignity, "Thank you so much"—and a few minutes later fall head over heels for retake after retake, until his knees and knuckles were bleeding. "Already a casualty, and the day yet so young," Peter would murmur—and then, before anyone else could pipe up with it, he'd add, "I know—this is TV, it isn't Metro."

Dear Phoebe debuted on Friday evening, September 10,

1954, opposite stiff competition: *Our Miss Brooks* on CBS and *Boston Blackie* on ABC. It won favorable reviews; *TV Guide* said the show "boasts what is probably the most absurd situation of any situation comedy on TV, and we use the word boasts advisedly. The show is good fun, thanks to a fine cast, spritely dialogue and some zany plot lines. Lawford is wonderful . . ."

Philip Minoff in *Cue* opined that "the fastest and cleverest of the myriad situation comedies on the channels continues to be the Peter Lawford starrer *Dear Phoebe*. Reminds us strongly, in zip and flavor, of the movie *His Girl Friday,* which, as you'll recall, had Cary Grant and Rosalind Russell speaking at an average of 200 words per minute to make the film the fastest-paced in history."

The show did well in the ratings; Peter said they expected a thirteen rating and got a twenty-two. "That was a happy surprise, because *Our Miss Brooks* has a twenty-two. Then we went up to twenty-five. *I Love Lucy* has a fifty-two." Alex Gottlieb was pleased. "I think we're proving that viewers, as well as sponsors, don't necessarily insist that every show on the air be patterned after the most successful show. My hunch is that Pete is going to wind up as a real TV matinee idol."

He didn't, and Peter blamed Gottlieb. The show was doing well enough to keep the network and the sponsor happy, and could have been renewed beyond the forty episodes and reruns aired between September 1954 and September 1955. Peter, however, endured a worst-case scenario of the problems a TV producer can face, and he decided to call it quits after one season.

"Gottlieb was Billy Rose's brother-in-law," Milton Ebbins explained. "When we were in the midst of negotiating the deal, Peter and Pat put up their share of the money for the pilot, but Gottlieb never put up his share. I kept pressing him. He'd say, 'Goddammit, my brother-in-law's got more money than Joe Kennedy!' I'd say, 'Alex, where's your money?' "

According to Ebbins, Gottlieb raised part of the money by borrowing it from the owner of the film lab hired to process *Dear Phoebe* episodes, and this didn't sit well with Peter. "He wanted out of the commitment, because things had gotten off on the wrong foot. The network persuaded him to stick it out. But when we started filming, Gottlieb was terrible. We finally barred him from the set."

Joe Naar and Peter soon found themselves in a confrontation with the producer. "Peter had a fight with Gottlieb," recalled Naar, "and the next thing I knew I was in a fistfight with him myself. I really didn't do anything except protect myself. I reached out my left hand and I dropped him. I'm an ex-fighter. There was going to be a lawsuit and I almost lost my job over it."

So Peter decided to let *Dear Phoebe* die after one season. Pat bought out Alex Gottlieb's interest in the show for fifty thousand dollars, and she and Peter owned the rights to the tapes, but nothing was done with them except for one season of afternoon reruns in 1957. Peter dabbled a bit more in television over the next few years, appearing on Jimmy Durante and Esther Williams spectaculars and in episodes of dramatic series. Before the decade was out he would make another venture into series television.

First, however, there was a new, unaccustomed—and uncomfortable—role for Peter: fatherhood.

PAT DISCOVERED four months after the wedding that she was expecting a baby—a happy occasion for most people, but especially so for a woman to whom family ties were so important. Joe and Rose had only one grandchild by a daughter, Eunice's son, Robert Sargent Shriver III, born four days after Peter and Pat's wedding. Thus, the reaction among the Kennedys to Pat's pregnancy was joyous.

Peter Lawford, on the other hand, wasn't entirely thrilled. He admitted at the time that the thought of himself as a father gave him "a very strange feeling." It made him feel older and less independent, and he found both sensations unpleasant. His bosses at MGM had pounded into his head the notion that to marry too young would adversely affect his career and that fatherhood would do it even greater damage.

Phyllis Kirk, the actress, who had known Peter during his last few years at MGM and remained a lifelong friend, explained the thinking. "It was the Hollywood idea of what a leading man was. The role of fatherdom connoted age. That's all part and parcel of that whole Hollywood thing: that you were forever young, forever good, forever handsome, forever the hero, and therefore you must never take parts—much less a life—that had to do with being other than that. For all those reasons, Peter probably didn't want to be a father."

This may be why it was so difficult for him to cope with Pat's pregnancy. It had been a hard enough adjustment for him to be married, to accommodate a woman into his everyday life. The pregnancy made it all the worse. Peter spent long hours away from home working on *Dear Phoebe,* and at night he often slept alone in his own bedroom. He forgot his and Pat's six-month anniversary until she brought out a cake in front of some friends she'd invited over. "It's our anniversary?" Peter asked, puzzled.

"Yes," Pat replied. "Six months!"

"It seems like thirty years," Peter muttered.

As Pat entered her seventh month, Peter went to Milt Ebbins with a startling request. The Lawfords were renting a two-bedroom redwood house on the beach at Malibu, with both a farmhouse feel and a twenty-four-foot window facing the ocean.* It was a forty-five-minute drive to and from the *Dear Phoebe* soundstage at American National Studios on Santa Monica Boulevard in Hollywood, and Peter decided he didn't like making the trip every day.

Ebbins and his wife, the former singer Lynne Sherman, were renting a house on Outpost Drive above Hollywood Boulevard, just a few minutes from the studios, and Peter knew that it had a separate suite of rooms on the first floor that Milt and Lynne didn't use. Peter asked him if he could sleep there whenever he was filming *Dear Phoebe.*

"Peter started staying with us during the week," Ebbins recalled. "He only went out to Malibu on the weekends. Now here's a man who has a pregnant wife at home, right? She was very upset, but he wouldn't change his mind. I said to him, 'Dammit, Peter, you've *gotta* go home. This is terrible.' He just dismissed it and said, 'I don't wanna go all the way out there.'

"He couldn't cope with the fact that she was having a

---

*When they were first shown the house, Pat learned that her father had rented it in the 1920s—as a love nest for him and Gloria Swanson. She took it anyway.

baby. He was a strange duck, Peter. I don't think he liked children. My wife and I would prepare dinner for ourselves and we'd give some of it to Peter—he was like a boarder."

Finally, Pat showed up at the door. "If you're not going to come out to the beach," she told Peter, "I'm going to move in here." She did so, then and there. But only for a while; she soon took off on a skiing trip to Canada. Peter's friends were alarmed—wasn't he worried about the baby? "Certainly not," he replied. "Pat's very good on skis." When he was reminded that even the best skier can fall down, Peter responded, "You can fall down anywhere."

Pat's trip didn't cause her pregnancy any problems, but she did go into labor early, and on March 29, 1955, she gave birth to a six-pound-thirteen-ounce boy. Peter had long wanted to name his firstborn Christopher whether the child was a girl or a boy. "It's being done in England," he explained. "They call girls 'Christopher' over there." Pat concurred. On April 25, the child was christened Christopher Kennedy Lawford by Francis Cardinal McIntyre.

Christopher's birth gave Peter his first real taste of the insularity and protectiveness of the Kennedys. Of her twenty-eight grandchildren, Rose Kennedy related in her autobiography, the family nurse, Luella Hennessey, had been on hand "to take care of twenty-seven of them from birth"—meaning that an emissary of Rose Kennedy's was present at every one of her grandchildren's births save one.

The exception was Christopher Lawford—but in his case it was Rose herself who was in attendance. "Christopher . . . came a few days early," Rose wrote, "and I was visiting Pat and Peter at that time, so I took charge and took care of him."

Rose Kennedy "took charge," apparently, whenever she came to visit the Lawfords. Dolores Naar, then married to Joe Naar, became quite close to Peter and Pat. "There was no question that Peter was no longer the head of that household when Pat's mother was there," she recalled. "It was not a situation designed to make a son-in-law happy, and Peter was no exception."

If Peter had found the idea of fatherhood disquieting, he admitted that "the feeling is even stranger now that the event has occurred." He was edgy and short with Pat; the baby's lusty crying so upset him that Pat rented an apart-

ment two doors away for Christopher and his nanny to stay
in.

AT FIRST, Pat didn't know about Peter's adulteries. With
hindsight, however, she might have suspected them earlier
because their sex life hadn't been good from the start. Pat
had been raised by her obsessively religious mother to believe that sexual intercourse was a sin except within marriage, and even then that its sole purpose was procreation.
She was a virgin when she married Peter, a man who had
had sexual relations since the age of ten, had frequented call
girls, and whose preferred sexual satisfaction was not
achieved via the missionary position. The Lawfords had sex
far less frequently than Peter would have liked, and when
they did it wasn't completely satisfying for him. He later
told Arthur Natoli, an associate, that Pat would cross herself
before each and every sexual encounter they had.

His response to these frustrations—worsened by Pat's
unavailability to him during her pregnancy—was to dally
with other women. According to Milt Ebbins, "Peter had
alliances while Pat was expecting. Fast ones, not with anybody famous. He wouldn't get involved in anything serious.
He was too smart for that. He wasn't gonna take any
chances with the Kennedys around—he was scared to death
of the Kennedys."

With good reason, Jeanne Carmen discovered. Marilyn
Monroe had fallen out of close touch with Peter, but her
friend Jeanne was still quite friendly with him. "Peter would
come by my house or I'd meet him for coffee, things like
that," she recalled. "He'd call me from his car phone and
tell me to look out the window—that was when telephones
in cars were very rare. He'd sit there and wave to me like
a kid."

Peter and Jeanne never did have a sexual relationship—
she was still bemused by the fact that Peter had never made
a pass at her—but someone suspected they might be having
an affair. "I guess Pat thought we were getting too friendly,"
Carmen said, "because I got a call from the Kennedys' attorney. He told me, 'I've been asked to tell you to stop seeing
Peter Lawford. If you don't, you'll live to regret it.'

"Well, I knew the Kennedys were tough and that my
ass would be grass if I continued the relationship with Peter

You don't go up against the Kennedys. I knew that because I knew people who had tried to go up against them. So at that point I stopped seeing Peter."

Peter was furious when Jeanne told him why she could no longer see him. He was beginning to feel overwhelmed by the enormous Kennedy presence in his life as it was, and now he felt as though Big Brother—or Big Father—was watching his every move. He didn't like the feeling that he was slowly, inexorably losing control over his life.

He sometimes felt suffocated by the sheer number of Kennedys and the intensity of their loyalty to one another. "I had never known a family like the Kennedys," he said. "The rough-and-tumble of a large gregarious family was completely foreign to me, and I became—by marriage—an outsider in an almost overwhelming situation."

He was particularly so because, unlike Joe Kennedy's other sons-in-law, Peter never became part of the family business. Eunice's husband, Sargent Shriver, and Jean's husband, Stephen Smith, both became involved in the Kennedy financial and political empires; Peter couldn't have cared less about the former and played only a peripheral role in the latter. But it was more than that; Peter felt himself alienated even from the family's recreation. "The secret," Peter said, "was participation. But I'd never played touch football in my life. And that family had a team in and of themselves."

"Peter hated to go to Hyannis Port," Milt Ebbins recalled. "He stopped going alone after a while—he wanted me to come with him. Because otherwise he felt totally isolated. He just didn't like that atmosphere—that big family. At one time they *rang a bell* for dinner. And we'd sit down at this long boardinghouse table, the women would come out with pitchers of milk and big tubs of butter and hot bread and creamed fish and mashed potatoes, and they'd all jump on it. Peter couldn't take that. It seemed almost barbaric to him. He just sat there.

"Jackie introduced Jack to French cuisine, and of course Peter loved that. She and Peter both felt like outsiders in that family. That's why they got along so well. They were close all his life. They understood each other."

The power the Kennedys generated was awesome, Peter found. "When it was in full swing it was like a juggernaut. I used to find excuses not to go." Joe Kennedy, though, was sympathetic: "The old man watched this, and later he said to me, 'I know what you were going through.' "

Even in his own home, Peter was made to feel like an outsider by the Kennedys. "When anyone from the family was there," Dolores Naar remembered, "everybody else in the room was excluded—including Peter. He was always trying to find a way to work his way into that family. But he was the outcast. If Peter had had more self-esteem, that could have been a good thing. He could have retained his individuality. But it worked the other way for him. He felt the Kennedys looked down at him. He always felt inadequate because he wasn't as well educated as they all were. They were as sharp as tacks, those people. It really was a constant struggle for Peter—just to keep his head above water."

Peter hated these feelings of inadequacy, and one way he could assert himself was by having extramarital affairs. It was a pattern that would repeat itself again and again in the Lawford marriage: Peter's self-assurance would be worn down by the Kennedys, and he would attempt to bolster it by accepting many of the sexual invitations he constantly received from women.

Pat Lawford tolerated much more from her husband than most women would have; she had learned her mother's lessons well. Rose Kennedy had been aware of her husband's infidelities, but had chosen to ignore them. "In all the years that we have been married," Joe said of Rose, "I have never heard her complain. Never. Not even once. That is a quality that children are quick to see."

The Kennedy girls had been taught through the relationship of their parents that the man was the master of the house, that his will was law, and that any breaking of the marriage vows was to be silently acquiesced to by the wife. Pat had been too young to comprehend what was happening when Gloria Swanson had visited Hyannis Port in 1929, but she surely realized at some point in her life that Rose had welcomed her husband's mistress into her home without protest.

At the beginning of her marriage, Pat was every inch her mother's daughter. As Dolores Naar recalled, "Pat was so in awe of Peter. He was a movie star and a beautiful man and *she got him*. She really wanted to look up to that man." At that point, Milton Ebbins saw, Peter ruled the roost. "She looked up to him, did everything he said. Boy, did *that* change! Peter was essentially a weak man, and the minute Pat saw that, *pow*! You show weakness to the Kennedys and you're in trouble. The larger she and her family loomed in Peter's life, the weaker he got. And the weaker he got, the stronger she became. The guy never had a chance."

Ultimately, Pat Kennedy was far less willing to be a long-suffering wife than her mother had been, but she stuck it out with Peter, as much because of her Catholicism and their children as because of her love for him.

There were good times along with the bad, of course. When Pat and Peter were getting on well, were on the same wavelength, they were able to recapture some of the heady romance of their courtship. And Pat still harbored deep in her heart the belief that Peter would come around, would be more faithful, would become a better father. She convinced herself that she and Peter would grow more compatible as their marriage evolved, that they could triumph over every obstacle thrown in their way.

But over the next few years, Pat's hopes sagged under the weight of reality. The Lawford marriage floundered; their relationship became more and more strained. Then, in 1956, John F. Kennedy's political star began the meteoric rise that would lift him to the summit of world power four years later. Peter and Pat's lives became so exciting that it was possible for them to ignore for long periods of time the fact that their marriage wasn't working.

SEVENTEEN

IF PETER Lawford's public eclipse by the Kenned[ ]
family can be said to have begun at any one moment, [ ]
was when Jack Kennedy decided to run for the 195[ ]
Democratic vice-presidential nomination. Kennedy had bee[n]
one of the party's brightest young stars since his election [ ]
the Senate in 1952, and the publication of his Pulitzer Prize[-]
winning collection of biographical essays, *Profiles in Cou[r-]*
age, had singled him out as one of that rarest of breeds—
an intellectual politician.

Jack Kennedy had long been intrigued by Hollywood—
by the business of it, the art of it, and the sexuality of [ ]
He often made what he called "hunting expeditions" to L[os]
Angeles, where he would woo beautiful women, from aspi[r-]
ing unknowns to major stars like Gene Tierney and Jun[e]
Allyson. He was fascinated by how sexual dynamism in Ho[l-]
lywood translated into power—and vice versa. His frien[d]
Chuck Spaulding recalled that " 'charisma' wasn't a catch[ ]
word yet, but Jack was very interested in that blinding ma[g-]
netism these screen personalities had. What exactly was *i[t]*
How did you go about acquiring it? Did it have an impa[ct]
on your private life? How did you make it work for you[ ]
He wouldn't let go of the subject."

Jack Kennedy later used much of what he learned [to]
great political advantage, but his main interest early on w[as]
sexual conquest. With his boyish good looks and keen min[d]
he had never had trouble attracting women, in Hollywoo[d]

or elsewhere, but his sister's marriage to Peter Lawford afforded him additional entree to moviedom's most gorgeous
females.

Of all his in-laws, Peter got along with Jack the best.
Jack had no problem with Peter's being English; he had
strongly supported his sister Kathleen's decision to marry a
nobleman, and remained despite his father's
debacle as ambassador to the Court of St. James's. His first
book, the highly acclaimed *Why England Slept,* chronicled
the events leading to Britain's entry into World War II.

Jack admired Peter's savoir faire, his cultured manner,
his sartorial elegance, and he knew that Peter was someone
he could learn from. The Kennedys lived up to the stereo-
type of the rambunctious, all-American Irish family (and
provoked Lady Lawford's disdain because of it), but of them
all Jack was the only one who aspired to old-world sophistication. His decision to marry a debutante, Jacqueline Lee
Bouvier, the daughter of socialites Janet Lee and John
"Black Jack" Bouvier, was motivated largely by her continental flair, her knowledge of French, her impeccable etiquette. She was just the kind of wife the ambitious Jack
Kennedy wanted the world to see on his arm.

The friendship between Jack and Peter, however, was
based on more than that. Both men had a lusty appetite for
women, and neither felt constrained by his marriage vows
to curb his desires. Once Peter became a part of the Kennedy family, he was happy to help the newlywed Jack on
his Hollywood "hunting expeditions." One of the women
Peter made sure Jack met was Marilyn Monroe.

In the summer of 1954, Peter arranged for Jack and
Jackie to be invited to the agent Charles Feldman's home
for a party. Peter knew that among the guests would be
Marilyn Monroe, the most talked-about woman in the world
that year, and her husband of six months, former New York
Yankee baseball great Joe DiMaggio. Their marriage was
already on the rocks, and it would end a few months later,
destroyed by DiMaggio's jealousy and Monroe's unwillingness to give up her burgeoning career, as DiMaggio insisted,
and be a housewife.

DiMaggio's mistrust of Marilyn's fidelity was usually
unfounded, but in the case of Marilyn and John F. Kennedy,
his suspicions were justified. Bob Slatzer was a Paramount

publicity and rewrite man who had had an on-again off again romance with Monroe since 1946. They had gotten married during a carefree weekend in Tijuana in 1952, but according to Slatzer, pressure from Marilyn's studio, and her own second thoughts, led them to have the marriage annulled and the records destroyed. Marilyn told Slatzer about the party at which she first met Jack Kennedy, and a few weeks later Feldman related essentially the same story to him. "She had to talk DiMaggio into going," Slatzer recalled, "because he hated Hollywood parties. When she was introduced to Kennedy he said to her, 'I think I've met you someplace before,' and she told me that she thought she might have met him in the forties when he used to stay out here with Bob Stack."

Marilyn said she felt uncomfortable at the party because Jack Kennedy stared at her the entire evening. "I may be flattering myself," she giggled, "but he couldn't take his eyes off me." Charlie Feldman noticed that Jackie saw what Jack was doing, and she was getting angry. Joe DiMaggio was aware of what was going on, too. Every few minutes he would grab Marilyn's arm and say, "Let's go! I've had enough of this!" Marilyn didn't want to leave, and Feldman recalled that "they had words about it."

The DiMaggios did leave early, but sometime before that Marilyn gave Senator Kennedy her phone number. The next day Jack called, and DiMaggio answered the phone. When he asked who was calling, Kennedy said, "A friend." DiMaggio hung up in Jack's face and started to grill Marilyn about who it was, because he hadn't recognized Kennedy's voice. The next time Marilyn saw Kennedy, he said, "I guess I shouldn't call at certain times, huh?"

Marilyn told Bob Slatzer that she and Jack Kennedy didn't "get together" until after her divorce from DiMaggio early in 1955. She began to spend a good deal of time in New York during this period, and occasionally, when she and Jack were both in the city, they would meet.

A few months after the party at Charlie Feldman's, Jack was hospitalized for surgery to alleviate a chronic back problem. Visitors to his room were amused by a color poster of Marilyn Monroe he had taped to the wall, in which she wore blue shorts and stood with her legs spread widely apart. Kennedy had hung the poster upside down.

*   *   *

KENNEDY ALMOST died after the surgery; he was given the last rites of the Catholic Church while lying in a coma. But he rallied and emerged from the ordeal a stronger, more ambitious man—and a more impatient politician. While recuperating in Palm Beach he wrote *Profiles in Courage,* and the rise in his national political star prompted by the book's critical plaudits made him think seriously about higher office.

That one of his sons would achieve the presidency had long been a dream of Joe Kennedy's; when Joe Junior was killed, Kennedy transferred his expectations to Jack. The odds were long: not only had a Catholic never won a presidential election, but Jack Kennedy was a freshman senator with little experience in international affairs and was barely above the constitutional minimum age to hold the office. By 1960, the Kennedys felt, Jack could overcome these disadvantages, and their master plan was to orchestrate the rise in his reputation and popularity until his nomination had become a virtual inevitability.

At the 1956 Democratic convention in Chicago, which was poised to nominate Adlai Stevenson for a second race against President Dwight D. Eisenhower, Jack was scheduled to narrate a documentary that would open the convention, *The Pursuit of Happiness*. The film was produced by Dore Schary, and for the first time, John F. Kennedy was able to utilize his brother-in-law's show business ties to further his career. Schary remembered that Kennedy flew to Los Angeles to confer with him about the film: "I went down to call for Senator Kennedy at the Lawfords' home [in Malibu]. We ran the film alone for Senator Kennedy, and he thought it was wonderful." With input from Pat and Peter, Jack suggested some changes in the narration script, which Schary made.

The film and Jack's narration were so well received that Kennedy was asked to make the principal nominating speech for Stevenson. His brilliant oration—he rewrote a draft by Arthur Schlesinger that Stevenson's aides had supplied to him—catapulted him into the national spotlight, and suddenly the talk was that Jack Kennedy would make a splendid vice-presidential nominee.

He agreed. He decided to fight for the nomination, which he saw as a stepping-stone to the respectability he would need to run for president in 1960. Joe Kennedy argued against the race, afraid that Stevenson's all but certain loss to the popular Eisenhower would damage Jack's reputation as a winner. Jack felt that a second Stevenson defeat would not be blamed on him and that a well-fought national campaign would gain him tremendous name recognition and temper him for the 1960 battle as nothing else could.

Kennedy hoped Stevenson would take the traditional route and choose him as his running mate, thereby making his nomination by the delegates a mere formality. Instead, Stevenson threw the decision to the convention floor without a recommendation, allowing the Democrats to choose for themselves among Kennedy, Tennessee senator Estes Kefauver, who had a strong political organization forged in his primary campaign against Stevenson, and Minnesota senator Hubert Humphrey, a bright new face in the party's liberal wing.

Stevenson's action earned him Kennedy's enmity and left Jack with only twelve hours to campaign. Jack and Bobby surged into action, but they were unprepared—so much so that when Jackie walked into the Kennedy headquarters early the following morning, Bobby looked at her balefully and asked, "Do you know anybody in Nevada?"

She didn't, but she suggested Bobby call Peter in Malibu—Peter knew Jimmy Durante, and didn't Durante perform in Las Vegas? Bobby called the Lawford house and woke up Peter and Pat, who was eight months and three weeks pregnant. Peter told Bobby that he knew Wilbur Clark, the owner of the Desert Inn. Clark, it turned out, was the chairman of the Nevada delegation, and Bobby asked Peter to give Clark a call because "We need Nevada's votes, and I don't think we'll get them unless you can persuade Clark to change his delegates' minds."

Peter called Clark, and that evening thirteen of Nevada's fourteen votes went to Kennedy on the second ballot, putting him within thirty-eight votes of the nomination. Jack ultimately lost to Kefauver, but afterward he made an eloquent appeal for unity and left the convention a much stronger—and more famous—politician. He campaigned hard for Stevenson, all the while gaining more recognition and collecting political IOUs that he could cash in for the 1960 campaign. With Stevenson's defeat in November, John

F. Kennedy quickly became the front-runner for his party's next presidential nomination.

A WEEK after the convention ended, on August 25, Pat gave birth to the Lawfords' second child, a girl they named Sydney, after Peter's father, in the unisex British tradition Peter favored. A month later, Peter purchased the home that he, Pat, and their children would share for the next eight years. It was a house with a celebrated past, and within a few years the Lawfords' occupancy of it would make it one of the legendary houses in show business history.

The dwelling was Louis B. Mayer's Santa Monica beachfront mansion that Peter had first visited as a wide-eyed fifteen-year-old during one of Mayer's Sunday brunches. Mayer had purchased it in 1932 and spent nearly a million dollars to turn it into a surfside Xanadu. A ten-thousand-square-foot neo-Spanish building on two lots, it featured a dozen rooms, four bedroom suites, an elevator, a theater-sized projection screen that pulled down from the ceiling in the living room, a guest house, and an enormous swimming pool yards from the Pacific Ocean.

Mayer had spent seventy-five thousand dollars on imported Italian marble that he installed around the pool and fireplaces and throughout the master bedroom. The Mayer house became one of the social centers of Hollywood, a fitting den for the MGM lion and his cubs, and a "second home" to such movie greats as Clark Gable, Jean Harlow, Spencer Tracy, and Katharine Hepburn.

When Mayer's wife, Margaret, divorced him in 1947, she won a three-million-dollar settlement that included the mansion. Ill and a recluse, Margaret was unable to keep the place up; when she died in 1955 it was badly in need of repair.

The photographer Don Pack remembered walking along the beach with Peter in the early fifties when Peter pointed to the Mayer house and said, "Someday I'm going to buy that." On September 27, 1956, he did, from the estate of Margaret Mayer—for a purchase price of ninety-five thousand dollars.

The enormous amount of money Mayer had put into the house over the years meant little to its resale value. In the fifties the population of Southern California was still relatively small, and there wasn't the kind of frenzied competition for housing that later developed with the area's population boom. Most wealthy home buyers didn't want to live in Santa Monica, even at the beach; they preferred Beverly Hills or Malibu. Property values around the Mayer house kept its value low, and because its upkeep had been neglected, it was something of a white elephant, a "fixer" in today's real-estate parlance. After he bought the house, Peter spent twenty-two thousand dollars to repair the plumbing alone.

The house gave the Lawfords the kind of privacy they could never have had in Beverly Hills, where their house would have been one of the stops on the bus tours of movie stars' homes. Most of the houses like Peter's that fronted on the ocean along the Pacific Coast Highway looked modest from the street; it was only once one was inside that their lavishness became apparent. Peter's neighbors were doctors, lawyers, and other professional people with enough income to afford big houses in Santa Monica, but without the wherewithal to live in the "better" neighborhoods of Malibu and Beverly Hills. Although Pat did have that kind of money, Peter was more comfortable here—because the house was right next to State Beach, where he could surf and play volleyball with his friends.

Peter made the mortgage payment every month, but Pat paid for most of the renovations. (In the late fifties General Electric installed a completely new kitchen in exchange for a commercial endorsement from Peter.) Within a few years the house was both palatial and comfortable, both elegant and lived-in. Pat installed a playground and built a playhouse for the children and furnished the bedrooms in art deco and the den with cozy overstuffed sofas. The living room served as a sprawling entertainment center.

Bonnie Williams, a secretary to Joe Kennedy who later worked for Peter, recalled the house as "typically Kennedy. Kennedy homes are all big and beautifully done, but comfortable. Peter loved it. He spent a lot of time in that large formal living room, and I can just see him on the couch with his feet up, talking on the telephone."

After the November election, Jack Kennedy came to spend a few days with Peter and Pat in their new home and recover from the rigors of the campaign. As he sat on the patio at twilight, the ocean waves lapping gently at the shore just yards away, Jack spoke to Peter about what an exhilarating experience it had been to travel from state to state in support of various Democratic candidates and how encouraged he had been by the public's reaction to him.

"You have no idea, Peter," he said, "how nice it is to hear people say, 'There goes John Kennedy.' They don't say, 'There goes Peter Lawford's brother-in-law' anymore. I'm really getting an identity of my own."

WHILE PETER felt alienated from the Kennedy family, Pat had problems of her own with Peter's close network of friends. Dolores Naar felt that "it was tough for Pat, having Peter's buddies running through her living room all the time with their surfboards, yelling, 'Surf's up!' Peter was very close to these men. Every Saturday and Sunday he was out on the beach.

"Joe and Peter and the rest of the guys had their own little dialogues going on. I used to go with Joe when we first got married, but after a while I stopped because I realized it was just a gang of guys who wanted to be together. Pat didn't participate; she'd just do whatever she wanted to do."

Peter Sabiston thought that Peter's reluctance to "cut the cord" with his bachelorhood friends stemmed from his unfulfilling relationship with his wife. "He would always try to include some friends, whether it was me or Joe Naar or Dick Livingston, in whatever he did, because he didn't have much fun with Pat in a one-on-one situation."

Pat disliked Peter's beach friends, and they, for the most part, reciprocated her ill will. They saw her as cold, aloof, difficult to get close to. Dolores Naar's recollection of her first exposure to Pat was fairly typical. On her first date with Joe he took her to Peter's house—but she didn't know that's where they were going. Just before they arrived, Joe told her who his friend was and warned her, "He and his wife will probably ignore you, but it doesn't mean anything."

Dolores braced herself, but she found Peter charming. "He was in his swim trunks. What a beautiful man, with such a warm smile! But Joe was right about Pat. She was reading the newspaper when I came into the room, and she didn't even look up at me." Dolores would become one of only a handful of Peter's friends who managed to get close to Pat, but even she never fully understood her. "Pat was so complex. She could be the warmest, she could be the most hostile, she could be the most indifferent. And you had to kind of read her. She never sought my advice—she's not that kind of woman. She's very private."

Peter Sabiston never forgot an incident with Pat, one that left a bitter taste in his mouth. "Pat wanted to buy Peter a diving board for his birthday, so she asked me if I knew anyone who could lend her a station wagon so she could go out to the [San Fernando] Valley and pick it up. I borrowed a friend's car and let her use it. On the way out there, she was involved in an accident. Did about eight hundred dollars' damage. And she refused to pay for it! She said I should have my friend pay for it. I said, 'How dare you! What do you mean have my friend pay for it? He was nice enough to lend you the car. The least you can do is return it to him in the same condition it was in when you borrowed it!' She didn't see it that way. She simply wouldn't pay. I almost ended our friendship over it. Peter finally wound up paying for it."

When Pat did show her warm, friendly, generous side, it was usually to Peter's Hollywood friends. Still an enthusiastic movie fan, she loved meeting Judy Garland, Jackie Cooper, Lauren Bacall, Humphrey Bogart, Martha Raye, Jimmy Durante, and dozens of other celebrities who were close to Peter. If Pat wanted to meet a movie star or two, all Peter had to do was invite them to dinner. Usually, they accepted.

Several nights a week the Lawfords had a small group for dinner and games—sometimes poker, sometimes charades, sometimes a board game. Usually there was a current-events quiz, something Pat had been brought up with; she and her siblings had been questioned about world events by their father every evening at dinner.

Meals were prepared by the cook, but sometimes Pat or Peter would give it a go. "Pat made one of the all-time great beef stews," Milton Ebbins recalled. "She'd serve a salad, some crusty French bread, and this terrific stew, and boy, nobody complained. She was a great hostess, too."

Peter wasn't a bad cook either, his friends agreed, although he had a maddening habit of making whatever he wanted to eat whether his friends liked the dish or not. On one such occasion, Martha Raye watched him put a plate of food in front of her, then stood up and screamed, "Jesus Christ! Are we having liver and bacon and Brussels sprouts *again*! Don't you realize we think it *stinks*!"

With people she knew and liked, Pat sometimes let her hair down to the point of childishness. "One night, there were eight of us sitting around the dining room table at Pat's house," Dolores Naar recalled. "We helped ourselves at the buffet, then sat down at this beautifully set table with wine, and the meal was wonderful. Then for dessert the girl came in with a platter of ginger snaps and something struck Pat funny. She took a bite out of one of the cookies, then she threw it at Peter. Soon we were all throwing these cookies at each other. Pat used to do things like that."

The one performer Pat was most eager to meet, Frank Sinatra, never accepted an invitation from Peter Lawford. Pat begged her husband to patch up his rift with Frank, but Peter had already made a number of unsuccessful attempts and didn't want to subject himself to the humiliation of Frank's cold rejection again. So Pat took matters into her own hands. She was having lunch with Molly Dunne one afternoon, and when Molly mentioned that she had a date with Frank Sinatra that night, Pat's eyes lit up. "Call him and tell him I want to invite him over for dinner!"

"Call him yourself," Molly replied. Pat did—and pretended to be Molly in order to get through to him. When he got on the line and found out it was Pat, he was furious. He not only refused her dinner invitation, but shouted at her before hanging up, "Tell Mrs. Dunne that I'm busy tonight!"

Molly did try to intervene between Peter and Sinatra. "Frank would have me in tears because he would refuse to have anything to do with Peter, who was my best friend. I asked him why and you know what he said? 'Any guy who would stiff a hooker is a real jerk.' "

PETER BECAME concerned about money in the second half of the fifties; he was doing only sporadic TV work, and his finances were tight. It was these worries, ironically, that led him into a serious blunder that probably cost him once and for all the major stardom that had always seemed just one step ahead of him—and the financial independence that would have come along with it.

In 1958 the producer Albert R. "Cubby" Broccoli offered Peter the leading role in a series of films he planned to make based on Ian Fleming's James Bond spy novels. Broccoli thought Peter would be perfect to play the handsome, soigné Englishman with an eye for beautiful women, a love of gadgetry, and a distaste for criminals. But the idea of playing a British spy reminded Peter uncomfortably of all those cloak-and-dagger scripts he had rejected before *Dear Phoebe,* and the success of the films was by no means guaranteed. Broccoli was not a powerhouse producer; he'd done just seven unmemorable films to that point.

Worse, Broccoli was able to offer Peter only twenty-five thousand dollars per picture and wanted him to commit to the entire Bond series he planned—at least five films. Peter's minimum asking price at the time was seventy-five thousand, and he didn't want to take such a severe cut in pay. The five-picture stipulation, Peter said later, would have given him pause at any price. "I thought it would have tied me up too far in the future."

It seemed like the right decision at the time, but in retrospect it was the worst of Peter's several professional missteps. When the first Bond film, *Dr. No,* was released in 1962, it became an enormous box-office hit and spawned an endlessly lucrative Bond series that made a legend of Sean Connery, a young Scottish actor with three minor films to his credit. There's no reason to assume that the picture would not have been as big a hit with Peter in the lead role; and if it had been he would have been in a strong position to renegotiate his contract with Broccoli for far more money and a share of the profits in the subsequent films. Most important, it would have made a superstar of Peter and allowed him to carve out a niche for himself quite distinct from the rising Kennedy phenomenon. It was a missed opportunity that remained one of his great regrets.

At the time, however, Peter's best course of action appeared to be another television series. In a wry twist, it was MGM that approached him with the idea. Of all the Hollywood studios, Metro had disdained television the longest, but early in 1958 the studio was in deep trouble. At the end of its fiscal year in August 1957, it had suffered a loss for the first time in its history. Now, MGM looked on television as its salvation, and with good reason: when Peter began work on his series it was the only production on the lot.

Metro's idea was for Peter to do a small-screen version of their famous series of six *Thin Man* movies that had starred William Powell and Myrna Loy as Nick and Nora Charles, an urbane couple who solve crimes, bicker wittily, and drink heartily. (In one of the films, Nora enters a bar where Nick has been imbibing for some time. She sits down next to him and asks, "How many has he had?" The bartender replies, "Six." Without missing a beat Nora says, "Set 'em up.")

Peter liked the idea, especially when MGM agreed to give him twenty-five percent ownership of the show. The Colgate-Palmolive Company signed up as the sponsor, and statuesque, stylish Phyllis Kirk joined the cast as Nora. John Newland got the nod to direct the first ten episodes.

According to Peter, who was now 34, the studio wanted him to be a replica of William Powell. "Once I had signed for the part," he said, "I got a call from makeup. I couldn't imagine what it was. When I got there they put a homburg hat on me, grayed my hair a bit, added a small mustache, and even suggested I add a little padding to my beltline. They were actually trying to get me up like William Powell!" He balked loudly. "Get Powell if you want!" he shouted at Eddie Mannix. Later he said, "I wasn't about to follow William Powell. I'm not that crazy. Besides, I wanted some identity of my own."

So did Phyllis Kirk, who made it a point not to watch the *Thin Man* movies so she wouldn't pick up any of Myrna Loy's characteristics. She and Peter were, on and off the screen, never anything but themselves: Peter the light, devil-may-care leading man, Phyllis the sophisticated New Yorker, a former model and stage actress just a tad disdainful of Hollywood. From the beginning, the impression was that they mixed about as well as oil and water, and a number of people believe to this day that he intensely disliked her.

Indeed, Phyllis Kirk was an acquired taste for Peter. They had met in 1950 when Phyllis, just put under contract to MGM, did a few scenes in *Please Believe Me*. "Peter was the star of this film," she recalled, "and he was terribly kind to me. He was so gentle and gave me little tips—he was wonderful. I will never forget that first encounter with him, because he was so generous. The best part of Peter was very kind."

On the *Thin Man* set, however, Kirk's reserved demeanor often rubbed Peter the wrong way, and it brought out some unpleasant behavior on his part. Except for Kirk, it was an all-male company, and Peter led the cast and crew in continual razzings of her that sometimes drove her to distraction. Eventually, everyone joined in. Bill Asher was a well-regarded TV director (*I Love Lucy*) who took over from John Newland, and he remembered that he once needed a frightened reaction shot from Kirk and did "a terrible thing. She was supposed to react to someone coming through the door, and I told her to reach behind her at the same time into a cigarette box. I put a mouse in the box, and everybody knew it except her. She reached back and what a reaction! She let out a scream and got so mad, she was throwing things at us."*

Peter enjoyed doing wicked send-ups of his costar's more distinctive characteristics. He would hold a comb across his forehead to mock her signature bangs or walk across the soundstage in the tiny mincing steps she was forced to take in her stylish but confining midcalf-length skirts. His tauntings rarely let up. During an interview with a *TV Guide* reporter, Phyllis mentioned that her birthday was coming up soon and said, "I'll be twenty-eight." Peter glanced at her and said, "Around the *waist* you'll be twenty-eight."

Whenever the script called for Peter to do a scene holding Asta, the couple's famous terrier, Kirk recalled that "he would, on the fourth word of the scene, hand me this forty-five-pound mass of muscle and sinew and bone and I would have to hold this monster throughout the scene. Like a trouper, I would do the whole scene holding this dog."

She was a good sport about all this and she harbored no ill will. "It was like having a group of pesky brothers

---

*Phyllis Kirk wasn't alone as the victim of practical jokes. At a wrap party at the end of *The Thin Man*'s first season, everyone exchanged presents. When Peter opened his, he found a chicken claw inside the box. "It was cruel to make fun of his bad hand like that, but he laughed harder than anyone," assistant director Paul Wurtzel recalled. "He could take it as well as dish it out."

who were always trying to upset my dignity a little bit. I was probably terribly proper in their view. I was also somewhat separated, in the sense that I did not party and my personal life was my personal life. That used to drive Peter crazy. He couldn't understand anyone who had this sort of other life that didn't have to do with everything that was going on in Hollywood."

The main reason many people feel that Peter disliked Phyllis was a curious conversation he had with John Newland a few episodes into the series. Newland was directing Peter in a bedroom scene with Phyllis, and he asked them to kiss. Afterward Peter approached Newland and said, "I'm not going to do this. I don't want to kiss Phyllis. I like her, but I don't want to do that. And I don't have to."

Newland looked at him blankly. "What are you talking about, Peter?"

"My contract says that I don't have to get involved in any kind of overt sexual level in this show."

Newland replied, "Well, Jesus, okay," and went to talk to one of the producers. "Peter tells me that he has a clause in his contract that he not be required to kiss and touch Phyllis Kirk," Newland told the man. "Now, how can I do the show like that?"

"Oh, you know Peter," the producer replied. "Just do the best you can."

Newland asked if there really was such a clause in the contract. There wasn't. But rather than go back to Peter and confront him about it, Newland tried to choreograph the ten episodes he directed so there would be no physical contact between Peter and Phyllis.

Why did Peter make such a strange demand, that actors playing man and wife never kiss each other during a series? Phyllis Kirk believed the only explanation was that Peter had a very bizarre sense of humor: "Depending on what day of the week it was and what time of day, Peter was apt to say anything." It could also have been that Peter overreacted in a desire to avoid doing anything in front of millions of television viewers that would embarrass his wife or her family in an era of strict morality codes. Paul Wurtzel recalled that "we had one scene where they had to be in bed together, discussing something. Because of the network censor we had to reshoot it with them in separate beds."

Later in the run of the series, the code restrictions were

loosened, and Peter and Phyllis kissed whenever it seemed appropriate. Phyllis recently viewed a *Thin Man* episode that "showed me and Peter sitting on the same bed, kissing. Now, on television in those days you did not do passionate, slobbering, current-day kisses. But it was certainly a kiss and it didn't look to me as though either one of us abhorred what we were doing."

THE TROUBLESOME chemistry between the two stars, it developed, was only one of the problems that plagued *The Thin Man* once it debuted over NBC on Friday, September 20, 1957, in the nine-thirty P.M. time slot. Critical reaction was scathing. Jack O'Brien's comments in the New York *Journal American* were typical. Under the headline "A Fat Chance for Thin Man," O'Brien complained that "everyone connected with the TV version of *The Thin Man* seemed to have absolutely no notion what its old effervescent movie joke was about. Its writing was dogged and dull, the performance of Phyllis Kirk ditto, the direction sluggish, the mood leaden and dense. Peter Lawford, a practiced and recognized professional at light comedy, enjoyed neither lightness nor comedy in his script this time, for whatever the high proficiency of even so effective a light romantic comedian as Lawford, the play still is the thing, and this thing was not a play, not a comedy, nor even a farce, except for being a joke on its own self. It will have to improve."

Peter had complained from the beginning that the show didn't have enough comic elements. "I screamed for comedy," he said, "but they insisted on making mystery the most important thing. Then, the notices came out pointing up that we were short on whimsy." Even when comedy was added, however, the scripts often left a lot to be desired. "Peter and I were dreadful in script conferences," Phyllis Kirk recalled. "We'd sit with the writers and be terribly insulting. My feeling was—it can be as cute as they want it to be, but if it ain't actable, fellas, forget it."

Advice started to come in on how to improve the show, in one instance from no less an authority than William Powell himself. Peter told the story of asking Powell what he thought of the series: "Mr. Powell's theory—and I agree with it wholeheartedly—is that what's lacking in the Thin Man as I play him is his quality of tipsiness. The original character was half stiff all the time. He went through life on a pink cloud and Powell played him that way. But we're limited because of TV. In the premier episode, I mixed martinis and we got over four hundred letters, mostly from the South, some demanding that we drink milk! Can you see me mixing a chocolate milk?"

If Peter was compelled not to tipple on the show, he felt no such constraints offscreen. Paul Wurtzel recalled that "every day when we'd break for lunch, Bill Asher and I would go up to his dressing room and we'd call the commissary and they'd bring whatever you wanted. We'd drink gin and Dubonnet, straight. Nobody would get smashed, but you'd have a couple of cocktails and eat lunch and you'd go back to the set and you could hardly move."

John Newland and Don Weis, who also directed some episodes, had found themselves unable to join the lunchtime drinkers. "I went once," Newland says, "and never went again. I never drank during lunch because it made me too slow. Peter drank a lot. And what amazed me about him was that he could drink three or four martinis and later not miss a mark or a beat. It never affected one moment of any shoot on any day."

There was a lot of pressure on Peter filming *The Thin Man*. The production schedule was grueling—two shows every eight days with only Sundays off—and workdays were so long Peter complained that "I meet myself coming home every night." He was worried about the scripts and worried about the ratings, which were mediocre despite weak competition. Still, he always kept an eye out for the girls. He often asked Paul Wurtzel, "You know any dames? Let's get some dames." Wurtzel told him he didn't know any dames—"My life and the studio, I kept them separated"—but tried to help Peter round somebody up. "Here's Peter Lawford, the great romantic guy who can get any woman he wants, and one night I sit there for an hour trying to figure out who might know some hookers for him."

By now, Peter was convinced that the problem with *The Thin Man* was a lack of on-screen chemistry between him and his costar. Before the second season began, he spoke to an executive of Colgate-Palmolive: he wanted to replace Phyllis Kirk with the British actress Hazel Court, whom he thought more sensuous than Phyllis. "Everybody else thought Phyllis was sensational on the show," Milt Ebbins recalled. "She got a lot more publicity than Peter ever did, and the sponsor told Peter that without Phyllis there'd be no show. So he had no choice. He backed off."

A number of attempts were made to save *The Thin Man*. The show had already used three talented directors when its desperate producer, Sam Marx, suggested that George Cukor try his hand at a few episodes. Cukor, intrigued by a medium in which he'd never worked, was interested. "George came to help us and he was marvelous as always," Phyllis recalled. "He was such a master at getting people to loosen up and extend themselves, and that's what that was all about—just to get us out of a kind of rut."

Paul Wurtzel recalled that "George did try to help. He never directed a whole episode, though, only a couple of shots. He said, 'I don't know how to help this show.'"

There was the rub—*The Thin Man* was beyond help. It faced much stiffer competition its second year when *77 Sunset Strip* was scheduled against it on ABC and became not only a hit series but a pop trendsetter. When Colgate-Palmolive withdrew its sponsorship at the end of the second season, NBC canceled the show.

Despite the indignities she was subjected to on the set, despite everything, Phyllis Kirk harbored no regrets. Often approached by fans who remember the show fondly, she recalled that "I had a wonderful time doing *The Thin Man*. Peter was a marvelously generous actor. He taught me a lot; he never hogged a scene. We had a lot of fun doing that series. We had bad days, too. Peter could be cranky, even bitchy. So could I. There were days when we would *snarl* at each other, like a brother and sister—which, incidentally, was always how I viewed our relationship. I was very fond of him."

Peter was galled by his second failure in what many still considered a third-rate medium (so called, according to Ernie Kovacs, "because it is neither rare nor well done"), but he had little time to dwell on it. His movie career was about to be revived at an unlikely studio, MGM, and by an unlikely benefactor—Frank Sinatra.

EIGHTEEN

FRANK SINATRA had not spoken to Peter Lawford for almost five years. He would decline an invitation if he knew Peter was expected at a party; if he somehow found himself at a function with Peter, he'd do fancy footwork to avoid running into him. But despite his rude rebuff of Pat's attempt to meet him, she hadn't given up. "Like most women," Peter said, "she was mad about Frank."

It was Rocky and Gary Cooper who set the stage for the rapprochement between Sinatra and Peter that made Peter a member of Sinatra's celebrated "Rat Pack," the mainstays of which were Dean Martin, Sammy Davis, Jr., and Joey Bishop. More sporadic participants included Shirley MacLaine, Juliet Prowse, Angie Dickinson, Tony Curtis, and Janet Leigh. Also known as "The Clan," the group became the focus of inordinate public attention in the late 1950s.

A Democrat, Sinatra had performed at the party's national convention in 1956 and was well aware of John F. Kennedy's political potential. Jack was already the front-runner for the 1960 nomination, and as Peter put it, "Frank could see a bandwagon coming." Access to political power was very important to Sinatra, the son of Italian immigrants. Insecure, emotionally scarred by his childhood tauntings as a "dago" by playmates in Hoboken, New Jersey, Frank wanted nothing more than to "show them." It wasn't

enough that he had been the idol of millions of bobbysoxers and had won an Academy Award. That was just show
business. To be an associate—maybe even a friend—of the
president of the United States, that was *real* achievement.
The prospect of it was enough to move Sinatra to a very
uncharacteristic action—he swallowed his pride and set
things right with Peter Lawford.

At the Gary Coopers' on a hot, dry August evening in
1958, Pat, six months pregnant, sat next to Sinatra at the
dinner table. Peter was held up with *Thin Man* shooting,
and when he arrived about an hour late he saw that Pat and
Frank were engaged in convivial conversation. "Pat and
Frank hit it off beautifully," Peter said. But when he took
his place at the table, Sinatra looked at him and said to Pat,
"You know, I don't speak to your old man."

That was enough to break the ice, and the rest of the
evening progressed pleasantly. Pat followed up the next
week with a dinner invitation to Sinatra, which he accepted,
and before long the three were fast friends. Pat was now
completely smitten with "Ol' Blue Eyes." As Peter said,
"There's no one in the world who can be more charming
than Frank when he wants to be."

When the Lawfords' third child, a girl, was born on
Tuesday, November 4, she was named Victoria Francis—
Victoria because her uncle Jack had been elected to a second
term in the U.S. Senate that day, and Francis after Francis
Albert Sinatra. The reconciliation was complete.

It would take another year, though, before Frank apologized to Peter for his behavior over what he now realized
was a misunderstanding about Ava Gardner. In Monaco
with Peter and Pat for a benefit thrown by Princess Grace,
Frank persuaded the Lawfords to follow him to Rome,
where he hoped to be reunited with Ava—he was still carrying a torch for her. "Ava very effectively dodged him,"
Peter said, and Frank found himself in his hotel room in
the middle of the night drinking with Peter and Pat. "Frank
and I were pretty drunk," Peter recalled, "and about three
in the morning Pat said, 'I give up on you guys,' and went
to bed.

"Frank was hurt as hell about the way Ava had been
ducking him. I don't know whether he sensed the compassion I felt for him, but suddenly he looked up from his drink

bleary-eyed and said, 'Charlie'—which was the nickname he always used for me—'I'm sorry. I was dead wrong.'" This rare display of Sinatra humility touched Peter, and he responded, "Hey, I know it takes a lot for anybody, especially you, to say that. Let's not do that again. What a waste of time!"

"We got on like a house on fire after that," Peter said. "But even as close as we got, I never had a feeling of permanence. I knew you could never rely on this impulsive, explosive, gregarious, generous, charming, petulant man for a real friendship." For the next four years, however, Sinatra became one of the vortexes of Peter's life. He deeply admired him and was fascinated by his talent, his charisma, his scrappy street-fighter courage, his power in Hollywood.

"This is such an *enormous* talent," Peter told a reporter about Sinatra at the time. "[His] energy is some kind of magic that a lot of us wish we had. We're all attracted to him because of that." To another journalist, Peter said, "I don't want it to sound phony, but I consider it a privilege to live in the same era Frank's in. I *do*. I think he's a giant; a fantastic human being. Apart from that vast talent—we don't have to talk about that—he's got qualities of energy, imagination, kindness, thoughtfulness, awareness, all those qualities you try to find in yourself and hardly ever do."

Clearly, Peter had passed the litmus test for membership in the Rat Pack—total obeisance to its leader. "I used to feel kind of sorry for Peter," Arthur Julian, the producer friend of his, recalled. "He felt that being accepted by Sinatra was so important. He always had an acceptance problem."

Just as Sinatra's rejection of Peter had been total, his reacceptance of him was all-encompassing. In the next few years they made movies together, appeared onstage together, played together, drank together, drove matching Dual-Ghias, enjoyed women together, traveled together, relaxed together. They became partners in the Cal-Neva Lodge, a Lake Tahoe hotel and casino, and in a Beverly Hills restaurant, Puccini.

The restaurant offered great Italian food and live entertainment at the piano, and it became very popular with celebrities who wanted to associate themselves with Sinatra's show business power and Lawford's potential political power. Peter never put up any money for his share of the business. To Sinatra, the cachet that Peter's class and in-laws brought to Puccini was investment enough.

THEY CLAIMED never to have called themselves the "Rat Pack" and professed distaste at the term, blaming it on *Time* magazine. Nominally, at least, Sinatra's crew had its genesis in Humphrey Bogart's "Holmby Hills Rat Pack" in the early fifties. Bogart's group had been far less stylized than Sinatra's; according to Bogie, they existed "for the relief of boredom and the perpetuation of independence." Bogart's wife, Lauren Bacall, said they were devoted to nothing more than "drinking a lot of bourbon and staying up late . . . and you had to be a little musical."

Sinatra had been a member of Bogart's group, along with Judy Garland and her third husband, Sid Luft; the literary agent Irving "Swifty" Lazar; the restaurateur Mike Romanoff; Jimmy Van Heusen; David Niven; and the singer and author of the "Eloise" books, Kay Thompson. Kay later said of the group, "We were all terribly young and terribly witty and terribly rich and old Humpty Bogus was the head of it." When Bogart—whom Sinatra worshiped—died in 1957, Frank took over as leader. Most of the original members dropped out (Lauren Bacall among them after Sinatra broke off an engagement to her) and Sinatra brought in Dean, Sammy, and Joey as the stalwarts of the new group. Soon, Peter became the "fifth Musketeer."

Asked about Sinatra's version of the Rat Pack, Thompson said, "Oh Lord! I'd love to be in it. I'd be devastated. They're darling people, adorable people, and I adore them. I adore Peter and I'm mad for Frank. Anybody who doesn't respond to Frank is a nut!"

Peter not only responded to Sinatra, but to the whole idea of "belonging" that the Rat Pack offered him. It gave him entree into a whole community of performers he admired, which had been off-limits to him when he and Sinatra were on the outs. His closeness to Sinatra gave Peter a certain aura, made him a more important figure in the industry. And that helped him hold his own in his struggle for identity within the Kennedy family. As Jack's political star rose, and Peter's career floundered, Peter needed a buoy to keep his head above water. The Rat Pack provided it.

Before long, the intense interest of the press and public in "The Clan" again elevated Peter to star status in America. Articles syndicated in newspapers around the country analyzed every aspect of its members—their style, their language, their latest high jinks, their latest feuds, who was "in" last week, who was "out" this week. Richard Gehman, who wrote a book on the subject, said of the Rat Pack in the *American Weekly*: "For some reason that perhaps only a social historian of the future will be able to explain, no group of male human beings . . . excites, fascinates and dazzles—and at times exasperates—the American public quite as much as Frank Sinatra and his friends."

Even their detractors had to admit that the Rat Pack was a *colorful* group. They developed a style distinctly their own, the hallmark of which was "cool." They'd carry a martini in one hand and a cigarette in the other, putting either down only long enough to snap their fingers when a jazz beat moved them. They drove expensive cars with telephones, flew in private planes for weekends in Palm Springs, stayed in penthouses in hotels that only they knew even *had* penthouses. And always they were surrounded by beautiful young women who hung on their every word, laughed at all their jokes, and gave the distinct impression that they were there to serve.

They developed a mode of expression all their own. Women were "broads," a term that could be derogatory but was usually a compliment—"She's a great broad." Anything boring was "dullsville," anything exciting "a gas." Close friends were always called "Charlie," usually with a descriptive modifier. Milt Ebbins was "Charlie Bluecheese" because he never had a tan, and Peter was alternately called Charlie the Seal, because of a cigarette cough, and Charlie Pentagon or Charlie Washington because of his wife's family. (Later Sinatra dubbed him, more cleverly, "Brother-in-Lawford.")

Frequently used Rat Packer terms were "bird" and "clyde," the former referring to a man's frontal anatomy and the latter to his posterior. "How's your bird?" was a greeting much employed, and "I'm up to my clyde in work" was a frequent complaint. The Rat Packers loved to use these code words in the presence of outsiders who had no idea the boys were talking dirty. Tom Allen, in the Sunday edition of the New York *Daily News,* pointed out, "Child psychologists would note that kids like to do this, too, but they usually grow out of it by the time they're teenagers."

There were other bizarre locutions. At Sammy Davis's 1961 wedding to Mai Britt, Pat asked him, "How do you feel, Chicky Baby?" Davis replied, "Man, I'm electric!"

Peter soon adopted this self-consciously hip language himself. In an interview with Stephen Birmingham, Peter spoke of his annoyance at constant questions about the Rat Pack and described an encounter he'd had with a French journalist: "Like, we were getting off the boat the other day in Le Havre, and this French dame—this French reporter—comes up to me and says, *'Êtes-vous un Rat?'* Luckily, I speak French, but I don't dig *'Êtes-vous un Rat?'* She's asking me, am I a Rat? I don't dig. Then I dig. She's asking me about the Rat Pack, you dig? But there's no word in French for Rat Pack, you dig?"

"I told him I dug," Birmingham commented wearily.

It was clear that Peter had taken up many of Sinatra's mannerisms—and there were those who wished Peter had chosen someone a bit more deserving of such slavish emulation. For in addition to the admirable qualities about the man that Peter enumerated so dutifully, there was Sinatra the boozer, gambler, barroom brawler, and womanizer.

Peter wasn't much of a gambler himself, and he always avoided a fight, but he admired Sinatra's pugnacity, and he felt more secure when Frank was around. It was his efforts to keep up with Sinatra's drinking, however, that most harmed him. Sinatra always had a drink in his hand, but keen-eyed observers noticed that he would sip it slowly, put it down three-quarters full, take another drink, then do the same thing with that one. Peter, on the other hand, would drink an entire glass quickly and then reach for another.

There were other negatives about Sinatra that Peter was aware of but glossed over in his desire to be "in" with the Rat Pack. Sinatra cultivated friendships with the most notorious gangsters in the country. Theirs was the bloody flip side of the power that Jack Kennedy coveted in Washington, and Sinatra was equally impressed with it—impressed by the dons' wealth, their power, their fearlessness, the respect they commanded even from powerful members of legitimate society.

Sinatra grew especially close to Sam "Momo" Giancana, the head of the Chicago Mafia—a man who had, by 1960, ordered two hundred torture-murders of men who had crossed him or gotten in his way. Giancana controlled virtually all of the bookmakers, prostitutes, loan sharks, and extortionists in Chicago and owned interests in the Riviera, the Stardust, and the Desert Inn hotels in Las Vegas.

Arrested over seventy times, Giancana had served time in prison on a variety of charges, among them murder, assault with intent to kill, contributing to the delinquency of a minor, burglary, and bombing. He was a small, dapper man who wore sharkskin suits, fedora hats, silk shirts, alligator shoes—and a star sapphire pinky ring given to him as a gift by Frank Sinatra.

Peter lived with this aspect of Sinatra, but he didn't like it. "Frank never called [Giancana] or any of his killers Mafia," Peter told Sinatra biographer Kitty Kelley, "but they were Mafia all right. . . . Because of Giancana, he kowtowed to the Chicago mob. Why do you think Frank ended every one of his nightclub acts by singing 'My Kind of Town Chicago Is'? That was his tribute to Sam, who was really an awful guy with a gargoyle face and weasel nose. I couldn't stand him, but Frank idolized him because he was the Mafia's top gun. Frank loved to talk about 'hits' and guys getting 'rubbed out.' And you better believe that when the word got out around town [Hollywood] that Frank was a pal of Sam Giancana, nobody but nobody ever messed with Frank Sinatra. They were too scared. Concrete boots were no joke with this guy. He was a killer."

Giancana's tough-guy persona impressed Sinatra mightily, and he tried his best to emulate it. With his temper already dangerously violent, an angry Sinatra could now be a fearsome sight indeed—and his rage might be directed at anyone, anytime.

"You have no idea of that temper," Peter said years later. "He can get so mad that he's driven to real violence, especially if he's been drinking. I know. I've seen it. One time at a party in Palm Springs, he got so mad at some poor girl that he slammed her through a plate glass window. There was shattered glass and blood all over the place and the girl's arm was nearly severed from her body. Jimmy Van Heusen rushed her to the hospital. Frank paid her off and the whole thing was hushed up, of course, but I remember

Judy Garland and I looking at each other and shivering in fright at the time. I did everything I could to avoid setting off that temper."

Peter had "set off that temper" with the Ava Gardner misunderstanding, and no one, not even Sinatra's closest friend, was safe from it. If anyone failed to accord him the proper respect—which usually meant hoisting him on a lofty pedestal—he was sure to be ostracized from the group. "Frank is not a forgiving person," Joey Bishop said. "There was a time he didn't talk to Sammy, didn't talk to Dean, didn't talk to me. I was able to make up with him after he almost drowned in Hawaii. I sent him a wire—'You must have forgotten who you were. You could have walked on the water.' I got a call from him the next day, like nothing had happened between us."

It took Sammy Davis, Jr., almost a year to get back into Sinatra's good graces after he gave an indiscreet radio interview in Chicago in 1959. "There are many things [Frank] does that there are no excuses for," Davis told Jack Eigen on the air. "Talent is not an excuse for bad manners. . . . It does not give you the right to step on people and treat them rotten. That is what he does occasionally."

Davis didn't stop there. He was asked who he thought was the number-one singer in the country, and he replied that he was. "Bigger than Frank?" Eigen asked. "Yeah," Davis replied.

Sinatra was livid, not only about Sammy's remarks but because he had made them in Chicago in front of his Mafia cronies. Milt Ebbins recalled that "Frank had made sure Sammy got hired for a World War II film he was planning for MGM, *Never So Few,* for seventy-five thousand dollars. It hadn't been easy to get him in the picture in the first place. Frank met with the producers and they told him, 'Frank, there were no Negroes in the Burma theater.' Frank told them, 'Now there are.' So Sammy got hired. The studios wanted Frank so badly they'd agree to practically anything. He had that kind of power."

The *Never So Few* script had been rewritten to include Sammy, but after the Chicago interview Frank, at another meeting with MGM executives, told them, "Davis is out." They didn't ask him why. When he suggested that Steve McQueen replace Sammy, they agreed, and the script underwent another revision.

"You wanna talk destroyed?" Ebbins said. "Sammy Davis cried from morning to night. He came to see us when Peter was at the Copacabana, appearing with Jimmy Durante. He said, 'I can't get Frank on the phone. Can't you guys do something?' Peter told him, 'I talked to Frank but he won't budge.' Sammy never did the picture, never got any money. He could have sued because he had a contract, but he didn't dare. You don't sue Frank Sinatra."

"Sammy was quite lucky," Peter said. "Frank let him grovel for a while and then allowed him to apologize in public a few months later." But by then Davis was irrevocably out of *Never So Few*. As the film's start date neared, Sinatra added Peter to the cast, handing him his first big screen role in more than six years.

NINETEEN

"WHEN SINATRA, the king of Hollywood, makes a movie," Tom Allen wrote in 1960, "he is producer, star, and—as self-appointed casting director—personnel man for his pals." Sinatra's influence in the casting of Peter Lawford in *Never So Few* is a good example of the kind of power he wielded in Hollywood.

The picture was a World War II adventure set in the Burma theater. The ravishing Italian actress Gina Lollobrigida provided Sinatra's love interest, and Frank wanted Peter to play the relatively small part of Captain Grey Travis, a medic. Peter was eager for the role and told Milt Ebbins, "Go make a deal." Ebbins and Peter Shaw, who worked with Peter's agent at William Morris, set up an appointment with Benny Thau, a vice president and head of talent at MGM. "Thau was a low-key executive," Ebbins recalled. "Very soft-spoken. He'd say, ever so gently, 'How are you, Milt? Is everything okay? How's Peter doing? Is he all right?' But you had to watch out for guys like that, because they're the ones who'd kill you in a negotiation."

When Ebbins and Shaw were ushered into Thau's office, Thau sat behind his huge desk and made amiable small talk with his two visitors, never broaching the subject of the meeting. Finally Shaw said, "Listen, we want to talk about *Never So Few* and Peter Lawford."

A gentle sympathy inflected Thau's voice. "I must tell you—this is a very low-budgeted part."

236

Ebbins's eyes grew ingenuously wide. "Really? How low?"

"Well, it's three weeks of work and we think it's worth about fifteen hundred dollars a week."

Ebbins was aghast. "What? You've gotta be kidding!" he cried. Shaw sat dumbfounded.

When Ebbins told Thau that that wasn't nearly enough, Thau asked him, "What do you want?"

"We want seventy-five thousand," Ebbins replied.

Without another word, Thau pressed a button on his desk. "In a flash, in came Eddie Mannix," Ebbins recalled. "Mannix used to be a bouncer at Palisades Park in New Jersey, and Nick Schenck had brought him out here in the forties to take care of trouble at the studio and he became a top executive. He was a terrific Irishman—Gable and all the male stars loved him because he was a man's man and one of those real outgoing guys. He was a wonderful man—but a tough son of a bitch."

Mannix looked at Shaw and Ebbins and said in his gruffest voice, "What's going on here?" When Thau told him, he said, "What the hell do you want that part for? Jesus Christ, it pays nothing!"

Ebbins said, "What do you mean? It's a good part—it goes all through the picture. We think it's worth seventy-five thousand dollars."

Mannix blanched and looked at Thau. "I'll tell you what," Thau said finally. "We'll pay you twenty-five thousand."

Ebbins held firm for seventy-five thousand, and Thau grew impatient. To him, Peter Lawford was a two-thousand-dollar-a-week contract player the studio had let go and who had made just one movie since. Now he wanted seventy-five thousand dollars for three weeks' work? "I think you're nuts," Thau said. "You're crazy to risk losing this picture. This is a Frank Sinatra picture, with Gina Lollobrigida."

"Well," Ebbins said, "I guess I'll have to go back to Frank and tell him we can't do the picture."

"What do you mean?" Mannix asked.

"Eddie, Frank Sinatra told me to come here and see you guys. He wants Peter in the picture. And now I gotta go tell him Peter's not gonna be in it."

"How are you gonna tell him?"

"I'm gonna tell him that you won't pay the money he wants."

Mannix sat silently for a few seconds, then said quietly, "Well, let's discuss this again—later."

Ebbins reported the details of the meeting to Sinatra, who told him, "It isn't such a big part, but fuck 'em. Hold out for more money—you'll get it."

"So we held out," Ebbins recalled, "and we got something like forty or fifty thousand dollars, which was really pretty good. Mannix and Thau weren't too happy, but we were pleased as hell."

Never So Few was filmed on the MGM lot without incident, and it opened in New York in January 1960 to mixed reviews. Arthur Knight summed up the general reaction in *Saturday Review*: "What might have been an explosive and searching drama turns out to be just another war adventure film." Peter received no special attention from the critics, who saw the movie as Sinatra's and Lollobrigida's show, something for which Peter was grateful, since *Never So Few* was a box-office bomb. It cost $3.48 million to make and left MGM with a net loss of $1.15 million.

LONG BEFORE *Never So Few* was released, Peter and Sinatra had already signed to do another picture together and this time it was Peter who initiated the project. In 1955 he had run into Gilbert Kay, an assistant director, on the beach in front of his house. "He told me the story of *Ocean's 11*," Peter explained. "He had acquired it from a gas station attendant, who was one of twenty-five men to dismantle some valuable radio equipment in Germany during the war and carry it piece by piece out of the country. We thought the idea could be applied to a fictional story for a movie [about a group of war veterans who] rob six gambling casinos simultaneously in Las Vegas on New Year's Eve when the lights go out."

Peter was interested, but Kay wanted to direct the film and Peter told him he couldn't guarantee that. So Kay shopped the script around Hollywood. He was unsuccessful and he returned to Peter four years later willing to sell the property outright. Peter was confident he could interest Sinatra in making the movie, so he and Pat paid five thousand dollars apiece to purchase an option on it.

When Peter told Sinatra the story—Frank would play Danny Ocean, the leader of eleven men who pull off this intricate Vegas heist—"he flipped," Peter said. Sinatra envisioned it as a vehicle for the Rat Pack, and his interest in the project gave it new life. He owed Warner Brothers a picture, and when Jack Warner read the script, his reported reaction was, "Let's not make the movie—let's pull the job."

Warner agreed to pay fifty thousand dollars for the script, ten thousand of which went to repay Peter and Pat. Once Warner Brothers bought the movie it became Frank Sinatra's film, and he stood to make the most money on it. But it had been Peter's baby, and Sinatra appreciated that. Once again, he saw that Peter was well taken care of financially.

"Peter and I went to Burt Allenberg, who was Sinatra's agent," Milt Ebbins recalled. "He was one of the greatest agents of all time—he had handled Gable, Lombard, Cary Grant. A big-time agent. Brilliant. He was putting together the deal for Ocean's 11. He had a commitment from Warner Brothers, so he could do anything he wanted—he and Frank could cast the film, decide who got what salary, decide who got what percentage of the profits.

"Allenberg was shrewd. Peter and I sat there and listened to him bad-mouth the movie. He said, 'What do you want to do this picture for?' He was trying to downgrade Peter's position so we wouldn't ask for as much money as we might have."

Peter remained silent while Ebbins did the talking, saying that since Peter was the one who had found the property, he should be compensated for it. Then he grandly asked for one third of the film's profits. "It was a real shot in the dark. I had no strength at all. I was fighting a losing battle. Warner had no obligation at all to involve Peter in this picture."

But Ebbins acted as though his position were much stronger, and he further told Allenberg, "I want you to consider Peter to act in this picture with the other guys."

Allenberg's reply was chilling. "Is that a deal breaker?"

Ebbins remained stone faced and avoided Peter's gaze. "Let's not say it's a deal breaker. Let's just say Frank wants Peter to do the picture."

Allenberg replied, "Let me talk to Frank about this,"

and ended the meeting. A few days later, he called Peter and Milt back into his office and offered them 16 2/3 percent of the film's gross profit (after only its negative costs were deducted) and agreed to hire Peter to act in the picture for a fee of fifty thousand dollars—"a *great* deal," Ebbins recalled. And indeed it was: the film was a big hit, and Peter and Pat netted a $480,000 profit, out of which they gave Ebbins two points in appreciation.

Ocean's 11, as Peter's friend Roy Marcher put it, was "a ten-million-dollar home movie." In addition to Frank, Peter, Sammy, Dean, and Joey Bishop, the film featured old Sinatra friends like Cesar Romero, Richard Conte, and Henry Silva, and the latest Rat Pack "broad," Angie Dickinson. The director, Lewis Milestone, was suggested by Peter and was an excellent choice, in Joey Bishop's opinion: "It would have taken a great director to have been able to take this gang of people and get a good picture out of them. He had to be as *little* a director as possible and still get his points across when the time came."

He also had to good-naturedly tolerate a great deal of unprofessionalism. Sinatra's cool, laid-back style and aura of disinterest created an extremely casual air on the *Ocean's 11* set, and at times the motion picture took a backseat to other considerations. None of the Rat Pack was ever available for shooting before noon, because every night they held what they called their "summit meeting" at the Sands Hotel—a performance in the Copa Room in which the five of them sang, told jokes, danced, kidded each other, and generally acted like carefree fraternity brothers.

Frank Sinatra owned a piece of the Sands, and the Copa Room had been built for him. Every night twelve hundred people bought tickets, and eight hundred more were turned away, for shows that were, one reporter said, "of gaping brilliance."

"I couldn't wait to get to work," Peter later said. "Everybody was flowing on the same wavelength. It was so much fun. We would do two shows a night, get to bed at four-thirty or five, get up again, and go to work on a movie. We'd finish filming, go to the steam room, get something to eat, and start all over again—two shows. They were taking bets we'd all end up in a box."

Most nights, all five performers appeared on stage, but

sometimes one or two might be too tired to make it. On rare occasions, only one performer would show up. One show began with the Copa's MC asking over the loud-speaker, "Who's starring tonight?"

Joey Bishop's world-weary voice replied, "I dunno. Dean Martin is drunk, Sammy Davis hadda go to da temple, Peter Lawford's out campaigning for his brother-in-law."

"What's Frank doing?"

A knowing snicker. "Just say—somebody will go on."

The shows were never exactly the same; although they were carefully prepared, a good deal of the material was thought up at the last minute by Bishop, the comedy writer of the group, or improvised by the others onstage. Always there was booze and booze jokes; a typical show at the Sands would begin with Dean and Sammy wheeling out a bar full of drinks while Joey announced to the audience, "Here they are, Haig and Vague." In the middle of a routine Sammy might turn to the audience and say, "You can get swacked just watching this show."

There was a lot of mutual ribbing. Frank would take a drink and launch into a song, then Joey would interrupt him. "Don't sing anymore, Frank. Tell the people about the *good* work the Mafia is doing."

"Nobody could get away with that but me," Bishop recalled, "because I looked as though if Frank just looked at me I'd wither." In one show, while Dean was singing, Peter, Sammy, and Joey walked onstage wearing tuxedo jackets and boxer shorts—with their pants folded over their arms. "We walked across the stage as if we were discussing business," Bishop says. "It got a scream—three guys in their shorts."

Oftentimes one or two of the group would stand off-stage and heckle. Robert Legare wrote in a *Playboy* article on the shows, "Without fail, the Summiteers tried to break one another up with off-stage heckling and ad-libs that were often funnier than the on-stage material. When they succeeded, which was often, the audience lapped it up . . . every gag, every gesture, every amble across the stage by a star, had the whole place rocking with wild glee."

The Rat Pack's self-deprecating humor was often hard-edged—as when Dean Martin picked up Sammy Davis, Jr., and announced, "I'd like to thank the NAACP for this trophy," or when Sammy told Peter, "I know your kind. You'll dance with me but you won't let your kids go to school with me."

Still, only once did Joey Bishop feel they'd crossed the line into bad taste—when Frank and Dean, improvising, started to call each other "dagos." Bishop walked off the stage, and after the show Sinatra asked him, "What the hell happened to you?"

"Frank, what happens after you leave the stage and somebody calls you a dago?" Bishop replied. "You're not gonna like it and they're gonna say, 'Well, I heard you say it yourself onstage.' I don't know how to act out there when you start that stuff. Am I supposed to think it's camaraderie? I can't stand out there on that stage while you're doing dago, dago, dago."

Martin and Sinatra never used the word onstage again. "If you tell Frank something and you're right," Bishop said, "then you're home free."

One of the reasons the "summit" shows were so popular was that audiences sensed they were seeing the Rat Pack as they really were, that they had been made privy to how these men behaved with each other offstage. In many respects that was true. Dick Livingston recalled spending a few days in Vegas and catching the shows. "The morning after every show, we'd all get into the sauna at the hotel, and Sinatra would order twenty gin fizzes that the waiter would bring right into the sauna. Dean would wander in with a hangover and say, 'Even my hair hurts.' Then Sammy would come in with a white towel wrapped around his middle and Frank would say, 'Sammy, you can't come in with that towel. There's a brown towel out there for you.' It was like they were still onstage, and it was fun, really fun."

The Rat Pack shows were Las Vegas's biggest draw for the two months of *Ocean's 11* filming in the winter of 1959–1960. Sinatra and Martin, who both owned a piece of the Copa Room, made between seventy-five thousand and a hundred thousand dollars a week for their labors. The rest of the Rat Pack pocketed about twenty-five thousand a week—a lot more money than Peter could have made doing virtually anything else.

Peter, of course, was the odd man out in this high-powered talent pool. A joke around Vegas at the time had a group of conventioneers headed for the Sands and wondering which of the Rat Pack would be onstage that night. "With our luck," one of them grumbles, "it'll be just Peter Lawford."

"Peter held his own," Joey Bishop recalled, "but he was well aware that a lot of people wondered, 'What is he doing up there with those four guys?' I mean if you could take anybody away from the show without hurting it, it would be Peter. He must have sensed that the only reason for his being there was his relationship to Jack Kennedy. And that would make anyone feel ill at ease."

On February 7, Jack attended the show. A month earlier, he had announced his candidacy for president and he was gearing up for the first few primary showdowns. When Sinatra introduced Kennedy to the audience, Dean Martin watched the handsome young candidate as he stood and acknowledged the crowd's applause. Then Martin turned to Sinatra and asked, "What did you say his name was?"

TWENTY

IN THE EARLY FALL of 1959, Milt Ebbins was having dinner with Peter and Pat in their Santa Monica house. It had been a pleasant evening, good food and wine mixed with conversation about show business and politics while the strains of Sarah Vaughan's "Broken-Hearted Melody" lilted from the stereo console. Ebbins noticed that Peter was drinking a little more than usual, but he seemed to be okay.

As Ebbins remembered it, "Everything was fine at first. Then, for no apparent reason, Peter turned on Pat. His whole face changed, his lip curled, he started to abuse her verbally. It was terrible to see. She sat there and took it for a few moments; then she just got up, said 'Good night,' and went upstairs. I didn't know what to say. Peter could be like Dr. Jekyll and Mr. Hyde—especially when he was drinking."

The scene wasn't an isolated one. While Peter's career continued on an upswing, his home life deteriorated. More and more he and Pat found it difficult to be together. They spent lengthy periods apart, she in Hyannis Port with the children, he at home in Santa Monica. On the rare occasions when Pat was home, she and Peter surrounded themselves with friends. On most weeknights and every weekend the house was overrun with Peter's beach buddies, Pat's political associates, Peter and Pat's show business pals. A house full of company would keep the Lawfords in a genial mood, but even when they were in a good frame of mind, according to Peter Sabiston, "there was very little affection between the two of them. No hand holding or embracing or anything like that." Nor were the Lawfords usually demonstrative in a negative way, but on occasion they would slip. "There was some bickering," Sabiston recalled. "They both had sharp tongues."

Dolores Naar added, "Because we were so close to them, we could see the hostility when she talked to him, we could hear the little snide remarks, the put-downs."

A general assumption about Peter and Pat's marital problems is that they were created solely by his drinking and philandering. Their close friends knew that the situation was more complex. Joe Naar observed that "Pat made Peter feel like a second-class citizen," and Dolores Naar added, "He just didn't fit in with the political side of her. He was trying to find a place, trying to be needed and important. But Pat always kind of put him down. So he would see other women. And that's why things started to fall apart. But I'm not sure what came first. Maybe Pat treated him that way *because* he was seeing other women."

It was truly a vicious circle. Pat in love with Peter but caught up in the whirlwind of her obsessively political family; Peter in love with Pat but feeling emasculated in the presence of her powerful brothers and seeking reassurance from other women; Pat angered by Peter's womanizing, pulling herself farther away from him and putting him down, which made him feel even less worthy.

For that reason and others, Peter's sex life with Pat was more unsatisfactory than ever for him. Peter told Jackie Cooper's wife, Barbara, that "after Pat and I have sex, if I want to talk about it the next morning, she'll have *none* of it. It's over, done with, that was her job and she'd done it."

"There was reason for Peter to philander," Joe Naar thought. "Pat was very manipulative. I think she provoked things. I don't know if she fell out of love with Peter or if she thought she was too good for him or what. But it was clear that she provoked the incidents of infidelity and he reacted to the provocations in the best way he could to keep his self-respect and dignity."

Pat alternated between sanguinity and anger about Peter's affairs. She knew about his penchant for prostitutes. According to Milt Ebbins, "Peter was the whore's delight. Every time we traveled, every place we went, there were all these hookers. It was cheaper for him to do that. You have to wine and dine girls. Peter never wanted to get involved. It was easier to have call girls than to try and romance somebody. So he always liked hookers. They were high-class hookers, of course, not girls off the street."

Sometimes, Peter did "get involved"—he had a brief fling with Kim Novak in the late fifties and for a time kept a mistress in New York. If Pat found out about a particular dalliance, she would sometimes confront Peter angrily, but more often she simply let him know very coolly that she was onto him. She took the latter course one evening when Peter came home from filming. Pat fixed him a cocktail, and as she handed him the drink she said evenly, "You'll have to get rid of that girl in New York." Peter looked at her slack-jawed and she went calmly about her business.

It was around this time that Peter began to suspect Pat of having an affair, and he paid a visit to Fred Otash, the former LAPD vice squad officer who had killed the *Confidential* magazine story about Peter's penchant for prostitutes and who was now a private detective. "Peter came to me one day in 1959," Otash recalled, "and asked if I had anything that he could use to make secret recordings. I gave him a Magnet-O-Phone and showed him how to use it."

Peter kept the eavesdropping device for over a month and told Milt Ebbins he thought Pat was "seeing other guys." Ebbins recalled Peter telling him that he had "picked up the phone one time and heard her talking to one of them, telling him what she'd like to be doing to him and all that. But she made no bones about it. It was no big secret. She didn't say she was going to visit an aunt. By that time the marriage was in trouble, so Peter knew what was happening."

Peter and Pat never seriously considered divorce at this time, for a variety of reasons, her Catholicism chief among them. A divorce not only would have damaged Pat's position in the church, but could have affected her brother's hopes of becoming the first Catholic president of the United States. And there were, of course, the children.

Christopher was now four, Sydney three, and Victoria one, but Peter's talent for fathering had not improved with time. "Peter didn't know how to treat his children," Dolores Naar said. "When they would come down from their naps, they would come up to him and kiss him and he'd rub their backs as he sat in his lounge chair out by the pool and give them a kiss. But that was it. I never saw them sit on his lap; I never saw him running or playing with them."

Peter's upbringing had left him emotionally ill-equipped for parenting, and he was incapable of being a "pal" to his son. More often than not, it was his friends who did fatherly things with Christopher; Dick Martin, the comedian, recalls that he, not Peter, taught the boy how to swim in the Lawfords' Olympic-size swimming pool. And it was Peter's old Freed Unit friend Leonard Gershe who would regale Christopher with stories he'd make up on the spot.

Both Peter and Pat had grown up in households in which children were raised primarily by governesses, and Pat shared Peter's hands-off attitude toward the children. They had a nanny who took care of them; the children had their time with their mother and their father for an hour or so in the evening, and then it was up to bed. "To tuck the children into bed meant nothing to Pat," Dolores Naar observed. "To be there when they took their naps meant nothing; she could go on a six-week trip around the world and that meant nothing. That's how she grew up. Her parents traveled a lot."

When she *was* with her children, Pat sometimes seemed short on patience with them. Leonard Gershe recalled that "when the nannies weren't around and Pat had to deal with the kids herself, she'd push the clocks ahead an hour so they'd go to bed an hour early. She couldn't take them any more than that."

For his part, Peter did *try* to be a good father, Dolores Naar believed. "Peter was always very gentle with his children. They knew that he wasn't the kind of dad that they could jump on his back or whatever. It was all very restrained. He would stroke their back or pet their hair. He had a softness and a warmth with the children. You knew that he really loved them, but he didn't know what to do with them."

*   *   *

PETER DIDN'T see much of his children in any event
between the summers of 1959 and 1960. In quick succession, he'd made *Never So Few* and *Ocean's 11*—and his next
movie, offered to him independently of Frank Sinatra, would
take him to Israel, eight thousand miles from home, and put
him under the direction of the formidably Teutonic filmmaker Otto Preminger.

Preminger was one of Hollywood's most flamboyant
producer-directors, with *Laura, The Man with the Golden
Arm,* and *Anatomy of a Murder* to his credit. His new film
was the movie version of Leon Uris's best-seller about the
genesis of the Jewish homeland, *Exodus,* and Peter was to
be part of an impressive all-star cast that included Paul Newman, Eva Marie Saint, Sal Mineo, Ralph Richardson, and
Lee J. Cobb. It was a motion picture "event," and Peter
didn't want to do it.

"I couldn't get Peter to sign the contracts for *Exodus,*"
Milt Ebbins recalled. "He'd agreed verbally to do the picture, and Preminger kept asking me for the contracts back.
He'd call me and say, 'Milt, vere are ze contracts? I've got
to have ze contracts!'"

When Ebbins asked Peter why he was so reluctant, he
replied that he didn't want to go on location to Israel, a
new country where even the best hotels offered few ameni-
ties. Worse, he had heard that it was forbidden to light a
match on Saturday. A heavy smoker, Peter shuddered at the
thought.

His manager reminded Peter that he had already told
Preminger he would do the picture, and he couldn't back
down. He persuaded Peter to sign the top pages of each of
the four copies of the contract. After he initialed the inside
clauses on the first contract, he refused to do so again on
the other three. Ebbins had to do it for him.

Peter was wary, too, of Preminger, an autocratic task
master often referred to as "der Führer." He asked his
friend David Niven, who had worked with Preminger, for
advice on how to handle him. Over lunch at Romanoff's
Niven spelled out his formula for a successful working relationship with Otto: "There is only one way to handle Preminger. If you get into an argument with him, walk up to
him, put your face right up against his—nose to nose—and
scream, '*Fuck you, Otto!*' And you'll win. But remember

it's gotta be nose to nose. Stand right in his face and yell as loud as you can, *'Fuck you, Otto!'* Then you'll have no problems with him."

Peter never had to use Niven's advice; he and Preminger got along well. The director, in fact, seems to have been a pussycat when it came to Peter. When Preminger chartered an airplane to transport the cast and crew from one location to another, Peter sat in the first-class section with his erstwhile best man, Bob Neal, who had agreed to accompany him when Ebbins came down with the flu. Neal, who by now had quite a reputation as a fun-loving millionaire, sat in the last remaining first-class seat while Preminger, who had paid for the plane, sat in the tail section.

Finally the director came up front and said to Peter, "Vy do you bring zis playboy vit chou?" In his usual flip manner, Peter responded, "For laughs, Otto. You wouldn't know." Preminger spent the rest of the flight in the rear of the plane.

Although Preminger didn't live up to Peter's fearful expectations, the location shooting did. Most of Peter's scenes were filmed on Cyprus, and his hotel room featured a bare light bulb hanging by a cord from the ceiling and enormous black bugs in the closet. But the filming of *Exodus* was uneventful. Peter played an English officer he described as "a real stinker. He's anti-Semitic and does a lot to keep the Jews from getting into Israel." The rare opportunity to play a heavy did have its appeal for Peter despite the thankless nature of the role.

The film racked up an impressive seven million dollars in box-office grosses and three Oscar nominations (Ernest Gold's sweeping musical score won). But it was panned by most critics. Although some of the performances were singled out for praise (notably, Sal Mineo's), Ronald Bergan's comments about the film were typical. He called Dalton Trumbo's script "simplistic" and "all-things-to-all-men" and thought the movie contained "little passion, depth or sweep. What it had were stereotypes, sanctimony and schmaltz."

And it was *long*. Comic Mort Sahl provided what has remained the last word on *Exodus* at an industry screening in the fall of 1960. Three hours into the film, Sahl stood up, turned to Preminger, and pleaded, "Otto, let my people go!"

Peter returned to Los Angeles in late June 1960. He had had a clause inserted in his contract that guaranteed he would be able to return to the United States by July 1—in time for the Democratic National Convention. He wanted to make sure to be on hand when, if luck continued to smile, John F. Kennedy would be nominated as the Democratic Party's candidate for president.

TWENTY-ONE

ON JANUARY 2, 1960, forty-two-year-old Jack Kennedy stood under television and newsreel lights in the Senate Caucus Room and declared, "I am announcing today my candidacy for the presidency of the United States."

He had spent most of his life preparing for that moment, wearing the mantle of presumption to greatness that had been his since the death of his brother Joe. But Kennedy found that presumption and reality were two different things when he began his campaign for the Democratic nomination. He was the youngest man ever to seek the presidency; many observers viewed him as callow and inexperienced. Moreover, Catholicism had always proved an insurmountable barrier to winning the nation's highest office.

Jack Kennedy had been fascinated with the entertainers he'd met in Hollywood, and he became convinced that they could make a real difference to his prospects. They were, of course, extraordinarily wealthy and thus highly attractive from a purely fund-raising point of view. More important, Kennedy sensed that the charisma he'd found so magnetic in them, their popularity and larger-than-life images, could be used to enhance his own appeal.

Kennedy wasn't the first presidential candidate to attempt to woo Hollywood stars to his cause. But he *was* the first to do it to such an extent—and, as Peter Lawford's brother-in-law, the first to do so from an insider's vantage point. One of Jack's earliest campaign strategies was to uti-lize Hollywood celebrities, not just to raise money behind the scenes but to campaign publicly to get out the Kennedy vote.

Two years before he announced his candidacy, he had made his first overture to a celebrity for support. Visiting the set of *The Thin Man,* he had spent several hours in discussion with Phyllis Kirk. Director Don Weis thought that Kennedy was "really in heat for Phyllis," but she re-called their discussions as purely political: "My theory at the time was that actors should not stump for candidates, be-cause it was unfair. There are a lot of people in this country who are very influenced by their idols saying jump through this hoop or vote for Genghis Khan. I felt you could work behind the scenes, but you don't have to go out and hog-wash the country into thinking that they should vote for the candidate you're voting for."

Kennedy listened to Phyllis's argument and said, "I dis-agree. I think someone like you should become very actively involved." After hours of discussion, Kennedy swayed her to his way of thinking, and four months later she decided to lend her name to an advertisement—for Adlai Stevenson for president. The day the full-page newspaper ad appeared, Kirk got a phone call from Senator Kennedy. "I want to congratulate you for joining the fray," he said. "I think it's wonderful that you're putting your name on the line. This, however, is not exactly what I had in mind."

Phyllis Kirk eventually came around to Kennedy, as did almost all of Peter's Hollywood friends. Sammy Cahn remembered running into Jack at a party before he'd an-nounced his candidacy. Kennedy asked him, "Could you write me a campaign song?" Cahn replied, "What are you running for?" When Kennedy told him, he offered to write new lyrics for his Oscar-winning song "High Hopes," which Frank Sinatra had sung in the 1959 film *A Hole in the Head.* The reworked ditty became the Democrats' 1960 theme song:

K-E-double-N-E-D-Y,
Jack's the nation's favorite guy
Everyone wants to back Jack,

Jack is on the right track.
And he's got HIGH HOPES,
He's got HIGH HOPES,
He's got high-apple-pie
-in-the-sky hopes.

A series of Los Angeles fund-raisers, at which contributors were entertained by Frank Sinatra or Sammy Davis or Judy Garland and then heard the candidate speak about his vision for America, netted hundreds of thousands of dollars for the primary campaign. Evie Johnson remembered one at the Lawfords' beach house: "Peter had rounded up quite a good group, and they entertained. Judy sang. Teddy Kennedy was there, and he did a belly dance for us, kind of like a hula. We all got sort of crazy."

Frank Sinatra committed himself totally to the goal of making John F. Kennedy the next president of the United States. He rechristened his group of followers the "Jack Pack," sang about "that old Jack magic," and worked tirelessly to raise money for the Kennedy campaign. "Frank snapped his fingers, and people fell into line," Milt Ebbins recalled. "He'd get on the phone to somebody and before you knew it he'd be saying, 'Gotcha down for ten thousand,' and that would be the end of it. Frank was fantastic. Peter didn't do as much for Jack's campaign as Frank did, but it was Peter who brought Frank to Jack in the first place."

Sinatra offered to round up the Rat Pack and sweep into West Virginia to do the same thing for the Kennedy primary campaign there that he'd done in Hollywood. But Jack Kennedy was nothing if not a savvy politician. He knew that Sinatra's personality and manner would go over far less well in a small, parochial state than it did in Beverly Hills and Las Vegas, and he'd heard stories about the last time Sinatra and his band of merrymakers had descended on a small town.

Sinatra, Dean Martin, and Shirley MacLaine had spent several months in Madison, Indiana, for the filming of *Some Came Running* in 1958. Martin and Sinatra were rarely without a drink in their hand, and on one occasion Sinatra roughed up a sixty-six-year-old hotel clerk for getting a hamburger order wrong. Another time, riding a bus, Sinatra smiled and returned the townspeople's waves of greeting through a window—all the while muttering things under his breath like "Hello there, hillbilly!" ... "Drop dead, jerk!" ... "Hey, where'd you get that big fat behind?"

And so Sinatra was kept out of the West Virginia campaign—but only in person. FBI wiretaps reveal that he apparently disbursed large mob donations in West Virginia that were used to pay off election officials. And in a more indirect but no less important contribution, Sinatra introduced Jack to one of his recent conquests, Judith Campbell, a vivacious twenty-five-year-old Irish brunette with limpid blue eyes—a "nicer" Liz Taylor, as Jimmy "the Weasel" Fratianno, a Los Angeles mafioso, called her.

A recent divorcée, Judy Campbell had run into Sinatra at Puccini one night in November 1959. They'd met once before, but this time Frank showed strong interest in the young woman. He invited her to join him on a trip to Hawaii a few days later with Peter and Pat, and it was in Honolulu on November 10 that their affair began. At first Judy found Frank charming and attentive, but his mercurial temperament soon gave her second thoughts. She called off the romance when Sinatra invited her to his Beverly Hills home and expected her to participate in a *ménage à trois* with him and another woman.

They remained friends, however, and Frank invited her to Vegas to see some of the "summit" shows during the filming of *Ocean's 11*. It was there that Sinatra introduced her to Jack Kennedy and his twenty-eight-year-old brother Ted, who was western states coordinator for the campaign.

Ted Kennedy made a pass at Campbell, which she rejected, but one month later, on the night before the New Hampshire primary, she began a sexual affair with the candidate. "It was amazing to me that he could be so relaxed on the eve of the first primary of his presidential campaign," Campbell later said, "but unbelievably, he didn't mention New Hampshire once during our entire night together."

Jack Kennedy was certain he'd win New Hampshire, but he was deeply concerned about his chances in West Virginia, and when Campbell told him that Sinatra had just introduced her to Sam Giancana, Kennedy asked if she would arrange a meeting between them. When Judy asked why, Jack replied, "I think I may need his help in the campaign."

Kennedy and Giancana met at the Fontainebleau Hotel in Miami Beach, and although the subject of their conversation remains unrecorded, Giancana apparently agreed to use his "influence" with West Virginia officials in order to ensure a Kennedy victory there. Kennedy may or may not have offered anything concrete in return, but it soon became clear that Giancana expected that if Jack won the presidency, the federal government would "go easy" on organized crime. It wasn't an unreasonable assumption.

Giancana sent one of his cronies, Paul "Skinny" D'Amato, into West Virginia to "convince" the sheriffs who controlled the state's political machine to "get out the vote for Kennedy." D'Amato did so by agreeing to forgive gambling debts many of the men had incurred at his 500 Club in Atlantic City, and he handed others cash from a fifty-thousand-dollar war chest set up for the purpose with Mafia donations.

Jack Kennedy beat Hubert Humphrey handily in West Virginia, ending the Minnesotan's candidacy and defusing the religion issue once and for all by winning in an overwhelmingly Protestant state. In July he came into the Democratic National Convention with victories in all seven of the primaries he had entered, and he was just sixty-one votes short of the nomination. Serendipitously, the convention was held in the Los Angeles Sports Arena, putting Kennedy's show business supporters smack in the middle of the action. The night before the convention's July 11 opening, the Democratic Party staged a hundred-dollar-a-plate fund-raiser at the Beverly Hilton Hotel attended by twenty-eight hundred people. The Rat Pack and other of Hollywood's biggest names were present—Judy Garland, Angie Dickinson, Milton Berle, Joe E. Lewis, George Jessel, Mort Sahl, Janet Leigh, and Tony Curtis among them.

Judy Garland sat at the head table next to the candidate; Frank Sinatra sat a few chairs down with some of the other presidential hopefuls—Senators Lyndon Johnson of Texas and Stuart Symington of Missouri, and the potential draftee Adlai Stevenson.

The next day, Frank, Sammy, Dean, Peter, Janet Leigh, and Tony Curtis led the hundred thousand people jammed into the Sports Arena in a rousing rendition of "The Star-Spangled Banner" to open the convention. A few bars into the song, members of the Alabama delegation, seated close to the stage, began to heckle Sammy Davis with vicious racial epithets. His face burning with hurt and anger, Davis forced back tears. Sinatra tried to buck him up, whispering, "Those dirty sons of bitches. Don't let them get to you, Charlie!" Davis finished the song, but he didn't take his seat with the others once the convention was gaveled to order.

Alabama was one of the uncommitted delegations that Jack needed to guarantee a first-ballot victory. It was left to Peter to swallow his anger two days later and try to charm a group of men he considered bigots. "I will leave the speechmaking to the politicians," Peter said on air as TV cameras followed him into the delegation, "but I did want to shake hands with all these people and talk to them as friends."

Throughout the week, Sinatra and the Rat Pack roamed the convention floor, ignoring barriers and restrictions, and cajoled recalcitrant delegates to join the Kennedy cause. Conscious of the cameras, Sinatra painted his bald pate black so it wouldn't be obvious under the TV lights.

After the first convention session, Jack Kennedy retired to his suite at the Beverly Hilton Hotel and spent some time with Judy Campbell. (Jackie had stayed home because she was six months pregnant and had a history of problem pregnancies.) Apparently Jack had never compared notes with Sinatra about Judy, because he tried, as Sinatra had, to talk her into a three-way—"with a secretarial type in her late twenties," as Campbell recalled it. "I know you," Jack told her. "I know you'll like it." Just as she had with Sinatra, Judy refused.

For the rest of the convention, Jack Kennedy's sexual amusement was provided by Marilyn Monroe, who was preparing to begin work in Reno on *The Misfits,* written by her husband, the playwright Arthur Miller, and costarring Clark Gable. Miller and Monroe, dubbed "the Egghead and the Hourglass," had wed in 1956, but the marriage had been in trouble for several years, and Marilyn was just emerging from an affair with the French singer and actor Yves Montand, the costar of her most recent film *Let's Make Love.*

Jack Kennedy and Marilyn Monroe had continued to rendezvous occasionally in New York throughout the 1950s. Whenever a rift developed between Monroe and Miller, she would drive into Manhattan from their Connecticut farm-

house and stay at her East Fifty-seventh Street apartment.
If Jack was in town, she would meet him in his suite at the
Carlyle Hotel. Now, with her marriage on the rocks, Marilyn
was in Los Angeles without Miller, and Kennedy's large
contingent of Hollywood supporters made her far less con-
spicuous in Kennedy's company than she might have been.
The second night of the convention, Marilyn dined with
Jack, Peter, and Kennedy aide Kenneth O'Donnell at
Puccini.

Before dinner, Marilyn and Jack had apparently been
intimate, because Marilyn giggled to Peter that Jack's
performance earlier had been "very democratic" and "very
penetrating." According to Marilyn's long-time maid, Lena
Pepitone, Kennedy was "always telling her dirty jokes,
pinching her, and squeezing her. . . . She told me that [he]
was always putting his hand on her thigh." This evening at
Puccini, apparently, he continued northward, running his
hand farther under Marilyn's dress. "He hadn't counted on
going that far," Marilyn laughed to Lena. When he discovered she wasn't wearing any panties, "he pulled back and
turned red."

If the candidate seemed confident and at ease, his advis-
ers and family were less tranquil. He was within reach of
the nomination, but until it was officially his, anything could
happen. The greatest threat was the tremendous emotional
attachment many of the delegates—even those pledged to
Kennedy—still felt for Adlai Stevenson. When Stevenson
said he would allow his name to be placed in nomination,
the Kennedy camp verged on panic. Iowa delegate Arthur
Thompson recalled seeing Pat Lawford just outside the convention hall during a thunderous demonstration for Stevenson. "She was walking back and forth in what I would
describe as a very nervous manner, smoking a cigarette, and
with further evidence of nervousness. She walked [into the
hall] several times to take a look at the proceedings, then
back out again to catch some of it, as I was, on the loud-
speaker. I've called that since the 'Kennedy faction's moment of uncertainty.' "

Jack Kennedy seemed unfazed. "Don't worry, Dad," he
told his father. "Stevenson has everything but the votes."
He was right. By the time the roll call reached Wyoming,
Jack was within a few votes of a first-ballot victory. Ted

Kennedy pushed his way through the crowd to the chairman of the Wyoming delegation and shouted above the din, "You have in your grasp the opportunity to nominate the next president of the United States. Such support can never be forgotten by a president." The gambit worked—the chairman announced all fifteen of Wyoming's votes for John F. Kennedy.

The hall erupted once again, this time in acclamation for the nominee of the Democratic Party. Frank Sinatra and the Rat Pack celebrated wildly, patted each other on the back, glad-handed strangers. "We're on our way to the White House, buddy boy," Sinatra yelled to Peter, a smile beaming from his face like a sunburst. *"We're on our way to the White House."*

TWENTY-TWO

THE DEMOCRATIC nominee began his race for
president as a distinct underdog. His opponent, Vice-
President Richard Nixon, had served for eight years
under one of the most popular presidents in history, had
traveled the world as Dwight Eisenhower's representative,
had debated Soviet premier Nikita Khrushchev. Although
he was just four years older than Kennedy, Nixon was
viewed by many Americans as far more experienced, far
more to be trusted with the great power of the office he
sought.

Kennedy needed to prove himself as qualified for the
presidency as Nixon was, and he was given a golden opportunity to do so when the Vice-President agreed to a series
of nationally televised debates. The encounters would put
Kennedy on an even footing with Nixon before either uttered a word, and they would give him and his campaign
themes the kind of exposure he couldn't have bought for
millions of dollars. If Kennedy merely held his own in the
debates, he would come out ahead.

In preparation for the first confrontation, Jack Kennedy
turned to the person close to him who had had the most
experience in the medium he needed to conquer—Peter
Lawford. Peter was thrilled that there was finally something
he alone could offer the campaign. He gave his brother-in-
law some general advice—"make sure you wear a dark suit,
a blue shirt, and the darkest makeup that still looks natu-

259

ral"—and then he told Jack something that may well have won him the election: "Don't be afraid of the camera. Look directly into it, as though it were a friend across the dinner table. You'll be making contact with millions of people at the same moment, but each one will feel as though you're talking only to him."

Kennedy's skillful use of the TV cameras in the first debate was, arguably, more important than any other single factor in the election. His self-assured good looks and his cool, steady eye contact with viewers contrasted starkly with the ill-at-ease, sweaty uncertainty of gaze from Nixon that made him appear shifty-eyed. The Vice-President's gray suit blended into the background and tended to wash him out; Jack Kennedy's dark blue suit, as Peter had told him it would, made him appear vivid, more forceful. Radio listeners scored the debate a draw; TV viewers gave the contest handily to the Democrat.

The debates helped Kennedy overcome the odds against him and draw even with Nixon in the public-opinion polls. And Peter was able to help Jack in another small way using television. Throughout the primaries and the general election campaign, Peter made frequent guest appearances on shows like Frank Sinatra's and Perry Como's, often getting in a good word for the Kennedy campaign. There had been some controversy about the issue of equal time over the airwaves, and a lot of people wondered how he got away with it.

"You can't ask me how I 'get away' with plugging Kennedy on TV," Peter told a reporter, "because in all honesty I have never taken it upon myself to do so. In every instance, the Kennedy lines were written in for me by the show management. I could easily understand how this would happen on the Sinatra show, but I must say I was a little surprised when it came up on the Como show. I thought it was marvelous nevertheless. After I did the show I went home and wrote a note of thanks to Perry. I said, 'If ever our man gets into the White House, I'm sure he'll make you ambassador to Rome.' "

Kennedy's conquest of television notwithstanding, there was still great uncertainty about the outcome of the election, and the Hollywood contingent of the campaign didn't let up. In September, Frank Sinatra left for Hawaii to film *The*

Devil at 4 O'Clock, costarring Spencer Tracy. Peter joined him there for a series of Kennedy fund-raising concerts at Waikiki Beach, at Hilo on the big island of Hawaii, and on Maui, where Sinatra was filming. "We hit all the islands," Peter recalled, "just the two of us. I'd smile and Frank would sing, picking up local bands along the way."

The largest of the events was a "Koncert for Kennedy" at the Waikiki Shell on October 2, where Sinatra sang fourteen songs to an audience of over nine thousand. Peter spoke briefly to the crowd, offering mostly wisecracks: "It's not true that I'm for Kennedy because I want my brother-in-law out of the house." He introduced Sinatra as "our next ambassador to Italy," but the singer demurred, saying, "I just want to run the Miss Universe contest."

As Kennedy's campaign rolled along, Democrats began to smell victory, and the crowds at his public appearances swelled to sometimes unmanageable sizes. On October 26, Janet Leigh, Tony Curtis, Sinatra, and Peter joined the candidate at a huge rally in New Jersey, Sinatra's home state. Nearly forty thousand avid Democrats attended. Peter was the master of ceremonies, Sinatra sang, Leigh said a few words. Then the candidate delivered a stirring oration, and the throng grew so frenzied that fifteen women fainted and a man had to be carried out of the arena over the heads of the crowd.

ON ELECTION DAY, November 8, Jack Kennedy received at least one vote that no other candidate before him ever had—Peter Lawford's. In order to vote for his brother-in-law, Peter had studied to become a citizen of the United States in the early spring of 1960, and on April 23, as Kennedy campaigned in West Virginia, Peter stood along with six hundred other people in Los Angeles, raised his right hand, and pledged his loyalty to America. "It's the one thing in the world I wanted most," Peter said afterward. "I was never so frightened in my life as when I took the examination. I kept saying to myself, 'Suppose I fail?'"

A few hours after his swearing-in, Peter got a telegram from his sisters-in-law Joan and Ethel: "Congratulations and welcome to America. However, hold your passport till after West Virginia, and if Hubert wins, we'll all go back to England with you."

Now, Peter was able to vote for Jack in the general election, and he did so by absentee ballot because he planned to be in Hyannis Port to wait out the election results with the rest of the family. He joined Jack for the last Kennedy rally of the campaign in Boston Garden on Monday night, November 7. Jack introduced several members of his family before getting to Peter, who elicited the loudest response of all. "You're very popular in Boston, Peter," the candidate commented as he heard the crowd cheer for his brother-in-law.

By four A.M., when Peter and Jack went to bed at the Kennedy compound in Hyannis Port, the election results were still in doubt. CBS News had projected Nixon the winner early in the evening, then changed its mind. At five forty-five Bobby Kennedy got word that Michigan had finally gone for Jack and put him over the top in the electoral college. When the candidate arose at nine o'clock he was told he was the president-elect.

By then the press had descended on the compound, and so had the Secret Service. When Jack took a stroll along the beach that fronted the Kennedy property, he was trailed by armed guards—protection he would come to hate and try to elude whenever possible. Then Vice-President Nixon conceded the election and dozens of Kennedys and their friends piled into a caravan headed for the Hyannis Armory to see Jack meet the press for the first time as president-elect.

The 1960 presidential election had gone to Kennedy by a mere 118,574 votes out of more than sixty-eight million cast, and some observers felt that the Democrats hadn't won it fair and square. Peter's FBI file contains a copy of a letter sent anonymously to President Eisenhower shortly after the election by a disgruntled New York Republican.

"My suspicions concerning possible election fraud on a national scale by organized crime grow stronger and stronger," the correspondent wrote. "When I first saw Frank Sinatra and his well-known 'Rat Pack' on the Kennedy bandwagon, I didn't like the 'odor of things.' Sinatra is well known in show business as being buddy-buddy with the syndicates of crime throughout the world, and these people stop at nothing. . . . They treated the last election as they would a horse race with very heavy betting. Peter Lawford who is Kennedy's brother-in-law had $50,000 bet on his winning . . . this is peanuts [compared] to what the mob had bet on a Kennedy victory. These include the top juke box operators, pinball game specialists and the like—you see, *machines are their business*. Therefore, could it be possible that in addition to 'fixing' votes in other ways, they could do something to voting machines that would register only one out of every three or four votes for Nixon? In Chicago they really went all out, as you can tell by looking at the returns in that city. . . ."

Ovid Demaris, a Mafia specialist, analyzed the 1960 Illinois results and found that although Nixon had won 93 of the state's 102 counties, he lost Illinois by 8,858 votes—because of a huge Kennedy majority in Cook County, which includes Chicago. A partial, unofficial Republican recount of the Cook County vote reportedly turned up an extra 4,539 votes for Nixon, but an official recount was blocked by Chicago's Democratic mayor, Richard Daley. Indeed, the Chicago Mafia boss, Sam Giancana, boasted that he had been responsible for Kennedy's victory.*

Eisenhower urged his Vice-President to contest the election results, but Nixon declined. In his memoirs, Nixon wrote that he did so to avoid dividing the nation, but he may have had less noble motives. A careful investigation would surely have uncovered local fraud that benefited the Republican ticket as well. And Nixon was aware that Bobby Kennedy knew but had decided not to leak the fact that Nixon had sought psychiatric counseling in the 1950s.

That was the Kennedy camp's ace in the hole. Not only did it make Nixon think twice about demanding a recount, but it kept him from releasing information during the campaign that would have destroyed his opponent's candidacy—that Jack Kennedy was an adulterer. Had he chosen to use it, Nixon had more than enough information on the Kennedys—information obtained through wiretaps that Fred Otash had installed in the Lawford home in 1959. Otash had been approached, by his own account, by "some people within the Republican Party who were trying to find things

---

*Even if Kennedy had lost Illinois, however, he still would have won the election.

out about the Kennedys. It was a political bugging to try to develop a derogatory profile on the Kennedys. Not regarding women, that came later. Just some inside information about what they were doing generally, their strategy for the 1960 campaign, that sort of thing."

IT WAS SOMEHOW fitting that one of the first controversies surrounding John F. Kennedy as he prepared to take office swirled around Frank Sinatra and Peter Lawford. The imbroglio, a tempest in a teapot if ever there was one, erupted when the two men arrived in a cold, blustery Washington the second week of January 1961 to begin preparations for a fundraising gala to be held the night before Kennedy's inauguration. They had flown in from Los Angeles on the President-elect's private plane, *Caroline,* and as they stepped off the aircraft along with a dog wearing a black sweater, they were met by a uniformed airman and whisked off in a maroon limousine to the National Guard armory.

This riled Iowa Republican congressman H. R. Gross, who lambasted the Pentagon for providing "taxi drivers and handmaidens" for Sinatra and Lawford. "If there is nothing more important for some of our military than to serve as lackeys and wet nurses," Gross huffed, "we had better give immediate attention in Congress to a reduction of personnel in the military establishments."

A Defense Department spokesman assured Gross that it wouldn't happen again. Sinatra and Peter, after muttering a few choice words about the congressman, set about planning a star-studded event that would, in Peter's words, bring in "the biggest take in show business history for a one-nighter."

The chief purpose of the gala was to raise two million dollars to erase the Democrats' campaign debt, and there was little doubt that it would succeed. By December 7, all seventy-two available boxes had been sold—at ten thousand dollars apiece; one of them was bought by Joe Kennedy. And the fourteen thousand additional armory seats were going fast at a hundred dollars each. "We will net more than 1.9 million," Peter said. "It will be the first time in history a man has gone into the White House out of debt after a campaign. Adlai Stevenson still is five hundred thousand dollars in debt from his last campaign. He's been trying to pay it back with speaking engagements. The show we're putting on may also pay up Adlai's expenses."

The revue, Peter said, would comprise "songs, dances, sketches, and comedy. Almost everything will be new material." Set to appear were Sinatra, Sammy Davis, Jr., Dean Martin, Tony Curtis, Janet Leigh, Shirley MacLaine, Harry Belafonte, Milton Berle, Nat King Cole, Red Skelton, Bill Dana, Alan King, Mahalia Jackson, Bette Davis, Ella Fitzgerald, Gene Kelly, Juliet Prowse, Louis Prima and Keely Smith, and Nelson Riddle's Orchestra. Joey Bishop would serve as master of ceremonies.

From the outset, there were nothing but problems. Dean Martin couldn't wriggle out of a movie commitment and had to leave the show. Shortly after the election, Sammy Davis had wed the blond Swedish actress Mai Britt, and he was afraid the interracial marriage would cause a repeat of the humiliation he had suffered at the convention. He declined to appear.

Eager to have as many star names as possible at the gala, Peter prevailed on the Broadway producer Leland Hayward to close *Gypsy* for one night, on January 19, and release Ethel Merman so that she could appear in the show. He did the same with *Becket* to free up Sir Laurence Olivier and Anthony Quinn. Peter told a reporter that he was "overwhelmed" by the willingness of stars to appear at the gala. "We just call them and they say, 'What time do you want me?' Sometimes, when some of us get together, we say it's going to be kind of hard to concentrate full time on our jobs again."

The logistics of it all were extraordinary. Peter reserved the entire tenth floor of the Statler Hilton Hotel for the gala's personnel and their spouses; security guards were posted at the elevator so that no one without a pass could get off at that floor. "Only Jack himself could walk down that corridor uninvited," said one burly guard.

Reservations had to be made for hotel rooms and transportation; everything had to be synchronized to maximize rehearsal time, and Sinatra and Peter did it all. Bill Asher, who directed the taping of the show, said, "Frank was brilliant, really wonderful. He *was* the producer—it wasn't just honorary. And Peter was brilliant, too, very helpful in the structuring of the show, in the preparation of the written material people were doing. He made a big creative contribution. His only contribution to the show itself was to introduce Frank. It was a hectic time. The enormity of it kind of blows everything away, because you're so insignificant—even though you're important as the director of the gala. But what was going on in the country, the emergence of this man Jack Kennedy—that was awesome."

AROUND NOON the day of the gala, it began to snow. By nine P.M., the show's scheduled starting time, the National Guard was plowing the streets, which were covered by six inches of snow and waist-high drifts. The storm caused chaos. Most of the performers were late, and many of them were forced to appear in their rehearsal clothes because there was no way for them to get back to their hotel rooms and change. By ten-thirty all the performers were present, but the President-elect still wasn't, and neither was half the audience.

The tension got to Sinatra. He drank heavily and threw temper tantrums throughout the evening, usually raging against Peter. "I don't remember what it was about—something to do with nothing," Bill Asher recalled. "But Frank was really into the juice that night, and he got mad at Peter. We had a lineup of people in the show on a big bulletin board, and Frank kept coming into the room screaming, 'Fuck Lawford! I'm not gonna do this show. I'm out!' and then he'd pull his name down off the board. Every time he did it I'd stand behind him and put his name right back up."

Finally, at ten-forty-five, with the armory still only half full, Jack and Jackie arrived. After they were escorted to their seats, they stood and acknowledged the cheers of thousands in the enormous building. Bob Neal remembers the moment well. "Jack was up on the second floor, on a kind of balcony. I was standing below with my date, Tippi Hedren, who was the gorgeous blonde from *The Birds,* and my sister Puddin', who wasn't bad at the time either. By God, Jack's looking directly at *us* and waving! There were four million people in the place and he's waving at us. I'm sure he was just trying to figure out who I was with. He had an eye for the girls, I'll tell you!"

The show, for all its potential for disaster, went off

without a hitch. Joey Bishop opened the proceedings with
a question for Jack: "Now that you've been elected, Mr.
President, how do I get that bumper sticker off my car?"
Ethel Merman sang in her street clothes; Juliet Prowse, all
legs, wowed the audience with a stunning dance routine.
Fredric March gave a dramatic reading of Lincoln's farewell
address, and Laurence Olivier stirringly read an original
piece he had written about what John F. Kennedy meant to
the United States. While Frank sang the moving ballad "The
House I Live In," Jackie Kennedy bit her lip to keep from
crying, and when he finished she dabbed at her eyes with a
handkerchief.

The three-hour show was a rousing success, and when
it was over Jack addressed the audience from the stage. "I
know we're all indebted to a great friend—Frank Sinatra.
Long before he could sing, he used to poll a Democratic
precinct back in New Jersey. That precinct has grown to
cover a country. . . . You cannot imagine the work he has
done to make this show a success.

"A great deal of our praise and applause," the President-elect went on, "should also go to the coproducer, my
brother-in-law Peter Lawford. He has been a citizen of this
country less than a year, but already he has learned a citizen's delight in paying off a political debt. . . . I want Frank
and Peter to know that we're all indebted to them, and
we're proud to have them with us."

The next day, when John F. Kennedy and Lyndon B.
Johnson were sworn in as President and Vice-President,
Peter wasn't among the family and dignitaries seated behind
them on the dais. Throughout the inaugural week, Peter and
Pat had been estranged; she did not stay with him in his
hotel suite at the Statler Hilton, as every other spouse had
done. Leonard Gershe, who had written special material for
the gala, recalled watching the swearing-in with Frank in his
suite. "Peter came in, still in his bathrobe. I thought that
was strange. Frank didn't want to go—it was something like
twelve degrees below zero, and he could just as well watch
it on TV. But Peter was JFK's brother-in-law. He should
have been there. But something had happened and he stayed
away."

Peter did attend a "Reception for President and Mrs.
Kennedy's Families" immediately after the inaugural parade,

the first held by the new President in the White House.
Over 150 Kennedys and Fitzgeralds and Bouviers and Lees
and Auchinclosses (Jackie's stepfather's family) milled about
the enormous state dining room. "Jesus Christ," Joe Kennedy muttered, "I didn't know Jackie had so many goddamn
relatives." Pat and the President's other sisters scurried to
explore the White House's myriad rooms, running up and
down the stairs like children.

Jackie's cousin John H. Davis watched the proceedings
with a keen eye. "Peter Lawford," he later wrote, "was
going around shaking hands with everybody as if *he* had
just been elected President."

IN BETWEEN the numerous inaugural parties held
throughout the day and night of January 20, Frank Sinatra
sent his valet, Tony Consiglio, to fetch Milt Ebbins and
bring him to his suite. Ebbins walked into Sinatra's bedroom
and saw Juliet Prowse, who would be briefly engaged to the
singer the following year, sitting on the bed. "What does he
want?" Ebbins asked. Prowse shrugged and gestured toward
the bathroom, where Sinatra was shaving. Ebbins walked
over to the doorway. "Yes, Frank, what is it?"

Sinatra put down his razor and turned to Ebbins.
"You'd better talk to that friend of yours."

"What do you mean?"

"If Peter doesn't watch his ass, he's gonna lose his
old lady. You'd better tell him to wise up and get his act
together."

"Frank, can't you help?"

Sinatra leaned closer to the mirror and pulled the razor
up along his jawline. "Shit, I'm not his keeper. You just tell
him to watch himself or he's going to lose everything."

PART FOUR

HOLLYWOOD/
WASHINGTON
BABYLON

"Can't you just see
me as First Lady?"

—Marilyn Monroe
to Jeanne Carmen

TWENTY-THREE

NOT LONG after his brother-in-law was inaugurated as president, Peter Lawford was sitting in the Beverly Hills office of the production company he had recently formed. He and several high-level Hollywood moguls were discussing a film deal, and Peter was arguing for the salary and the billing he wanted.

Peter's secretary buzzed the telephone line on the conference table. He frowned and pressed the intercom button. "I told you to hold all calls."

"It's President Kennedy, sir."

Peter glanced across the table as the executives sat up, impressed. "Tell him I'll call him back," he said, and released the button.

Jack Kennedy's ascension to the highest office in America elevated Peter Lawford's stature as no achievement of his own had ever done. Virtually overnight, he gained an aura of importance that few Hollywood performers had ever equaled. As never before, he was in demand for interviews, television guest stints, and film roles. Major magazines and newspapers featured stories on the Lawfords, calling them "the Hollywood branch of the Kennedy family." *McCall's* magazine interviewed Peter in depth about his relationship with the President, and *Cosmopolitan* featured him and Pat on its cover—the first time Peter had appeared on the cover of a general-interest national magazine.

The *Cosmopolitan* article, written by Stephen Birmingham, deftly summed up the perceptions most people held of Peter Lawford at this time. It detailed a whirlwind week during which he and Pat "whoop[ed] it up at a Hollywood party with a group of the town's most notable, and noisiest, luminaries"; were "demure and decorous" at a high-society dinner party in New York; and relaxed "over an informal supper at the White House with the President of the United States and his wife."

"To the average man or woman," Birmingham noted, "an evening in any one of these three worlds, once in a lifetime, might seem so tantalizingly remote as not to be worth wishing for. To Peter and Patricia Lawford, this is their life."

Journalists recorded dutifully that Peter usually wore velvet slippers with gold foxheads sewn across the vamp, and liked to play golf in his bare feet—even when he played with the President—until the club passed a resolution forbidding it. "Peter," said a friend, "is a very loungey kind of guy."

Like many reporters before him, Birmingham had no doubts that the Lawfords were as carefree as any couple could get. "Everything they do seems almost irritatingly *easy* for the Lawfords," he commented. "They seem to have reached top positions in all sorts of heady areas with no more effort than the sun expends when it rises in the morning. . . . When a friend remarked that leading any of [Peter's] three lives might seem enviable and out of reach for most Americans, he shrugged—'Just an accident.'"

Peter maintained that nonchalance whenever he was asked his feelings about being the President's brother-in-law. Even before the inauguration, columnists wondered about Peter's potential role in the Kennedy administration. Some of the speculation was silly, like the suggestion that he be named ambassador to Great Britain. Others were more plausible. President Eisenhower had appointed the actor Robert Montgomery as his "presidential television adviser," and rumors were rife that John Kennedy would do the same with Peter. Peter scoffed at all the talk. When Earl Wilson, the columnist, asked him if he planned to move into the White House, he replied, "And do what? Be court jester?"

Still, Peter took full advantage of the extraordinary perquisites that came with being the President's brother-in-law.

As he had at the inauguration, he sometimes acted as though he were president. He commuted on *Air Force One* and hopped into helicopters to make the few-mile trip from Santa Monica to Hollywood. He turned the presence of Secret Service men, there to guard the President's life, to his own benefit; they complained that he was always telling them, "Boy, bring my bags" and "Fetch me a drink." One agent testily told a reporter, "We don't mind wet-nursing [the President's daughter] Caroline, but we have to wet-nurse Lawford, too."

Peter didn't always use his influence with the White House just for his own benefit; sometimes he made generous gestures for his friends. When Gary Cooper lay dying in 1961, he was pleasantly surprised by a call from President Kennedy to wish him well. "I'm sure," Rocky Cooper recalled, "that Peter's fine English hand was behind that one."

In a lengthy interview with reporter Vernon Scott published in *McCall's* magazine, Peter described a typical visit of his to the White House. "Even upstairs, in the President's private quarters, an overwhelming aura of history overcomes you. As overnight guests, we are assigned to the Queen's Room, a simple chamber with a four-poster bed so huge I have trouble climbing into it. The furniture in the family rooms I like to refer to as Early Comfortable—modern and traditional pleasantly in accord, lots of chintz, and, of course, brilliant paintings everywhere. Most of the taste is Jacqueline Kennedy's, and it's impeccable."

Rather than use the gold service reserved for state affairs at their private dinners, Peter said, the Kennedys dined on china emblazoned with the Great Seal of the United States. "Each piece of silver is simply engraved 'The President's House.' And I haven't pocketed a single fork or spoon as a memento yet, although I won't say I haven't been sorely tempted!"

His most memorable visits to the White House, Peter averred, were those at which he and Pat were the First Couple's only dinner guests. "I recall one such evening," he said, "a warm night. JFK returned from his dip wearing slacks, an open sports shirt, and a jacket. Jacqueline and Pat were in blouses and Capri pants. . . . The President kissed his wife, asked about the children, and wanted to know how Jacqueline had occupied her day. He noticed, and complimented, her hairdo and Pat's new pants. This led to a discussion of fashions, and JFK seemed completely informed on the subject.

"The hi-fi softly played classical music as we sat down. Jacqueline, who is somewhat reserved even in small groups, is a fascinating conversationalist when drawn out, and her husband knows how to do this. The President, grinning mischievously, switched the conversation to [me]. He loves to kid me, and I enjoy it as much as he does. I got a good going-over, with Jacqueline and Pat joining the fun."

Jack *did* enjoy ribbing Peter, and he did it as often as possible. On a visit to the Santa Monica house, the President noticed a photograph on a wall of himself with Peter aboard the Kennedy yacht. Peter was in the bathroom, but when Jack yelled, "Peter, come here immediately!" he was next to him in a flash. "When he wanted to make his voice sound authoritative, it did," Peter said.

"Peter," Kennedy said, pointing to the framed eight-by-ten of the two of them immersed in conversation, "there's something wrong with this picture." Puzzled, Peter looked closely at the image and said it seemed perfectly fine to him.

"Nobody's going to believe that picture," Jack finally said, savoring his punchline, "because it looks like I'm listening to your advice."

Peter enjoyed stringing Milt Ebbins along in much the same way. On a flight to Washington aboard *Air Force One*, a Secret Service man asked Ebbins for his business card. When he took out his card case, Milt realized there was a stick of marijuana in it. A few months earlier, he and Peter had been in Birdland in New York to hear Count Basie. "Some guy came up to Peter and said, 'Man, I love you, you're great,' and slapped something into his hand," Ebbins recalled. "Peter held on to it and came back to the table and said, 'Jesus, that guy just gave me a stick of shit.'"

Penalties for possession of marijuana were harsh in 1961, and Ebbins said to Peter, "Jesus Christ, give that to me." He slipped the joint into his card case, planning to drop it into the toilet. "I didn't want anybody arrested for marijuana possession," Ebbins recalled. "There were undercover cops everywhere." But he never got the chance that evening to dispose of the cigarette, and because he wasn't a pot smoker he forgot he had it until that moment aboard

Air Force One. After he handed his card to the Secret Service man, he whispered to Peter, "Jesus, I've got marijuana in here. If they find me on *Air Force One* with a stick of shit there's gonna be hell to pay!"

Peter knew that there was probably no safer spot on earth at that moment, but he fed his manager's fears. "You're right, Milt," he said. "You'd better get rid of it quick! Jesus, that's all we'd need."

Ebbins was frantic. "I know, I'll throw it in the can!"

"Don't do that!" Peter exclaimed in mock alarm. "They examine *everything* on this plane when it lands. They'll find it!"

Realizing at this point that Peter was putting him on, Ebbins threw the stick of marijuana into the toilet. When he returned to his seat, Peter said, "If they find it, they damn well better not blame me, that's all I can say."

Jack Kennedy's joshings of Peter, like Peter's of Ebbins, were rooted in deep affection, even regard. The historian Arthur Schlesinger, Jr., one of the President's most trusted aides and speech writers, came to him one day and asked for Kennedy's permission to write film criticism for the publication *Show*. Kennedy said it was okay with him, "as long as you treat Peter Lawford with respect."

Jack Kennedy liked Milt Ebbins for precisely that reason: he treated Peter Lawford with respect. The Kennedys had come to expect Ebbins to be with Peter most of the time; they laughingly referred to the two of them as Tweedledee and Tweedledum. Most of them liked Milt and appreciated his gentlemanly, caring manner and his wonderful way with a story.

ONE OF Jack Kennedy's great talents was his ability to draw on the talents and expertise of others. He surrounded himself with "the best and the brightest," intellectuals like Schlesinger and Theodore Sorensen who complemented his own mental acuity and made his administration one of the brainiest in history.

In that company, of course, Peter Lawford was outclassed. But the President knew that there were things he could learn from Peter that no one else in his inner circle could teach him. He'd sought his help with the televised debates with Nixon, and his concern for how he looked on television continued after his election. But there were other things he admired Peter for as well: his sophistication, his savoir faire, his sartorial flair. Kennedy appreciated Peter's sense of style—and he wanted to learn from it.

Milt Ebbins recalled the President, in the White House, emerging from his bedroom dressed for a reception for West German chancellor Konrad Adenauer. He asked Peter if he looked okay; when Peter replied that a different tie would go better with his suit, Jack went back to his closet and chose another one more to Peter's liking. On another occasion Jack took Peter's suggestion for a hairstylist, a young man just out of beauty school named Mickey Song, who had worked for Eva Gabor and Merv Griffin. As Song remembered it, "Merv liked what I did, and he really built me up to Peter."

Song's first encounter with Peter Lawford was memorable. "I came into the house and Peter called out that he'd only be a minute. When he came out, he was stark naked. I had the feeling he was testing me, you know, because I was a hairdresser. I guess he wanted to make sure I wasn't going to come on to him or something. I just turned away and started going through my stuff."

Later, as he was cutting Peter's hair, Song sensed that he was being tested again. "Peter kept asking me all these questions about the other celebrities I had worked on. He was really eager for gossip. But my intuition told me that he was trying to see whether I'd talk about *him* to my next client. So I kept saying that I really didn't know anything about anybody."

Peter was pleased with his haircut, and Song apparently passed the test, because Peter suggested to both Jack and Bobby Kennedy that they use him. "The President had very thick, heavy hair," Song recalls, "and on television it photographed like a toupee. They needed somebody to cut his hair differently, but they didn't want to use anybody famous, because they were afraid he'd exploit the association for publicity. Plus they had been having trouble with people who worked for them doing tell-all articles."

The next time Song came to the Santa Monica house to cut Peter's hair, Peter told him, "There's someone upstairs whose hair I want you to cut next." Song went upstairs and met Bobby, and he was amazed when the attorney gen-

eral did exactly the same thing Peter had done: he appeared
before him naked at first and then tried to get him to gossip
about others.

"Once again I didn't react, and I told Bobby that I
never speak about any of my clients to anyone. That pleased
him, and finally I found myself cutting the President's hair."
On that occasion, Jack Kennedy greeted him with a towel
around his waist and allowed Song to see him naked before
putting on a robe. During the haircut, the President tried
to pry gossip out of Song. "It astonished me that all three
of them did the same thing," Song recalled, "but later when
I thought about it I realized that Bobby and Peter were just
emulating Jack. And I also realized that with the President,
it wasn't calculated. He was just real nonchalant about
things, and he loved to hear show business gossip."

The President continually sought Peter's advice about
his appearance. When Jack made his first major televised
address to the nation as President in 1961, Peter was in Las
Vegas, appearing with Jimmy Durante in a two-man show at
the Desert Inn. During the engagement, Peter was officially
registered in a spacious penthouse suite that was essentially
his Vegas headquarters and was usually overrun with hangers-on.

To gain some privacy, Peter had booked another room,
across the hall from the suite, to which no one had the
phone number. There, he could take a nap or watch television and be left undisturbed. Bob Neal, who was staying in
the suite, recalled one evening when he joined Lawford in
this "getaway room." Peter was lying in his bed, nodding
off as he watched television. Neal began dial flipping. He
decided to bypass a Frank Sinatra movie and then saw that
President Kennedy was addressing the nation. "I started
watching Jack's speech, and got absorbed in it. After a few
minutes, I looked over, and Peter had fallen sound asleep."

A few minutes after the President's talk was over, the
phone in Peter's room rang. Peter awoke with a start, stared
at the phone, and then looked at Bob Neal. According to
Neal, "That phone *never* rang! I said, 'It must be a wrong
number.' So we let it ring. But it was persistent. Finally
Peter said, 'Well, you answer it, Bob. They don't know your
voice.' "

Neal picked up the phone, and heard the unmistakable

accent: "I want to speak to Peter Lawford right now." Neal replied, "Just a minute, sir," and handed the receiver to Peter. "When I said that," Neal recalled, "Peter knew exactly who it was. Jack Kennedy was probably the only person in the world who could have gotten through on that line.

"Peter sat straight up in bed and grabbed the phone. He kept saying, 'Yes, sir. Yes, sir. Yes, sir.'"

As he listened, Peter covered the mouthpiece with his hand and whispered frantically to Neal, "What did he talk about? How did he look?" With Neal's sotto voce coaching, Peter responded to Jack's questions. "Yes, sir, it went just fine. Your makeup looked good. Your delivery was strong. No, sir, the speech wasn't too long."

"Peter managed to stumble through the call," Neal recalled. "And afterward he was just drained. It really hit him hard. He didn't want the President to know he hadn't watched him. He was fast on his feet, though—he managed to improvise his way through it. After that, he paid more attention whenever Jack was on television."

As perceptive as Jack Kennedy was, he surely sensed that Peter had not paid close attention to his address, and he soon came to realize that very little of the Kennedy family's political intensity was ever likely to rub off on his brother-in-law. Peter was uninterested in world affairs and had a lazy streak. If Jack Kennedy had thought he could change that, he learned otherwise.

When Warner Brothers set out to make a movie version of Robert J. Donovan's book *PT 109,* recounting Jack Kennedy's World War II heroics when he rescued his men after a Japanese destroyer cut their PT boat in half, Kennedy quite naturally turned to Peter for advice. Visiting the President at a retreat he occupied for a time in Virginia, Peter found the script of *PT 109* on his bed with a note from Jack: "Please read and be prepared to discuss at eight-thirty A.M."

Peter had had too much to drink that evening, and although he started the script he couldn't keep his eyes open and fell asleep about a third of the way through it. The next morning, as the President prepared to be whisked back by helicopter to the White House, he asked Peter for his reaction to the script. When Peter explained what happened and said he had liked as much as he had read, Jack just smiled and left. He never asked Peter for any further input on the production of *PT 109*.

IF PETER wasn't much help to President Kennedy on some fronts, he was *very* helpful in another respect. Bill Asher recalled Jack, just after his election, checking out some girls in bikinis on the beach in front of Peter's house. "I'm gonna have to give all that up when I become President," he said ruefully. "I hope it's worth it."

Thanks in large measure to Peter Lawford, Jack didn't have to "give all that up." He could always count on Peter to have a beautiful girl in tow whenever he visited the White House without Pat (which he often did). Kennedy had always had ample opportunity for sexual escapades while traveling, of course, but what surprised and delighted him was how easy it was to frolic within the White House itself.

He carried on concurrent dalliances with two of his secretaries, who came to be known to the Secret Service as Fiddle and Faddle. Milt Ebbins recalled sitting in the Oval Office with the President and Peter and expressing amazement that Jack was so nonchalant about having sexual liaisons in the White House. "Aren't you afraid that Jackie will come back earlier than you expect and catch you with these broads?" Milt asked him. Jack smiled. "Jackie can't get within two hundred yards of this place without my knowing about it," he replied.

Jack and Jackie spent a good deal of time apart, which allowed the President breathing room when it came to chasing after what he called "poon," a crude term popular among Navy men to describe a woman's sexual anatomy. But Jackie, like Pat, rarely missed much when it came to her husband's philandering. "Jackie knew the score," her friend Truman Capote said. But, again like Pat, she closed her eyes to much of it and gave her husband tremendous leeway. As Jackie confided to a friend, "I don't think that there are any men who are faithful to their wives."

Jackie's father, John "Black Jack" Bouvier, hadn't been—nor, certainly, had Joe Kennedy. Both Jackie and Pat had been taught, by example, to accept a husband's extramarital activities if the marriage—and appearances—were to be preserved. Thus both Jack and Peter were given wide latitude by their wives when it came to "getting tail," as Jack also liked to put it, and their pleasure in the chase was what they most strongly had in common. Whenever he was in Washington, Peter would keep an eye out for pretty young women to bring to the White House. One of these was Susan Perry, a "stunning blond" twenty-one-year-old receptionist in the office of Senator Jacob K. Javits, a New York Republican. She caught Peter's eye early in October 1961, and he, seeking to impress her, invited her to dine with him and the President. Expecting a large gathering, Perry accepted.

When she arrived with Peter at the White House family quarters, she was puzzled to find only the President, one of his longtime aides, and another attractive woman who was introduced as a Soviet translator. As the evening progressed, Susan mentioned to the woman that her dress had ridden suggestively up her thigh. "So what?" she replied. After dinner, Peter left with Susan and the aide, leaving the beautiful Russian with the President.

The next day, worried, Peter telephoned Senator Javits's office and pleaded with Richard Aurelio, Javits's press secretary, not to alert the press to the intimate evening their receptionist had witnessed at the White House. Aurelio assured Peter that he had no such intention.

The story began to circulate around Washington nonetheless, and a few weeks later, *The New York Times* carried an account of the evening, complete with Peter's photograph. No mention was made of the Russian translator or of the fact that no wives were present, and the gist of the article was Susan Perry's "Cinderella story" of dining with the President "at the invitation of a handsome movie star."

It was easy to read between the lines of the *Times* article; Miss Perry was a "pretty young receptionist" who had "attracted the attention" of Peter Lawford; she had "blushingly accepted" his invitation to the White House. When Jack Kennedy saw the *Times* that morning, he got on the phone to Peter in a flash. "Damn it, Peter, how did that happen? Is that girl crazy?"

Peter attempted to stammer an explanation, but Kennedy cut him off. "Look, Peter, the word is out in this town that I'm doing it to every girl who walks. I'm going to get blamed again—and you're the one who was with her. What

THE DARK SIDE OF GENTILITY

May Lawford with two-month-old Peter in Beaulieu, France, November 1923. May later said, "I hate babies. . . . Peter was an awful accident." (COURTESY MILTON EBBINS)

The Lawford ancestral home, in Toddington. While in England, Peter and his parents divided their time between this house and a flat in London.
(COURTESY WILLIAM NOAD)

(*Below*) Lieutenant Sydney Lawford (*seated, center*) of the Royal Fusiliers regiment, circa 1900. Lawford's heroism in World War I led King George V to knight him.
(COURTESY W. NOAD)

Four-year-old Peter at play in Hove, England, in 1927. By this age he had decided he wanted to be an actor, not a soldier. His father wasn't pleased. (COURTESY M. EBBINS)

On the beach at Deauville with his parents in 1928. The Lawfords had fled to this French watering spot in 1924 when the scandal of their divorces erupted in London. (COURTESY M. EBBINS)

May and Sir Sydney attend a polo match at Le Touquet in 1929. He was sixty-four; she, forty-six. Peter later said of his parents, "I adored him and loathed her, from a very early age."
(COURTESY M. EBBINS)

Peter at Vichy in 1928. His first language was French, and his mother called him "Pierrot." Privately, she dressed him as a girl until he was eleven.
(COURTESY M. EBBINS)

Peter makes his film debut at seven with Leslie Fuller in *Poor Old Bill,* 1931. His acting career was derailed when his relatives threatened to disinherit him. (COURTESY ACADEMY OF MOTION PICTURE ARTS AND SCIENCES)

The Lawfords traveled around the world several times before Peter was fourteen. Here *(left)*, he and Sir Sydney wear identical bathing suits in Ceylon, circa 1932. (COURTESY M. EBBINS)

Peter and his father prepare to ride an elephant in India, circa 1933. Because May Lawford's father and grandfather spent a combined eighty years in India, her in-laws suspected she had some Indian blood. (COURTESY M. EBBINS)

In Tahiti in 1933, Peter tried his hand at canoeing. He loved the months he spent there: "It was a boy's paradise."
(COURTESY M. EBBINS)

(Below) At the Royal Hawaiian Hotel, November 1934, the Lawfords pose in their tropical whites during a nine-month stay in Honolulu. The islands remained a favorite vacation spot for Peter all his life.
(UPI/BETTMANN)

During the family's long sea voyages, Peter would appear in shows and skits. Once, he disguised himself as a girl and won a mother-daughter talent show with May. (COURTESY M. EBBINS)

By nine, Peter had developed into a beautiful boy, and around this age he had the first of a series of sexual encounters with adults—both male and female. (COURTESY M. EBBINS)

THE MGM YEARS

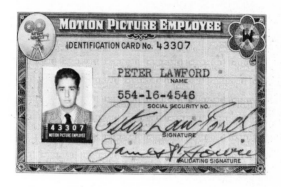

Peter's studio ID card, issued in 1942 when he was eighteen. (WARDER HARRISON COLLECTION)

MGM experimented with "looks" for Peter at the start of his career. An attempt at slicked-back ultrasophistication in 1942 *(left)* quickly made way for the more natural boy-next-door look of 1943. (MGM)

On the set of *A Yank at Eton* (1942) Peter pals around with Freddie Bartholomew *(left)* and Mickey Rooney. Peter knew nothing about an indiscreet Bartholomew remark to the British press about Peter's parentage that had kept the Lawfords from returning to England in 1938. (MGM)

Peter's portrayal of Irene Dunne's dying son in *The White Cliffs of Dover* in 1944 won him critical praise. (MGM)

An eight-month affair with Lana Turner in 1944 left Peter hopelessly in love—and heartbroken when she suddenly broke it off. (PICTORIAL PARADE)

There was no love lost between Peter and his *Son of Lassie* costar. "Lassie was a vicious bastard!" he said. (MGM)

(Left) Peter was one of the most sought-after escorts in Hollywood in the 1940s. Here, he and Lucille Ball make the scene at the Clover Club, November 1944.
(AP/WIDE WORLD)

(Left) Peter seems smitten as he and Anne Baxter look into each other's eyes at the Hollywood Palladium, December 1943.
(UPI/BETTMANN)

A romance with Judy Garland evolved into a volatile, lifelong friendship. Here, they dance at the Mocambo, circa 1948.
(CULVER PICTURES)

(Left) Ava Gardner was one of Peter's brief affairs. Here, the couple attend the opening of Alfred Hitchcock's *The Paradine Case,* January 1948.
(CULVER PICTURES)

When Peter wasn't on a set or in a nightclub, he was at the beach, where he surfed, exercised, and played volleyball.
(UPI/BETTMANN)

The Lawfords at home, 1945. Although this was a posed gag shot, the expression on Peter's face was similar when he learned that May had told Louis B. Mayer she feared Peter was a homosexual. (MGM)

June Allyson kisses Peter in a *Good News* publicity shot, 1947. Peter's feelings toward the actress weren't always so affectionate. (MGM)

Peter gave sixteen-year-old Elizabeth Taylor her first real screen kiss in *Julia Misbehaves,* 1948. She adored him, and her mother wanted them to marry. But Peter was nervous about her age and resisted her charms. (CULVER PICTURES)

Frank Sinatra and Peter became pals in the forties, but in 1953 the singer broke off the friendship when he suspected that Peter had rekindled his affair with Ava Gardner, Frank's estranged wife. (PHOTO BY LEO BORR)

Sporting a mustache he grew for *Kangaroo,* Peter escorts the international socialite Sharman Douglas to a Hollywood party, 1950. He broke off their engagement after only four days.
(MOVIE STARS PARADE)

On the way to film *Kangaroo,* Peter met Jean MacDonald, a society columnist, in Honolulu. They too became engaged, but once again the romance fizzled.
(PHOTOFEST)

Judy Holliday and Peter had an affair during the filming of *It Should Happen to You,* in 1953. He dumped her abruptly— because he had met the woman he wanted to marry.

Peter and Patricia Kennedy celebrated their marriage in New York on April 24, 1954. (UPI/BETTMANN)

The enormous crowd outside St. Thomas More's Church
threatened to turn into an unruly mob as the Lawfords
emerged after the nuptials. (UPI/BETTMANN)

Christopher Lawford, Peter's first child, is christened, 1955.
With Peter and Pat are *(left to right)* Joe Kennedy, Francis
Cardinal McIntyre, Peter Sabiston, and May Lawford. May's
expression sums up her deep disdain for the Kennedy family.
(UPI/BETTMANN)

Peter's two 1950s TV series met with mixed success. *Dear Phoebe,* a sitcom with Marcia Henderson in which he played an advice-to-the-lovelorn columnist, was well reviewed but lasted just one season in 1954. (PICTORIAL PARADE)

In *The Thin Man,* Peter and Phyllis Kirk played Nick and Nora Charles, husband-and-wife detectives seldom without their dog, Asta. The comedy-drama was panned by critics, but found an audience and lasted two seasons between 1957 and 1959.

The "Rat Pack," 1958. As John F. Kennedy's political star ascended, Frank Sinatra *(center)* deigned to allow Peter into his "clan," which also included *(left to right)* Sammy Davis, Jr., Joey Bishop, and Dean Martin. (PHOTO BY DON PACK)

Between the filming of *Ocean's 11* and the sold-out Rat Pack "summit" shows at the Sands Hotel in Vegas, the Clan hung out in the steamroom, where they drank and ribbed each other constantly. (PHOTO © 1960 BOB WILLOUGHBY)

Father's Day, 1959: Peter poses with his children in the playground of their beach house in Santa Monica. *Top to bottom:* Victoria, seven months; Christopher, four; and Sydney, three. (COURTESY W. NOAD)

(*Below*) On November 8, 1960, John F. Kennedy was elected president. The next day, at the Kennedy compound in Hyannis Port, Peter and his sisters-in-law Eunice, Ethel, and Joan (*left to right*) celebrate. (PAUL SCHUTZER/*LIFE* MAGAZINE © TIME WARNER, INC.)

Peter chats with Jacqueline
Kennedy before the
inaugural gala, January 20,
1961. He and Frank Sinatra
coproduced the event, which
was rife with problems.
(PAUL SCHUTZER/*LIFE
MAGAZINE* © TIME WARNER, INC

Peter and the president sailing
off Hyannis Port, 1961.
When Jack Kennedy saw this
photo he kidded Peter that
no one would believe it
because "it looks like I'm
listening to your advice."
(SANDERSON/SHOOTING STAR)

Peter and Pat on the French location of *The Longest Day,* 1961
Peter played the British war hero Lord Lovat, and was hired
for the part mainly because Darryl Zanuck, the producer, knew
he would be able to help get the U.S. Army's permission to
use military personnel and equipment in the film.

The Lawford beach house *(center)* often served as the Western
White House. This photograph was taken August 20, 1962,
during a presidential visit. (UPI/BETTMANN)

On May 19, 1962, Peter introduced "the late Marilyn Monroe" at a birthday party for the president at Madison Square Garden. Marilyn's sexy rendition of "Happy Birthday" left the crowd cheering—and Kennedy grinning. (UPI/BETTMANN)

November 22, 1963: Peter and Milton Ebbins rush from a helicopter to the Lawford house after hearing the news that President Kennedy had been assassinated. (AP/WIDE WORLD)

Peter comforts his seven-year-old daughter Sydney as they join
(*left to right*) Lady Bird Johnson, Robert Kennedy, Jean Smith,
President Johnson, Pat, Caroline Kennedy, and Jacqueline
Kennedy at President Kennedy's funeral on November 25, 1963.
(UPI/BETTMANN)

Peter returned to work immediately after the funeral, rejoining Jimmy Durante on stage in Lake Tahoe, and was criticized. (JOHN LOENGARD/*LIFE* MAGAZINE © TIME WARNER, INC.)

Carroll Baker as Jean Harlow and Peter as Paul Bern in a scene from *Harlow*, 1965. The filming was an emotional strain on him. (PICTORIAL PARADE)

A harrowing moment in *Dead Ringer* (1964) when Peter, playing Bette Davis's conniving lover, is attacked by a vicious dog. (PHOTOFEST)

Peter's joint Hawaiian vacation with Jackie Kennedy in June 1966 sent his ex-wife, Pat, into a fury. With them *(top to bottom)* are John Kennedy, Jr., five; Christopher, eleven; Caroline Kennedy, eight; and Sydney, ten. (SANDERSON/SHOOTING STAR)

Sammy Davis, Jr., was the only Rat Packer who remained close to Peter after his final falling-out with Sinatra in 1962. Here, they do a soft-shoe routine on TV's *The Hollywood Palace,* 1967. (PICTORIAL PARADE)

Peter attempts to escape the clutches of Gina Lollobrigida in their 1968 movie *Buona Sera, Mrs. Campbell*. Off the set, Peter said, the scene was repeated for real in Gina's Rome villa. (PHOTOFEST)

Model Geri Crane accompanies Peter to London for the filming of *Salt and Pepper*, 1967. Their relationship lasted three years. (POPPER PHOTO/PICTORIAL PARADE)

Peter, forty-eight, and Mary Rowan, twenty-one, are married in
Puerto Vallarta, October 30, 1971. Flanking them are best
man Christopher Lawford, sixteen, and bridesmaid Toni Stabile.
Peter's drinking, drug use, and womanizing quickly put the marriage
in trouble, and the couple separated in 1973. (AP/WIDE WORLD)

Peter's flagging career in the mid-1970s left him with little choice
but to do silly TV shows such as this one with Dick Clark,
Las Vegas Celebrity Secrets, in September 1974.
(PICTORIAL PARADE)

June 26, 1976: Stoned on vodka and Quaaludes, Peter, fifty-two, takes his third wife, Deborah Gould, twenty-five, in Virginia. The next day, he couldn't remember getting married, and within a few months Deborah had gone home to Miami. (UPI/BETTMANN)

Christopher Lawford, twenty-eight, was graduated from Boston College Law School in 1983. Flanking him *(left to right)* are Sydney, twenty-seven; Pat; Victoria, twenty-five; and Robin, twenty-two. (PHOTO BY BRIAN QUIGLEY)

Later in 1983, Peter gave Sydney away in marriage to Peter McKelvy. He hadn't wanted to attend the wedding, and fell down, drunk, during a rehearsal. (PHOTO BY BRIAN QUIGLEY)

Pat Seaton, twenty-five, and Peter, sixty, in April 1984. Companions since Seaton was seventeen, they were wed in July 1984. Peter died five months later, on Christmas Eve. (PHOTO BY GEORGE RICHARDSON/BORSARI)

A debonair portrait of Peter from his last picture, a European TV movie entitled *Where Is Parsifal?* The film was shown after Peter's death.

is Jackie going to say? Tell me that! It was damn bad judgment. We won't let that happen again." He hung up.

Peter did let it happen again. The situation was similar: a pretty young girl, a Lawford invitation, a private dinner *sans* wives. Early in the evening, the President asked the young lady what she did for a living. "I work for Senator Goldwater," she replied ingenuously.

The tone of the evening changed in a snap, and after the woman was sent on her way in a cab, the President dressed Peter down once again. "For God's sake, Peter! She works for *Barry Goldwater*! He's probably gonna be my opponent in 1964! Do you know what he could do with information like that? Don't you find out who people work for before you bring them up here? *Jesus!*"

AS HE COULD in so many other areas, the President was able to steal Peter Lawford's thunder with women as no one else ever had. If Peter's friends had discovered that no girl of theirs was safe around him, Peter quickly learned the same thing about Jack.

Bob Neal, widely renowned as a playboy, was happy to be third Musketeer when he was with Jack and Peter. He recalled a cocktail party at the Manhattan apartment of Earl E. T. Smith, who had been President Eisenhower's ambassador to Cuba.

Peter brought Neal and Milt Ebbins to the party, which included many of the President's closest associates, among them his aide Dave Powers and his brother-in-law Steve Smith. Neal saw the President sitting on a couch flanked by two young women. Peter greeted Jack and shook his hand; Ebbins and Neal followed suit. As he pumped Bob's hand Kennedy said to him, "My God, Bob Neal. That's the man we'd all like to be."

A few minutes later Peter pulled Neal aside and they went out on a balcony overlooking Central Park. "What was he talking about, you're the man everybody wants to be?"

"I don't know," Neal replied. "Why don't you ask him?"

Ebbins overheard the question and answered it for Peter. "Jack's heard about all the great-looking girls Bob's been dating lately."

"Oh," Peter said. "I get it."

A few minutes later, Peter walked up to Neal and whispered, "You see that guy over there? He's with a *beautiful* girl from South America." Neal had indeed seen her.

Peter's voice turned conspiratorial. "He's had about twelve drinks too many. Why don't we separate them?"

"Good idea," Neal replied. "How do we do that?"

"Let's get them into the elevator first, and we'll figure it out once we get down on the ground."

Within minutes, Peter and Bob were in Ambassador Smith's private elevator with the hapless man and the girl from South America. Just as the elevator operator started to close the doors, they heard a commanding voice—"Hold the elevator!"

"The operator stuck his head out of the door and here came the President," Neal recalled. "He strolled into the elevator and looked at Peter, then at me. 'Well now,' he said, 'where do you two fellows think you're going?' Peter looked at me and then said, 'Well, sir, it's past our bedtime and we thought we would go back to our hotel.'

"Jack replied, 'You're exactly correct.' Then he turned to the gorgeous girl and said, 'Young lady, would you join me for a drink at the bar?' She said, 'I'd be delighted to, Mr. President,' and off they went. We two jerks wound up on Fifth Avenue with a guy who couldn't find the floor with his hat. The President knew what we were doing."

And the President always made sure that nothing similar happened to him. During a visit to the Lawfords' in Santa Monica, Kennedy discovered that a certain friend of Peter's was in the house. "Either he goes or I go," he told Peter.

"But Jack," Peter pleaded, "he's one of my best friends! What am I going to say to him?"

"I don't care, just get rid of him." The President started to change out of his bathing suit and back into street clothes, prepared to leave. Peter grabbed Milt Ebbins, who'd been watching all this, and pulled him into an adjoining room. "What am I going to do, Milt?"

"You've got to tell the guy to leave. Make up some excuse. You can't let the President of the United States leave here because you don't want to insult your friend."

Peter made an excuse about security considerations, and his friend left. What had the man done to so offend the leader of the free world? During Kennedy's last visit to California, the hapless fellow had made a pass at one of Jack's girls.

FOR THE FIRST two years of the Kennedy administration, Pat and Peter's beach house was essentially the Western White House. Officially, the President stayed at the Beverly Hilton Hotel, but he spent his days relaxing by his sister and brother-in-law's pool. The presidential flag flew over the property, and Jack's helicopter would land on the sand in front of the house—much to the Lawfords' neighbors' dismay, because their pools filled with blown sand after each landing and takeoff.

A week before one of the chief executive's visits, Secret Service men would invade Peter's garage and turn it into a communications center—a huge bank of dials and knobs and flashing lights that kept Kennedy in contact with the world. His guards shadowed Kennedy wherever he went, and he enjoyed giving them the slip whenever possible. In Palm Beach, he had skulked out the back of a drugstore with the help of a clerk. On one visit to Peter's house, Jack casually asked Milt Ebbins, "Would you go inside and tell one of the guys in the garage that I'm going for a swim?"

Ebbins said yes, and added, "Will you wait until I get back?"

"Sure," Jack replied. "I'll wait."

"I went inside," Ebbins recalled, "and of course Jack went into the water by himself. The guys in the garage were standing there—*real serious*. I said, 'Listen, guys, you'd better get out there—your boss is going in the ocean.'"

The Secret Service men cried, "What!" and jumped up, grabbed their guns, and ran outside. Two of them waded into the water, fully clothed. By now the President was surrounded by people, amazed that it was him. "My God! It's Jack Kennedy!" one woman screamed. The following day, a photograph was wire-serviced around the world showing Jack on the sand in his wet bathing trunks surrounded by dozens of beaming beachgoers.

The next time the President came to Peter's house, Ebbins saw a change: "I drove up to Peter's garage and all the Secret Service guys were there, and two of them were completely dressed in frogmen outfits—goggles, flippers, tanks! It was very funny. But it *was* dangerous what Jack did. How the hell do you know who's looking for him around that house? He wasn't even supposed to swim in the pool without the Secret Service checking it out first—they were afraid someone might wire it up to electrocute him."

Kennedy refused to be intimidated by the dangers of his job. He took risks—recklessly, some say—in order to live as normal a life as possible. When he was at Peter Lawford's house, he was there to relax and have a good time—and Peter saw to it that he did. Whenever Jack visited when Pat was away, Peter could be counted on to throw a party for him that included, in addition to Peter's show business friends, lovely young starlets, models—and hookers. After an evening of partying, Jack would choose one or two of the prettiest and return with them to his hotel suite. Some of the parties at Peter Lawford's house—those peopled by a great many beautiful young women and a great many older married men—became legendary.

A number of Peter's female associates found them offensive. Jeanne Martin, Dean's wife, told Anthony Summers, a biographer of Marilyn Monroe, that "it was a nasty business—they were just too gleeful about it, not discreet at all . . . the things that went on in that beach house were mind-boggling."

To Peter Dye, the Lawfords' next-door neighbor, it was "nothing but *La Dolce Vita* over there. It was like a god-damn whorehouse. And Jack Kennedy hustled my wife. He wanted her to go to Hawaii with him. It was the most disgusting thing I've ever seen."

Bonnie Williams, Peter's secretary, refused to attend these ersatz bachelor parties at the Lawford place. "[The director] Dick Donner was always trying to get me to go with him," she said. "He would tease me about wanting to take me to an orgy. I didn't partake in any of that, but I know I heard of some of them. I've heard some pretty wild stories. Peter told me about one real wild party where somebody was running about in the nude and cavorting around and I don't know what-all they did. I never was much for that kind of thing, and I could see where you could get yourself headed in the wrong direction if you got started with it."

Pat heard about what sometimes went on at her house, but she was more curious than angry. Joe Naar recalled that "Pat would ask me questions like, 'Do orgies happen? Tell me about them.' I hadn't been present at any, so I couldn't tell her. But I knew she was hungry for details."

IN HIS *Cosmopolitan* article, Stephen Birmingham quoted an anonymous friend of the Lawfords' who enumerated the pros and cons of being related to the nation's chief executive. "The fact is that both Peter and Pat are terribly impressed with the President, and with their relationship to him. They're deeply in awe of him—as a president and as a man. [But] they're both realizing more and more that they live in a fishbowl—that everything they say or do will somehow, indirectly, be related to the White House. . . . They see that they can no longer live lives of their own, the way they once did."

It was clear that while his brother-in-law's presidency hoisted Peter's stature, it diminished it at the same time. The light from the brilliant sun that was Jack Kennedy obscured as much as it illuminated. The odd little *pas de trois* that Peter and Jack had danced with the public's perceptions of them over the years had now come full circle. Jack had been pleased after the 1956 convention when he was no longer being called "Peter Lawford's brother-in-law." Now, a few months after Jack's election, Peter ruefully told a reporter, "A strange thing has happened since he became President. I seem to have lost my identity. There was a time when I'd be rushing through an airport and I'd hear someone say, 'There goes Peter Lawford!' Now, for some reason, people have trouble remembering my name, and it's 'There goes . . . you know, what's his name . . . the President's brother-in-law!' "

TWENTY-FOUR

FROM HER well-worn Queen Anne wingback chair, drinking Southern Comfort and stroking her tomcat, Amber, Lady Lawford could look around the living room of her one-bedroom cottage in West Los Angeles in 1961 and see her life pass before her. At seventy-eight, she had little more than her memories, and she surrounded herself with reminders of grander times that lined the walls and covered most available surfaces. There were autographed pictures of the king and queen of Belgium, portraits of the Duke of Windsor, Charles de Gaulle, and Benito Mussolini, glass-negative prints of her parents and grandparents, and movie magazine covers with her son's handsome face smiling out from them.

A glass case lined with blue velvet housed Sir Sydney's medals and commendations, and his rifle and sword hung on the wall. A faded Christmas card from King George and Queen Mary held a place of honor on a side table.

Like a sleeping giant, May had been relatively quiet since Peter's wedding. He had set her up in a small house on Kelton Avenue in West Los Angeles, paid her rent, and given her one hundred fifty dollars a month to supplement the fifty-two-dollar monthly check she received from Sir Sydney's pension. Once again in "reduced circumstances," May lost none of the grandness and hauteur she had honed over the years. She called her tiny, cluttered living room "my drawing room." She served visitors four o'clock tea, with

286

finger sandwiches and scones, on a silver tray that was, she said, a gift from King George. She never abandoned her aristocratic airs and still insisted on being called Lady Lawford. "I used to take her to lunch," Milt Ebbins recalled, "and she was the ultimate lady. Grand manners. She used to eat at Clifton's in Century City all the time. They called her Lady Lawford. In a cafeteria! She *was* a grand lady."

She was also a lonely and frustrated one. She had little to do, her creative talents stifled, her wit with no outlet, her financial situation barely tenable. She was getting drunk now more and more frequently. Peter hated to be around her when she was drinking, reminded as he was of his childhood traumas and the time at the Sunset Boulevard house when he'd awakened in the middle of the night and found his mother lying spread-eagled on the hallway floor, passed out.

May had begun neurotically to fixate on herself, her problems, her physical ailments. She had suffered from arthritis since girlhood, and in the mid-1950s it had taken a severe turn for the worse. Her doctor told her that her repeated attacks were "more in my head than anywhere else" and suggested that May become more active. "Do something you like doing, and maybe it will get better," he said. "You need to do something besides just stay home and stroke the cat."

She also needed extra money; two hundred dollars a month was barely subsistence for her. And so Lady Lawford decided, in her mid-seventies, to make a serious attempt at an acting career. "I will not merely sit and wait for those pearly gates to open," she declared by way of explanation. May had played a few small film roles at MGM during the previous decade, calling herself either Lady May Lawford or Mary Somerville, but she had never thought of acting as a potential career. Now, she professed, she did.

She signed on with the Virginia Doak agency, then prepared a portfolio of photographs of herself in a variety of guises—a stern Mrs. Danvers–like housekeeper, a formidable businesswoman, an elegant dowager, a frightened, sad old woman. Her résumé noted that she could ride Western and English saddles, spoke French, German, and some Hindustani, could drive a team of four horses, and was a crack shot.

When Peter got wind of her plans, he was not happy.

"Peter put both feet down against it," May said. "He's such a damned nuisance. It's really none of his business." She went ahead, and with some success. She was, as one of Peter's friends noted, "right out of Central Casting." She *was* a perfect "type," but she put a few restrictions on the roles she would accept. "I won't play Peter's mother," she said, "and I won't play society matrons. The best thing for me to do is concentrate on a bottle of gin and a red nose— that's the kind of role I prefer." Instead, she got a television role as Roddy McDowall's mother in a *Matinee Theatre* production and a bit part on *Climax!* When the latter, her first assignment, was aired she watched it alone in her living room with her cat. She didn't know, she said, whether her son had tuned in to watch her performance.

One of May's jobs in 1957 was a small part on *The Thin Man,* an assignment Peter did not want her to have. But the show's sponsors convinced him that it would be a strong publicity angle for the show and would soften some of the negative press that May's outspoken comments about his opposition to her acting career had created. Indeed, shortly before May's *Thin Man* episode aired, *TV Guide* ran an article entitled "A New Career at Sixty" (May always lied about her age) in which the author noted Peter's reservations about his mother's career plans and added, "Apparently all now is friendly between the two, inasmuch as Lawford hired her for *The Thin Man.*"

"I don't want to cash in on Peter's name," May told the reporter. "True, here I'm known as Peter Lawford's mother, but in England, Peter is known as Lady Lawford's little boy." She told another journalist that she hoped to continue working steadily. Always one to preserve appearances, however, she added quickly, "I hope I don't take a part away from some actress who needs the money."

May's hopes of a lucrative new career were soon dissipated. There weren't many jobs for a woman her age, and there was fierce competition from far more established actresses for the roles that were available. But May refused to accept that reality. When acting jobs became scarce, she blamed the great bogeyman in her life—the Kennedys. "I used to get one or two small parts in American TV," she told a British reporter, "but since Peter married into 'America's Royal Family' there haven't been any."

May again and again complained that Peter, the Kennedys, and the Rat Pack were actively preventing her from winning roles, that they "fixed it up so that no agent offers me anything." In her autobiography, she tells an elaborate story, undated, of going to a party while Sir Sydney, ill with influenza, stayed home. During the evening she was approached by "some little Jew, an agent," who introduced her to a producer. The man loved May's presence, and her pronunciation of "Worcestershire sauce," and he offered to give her "a test."

The next day, she went to MGM, where the producer "raved over my reading and over my posture and regal carriage." He asked May if she objected to doing television commercials, and when she said she didn't he offered her a contract at one hundred dollars a week for an "indefinite" period.

"Well," May said, "that will buy the cats some liver. Where do I sign?"

No sooner had she said this, May claimed, than the studio door opened and Pat Lawford entered. She was "a bit aghast" when she recognized May, and a few minutes later she and the producer went into another room. When they emerged, the man told May he was sorry that things couldn't be arranged after all: "The studio limousine will await you out front to drive you home."

There are a number of problems with this story. Sir Sydney died in February 1953, and Peter did not marry Pat Kennedy until April 1954. (He didn't even begin to court her until November 1953.) That Pat Kennedy would walk into an MGM audition before she married Peter (or at any time for that matter) is highly unlikely. And the question must be asked—why would Pat object to Lady Lawford making some extra money doing commercials? She saw no shame in product endorsement—she, Peter, five-year-old Christopher, and four-year-old Sydney would soon appear in a print ad for Kodak cameras.

What really happened—or whether anything happened at all—is difficult to tell. In her later years, May began to fabricate stories that justified her growing hatred of the Kennedy family; she blamed them for everything wrong with her life. She harangued anyone who would listen on the subject of the Kennedys' heritage, their breeding, and their manners. Most of all, she complained bitterly about their treatment of her. She ranted that she had discovered a silver tray "handed down in my family from Queen Anne" that she had given Peter and Pat as a wedding present "leaning against the wall on the dirty floor of Peter's garage."

She never got to see her grandchildren, she claimed; she wasn't invited to christenings, and as the children grew older they were never brought to visit her. "Pat says it's too far for them to come—even though they're always going off to the East Coast and overseas. Pat rings me up occasionally and asks me over to see the children, but when I get there she runs away to telephone or write letters. My grandchildren don't know me very well. When I told Sydney that I was her grandmother, she replied, 'Oh, no, you're not. My real grandmother is in Boston.' "

May's antipathy toward the Kennedys reached a crescendo during the 1960 presidential campaign. Because of her acid tongue and ill-disguised disdain for them, the family wasn't about to allow her access to any forums in which to spout off and hurt Jack's chances of winning. When May asked her daughter-in-law to get her a ticket to one of Jack's fund-raisers, Pat allegedly replied, "If I can find someone to let you sit at their table."

"I didn't think it would be much fun sitting alone," May later said, "so I didn't go. I should have though, it would have forestalled endless calls asking why I wasn't there." A reporter from the *Times* of London asked her why she never appeared at Kennedy functions. She replied that she didn't know, except that the Kennedy family "is not too hot on etiquette or protocol." An hour later, the reporter called May back and apologized: he had checked with the Kennedys and was told that she had been "bedridden for years."

May didn't cause any trouble during the election. Privately she stewed, she seethed, she threatened to rent an elephant and ride it down Wilshire Boulevard with a banner across its hide reading "Vote for Nixon."* Publicly, how-

---

*Of course, she never did so, but this is one of those stories that both she and Peter exaggerated over the years until, in the retelling, her threat had turned into an action.

ever, May remained silent—until December 12, 1960. On that day, she took a job at the Tibor Designers jewelry shop in Beverly Hills, and someone alerted the press to the news. The next day, headlines around the country read, "Lawford's Mother Has $50-a-Week Job."

"I find it very difficult to live on what I have," May told the wire service reporters, finally honest about her personal situation. "Now that I'm an old lady I've accepted an offer to work for Mr. Tibor's jewelry establishment. Unfortunately, Mr. Tibor has no first name. But he's Hungarian. He sells bracelets and things for as much as four thousand dollars. And I get five percent of all my sales."

She intimated that her son and in-laws had neglected to care for her properly, and she complained anew that she had lost acting roles because of them. "The Kennedy people and I do not see eye-to-eye about anything. They're Irish—and ever since we English sent the Black and Tans over and beat the bejabbers out of them, the Irish have despised us." Then she delivered the coup de grace: "If I had been an American citizen during the election I would have voted for Richard Nixon."

One week after she took the job at Mr. Tibor's, May was once again unemployed—and once again spoke out, hinting darkly to reporters that sinister forces were at work. "There is something behind all this," she told the writer Pete Hamill. "And I mean to find out what it is. The atmosphere at the store Friday was so cold I needed wool socks. Mr. Tibor told me, 'This political thing is affecting my business. I can't afford to be involved.' He told me he was losing business because of my differences with the Kennedys."

May suggested that her forced departure from Mr. Tibor's was part of a larger conspiracy against her. "I was supposed to do a local television show, but someone of political power swooped down and botched the thing. Also, this week someone called an ambulance, a police car, and heavens knows what-all to my home. One morning, I was lying in bed when a man crashed through a screen window. I sat up and shouted, 'Who the hell are you?' He said they'd had a report that I had died of a heart attack, and then he left."

Peter, in the midst of planning the inaugural gala, was mortified by May's outbursts, and so were the Kennedys.

Joe Kennedy telephoned Peter and barked, "You've got to find some way to shut down your mother."

"She's my *mother*, Mr. Kennedy. I can't kill the woman."

"No," Joe replied. "But I can." He then told Peter, "Slip her some cash. Pay her off. She'll quiet down. If you don't, I will."

"Joe Kennedy plainly didn't know my mother," Peter later said. "No amount of money in the world would have bought her silence."

When a friend of Peter's told him around this time that he had run into May, Peter muttered, "Was she floating facedown or face-up?" But the attempt to silence May, when it came, was far more civilized than that. She received a call from a man asking her to meet him in the lobby of the Beverly Hills Hotel for a "business interview." When she did, she claimed, he offered her a thousand dollars a month, a car, three maids, and ten percent of his book publishing business if she would agree to live permanently in Cannes. "I stalled and asked a friend to investigate," May said. The friend's finding: "The Kennedys want you out of their hair."

Milt Ebbins confirmed that May was urged to leave the country, but added that, as usual, she grossly exaggerated the circumstances. "Somebody might have said to her, 'May, your arthritis is bad, why don't you go and live in Cannes? It's warmer there.' And they probably offered to take care of her expenses. That's all."

In any event, May refused to leave the United States, and she escalated her diatribes against the Kennedys. A few months later she appeared on the LA talk show of the right-wing commentator Paul Coates and reiterated her disagreements with the President's family.

"The night I went on the Paul Coates program," May later said, "I was kept awake by prowlers till I opened my window and told them to go or I would come down and beat them up—and remember I was British and afraid of nothing! In the morning when I went down to get breakfast and water my flowers I found the water hose cut to pieces, mud thrown on the house, and several pots of flowers destroyed. My small black cat was missing. I am helpless in the face of such treatment."

May lashed back in the only way she knew how—with her tongue and her quill. She threatened to write a book

about Peter and the Kennedys, in which she would publish
pictures of Peter, "who fancied himself a girl," dressed in
female attire. She began to write the book, and a few months
later she told friends that Peter had hired men who broke
into her house and stole the manuscript and photographs.
Verbally, she continued to express doubt to everyone within
earshot about Peter's sexual inclinations.

She wrote vicious notes to Peter about the Kennedys.
She sent him a May 20, 1961, press clipping from the *Irish
Times* about two cousins of President Kennedy's who had
met America's ambassador to Ireland, E. G. Stockdale,
when he visited New Ross. She typed above it, "Rumor has
it that these ladies were found living on a dirt floor in the
most primitive aboriginal Irish condition. . . . I always knew
the Kennedys were bogtrotters, but never dreamt they were
as low on the social scale as these Irish cousins suggest! I
understand they have frothy brogues which they spit out
between their false teeth!"

Drinking, angry, she fired off "To Whom It May Concern" letters to columnists, reporters, politicians, and movie-
industry people berating Peter and the Kennedys for "giving
money to dirty, filthy niggers" while she was without enough
food to eat. She charged that her telephone had been
tapped, that the Kennedys were keeping her a virtual prisoner, and that her life was in danger.

She told Hedda Hopper, in an interview the gossip
columnist never published, that she had been having some
"trying" experiences. She didn't know who was behind
them, but she hinted it might have been Sinatra's "hood-
lums." Ambulances had been sent to her door, she said, and
one medic told her that she'd been reported dead. She had
received threatening phone calls in the middle of the night,
May concluded, telling her "We are coming over to cut your
throat."

How much of this was fact and how much the ravings
of an embittered, alcoholic woman? It's certainly possible
that any number of people might have wanted to suppress
Lady Lawford's more vengeful impulses by stealing an in-
flammatory manuscript, or even to harass and intimidate her
until she agreed to leave the country. But the credibility of
many of her charges is made suspect in light of the increasingly fanciful scenarios she had begun to create.

"She was saying such crazy things after a while," Milt

Ebbins recalled. "She said the Kennedys abducted her and took her to a motel, where she was beaten and injected with drugs." Late one night Ebbins was jarred awake by the shrill jangle of his telephone. It was May. "They're on my lawn, Milt," she shouted, extremely agitated, "and I've got a shotgun! So help me God I'm gonna kill them!"

Ebbins sat bolt upright in his bed. "*Who's* on your lawn, May?"

"Frank! And Sammy! And Dean! And if they come in here and try to hurt me I'm gonna kill them! I killed people in India and I'm gonna shoot all three of them!"

"May, please, calm down," Ebbins pleaded. "Don't do anything until I get there."

He dressed quickly and drove over to May's. There was no one on the front lawn. He looked around the grounds and saw nothing out of the ordinary. When he knocked on May's door, she wouldn't open it. He soothingly told her that no one else was there. "Are you sure?" May asked him.

"Yes, May. It's only me. Open the door."

After she let Ebbins into her living room, May stood in front of him, stock-still, holding a twenty-two-caliber pistol in her hand. "If they come in here," she said, "I'm gonna shoot them. My husband gave me this and I know how to use it."

Ebbins tried to calm her. "May, relax. There's nobody there."

"They must have gone, but they *were* there."

"I believe you, May. Give me the gun, okay?"

"Why?" She peered at him suspiciously.

"Just let me look at it."

Warily, she handed Milt the gun and he uncocked it. There were no bullets, there was no firing pin. He handed the firearm back to May.

"She wasn't insane," Ebbins concluded. "She was an alcoholic and I think it just burned a hole in her brain. Don't forget, here's a woman who lived the good life. She had money, she hobnobbed with royalty. She had been a creative woman who had written and acted. Then she finds herself without a husband, on the dole, unable to work, her son and daughter-in-law wanting nothing to do with her. It all combined to send her over the edge."

TWENTY-FIVE

For almost a year, since the completion of *Exodus*, Peter had not worked, either in movies or on television. This was entirely by choice. First he had been preoccupied by the election, then the preparations for the inaugural, and then simply the heady enjoyment of his singular position as brother-in-law of the President and all the "perks" that came with it.

His income from the box-office receipts of *Ocean's 11* would have allowed him to coast for at least another year, but by the spring of 1961 he was ready to get back to work. Frank Sinatra was set to go with *Sergeants 3*, the second of a proposed five pictures to star the Rat Pack boys. Each film would grant the highest profit participation to one of the members, beginning with Frank, then Dean, Peter, Sammy, and Joey Bishop.

Sergeants 3, a comedic remake of *Gunga Din* with a western setting, was filmed in the rugged desert of Kanab, Utah. In sharp contrast to the bacchanalian nightlife Las Vegas offered during the filming of *Ocean's 11*, Kanab provided Sinatra and company no nocturnal entertainment whatsoever. They played cards, watched Laurel and Hardy movies, imported hookers, and complained about how bored they were. "There was a Dairy Queen that was open until eleven o'clock," Joey Bishop recalled. "My advice to everybody was to get two scoops, because after that there wasn't a goddamn thing to do!"

So that his group could entertain each other more handily, Sinatra had the hotel install a door between each of the rooms on the floor they occupied. The considerable expense of this construction was charged to the film's budget.

Peter's year of leisure had left him heavier than he had ever been in his life. He was now thirty-eight, and food and booze turned into fat on him much more readily than they had when he was younger. He had stopped the more vigorous athletic pursuits like surfing and volleyball that had burned calories, and when he arrived in Kanab he was thirty pounds overweight. Ken DuMain, who once again was hired as Lawford's stand-in, was shocked when he first saw him: "His face was very puffy and full, and his body was much heavier than I had ever seen it. He was drinking and partying all the time, and it showed." Even the President had noticed it. "You've really let yourself go," Jack told Peter. "I'd hate to see you eat your way out of show business."

Every evening, the cast would gather with director John Sturges in the basement of the local schoolhouse to view the day's rushes. "Whenever Lawford came on-screen," DuMain recalled, "Frank would say, 'There's fat boy.' Well, Peter wasn't happy about it. He started taking Dexedrine to lose that weight, and it worked. After the first third of the picture, he was back to looking like the Peter Lawford of old. So he looks both heavy and slim in the movie."

Peter's bad arm caused him some problems. As DuMain recalled, "there were a couple of scenes that I had to do for him where he runs and climbs a ladder on the side of a building. He said, 'I can't do that—my arm's not strong enough.' So I'd climb the ladder and they'd use long shots or shots from behind."

A few days into filming, Peter told DuMain that he had spotted a "pretty little extra girl" he was eager to meet, and since DuMain knew her, could he introduce her? The next day, walking with the girl, DuMain saw Peter studying his script and brought the girl over to him. "I introduced them and they started talking, at which point I discreetly walked away and left them alone." At the end of the filming, Peter sent DuMain a note: "Dear Kenny: Thank you again so much for all the little extras—and I don't mean people!"

DuMain was soon to learn that the "pretty little extra

girl" wasn't Peter's only sexual divertissement during the filming of *Sergeants 3*. Early one morning, a call came through for Lawford, and DuMain took it. Jackie Kennedy was on the line. "I raced across the compound to Peter's cottage," DuMain recalled, "and rapped on his door. He opened it and I saw that there was a girl in his bed. It was Joan Arnold."

Joan Arnold was the lovely blond daughter of the head of MGM's camera department. She worked as a secretary for Peter at Chrislaw, the production company he and Milt Ebbins had formed earlier that year, and she had come to Kanab to spend the weekend with him. They had been sexually involved intermittently for several years. According to Ebbins, "There was an alliance whenever he wanted it. She was a terrific girl, a great secretary. She liked to drink, and she'd pour drinks for Peter and herself at lunchtime."

Ebbins feared that Joan's "alliances" with Peter put her in jeopardy. "I used to say to her, 'Joan, you're gonna get your ass in a sling.' But she was very closemouthed. She never once admitted to me that she and Peter were involved. But I knew for sure because once Joan came with my wife and me and me and Peter up to Tahoe. I couldn't sleep one night and I went into Peter's bedroom. There they were in bed together."

Despite these warnings, Joan continued to dally with Peter "whenever he wanted it" because she was in love with him, and she told DuMain she felt Peter would someday marry her. But the relationship came to an abrupt end some months later. While Pat was away, Peter gave a dinner party, and among the guests were Joan Arnold and Joe and Dolores Naar. That Joan was present wasn't surprising; she frequently worked at the house. What raised Dolores's eyebrows was that when she and Joe left, Joan Arnold was the only guest still there.

When Pat returned from her trip, she paid an unannounced visit to the Chrislaw offices. Ebbins remembered it vividly. "She came in and she had a face like Peter's when he gets angry—like a lion. She didn't even look at Joan or say anything to anybody—she just stormed into Peter's office."

The minute Pat left, Peter went into Milt's office and told him to fire Joan Arnold. Ebbins was aghast. "You're crazy! Fire her? She's the best secretary in the world. Why should we fire her? For what reason?"

"I don't need to give you a reason," Peter growled. "Just fire her."

"Yes you do need to give me a reason, because otherwise I'm not going to do it."

"My wife's gonna drive me crazy unless we fire her."

"Yeah," Ebbins shot back, "and it's your fault! What the fuck is the matter with you? Why didn't you just deny it? You'll destroy this woman if you fire her."

"Do you want me to do it?"

"Yes!" Ebbins shouted—and walked out of the room.

Of course, it ultimately did fall to Milt to let Joan go. "It was hard for me, and it was a terrible blow for her. She'd been there for years; she was his lover." Milt told her she'd been stupid. "You go to a party with Dolores Naar, who's a pipeline to Pat, and you're the last person to leave? Why didn't you pretend to leave and come back?" But even at this point, Joan wouldn't admit to anything. "What are you talking about?" she asked. "Nothing happened!"

"Getting fired from Chrislaw destroyed Joan Arnold," Ebbins recalled. "Her heart was broken. Peter just sat there and let his wife destroy this woman, who was a great secretary and a great friend. She died of cancer several years later."

SERGEANTS 3 didn't advance the careers of anyone involved in it. The public was indifferent, the critics hostile. Typical were Thomas Wiseman's comments in the London Sunday Express: "Sergeants 3 gives the impression of having been made for the private amusement of members of Sinatra's Hollywood clan, the Rat Pack—which has the motto: 'If you're in you're very, very in, and if you're out you're dead, Daddyo.' The Clan may find it all quite hilarious. But to an audience that is not 'in,' the joke looks almost as thin as Mr. Sinatra.... The film works neither as a straight Western, nor as a 'spoof' of the genre. To string together all the corniest situations from previous Westerns does not in itself constitute satire. This time the Rat Pack is very, very out, not to say dead, Daddyo."

Happily for Peter, his next two movies were far better received. But both of them slapped him in the face with a new and unpleasant realization: he was being hired not for his talent or box-office draw, but for what his brother-in-law could do for the production. It was easy to dismiss the offers from fly-by-night producers, Peter said. "You know, the kind of thing where the picture is shot in Siam and the music recorded in Greece and the voices dubbed in New York and then the producer puts up a billboard: 'Starring the President's brother-in-law.' So you ignore those deals, right?"

Harder to ignore was the formidable Darryl F. Zanuck, who for seventeen years had been the head of production at Twentieth Century-Fox and was now an independent producer. *The Longest Day* was to be his epic saga of D-Day, the decisive Allied invasion of Nazi-held France. Zanuck had hoped to use American servicemen stationed in France as extras, and he wanted access to the Army's tanks and landing boats. Permission, however, was denied him. Again and again, he asked for special dispensation. Again and again the Army turned him down. Then, he hired Peter Lawford to play Lord Lovat, a flamboyant Scottish commando leader.

Shortly after he signed for the role, Peter had dinner with Zanuck, whose favorite expression was "Don't say yes until I'm finished talking!" The mustachioed, cigar-chomping mogul wasted no time telling Peter about his problems with the Army. It was a situation, he said, that threatened the very production of *The Longest Day*. "The soldiers and equipment are already there, Peter, and I'm willing to pay for everything, but they keep turning me down."

Peter listened quietly and then said simply, "Let me see what I can do." Within a few days, all of Zanuck's requests had been granted. Zanuck had sensed that if Peter wanted to, he could intercede with the Kennedy administration to help Zanuck get what he needed—and he was right.

Peter was due in France for the filming of his sequences late in August 1961. On July 2, Pat gave birth, a week overdue, to a five-and-a-half-pound baby girl. "Well, it finally arrived," she wrote to her parents, who were vacationing on the French Riviera. "Red hair and the longest fingers I've ever seen. So maybe she'll have Dad's brains, too!"

Friends of the Lawfords had barely had time to get

used to the fact that Pat was pregnant. Leonard Gershe recalled with some wonderment that on Sunday, June 25, he was playing tennis with Pat at Janet Leigh and Tony Curtis's house. After the game, they sat around the pool and discussed plans for dinner the following week. "I can't come," Pat said. "I'm going into the hospital Thursday."

"What do you mean you're going to be in the hospital?" Lenny asked. "What's wrong?"

"I'm having a baby," Pat replied nonchalantly.

Gershe thought she was kidding. "She hadn't said anything; she wasn't showing. She was playing *tennis,* for God's sake. Maybe her clothes were a little loose, but when a woman's going to have a baby in a week, you can usually tell. But none of us, her closest friends, even knew. I mean this was kind of pathological really—a psychotic need for privacy."

Robin Elizabeth Lawford was christened on July 8 at St. Monica's Church. Peter and Frank Sinatra met Robert Kennedy at LA International Airport that morning and drove him to the church, where he served as Robin's godfather. Her godmother was Rocky Cooper ("Pat ran out of Catholic friends," Rocky said). May Lawford was invited to the christening, she said, only because there had been such "bad publicity" over her exclusions from the previous two.

At the end of July, with Robin not a month old, Pat flew to Washington to stand in for Jackie as hostess at a White House function. She then spent a week at Hyannis Port before flying to Nice to join her parents at their home in Antibes for several weeks of vacation.

Peter had left a week earlier for Paris with Frank Sinatra, Dean Martin, Jimmy Van Heusen, Mike Romanoff, and Milt Ebbins. Dean was en route to Germany; the rest of the group planned to rent a luxury yacht and meet up with Bob Neal, Porfirio Rubirosa, and his wife, Odile.* The group would then join Pat and her parents for a Mediterranean cruise.

Bob Neal was charged with finding a suitable yacht—

*Rubirosa, an international playboy and race-car driver, was the former son-in-law of Dominican Republic strongman Rafael Trujillo. In 1953 he married Woolworth heiress Barbara Hutton, his fourth wife, and left her fifty-three days later. The divorce netted him millions.

big, Peter told him, with at least four staterooms—which Neal, Peter, Sinatra, and Rubirosa would share the expense of renting. Neal found one "particularly suited," he thought. "It had four double master staterooms, so nobody could scream about being in the crew's quarters or something. It was 110 feet long and had a crew of seven. I cabled the name of the boat and the information to Paris, and I got a wire back from Frank: 'Get a *big* boat, will ya?'"

Neal went back to the rental agent and asked for the biggest yacht available. He was told that would be the *Hiniesta* at 175 feet. "She's old," Bob was told, "but she's been redone beautifully. The problem is, she's a steam yacht." The agent went on to explain that the boat ran on water and that every two days or so they'd have to take it back to port and reload it. Bob said that didn't matter and reserved the yacht, leaving an eight-thousand-dollar deposit. He then ordered the finest food and liquor—Dom Pérignon champagne, caviar, the thickest steaks, and the freshest seafood—for a cruise that might add to its cargo of VIP passengers Stavros Niarchos, the Greek shipping tycoon and his wife, Tina, the ex-wife of Niarchos's rival Aristotle Onassis.

The plans started to unravel in Paris when Peter, Frank, Dean, Mike Romanoff, and Milt Ebbins attended a cocktail party in honor of the publicist Henry Rogers. Among a plethora of beautiful women was a particularly striking young model, and Dean Martin, dazzled, homed in on her immediately.

Then Ebbins saw Peter start to make a move on her. "I knew Martin was dead. If Peter wanted a woman, he got her. He told me he was going to take the girl home. I said, 'You're kidding! You're gonna take her away from Dean?' He said, 'I'm not taking her away if she wants to come with me.'"

When Dean asked the young woman if she'd like to have dinner with him after the party, she said, "I'm very sorry, but I have another engagement." Peter left the gathering with the girl, and as the rest of the Sinatra party sat in the back of a limousine on the way to dinner, acrimony surfaced. "Your friend's a real nice guy," Frank said to Ebbins. "I don't think that was too goddamn nice," Jimmy Van Heusen piped up. And Dean Martin asked plaintively, "What ever happened to one for all and all for one?"

Sinatra's anger was aggravated the following night when

he went to dinner with Peter, the President's press secretary Pierre Salinger, and a few others at San Francisco, a posh Parisian restaurant. After a meal freely lubricated by alcohol, Salinger excused himself to go to the restroom, and Peter went over to the bar to order another drink. When Salinger returned, he joined Peter at the bar, where they remained in a tête-à-tête for several minutes.

Sinatra sat at the table and fumed. Finally he got up and confronted Peter and Salinger. "You guys having a private conversation? What are you talking about that you can't say in front of me?" Peter tried to explain that they hadn't meant to exclude him, they had just gotten caught up in a conversation, but Sinatra was not placated. He left a few minutes later.

According to Bob Neal, "Frank had enough booze in him that he'd manufactured in his mind the idea that they thought he wasn't good enough to be included in White House discussions or some nonsense like that." The next day, Sinatra was scheduled to arrive in Nice for the yacht cruise, and Neal went to meet his plane. The singer wasn't on it. When Neal called him in Paris, Sinatra yelled into the phone, "I'm not going on any goddamn cruise with that lousy bastard!"

Neal, in the dark about the night before, asked, "Which lousy bastard is that, Frank?"

"Fucking Lawford! To hell with him! I'm going to Germany with Dean!"

Now Neal had a problem: Sinatra was supposed to have paid his share of the expense of the cruise: $5,870. He called Peter, who told him, "The son of a bitch has to pay, whether he comes or not. You call Jack Entratter in Paris. He'll give you the money." Neal called Entratter, the manager of the Sands Hotel in Las Vegas and a close associate of Sinatra's, and he got hold of Frank. Sinatra's reply: "Pay the son of a bitch!"

Finally, the remaining merrymakers gathered to board the *Hiniesta,* and there was great consternation at the sight of it. To Bob Neal it was "the worst-looking damn vessel you ever saw. It looked like the Leviathan." Once everyone boarded, however, they felt better, much to Neal's relief: "It was beautiful inside. They'd really done a great job of refurbishing the thing."

Loaded up with "eight thousand million gallons of water," as Neal put it, the yacht began its chug through the Mediterranean, picking up Pat and her father along the way. Bob Neal found Joe Kennedy a very amusing man. "We were coming up on St. Tropez, and I said, 'Oh, look, Mr. Kennedy, those two girls on that boat over there have no bras on.' He yelled, 'Where? Where?!' and almost went over the side trying to get a look at them."

On the second day, Peter, Pat, and friends were invited to lunch with Stavros and Tina Niarchos by their pool, which lay nestled among rocks in the Mediterranean Sea. (Their house sat atop a seaside cliff two thousand steps above the pool.) Pat didn't want the Niarchoses to see the *Hiniesta.* "You can't park this goddamn scow where they can see it," she told Neal. The crew dropped anchor just out of sight behind a jutting cliff, and the passengers took a shore boat to the Niarchos dock. Tina kept asking, "Where's your yacht?" Neal told her, "Tina, you won't believe this, but the yacht had to go back to Nice to take on some more water."

"Water?" Tina said, frowning. "Why do you need water? You've got Perrier, Scotch, champagne—"

Niarchos interrupted. "What *is* the thing?"

"It's a steam yacht, Stavros," Neal replied. "Built about 1902."

"What an interesting relic. What does it look like now?"

"It looks great," Neal told him. "It's really beautiful inside."

To everyone's relief, that ended the discussion. "Stavros never did see the thing, thank God," Neal said.

DURING THE cruise, Pat and Peter received word via cable that Robin, five weeks old, had been rushed to the hospital after choking. The baby, they were told, was doing fine, and they decided not to cut their trip short. Three days later, another cable came: Robin had been readmitted to the hospital with an intestinal blockage that might require surgery. The Lawfords decided to return home immediately and caught the first flight from Nice to London, where they could make the fastest connection with a flight to Los Angeles.

When a reporter at Heathrow Airport told Pat that Robin was about to go under the knife, she gasped. "That's news to me!" She and Peter were taken to a private lounge where they placed a call to the White House. They spoke to presidential physician Dr. Janet Travell, who was in close contact with Robin's pediatrician, Dr. Gilbert M. Jorgenson. Travell informed them that Robin suffered from pyloric stenosis, an overgrowth of muscular tissue that had blocked her intestine. It was not an uncommon ailment in infants, Travell said, and shouldn't be a problem if it was removed immediately. Both she and Dr. Jorgenson agreed that surgery was necessary, and Pat gave her consent.

When she left the lounge, reporters noted that Mrs. Lawford was near tears. "My baby's going to have an operation in five or six hours," she told them. She was asked how serious it was. "Serious enough," she replied.

On the twelve-hour flight from London to Los Angeles, the Pan American pilot kept the Lawfords informed of Robin's progress. They heard in midflight that the operation was a success, and when the plane landed at Los Angeles, Milt Ebbins (who had returned from Paris a week earlier) confirmed that "the baby is doing beautifully." Peter told the press, "I guess you can realize how worried Pat and I were, and we are pleased and happy that Robin is all right."

There was a great deal of criticism, particularly in the British press, of the Lawfords' decision to leave a month-old baby and go on vacation (much as there would be years later when the Duchess of York left newborn Princess Beatrice for a vacation in Australia). Peter and Pat never answered the criticism, and things weren't made any better by a White House announcement on August 18—with Robin still hospitalized—that Pat planned to join her sisters Jean and Eunice for a private visit to communist Poland "if the baby continues to make progress."

Pat decided against the trip to Poland, even though Robin's recovery appeared to be complete. Instead, she joined Peter on August 26 as he flew back to France for the start of principal photography on *The Longest Day*.

TWENTY-SIX

THE FILMING of *The Longest Day* began on a resonant note for Peter. As he flew in a helicopter between locations along the French coastline, he noticed a partially sunken ocean liner near the shore, listing at a forty-five-degree angle, waves lapping against its main deck. He stared silently down at the sight for a few moments as the chopper's blades whirred above him. Then he asked the pilot to swoop lower and hover above the ghostly hulk. "See that ship down there?" he asked Milt Ebbins, who was seated beside him.

"Yeah, it's pretty big," Ebbins replied. "Must have been sunk in World War II. Do you know which one it is?"

"Yes," Peter said quietly. "It's the *Champlain*. My parents and I sailed across the Atlantic on that ship once, when I was a kid." The pilot lowered the helicopter as close to the water as possible, and the vessel's name became visible despite the heavy buildup of barnacles on its side.

"Sure enough," Ebbins recalled, "there was the name—*Champlain*. It was an eerie experience. Peter was very quiet as we got back up in the air and proceeded down the coast. It was almost as though the condition of that ship symbolized his childhood in some strange way."

Even more uncanny was the experience of British actor Richard Todd, who worked beside Peter for Zanuck's recreation of the D-Day crossing of the Orne river that created a crucial linkup with airborne forces and helped the Allies to victory. Todd had taken part in the actual battle. "As the film unit gathered for the first shots around Pegasus Bridge," Todd recalled in his autobiography, "I had a distinct feeling of déjà vu. Here I was, dressed and equipped exactly as I had been seventeen years before, on ground that would forever be stamped on my memory, and surrounded by young British soldiers indistinguishable from those who had been with me on D-Day."

Todd was portraying John Howard, who had led the glider attack on Pegasus Bridge. "At one point in the film I (as John) was seen in brief conversation with an officer of the Parachute Regiment who was meant to be me, so I was in effect standing beside myself talking to myself."

This eerie verisimilitude was exactly what Darryl Zanuck wanted. Ken Annakin, who directed these sequences, recalled that "I've never known a producer so anxious to have a film made with as much truth as possible."

The attitude rubbed off on Peter in his portrayal of Lord Lovat, the man who had led the British forces across Pegasus Bridge. Lovat was a somewhat comic figure who had a bagpiper follow him into battle, wore turtleneck sweaters and berets, and used a hunting rifle instead of an army rifle. He was an oddball, but he was also completely fearless. In the course of the war he had his stomach blown out but survived; and he became one of Britain's most beloved World War II heroes.

Zanuck invited him to advise the production, and Peter gladly accepted advice from Lovat, who watched the filming from the sidelines. "Peter did try to imitate Lovat's mannerisms," Annakin said. "Lovat was a great traditional Scottish chieftain, a man who clearly had a natural power over people, and I think Peter fell into that very well."

Lovat nodded in approval as he stood beside Annakin and watched Lawford's performance unfold. "Yes, he looks fine," Lovat said, "but he doesn't walk like me at all." Annakin told him he shouldn't expect an actor to be a perfect duplication of him, but that all of the action Lovat had described to the filmmakers was being replicated exactly.

Lovat's attention, though, wasn't always on Peter. Milt Ebbins and Pat were standing beside him one day watching a take. Milt watched Lovat "make a play for Pat you wouldn't believe. He was so overt, it was ridiculous. She was laughing. He said, 'Say, Pat, let's you and I go have a drink somewhere, quietly. We can send Milt back with the car.' Pat said, 'Are you kidding? I have a husband! Remember him?' Lovat replied, 'So what? I'm married, too.' Nothing ever came of it, of course. Pat thought it was just hysterical."

Less amusing was a near tragedy on the Île de Ré in France's Bay of Biscay, where the film crew re-created the British landing at Normandy Beach. American troops were conducting landing maneuvers there, and—thanks to Peter's influence—Zanuck had received permission to join the exercises, saving his production a great deal of time and money.

It was a very involved shot for Ken Annakin. "Everything was going on. A German plane was to pass down the beach, strafing people, there were about four thousand troops on the beach doing various things, fires had to be started, shells were bursting, and amid all this these landing craft had to come in."

Zanuck had instructed Annakin that he wanted the soldiers to jump off the landing craft's ramp into waist-high water, holding their rifles aloft, "so that you could clearly see them coming gallantly ashore." Annakin huddled with the landing craft's sergeant in command to find out how long it would take after the craft started toward shore for the ramp to be lowered enough so that the men could jump safely into the correct depth of water.

They ascertained that it would take sixteen seconds, and rehearsed it six times. Each time it took exactly sixteen seconds from Annakin's cue until the landing craft came close enough to the shore for the men to step off the ramp as it was lowering. Annakin set up the final take—a process that took five hours. Finally, they were ready to go and Annakin gave his cue and began to count from one to sixteen. When he reached three, the ramp abruptly lowered. Peter and a hundred commandos went straight down and vanished into eight feet of water.

At first, Peter later told Annakin, he expected little trouble getting back to the surface. But he hadn't pulled the zipper of the wet suit under his clothes all the way up to his neck because he thought he'd be wading through water only waist-high. The rubber suit began to fill with water, pulling him down, and his frantic efforts to reach the surface were hindered by his weak right arm. He couldn't see a thing and started to panic. After a few seconds that seemed like an eternity, Peter got close enough to the shore to lift his head above the surface of the water.

"Peter could have drowned," Annakin said, "but he managed to struggle ashore, as did the queen's bagpiper, and they went onto the beach in ragtag form—probably just as the soldiers had done in wartime. I wanted to use that first take because I thought it was more realistic, but Zanuck wanted it filmed in exactly the heroic fashion he'd planned. So we redid it two days later, again taking five hours to set the whole thing up—but this time we used a different guy to lower the landing ramp."

The Longest Day was exactly what Zanuck promised it would be—an "event" picture, a "gigantic and fascinating film," as Tony Thomas put it. London's *Sunday Express* gave Zanuck his most treasured compliment with the observation that "It s so realistic a stalls seat feels like a fox hole." The film received five Oscar nominations, including best picture, and won twice, for best black-and-white cinematography and best special effects.

Peter's performance was singled out by American critics as one of the best in the film, but their British counterparts were unimpressed; most felt Peter had played Lovat "badly." About the kindest observation to be found in Britain was offered in the *Sunday Express* by Leonard Mosley, who as a reporter during the war had parachuted onto Normandy Beach alongside Richard Todd: "Mr. Lawford has never been my idea of an actor. He has not so much a poker face as a cast iron face. This, curiously enough, makes him just right for the part of Lovat, an imperturbable hero if ever there was one."

Ken Annakin felt that the criticism directed at Peter was sour grapes. "Even though the Americans looked upon Peter as British, the British looked upon him as American. Traditionally, when an American plays a revered British figure, none of the Brits like it very much. I think Peter was very good. He captured Lord Lovat's *spirit*."

PETER RETURNED home in October 1961, just in time to begin work on his second picture for Otto Preminger, *Advise and Consent,* based on Allen Drury's controversial best-seller about sex and chicanery in Washington. Still another "event" picture, it featured an extraordinary cast: Henry Fonda, Don Murray, Charles Laughton, Walter Pidgeon, Franchot Tone, Burgess Meredith, George Grizzard, and Lew Ayres.

Once again it was a production that needed assistance from Peter, and he had no illusions about why he was hired to portray a playboy senator. "I know the reason they want me on the picture," he told Ken DuMain. "They want to do some shots inside the Senate building and they figure I can be instrumental in getting it done."

Actually, Preminger had higher hopes than that. What tremendous publicity for his film, he reasoned, if his scenes of a president in the Oval Office and the private White House quarters could be filmed on location—in John F. Kennedy's office and living room. Once again, one phone call from Peter to Jack was all it took to smooth the way. The President—still such a movie buff that he would call Peter to discuss the British box-office receipts of *Ocean's 11*—thought it would be fun to have a movie crew around for a few days, and he granted Preminger permission to film in the White House.

Peter's casting as a young, good-looking, womanizing senator "more interested in coos than bills" (as Helen Markel slyly put it in *Good Housekeeping*) raised a few eyebrows among reporters, who knew Jack Kennedy's reputation and thought the character a little too close for comfort to Peter's brother-in-law. Was the President, Peter was asked insinuatingly, upset by his latest role? "It's a lot of rubbish," he replied testily. "I just don't know how people can say things like this! That role couldn't possibly reflect on the President. I saw him over the weekend, and he had just started reading the book on which the film is based. He asked me in a friendly way if I had a good script. That didn't sound as though he were displeased."

Quite the contrary; Kennedy was delighted. After the first week of filming in the basement of the Senate Office Building, he invited Preminger and the entire cast to lunch at the White House. It was a memorable afternoon for everyone. They would have been excited under any circumstances to dine with the President of the United States, but they were particularly so because of their immersion in a movie about the presidency and congressional politics. Some observers noted wryly that Franchot Tone, playing the President, seemed more "presidential" than the youthful Jack Kennedy.

The day was memorable for Otto Preminger for another reason altogether. After the luncheon, Kennedy asked Milt Ebbins to come to his office. Pierre Salinger was with the President, and the first thing Jack said was, "I know you can do this, Milt."

"Do what, Mr. President?"

"I want you to tell Otto Preminger that he can't shoot in the White House after all."

Ebbins's face went white. "Oh, Jesus Christ, Jack! He's all set to go, he's got the cables, the equipment—"

"Jackie won't let him in here," Kennedy explained. "She doesn't want all those cables lying around. It's out of the question. You've gotta tell him. You and Pierre talk to him."

Salinger and Ebbins went down to Pierre's office to call Preminger. Neither of them wanted to be the one to break the news, but Salinger did so. *"Vat?"* Preminger exploded. "You must be crazy! I am hready to shoot! Vat iss diss, a *joke?*"

Ebbins took the phone from Salinger. "Listen, Otto, this is Milt. Forget it, it's off."

"Who iss diss?"

"It's Milt Ebbins. You can't shoot—"

"Get off diss telephone! Who vants to talk to you?"

"Otto, it's out, finished, over—"

"Vat do you mean—you have de authority to tell me diss? *You* are hrepresenting de *President?*"

"Yes, I have the authority to tell you . . . it's out!"

"Do you know vat you are doink to me?"

"It's not me, Otto, it's Jackie; she doesn't want you to shoot in the White House."

"Let me talk vit her—"

"No, Otto, it's *out,* finished, *kaput.*"

Preminger was furious, and from that point on his attitude toward Peter changed markedly. In the middle of Helen Markel's interview with Peter on the set, Preminger thundered across the Senate cafeteria, "Mr. Lawford, ve are *vaiting* for you. Vy must you *alvess* be answering qvestions, qvestions, *qvestions?*"

Once Peter began the scene, an exchange with Charles Laughton, Preminger instructed Laughton to hold his hand higher during an angry gesture. Laughton told the director that if he held his hand that high it would cast a shadow across Peter's face.

"Dot iss not your problem, Mr. Laughton," Preminger sneered.

"But Mr. Lawford has pointed out to me that it *is* his," Laughton replied in his best House-of-Lords baritone.

Later, when an actor sought the director's help in conveying an air of haughty disdain, Preminger told him: "Simply take lessons from Mr. Lawford."

Preminger didn't just make the working atmosphere chilly for Peter; he took a director's ultimate revenge and edited him out of the picture. After an early establishing scene that leads a viewer to expect that Peter will be a major character in the film, he is seen only fleetingly, his part so truncated that one comes away wondering why the character exists at all.

Advise and Consent was a popular picture, well reviewed as a political soap opera produced for the masses with a veneer of weightiness that made it seem like an "important" movie. As critic Dwight MacDonald observed of Preminger, "No one is more skilled at giving the appearance of dealing with large controversial themes in a bold way, without making the tactical error of doing so."

The success of *The Longest Day* and *Advise and Consent,* and the barrage of publicity he received over his participation in them, were Pyrrhic victories for Peter. He was uncomfortable with the knowledge that he had been hired for both films primarily because he could provide the producers with something they needed. None of the press reports alluded to this specifically, but there was a widespread perception that Peter's new status as "First Brother-in-Law" was responsible for the resurgence of his career.

Peter bristled whenever a reporter broached the subject. One British reporter observed scathingly, "Peter Lawford, well known now as the actor husband of President Kennedy's sister, may inspire drama students with a new dictum: if you want to get ahead, get a head of state."

"People seem to forget," Peter responded, "that I have been in this business for twenty years. I had a career before I ever met Pat Kennedy." But then he muttered an aside that seemed to prove the reporter's point: "If you could call it a career."

But Peter couldn't win. Even with the power of the White House behind him, he wasn't offered starring roles, and his willingness to open doors might just as easily blow up in his face, as it had with Preminger. He was not the man who made the decisions; rather he was at the mercy of forces and personalities beyond his control.

Despite some solid performances in a variety of roles, Peter wasn't able to shake the general impression that he was a lightweight. Joe Kennedy had turned to Bill Asher some months earlier and said, "Peter's not a very good actor, is he?" Asher protested that he thought Peter was a very good actor indeed, but Kennedy didn't seem to buy it.

Once again Peter Lawford was one of the smallest fish in a very big pond, and reporters wouldn't let him forget it. One woman journalist said to him, "Your pictures are getting bigger." As he started to offer a gracious thank-you, the woman interrupted: "But your parts are getting smaller."

Peter gave her a sharp look. Then he smiled wanly and said, "Touché."

ONCE PETER completed principal photography on *Advise and Consent* in mid-December, he flew directly to Palm Beach to spend the Christmas holidays with the Kennedys. An extended visit with his in-laws was not one of Peter's favorite pastimes, but now that Jack was President, Peter enjoyed being in his company more than ever. Bob Neal observed that "Peter was very impressed with the office. Everyone was, of course, but Peter more so. He was in awe of Jack."

Being with the Kennedys, however, caused Peter no end of ego battering. Driving off the Kennedy grounds, he saw a crowd of people wave from across the street. He waved back—only to hear what they were really interested in when they shouted: "Where's Jackie?"

The Kennedy family's holiday joy was short-lived. One week before Christmas, Joseph Kennedy felt faint while playing golf and could barely walk back to his car. At home, he took to his bed, where he lay ashen faced, unable to move. Rose Kennedy told the servants she was sure he'd be all right—and that in any event, "there is nothing I can do but pray." She then kept an appointment for a golf game of her own. A few hours later, Kennedy's niece Ann Gargan called an ambulance and Joe was rushed to St. Mary's Hospital.

He had suffered a massive stroke and was, in the words of family friend LeMoyne Billings, "one breath away." Joe was hooked up to life-support systems, and his doctor told the family that even if he recovered, his body would be useless to him. Briefly, that first night, the family considered pulling the plug on the life supports. It was Bobby who finally vetoed the idea. "No, let him fight for his life."

Joe's condition remained stable through Christmas Eve, when he developed pneumonia. Doctors performed a tracheotomy the next day to relieve congestion in his throat and chest. While the children's Christmas morning was kept as normal as possible, the adults attended mass in the chapel at St. Mary's Hospital, where they prayed for the patriarch's recovery. The Associated Press wired a photo across America of a doleful Peter and Pat leaving the hospital after a visit to her father's bedside.

Joe Kennedy lived another eight years, but he remained completely incapacitated. This once powerful, vibrant man was confined to a wheelchair, completely paralyzed on his right side. He drooled from the corner of his mouth, he was no longer able to speak intelligibly, and the muscles of his right arm contracted until his hand had tightened, much like Peter's, into a claw. His grandchildren were so frightened by this apparition that had once been their imposing grandfather that they ran away from him in tears.

Now, Rose Kennedy packed mourning clothes for herself whenever she traveled, just in case. Frank Saunders, the Kennedy chauffeur, said that whenever Rose entered Joe's room, he became visibly upset. "Before, he had been the Supreme Being in the Kennedy house," Saunders said. "But after the stroke it was like a little smile came over her face, as if to say, 'Gotcha now!' "

AFTER A subdued New Year's Eve celebration in Palm Beach, Peter flew to New York to rehearse and tape his starring role in an NBC-TV *Theater 62* version of *The Farmer's Daughter,* the 1947 RKO film that had won an Oscar for Loretta Young. The charming fable concerned a simple

Swedish farm girl from Minnesota who joins the household of an urbane congressman and tries to influence his political views. Eventually she runs successfully for Congress herself, and wins her employer's heart in the process.

Lee Remick, cast to play the farmer's daughter opposite Peter's congressman, was a highly touted twenty-seven-year-old newcomer with six prestigious movies to her credit. In *The Farmer's Daughter,* which was aired on January 14, Remick looked like a petite version of Marilyn Monroe.

Peter and Lee hit it off instantly. "He was very nice and funny and charming," Lee remembered. "We had a lot of laughs making it. Peter had that lovely kind of easy charm. I remember being a teenager and seeing him in movies. I thought he was terrific."

According to Milt Ebbins, Peter soon became involved in a "full-blown affair" with Lee Remick, despite the fact that she was married and had two children. "He was on the phone to her constantly," Ebbins recalled, "and she used to come up to see him at the Savoy Plaza, where he was staying during the filming." When Milt came to visit Peter at the Savoy, he found him uncharacteristically eager for his manager's stay to be a short one. "Usually Peter wanted me to stay with him as long as I could. But he asked me, 'How long are you going to stay? Just a few days, right?' The reason was that he was using his suite as a trysting place for him and Lee and I was putting a crimp in his style."

When Peter and Lee returned to Los Angeles, Peter confided in Ebbins that "this is a lot more serious than you think."

"Are you kidding?" Ebbins replied, nonplussed.

"Yes, I'm telling you, Milt. I may marry this girl."

Before long, Peter and Lee's feelings for each other became so obvious that Hedda Hopper ran a thinly veiled "blind item" in her nationally syndicated column that her personal files confirm was about Peter and Lee: "The big news in Hollywood is a romance that can't be put into print. I don't like blind items, but I guarantee if this one hits the papers it will curl hair from Washington to Santa Monica."*

---

*Lee Remick denied having had an affair with Peter Lawford.

Four days later, Hopper wrote, "Regarding my blind item of the other day about Hollywood's most hush-hush romance, the two parties evidently don't seem to care who knows. They dined in a popular restaurant, and if he's not careful he may lose his million dollar baby."

Peter soon confided in Bill Asher, as he had in Milt Ebbins, about his feelings for Lee. "Things got pretty heavy," Asher recalled. "He told me he was thinking of asking Lee to marry him. I got on him about it. I said, 'You must be a lunatic. Cool it!' But he didn't want to cool it—not at all."

Peter began to press Lee to marry him. Again and again he asked her, but she remained noncommittal. Peter later said that when he posed the question once more on the telephone, Lee told him she would give him an answer—in person. Peter booked a room at the Beverly Hilton Hotel and Lee made a date to meet him there the following evening.

"This is the big day," he told Ebbins the next morning, clearly confident that Lee's answer would be yes.

Peter and Lee remained in his suite for two hours before Peter called Milt Ebbins and asked him to come up. "Lee had left," Ebbins recalled, "and Peter was crushed. He said she had turned him down. She told him that she loved him and wanted to be with him, but she could never leave her husband because he would take her children away from her, and she couldn't bear that. She told him, 'Peter, it has to end. I can't break up my family.' "

As she had with so many of Peter's affairs, Pat became aware of the one with Lee Remick. A few weeks after Hedda Hopper's "million dollar baby" item Peter and Pat threw an extravagant party at the beach house and invited Lee and her husband, Bill Colleran. As the guests began to arrive, Pat remained near the front door so that she could greet everyone. When she opened the door to the Collerans, Lee put out her hand and said, "Hello, Pat. I'm Lee Remick."

Without missing a beat, Pat replied, "And I'm the million dollar baby."

TWENTY-SEVEN

EARLY IN the evening of April 28, 1961, Judy Campbell sat on the edge of the bathtub in her suite at the Ambassador East Hotel in Chicago and waited. In the next room, the President of the United States was meeting with Sam Giancana, and Judy wanted to give them some privacy. She stayed in the bathroom for about twenty minutes; when the meeting was over and both men were preparing to leave, Jack Kennedy apologized to Judy for not being able to remain with her. He was on his way, he said, to address a Democratic Party dinner.

After Kennedy's election as President, he had continued both his sporadic affair with Judy Campbell and his business association with Sam Giancana. Now, the assistance that the Mafia *capo di tutti capi* (boss of all bosses) could offer Kennedy was far more sinister than a few stolen votes. The April 28 meeting in Judy Campbell's hotel room followed by just eleven days a major humiliation for the young Kennedy administration: the aborted Bay of Pigs invasion, a botched attempt by CIA-backed Cuban nationalists to oust the tiny country's Communist dictator, Fidel Castro. President Kennedy told the nation that he took full responsibility for the failure of the operation.

He didn't intend to fail the next time. Ridding America of the threat of a Soviet-controlled government ninety miles from Miami Beach became a major priority of the Kennedy White House. To achieve that goal, Operation Mongoose was put into effect: a White House–directed undercover effort to oust Castro by any means available. These included sabotage, the fomentation of dissent, guerrilla warfare, propaganda—even assassination.

Testimony before the Senate Committee on Intelligence in 1975 by a number of Kennedy administration officials, including White House aide Richard Goodwin and two former directors of the CIA, John McCone and Richard Helms, confirmed that "liquidation" of Fidel Castro had been discussed at top-secret meetings about Operation Mongoose. CIA attempts to kill Castro, his brother Raul, and Che Guevara by poison pills and exploding cigars had failed or been aborted by April 1961. In June, Los Angeles–Las Vegas *capo mafioso* Johnny Roselli organized an assassination team to ambush the Cuban dictator. That effort also failed.

Whether John Kennedy had direct knowledge of these attempts on Castro's life has been a matter of speculation for years. The Intelligence Committee's hearings, while revealing that a lax moral climate prevailed in the Kennedy administration, were not able to say definitively whether the U.S. government's murderous exercises were directly sanctioned by the President. But John F. Kennedy was not a leader who distanced himself from his administration's activities. It is likely that he was aware of the CIA efforts to kill Castro and of the recruitment of mob figures to carry out the plans. Now, with the revelations of Judy Campbell, it appears that Kennedy personally orchestrated at least some aspects of both these elements of Operation Mongoose.

Campbell, in a *People* magazine interview in 1988, said that she arranged ten meetings between Kennedy and Giancana and acted as their courier, carrying plain manila nine-by-twelve envelopes among Kennedy, Giancana, and Roselli: "There was no writing on them . . . nothing. They were sealed but not taped. They weighed about as much as a weekly magazine and felt as if they contained papers." Campbell said she never considered opening them to see what was inside.

Campbell, who had solid documentation of her travels and was well represented on White House telephone logs, claimed never to have pondered the implications of what she was doing. She was, she said, a naive twenty-six-year-old who didn't know exactly what business Sam Giancana

was in. "Sam was one of the nicest, kindest people I knew,"
she said. "I didn't know he was a murderer. I wouldn't have
believed it." She added that she didn't figure out what she
had gotten herself involved with until she was called before
the Senate Intelligence Committee in 1975. "It finally
dawned on me that I was probably helping Jack orchestrate
the attempted assassination of Fidel Castro with the help of
the Mafia."

It is clear that Jack Kennedy, who was gaining a reputation for recklessness, was playing a particularly dangerous
game. And his utilization of mob figures didn't stop with
international intrigue; on at least one occasion he accepted
their help in extricating himself from a potential scandal.

Early in 1961, a twenty-one-year-old man named Robert
Westbrook, set out to sue his wife, a starlet named Judi
Meredith, 24 for divorce, citing adultery. Westbrook's stepfather, Peter Fairchild, a restaurateur, hired Fred Otash to
assemble evidence that Judi had had sexual affairs with a
number of men in Hollywood. When the complaint was
prepared for submission to the court, the men were listed
as "Dean Martin, Jerry Lewis, Frank Sinatra, etc. etc. etc."

Word got out that one of the et ceteras was President
Kennedy, and before long Otash got a call from Johnny
Roselli. He wanted to meet with Otash at the Brown Derby
restaurant in Hollywood—"at the request of the attorney
general." Warily, Otash agreed.

"I'm sitting there with Johnny Roselli," Otash recalled,
"and two FBI men are covering the meeting. Roselli says to
me, 'Listen, Otash, you've got yourself a problem. You're
in trouble. You're fucking around with the White House
here. What's this shit that you're gonna name Jack Kennedy
as a corespondent in Judi Meredith's divorce case? How can
you name the President of the United States in a divorce
case?'

"I said to him, 'He fucked my client's stepson's wife,
that's how! Who the fuck is that cocksucker! Who are you
representing, anyway?'*

"He said to me, 'I'm representing the Kennedys.' I said,

---

*Judi Meredith has denied that she ever slept with Jack Kennedy.

'Are you kidding me?' I couldn't believe my ears—here's Roselli, a guy who's a fucking *mobster,* intervening on behalf of the White House. I used to have the prick under surveillance. I used to put guys like him in jail, and now he's representing the *President.* I'm sitting there thinking, *Wait a minute. What is this bullshit?*"

There were other meetings, at least one of which Sam Giancana attended. Roselli asked Otash what it would take to "straighten things out." Otash replied, "Very simple. Judi wants a hundred thousand dollars. Her husband isn't gonna give her shit, because I'm gonna name Frank Sinatra as a guy who was fucking her, Sammy Davis as a guy who was fucking her, Dean Martin as a guy who was fucking her, Jerry Lewis, Jack Kennedy. My client's stepson has a real case for divorce, and he ain't giving her a dime. Why don't you have the Rat Pack throw a charity show, give Judi the money, and the case will go away."

By the morning of the court hearing on the Westbrook divorce, nothing had been resolved. "I went into that courtroom," Otash says, "prepared with the documents to have the complaint amended and name John Kennedy. I'm in the judge's chambers and I've got all the papers and all of a sudden somebody hands a check to Judi's lawyers. And the matter is settled. She got what she wanted. She sure as hell didn't get it from her husband. She got it from somebody else."

Giancana, Roselli, and their fellow mobsters understandably expected that with their various assistances to the Kennedy administration, the FBI would turn a blind eye to their illegalities. Bureau wiretaps in December 1961 recorded this exchange between Giancana and Roselli concerning the mob donations to the Kennedy campaign:

ROSELLI: Sinatra's got it in his head that they [the Kennedys] are going to be faithful to him [and, by extension, the mob].

GIANCANA: In other words then, the donation that was made . . .

ROSELLI: That's what I was talking about.

GIANCANA: In other words, if I ever get a speeding ticket, none of those fuckers would know me?

ROSELLI: You told that right, buddy.

Giancana hadn't told it right at all. Not only did J. Edgar Hoover's men not lessen their campaign against the Mafia, they dramatically increased it. Attorney General Robert Kennedy had set as one of the highest priorities of his department the destruction of what he called "the enemy within," and said, "I'd like to be remembered as the guy who broke the Mafia." Kennedy authorized surveillance, harassment, and wiretaps of Giancana, Roselli, and dozens of other mob figures.

On February 27, 1962, Hoover sent Robert Kennedy a memorandum that outlined some of the information the Bureau's surveillance had revealed: Judy Campbell had made phone calls to both Sam Giancana and the White House. The White House calls, Hoover told Bobby, were apparently being made to the President's secretary, Evelyn Lincoln. Bobby undoubtedly told his brother about the memo, but the relationship between Jack, Judy, and Giancana didn't stop. Hoover, informed that Campbell's calls to the White House had not ceased since his memo to Bobby Kennedy, met with the President on March 22 to tell him that his department was aware of his affair with Campbell and of her relationship with Giancana.

Kennedy was furious. He intensely disliked Hoover, the sixty-six-year-old, staunchly right-wing self-styled protector of American values who had been entrenched as either assistant director or director of the FBI for forty years. Jack looked upon Hoover as a dangerous personal foe; when Judy Campbell told Jack that she was being followed by FBI men, he told her, "Ignore them. It's just part of Hoover's vendetta against me." Now, the director had information he could use as an ace in the hole if Jack and Bobby tried to oust him as head of the Bureau. Still, the President did not sever his relationship with either Judy Campbell or Sam Giancana. When Judy expressed concern about the FBI surveillance of Giancana, Jack told her, "Don't worry. Sam works for us."

The stepped-up FBI campaign against organized crime

infuriated mob leaders across the country, who accused Jack Kennedy of betrayal—he had accepted their help and then allowed them to be harassed. They made repeated attempts to convince the administration to "lay off," often through Frank Sinatra, who begged Peter to "convince Bobby to lay off Sam." Eager to please Sinatra, Peter agreed. He flew to Washington and met with Bobby in his Justice Department office.

The attorney general listened stonily as his brother-in-law pleaded Giancana's and Sinatra's case. Peter reminded Bobby of their contributions to the Kennedy campaign and asked if he couldn't just ease up a little bit. To no avail. By now his anticrime campaign had become an obsession with the attorney general, whether or not his brother was in bed with the mob. And Peter Lawford may have been the worst choice to plead the mob's case—Bobby and Peter had little use for each other, and both of them knew it. The essence of Bobby's response was that Peter should mind his own business.

Peter went back to Sinatra, and Sinatra went back to Giancana, with a wholly unsatisfying report. The mob gradually came to realize that Sinatra was not as tight with the Kennedys as he had boasted he was. An FBI wiretap of a December 6, 1961, conversation between Giancana and Roselli revealed their growing anger with Frank's unfulfilled promises.

GIANCANA: One minute he tells me this and then he tells me that and then the last time I talked to him was at the hotel in Florida a month before he left, and he said, "Don't worry about it. If I can't talk to the old man [Joe Kennedy], I'm gonna talk to the man [President Kennedy]." One minute he says he's talked to Robert, the next minute he says he hasn't talked to him. So, he never did talk to him. It's a lot of shit. . . . Why lie to me? I haven't got that coming.

ROSELLI: I can imagine. . . . Tsk, tsk, tsk . . . if he can't deliver, I want him to tell me: "John, the load's too heavy."

GIANCANA: That's all right. At least then you know

how to work. You won't let your guard down then, know what I mean? . . . When he says he's gonna do a guy a little favor, I don't give a shit how long it takes. He's got to give you a little favor.

With Sinatra failing to come through for them, the mob's pressure on Peter became more direct. It was around this time that Milt Ebbins was sitting with Peter in Jimmy Durante's dressing room at the Copacabana, where Jimmy and Peter were appearing together. "In walks Jimmy," Ebbins recalled, "with two of the meanest-looking guys you've ever seen in your life. With these big-brimmed hats. Jimmy said, 'Peter, I want you to meet my friends, Louie and Joe.'

"Peter looked up at them. I thought they were going to kill us. Poor Jimmy was scared to death. One guy says, 'Hey, Lawford! Can't you get Bobby Kennedy to lay off us, for crissakes? You're his brother-in-law. Tell him to lay off!'

"Peter started to stammer and I told them that Bobby would probably work twice as hard against them if Peter went to plead their case. The guy said, 'Maybe he's right,' and they left.

"Peter said, 'What was that?' Then he got tough and said, 'Boy, I was watching those guys!' I said, '*You* were watching them? They'd chew you up and spit you out.'

"Jimmy Durante said, 'I'm really sorry. When those guys come in, forget it, you do what they want. I'm sorry.' "

The feeling on Ebbins's part that "they were going to kill us" wasn't that far off the mark. In another wiretapped conversation, Johnny Formosa, one of Giancana's henchmen, told his boss, "Let's show 'em. Let's show those asshole Hollywood fruitcakes that they can't get away with it as if nothing's happened. Let's hit Sinatra. Or I could whack out a couple of those other guys. Lawford and that Martin, and I could take the nigger and put his other eye out."

Other mafiosi, the FBI discovered, had made threats on the life of the President as well, a fact that J. Edgar Hoover never revealed to the Kennedy brothers. But both Bobby and Jack did feel the heat of possible public disclosure of the administration's ties to organized crime in March 1962. Rather than end those ties, however, Bobby decided that the best course of action was to distance the presidency from the most visible link between the government and the mob: Frank Sinatra.

SINATRA HAD reveled in his relationship with the Kennedy White House. For months after the inauguration, he had insisted that friends listen—over and over again—to a recording of John Kennedy's tribute to him at the gala. He loved it when Hollywood moguls asked him, "What do you hear from the White House?" Like Peter, if the President called him while he had influential visitors, Frank would feign nonchalance and boast that the President always sought his advice.

Just as he had in Paris when he thought Peter and Pierre Salinger had excluded him from a conversation, Sinatra would become enraged whenever he felt slighted by the Kennedys. Again and again he renounced his friendship with the President's family, then curried favor to get back in their good graces. Early in 1961, Bill Asher was preparing a tape of the inaugural gala for presentation on NBC television. "It was never aired," Asher related, "because of equal-time considerations or something, but in the process of editing it we decided to put a frame around it, and Frank agreed to have us shoot some new footage of him to include at the beginning and the end.

"Then there was some rift between Frank and the Kennedys, and Joe Kennedy called me and said, 'I want you to take Frank Sinatra out of every inch of that show—I don't want his face anywhere in it.' It wasn't easy—Frank was a big part of that show—but I managed to do it."

Ten days later Joe Kennedy called Asher and told him to put Frank back in. Asher did. Then he called again and told the director to take Frank out. Finally, Asher had had it, and told Joe: "Mr. Kennedy, you might not be aware of this, but I work for a living, and I can't do this anymore. I'm sorry."

Finally the souvenir tape of the gala was complete—with Sinatra in it—and Joe Kennedy asked Peter to bring it to Palm Beach so that he could see it. Peter and Milt Ebbins flew down and showed Joe the film, and when Sinatra found out about it he exploded.

"Frank went crazy," Ebbins recalled. "He thought this was some kind of big premiere for the film of the inaugural, and that he should have been invited. I tried to explain that it was a spur-of-the-moment private showing for Joe Kennedy. He screamed at me, 'Then why the fuck were *you* there, Ebbins?' I said, 'I go everywhere with Peter, Frank; you know that.' Well, he stayed mad a long time over that one.''

Frank got over it when he was invited aboard the Kennedy yacht *Honey Fitz* in September. He arrived in Hyannis Port with a case of wine, a dozen bottles of champagne, and two loaves of Italian bread. The presidential flag flying over the Kennedy compound revealed that John F. Kennedy was there. Frank regaled the other guests, who included Peter and Pat, Ted Kennedy, and the Rubirosas, with stories of his audience with Pope John XXIII in Rome. "All your friends in Chicago are Italian, too," Peter said, laughing.

It wasn't just Sinatra's ego that thrived on his association with the First Family; his pocketbook benefited too. In 1957, Frank had signed a three-million-dollar deal with ABC for a television series (one that was occasionally aired opposite *The Thin Man*). To save Frank money on his taxes, the fee was to be deferred over several years. When the show was canceled, the Internal Revenue Service disallowed the deferral and insisted that Sinatra pay taxes on the money as though it had all been paid to him in the first year.

The IRS hit Frank hard, assessing daily penalties and interest on the additional amount they were demanding, and he was unable to pay the taxes. Frantic, he asked for Joe Kennedy's help. Peter set up an appointment with his father-in-law for Frank and his attorney, Mickey Rudin. Joe knew how to bend, work with, and circumvent many of the tax laws, and he gave Sinatra advice that reduced the tax bill to sixty-five thousand dollars, saving him over a million dollars.

But by 1962 Sinatra's friendship with the President's family had become a public embarrassment for the administration. Above and beyond Frank's mob ties, which might explode in the Kennedys' faces at any minute, they soon came to realize that Sinatra was a lightning rod for criticism. There was so much negative publicity about the yacht trip that Pierre Salinger felt compelled to deny that Frank had been in Hyannis Port as a guest of the President. Rather, he said, Frank had come to review Bill Asher's souvenir recording of the inaugural gala with Joe Kennedy.

Peter's membership in the Rat Pack had whipped up bad press, and he was continually forced to defend himself against criticism that his Hollywood antics were beneath the dignity of a brother-in-law of the President of the United States. "There is no 'clan,'" Peter protested. "There is only a group of people who enjoy getting together. I mean, it makes us sound like children—like we all wear sweatshirts that say 'The Clan' on the back and Frank with a whistle around his neck. They make us sound so unsavory."

The problem, of course, was that many of Sinatra's associates *were* unsavory, a fact that hit very close to home with Peter when Puccini failed for that very reason. Among the restaurant's regular clientele was Sinatra's friend Mickey Cohen, who had been the head West Coast mafioso since Bugsy Siegel's murder in 1947. One evening in 1961 the squat, glowery Cohen walked into Puccini and saw comedian Red Skelton's manager dining with actor George Raft.

"Mickey Cohen was very good friends with Red Skelton," Milt Ebbins recalled, "and there were rumors that Red's manager was having an affair with Red's wife. Cohen saw this guy, walked over to his table, jumped up on the booth, and started kicking him. Raft tried to stop him and Cohen hissed, 'You shut up, Raft, or you know what you're gonna get.'"

Skelton's manager wound up in the hospital, and the incident made the newspapers. "From then on," Ebbins says, "the restaurant was filled with police department undercover guys every night, and nobody wanted to eat there anymore. It was a terrific restaurant, but now everybody looked on it as a hangout for Sinatra's Mafia friends and they were scared to come to it."

Bobby Kennedy saw that Sinatra's links to the mob had become uncomfortably public and that assumptions could be made about the President's relationship with Sinatra. At a staff meeting, one of the Justice Department's young attorneys complained to Bobby, "We are out front fighting organized crime on every level and here the President is associating with Sinatra, who is in bed with those guys."

The attorney general asked the lawyer to prepare a full report for him, but he was well aware of Sinatra's associations, and he knew that the time had come to sever ties with the singer.

*   *   *

TWO MONTHS earlier, in January 1962, Peter had made a request of Sinatra: the President was coming to Southern California on a political trip in March. Could Jack stay at Frank's Palm Springs house for a few days?

Could he? Sinatra immediately began a massive construction project designed to make the property suitable as the Western White House. He built separate cottages for the Secret Service men, installed a communications bank with twenty-five extra telephone lines, poured a huge concrete heliport, and had a solid gold plaque inscribed "John F. Kennedy Slept Here."

"It had been kind of a running joke with all of us in the family," Peter later said. "He even erected a flagpole for the presidential flag after he saw one flying over the Kennedy compound in Hyannis Port. No one asked Frank to do this."

A few weeks before the trip, Bobby prevailed on the President to break off his public ties with Frank Sinatra once and for all. "Sam Giancana has been a guest at that same house," the attorney general told his brother. "How is it going to look? There are too many people who know about Sinatra's ties to these guys. We can't take the risk, Jack."

Jack liked Sinatra and thought Bobby was being an alarmist. "What difference does it make?" he asked. Bobby argued forcibly about the sensitivity of the situation, and the President finally was persuaded that it would be better for him to stay elsewhere. Bobby telephoned Peter and told him to let Frank know that the President's plans had changed.

Peter could feel the blood drain from his face as he listened to Bobby's words. He knew what Sinatra's reaction would be, and he didn't want to witness it. He tried to persuade Bobby to keep the President's plans just as they were; when he could not he called Jack and tried to appeal to the President's affection for and gratitude to Sinatra. It didn't work. "I can't stay there while Bobby's handling the investigation [of Giancana]," Jack told the frantic Peter. "See if you can't find me someplace else." Peter protested that Frank would be extremely upset. "You can handle it, Peter," Jack replied. "We'll take care of the Frank situation when we get to it."

Given an unenviable task, Peter was, he admitted, frightened. He telephoned Sinatra with the news, using as an excuse the Secret Service's concerns about security short-comings on his property. Sinatra was devastated. After Peter's call he muttered to himself again and again, "What am I gonna tell my kids?" He put a call through to Bobby, hoping to change the decision. The attorney general bluntly told Sinatra the truth—that his questionable associations made it impossible for the President to stay at his house.

"Frank was livid," Peter said. "He called Bobby every name in the book and then rang me up and reamed me out again. He was quite unreasonable, irrational really. [Frank's valet] George Jacobs told me later that when he got off the phone, he went outside with a sledgehammer and started chopping up the concrete landing pad of his heliport. He was in a frenzy."

Sinatra's anger grew when he learned that Jack had decided to stay at Bing Crosby's nearby estate. "He felt that I was responsible," Peter said, "for setting Jack up to stay at Bing's—the other singer and a Republican to boot. Well, Frank never forgave me. He cut me off like that—just like that!"

Although he had had nothing to do with either decision, Peter took the brunt of Sinatra's fury. The singer refused Peter's phone calls, told associates that he wanted nothing more than to punch him in the face, and wrote him out of two upcoming Rat Pack movies, *4 for Texas* and *Robin and the 7 Hoods*. (For the latter film, Frank hired Bing Crosby!)

Sinatra did agree to see Milt Ebbins, who went to Frank's office and spent three hours pleading Peter's case. Ebbins told Sinatra that Peter was "innocent," that it was Bobby who had made the initial decision that Jack shouldn't stay at his compound, and that it was Jack's golfing partner Chris Dunphy, not Peter, who had arranged for Jack to stay at Bing Crosby's house. He also leveled with Sinatra and told him the reversal of plans had been prompted by the fact that Bobby was investigating some of the singer's friends.

"None of it worked," Ebbins recalled. "Frank just wrote Peter off. And Peter was destroyed. He loved Frank. He loved being a part of the Rat Pack. And all of a sudden he was on the outs. Not only did he lose the Rat Pack movies, but a lot of other opportunities as well—I know we lost a couple of Billy Wilder pictures."

Peter tried desperately to get back into Sinatra's good

graces. When the President arrived in Los Angeles, Peter asked him to "give Frank a call." Ebbins put the call through, and Sinatra's valet thought it was a joke. "Ebbins has gone off the cliff," he told Frank. "He says the President wants to speak with you." Ebbins put Jack on the line and he had a pleasant, inconsequential chat with Sinatra. There was no mention of what had transpired, and Sinatra wasn't much mollified by the call. A few months later, Peter and Milt were at the White House, and Ebbins suggested that Peter ask Jack to invite Sinatra for a visit. "I can't go to the President of the United States and say, 'You gotta invite Frank Sinatra to the White House,'" Peter protested. "All right," Ebbins replied, "we'll both do it."

Ebbins did the talking. "Jack," he began, "would it be possible to invite Frank here for lunch? He was such a good friend."

"Okay," the President responded. "We'll have a big Italian dinner here on Monday." Ebbins relayed the invitation to Frank, who was hesitant at first but agreed to fly into Washington for the soiree. Ebbins made arrangements to have Sinatra picked up by helicopter at Dulles International Airport and flown to the White House. Sinatra had been there before, but always secretly; he used a back entrance to avoid reporters. The same precautions would have to be taken this time—and the dinner was possible only because the First Lady was out of town. "Jackie hates Frank and won't have him in the house," Jack had told Peter.

In Sinatra's honor, Kennedy flew in an Italian chef from New York who prepared veal piccata and fettuccine Alfredo. But the afternoon of the dinner, the singer's secretary, Gloria Lovell, called Milt Ebbins to say that Frank was ill and couldn't attend. "Isn't there some way he can make it?" Milt protested. "This is the President of the United States. If he's *dying* he's gotta come." No, Lovell said, Frank had the flu and was really too ill to make it.

The dinner party went ahead without Sinatra. A few days later, Lovell told Ebbins the real reason Frank hadn't been able to come: Marilyn Monroe, with whom he was having an affair, was depressed and had wandered out of his house and disappeared. "He spent the whole day looking for her," Lovell said. "He was worried sick that she was going to hurt herself. That's why he didn't go to the dinner."

Later, Sinatra got another invitation to the White House, this time for lunch, and things went off without a hitch. But he never again had a good word for Peter Lawford. It was clear that while Sinatra had forgiven all his other cronies their trespasses, he was not going to allow Peter back into the inner sanctum. Beyond all else, it was clear that Frank Sinatra no longer *liked* Peter Lawford.

The Sinatra debacle sent Peter reeling into a depression, one punctuated by bouts of heavy drinking. The whole sordid incident reinforced in him the feeling that his life was out of his own control, and it impressed on him anew the negative aspects of being related to the President. He felt diminished by the loss of so central a relationship in his life, felt his financial security undermined by the career roadblocks Sinatra had already begun to set up against him, and felt his physical safety threatened by the mob's fury against the Kennedys and the Rat Pack.

Matters went from bad to worse. Added to Peter's myriad of troubles was a new one: just as Sinatra had been weeks before, Peter soon found himself "worried sick" about Marilyn.

TWENTY-EIGHT

M ARILYN MONROE emerged from the bedroom of her Spanish-style home on Fifth Helena Drive in the Brentwood section of Los Angeles before nine A.M. on the morning of Saturday, March 24, 1962. Normally, she slept past noon, but this was an important day. Marilyn had asked her housekeeper-companion, Eunice Murray, a lay psychiatric nurse recommended by her therapist, Dr. Ralph Greenson, to tell the workmen who were renovating the house not to come on the twenty-fourth. "I'm going on a trip," Marilyn offered by way of explanation, "and my hairdresser's coming to help me get ready."

At eight A.M., the plumber arrived unexpectedly with a crew of men to install a new hot-water heater. Mrs. Murray told them to proceed, not expecting Marilyn to arise for hours. When she was up less than an hour later, Eunice was certain Marilyn would be angry, but she was in too good a mood for that. "I'll go over to the Greensons' to have my hair washed," she chirped. "It's all right."

Several hours later, Marilyn returned and dressed for the trip. At noon, Peter Lawford arrived to pick her up. "Peter paced back and forth," Mrs. Murray recalled, "while Marilyn put the finishing touches on her attire." Nearly an hour later, she was ready—and wearing a black wig over her new hairdo. Peter and the disguised Marilyn drove to Palm Springs—to spend the weekend with John Kennedy at Bing Crosby's house. The President planned to relax and

330

throw a party Saturday evening to meet some of the Southern California Democratic politicos. It was a semipublic occasion, but Marilyn Monroe was a somewhat more private guest.

Philip Watson, later the Los Angeles County assessor, was invited to the Crosby compound that night, and he soon discovered that there were in fact two parties—one at poolside and a smaller, more exclusive one in the President's cottage. Watson, running for assessor, was invited to the smaller gathering and saw that Marilyn Monroe was there. He wasn't particularly surprised; he had seen Marilyn with the President at another party at the Beverly Hilton Hotel the previous November. What astonished him now was how little effort either made to disguise their intimacy.

As Watson remembered it, "The President was wearing a turtleneck sweater, and she was dressed in kind of a robe thing. She had obviously had a lot to drink. It was obvious they were intimate, that they were staying together for the night."

On Sunday, Marilyn telephoned her masseur, Ralph Roberts. During Marilyn's rubdowns, she and Roberts often discussed anatomy, a subject Monroe had studied while developing her body as a young starlet in the late 1940s. The last time they'd met, Marilyn had asked Roberts to give her a refresher course in preparation for her sojourn with the President. She was giving "my friend" a massage, Marilyn told Roberts when she called him from Palm Springs, and they disagreed about the position of certain muscles in the body. "I'm going to put him on the phone, and you can tell him."

Roberts soon heard the unmistakable Boston twang of John F. Kennedy. "I told him about the muscles, and he thanked me," Roberts recalled. "Of course, I didn't reveal that I knew who he was, and he didn't say." Later, Marilyn told Roberts that she had told the President that Roberts could give him a better massage than she could. "He said that wouldn't really be the same, would it?" Marilyn recalled. Then she giggled. "But I think I make his back feel better."

A YEAR earlier, living in New York, Marilyn had hit rock bottom. She was depressed over the failure of her marriage to Arthur Miller and the death of her girlhood idol Clark Gable, with whom she had just starred in *The Misfits*. She had suffered from severe insomnia and had been taking ever-increasing doses of barbiturates to help her sleep. "She took so many pills to get to sleep at night," recalled John Houston, the director of *The Misfits*, "that she had to take wake-up pills to get her going in the morning—and this ravaged the girl."

She had fallen deeper and deeper into a maelstrom of drugs and alcohol. As the grip of depression tightened around her, she became convinced that at thirty-five she was too old to continue as a sex symbol, that two box-office failures in a row meant her career was over. She despaired of ever having a happy marriage after three divorces—or a much-wanted child after three miscarriages.

Just before Christmas 1960, Marilyn had read that some of Clark Gable's associates blamed her for his death, citing the delays and headaches her emotional and marital problems had created on the Nevada *Misfits* location. Gable, in fact, had said a few days before filming ended, "What the hell is that girl's problem? God damn it, I like her, but she's so damn unprofessional. I damn near went nuts up there in Reno waiting for her to show. Christ, she didn't show up until after lunch some days. I'm glad this picture's finished. She damn near gave me a heart attack."

The day after the picture wrapped, Gable had suffered a massive coronary. As a girl in an orphanage, little Norma Jeane Baker had fantasized that Clark Gable was her father, and the thought that she might have hastened his death was devastating. One evening Lena Pepitone, Marilyn's maid, came into her bedroom and found her, disheveled and wearing only a terry cloth bathrobe, leaning out of her high-rise apartment window. Pepitone rushed across the room, grabbed Marilyn around the waist, and pulled her back in. "Lena, no," Marilyn sobbed. "Let me die. I want to die. I deserve to die. What have I got to live for?"

Pepitone convinced Marilyn to call Joe DiMaggio, with whom she had remained friendly. They talked for an hour, and Marilyn's mood improved. "Gee," she said to Lena, "how could I have been so crazy? I just lost control for a second. I didn't know what I was doing." When Lena teased her about looking too sloppy for a suicide attempt, Marilyn laughed. "I thought about dressing up. I did . . . really. But my hair's a mess anyway, so I figured, what the hell?"

Marilyn had soon fallen once again into a downward spiral, and less than two months later, her New York psychiatrist, Dr. Marianne Kris, persuaded her to enter the Payne Whitney Psychiatric Clinic in Manhattan. Expecting a cushy rest cure designed to wean her from alcohol and sleeping pills, Marilyn was shocked by her treatment after she signed in as Faye Miller.

What Marilyn didn't know was that she was being admitted as a potentially self-destructive patient. When she was brought to her room, all her personal property, including her clothes, was confiscated. There were iron bars across the windows; all sharp objects had been removed from the room. The bathroom had no door, and the mirror over the sink was made of polished chrome rather than glass. There was, in short, nothing in the room that she could use to injure herself.

The door to her room locked from the outside, and in the middle of it a small shatterproof pane of glass covered by iron bars allowed passersby to check on her at will. No visitors were permitted to see her. She felt like a caged animal, abused and abandoned; she knew that orderlies and janitorial staff were peeping through the window to gawk at the most celebrated sex symbol in the world.

As Marilyn sat in her stark room and stared at the iron bars on the windows, her worst nightmare—the fear she had fought all of her life—seemed to be coming true. Her grandmother had died in a mental hospital. Her mother had been institutionalized for most of her life. Was she going insane, too? The thought soon sent her into a paroxysm of hysteria.

She began to pound on the door, screaming, "Open this door! Let me out! Please! Open the door!" Finally she stripped herself nude and stood screaming in front of the window. She was taken to a maximum security ward, where she threw a chair through a window and was put into a straitjacket. "They had me sedated," she later told a friend. "At night there was a steady procession of hospital personnel, doctors and nurses, coming to look at me. There I was, with my arms bound. I was not able to defend myself. I was a curiosity piece. . . ."

Finally she was allowed a phone call. She telephoned Joe DiMaggio, a man of considerable influence in New York. DiMaggio was able to get Marilyn released from Payne Whitney and moved to Columbia Presbyterian Medical Center, where she was treated as a normal hospital patient and slowly weaned of her addiction to sleeping pills.

Within a year Marilyn had bounced back, and by early 1962 she had begun a new life in California. Although she had kept her New York apartment, she purchased the first house she had ever owned in Brentwood, about a fifteen-minute drive from Peter's house, and was now spending most of her time in Los Angeles. She strengthened her friendship with Peter, often visiting with him and Pat in Santa Monica, and Peter's friends found themselves charmed by her.

"One night Marilyn came to dinner," Dolores Naar recalled. "She was late as usual, and she arrived looking very disheveled. She had on a pair of pedal pushers from Jax, which was the only really hot store in LA at that time. She had a soft voice and that little-girl quality and there was a shyness about her." As the group drank cocktails before dinner, Pat put the original-cast album of the current Broadway hit *How to Succeed in Business Without Really Trying* on the stereo. " 'I Believe in You' was the big hit at that time," Dolores recalled, "and Marilyn and Pat and I were all doing our dance versions of it. Marilyn was singing and dancing sensually to the music and had the most charming way about her, very innocent, fragile. Not fragile physically, but fragile—like you could destroy her if you said boo."

In the late spring of 1962 Marilyn made preparations to begin her first movie in nearly two years, *Something's Got to Give,* took trips to Mexico to buy furnishings for her new house—and intensified her affair with Jack Kennedy. That the most powerful man in the world—and the handsomest head of state—found her desirable bolstered Marilyn's precarious self-esteem, made her feel that she hadn't lost the sexual allure that had made her a movie idol. Like a little girl at play, she delighted in disguising herself for their trysts and fantasized that Jack would divorce Jackie and marry her. "Can't you just see me as First Lady?" she asked Jeanne Carmen.

Carmen recalled that Marilyn studied world politics so

that she could hold her own in a conversation with the President and make herself a more suitable candidate for his wife. "She wanted to learn, so in case she got to be a great lady, she could go out there and *act* like a great lady. It may seem silly of her, but Nancy Reagan did it, didn't she? And she was never more than a starlet in Hollywood."

While Marilyn had seen Jack Kennedy only at intervals since their first meeting in 1954, by early 1962 she was trying to be with him as often as possible. They saw each other whenever Jack was in California, and on at least two occasions during the spring of 1962, Marilyn made a special trip to New York to be with Kennedy.

The first was a black-tie dinner party in the President's honor given by Fifi Fell, a socialite, in her Park Avenue penthouse. Among the two dozen guests were a number of presidential aides, Ambassador Earl Smith, Peter, Milt Ebbins, and Marilyn. Around seven o'clock, Ebbins and Dave Powers were dispatched to pick Marilyn up at her apartment and bring her to the party. "We got there at about seven-thirty—dinner was at eight—and she wasn't ready," Ebbins recalled. "Powers didn't want to wait for her, so he told me to stay and went back to the party, then sent the limousine back for us."

As Ebbins sat and waited, he noticed that everything in the apartment was white—the rugs, the ceilings, the walls, the furniture, even a piano. At eight o'clock, Marilyn's maid told Ebbins that her hairstylist, Kenneth, was finishing up Marilyn's hair. "She should be out very soon." At eight-fifteen, the phone rang, and Ebbins picked it up. It was Peter. "Where is she? The President's here. Everybody's waiting!"

"She's not ready yet. I'm sitting here waiting for her."

"C'mon," Peter shouted. "Dinner's practically ready!"

At eight-thirty, the maid announced to Ebbins that Marilyn was done with Kenneth and should be out in just a few minutes. By nine o'clock, there was still no Marilyn. Peter called again. "You son of a bitch!" he screamed. Ebbins could hear Dave Powers in the background, threatening him with physical violence.

By nine-thirty, Ebbins couldn't take it anymore. He opened Marilyn's door and walked into her bedroom. He saw her sitting at her vanity table, naked, staring at herself in the mirror. "Marilyn, for crissakes," he said. "Come on! The President's waiting, everybody's *waiting*."

Marilyn looked at him dreamily. "Oh," she said finally. "Will you help me on with my dress?"

"So I'm watching this giant international movie star standing there stark naked in her high heels," Ebbins recalled. "She puts a scarf over her hair so it won't get mussed and pulls this beaded dress over her head. This dress was so tight it took me ten minutes to pull it down over her ass! She says, 'Take it easy. Don't tear the beads.' I'm on my knees inching this dress down over her ass and my face is right at her crotch. But I'm not thinking of anything but getting her to that goddamn party."

Finally, at ten o'clock, Monroe was ready. Ebbins was astounded. "Whew, did she look sensational—like a princess. I said to her, 'Jesus Christ, you sure are pretty.' She just said, 'Thank you.'"

Marilyn put a red wig over her hair, slipped on dark glasses, and rode in the limousine with Milt to Park Avenue. When they arrived, over fifty photographers were milling around the lobby of the building, hoping to capture some of the celebrities attending the party upstairs as they left. Not one of them recognized Marilyn. When she got off the elevator three Secret Service men watched her slip off the wig, touch up her hair, take off the glasses and become Marilyn Monroe again.

As she and Ebbins entered the apartment, Jack Kennedy had his back to them. He turned around, smiled at Marilyn, and said, "Hi!" She sashayed up to him and he took her arm. "Come on," he said to her. "I want you to meet some people." As they walked away, Marilyn looked back at Milt Ebbins and winked.

For a few seconds, Ebbins thought he was in the clear. Then someone grabbed him by the back of the neck and pulled him into a bedroom. It was Peter, red with fury. "You son of a bitch!" he hissed, and raised his fist, measuring Milt for a punch. Dave Powers grabbed Ebbins by the collar and tore open his shirt at the neck.

Ebbins managed to calm the two men down, and it was then that he learned that there had been no dinner. "Everybody just ate hors d'oeuvres and drank and got blind drunk and happy as larks," he recalled being told. "Nobody cared about dinner after a while. They told me the chef tried to jump out the window. Here he had cooked a fabulous dinner for the President of the United States and nobody ate it!"

MARILYN'S REPUTATION for tardiness became a running gag at a star-studded fund-raising gala in Madison Square Garden on May 19, 1962, held to celebrate the President's upcoming forty-fifth birthday. Attended by fifteen thousand loyal Democrats, the extravaganza featured Jack Benny, Henry Fonda, Ella Fitzgerald, Peggy Lee, and Maria Callas, among others.

It was Peter's idea to have Marilyn Monroe sing "Happy Birthday" to Jack as the evening's finale. It would be the first time Monroe would perform before a live audience since 1954, when she entertained American troops in Korea during her honeymoon with Joe DiMaggio.

Marilyn asked her favorite designer, Jean-Louis, famous for the flesh-colored gowns he'd created for Marlene Dietrich, to design something similar for her, a dress that would look like "a second skin." Made of flesh-colored mesh studded with rhinestones, the gown cost five thousand dollars and had to be sewn on. Marilyn wore no underwear beneath it.

Mickey Song, who had cut Jack's and Bobby's hair for the occasion, begged Bobby to let him have a shot at Marilyn Monroe's hair. "She didn't want me to work on her, because she didn't know me. But Bobby convinced her. I didn't know if I'd get the chance until she showed up backstage at Madison Square Garden. Her hair had been set, but it needed some finishing touches."

Song applied them in Marilyn's dressing room, and he added a sensational flip curl on Marilyn's right side, an effect he achieved by teasing her hair from beneath "and using lots of hair spray" to keep the curl in place.

"While I was working on Marilyn," Song recalled, "she was extremely nervous and uptight. The door was open and Bobby Kennedy was pacing back and forth outside, watching us. Finally he came into the dressing room and said to me, 'Would you step out for a minute?' When I did, he closed the door behind him, and he stayed in there for about fifteen minutes. Then he left, and I went back in. Marilyn was all disheveled. She giggled and said, 'Could you help me get myself back together?' "

As showtime approached, Marilyn grew terrified—not

only of performing live, with no chance for retakes, but of singing in front of the President and other high government officials. With the show's producer, Richard Adler, she had endlessly practiced the familiar verse to "Happy Birthday" and a special stanza written especially for Kennedy. She had had trouble remembering the new material, and Adler warned the President that Monroe might flub some lines. "Oh, I think she'll be very good," Kennedy responded.

As she waited in the wings to go on, Marilyn's nervousness threatened to undo her. She had been drinking to fortify herself, and by this point she was visibly tipsy.

With Peter onstage as an ad hoc master of ceremonies for the purpose of introducing Marilyn, the preplanned running gag began. As the President sat near Bobby and Ethel Kennedy (Jackie spent the day horseback riding in Virginia), Peter gave Marilyn her first of several introductions: "Mr. President, on this occasion of your birthday, this lovely lady is not only pulchritudinous but punctual. Mr. President— Marilyn Monroe!"

A roar arose from the audience, but Marilyn didn't appear. Peter shrugged theatrically and walked offstage, and several other acts came on to perform. Then Peter returned for another go, calling Marilyn "a woman about whom it may truly be said—she needs no introduction." A drumroll announced her entrance—but again there was no Monroe.

After a long pause, Peter continued. "Because, Mr. President, in the history of show business, perhaps there has been no one female who has meant so much . . . who has done more . . . Mr. President, the *late* Marilyn Monroe!"

Cheers rocked the Garden as Marilyn, panicking and being pushed from the wings by Milt Ebbins, appeared onstage. Swathed in white ermine, taking tiny mincing steps that were all she could manage in her skintight gown, she sidled up to Peter, who removed her fur and exited stage left. The thousands of rhinestones on Marilyn's dress reflected the spotlights and made her seem more a celestial vision than a human being.

She stood silently in front of the microphone for several long moments, collecting herself. Then she breathed heavily, eliciting more cheers. After flicking the microphone with her finger to make sure it was working, she began to sing "Happy Birthday" as it had never been sung before. Slowly, breathily, sensually, Marilyn made the song seem somehow suggestive, particularly when she intoned, "Happy Birthday ... Mr. Pres ... i ... dent ... Happy Birthday ... to *you*."

The performance came off without a hitch, just as Jack Kennedy had predicted. "The President was a better showman than I was," Richard Adler admitted. "But you couldn't hear [her singing] anyway. For the crowd was yelling and screaming for her. It was like a mass seduction."

At the conclusion of the song, Marilyn urged the audience to join her ("C'mon, everybody, Happy Birthday!") and a huge cake was wheeled onstage. Within a few minutes, the President was at the microphone. "I can now retire from politics," he told the crowd, "after having had 'Happy Birthday' sung to me in such a sweet, wholesome way."

Later Marilyn attended a private party in the President's honor given by Arthur Krim, the head of United Artists. There her glittery presence mesmerized the male guests, who in addition to the Kennedy brothers included Vice-President Johnson, Adlai Stevenson, and Arthur Schlesinger. Stevenson wrote a friend that Marilyn was wearing "skin and beads. I didn't see the beads! My encounters [with her], however, were only after breaking through the strong defenses established by Robert Kennedy, who was dodging around her like a moth around a flame."

Schlesinger later wrote, "Bobby and I engaged in mock competition for her; she was most agreeable to him and pleasant to me—but then she receded into her own glittering mist. There was something at once magical and desperate about her. Robert Kennedy, with his curiosity, his sympathy, his absolute directness of response to distress, in some way got through the glittering mist as few did."

After Krim's party, Marilyn was whisked into the Carlyle Hotel to spend a few hours alone with the President. It would prove to be their last rendezvous.

BY JUNE 1962, Marilyn Monroe was as emotionally needy as she had ever been in her life. She once again was caught up in a spiral of insecurity, depression, alcohol, and drugs. She had just been fired from *Something's Got to Give* because of repeated lateness and absences. They were caused, she said, by illness, but her Twentieth Century-Fox bosses mistrusted the excuse and pointed to her flight to New York to sing for the President as proof that she wasn't as ill as she claimed. Headlines across the country screamed, "Marilyn Gets the Sack," and now it wasn't only her irrational fears that suggested her career might be over—commentators were speculating about the same thing.

Worse, Marilyn's involvement with John Kennedy, initially a euphoric high, had left her feeling abused. She had realized that to Kennedy she was, like so many other girls, little more than another piece of "poon," and it hit her like a fist in the face.

Jeanne Carmen had often been present at the Lawfords' with Marilyn and Jack Kennedy, and she hadn't liked what she'd seen. "Peter introduced me to the President at the beach house. He was the go-between. I like that term better than 'pimp.' It was so easy for Peter because he had that house and that made it easy for everyone. I was always amazed, though, at anybody coming there, especially the President, because it wasn't a totally private house. There were houses right next door."

Like college fraternity brothers with a sexy coed, Peter and Jack had become more brazen with Marilyn as time went by. At first, she had been part of a small group to dine with the President at the beach house, and he would take her back to his hotel at the end of the evening. But before long, as Mrs. Dean Martin recalled, they got a little too "gleeful" and "not discreet at all." Peter had once telephoned Marilyn to invite her to a party, and she asked who else would be there. Among the names he gave her, she recognized two high-priced call girls. She coldly declined the invitation.

Jeanne Carmen knew that Marilyn was "extremely offended by stuff like that. Whenever they treated her that way, she'd be so upset she wouldn't want to speak to any of them ever again. It wasn't that they thought of Marilyn in that way, it was just carelessness. They didn't stop to think that she would be offended."

Jack Kennedy's cavalier treatment of Marilyn left her alternately clingy, belligerent, and despondent. Her Los Angeles psychiatrist's son, Daniel Greenson, now a doctor himself, remembered going to see Marilyn that summer when his father was out of the country. "This woman was desperate. She couldn't sleep—it was the middle of the afternoon—and she said how terrible she felt about herself, how worthless she felt. She talked about being a waif, that she was ugly, that people were only nice to her for what they could get from her. She said life wasn't worth living anymore." Milt Ebbins tried to cheer Marilyn out of one of her depressive moods by telling her, "C'mon, Marilyn, you know everybody loves you." She replied, "Everybody doesn't love me. The only ones who love me are the guys who sit in the balcony and jerk off."

Marilyn was devastated when Jack Kennedy tried to distance himself from her. She began to call him at the White House and wrote him what Peter termed "rather pathetic letters." But if Marilyn hoped for some help from Peter, she soon realized it wouldn't be forthcoming, as he too began to avoid her. "I wonder where the hell Peter is?" she asked Jeanne Carmen. "I haven't been able to reach him for days." Increasingly now, Carmen noted, Peter was making himself scarce: "Peter would disappear on you when he didn't want to talk."

The President was also unavailable to Marilyn; her letters and phone calls to him went unanswered. Finally—appalled at being ignored—she threatened to reveal the affair to the press. This had the hoped-for effect: Jack responded. He sent Bobby to Los Angeles to talk to Marilyn and soothe her feelings.

According to Peter's third wife, Deborah Gould, Peter told her that Bobby's mission as messenger for his brother marked the beginning of an affair between him and Marilyn. They had been sexually intimate a few times before the encounter in Marilyn's dressing room at Madison Square Garden, but now they found themselves deeply drawn to each other—Marilyn out of a kind of desperate transference of her affection from Jack to Bobby, and Bobby because his physical attraction to Marilyn was now joined by a deep compassion for her suffering, that "directness of response to distress" that Arthur Schlesinger had observed in him.

This affair, by all accounts, was far more serious than the one between Marilyn and Jack, and it developed quickly. Bobby began to spend more time in Los Angeles, always seeing Marilyn, often at the Lawfords' house. Lynn Sherman, a neighbor of Peter's,* noticed that "there were many

---

*Not the Lynne Sherman married to Milt Ebbins.

rendezvous there. The official car used to drive up, and you knew Robert Kennedy was in town, and then the help would come in and say, 'Marilyn's arrived.' ... Sometimes I'd notice Bobby and Marilyn go out through the patio to the beach to walk."

Chuck Pick, a twenty-year-old parking attendant at Romanoff's whom Peter had befriended two years earlier, recalled working a party at the Lawford house one night. "Marilyn was there, and so was Bobby. One of the Secret Service guys said to me, 'You have eyes but you can't see, you have ears but you can't hear, and you have a mouth but you can't speak. You're gonna see a lot of things, but you have to keep quiet.'

"I didn't know what he was talking about, but a little while later I guessed. The party was breaking up, and Marilyn and Bobby were leaving together. I brought around his white 1956 T-bird and Marilyn got into it and I just sat there—I guess I wanted to sit next to Marilyn Monroe for as long as possible. Finally Bobby said, 'Okay, you can get out now,' and he got in and they drove away."

The Lawfords' next-door neighbor Peter Dye recalled Marilyn's telling him that she was "nuts" about Bobby. "Absolutely crazy. But it wasn't a physical attraction for her. It was more mental. Because she was depicted as a dumb blonde. You always want what you don't have, and Bobby was a bright guy. That's what turned her on."

Jeanne Carmen, who lived in the apartment building on Doheny Drive in Beverly Hills where Marilyn kept an apartment even after she purchased her home, remembered being at Marilyn's place once when Bobby Kennedy dropped in. "He was very surprised when I answered the door, and it seemed as though he was going to turn around and leave. But Marilyn came out of the bathroom with her robe on and her hair wrapped in a towel and she jumped into his arms and they kissed. Then we sat down, and they were kind of like two kids in love."

Marilyn had kept a diary for years, mostly to remind herself to do things and bring some organization to her sometimes jumbled affairs. Now, with the attorney general of the United States spending so much time with her, she began to jot down notes of the things she and Bobby discussed—especially after he complained that she didn't remember half the things he'd told her.

"She wanted so much to be a part of his world," Jeanne Carmen recalled. "Again, she thought Bobby would be her passport to becoming a great lady. I saw the stuff in Marilyn's diary—things about Jimmy Hoffa [the corrupt Teamsters Union leader Bobby was investigating] and Fidel Castro. It didn't mean anything to me because I was just a stupid young girl and couldn't have cared less if they all killed each other."

It seemed unlikely to Jeanne, however, that Bobby had confided in Marilyn about sensitive issues as much as her diary notations seemed to indicate. "She told me she made notes of things he told her, but you never know when your girlfriends are telling you the truth. I can't imagine him talking to her about that stuff—she wouldn't have known what he was talking about. It would have gone in one ear and out the other.

"I think she made those notes when he was talking on the telephone, in the hope of having something to talk to him about later. She'd write down big words and try to learn them so she could use them correctly later on. It probably never occurred to Bobby that she was listening to his conversations."

Neither did it occur to him, at first, that anybody else was. But by late July 1962, he, Jack, and Peter became aware of the fact that Peter's beach house, and both Marilyn's house on Fifth Helena Drive and her apartment on Doheny, were bugged. The Kennedy brothers' affairs with Marilyn Monroe, they both now realized, had left them extraordinarily vulnerable. The enemies the Kennedy administration had made—from the Mafia dons they had betrayed, to the pro-Castro forces whose leader they had attempted to kill—were not lax in collecting as much evidence of Kennedy malfeasance as possible, in the hope of retaliation.

Suddenly, Robert Kennedy's relationship with Marilyn Monroe had become dangerous—and Bobby knew he would have to end it.

TWENTY-NINE

MARILYN WAS frightened. She sat on the beach at Point Dume, north of Los Angeles, bundled against the growing chill and watching the remains of a blazing mid-July sun disappear behind the Pacific Ocean. Her companion, her old friend Bob Slatzer, listened as she poured her heart out about Bobby Kennedy, wondering why he wouldn't return her phone calls. To Slatzer's astonishment, Marilyn then said that the attorney general had promised to marry her. Slatzer tried to reason with her, tried to explain that there was no possibility that the President's brother, a staunch Catholic with seven small children, would risk such a scandal. Marilyn began to sob. "Then you're saying . . . that maybe . . . he never even meant it?"

Slatzer nodded, and Marilyn's mood, as it often did in connection with the Kennedys, changed from sadness to anger: "I was good enough to be around when he wanted to see me!"

Slatzer strongly urged Marilyn to forget the whole thing, put the Kennedys behind her, and go on with her life.

After a few moments of silence, Marilyn said, "You know something? What really has me scared is all the strange clicks and sounds I've been hearing on my phone lately. That's why I called you from a pay phone. I don't know what to think."

She had good reason to be afraid. By now, her house, like Peter Lawford's, was thoroughly bugged—a maze of electronic eavesdropping lines intermingled with the telephone wires throughout her attic. The installations allowed surveillance experts to listen both to her telephone conversations and to the activity in her bedroom through a hidden microphone.

The equipment had been in Monroe's house since March, shortly after Arthur James, a real estate agent and friend of Marilyn's, received a call from an emissary of Carmine DeSapio, the New York Tammany Hall politician with ties to the Mafia and Jimmy Hoffa, who wanted to "get" Bobby Kennedy in retaliation for his dogged investigation of Teamsters Union corruption. "The request," James told Anthony Summers, the Monroe biographer, "was that I should get Marilyn away from her house for a while. . . . They wanted her place empty so they could install bugging equipment. I knew about Marilyn's relationship with Robert Kennedy—she had told me—and that was evidently the reason for wanting to bug her."

According to Fred Otash, there were a number of people besides Jimmy Hoffa on whose behalf Marilyn Monroe's and Peter Lawford's houses were bugged. Initially, in 1959, "certain elements" of the Republican Party had hired Otash to bug Peter's house for purely political reasons. "Later," recalled Otash, "when things started developing with Giancana and Roselli and the Kennedys, there were other electronic devices installed by other people for other reasons. Now you're developing another profile to embarrass the White House, because now the Kennedys are in power. Now they're fucking over a lot of people who are taking great offense at what they're doing. You've got the Teamsters who had a hard-on for them, organized crime who had a hard-on for them, the FBI who had a hard-on for them. You had the CIA who wanted to neutralize them because they didn't want them to take over control of the agency. And the Republican Party was still interested in a derogatory profile, because they wanted them out after four fucking years."

For over two decades, Otash refused to say whether or not the Kennedys had been under surveillance, but when several of his deputies began to speak out, he joined them.

"I would have kept it quiet all my life," Otash said. "But all of a sudden I'm looking at FBI files and CIA files with quotes from my investigators telling them about the work they did on my behalf. It's stupid to sit here and deny that these things are true. Yes, we did have the place [Lawford's house] wired. Yes, I did hear a tape of Jack Kennedy fucking Monroe. But I don't want to get into the moans and groans of their relationship. They were having a sexual relationship—period."

According to Otash, Bernard Spindel, an East Coast wiretap specialist, approached him in the last months of Marilyn's life about bugging the star's house for a client Spindel would not name. "Spindel came out to California and wanted me to engineer the wiring of her home, the placing of illicit devices in the bedroom and wiretaps on the phone ... and I said, 'No, I don't want to be any part of that.' He said, 'Well, can you give us some support, some personnel?' And I said, 'Yes, I can.'"

Marilyn, it turns out, was already bugging herself. She had gone to Otash and asked him to give her electronic equipment with which she could bug her own telephone. "I have no idea why she wanted to do this," he said. "Maybe she wanted to have something she could hang over Bobby's head."

The Kennedy hairstylist Mickey Song learned that Marilyn was bugging herself from two conversations he had—one with Marilyn and one with Robert Kennedy. Late in July, Marilyn summoned Song, who happily assumed she wanted him to style her hair. When he arrived at her home, he was taken aback to find that she didn't want her hair done. Instead, she pumped Song for information about the Kennedys. "She figured who else would know more about what's going on than a hairdresser," Song said. "She was used to that at the studios, so she came right to the source."

Marilyn asked Song about both Bobby and Jack—where they had been, whether he had ever seen them with other women. "I didn't want to get involved, and I remembered how Peter, Bobby, and Jack had tested me to see if I was a gossip, so I kept telling her, 'I don't know ... I don't know.'

"She knew I was being evasive, so she said, 'Don't you want to help me?' I said, 'I don't want to get involved.'

Then she told me that the Kennedys were using me just as they were using her. She tried to make us comrades against the Kennedys. I just said, '*I'm* not being used. They're treating me great.' "

Song told Marilyn nothing, and a few weeks later, after Marilyn's death, he was glad he hadn't. "I saw Bobby and he said to me, 'You're always defending the Kennedys, aren't you? That's good.' I just thought he'd heard something about me from someone, but then he said, 'I heard a tape Marilyn made of you a couple of weeks ago.'

"I was stunned. I had no idea she was taping me. I guess she was trying to get something on them, to keep them in line. At the time, I didn't really care about Marilyn and the Kennedys. Now, I think she was abused. They played with her, and they tired of her, and I think they found her a lot of trouble to get off their hands. She wasn't going to go that easily."

By mid-July, both Kennedy brothers knew that their affairs with Marilyn Monroe had put the administration in great jeopardy. According to Otash, a disgruntled former employee of his had tipped Peter off about the bugging devices in his house. Suddenly it was clear that any number of Kennedy enemies could have gathered damaging information about the President and the attorney general—information that at the very least could be used to influence sensitive decisions or, in a worst-case scenario, might bring down the Kennedy presidency.

Robert Kennedy's first gentle attempts to extricate himself from the Monroe affair were unsuccessful. Marilyn reacted badly, refusing to accept the end of the romance without an adequate explanation. "He should face me and tell me why," she said. "Or tell me on the phone. I don't care. I just want to know *why*." A reason was not forthcoming, and Marilyn called Bobby repeatedly to get one. He changed his private office telephone number, forcing her to place calls through the Justice Department switchboard. The calls—her phone records reveal eight in a little over a month—went unanswered. Angry, Marilyn called Bobby at home for the first time, and he was furious with her.

Matters continued to worsen, and Marilyn finally turned to Pat Lawford for help. According to Jeanne Carmen, Marilyn never blamed Peter for involving her with the

Kennedys. "He was always the good guy. Peter could do no wrong as far as she was concerned."

Marilyn told Bob Slatzer that she had spoken to Pat Lawford about her problems with Bobby. "Pat told her that she really should forget it, that she should ignore Bobby's promises. She told Marilyn something like, 'Bobby's still just a little boy. But you have to remember he's a little boy with a wife and seven kids.' She told Marilyn that marriage to Bobby was out of the question. She also said that part of the reason Bobby broke off with Marilyn was tremendous pressure from his mother, Rose. She strongly disapproved of Bobby and Jack's behavior. Rose laid down the law to Bobby about Marilyn about a week before he broke things off with her."

Peter and Pat had watched Marilyn's disintegration with alarm. She was taking more and more pills to sleep at night, drinking champagne earlier and earlier in the day to elevate her moods. Her fears of aging, of losing her appeal, had been so badly exacerbated by her firing from *Something's Got to Give* and by her rejection by the Kennedy brothers that she was now chronically depressed. Increasingly, she was "letting herself go." Bill Asher remembered playing volleyball at Peter's when "Marilyn came out of the house, and it was so sad. She was wearing slacks and she had a slit in the back of her pants. She had lost all of her sense of respect for herself. By then she was unkempt and dirty and wobbly on her legs."

Don Pack, the photographer for the Santa Monica *Evening Outlook* who had befriended Peter, recalled seeing Marilyn passed out on Peter's sofa one evening. Later, Peter spoke of awakening one early morning to find Marilyn, who was sleeping over at his house, standing at a balcony railing and staring at the swimming pool below, as if she were contemplating jumping. At closer range he saw that she was crying. "I led her in and made breakfast, and Pat and I consoled her for hours. She was completely down on herself, talked about how ugly she felt, how worthless, how used and abused."

In the hope that a change of scenery might do Marilyn some good, Peter and Pat brought her in late July to the Cal-Neva Lodge in Lake Tahoe, a casino resort allegedly co-owned by Frank Sinatra and Sam Giancana. It was a disastrous weekend during which, according to restaurateur Mike

Romanoff's wife, Gloria, "they were all drinking a great deal." Marilyn told Gloria that she had become so immune to the effects of barbiturates that they no longer worked for her except in large doses. "So she'd begin about nine in the evening, and build up that lethal combination of booze and pills."

Employees of the Cal-Neva Lodge recall a depressed, withdrawn Marilyn Monroe, so afraid of being alone that she left her telephone line open to the casino switchboard when she went to bed. It was this open line that saved her life on Saturday night. The operator heard labored breathing and alerted Peter and Pat, who rushed to her room and found Marilyn on the floor, drugged, barely conscious, apparently having fallen out of bed. They revived her with coffee and long walks around the room.

Mae Shoopman was the cashier at Cal-Neva, and she recalled that Marilyn's close call was an accidental overdose. "There was no suggestion of a suicide attempt. She just couldn't sleep and took more pills than she should have."

On the trip back to Los Angeles, both Marilyn and Peter were drunk. (Pat had flown from Tahoe to Hyannis Port for a visit with her family.) The airplane pilot's widow, Barbara Lieto, recalled that Peter got into a nasty argument with her husband, Frank Lieto, over where the plane should land, insisting that the pilot touch down at Santa Monica Airport even after being told the airport was closed.

After landing at the LA airport, a staggering, barefoot Marilyn went home in a limousine and Frank Lieto and two other crew members gave Peter a ride to Santa Monica. Peter further angered Lieto when he insisted that he stop the car, although it was after midnight and they were only a few blocks from the beach house. Peter hopped out and stepped into a phone booth, where he spoke to someone for half an hour while the others waited for him with growing impatience and wondered why he couldn't have made the call from his own telephone, minutes away.

The reason, of course, was that his phone was bugged, and what Peter said during the thirty-minute conversation was of a very sensitive nature. He was warning Robert Kennedy that Marilyn Monroe had begun making threats—threats that, given her highly unstable condition, could not be taken lightly.

The most disturbing of them was Marilyn's ultimatum

that unless she heard from Bobby, unless he explained to her face-to-face why their relationship was over, she would hold a press conference and reveal their affair. She hinted to Peter that she had tapes of herself and Bobby, tapes she would play to prove what would be a startling revelation. It was the knowledge that Marilyn had bugged Bobby and might use the tapes against him that led Peter to make his frantic late-night dash to the telephone booth.

Did Marilyn seriously consider holding such a press conference, which would have created a scandal that could have toppled the administration and might have ended her own career? Or was she bluffing? Marilyn talked about it to Jeanne Carmen, and she believed Marilyn *was* serious. "She would have gone through with it. Because she didn't realize the seriousness of it. She wasn't the type of person who played games or bluffed. She was like a hurt little girl and she wanted to *get even*."

MARILYN WAS now reaching out for any kind of psychological anchor. Her near-daily sessions with her psychiatrist were not enough to ease her pain, and she constantly telephoned friends, indiscreetly telling them about her travails with Bobby. From phone booths, she called Arthur James to complain that Bobby had "cut me off cold." On August 3, she called her old friend from the time she'd been married to Arthur Miller, poet Norman Rosten. He thought her voice sounded frenetic and unnatural, and it worried him. She called Anne Karger, the mother of an early lover, to whom she sounded depressed. She told Karger she was going to marry Bobby Kennedy. Incredulous, Karger pointed out the absurdity of that notion. Marilyn quietly replied, "If he loves me, he will."

Peter tried his best to keep Marilyn calm and rational and prevent her from carrying out her threats against his brothers-in-law. On Thursday, August 2, she attended a gathering at his house. Peter's friend Dick Livingston remembered her vividly that night. "She came in carrying her own bottle of Dom Pérignon champagne. She drank it over little ice cubes from Peter's ice-cube maker. She had on the damnedest outfit—a pair of hip-huggers with a bare midriff that revealed her gallbladder operation scar and a Mexican serape wrapped around her neck. She was absolutely white, the color of alabaster."

When Livingston said to her, "My God, Marilyn—you ought to get some sun," she looked at him and whispered, "I know. What I need is a tan . . . and a man."

The next night, Friday, August 3, Peter took Marilyn to a local restaurant to dine with him and Pat Newcomb, one of Monroe's press agents and an intimate friend. Once again Marilyn became badly intoxicated, so much so that she failed to recognize Billy Travilla when he came over to the table to say hello. Travilla had designed Marilyn's clothes in eight of her biggest hits, and created her most famous outfit, the pleated white dress that swirls up around her in *The Seven Year Itch*. "She looked at me with no recognition at all," Travilla recalled. "Then all of a sudden she said, 'Billy!' I left the table very hurt and upset."

Marilyn returned home that evening drunk and determined to talk to Bobby Kennedy. She had made her last call to the Justice Department on the previous Monday, July 30—a call that lasted eight minutes, according to her phone records. Whether she spoke to Bobby or to his secretary, Angie Novello, is unknown, but she was clearly left unsatisfied. After Bob Slatzer told her that Bobby was due in California at the end of the week, she called Peter to ask where Bobby would be staying. Peter told her to call Pat in Hyannis Port. Pat told her that Bobby had a reservation at the St. Francis Hotel in San Francisco, along with his wife, Ethel, and four of his children.

The late New York *Daily News* reporter Florabel Muir, according to her former assistant Elizabeth Fancher, was one of a handful of journalists who attempted to re-create Marilyn's last days after her death. Muir paid an operator at the St. Francis for information and was told that Marilyn called Bobby several times during the day on Friday, August 3, and left messages. As far as the operator knew, the calls were not returned.

Now, in the late night hours of August 3, while Pat Newcomb slept over in another bedroom, a drunk, angry Marilyn called the St. Francis and left yet another message. Then she took some of the Nembutal sleeping pills that the Vicente Pharmacy had delivered to her earlier that day, and tried to go to sleep.

She was unsuccessful. As she told Jeanne Carmen early the next morning, she was disturbed repeatedly throughout the night by a series of anonymous telephone calls. The caller, a woman, kept repeating the same words: "Leave Bobby alone, you tramp. Leave Bobby alone." The calls didn't stop until five-thirty A.M. "Marilyn said she couldn't tell who it was," Carmen said. "She didn't think it was Ethel—she said she'd recognize Ethel's voice—but she did think it was somebody Ethel had put up to it. She said the voice did sound kind of familiar, but she couldn't place it."

Deeply rattled, Marilyn couldn't get to sleep even after the calls stopped, and by daybreak she was exhausted. She called Jeanne Carmen and suggested Carmen come over with a bag of sleeping pills and drink some wine with her. "We were sleeping-pill buddies," Carmen recalled. But she was busy that day and begged off.

THE MURKY DETAILS of Marilyn Monroe's last hours alive, and of Peter Lawford's involvement in them, have fueled speculation for three decades. Many of the principals are dead, and others have steadfastly refused to speak about these events. In recent years, however, the fog has begun to lift. More and more witnesses have come forward for the first time, and many participants have changed their stories, admitting that the rumors they had denied for years were in fact true.

It is now possible to re-create a plausible scenario, based on eyewitness accounts, of the events that led up to Marilyn's death. She was clearly frantic after her harrowing night of telephone harassment. Mrs. Murray's son-in-law, Norman Jeffries, who was doing some of the renovation work on Marilyn's home, recalled his shock at her appearance that Saturday morning: "She looked sick, desperately sick—not only in the physical sense—and I thought there must be something terribly wrong. She must have taken a lot of dope or something, or maybe she was scared out of her mind. I had never seen her look that way before."

Peter, concerned about Marilyn the night before, became alarmed at her condition that morning after talking either to her or to Pat Newcomb. Marilyn had demanded that Bobby tell her face-to-face that their relationship was over, and Peter realized that the situation was now so volatile that Bobby would have to do just that.

For years Peter would deny that Bobby was even in California that weekend, but contemporary newspaper reports and eyewitnesses prove that he was in San Francisco. One of Peter's neighbors, Ward Wood, places Bobby in Los Angeles on Saturday afternoon. And there are other accounts, secondhand but made compelling by their number, of Bobby's presence.

Sam Yorty, then the mayor of Los Angeles, recalled, "I do know that Bobby Kennedy was in town that day. He was staying at the Beverly Hilton Hotel. This was all told to me by the [Los Angeles] police chief, [William] Parker. He was very adamant that Kennedy was seen at the hotel the night of Marilyn's death."

LAPD chief of detectives Thad Brown told associates he knew Bobby was in Los Angeles that day, as did former deputy DA John Dickey. And according to both Marilyn's former business partner Milton Greene and Peter's third wife, Deborah Gould, Peter admitted to them that Bobby was in LA and that he went to see Marilyn.

Frank Neill, a former employee of Twentieth Century-Fox, later stated that Bobby arrived by helicopter at a landing pad near the studio's stage eighteen, which was often used by the Beverly Hilton Hotel for that purpose. A confidential police source supports this story.

A number of surveillance experts—among them Fred Otash and Bernard Spindel's aide Earl Jaycox—have stated that they listened to some of the tapes made at Monroe's home, including one recorded on the day she died. Their accounts of what is contained on the tapes are remarkably similar. A third (anonymous) source who listened to Spindel's tape is quoted by Anthony Summers in his Monroe biography, *Goddess*. His version, similar to the others, added an element that is especially interesting in light of the new information revealed to this author by Fred Otash and Mickey Song about Marilyn's bugging of herself and Bobby's knowledge of it. "First," the source told Summers, "you could hear Marilyn and Kennedy talking. It was kind of echoey and at a distance. . . . Their voices grew louder and louder. They were arguing about something that had been promised by Robert Kennedy. Marilyn was demanding an explanation about why Kennedy was not going to marry her. As they argued, the voices got shriller."

Bobby apparently had just learned about Marilyn's own wiretaps and was looking for a recording device or microphone. "He was asking again and again, 'Where is it? Where the fuck is it?' " The tape ended with the sound of a door slamming and then resumed, this time with another voice in addition to Marilyn's and Bobby's. Summers's source didn't recognize the voice, but was told by Spindel as they listened to the tape together that it was Peter Lawford's. "RFK was saying words to the effect, 'We have to know. It's important to the family. We can make any arrangements you want, but we must find it.'

"Apparently, he was still looking for the recording device. Then they apparently came close to where the transmitter was. There was a *clack, clack, clack* on the tape, which Bernie said he thought was hangers being pushed along a rail. . . . Kennedy was screeching, and Lawford was saying, 'Calm down, calm down. . . .' Monroe was screaming at them, ordering them out of the house."

Then, according to the source, there were "thumping, bumping noises, then muffled, calming sounds. It sounded as though she was being put on the bed." Two other people confirm the existence of this tape. Michael Morrissey, a Spindel employee who is now a Washington lawyer, listened to a few minutes of the recording and heard a bang or thump, as though someone were falling. And Bernard Spindel's doctor, Henry Kamin, said Spindel told him about the tape, described a "violent incident" on it, and was "very nervous" about having it in his possession.

Bernie Spindel's Monroe tapes were seized during a raid on his home in 1966 by New York district attorney Frank Hogan's office. Spindel told *Life* reporter John Neary, "Hogan really did Kennedy a favor by pulling the raid. They stole my tapes on Marilyn Monroe and my complete file." Spindel's lawyers sued to recover the seized materials, stating in their suit that among the items they sought to have returned were a "confidential file containing tapes and evidence concerning circumstances surrounding, and causes of death of Marilyn Monroe, which strongly suggests that the officially reported circumstances of her death are erroneous." The suit failed, as did a later one by Spindel's widow.

The FBI says that it routinely destroyed its investigative file on Spindel, but at least one document still exists to reveal that a confidential source had informed the FBI of what Spindel's tapes contained. More than half of the document is blacked out, but this remains: "He also said that Senator Bobby Kennedy was present at the time Marilyn Monroe died and ———— wanted to 'get' Bobby Kennedy off his back ———— could do so by listening to the various recordings and evidence ———— concerning Bobby Kennedy's presence there at the time."

THIRTY

IN THE decades since Marilyn Monroe's death, there has been so much obfuscation, so much evasion, so many lies told about the circumstances that many people have come to believe that Robert Kennedy and Peter Lawford were directly involved with her death, that they may even have murdered her to keep her from revealing her involvement with the Kennedy brothers. The confidential source who listened to the Spindel tapes, for instance, believed that when Peter and Bobby left Marilyn's house on Saturday afternoon she was dead.

There was, without question, a cover-up, and Peter Lawford was a part of it. But the weight of evidence points only to a cover-up of Marilyn's relationships with the Kennedy brothers, not of her murder. It is virtually certain that Robert Kennedy did not see Marilyn again after his last visit to her house, and Marilyn was still alive throughout the evening hours of August 4. She spoke on the telephone to a number of people that night, including a studio hairdresser, Sidney Guilaroff, at nine-thirty; a recent lover, José Bolanos, between nine-thirty and ten; and Jeanne Carmen at ten.

While it is possible that Kennedy returned after ten that evening, he did not do so in the company of Peter Lawford, who is firmly placed in his home between the hours of seven P.M. and one-thirty A.M. by several friends and a maid who were with him that evening.

Much more likely is that Marilyn was overwhelmed by

a crushing depression after Bobby and Peter left her house that afternoon. At four-thirty she urgently telephoned her psychiatrist, Dr. Ralph Greenson, who made a highly unusual weekend house call. The actress was extremely disturbed when Greenson came to see her. He found her, he later told the suicide prevention team that investigated her death, "depressed and drugged," "furious," and "in a rage." Circumspectly, Greenson said only that Marilyn had been involved sexually with "important men in government" and was feeling "rejected by some of the people she had been close to."

Greenson spent two and a half hours with Marilyn, after which he felt that he had calmed her down. But she remained depressed. The friends who spoke to her later in the evening say that she sounded sad and groggy, her words slurred, her responses slow.

Peter had planned a dinner party Saturday night with Marilyn and a few other friends, including the Naars, George "Bullets" Durgom, an agent friend of his, and Milt Ebbins. Despite the earlier scene with Bobby, Peter still hoped Marilyn would come, and at six o'clock he called Joe Naar, who lived near her, and asked him to pick her up on his way over. Around seven-thirty, just as the Naars were leaving the house, they got another call from Peter. Marilyn wasn't feeling well, he told them, and wouldn't be coming.

Peter didn't tell the Naars, but he was deeply disturbed by the conversation he'd just had with Marilyn. She had sounded terrible. "I could hear the depression moving in on her," he would say later. "Her voice sounded slurred, she seemed to be slipping away. She didn't understand everything I said." Peter told LA Police Department investigators in 1975 that he began to yell at her, to give her a "verbal slap in the face," but that she had simply said, "Say good-bye to Pat, say good-bye to the President, and say good-bye to yourself, because you're a nice guy." Then there was silence, as though Marilyn had not hung up but had just put the receiver down—or dropped it.

Concerned, Peter called back fifteen minutes later, but heard only a busy signal. Around eight, after several more attempts met by nothing but the busy tone, Peter called the operator to check on the line. He was told that no one was speaking on the telephone and it must be out of order.

Now Peter was deeply worried. He knew that Marilyn had very good reason to be depressed, even suicidal. Most people would have jumped in their cars and sped to Marilyn's house. But Peter Lawford was not a decisive man. He rarely took action without conferring with someone, and this night, because of the sensitive nature of Marilyn's relationships with his brothers-in-law, Peter was especially reluctant to involve himself before he sought some advice. Instead of rushing to Marilyn's aid, he picked up the telephone.

The first person he called was Ebbins, who earlier had begged off the dinner party. "Milt, a very strange thing just happened," Peter told him. He then related Marilyn's series of good-byes and said he wanted to go over and see if Marilyn was okay.

"For God's sake, Peter, you're the President's brother-in-law," Ebbins told him. "You can't go over there. Your wife's out of town. The press will have a field day. Let me get in touch with Mickey Rudin [Marilyn's attorney]. It's better to let someone in authority handle this."

Ebbins telephoned Rudin at about eight-fifteen and got his answering service. The service located Rudin at a cocktail party at the home of Mildred Allenberg, the widow of Burt Allenberg. The lawyer called Ebbins back at about eight-thirty. When Milt explained what had happened, Rudin told him to sit tight while he telephoned Eunice Murray, the lay psychiatric nurse who often spent the night at Marilyn's home.

Around nine, Rudin called Mrs. Murray at Marilyn's house. According to her, the attorney inquired as to Marilyn's welfare but did not tell her of Ebbins's inquiry or suggest that there was any reason to suspect trouble. Murray, knowing Marilyn was in bed and having no reason to think all was not well, told Rudin that as far as she knew Marilyn was fine. (Murray later said that she was out of the house for part of the afternoon and although she knew Bobby Kennedy had been there, she was not aware of an argument between him and Marilyn.)

In 1962, Rudin was interviewed by police investigators. (He has refused all requests for interviews on this subject since.) At that time, according to the interviewer's report, Rudin said that after speaking to Mrs. Murray he believed that "Miss Monroe was suffering from one of her despondent moments" and that he had "dismissed the possibility of anything further being wrong."

Rudin then called Milt Ebbins back to tell him that there was no cause for worry. "Milt," he said, "you know there isn't anything in the world I wouldn't do for Marilyn. Please don't be concerned about her."

"Well, Lawford's very worried," Ebbins replied.

"You just tell him what I said."

Ebbins called Peter, who told him that he wanted to hear directly from Rudin. When Rudin called Peter he said, "Believe me, she does this all the time. If there was any reason to be alarmed, we'd be way ahead of you because Mrs. Murray would have called us. But she does this every night."

Still, Peter told Milt he wanted to go over to Marilyn's. Finally Ebbins said to him, "So go. Get in your car and go. I can't stop you." But Peter didn't go. Instead, he made more phone calls. One of the calls, according to Dr. Robert Litman, one of the members of the suicide prevention team, was to Washington. Another was to Bill Asher, who gave him the same advice Milt Ebbins had: "I don't know, Peter. You're the President's brother-in-law. We don't want to break into Marilyn's window and find out something's happened."

While all this was going on, Peter did an excellent acting job in front of his guests. "I picked up on nothing," Dolores Naar recalled. "Except that during the evening there was a call and Peter said, 'Oh, it's Marilyn again'— like she does this all the time. His attitude didn't change. It was a very light, up evening." Erma Lee Riley, Peter's maid, agreed: "There wasn't a word of worry about Marilyn."

But by the time the Naars left the Lawford house at around eleven, Peter was very drunk—and still concerned about Marilyn. Shortly after the Naars arrived home, Peter telephoned and asked Joe to go by Marilyn's house and check on her. Joe, who had already undressed for bed, put his clothes back on and was headed out the door when Peter called again. "He said that he'd spoken to Marilyn's doctor," Dolores recalled, "and he had said that he had given her sedatives because she had been disturbed earlier and she was probably asleep, so don't bother going. He said, 'You'll just wake her up.' "

These were an odd pair of telephone calls in an evening replete with oddities. Why did Peter, who had been worried about Marilyn since seven-thirty, wait until the Naars had returned home to indicate any concern to them over Marilyn? And why did he first ask Joe to go over to Marilyn's (after being told by Mickey Rudin that she was okay) and then, just a few minutes later, tell him *not* to go? Dolores feels that the two calls were "calculated to mislead us. Joe and I wondered, 'Why did he call us the second time and tell us not to go?' Maybe because by then he knew that Marilyn was dead."

Or dying. For Marilyn Monroe's press agent—traditionally the first person notified in a Hollywood emergency—did receive an urgent telephone call during a performance at the Hollywood Bowl. Arthur Jacobs and his fiancée, Natalie, were enjoying the Henry Mancini orchestra when they were disturbed about an hour before midnight. According to Natalie Jacobs, now Arthur's widow, the call was most likely from Pat Newcomb, who worked for Jacobs, and the news was that Marilyn Monroe was dead. "Pat Newcomb was the first one at the house," Natalie Jacobs insisted.

In light of the recollections of other witnesses, however, it is more likely that Arthur Jacobs was summoned because Marilyn had fallen into unconsciousness and could not be roused. Such a situation, demanding official medical assistance, would have required under any circumstances that Marilyn's press agent be alerted. Given the potentially explosive nature of Monroe's relationships, the greatest care needed to be taken.

If Pat Newcomb alerted Arthur Jacobs to Marilyn's condition, it is likely that she also alerted Peter. This would explain his abrupt about-face with the Naars. By now, Peter would have been very near panic. If Marilyn Monroe were to die, it would be impossible to keep reporters and photographers from descending on her house and discovering any number of items linking her to the Kennedys—her diary, her personal telephone book, perhaps even a suicide note. Peter could not have been anything but frantic at the prospect.

According to several sources, the extraordinary late-night events of August 4 finally pushed Peter Lawford into action. As Dolores Naar says, "Peter probably called Jack or Bobby and was told to take care of things—do whatever he had to do. And *do it yourself*—don't involve anybody else under any circumstances."

The first thing Peter did, from all appearances, was help Bobby Kennedy leave Los Angeles. According to LA police chief William Parker, Kennedy was seen at the Beverly Hilton Hotel on Saturday night, so he did not return to San Francisco immediately after he left Marilyn's house that afternoon. William Reed Woodfield, a photographer who had taken some of the last nude photographs of Marilyn during the filming of *Something's Got to Give,* embarked on an investigation of Marilyn's death with *New York Herald Tribune* writer Joe Hyams within a few days of the event. Woodfield heard that Bobby Kennedy had been rushed by helicopter from Peter's house to Los Angeles International Airport late Saturday night.

On a pretext, Woodfield gained access to the flight logs of the helicopter company Peter used most frequently. There, for the night of August 4, he found a notation that a helicopter had been dispatched to the Lawford house for a trip to the LA airport sometime around midnight. The next morning at nine-thirty, Robert Kennedy attended Sunday mass near San Francisco.

Hyams and Woodfield knew they had the makings of a sensational story. Hyams called Robert Kennedy's Washington office for comment and was told that the attorney general would be very appreciative if the story were not run. As Woodfield recalled it, "Joe said to them, 'It will eventually come out. Why don't you just say you were at Peter Lawford's?' We weren't saying that Bobby was involved in Marilyn's death. No one would have guessed from the story that Marilyn and Bobby were involved. Still they refused to comment and asked us not to do the story."

Hyams did file the piece with the *Herald Tribune,* but the paper decided to kill it. The reporting contained, they felt, potentially libelous innuendo about the President and his brother.

WHILE ROBERT Kennedy was leaving Los Angeles, there was a great deal of activity at Marilyn's house on Fifth

Helena Drive. By the time Arthur Jacobs arrived at the scene, an ambulance had been called. James Hall, a driver for the Schaefer ambulance service, remembered that he received the call on the way back from another within a few miles of Marilyn's house. "It took us only a few minutes to get to her house."

The official version is that when Marilyn was found, she was dead in her own bed, the telephone receiver in her hand. According to Hall, when he arrived with his partner, Murray Leib,* Marilyn was in the guest bedroom, not her own room, and she was comatose but still alive. "We had to move her," Hall recalled, "because you have to put the patient on a hard surface to do CPR or else the chest just sinks into the bed. We picked her up to lay her on the floor and we dropped her. I'll never forget it because she was the only patient I ever dropped. The coroner talked about an unexplained bruise on her hip—that's where we dropped her. Dead bodies don't bruise, so she was definitely still alive.

"I applied mouth-to-mouth resuscitation and she was coming around. Pat Newcomb was hysterical. She was trying to climb over us to get to Marilyn while I was working on her. She was screaming, 'She's dead! She's dead!' over and over again and I wanted to knock the crazy bitch on her butt. She was hampering what we were doing, but I don't think even a slap on her face would have calmed her down, she was that crazy.

"Just as Marilyn started coming around, this doctor arrived. I believe it was Dr. Greenson. He had a bag with him and he looked legitimate. He said, 'I'm her doctor,' and Pat Newcomb didn't say he wasn't, so I figured everything was okay because she never would have allowed anyone near Marilyn who didn't belong there. I yielded to him and he leaned over her, pushed her breast to one side, and gave her an injection in the crease of her breast.

"This guy was inept. He was very rough. I winced and thought, 'God, that must hurt.' Then I heard a pop. It was quite a snap. One minute later she was dead. For years I've

---

*Leib refused to discuss these events.

felt that she had been given an Adrenalin shot in an attempt to save her and it had failed. But now I don't believe it was an accident. I think the shot was intended to kill her."

Hall's story has been both partially corroborated and vehemently denied. Walter Schaefer, the owner of the ambulance service, confirmed that an ambulance *was* called to Marilyn's that night. Pat Newcomb said that she did not go to Marilyn's house until four in the morning, when she received a call from Mickey Rudin that Marilyn was dead. But Natalie Jacobs insists Pat Newcomb told her that she was the first person on the scene, and Natalie believed it was Pat Newcomb who called the Hollywood Bowl that evening.

Thomas Noguchi, the Los Angeles coroner who performed the autopsy on Marilyn, stated that he examined her body carefully for needle marks, using a magnifying glass, and found nothing. But according to a bill submitted by Marilyn's physician Dr. Hyman Engelberg to the Monroe estate, he gave her an injection the day before she died. Shouldn't Noguchi have noticed an injection mark that recent? Could he have missed another?

There is no way for Hall to know whether or not the injection he witnessed was intended to help or to kill Marilyn. Dr. Daniel Greenson, Ralph Greenson's son, vociferously defended his father. "He felt sorry for Marilyn Monroe, much more than most doctors feel for their patients. He brought her over to our house a lot because she didn't have a family. That's what she really needed, he said. My sister and I did a lot of things with her, played games. She was a nice person.

"Marilyn was dead when my father arrived at her house. He felt so awful that a patient of his killed herself. It really hurt him terribly, on a personal level. If he saw someone kill her, he certainly would have said something because he would want to relieve himself [of that burden]. I hate all this speculation, and especially that guy who says he saw my father plunge a needle into Marilyn's heart. That's ridiculous, and I've got to say that it hurts me."

The true cause of Marilyn Monroe's death may never be ascertained, what with all the loose ends and contradictory statements. Little of what has been said about what occurred that night has gone unchallenged—including reports of Peter Lawford's activities.

That Peter finally did go over to Marilyn's house in an attempt to remove any evidence linking her to the Kennedys, and then went to see Fred Otash, has been attested to convincingly by Otash, by an associate of his who prefers to remain anonymous, and by two of Peter's wives. Deborah Gould states emphatically, "Peter did say that he was the first one there that morning. He never admitted that he took a suicide note, but he didn't deny it either. I still believe to this day that he did."

Peter's last wife, Patricia Seaton Lawford, told the *Los Angeles Times* in 1985 that Peter told her he had gone to see Fred Otash sometime after Marilyn's body was discovered. "He approached Otash afterward," she said. "I don't know exactly what it was about, but I think it was to make sure that nothing would harm Peter's family."

That was, of course, an overriding concern. There can be no question that a massive cover-up began the moment Marilyn Monroe died, one that would have been necessary no matter what the cause of her death. It started with a several-hour delay in notifying the police and continued with carefully rehearsed versions of what happened from Mrs. Murray and Marilyn's doctors, versions that contain glaring inconsistencies and (it was later learned) evasions. It extended the next morning to the confiscation of Marilyn's telephone records by the FBI.

It is certainly plausible that Peter Lawford would do everything possible to protect the Kennedys and that he would have turned again to the person who had helped him with sensitive matters in the past—Fred Otash.

Milt Ebbins and several other of Peter's closest friends, however, firmly believe that Lawford could not have done any such thing. "Peter never did anything by himself," Ebbins said, an observation confirmed by many of his associates. "He would have called me to go over with him, or Joe Naar or Pete Sabiston—*nine people* he would have called. And even if he did go over there, why wouldn't he have told me about it afterward? He told me everything. He knew implicitly that I could be trusted."

It *was* uncharacteristic behavior for Peter, but the situation he found himself in was extraordinary, unprecedented—and dangerous. Dolores Naar's belief that Peter was told to do what he must—and not involve *anyone* he didn't have to—makes a great deal of sense under the circumstances.

Another of Ebbins's objections to this scenario concerns time. "I spoke to Peter at his house at one-thirty that night. Bullets Durgom told me he was there until one-thirty. At three o'clock I called Peter and there was no answer. He always disconnected the phone when he went to bed. He was very drunk when I spoke to him at one-thirty, and he couldn't have driven in that condition. I'm sure he passed out and that was that."

Time frames are notoriously unreliable in reconstructions of events long past, and rarely more so than in the mystery of Marilyn Monroe's death. Mrs. Murray gave times as widely disparate as midnight and three A.M. as the point at which she realized something was wrong; Dr. Greenson said he was alerted at three; Dr. Engelberg said it was eleven or twelve. Most of the people interviewed for this book are uncertain about times. The question, "Could it have been earlier?" was answered, "Yes. Or later."

That Peter did not answer his phone when Ebbins called him at three A.M. is not proof that he was in bed, passed out. He could just as well have been at Marilyn's house or at Fred Otash's. According to Otash, Peter was "half crocked or half doped" when he arrived at his door; no matter how drunk Peter was when he heard that Marilyn was dead, the news could have sobered him up enough to drive.

Ebbins believes that Peter did nothing but grapple with indecision that night. If he did more, it was only to protect the presidency of Jack Kennedy. Fantastic speculation aside, the most plausible verdict about the death of Marilyn Monroe is that it was a suicide—either intentional or accidental—and that a full-scale cover-up was immediately put into place to keep her relationships with the Kennedys from becoming public.

The investigation of Marilyn's death was hampered at every turn. Witnesses told contradictory stories but were never questioned under oath. Evidence was confiscated, even destroyed. Police interviewers noted that some of the principals were "possibly evasive," but none of them pressed for more complete answers. The police wanted to question Peter, a key participant in Marilyn's last days, but were told that he had left town on a trip and was unavailable. Investigators never followed up with him, although he had gone no farther than Hyannis Port.

There are many reasons why the Monroe cover-up was allowed to succeed. Chief among them was the immense power and popularity of the Kennedys. Many of the key figures in the investigation were Kennedy supporters, people who were willing to turn a deaf ear and blind eye to what they were learning, or even to obstruct justice. Local law enforcement officers could do worse than ingratiate themselves with the President of the United States; at least one Los Angeles police official hoped for an administration appointment. And J. Edgar Hoover was more than happy to assist in the confiscation of Marilyn's telephone records; with this kind of ammunition against the Kennedys he need never worry about their replacing him.

It took more than twenty years for the conspiracy of silence around the Monroe case to crack, and many people refuse to talk about it to this day. Some observers believe that those who maintained their silence were rewarded. Mrs. Murray, who began to change her story in 1985, took seven trips to Europe in the years immediately following Marilyn's death, and she was not a wealthy woman.

Pat Newcomb was rumored to have gone directly to the Kennedy compound in Hyannis Port and from there on an extended vacation. Truman Capote, a close friend of Monroe's, said, "The Kennedys didn't kill her, the way some people think. She committed suicide. But they did pay one of her best friends to keep quiet about their relationship with her. The friend knew where all the skeletons were, and after Marilyn died, they sent her on a year-long cruise around the world. For a whole year no one knew where she was."

Peter, for his part, was never put on tape as saying anything other than that Marilyn's death was a tragic accident that left him deeply remorseful that he hadn't gone to her aid immediately. He insisted until his death that Bobby Kennedy was on the East Coast the night Marilyn died and that the talk of affairs between Marilyn and the Kennedy brothers was nothing but "nonsense."

He repeatedly turned down large sums of money to tell the story. In 1976, he signed a contract with a New York publisher to write his autobiography for an advance of sixty thousand dollars, and was offered another hundred thousand dollars from the *National Enquirer* for serialization rights to the book. An editor worked with Peter in Palm Springs, but after two weeks the man gave up in despair and the publishers canceled the contract: Peter refused to talk about what they really wanted him to talk about—Marilyn and the Kennedys. "When Peter was desperate for money, practically destitute, he still wouldn't do it," Milt Ebbins recalled. "He was too fond of Jackie and her kids, too fond of Jack's memory, and too conscious of his reputation in his own kids' eyes to ever do something like that."

In 1984, Peter told the *Los Angeles Times,* "Even if those things were true, I wouldn't talk about them. That's just the way I am. Plus the fact, I have four children. I'm not going to embarrass them. I'm not going to embarrass the rest of the family."

To avoid "embarrassment" at the time of Marilyn's death, Peter proved himself a master of prevarication. There was a great deal of press speculation over the identity of the "mystery caller" to whom Marilyn was supposed to have been speaking when she died, telephone in hand. Peter "revealed" to columnist Earl Wilson that he had been. "She said she felt sleepy and was going to bed," Peter said. "She picked up the phone herself on the second ring, which leads me to believe that she was fine. She did sound sleepy, but I've talked to her a hundred times and she sounded no different."

In another interview a few days later, Peter claimed to know nothing of Marilyn's tortured emotional condition toward the end of her life: "If she had fits of depression, they were behind closed doors. She was not the kind to come moaning around with her troubles. She was always gay—she 'made' our parties when she came."

ON MONDAY, August 6, Pat Lawford flew back to Los Angeles from Hyannis Port to attend Marilyn's funeral. To the Lawfords' shock, they and all of Marilyn's other Hollywood friends were barred from the services by Joe DiMaggio, who had taken over the funeral preparations. The official reason, a spokesman for DiMaggio said, was that "if we allow the Lawfords in, then we'd have to allow half of the big stars in Hollywood. Then the whole thing would turn into a circus."

Peter was outraged at his exclusion. "The whole thing was badly handled," he said. "Marilyn had lots of good friends here in town who will miss her terribly and would love to have attended her final rites."

Joe DiMaggio's private response to Peter's published comment got closer to the truth about the snub: "If it wasn't for her so-called friends, Marilyn would still be alive today." It was a comment that hit home for Peter, as did another from Dr. Ralph Greenson when he was asked who—or what—bore responsibility for Marilyn Monroe's death: "There's enough blame for everyone to share."

Peter spent the rest of his life haunted by the knowledge that a large portion of that blame was his. He had brought Marilyn into the sexually charged, politically dangerous vortex of the Kennedys, a world with which she was emotionally unable to cope. He had watched ineffectually as she repeatedly courted death with drugs and alcohol. He had been instrumental in creating the situation that would finally send her over the edge. And after she called out for help, he vacillated for hours as her life slowly slipped away.

For years afterward, Peter would break into tears whenever the subject of Marilyn's death was raised. "I blame myself for the fact that she is dead," he told journalist Malcolm Boyes in 1982. In his 1984 interview with the *Los Angeles Times,* he said, "To this day I've lived with this. I should have got in my car and gone straight to her house. I didn't do it." At that point in the interview, he broke down and cried.

The most vivid example of just how much Peter was haunted by Marilyn's death occurred about a year after the event. In Judy Garland's Los Angeles house, Scottie Singer, her young secretary-companion, was watching television; Judy was in her bedroom. Suddenly Singer heard frantic pounding at the front door. She jumped up to open it, and Peter rushed in. "Where's Judy?" he shouted. "What's happened to her?"

"Peter, what are you talking about?"

"I've gotta get to her!" He pushed past the startled young woman and ran down the hallway. Frightened now, Singer stayed right behind Peter. He swung open Judy's bedroom door and found her lying deathly still, the telephone receiver in her hand. He looked at her and his face went chalk white. "Is she breathing?" They listened in silence, and in a few moments Singer said, "Yes, Peter, she's breathing normally."

Singer told Peter to come back into the living room with her, sit down, and have a drink. After about five minutes he had calmed down enough to explain himself to her.

"Peter told me that he was talking to Judy on the phone," Singer recalled, "and she had taken some sleeping pills. She fell asleep in the middle of the conversation and Peter just freaked. Can you imagine what a horrible ride that was for him, driving clear the hell out to Judy's house, terrified that she might have died—just like Marilyn."

THIRTY-ONE

A FEW MONTHS after Marilyn's death, Mickey Song, the hairdresser, was at a Kennedy family party. The President and First Lady were there, along with Bobby and Ethel Kennedy and a dozen other family members. Everyone was having a fine time, talking and laughing, when Song piped up. "You know who I really miss?" he said to no one in particular.

"Who?" someone in the group asked.

"Marilyn Monroe," Song replied.

The entire room fell dead silent. "They looked at me like, 'How could you bring that up?' " Song recalled. "I felt terrible. I really hit a sore point when I said that."

The death of Marilyn Monroe deeply shocked the Kennedy brothers. Their cavalier attitude toward women, their recklessness, their hedonism, their arrogance—all had contributed to the death of a fragile, sensitive soul. On August 5, Jack and Bobby Kennedy became older, wiser men.

Still, the family hubris was deeply ingrained. While the Kennedys felt bad about what had happened to Marilyn, they never blamed themselves. They needed an outsider to pin the rap on—however subtly. The scapegoat, of course, was Peter. While Jack remained friendly with him, most of the others in the family ostracized him. No matter that Jack and Bobby had pushed matters to an extreme. No matter that Peter had merely offered them an ambience they ardently sought. No matter that most of the Kennedys had

partaken of Peter's life-style to one degree or another—and
no matter that Pat, at least at the beginning, had been right
there with them. Peter became a symbol of all that had gone
wrong.

"Everything he went out of his way to do for them,"
Jackie Cooper said, "they held against him. Then they didn't
want him around. They cut him off. If he had been at Chap-
paquiddick he probably would have gotten blamed for that,
too."

The Monroe tragedy also marked the beginning of the
end for the Lawford marriage. Pat had turned a blind eye
to many of the excesses that Peter and her brothers had
committed in her beach house; she had sometimes even par-
ticipated in the drinking and merrymaking. Now, however,
this life-style had claimed a victim, a woman Pat had genuinely cared about. The revelries that had allowed Peter and
Pat to avoid their problems, that had made married life
bearable for a deeply estranged couple, were finally seen for
the destructive force they were.

Peter was wracked with guilt and sorrow over Marilyn's
death, tortured by his insidious censure by most of the Kennedys, miserable at the approaching dissolution of his marriage. He now found his best comfort in alcohol. Until the
summer of 1962, Peter had imbibed primarily to have a
good time, to be one of the boys, to loosen up. Occasionally
he would overdo it, but he hadn't been using liquor as a
crutch or an escape. Now he was.

So was Pat. And with both partners drinking heavily,
a tense marriage turned volatile. "They both became so dependent on booze," Peter Sabiston said. "They accelerated
their drinking tremendously." This sometimes tore holes in
the facade of public propriety they so assiduously tried to
maintain. Matty Jordan owned the Lawfords' favorite restaurant, Matteo's, on Westwood Boulevard, and he remembered nights when Peter and Pat would sit at their regular
table and "argue all the time. When they were drinking,
they'd get into a discussion and then things would snowball
and they'd wind up fighting. They'd try to keep it under
their breath, but you could tell what was going on." What
did they fight about? Matty is succinct: "He was fucking
around with broads."

That and so much else was wrong with the Lawford

marriage by early 1963 that Peter and Pat realized it was unsalvageable, and they decided that their only recourse was to divorce—despite the fact that there had never been so much as a legal separation among the Catholic Kennedys.

That spring, Peter and Milt Ebbins flew to Washington to break the news to Jack Kennedy. In the Cabinet Room, Peter sat on a window seat with his head in his hands and wept. He told the President that his marriage to Pat couldn't be saved, that the last thing he wanted to do was cause embarrassment for the administration, that he was "sorry, Jack, so sorry."

Kennedy put a comforting hand on Peter's shoulder. "Peter, listen," he said. "Don't worry about it. If it's going to happen it's going to happen. Let me tell you something— it's not all your fault. I know Pat better than you do."

As Peter sat sniffling, Jack added, "You and I will always be friends, Peter. You're not going to lose me."

"I'm worried about the publicity, sir," Peter said. "For you, I mean—"

"Ah, it won't be such a big deal."

At this point Ebbins, who had been standing silently by, spoke up. "Jack, I think you're wrong about that."

Peter jumped to his feet. "Goddamn you, Milt! How dare you contradict the President of the United States like that?"

"Wait a minute, Peter," Jack said, raising a hand to silence him. "What do you mean, Milt?"

"Jack, if we announce this tomorrow, there will be three pictures on the front page of *The New York Times* the next morning: Peter's, Pat's—and yours."

Kennedy glanced at Peter and turned back to Ebbins. Then he said quietly, "Maybe we'd better wait."

FOR THE NEXT two years, until after the 1964 presidential election, Peter and Pat Lawford were expected to remain married—in name only. It was a tremendous strain on both of them, especially since they decided not to tell anyone but their closest, most trusted friends of the decision, in order to avoid any leaks to the press. To keep the fiction of a solid marriage alive, the Lawfords often conducted elaborate charades of happiness, inviting their friends over for dinner and parlor games as they had for years.

"They would put on a show for people," Dolores Naar recalled. "She'd call him 'honey' and 'sweetie' and it was almost funny, because Joe and I knew that they hadn't spoken to each other in private for two weeks. It was easier for them to have people around than be alone together in the house and not speak to each other."

When they did speak to each other now, it was usually to argue—and their fights sometimes turned violent. After one, Pat threw Peter out of the house. "He was crying, it was real bad," Milt Ebbins recalled. "He took a few bags and checked into the Beverly Hilton Hotel. He was at the hotel for a while and he called up this girl he'd been seeing, a former dancer from Vegas. She came and stayed with him."

After a few days, Ebbins called Pat. Icily, she told him she didn't want to talk about it. Ebbins persisted. "Just let me tell you something, Pat. If you don't do something, you're gonna see headlines you wouldn't believe. If this gets out—and you know it's bound to—you're gonna see such a scandal your head will spin."

The line went silent for a few seconds. Then Pat said, "Tell him to come back."

A few months later, however, Pat tossed Peter out again—and this time her resolve was firm. Peter remained at the Beverly Hilton for several weeks, and it was during this period that he met Scottie Singer, who accompanied Judy Garland to a gathering in Peter's suite. They joined him and "five or six guys" who were playing poker. Singer didn't play but sat on the sidelines, chatting and catching up on her knitting. As the evening progressed, several of the men got angry with Peter for not paying attention to the game—he kept talking to and flirting with Scottie Singer. She was thrilled. "When I was a girl I cut Peter's picture out of *Modern Screen* and put it on my bedroom wall. Now here I was sitting across from him—and he was still a *gorgeous* man."

Later, as everyone got up to leave, Peter made a signal to Singer. He put his hand up to his face and used his thumb and pinky to mime a telephone receiver in order to get the point across that she should call him later. When Judy turned around and saw what he was doing, he pretended to be scratching his head. Singer called when she and Judy got home. "Peter wanted me to come back that night, but I told him I couldn't leave Judy alone in the middle of the night. I told him it would have to be some other time."

A few nights later, Singer excitedly drove to the hotel for a rendezvous with her girlhood heartthrob. The evening started off like a fairy tale. A romantic candlelight dinner, witty conversation, warm compliments from a man "I still had a huge crush on." After dinner, as though in a glorious dream, she found herself wrapped in the arms of Peter Lawford. "We were on the bed, just kind of hugging and kissing, and Peter turned off the lights. I was ready for the most wonderful night of my life."

After a few minutes, she heard the bedroom door open and looked up to see the silhouette of a woman standing in the doorway. The shadowy figure, moving slowly and sensuously, approached the bed and Singer discerned that she was a beautiful black girl. "I didn't know who she was or what she was doing there. Then she started to stroke my thigh and I figured out what was going on."

Singer had never been involved in a ménage à trois. "I was hurt and astounded and offended. I wanted to make love with Peter, not with Peter and some stranger. I was hurt that he didn't seem to think I'd be enough. At first I was afraid to say anything. I kind of closed my eyes and hoped that woman would go away. Finally I said, 'Peter, I can't deal with this. I want to be alone with you.'"

Peter realized he had made a mistake. "It's no problem," he said, and told the girl that Scottie wasn't comfortable with the situation. He thanked her and walked her out of the suite. When he returned to the bedroom, he apologized profusely. "I'm sorry. I should have asked." Singer was so flustered she cannot remember whether or not she and Peter resumed their lovemaking.

Singer saw Peter several more times, always in a one-on-one situation. A few months after their first date, he brought her to the beach house when Pat was out of town and proudly showed her photographs of himself with President Kennedy. Then the two sat and talked until far into the morning.

Toward daybreak, they lay together in bed. She held his hand as he tried to fall asleep. "It wasn't a sexual relationship that Peter and I had at this point," she recalled. "It was past that. He knew I cared a great deal about him, and he cared about me. He knew he could ask me to do whatever he wanted without feeling that I would think he was weird for asking me to do it.

"He asked me if I would squeeze his nipples. I said, 'Sure,' and as I was doing it he started to tell me that he felt guilty about sex. He said that ever since he was a little boy it had been drilled into him by his mother that sex was dirty, dirty, dirty. He said that having his nipples stimulated aroused him and gave him pleasure but he didn't feel guilty about it because that didn't involve his genitals. Those were the dirty parts."

IN MAY 1963, Milt Ebbins attended a birthday celebration for John Kennedy in Washington. The President sat on the dais, and in the audience were a dozen Secret Service men and over a hundred politicians eager to be photographed with the President for the next day's papers in their home states. Milt found himself pushed by the throng against a brick wall at the back of the room.

Jack spotted Ebbins from the stage, and as he stood up to leave he motioned for Milt to join him. Secret Service men cut a path through the crowd for him, and Jack put his arm around him as they started walking together amid a crush of bodies. "Then Jack stopped," Ebbins recalled, "which he wasn't supposed to do, because then he'd be a target for a shot. He turned to me and said something, and everybody started asking, 'What did he say? *What did he say?*' "

What the President said to Ebbins was, "When are you gonna get Peter a job?"

It wasn't up to Ebbins to get Peter a job—he had an agent for that—and he was too polite to point out to the President that the fact that Peter hadn't worked for nearly a year and a half was primarily because of his relationship to the White House. Frank Sinatra's subtle blacklisting of Peter over the Palm Springs issue had been very effective— a number of producers in Hollywood would not use him under any circumstances. Others, unconcerned about Sinatra but appalled by the situation surrounding Marilyn Monroe's last months, were also unwilling to hire Peter.

Of course, there *were* producers happy to use him, but even when he was offered work, he sometimes couldn't accept an interesting role because of his sensitive position as "First Brother-in-Law." This had happened early in 1962 when director Robert Aldrich wanted Peter for a costarring role in the Bette Davis and Joan Crawford thriller *Whatever Happened to Baby Jane?*

The script and cast appealed to Peter, and he agreed to make the picture. But two days later, he had second thoughts about the part: a sleazy, pasty, whining mama's boy, eventually played in a brilliant if off-putting performance by the character actor Victor Buono. It's hard now to imagine anyone but Buono in the role, and especially not Peter Lawford. It would have been, Peter realized, far too great a stretch for him—and the character's unsavory quality would have embarrassed the Kennedys.

In July 1963, though, Peter got another chance to work with Bette Davis in an equally intriguing film, *Dead Ringer,* this time in a role much more within his range: a manipulative gigolo and blackmailer. Peter was paid forty thousand dollars for five weeks' work, and brought to the role not only his patented good looks and charm but just the right dollop of malice. It was one of Peter's more effective performances, but it was not achieved without some difficulty. For the first time in his career, Peter's personal problems affected his professionalism, and Bette Davis, for one, wasn't pleased.

"It was a very tight shooting schedule," she said. "There were times when Peter was late in the morning, and sometimes he didn't know his lines. I knew he was having problems in his marriage and I knew he was drinking. But I wouldn't stand for that kind of unprofessionalism."

According to assistant director Phil Ball, Bette remained silent for a while, then she spoke to Peter about the matter. "He was tardy very few times after that," Ball recalled. For his part, Peter remembered Bette Davis only as "understanding, kindly, patient—even maternal, if that's the word. I suspect she felt sorry for me."

He was right. "Peter was a better actor than he got credit for," Davis said. "I thought he was very good in the film. But I could see that he was having some kind of trouble." Shortly after filming she confided in a friend that she was "sad" about him. "He's unfortunate, and it's too bad."

*　　*　　*

ALTHOUGH PETER hadn't acted for a long period before *Dead Ringer,* he hadn't been completely idle. In 1961, with the help of William Peyton Marin, the Kennedy family attorney, Peter and Milt Ebbins had formed a production company called Chrislaw, so called after Peter's six-year-old son. Ebbins was named executive vice president.

Almost immediately, the company had a major production deal with United Artists, whose head, Arthur Krim, was a close friend of Joseph Kennedy's. "Joe made a couple of phone calls," Ebbins said, "and we had a deal with UA. They gave us a suite of offices and a couple of secretaries, paid all our expenses, and agreed to finance our television and movie productions. It was a very lucrative arrangement."

By 1963, Chrislaw had developed *The Patty Duke Show* for television, starring the 1962 best supporting actress Oscar winner in a dual role as "identical cousins." Bill Asher, under contract to Chrislaw, directed the first thirteen episodes of the series, a hit that lasted four seasons.

Unsurprisingly, Peter wasn't deeply involved in the business aspects of Chrislaw; he left most of that to his partner. What intrigued him was finding interesting projects and casting them with compelling actors. "Peter was very active in the creative elements of Chrislaw," Bill Asher recalled. "He had ideas, he contributed. I brought everything to Peter for his input." Also involved was Joe Kennedy, who, even after his stroke, was kept abreast of things. Asher was often "summoned to Hyannis Port to show Mr. Kennedy what we were doing. I'd show him a book we wanted to option, a script we were doing, just so he would know what was going on."

Chrislaw's first big-screen production was a well-received crime saga, *Johnny Cool,* about a mob hitman known as "the delivery boy of death." Directed by Asher and starring Henry Silva in the title role, the film was praised by many critics as a stylish throwback to the golden age of gangster movies. It featured a gallery of Peter's friends in supporting roles: Sammy Davis, Brad Dexter, Richard Anderson, Joey Bishop, and Elizabeth Montgomery, who was married to Asher at the time. It was the opportunity to utilize good actors that brought Peter the most pleasure from producing. "It's wonderful to give actors jobs," Peter said, "to bolster them and bring back their faltering confidence. As an actor I know that when you get out on that stage, you expose *you*. And the older you get, the worse it gets; you're not sure of yourself."

In the case of *Johnny Cool,* Peter made a choice of leading man that seemed ill-advised. Henry Silva had appeared in small parts in *Ocean's 11* and *Sergeants 3,* but he had never carried a movie, and *Johnny Cool* required him to be on-screen for just about the entire film. It was a risk to cast him, and there was dissension, but Peter won out. "It was a low-budget movie, and I wasn't a star, so they could get me inexpensively," Silva recalled. "But there were a lot of other inexpensive actors he could have chosen. Peter believed in me, and gave me this extraordinary opportunity. I will always be grateful to him for that."

Peter's instincts about Silva proved correct. He was terrific in the movie, and when *Johnny Cool* opened on October 2, 1963, it did very well during its first seven weeks of release. A publicity stunt around the opening created some controversy. United Artists placed an ad in the *Los Angeles Times* and the Los Angeles *Herald-Examiner* inviting any past or present members of the Cosa Nostra to write for information about a special screening of the picture and received thirty-two responses.

UA refused police requests to see the replies and would not allow plainclothes detectives to attend the screening. *Variety* reported that "about 25 persons showed up, mostly jokesters but two or three who might have been for real. . . . At any rate, the combination of the teaser ads and all the news coverage created quite a local stir and a nifty plug for the picture."

Chrislaw's first foray into film production was on its way to being a big moneymaker—the picture went on to play at one Paris theater for over a year—and Peter and Milt couldn't have been more delighted. But seven weeks after its opening in America, the bottom fell out of *Johnny Cool*'s domestic box-office receipts. As Ebbins recalled it, "After November 22, Americans were in no mood to watch movies in which people were being shot."

PART FIVE

"MORE THAN HE COULD BEAR"

Rose Kennedy used to say,
"God never gives us more than we
can bear." God gave Peter Lawford
more than he could bear.

—Leonard Gershe

THIRTY-TWO

DURING THE first week of November 1963, Milt
Ebbins telephoned Chuck Pick, the personable
young valet car parker who frequently worked parties for Peter, and asked him to come immediately to the
Chrislaw offices in the William Morris Agency building to
"discuss something important" with Peter. Pick was reluctant to go, because he was studying for his classes at UCLA,
but Ebbins stressed that the summons was an urgent one.
Once Pick got to Chrislaw, he sat on a couch across the
room from Peter's desk and waited to hear what he had in
mind.

"I'm going to Tahoe," Peter told him, "and I need
someone to go with me."

Pick was puzzled. "What do you mean?"

"I need a person to take care of my needs."

The young man frowned and said nothing. "Over the
years," he explains now, "you hear stories about people—
everybody's gay, everybody's this, everybody's that. So I'm
sitting there and I had that question in my mind—what is
he *really* saying? I guess I had a look on my face like, 'Uh,
thanks a lot but I don't think I could do that.' And he said
to me—I'll never forget it—he said, 'It's okay.' He knew
exactly what was on my mind and I knew what he was
saying—'There's not going to be any hanky-panky.' We really didn't have to be explicit about it."

Relieved, Pick asked Peter what exactly it was that he

381

would be expected to do. "Well," Peter replied, "I just need someone to help me, like with my tuxedo, making sure everything's all right."

Pick hesitated. "I valet park, Peter, but I'm not a valet."

"No, I dress myself. I just need someone to *be* there."

Pick agreed to make the trip, even though he still wasn't quite sure what would be expected of him. "I never asked him why me, why there was no one else to go with him. At that point I think I became a paid friend. He lost a lot of friends when Sinatra wrote him off, but still I thought it was very odd that he needed me—a college kid—to go to Tahoe with him."

Peter had signed to appear with Jimmy Durante for two weeks at Harrah's in a revue the pair had staged sporadically at clubs around the country over the past few years. Peter had appeared with Durante at the Desert Inn in Las Vegas the previous December, and one reason they didn't return there is contained in Peter's FBI file. A memo dated January 2, 1963, quotes a Desert Inn official that Lawford "had run wild, had signed numerous charges that were not authorized, such as gifts, railway tickets, food, and etc., and that the hotel was now stuck with the bills. Durante brought Lawford into the show over the objections of the Desert Inn, and now Durante is very embarrassed about Lawford's actions." In May 1964, the hotel sued Peter for twenty thousand dollars.

Chuck Pick met Peter in the lounge at Harrah's on Sunday, November 17. Pick had a room in the hotel; Peter planned to stay in one of the guest houses of the hotel's owner, Bill Harrah. But after the first night Peter told Pick, "I don't like this arrangement, me in the house and you in the hotel. You're coming in with me." Pick thought the house was "a fabulous place. It was right on the lake, with maid service, a cook, the whole shot. We had a Rolls-Royce that I drove. It was incredible for me."

Monday evening, Peter brought the young man backstage to his dressing room before the first show. Pick had never seen Peter act, had never watched him rehearse, had never seen his TV shows. "I had no idea what it was he did. I heard the music come up onstage, and the show started. Jimmy Durante began the show by himself, then we heard, 'Mr. Lawford, you're on in a few minutes.'"

When the cue came, Peter stuffed a big silk handkerchief in his vest pocket and bounded onstage. "When he got out there," Pick recalled, "he just lit up. He and Durante did 'The French Lesson' and some comedy shtick and then they did a few dance steps together and seemed to have a great time. It was a fun show."

After he had seen the act a few times, however, Pick was struck by the fact that everything was rehearsed to the letter. It had all seemed so spontaneous to him that first night, but now every word was the same, over and over again: "Every gesture, every chuckle, was identical. I couldn't believe it."

Sharing a house with Peter Lawford, Chuck Pick got to know him very well—and he started to see the less sunny side of the man, traits in Peter that disturbed him. "He got up with a beer. Every morning I had to be sure there was a beer bottle by his bedside—I figured it was to settle his stomach. He'd have Bloody Marys in the morning, Tanqueray in the afternoon, Jack Daniel's at night. He'd get drunk, and that's when he'd get a little nasty. I'd have to say, 'C'mon, Peter—' But he didn't do it too much to me, because he liked me a lot. He wasn't sloppy, he'd be under control. I always thought a drunk would be falling down and drooling. I never saw him like that."

After a few nights in Lake Tahoe, Peter announced that he wanted to have a party and told Pick to invite as many chorus girls and dancers as he could. "That was one of my jobs—to go around and say, 'Hey, we're having a party tonight.' Peter hated to be alone. And he liked women, liked having them around. There was never anybody specific. But after a party, he might end up with a lady."

Occasionally, Peter would ask Pick to approach a young woman for him and say, "Peter Lawford would like to see you," but more often Pick would simply notice that Peter and one of the girls had discreetly slipped into a bedroom. Always, the next morning, Peter would not want the girls to stay. "He was nice about it, I never saw him treat any of them badly. But he made it clear that they were expected to go."

On Wednesday, November 20, Peter got a call from President Kennedy. During the conversation, Jack delightedly told Peter that Jackie had agreed to accompany him on a political fence-mending trip to Texas. She rarely made such trips, but this was a particularly important one, with the next presidential election less than a year away, and Jack knew that his wife's presence at his side would help make it a success. He had pleaded with her to come, and she had finally agreed. "Isn't that great, Peter?" the President said. "We leave tomorrow morning."

After Peter's show the following night, he and Pick threw "a little get-together with some people" that lasted until four in the morning. Peter didn't have a girl stay over that night; instead he sat up with Chuck until seven A.M. Friday and talked about Jack Kennedy.

"The sun was coming up," Pick remembered, "and Peter was telling me stories about the President. We just sat around talking, and Peter spoke about how much he loved Jack and how overwhelmed he would get sometimes just thinking that his brother-in-law was the President of the United States. I was really touched by how much Peter loved the man. He was so excited that he was going to be at the White House for Christmas."

Chuck and Peter finally went to bed at seven in the morning. About three hours later, Pick heard the doorbell buzz. "I thought, 'Where's the maid?' Then I figured she must have forgotten her key and it was her buzzing." He got up, opened the door to let the maid in, and groggily turned around to go back to bed. But then he realized that it wasn't the maid at the door but a man in a suit and tie he recognized as one of the vice presidents at Harrah's. "You have to wake up Mr. Lawford," the man said.

"I can't wake up Mr. Lawford," Chuck snapped. "What is it you want?"

Pick and the man from Harrah's argued back and forth a few times about disturbing Peter until, finally, the man said, "The President was just shot."

"What do you mean?"

"The President has been shot. You'd better wake up Mr. Lawford."

Chuck went into Peter's bedroom. "He was lying there. He was a very heavy sleeper, and normally, when I woke him, I'd have to shake him and yell, 'C'mon, Peter, wake up!' But this time I just kind of stood over him and put my hand on his shoulder and he opened his eyes and it was almost like he knew. He looked at me and I said, 'Peter, the President's been shot.' "

Peter cried, "Oh my God!" and leaped out of his bed. "There wasn't a second of disbelief," Pick recalled. "Just 'Oh my God!' and up. I ran out of the room and the guy from Harrah's was standing there. I said, 'We gotta go to Los Angeles immediately.' The man said, 'Mr. Harrah's plane is at your disposal. Whatever you need.'"

Peter came out of the bedroom and said, "Chuck, we've gotta leave *now*."

It seemed to Pick that the phone was ringing constantly, that everything was happening very fast. "We put the TV on and heard that the President had been shot in a motorcade in Dallas, but there was nothing about how badly he'd been hurt. Peter started making phone calls. He called Mrs. Lawford and Rose Kennedy, but the lines were busy and he couldn't get through. Reporters started gathering outside, and the police came and blocked off the house."

Peter rushed from room to room, trying to make telephone calls, stopping only long enough to listen to a few minutes of television news. But there was none; the commentators knew nothing of what was happening at Parkland Memorial Hospital, where the President had been rushed. Peter finally got through to Pat and then to Rose, but they too were in the dark about Jack's condition.

Peter had just said once again to Chuck, "We gotta get going," when the words from the television set caught his attention: "Here is a bulletin from CBS News." He turned to the screen and saw Walter Cronkite, looking stricken, make the announcement: "President Kennedy died at one P.M. Central Time in Dallas."

"Peter got up," Chuck recalled, "went into the kitchen, and threw up all over the floor. Just threw up, everywhere. Then he fell apart. He was lying on the floor, sobbing—he was crying so hard I didn't know what to do. I never witnessed anything like that in my life. I never saw a man break down the way he broke down. It was a terrible thing to watch. It scared me. I went over to him and he said, 'Leave me alone.'

"I was just a kid. I didn't know what was happening. I started crying, as much because of what I was seeing happen to Peter as because the President was dead. But I had to be okay because he was so bad. One of us had to be strong and keep it together, and I was it. I was the only person he could really hold on to."

Within an hour, Chuck and Peter were on the way to the airport. Later, Chuck didn't remember getting dressed. "I don't even think we brought our luggage. We just left. Peter didn't want to go through the crowd out front, but the police escorted us through it and took us to Tahoe airport and we took Bill Harrah's plane. There was a lot of crying and sobbing on that plane."

When they arrived at Santa Monica Airport, a helicopter awaited them. "We got out of the plane and ran to the helicopter and Milt Ebbins was there. It was just a three-person helicopter—there was only room for Peter, the pilot, and Milt. I said, 'Peter, I'll take a cab home. I'll be okay.'

"He said, 'No, no, I can't leave you like this.' I said, 'Just go.' Peter asked me if I'd call him when I got home. I said I would. And then they took off. I took a cab home and I called the house and told someone that if Peter needed me I'd be available."

BY THE TIME Peter and his manager arrived at the beach house, it had been overrun by reporters, curiosity seekers, and friends who had come to pay their respects. A priest and two nuns had been to see Pat, as had Dr. Charles Sturdevant, the chief of psychiatry at St. John's Hospital, who had put her under sedation.

Leonard Gershe wasn't sure if it would be appropriate for him to go by the Lawford house, but when he did he was told he was expected. "It was frantic," he remembered. "The phone never stopped—the White House calling, this person calling. The Naars were there, and the Dyes from next door, and people just kept coming in and out. Judy Garland was there. She was drinking and carrying on, going, 'Oh my God, I'll never sing "Over the Rainbow" to him again.'

"Pat didn't cry. She couldn't cry. She looked at you like she was almost autistic. But who could blame her? Your heart just went out to her. Peter was very strong. I remember him being in control. I think the fact that Pat was there made him keep it together."

While Peter made arrangements for the flight back to Washington for the funeral, Ebbins took a call from Le-Moyne Billings, the Kennedy confidant. Billings told Ebbins to let Pat know that he would be flying out to escort her back to the capital. Apparently, the Kennedys were prepared to exclude Peter from the funeral. "Lem," Ebbins told him, "let me call you back."

Ebbins went upstairs to talk to Pat. "She was in her bed, just lying there, staring straight ahead, everything drained out of her." He told her, as gently as possible, about Billings's call. Softly, she replied, "I'm going back with my husband." Ebbins called Billings back and no mention was made of the matter again.

At ten fifty-five that night, Peter, Pat, Milt, and seven-year-old Sydney boarded an American Airlines flight to Washington. (Eight-year-old Christopher didn't want to make the trip.) Ebbins could see that "Pat was so destroyed, she was like a zombie. She's not the kind of woman you ever think you'll see cry, but she cried on that plane. It was only a few seconds of tears every so often, though, and then she'd buck up and force herself to stop and her face would be strong again."

Purely by coincidence, Peter's frequent director Don Weis was on the same plane. Peter knew that Don's wife was seeing Dr. Max Jacobson, known as "Dr. Feelgood," a New York physician who had developed what he called a vitamin pill (sometimes an injection) that gave his patients energy and a sense of well-being. Both the President and Jackie had been regular "Feelgood" patients; Peter had had one injection and didn't like it. "There's something else in those shots besides vitamins," he had complained, and had never taken another.

Peter was right. The formula Jacobson had devised included amphetamines, "speed" drugs now known to be addictive and to cause mental and physical deterioration with prolonged use. In 1963, however, Jacobson's pills seemed like a panacea. Peter drank heavily on the plane, but Pat abstained, afraid alcohol wouldn't mix with her sedative. Peter asked Weis if he had any of Jacobson's pills, and Weis gave him one for Pat, who welcomed the release. "She got very happy on it," Weis remembers. "It was shocking. She acted silly. It was not the trip back you would expect from Pat Lawford. But it wasn't her fault. I gave her the pill."

THE LONG weekend of John Kennedy's funeral was like a surrealistic dream. Two hundred dignitaries from a hundred countries attended the rites, which were televised by satellite to virtually every country in the world—the first time in history that an event had been viewed simultaneously by the entire planet.

It was a majestic ceremonial good-bye to the man who had become, in less than three years in office, one of the most beloved presidents in history. A horse-drawn caisson bore his body to the Capitol rotunda on Sunday. On Monday a twenty-one-gun salute was fired, fifty jet planes flew overhead, and *Air Force One* dipped a wing in tribute. A requiem mass was celebrated at St. Matthew's Church, and an eternal flame was lighted over the grave into which he was lowered in Arlington National Cemetery. The First Lady, a widow whose dignity touched the world, was given the flag that had draped her husband's coffin.

What moved Milt Ebbins the most amidst all this pageantry, however, was a small moment he witnessed in the East Room, where the President's casket lay in state, flanked by guards representing the branches of the United States military. "Bobby came in," Ebbins recalled, "and threw his arms over the coffin and started talking to Jack. It broke my heart."

But the overriding motif of Jack Kennedy's funeral was of an Irish wake. "We had dinner in the White House every night," Ebbins recalled. "Jack's friends, Rose Kennedy, Ethel Kennedy. You'd never know it was a funeral. Jokes were being told at the table. Ethel was very funny. I tried to tell Pat about seeing Bobby in the East Room and she curtly cut me off—'We don't want to hear about that.' "

Peter was astonished by the merrymaking. "Everybody was up," he said, "drinking, smiling, and trying to make the best of it. There were even bad jokes about the costumes we were wearing. Not being Irish, I tried to get into the swing of it, but I was thoroughly destroyed. Looking back, I realize the way President Kennedy's death was handled was really the best way, even with the bad jokes. I think John F. would have looked on too much grief as unproductive."

THE TRAGEDY that brought much of the world together in grief didn't have the same effect on Peter and Pat. Publicly, they were united, walking alongside each other behind

Jackie, Bobby, and Ted as they followed the President's horse-drawn caisson. Privately, there was an impenetrable wall between them. They slept in separate bedrooms in the White House, and when Peter needed a woman's comfort, he didn't turn to Pat.

On Sunday night, at two in the morning, Peter asked Ebbins to come with him to get some air. He summoned the White House car and he and Milt went for a drive. After a few minutes, Peter told the driver to take them to the Shoreham Hotel. When Ebbins gave Peter a quizzical look, he told him, "I'm going to stop and say hello to Layte—she's in town overnight, switching planes."

Layte Bowden was a beautiful young stewardess who had worked on the *Air Force One* press plane and had the Secret Service code name "Mrs. Black." For over a year, she and Peter had had a sporadic affair, and it would continue for several more years.

"Do you think that's a good idea, Peter, going to see her in the White House car?" Ebbins asked.

"They don't know what the hell I'm doing," Peter replied. "How would they know? Pat's in the White House."

The car pulled up in front of the Shoreham. Peter got out and told Ebbins, "I'll only be a few minutes."

"That son of a bitch!" Ebbins recalled. "He kept me sitting in that car for an hour!"

On Tuesday, the day after the funeral, the Kennedy family repaired to Hyannis Port for their Thanksgiving holiday. All except Peter. With his estrangement from Pat, he couldn't see any reason to accompany them. Instead, he decided to resume his show in Lake Tahoe, where he had a contract at Harrah's and felt an obligation to Jimmy Durante. The Kennedys were displeased. The press criticized his action as unseemly. Many observers were puzzled.

Including Chuck Pick when Peter asked him to join him once again in Tahoe. "To this day I don't understand it," Pick said. "My mother kept asking me, 'Why is he doing that?' But I guess everybody else goes back to work, why shouldn't he? He just happened to be a performer. Peter wanted me to go back up there with him, and at that point I felt such a kinship to him—I want to say a love. There was a very special bond between us at that time because of what had happened in that house when we heard the news."

Pick was told to meet Peter at the LA airport in the Ambassador Room of TWA. "I got there and I saw Peter, with his back to me. I walked in and I was pretty shaken. He turned around and his first words to me were, 'I'm sorry I had to leave you at the Santa Monica Airport.' I can't tell you what that did to me. After all he had been through, he was still concerned about leaving me at Santa Monica Airport. I broke down and cried."

Peter completed the second week of the engagement, but things were very different. "It wasn't easy for him to sing those songs and be amusing," Pick recalled. "The show wasn't always good; he'd miss lines. He cried a lot backstage. There were no more parties; he didn't care about that. He'd just come home after the show, drink Jack Daniel's, and go to bed."

It took Chuck Pick a long time to get up the courage to ask Peter what had really happened that terrible day in Dallas. There were rumors of conspiracy, suggestions that the accused assassin, Lee Harvey Oswald, hadn't acted alone. There were dark hints that the Kennedy murder had been a Mafia hit, retaliation for Jack and Bobby's "betrayal" of the mob.

"You'll never know the truth of what happened in Dallas," Peter told Chuck. "You'll never know the truth." Pick tried to get him to explain himself, but he wouldn't. "I interpreted it as meaning that he knew what happened and few other people ever would," Chuck said.

Paul Wurtzel, the assistant director on *Dear Phoebe* and *The Thin Man,* remained friendly with Peter and became a student of the Kennedy assassination. Reluctant to query Peter, he nevertheless asked him to answer one question: "Did Oswald kill Kennedy or was it higher up?"

"It was higher up," Peter answered.

"I let it drop," Wurtzel said, "and I never asked him what he meant. I'm sure he wouldn't have said anything more to me. He still had kids and the family."

"JOHN F. would have looked on too much grief as unproductive." Still, Peter allowed his grief to overwhelm him, to affect every aspect of his life. His drinking now became virtually constant, his emotions often uncontrollable. He would break into sobs at the slightest provocation. He felt that his entire world had been snatched from him, and he didn't understand why. His grieving was so intense and so protracted that some of his friends lost patience with him.

One of them was Bill Asher. "We spent a lot of time with him after the assassination," the director recalled, "and it was very difficult. He was devastated—the crying jags! It was impossible to pull him out of it. Then he'd get belligerent. But mostly he would cry. I would stay up with him all night and talk to him. I said to him, 'Peter, you're not grieving for Jack Kennedy, you're grieving for you. You can't do that.' But life had dealt him the final killer blow. It just destroyed him."

Peter leaned more and more now on Chuck Pick, who frequently stayed at the beach house so that Peter wouldn't be alone. "He cried on my shoulder a lot. He'd come home late at night, drunk, and start crying and say, 'Why, Chuck, why?' What do you say to a man who's twice your age and he's supposed to be the wise one? He kept asking me why his life was falling apart. First he lost his friendship with Sinatra, then Marilyn died, then Jack was murdered. And his marriage was over."

Pick watched helplessly as Peter drank himself into a stupor night after night, sopped in alcohol and his own misery. "Sometimes he'd get nasty and I'd go home and think, 'What am I doing this for?' But he'd apologize the next day. I felt so sorry for him, after seeing what he went through that morning when Jack was killed, that there was nothing he could do to hurt me to the point that I would desert him. I wanted to be there for him, always."

THIRTY-THREE

O N DECEMBER 11, 1963, at eleven in the morning,
an envelope addressed to Peter was delivered to the
Lawford house in Santa Monica. Peter was in New
York, and Pat gave the letter to Milt Ebbins. Inside was a
note, crudely scrawled and misspelled as if by a backward
child: "Mr Lawfrod. Call Mr Sinatra at Mapas Hotel in
Reno. Tell him to call you back on untapped phone. Tell
him to play it cool because we have a spy. So if he don't
cooperate Jr. gets a 45 slug in his head."

Along with the note to Peter was one for Frank Sinatra,
in which he was told that his son, Frank Junior, who had
been kidnapped on December 8, was all right and would
be returned to him in exchange for two hundred thousand
dollars in fives, tens, and twenties. The money was to be
delivered by Peter at midnight on December 11 at the life-
guard station at Venice Beach.

Frank Junior was nineteen and aspiring to a singing
career like his father's, although his talents were more limited. Just before going on with his lounge act at Harrah's,
he had been abducted from his hotel room by two armed
men who had stuffed him into the trunk of their Chevrolet
and driven him through a blizzard to Los Angeles.

When the young man's father got the news in Palm
Springs, he telephoned Peter—the first time in almost two
years the two men had spoken. Sinatra asked Peter to call
Robert Kennedy and make sure that every resource of the

FBI was committed to finding his son. "There was no hello, no apology, nothing like that," Peter later said. Nonetheless, he called Bobby Kennedy, who had remained attorney general under the new president, Lyndon Johnson, and was told that the FBI would do everything within its power. Its agents would work around the clock; roadblocks had been set up at all state borders. "I know how Frank feels about me," Kennedy said to Peter, "but please tell him that everything is being done, and we'll get his boy back as soon as possible."

Peter was frantic over the kidnapping. FBI files indicate that he telephoned the New York bureau office repeatedly, seeking news about the investigation. An internal FBI memo dated December 10 (its sender's name is blacked out) noted that at around midnight on December 9 the New York office "received a call from Peter Lawford, who asked if there had been any developments in the Sinatra kidnapping case. Lawford called again about 3 A.M. and repeated the question. He appeared to have been drinking.

"Lawford called again this afternoon," the memo continued, "and asked about developments in the case. I told [the New York supervisor] he should tell Lawford very firmly that while we are investigating, there was no information that could be furnished to him, so as to discourage any further inquiries from him."

Alongside this last sentence, in the distinctive handwriting of J. Edgar Hoover, is the notation: "Right. Lawford is just a bum."

The ransom note mailed to Peter was postmarked before Frank Junior was released, but by the time it was delivered Frank Senior had received other word of the kidnappers' demand, paid the ransom, and been reunited with his son. The next day, the kidnappers were captured and most of the money recovered.

Sinatra threw a lavish party to celebrate his son's safe return. He invited the FBI men who had conducted the investigation, all the Rat Packers, Jimmy Van Heusen, Mike and Gloria Romanoff, his Palm Springs neighbors, and dozens of others. Peter was excluded, and Sinatra never again uttered a word to him.

FIVE MONTHS after the events in Dallas, the Lawford marriage remained in an uncomfortable state of limbo. Pat stayed in the East most of the time, returning to Santa Monica only when Peter was out of town. When she and Peter were together in California they would most often sit at home or in Matteo's and share alcohol and sorrow. "After Jack's assassination," Dolores Naar recalled, "night after night Pat would cry in her bed. She was always taking these big red capsules to help her sleep. The poor thing was absolutely devastated—I didn't know if she was going to survive."

Pat was able to pull herself together, but she didn't have the same success with her marriage. The problems she and Peter had had for most of their life together were only worsened by the tragedy they'd been through. Peter drank more and sought comfort with other women more often. "It got so bad," Bill Asher said, "that it was embarrassing to Patricia. He was doing dumb things—having affairs and drinking and taking drugs, and it got so that I knew there was no hope for the marriage."

But still the Lawfords were forced to remain married. President Kennedy's reelection, of course, was no longer a consideration in the timing of a Lawford divorce, but now there was a new factor: Bobby's decision to seek election as a U.S. senator from New York. He had stayed on as attorney general purely for the sake of continuity; he had long despised Lyndon Johnson and looked on his succession as a usurpation of his brother. Now, after a reasonable amount of time had passed, Bobby felt ready to move on.

Early in 1964, he began to reconnoiter for a suitable Senate seat. Massachusetts, the most likely state for him to represent, was out of the question because Teddy had succeeded Jack as a senator there in a 1962 special election. New York was the next clear choice; the Kennedys had lived there for many years, and despite a Democratic majority among registered voters, the state had two Republican senators. Still, the race wouldn't be an easy one, even with the groundswell of sympathy and affection for the Kennedys. New York wasn't Massachusetts, where the Kennedys were shoo-ins for just about any office they wanted. Bobby had never been elected to anything. And he would be running against a popular incumbent, Kenneth Keating.

Even if Bobby were to win, he would have to prove himself effective in the Senate as his own man, not merely

I didn't like. When I said I couldn't do what he wanted he got real nasty.

"I wanted to leave, but he wanted someone to stay with him until he went to sleep. He was taking Quaaludes. I sat downstairs in the living room and I didn't know how to get out of there. I was a little frightened. Finally at dawn I got a taxi and left."

A YEAR OF idleness since President Kennedy's murder had not helped alleviate Peter's grief. Everywhere he turned, there were reminders of Marilyn and Jack; magazine covers, newspaper articles, television documentaries. Even, sometimes, living embodiments. Chuck Pick recalled that before the November 1964 elections, Ted Kennedy was at Peter's house for a political fund-raiser: "Peter and I were in the den, and Ted was in the living room. We heard Ted say something and it sounded just like Jack. Peter broke down on the couch and started crying."

Milt Ebbins hoped that having Peter come to the Chris-law offices every day would take his mind off his sorrow, provide him with some immediate goals, give his everyday life some structure. It didn't work. The duties at Chrislaw—the company was now producing a film for Patty Duke called *Billie*—could be handled well enough without him, and there was really no one for Peter to answer to if he didn't show up. Bonnie Williams, now a Chrislaw secretary, recalled that "he was drinking a lot, and we had a great deal of difficulty getting him to come to work in the morning. Sometimes we had to go out to the house and help him get up."

A movie role, Ebbins hoped, would force Peter to pull himself together. In the fall of 1964, Martin Poll, the producer, hired Peter for his film *Sylvia* to play a wealthy man about to marry a beautiful, mysterious young woman played by Carroll Baker. The picture was unmemorable and did nothing to further the careers of anyone involved in it. Luckily, by the time of its release, Peter, Carroll Baker, and their director Gordon Douglas had all been signed to reunite in a much more interesting project: Joseph E. Levine's film version of Irving Shulman's *Harlow,* the controversial best-seller about the life of MGM's shimmering, sassy blond sex symbol of the thirties, Jean Harlow.

Carroll Baker, who had created a sensation in 1956 playing the sultry child-wife in *Baby Doll,* was being strongly hyped as the successor to Marilyn Monroe, who had long been considered the only actress who could do justice to Harlow on-screen. After her death, there was a vacuum in Hollywood that Carroll Baker and Carol Lynley were both trying to fill. Lynley, in fact, had been hired for a low-budget film of Harlow's life that was intended to compete with Levine's "official" version. Clearly, however, neither Baker nor Lynley had the complex allure of Monroe—or of Jean Harlow, for that matter.

Still, casting Jean Harlow was much less difficult than casting her husband, Paul Bern. Shulman had shocked readers with the tawdry details of Harlow's brief marriage to the forty-three-year-old MGM executive who—mortified and enraged by his sexual impotence—had first beat his bride with a cane on their wedding night and then, a few months later, killed himself after Harlow laughed at him when he entered her bedroom brandishing a dildo. (Five years later, Harlow herself was dead, a victim of uremic poisoning likely caused by a kidney injury she suffered when Bern beat her.)

Bern would be a thankless role, and certainly not one that most producers would think of Peter Lawford to play. But when the idea came up, Joe Levine and Gordon Douglas agreed it was just quirky enough to work. They did wonder whether Lawford would be willing to take such a big career risk.

He was. The drawbacks of playing so miserable a character were outweighed, in his view, by the sheer acting challenge of it. Acting challenges were not something Peter had been often asked to take on, and now that he was no longer concerned about being "a Kennedy" his options had expanded greatly. Most important, *Harlow* was a movie based on the most talked-about book of the year, produced by the hottest producer in Hollywood, and costarring the most publicized blond bombshell since Monroe. A major role in this film—even that of Paul Bern—could do nothing but bolster Peter's flagging stock in Hollywood.

Which isn't to say that Peter wasn't embarrassed to be playing Bern when the announcement was made. He felt it necessary to tell the press at a party Joe Levine threw to kick off the picture, "Thank goodness nobody can doubt me—I've got four kids."

What few could have suspected at the time was that enacting Paul Bern would be one of the most emotionally trying experiences of Peter's professional life. For the past several years, he *had* been grappling with impotency himself, a problem exacerbated by his drinking binges and anxieties. Playing Paul Bern was so deeply resonant an experience for Peter that it kept him in a fragile emotional condition throughout the filming in the early spring of 1965. Frequently he arrived on the set late, hung over, unable to remember his lines. Assistant director David Salven recalled that there was little sympathy for Peter when scenes had to be reshot again and again before he was able to recite the dialogue correctly. "At one point he needed cue cards. Everybody would say, 'If you drank sixty-five quarts of vodka every day, you'd have trouble remembering where to find the *studio*.' Some people would try to make excuses for him, and the usual reaction was, 'The fucker's drunk, that's all.' Nobody knew that he was impotent; nobody knew what he was going through."

Ken DuMain, who hadn't worked with Peter for several years, was his stand-in again for *Harlow,* and he was shocked at his condition. "When I came in, they were doing a scene in a restaurant with Carroll Baker and Peter, and he was in bad shape. He had been drinking, and he was hung over and his face was puffy. I felt very sorry for him. It's embarrassing when an actor blows his lines again and again."

The director called a break, and DuMain walked over to Peter. "Give me your script," he told him. "I'll go over your lines with you." The two men went outside and walked around the lot, rehearsing the sides of dialogue. "When we finished," DuMain recalled, "Peter told me that of all the telegrams he and Pat had received after President Kennedy's assassination, mine had touched them the most deeply. When we got back to the set, Peter went through the scene again and it was perfect. They printed it."

HARLOW, ALTHOUGH sumptuous to look at, was not a good film and was widely panned. It was a box-office hit, however, primarily because of the avalanche of publicity that surrounded it. Joseph Levine once said, "You can fool all the people all the time if the advice is right and the budget is big enough." Few critics were fooled by *Harlow* because although the budget was huge, the advice was abysmal.

Rather than tell the Harlow story as it actually happened, Levine, Douglas, and screenwriter John Michael Hayes opted for the clichéd Hollywood yarn of a virginal young girl thrown to the show-business wolves who triumphs on-screen but, in life, experiences tragedy and early death.

Because Joe Levine knew that Carol Lynley's rival version was in the works, *Harlow* was a very rushed production. John Michael Hayes had been brought in to "de-sexify" the original script by Sydney Boehm, and Carroll Baker was so grateful for his rapid rewrite that she gave Hayes one third of her fifteen percent profit participation in the picture. Editing was done on scenes that had already been shot at the same time that other scenes were still being filmed, and on the last day of production Neal Hefti, the composer, had already scored nine reels of music for the film. There was virtually no postproduction work.

Many of *Harlow*'s shortcomings can be attributed either to this rush or to the censorship restrictions of the day. Presenting Jean Harlow as the salty-tongued, sexually profligate woman she was would have created problems with the Catholic Legion of Decency that Joe Levine preferred to avoid. And certainly Paul Bern's sexual problems presented a thorny issue. The producers grappled with whether to show the events that preceded Bern's suicide—the centerpiece of the book—or merely refer to them.

Douglas did film Peter and Carroll in what the crew dubbed "the dildo sequence," but the scene ended up on the cutting-room floor, along with any other explicit evidence of the characters' sexual problems. According to participants in the filming, the sequence contained some of the best acting Peter Lawford had ever done. "The performance Peter gave as Paul Bern was brilliant," Carroll Baker recalled. "What I saw him do in that scene was really magnificent. He was touching, he was real. I was knocked out."

The one scene in the released version in which Peter is given free rein to emote—his final appearance in the picture—shows Bern begging Jean to give him another chance. "Help me over this," he pleads. "I'll go to a psychiatrist. Give me a chance—give me time."

Jean Harlow did try to help Paul Bern. She urged him to see a doctor, and she agreed to remain under the same roof with him so that he could save face. In the film version, she is not only unsympathetic but cruel. "Fifty million men, and I had to marry you," she snorts. When he pleads for her help she tells him, "I'm just an ordinary woman with the same ordinary fears and problems—"

"Then you should understand my problem," Bern says.

"I said *ordinary*!"

Now in tears, Bern says, "I couldn't live if I couldn't make it up to you."

"It's all so *sick*!"

"Please, Jean," Bern sobs. "Don't expose me to people for what I am."

Peter's performance of this exchange, enormously touching, caused the crew to burst into spontaneous applause when it was over. Milt Ebbins watched the scene being shot. "Peter wasn't acting," he recalled. "He was really feeling all those emotions."

THIRTY-FOUR

AS LATE as the winter of 1965, Peter harbored hope that his marriage could be salvaged. To him, a divorce from Pat would signify the end of his association with the Kennedys, would mark, with awful finality, the end of Camelot. Peter knew, of course, that those days were over, but something within him refused to accept fully that the glory was unrecoverable. Maybe, if he and Pat could reconcile, and Bobby ran for President . . .

But Pat pressed on with the divorce plans. With Bobby having been elected by a wide margin to represent New York in the Senate and having quickly established a national constituency, there was no longer, in her view, any reason to delay. She notified Peter that she wanted to draw up a separation agreement and then proceed with a divorce.

Jackie and Barbara Cooper were visiting Peter at the beach house when he telephoned Pat in Hyannis Port to ask her to reconsider. According to Jackie, "He wanted to get back together with her, and it was like, 'Wait until you see what I'm gonna say to her'—he was pretty sure he could convince her."

He never got the chance. Bobby intercepted the call, and the Coopers will never forget the one-sidedness of the conversation. "You mean, I'm never to see her again?" Peter said into the phone. "I'm never to call or come there? And she's never coming back here?"

When the conversation was over, Peter's eyes were filled with tears. Astounded by what she had heard, Barbara asked Peter, "How can you let your brother-in-law talk to you that way?"

Wiping his eyes, Peter softly responded, "When that family tells you you're not going to do something, you're not going to do it."

"Why?"

"Because you'll suffer sooner or later. You learn that very quickly. If they say don't do it, you don't do it."

On December 17, Peter and Pat signed a legal separation agreement. The document, never made public, granted "sole and exclusive" custody of the children to Pat, but allowed Peter to consult with her on the choice of schools they would attend—with the stipulation, "final selection of such schools shall be made by wife." Peter's visitation rights were limited to one Saturday or Sunday per month, with prior notification, if he was "living far away." If he lived nearby, he was allowed to visit the children one day every weekend. Once the children reached age sixteen, they would be permitted to visit their father, with "transportation expenses to be paid by husband."

All property belonging separately to Peter and Pat remained their own, and each waived any right to the other's estate. The Santa Monica house and contents were to be sold, and twenty-five thousand dollars of the proceeds, after the first mortgage was paid, was to be given to Peter, with the balance applied to a fifty-two-thousand-dollar second mortgage Peter had borrowed from Pat. Until the sale of the house, Peter was required to repay the debt to Pat in installments of three thousand dollars per year.

The agreement called for no alimony from either party and no child support payments from Peter. After he signed the document, however, Peter felt that he should have some financial obligation to his children. Pat told him that wasn't necessary, that she had enough money to take care of their every need. But he insisted, stressing that it was important to him that he contribute in some way to their well-being. Pat finally agreed that if Peter really wanted to he could pay four hundred dollars a month in child support.

Peter made the first two monthly payments and then never made another one.

* * *

ON DECEMBER 20, Pat and her four children joined Jackie, Caroline, and John Junior, along with Bobby, Ethel, and most of their children, for a Christmas ski holiday in Sun Valley, Idaho. The national press sat up and took notice, because rumors of an impending Lawford divorce had been swirling for months, and Sun Valley, with its short six-week residency requirement, had become the divorce mecca of America's socialites.

Pat would not confirm the rumors until she was ready to make an official announcement. To help shield her sister-in-law from reporters, Jackie Kennedy made herself uncharacteristically available to the press. One British journalist commented, "It was obvious that Jackie, who doesn't grant interviews, had done so to steer us away from the story we were really digging for."

The Kennedys left Idaho on January 5, 1966, but Pat stayed behind and took a suite at the Sun Valley Lodge in order to wait out the residency requirement. Now there was no denying it, and the Kennedy family attorney, William Peyton Marin, made the announcement of an "amicable separation." He said nothing about a divorce, but one clearly was imminent.

The encroaching finality of it unsettled Pat's resolve. She called Peter several times a day to ask him, "Why am I here? What am I doing?" Again and again she wavered; according to Milt Ebbins, Pat didn't really want to divorce Peter. "She still loved him. But in the end she had no choice. She knew that she couldn't live with Peter anymore. She hated hearing all those things about him all the time."

The day after Pat met the minimum residency requirement, she spent eight minutes on the witness stand in the courtroom of Judge Charles Scoggin to explain why she should be granted a divorce. Dressed in a simple black suit and black leather gloves, she sat with her head lowered most of the time, looking up only occasionally to answer questions. She charged Peter with mental cruelty and testified that her differences with him were irreconcilable. After testimony from the owner of the Sun Valley Lodge established Pat's residency, the divorce was granted.

The next day, Pat was back in New York—and having dinner with Peter. The New York press ran front-page photographs of the couple leaving the Colony restaurant and wondered if there was a reconciliation in the works. Peter simply said that he and Pat had gotten together "to discuss matters that involved the children."

What they actually discussed was the state of Peter's health. He had been having stomach cramps for over a year and had been told by a New York doctor that his liver was enlarged and he would have to stop drinking. He hadn't, and the cramps had grown worse. All this time, Peter had refused to undergo a full battery of diagnostic tests, but his discomfort was now so great that Milt Ebbins and Pat urged him to check into the Lahey Clinic in Boston, a Kennedy-endowed medical center within the New England Baptist Hospital. There, he would receive some of the best treatment in the world, all of it free.

Peter, worried about what the doctors might find, was reluctant, but he agreed to check into Lahey if Ebbins would accompany him. Dutifully, Ebbins went along, expecting to have a room of his own. Instead, Peter insisted that a second bed be brought into his room for Milt. "C'mon, Peter, you're a grown man," Ebbins told him. "I'll be nearby." But Peter wouldn't budge. "If you don't stay in my room with me, I'm leaving." Milt stayed, and when Ted Kennedy came by to visit one day he commented, "This doesn't look too good. Aren't people talking about you two guys in this place?"

At Lahey, Peter was under the care of Dr. John W. Norcross, one of the top liver specialists in the world. For three days he ran diagnostic tests on Peter to ascertain the cause of his stomach pain. When the tests were completed, a nurse approached Peter's roommate and asked to speak to him privately. "Mr. Ebbins," she said, "there's something awry with Mr. Lawford's tests. They're not coming out the way they should."

"What do you mean? What's wrong?"

"We think he's still drinking."

"He can't be," Ebbins said. "I'm with him all the time, and I haven't seen him touch a drop."

The nurse was insistent. "That's the only possible reason for the way the tests are turning out."

"Well, where are the bottles?"

"We looked for them in his room, but we can't find

any. Would you see if you can find them? We're absolutely certain he's been drinking."

Ebbins returned to the room, where Peter was lying on the bed, dressed in a hospital gown, watching television. After a few minutes had passed, Milt got up and went into the bathroom. "I had a hunch," he recalled. "I locked the door, took the top off the toilet tank, and there it was—a bottle of gin. I just put the lid back on and went to tell the nurse I'd found it. I didn't say anything to Peter."

The doctors confronted Peter, and when he came back to his room he screamed at Milt, "You dirty rat-fink bastard!"

Ebbins feigned innocence. "What are you talking about, Peter?"

"You told them about the gin, didn't you?"

Ebbins denied it, but Peter knew better. "He didn't forgive me for a long time, either," Ebbins recalled. After three more days of tests, Dr. Norcross asked to speak privately to Peter about the results. "You might as well let Milt hear it too," Peter said, "because I'll just tell him two minutes after you leave."

Norcross sat on a chair next to Peter's bed. "Mr. Lawford," he began matter-of-factly, "your liver is twice its normal size. If you keep doing what you're doing, you'll be dead in six months to a year of cirrhosis of the liver. It's just beginning in you, and it's a horrible death, believe me. The worst."

Peter looked stricken. "What do I have to do?"

"You have to stop drinking alcohol. You cannot drink for the rest of your life. We don't know why alcohol has this effect on the liver, but it happens to alcoholics."

Peter blanched. "Am I an alcoholic?"

"Yes," Norcross replied. "You're not a falling-down drunk, but you are an alcoholic."

"Can I have a glass of wine with dinner?"

"You can't even have a piece of rum cake. You have to stop drinking. But there is good news. The liver is a very regenerative organ. And we can bring it down to normal size with a very simple drug."

"What's that?"

"Vitamin A. If you stop drinking and take vitamin A, you'll be fine."

"That's great—"

"But believe me, if you continue drinking, you'll die."

Stunned by the severity of Norcross's warning, Peter resolved then and there to stop drinking. A few days later, he and Ebbins left the clinic. The first thing Peter did on the way home was stop at a bar and have a martini.

A FEW MONTHS later, Peter made plans for a trip to Hawaii. When he learned that Jackie Kennedy would be vacationing there at the same time, he wondered about the propriety of going. "Do you think it's okay?" he asked Milt.

"Why not?" Ebbins responded.

"Don't you think it'll look bad?"

"What are you talking about? Her kids will be with her."

Peter telephoned Jackie, with whom he had remained the friendliest of all the Kennedys, their bond as family outsiders still a strong one. He asked her if she would mind his being in Hawaii while she was. "Of course not," she told him. "In fact, why don't we fly there together?"

And so the plans were set for Peter and Jackie, in essence, to vacation together. She didn't seem to care about the inferences some might make about such an arrangement, and Peter put his own doubts out of his mind.

"It probably never even occurred to Jackie that it might look bad for her to travel with Peter," Ebbins recalled. "There was never any kind of an involvement between Peter and Jackie, other than that they genuinely liked each other. On the other hand, Peter told me that her sister, Lee Radziwill, made a big play for him once in the early sixties while they were strolling through Hyde Park in London. Peter said he turned her down because he had too much respect for her husband."

On June 5, Jackie flew from New York to San Francisco with her two children, Caroline and John Junior, and was joined there by Peter, Christopher, and Sydney. The next day a photograph was wired around the world showing Peter, Jackie, and the children descending an airplane ramp in Honolulu. Pat had given Peter permission to take the children on the trip, but she didn't know Jackie was going to be with him until she saw the picture in the newspapers.

Pat called Milt Ebbins on the telephone, very angry. "How dare he do that?" she shouted into the receiver.

"Pat," Ebbins replied, "Peter was planning to go there

anyway and so was Jackie. They decided to go together. So what?"

"She was so angry," he recalled, "that she just kind of growled. She thought that he was doing it for publicity or that people would misconstrue Peter's being with Jackie on vacation. She hung up and then she called me back and yelled some more. She was *livid*."

In Hawaii, Peter went to great lengths to see that Jackie enjoyed herself. He acted as her tour guide around the islands, took her and the children on camping trips, introduced her to his friends, and acted as her protector throughout her stay. A few days into the trip, he arranged a lavish garden party for Jackie at the Kahala Hilton, to which he invited his island friends and some of the most important people in Hawaii.

Jackie was hours late for the party, and one hundred and fifty of Honolulu's finest milled around under a broiling sun anticipating her arrival. "We were all dressed to the nines," Alice Guild recalled. "We waited and waited for her and started to sink into the grass with our high heels." When Jackie and her children arrived by helicopter, she was wearing sandals, a scarf, and a light shift, the kind a young woman might wear to the beach. According to Alice Guild, "Instead of her feeling embarrassed, one hundred and fifty guests were embarrassed because *we* were inappropriately dressed."

What surprised Peter's friends most about Jackie was that in private her voice was completely different from the soft, whispery voice that had fascinated the country during her televised tour of the White House early in 1962. Jean MacDonald was astonished that "she talked like you and me. I heard her with her children and it was so weird, because here was this totally normal mother's voice."

During the Hawaii trip, Jean and her husband, Bob Anderson, spent an evening with Peter at the beachfront house he had rented on Oahu. They talked late into the night, and Peter poured his heart out to them about the distress he felt at the recent events in his life. When Bob Anderson had to leave, he asked his wife to stay behind and "talk with Peter." She did, until seven in the morning.

They sat outside on a seawall in front of the house as the first rays of the sun started to appear over the water and talked about everything that had happened to Peter over the last few years. "I was struck by how concerned he was about what he had to offer his children," Jean recalled. "He was afraid that there was no role for him to play in their lives. He felt inadequate and overwhelmed by the Kennedys and their visibility and success. Everything his children needed could be provided for them by the Kennedys. He was afraid that his children wouldn't respect him because of that."

Jean tried to reassure Peter that there were a great many things he could offer his children. "I kept telling him what I had found in him that I thought was simply wonderful. I felt that he was an innately kind and good person. He was a great friend, understanding, someone you could sit down with and talk to and have a very meaningful, caring conversation. I felt that he had a solidness underneath that he could impart to his children."

Jean left Peter's house just as the sun cleared the horizon, uncertain whether her pep talk had made the impact she hoped it would. "I think he wanted to believe it, and he somewhat believed it. But he was losing confidence in himself as a person."

''I FOUND OUT who my true friends were after my divorce," Peter later said. "When I wasn't a part of the Kennedy family anymore, a lot of people I thought were my friends didn't come around anymore. I can't say it didn't hurt." Professionally, he discovered that the same thing was true. He had enjoyed some residual goodwill and sympathy after Jack's assassination, but it had faded by 1966, and the divorce eliminated the Kennedy connection that had buffered much of the enmity many in the business felt toward him. By then, Milt Ebbins found, Peter had become highly unpopular in Hollywood. "He burned bridges big time while Jack was President by adopting such a superior attitude. He stepped on a lot of toes, insulted important people in this town—and a lot of them wouldn't forgive him."

Peter found good film offers rare now—the combination of Sinatra's blackballing and the store of ill will against him proved a damaging one. What work he did get was provided by friends in the industry who remained loyal to him. He did two television guest shots in 1966, and had two minor film roles.

Sammy Davis was one of the few Rat Pack members

willing to buck Sinatra and associate with Peter, and he cast him in *A Man Called Adam* in a small role as the agent of a trumpet player addicted to drugs. "It was not a good movie and Peter was terrible in it," Milt Ebbins recalled. "He was fat—stomach out to here. He never should have done that movie. He got fifteen thousand dollars for it, I think. *God.*"

A more important movie but an equally small part followed in *The Oscar,* another glitzy Joe Levine drama purporting to show the raw underbelly of Hollywood. Stephen Boyd starred as an over-the-hill actor who finds himself Oscar-nominated and attempts to assure his victory—and his comeback—by ruthlessly spreading lies about his competitors. Art once again imitated life as Peter, who had just one scene, played an actor whose glory days were far behind him. When Boyd enters a restaurant, he is shocked to see that Lawford, an old friend who had once been on top of the heap, is now working as a maitre d'. Boyd offers his friend a small part in his next picture, and Lawford replies, "Look, I made the money. *I* blew it. New kids were arriving on every bus. So I died. I don't want to be dug up like some corpse and have to die all over again."

NOW, EVERY day held little deaths for Peter. He coveted film roles but did not get them. He was offered such insultingly small parts in minor pictures that whenever anything remotely reasonable came his way he accepted it in order to meet the bills.

And prodigious bills they were. Peter couldn't completely give up the trappings of wealth and power he had so enjoyed as John Kennedy's brother-in-law, and they were expensive. The most visible were the helicopters that landed on the beach in front of his house to shuttle him to and from the soundstages in Hollywood or to and from the airport. "I was chopper happy at the time," Peter later admitted, and he didn't like the drive out to the beach now any more than he had when he stayed in town weeknights to avoid it during Pat's pregnancy with Christopher.

It was more than that, though. Having a helicopter transport you was the ultimate status symbol in 1966, and for Peter it was a vivid reminder that he had been, for a while, a confidant of the most powerful man in the world.

"He wanted to put a helicopter pad outside his house," recalled Leonard Gershe, "until all the neighbors complained. It wasn't for the President, it was for him. For him! So he wouldn't have to drive to Warner Brothers."

Yet even this fragile symbol would be snatched from him. In June, copter pilot Hal Connors had landed amid swirling sand in front of Peter's house and picked him up for the trip to Los Angeles Airport and his flight to San Francisco on the way to Hawaii. When Connors returned, Santa Monica police arrested him for violating a city ordinance against such landings in residential areas. Connors protested that he had picked Peter Lawford up dozens of times before with no problem. Why, Connors asked, were they all of a sudden forbidding him to transport Peter as he had for years? A policeman replied, "Because Lawford isn't a Kennedy anymore."

THIRTY-FIVE

IN OCTOBER 1967, Peter and Sammy Davis roared through the streets of London's Soho on matching minibikes, dodging traffic and waving to gawking onlookers. Sammy's license plate read "SALT 1"; Peter's read "PEPPER 1." They were on their way to Alvaro's, a trendy discotheque on King's Road in Chelsea, and the club was having to turn away dozens of neck craners every week once the word got out that Lawford and Davis were regulars.

The pair were in London to star in *Salt and Pepper,* a James Bond takeoff developed by Peter for Chrislaw, and they set the English capital on its ear. "Swinging London" was the epicenter of the "youthquake" that was radically transforming the world's tastes in fashion and popular music. Peter and Sammy were much taken by all the experimentation with drugs, sexual freedom, and personal style. "It's stimulating, frightening, fun," Sammy told a reporter.

It was ironic that Peter and Sammy—old enough at forty-three and forty-one to be the parents of most of the "revolutionaries"—had become such a media rage. As one journalist noted, "Every newspaper from the *Sunday Times* to the *Daily Sketch* has come out with details of *Salt and Pepper.* . . . The entertainment columns of the daily press and feature pages of the color magazines are having a scoop day."

The excitement was created largely by the formidable reputations of the pair as former Rat Pack swingers and by

Peter's aura as the former brother-in-law of a martyred U.S. president. But there was another reason why Peter's presence caused a stir—as Graham Stark, one of *Salt and Pepper*'s British costars, recalled: "I always rather held the boy in esteem. He was a young Englishman who had gone to Hollywood, and anyone at MGM was a star to us. We grew up on Judy Garland, anything by Arthur Freed—and Lawford was involved. He actually kissed June Allyson onscreen—I could have killed him!"

At Alvaro's—where the two went every Saturday for lunch—Peter and Sammy were surrounded by some of the would-be hippest young people in London, who hung on their every word and treated them as entertainment icons. Before long the two men had co-opted the mod look for themselves. They wore their hair long, grew pork-chop sideburns (Peter's were gray), and donned Nehru jackets, bell-bottoms, and love beads. Peter had slimmed down again and wore blue jeans with a patch on the back that read, "Get your shit together." Peter and Sammy thought it all made them look more youthful and "with it," and many of their London admirers agreed. Others thought they were making fools of themselves.

Just as Peter and Sammy had adopted the self-conscious hipness of the Rat Pack, they now embraced the sixties mod style wholesale, complete with swinging parties, flower-child jargon, and experimentation with LSD and marijuana. Peter considered marijuana a godsend, a way to get high without drinking and further damaging his liver. Earlier, he had been adamantly opposed to any kind of drug use and had lectured Molly Dunne about its evils. "I was smoking marijuana long before Peter was," she recalled. "He didn't want me to smoke in the beach house. He'd say, 'Don't you smoke that stuff in here. Go outside!' And then he becomes this drug addict!"

Graham Stark went to some wild parties thrown by Peter and Sammy. "Sammy took up residence at the Mayfair in the Maharajah's suite and we were all invited up there at various times," Stark recalled. "There was a lot of action, girls falling out of cupboards. And why not? They were both big film stars and all those little darlings just loved them."

The "free love" aspects of the mod scene appealed mightily to Peter. Among the many pretty young women who "fell out of the cupboards" was one who belonged to Sammy. "Sammy had found this beautiful little model, a white girl," Milt Ebbins recalled. "He fell in love with her, and they were living together while they were filming *Salt and Pepper*. Peter stole her away. Sammy came to me and said, 'That fucker, I'll never talk to him again.' I asked Peter, 'What did you do?' And Peter replied nonchalantly, 'I stole his girl.' "

Peter and Sammy patched it up, and in between all the swinging, there was a movie to make. The idea for the film had come to Peter after a friend had referred to him as "salt" and Sammy as "pepper." He decided to turn it around and commissioned a script in which he would play Chris Pepper and Sammy would be Charlie Salt, a couple of nightclub owners in London who get involved in Bondlike intrigue, replete with comic bobbies, a car with a machine gun for an exhaust pipe, and all the requisite chases. Milt Ebbins got the go-ahead from United Artists executives for Chrislaw to produce the project after Michael Pertwee wrote a script they liked. Ebbins was named the film's producer, his first such assignment, and Sammy and Peter were named executive producers.

It was a difficult baptism for Ebbins. With a relatively small budget, he had hoped to film the London street scenes in Soho. But the congestion caused by sightseers prompted London police to ban the shooting and forced him to reconstruct Soho on the back lot at Shepperton Studios in Boreham at a cost of sixty thousand pounds ($144,000).

Ebbins was soon confronted with another, more serious problem. "Peter was the world's worst businessman," he recalled. "He always made decisions based on his emotions. He hired people because he liked them, not because they were necessarily right for the project." When it came time to hire a director for *Salt and Pepper,* Peter wanted Richard Donner, who at that point had directed only one minor film and some episodic television. Peter and Sammy had appeared in a *Wild, Wild West* episode Donner had directed, and Peter liked him.

Ebbins was skeptical, but when Peter insisted he agreed to hire Donner. "He's an incredibly successful director now," Ebbins recalled. "He's made *Superman, Lethal Weapon*—but in 1967 he wasn't ready. When the UA executives saw Donner's cut, they decided to reedit the film without his input. It cost us fifty thousand dollars to fix it."

According to Donner, the fault was not his. "I had a bad time on that film," he recalled. "Sammy and Peter were very undisciplined and there was a lot of cutting up. We'd have an eight o'clock call and they'd show up at noon, hung over from whatever it was they had ingested the night before. It was terrible for me, and I had no way of controlling them because they were the producers. What was I going to do, fire them?"

Donner quickly discovered that when Peter and Sammy did show up they usually didn't have much of an idea of what was in the script for the day's shooting. Instead, they would improvise conversations, do bits of business that had little to do with the plot. Donner decided to let them go off on as many tangents as they wanted. "I figured when I cut the picture I could just take all that extraneous stuff out. But then they fired me two weeks after we finished shooting. I was so angry at Peter at that point that if I'd found him it would have made the papers."

Despite everything, Donner and Peter remained friendly and later went into business together, with a group of other partners, in The Factory, an exclusive, trendy discotheque in West Hollywood. "There was a bit of hero worship in my feelings for Peter," Donner recalled. "The women just flocked to him. It was unbelievable. I always wanted to be a pilot fish to Peter's shark—you know, the little fish that hangs on to the shark and eats up anything that falls out of its mouth? Peter had so many gorgeous girls around him I was content with his overflow. I did very well through him."

Critical reaction was mixed when *Salt and Pepper* was released in September 1968. Most reviewers thought the film a waste of Sammy's talents, and the Los Angeles *Herald-Examiner* was hard on Peter for never seeming "quite sure as to whether he is supposed to be James Bond, Mr. Lucky or Peter Lawford." *Variety* summed things up by noting, "This is not a picture for thinking audiences."

But *Salt and Pepper* did well at the box office. It was number nine nationally its first week and set attendance records in some theaters—so good a showing that a year later Peter and Sammy were given the green light by United Art-

ists for a sequel, *One More Time,* again written by Michael
Pertwee and again produced by Milt Ebbins. In this version,
Peter would play not only Chris Pepper but his wealthy,
snobby twin brother, Lord Sydney, as well.

Richard Donner was never considered to direct *One
More Time,* because Peter had someone else in mind—Jerry
Lewis, who had been a friend since his days as half of the
Dean Martin and Jerry Lewis comedy team and who had
recently used Peter in his picture *Hook, Line and Sinker.*

Milt Ebbins's reaction to the suggestion, Ebbins recalled, was *"Jerry Lewis?"* United Artists was equally against
hiring Lewis, who hadn't directed a successful movie in
years, but Sammy and Peter were adamant, and in the end
the UA executives relented—after warning Ebbins, "You're
gonna have trouble."

The trouble began immediately. "Lewis came in to
work on the script," recalled Ebbins, "and he brought in a
writer who he paid to completely rewrite it. Then he threw
out the rewrite and hired Michael Pertwee, who wrote the
first script, to write another one. And all the time the cash
registers were ringing."

When the company arrived in London to begin shooting, Lewis told the producer he wanted to use three cameras. Although Ebbins knew that Jerry's idea would cost the
production three times the expense of one camera in film
alone, he agreed when Lewis promised to stay within budget. Then the director wanted to use the television system
whereby it is possible to look at each take as it's filmed.
"That's gonna cost us eighty thousand dollars!" Ebbins exclaimed. Milt called a meeting with UA executives over the
issue, and when Lewis promised to pay any cost overrun
out of his own pocket, UA approved the review-as-you-go
system. Once the cameras were installed, Ebbins asked
Lewis to test them before he began to shoot. "Milt," he
replied, "you're telling me about my business."

"Jerry," Ebbins pleaded, "just test the cameras. That's
all I ask." Lewis finally agreed that he would, but he never
got around to it, and he shot for half a day before he realized that there was something wrong with the lenses and he
hadn't gotten a single foot of usable film.

A few days later, as Lewis was setting up to shoot a
fight scene, the art director asked to speak to Milt. "My

Ebbins," he said, "I must tell you that Mr. Lewis insists on using antique furniture in this scene. Antiques cost a fortune and we can't insure them for what they're really worth, only what it would cost to buy newly manufactured furniture. I can make new furniture right here at the studio that will look just like antiques and nobody will know the difference."

Ebbins spoke to Jerry about it, and Lewis was furious. "Christ, Milt!" he exploded. "You're telling me how to do my goddamn job again!" Finally, after much cajoling, Ebbins convinced Jerry to let the art director make the "antiques."

"So he did the fight scene," Ebbins recalled. "In the first thirty seconds, a guy threw a punch and the other guy fell down and broke a table and three chairs! Luckily, the art director had made up some extras. Jerry Lewis didn't say a word to me."

The filming proceeded through one stressful confrontation after another, with Ebbins struggling to keep costs down and Lewis continually threatening to send them sky-high. After the principal photography was completed, Lewis insisted on editing the film without showing anyone a working print for review. The result, Ebbins remembered, was "awful. He had Peter and Sammy doing Martin and Lewis. Peter left the screening room, went into [United Artists executive] Herb Jaffe's office, and started to cry. Jaffe wanted to burn the negative."

The studio gave Ebbins the chance to recut the film himself, and he spent three weeks holed up with the editor. *One More Time* was finally released in June 1970, and at least one critic found it a "perfectly respectable, oddly endearing little film." The *Los Angeles Times* thought Peter's performance in the dual role his "best ... in quite some time." But the overriding reaction was summed up by the critic for the London *Sunday Mail: "One More Time* has one of those excruciating plots where everyone on screen is killing himself trying to be funny, and everyone in the audience is dying with embarrassment, disbelief and boredom."

IN THE FALL of 1967, immediately after completing *Salt and Pepper,* Peter traveled to Rome to appear with Gina Lollobrigida, Shelley Winters, Janet Margolin, Phil Silvers, and Telly Savalas in Melvin Frank's *Buona Sera, Mrs. Campbell,* a romantic comedy that would receive mixed reviews.

The shooting in Rome went without incident for Peter, but off-screen he became involved in romantic misadventures straight out of an Italian sex farce. The first of these involved his costar Gina Lollobrigida, who at forty had lost little of her voluptuous sex appeal or fiery Latin temperament.

During filming, the buxom seductress made a strong play for Peter. She invited him to her home for a romantic candlelight supper and made it quite clear that she was interested in more than just a friendly dinner. Nervous, Peter made a beeline for the door the minute he finished his dessert, leaving Lollobrigida to wonder what had gone wrong. Gina extended several more invitations to him, which he declined. "What's wrong with him?" she asked friends. "Or is there something wrong with me? What is it?"

Princess Ira von Furstenberg was more aggressive, but no more successful. Another formidable, lusty woman, she was the ex-wife of the Spanish prince Alfonso von Hohenlohe. During the 1960s, she made twenty-six Italian films, and a friend described her as a woman who would "rather be Marilyn Monroe than the queen of England."

The princess invited Peter to her palatial villa in Rome for dinner, and when he arrived, there was nothing but candlelight illuminating the entire house. After dinner, as Peter later told Milt Ebbins, "she went after me like a hawk. She got me on the couch and I couldn't get out of there!"

According to Ebbins, Lollobrigida and Furstenberg had scared off their prey. "Peter was petrified of strong, aggressive, larger-than-life women. He was afraid of not performing well. He could have had Liz Taylor, Marilyn Monroe, Gina Lollobrigida, but he was afraid. He couldn't risk going to bed with those women and having them get up and say, 'What the hell was that?' "

Younger, more submissive, star-struck girls who were likely to be impressed with Peter's stature and less likely to humiliate him in an awkward situation—these were the women who appealed to him. And Janet Margolin filled the bill on all counts. Pretty and slim, her long straight brown hair parted in the middle, Margolin had created a sensation in 1962 in her screen debut as an emotionally disturbed adolescent who falls in love with another troubled youth (Keir Dullea) in Frank Perry's *David and Lisa*. Her career would never fulfill that initial promise, but she would remain a well-regarded actress.

Peter was very taken with her, and the two were photographed holding hands during late-night strolls along the Via Veneto, he in a Nehru jacket and turtleneck sweater, she in a plaid skirt, sweater, and leather jacket. He was also seen about the same time (and wearing the same outfit) doing the town with the black singer Lola Falana, but Margolin was the girl who captured his heart.

Soon Peter was on the phone to Ebbins. He said that he was in love with Janet Margolin and was going to marry her. "Are you crazy?" Milt asked.

"This is the real thing, Milt!"

"Have you slept with her?"

"No, nothing like that."

"You must be nuts wanting to marry a twenty-four-year-old girl!"

"Well, maybe—but that's what I'm gonna do." Peter did propose to Margolin, and afterward he again called Ebbins. "Do you believe it?" he asked via transatlantic telephone. *"She turned me down."*

"What reason did she give you?"

"She didn't really say. I guess I'm too old for her."

Peter turned forty-four in September 1967, but he wasn't too old for many other younger women. His sexual and romantic involvements for the rest of his life were to be almost exclusively with girls half his age or younger—as young as seventeen in one case. This new predilection of Peter's may have begun as still another emulation of Frank Sinatra, who in 1966 married twenty-one-year-old Mia Farrow, the close-cropped, sylphlike star of TV's *Peyton Place*. ("I always knew Frank would wind up in bed with a boy," Ava Gardner sniffed.)

But there was clearly more to it than that. By now, Peter's sexual tastes had taken a distinct turn toward the kinky. Because of the ever-present threat of impotence, he preferred watching two women have sex to performing intercourse with either of them and risking embarrassment. He found that he could reach orgasm only after prolonged fellatio—sometimes several hours. And he had begun to experiment with sadomasochism. He feared that he could not broach these sexual activities to women like Gina Lollobrigida or Ira von Furstenberg without risking ridicule.

Young girls were a different matter. Everywhere he went, they buzzed around him like hummingbirds. They'd stare at him in restaurants and slip him their numbers as they walked by his table. Back in shape, still marvelous looking, he was attractive to women who had no idea who he was. For those who did know, the attraction was often irresistible.

When he made his choice the young woman usually felt very special indeed. Here she was, on the arm of a handsome man who had been next to greatness, one who treated her like a queen, was solicitous of her every whim. But what would begin as the biggest thrill of her life more often than not ended in disillusionment.

Arthur Natoli, a bluff, street-smart man, had replaced Chuck Pick as Peter's chauffeur-companion in 1967, and he was puzzled by Peter's sex life. "I used to call Peter's bedroom the Rocky Horror Room," Natoli recalled. "I always wondered just *what* went on in there."

Natoli got his answer when he introduced a young woman to his boss on the condition that if she slept with Peter, she would tell Arthur what went on. She promised she would.

The next morning, Natoli picked the girl up. "Boy, that was an experience," she said as she hopped into his car.

"What happened?"

"I don't know if I should tell you," she said.

"Hey! We had a deal!" Natoli protested. "Tell me!"

"Well," the girl began haltingly. "The first thing he did was put his pecker between his legs and close them, so it looked like he didn't have one. Then he told me to lick him there and pretend he's a girl. Then he wanted to watch me make it with another girl. That I didn't mind, but when he told me to tie him up and whip him, I walked out of the room. I'm not into that kind of stuff."

THIRTY-SIX

THERE WAS about it a distinct aura of déjà vu. The handsome bushy-haired young senator named Kennedy stood in the Senate Caucus Room and said simply, "I am announcing today my candidacy for the presidency of the United States."

With the exact words his brother had uttered eight years earlier, Robert F. Kennedy embarked on a challenge to Lyndon Johnson, a quest that had seemed, for the past four years, somehow inevitable. Jack Kennedy had said that he ran for president only because his older brother Joe had been killed. Now that Jack was dead, it was Bobby's turn, and after Bobby, Ted would step in. The Kennedy family had nothing if not a sense of destiny.

In many ways, however, Bobby's run for the presidency was anticlimactic. As Peter tellingly put it to a reporter, "With Jack, it was like going to your first prom. It was wonderful working for someone you really believed in. I'm afraid your second prom will never be as exciting."

It may have been his "second prom," but at least Peter was invited to it. Bobby knew that his former brother-in-law was still capable of rustling up celebrity support for his campaign just as he had for Jack's, and he asked for Peter's help. Despite the chilliness of their relationship, Peter agreed. He had long hoped in a nebulous, wishful sort of way that Camelot might be recaptured and that he might once again be part of the magic.

423

(He wasn't alone in that. When it looked as though Bobby's campaign might well be successful, Jackie Kennedy enthused, "Won't it be wonderful when we get back in the White House?" But when she overheard Jackie's remark, Ethel—who for years had resented the way her sister-in-law overshadowed her—gave her an icy look and said, "What do you mean *we*?")

Peter did his job. He brought dozens of celebrities into the Kennedy campaign, among them Lauren Bacall, Shirley MacLaine, Eddie Fisher, Natalie Wood, and Gene Kelly. He organized fund-raisers at The Factory, the West Hollywood discotheque he co-owned with Sammy Davis, Dick Donner, Paul Newman, Pierre Salinger, and Tommy Smothers, among others. (Newman, however, was an active supporter of another hopeful, Eugene McCarthy.)

Still, Peter was not involved as deeply with Bobby's campaign as he had been with Jack's. His efforts were limited to private California fund-raising; he did no traveling, made no speeches, never appeared with the candidate at whistle-stops. There were several reasons for this. One, of course, was Peter's uncomfortable association with the Hollywood excesses that Bobby wanted to forget and prayed would remain secret.

Another was the fact that Peter's presence was a reminder of the only divorce in the Kennedy family, a factor that could do nothing but hurt Bobby in a close election. A third reason was made evident by a full-page color photograph of Peter run by *Life* magazine in its May 10, 1968, article on the primary campaign. The photo, taken at a Kennedy fund-raiser at The Factory, showed Peter wearing shaggy Beatle-esque bangs, a black turtleneck sweater, and Indian beads, sitting at a table with a cigarette in his hand and both a mixed drink and a glass of white wine in front of him. It was a poor image even for a youth-oriented campaign; Bobby's advisors winced when they saw it and suggested that Peter's involvement be further limited.

Two weeks after Bobby announced his candidacy, President Johnson, beleaguered by protests against the Vietnam War, announced that he would not run for reelection—a wholly unexpected development that transformed the political landscape overnight. "I felt that I was being charged on all sides by a giant stampede," Johnson told his biographer,

Doris Kearns. "I was being forced over the edge by rioting blacks, demonstrating students, marching welfare mothers, squawking professors, and hysterical reporters. And then the final straw. The thing I feared from the first day of my presidency was actually coming true. Robert Kennedy had openly announced his intention to reclaim the throne in the memory of his brother. And the American people, swayed by the magic of the name, were dancing in the streets."

Bobby Kennedy's run for the presidency soon turned into what one reporter called a succession of "feeding frenzies." Much of the ardor stemmed from his brother's legacy, to be sure, but more and more of it was directed at him by people who saw in his face and heard in his words genuine compassion for them and their struggles. Those around Bobby worried about the emotionalism of his public appearances, his vulnerability to harm symbolized by his bleeding hands at the end of a day's campaigning. The candidate was fatalistic. "If they want to get me, they'll get me," he said. "They got Jack."

It soon became clear that Kennedy's quixotic quest for the Democratic nomination might very well succeed. Whether or not it would rested largely on the outcome of the California primary election on June 4 between Bobby and Eugene McCarthy. Bobby chose to spend election day at the beachfront home of John Frankenheimer, the director. This apparent slap in the face to Peter raised a few eyebrows, but Peter understood Bobby's need to steer clear. He proceeded instead with plans for a celebration at The Factory that would follow Bobby's hoped-for victory speech at his Ambassador Hotel election headquarters.

Around midnight, a contest that had been close all evening finally swung Bobby's way. He had won the most important primary in the country, and he now had the strongest possible momentum going into the Democratic convention in Chicago. Before he made his victory speech, he took a telephone call from his aide Kenny O'Donnell. "You know, Ken," he said, "finally I feel that I'm out from under the shadow of my brother. Now at last I feel that I've made it on my own."

Peter and Milt Ebbins watched Bobby's celebratory speech on television at The Factory. There would indeed be a victory party, and Peter couldn't help but feel pangs of the old excitement as hundreds of supporters cheered Bobby's last line—"Now it's on to Chicago and let's win there!"

A few minutes after Bobby left the podium, television cameras remained trained on the Ambassador ballroom as reporters began to interview Kennedy supporters. Suddenly, there was commotion, confusion. No one was quite sure what had happened. Some people thought they'd heard shots. Someone shouted, "He's been shot!" And suddenly the dread possibility of another disaster whipped Peter's attention back to the television screen.

He watched as the confusion grew into shouts of dismay. A commentator cried, unbelievingly, "Is it possible? Is it possible that Senator Kennedy has been shot?" The news cameras zoomed in again on the podium as Bobby's brother-in-law Steve Smith shouted frantically into the microphone, "Is there a doctor in the house?"

When he heard that, Peter turned to Milt and said, "He's had it." He then stood up and walked out of The Factory.

ROBERT KENNEDY, his head shattered by two bullets police said were fired by Sirhan Sirhan, an Arab angered by Kennedy's pro-Israel positions, lingered for twenty hours at LA's Good Samaritan Hospital. Jackie Kennedy, sedated and musing aloud about the church and death, flew in from New York; Lee Radziwill's husband, Prince Stanislaus, came all the way from London and joined the Kennedy family vigil.

Peter, who lived only a few miles from the hospital, did not. Instead, he went to Palm Springs to see a girlfriend, and Milt Ebbins was aghast. "Jesus Christ, Peter! How can you not go?"

"I just can't, Milt," Peter replied. "There's no place for me there."

Kennedy died at one forty-four A.M. on June 6, and a funeral mass was held at St. Patrick's Cathedral in New York on June 8. One hundred thousand ordinary citizens lined up for blocks outside the church for the chance to pass Kennedy's bier and pay their respects; during the service President Johnson and dozens of other dignitaries heard Ted Kennedy deliver an eloquent and moving eulogy. "My brother need not be idealized or enlarged in death beyond what he was in life," Ted said, his voice breaking, "[but] remembered simply as a good and decent man, who saw wrong and tried to right it, saw suffering and tried to heal it, saw war and tried to stop it. Those of us who loved him and who take him to his rest today pray that what he was to us and what he wished for others will someday come to pass for all the world."

Peter was invited to the funeral service, but his bad judgment on that occasion would result in his irremediable alienation from most of the Kennedy family. As he and Milt Ebbins checked into their hotel, Peter met a sexy young woman he wanted to impress. Despite the fact that the invitation to the funeral had been explicitly designated for only one person because of space constraints, Peter invited this young woman, a stranger, to accompany him to the rites.

Ebbins recalled what happened. "This girl went out and bought a black miniskirt, a black hat, and black gloves. Christ, the dress was so short it was *obscene!*"

As the three of them got into a cab to go to St. Patrick's, Ebbins said under his breath, "Peter, you're crazy— this broad—you *can't*! This is a *mistake*."

Peter saw that Ebbins was right. "You get out with her," he said.

"No way!" Ebbins replied.

When they reached the cathedral, Peter tried to distance himself from his companion, but she clung tightly to his arm, leaving no room for misapprehension about whom she was with. "She wouldn't let go of him," Ebbins recalled. "It was awful. The Kennedys were absolutely furious with him."

Pat Lawford was mortified by her former husband's behavior. She and the rest of her family looked on it as a deliberate insult to Bobby's memory, and they never forgave him. It was the final straw. If Peter had hoped ever to be accepted back into the bosom of the Kennedy family, the hope was now forever dashed.

That fact was made harshly clear to him a few months later, when he tried to place a telephone call to Ethel at her home in Hickory Hill and was informed by the operator that the unlisted number had been changed. He asked Milt Ebbins to call Sargent Shriver at the Kennedy Foundation offices in New York and get Ethel's new number for him.

When Ebbins called and explained that he was inquiring for Peter, Shriver refused to give him the number.

EVEN JACKIE Kennedy became unavailable to Peter, in October, when she left the country to marry the Greek shipping billionaire Aristotle Onassis. The former First Lady's decision to marry the often vulgar tycoon was viewed by many in America and abroad as a betrayal of her martyred husband, but Peter—though he did not attend the wedding on the island of Skorpios—was vocal in her defense. "What do people expect of her?" he said to a journalist. "To be a widow for the rest of her life? She's a human being, and she needs companionship and happiness just like all the rest of us. Wherever she finds that happiness, I'm all for it."

Pat Lawford, on the other hand, was never able to find marital happiness again. Although she had been tempted to revert to her maiden name, she kept the name Lawford, mainly for the sake of her children. After the divorce, she moved to Paris to be near Walter Sohier, a State Department lawyer she had been intermittently involved with since the early 1960s.

Leonard Gershe remembered his and Pat's interaction with Sohier after a party in 1961, when they went back to Walter's Georgetown home for a nightcap. The men were in black tie, and Sohier went upstairs to change clothes. Leonard and Pat loved practical jokes, and while they waited for Walter to come back down, Gershe hit on an idea. He scurried into the kitchen and got a bottle of ketchup. "I lay down on the floor," Gershe recalled, "and Pat poured the ketchup over me and stood there with her hair all a mess holding a knife over her head. He came down and saw us and didn't think it was at all funny. We were crying with laughter, and he was annoyed. So when I think of Walter Sohier all I can think of is his great sense of humor."

Nothing ever came of Pat's relationship with Sohier, and the same was true of Roger Edens. Leonard Gershe was Edens's companion, and he recalled that "Roger was very much in love with Pat. She was crazy about him, too—I don't know if she was in love with him, but she loved him."

Early in 1970, Pat and Edens were in New York to attend the opening of Gershe's play *Butterflies Are Free*. The night before, Edens told Pat that he was terminally ill with cancer. "She went mad," Gershe recalls. "She just lost all control. Her father had just died, and Jack and Bobby were dead, and she screamed, 'I'm losing another one!' Roger had to slap her to calm her down."

PETER MADE three movies in 1968, one of them abysmal, one mediocre, and one quite good. This last was *The April Fools,* Stuart Rosenberg's acerbic comedy of corporate morals and suburban marriages. Working opposite Jack Lemmon and Catherine Deneuve, Peter played—very well— a smug, smooth tycoon whose beautiful but neglected wife has a bittersweet affair with one of her husband's more hapless employees. It was Peter's best movie role in years. *Variety* thought that "Lawford is excellent in an unsympathetic part as the too-busy-to-bother husband of Miss Deneuve." And *Time* noted cleverly, "As played by Mr. Lawford, he is an untruthful narcissist with hair of chestnut brown and sideburns of Dorian Gray."

The April Fools should have led to further good film offers for Peter. It didn't, possibly because of the other two films he had in release at about the same time—*Hook, Line and Sinker,* a Jerry Lewis clinker in which he plays a doctor who convinces a patient to fake his own death for insurance purposes, and Otto Preminger's *Skidoo,* a disastrous all-star "mod" comedy about LSD, gangsters, and swinging hippies.

In December, Peter wrote to his agent, Abe Lastfogel, of the William Morris agency, to complain that very little had been done to get him quality work since his last letter on October 5, 1967. At that time, Peter wrote, he had felt encouraged by Lastfogel's reaction and was confident that the agent's belief in his potential would "seep down through the ranks. It makes me sad to report that this was far from being the case."

All his films since then, Peter pointed out, had come to him independently of William Morris, as had several TV shows and a four-day stint as guest host of the *Tonight* show. "I bore you with the aforementioned data," Peter went on, "simply to illustrate 'where it's at' and from whence the bread is coming!" He felt the "desperate need," he went on, for another agency to put an "imaginative force" to work for his benefit. He then informed Lastfogel that he was switching agencies.

The fault, however, lay not in the William Morris agency but in Peter Lawford. He had rarely been a box-office draw, and he had not—with the exceptions of *Salt and Pepper* and *One More Time,* which he had produced himself—been an "above the title" star since 1954.

Peter wasn't, of course, alone among notable MGM alumni in his career tribulations. With a few exceptions—Frank Sinatra, Elizabeth Taylor, Katharine Hepburn, and John Wayne among them—most of the stars of the "old days" were considered has-beens, relegated to occasional television work. The question "Whatever happened to?" became the cliché prelude to most mentions of the names June Allyson, Van Johnson, Cyd Charisse, Jane Powell, Kathryn Grayson, Gloria De Haven, and others.

A separate set of problems attached to Peter Lawford. He had made a lot of enemies in Hollywood; a number of directors, producers, and stars had refused to work with him under any circumstances for years. Now, as a tumultuous decade in Peter's life came to an end, he found himself looked upon by the "new Hollywood" as little more than a superannuated MGM second banana who had never had an excess of talent and whom they didn't much like anyway. If there had ever been a glimmer of hope that Peter could recapture the kind of power by association he had enjoyed while Jack Kennedy was President, it had been buried with Bobby.

THIRTY-SEVEN

THROUGHOUT THE 1960s, Peter had watched
with growing alarm the steady decline of Judy Garland, his closest female friend in the mid-1960s. She
was the only one of his MGM cohorts with whom he had
maintained so close an emotional bond, and for millions she
was the embodiment of the best that fabled studio had had
to offer.

But her long descent into drug and alcohol addiction,
her series of unsuccessful marriages, her personal and professional disasters, her weight gains and losses, and her suicide attempts were all emblematic as well of the stark reality
behind L. B. Mayer's sugarcoated vision of the world. Judy
was more an MGM product than Peter; her heights were
more spectacular, her depths more devastating. And yet
every time Peter looked at Judy Garland now, he saw something of himself in her.

She had, like him, a wry wit that could turn in a flash
into a lacerating rapier. As with him, her drinking and drug
taking made her unpredictable, apt to turn on a friend with
frightening ferocity over the slightest offense. Molly Dunne
remembered an occasion when Judy lit into Peter after they
had exchanged a few sharp words. "Judy had been drinking,
and she jumped up and started *screaming* at Peter. She said,
'You're a *lousy* actor! You were *never* a good actor! The
only reason you were at MGM was that all the *good* actors
were in the *war*!'

"Peter just sat there and took it. He never raised his voice. And of course that angered Judy all the more. She picked up her purse and hit him with it—whacked him across the head—and stormed out. The next day she called me and said, 'If you ever get tired of him you're always welcome to be my friend—you don't have to take this shit.' I think, though, that she finally did call and apologize to him."

Peter took a lot from Judy, as did many others; he knew that her mind had been warped by years of drugs and booze. In 1966, Joe and Dolores Naar had thrown a party for Pat to which Peter, at Pat's request, was not invited. It had created a rift between Peter and the Naars that lasted for years, but Dolores remembered it vividly for another reason as well: Judy's bizarre behavior.

The Naars had erected a huge tent behind their house and filled it with dozens of round tables; Roger Edens had strung small lights and orange blossoms from post to post within the tent and throughout the trees in the Naars' backyard, giving it a fairyland aura. The party was festive, with drinking and dancing followed by a sit-down dinner.

"Judy was seated at one table with her back to Pat, who was sitting at the next table," Dolores Naar recalled. "They hadn't exchanged two words all evening, but immediately after dinner, Judy stood up, picked up a glass of ice water, turned around, and poured it right down the back of Pat's dress.

"Pat never said a word. She just got up, turned around, saw who did it, and walked away. She went upstairs and we dried her dress with a hair dryer. To this day I don't know why Judy did it. Maybe she'd been stewing all night about Peter and Pat's divorce—who knows? You could never tell what was going through Judy's mind."

Judy's behavior grew more and more bizarre. One evening in the spring of 1966, she telephoned Peter, frantic and sobbing, and begged him to help her—something terrible had happened. Peter scrambled into his pants, jumped in his car "half in my pajamas," and sped to Judy's house. When she opened the door his heart almost stopped—her face was covered with blood. His legs feeling like rubber beneath him, he wrapped his arms around her and walked her over to a lamp, where he could see dozens of tiny cuts all over her face. "My God, Judy, what happened?" Crying again, Judy managed to say, "Mark went after me with a razor." (Mark Herron was her much-younger husband of less than six months.)

Peter helped Judy into the den and searched for antiseptic to dab on the nicks. He went through all the bathrooms but couldn't find a Band-Aid or antiseptic anywhere. "So I washed her face off with vodka," Peter said. "Then I found some BFI surgical powder and I put Judy's head back on the bar and put this powder on her face so that the cuts would coagulate."

He told Judy to stay put and headed down the hall to the bathroom to wash his hands. As he walked past Judy's maid Alma Cousteline's room, the door opened and she called him over. "I think I ought to tell you, Mr. Lawford," she whispered, "it wasn't Mr. Herron who did that—she did it herself. She was standing in front of the mirror in the hall with a razor blade in her hand, and she was cutting her face with it. She kept saying, 'Just look what that thing did to me!' I said, 'What thing?' and she said, 'Mark Herron,' and cut herself again."

"That was the kind of desperation she had," Peter said. "She wanted to let you know what kind of trouble she was in." But as with Marilyn Monroe, there was little Peter could do but watch the disassembly of someone he loved. "A lot of people I know who were terribly close to Judy washed their hands of her—they walked away. I several times would really get angry at her—anger out of sadness for her."

Peter did try to help. Early in 1969, he was in Philadelphia to cohost the *Mike Douglas Show,* and he asked Judy, who was there on a concert tour, to appear on the show. At this point, Judy's addictions had ravaged her, although she was not yet forty-seven. She was painfully thin, frail, and often unable to call up her voice; her audiences were never sure what they were going to see.

"Do they *really* want me?" she asked. "Of course they do," Peter assured her. Even so, he practically had to drag her out of her hotel to the studio. "She was in tears, all burned out," Peter said. "It destroyed you to watch all that talent dissolving into nothing. Poor, dear Judy."

During the filming of *One More Time* in London, Peter got a call from Milt Ebbins around noon on June 22. "Did you hear about Judy?" Milt asked.

"I hadn't heard," Peter said later. "Judy was dead. And

I was devastated." Her husband of six months, Mickey Deans, had found her in the bathroom of their London hotel room, sitting on the toilet, her head down on her chest. She had not tried to kill herself; the sleeping pills and alcohol had simply overwhelmed her tiny, emaciated body. She looked almost skeletal sitting there, as though the life had been ebbing out of her for years. And of course—as anyone would have seen who had stopped to take a long, hard look—it had been.

JUDY'S DEATH *was* devastating to Peter. He felt as though everything he valued was being cruelly snatched from him until he would have nothing left at all. He was bereft, wracked with survivor guilt. He both feared his own mortality and courted death with a what-the-hell attitude about drinking and drug taking that his friends feared was his own slow, subconscious suicide. He began acting in ways that were explicable only as the result of a desire to hasten his decline and justify his lifelong feelings of worthlessness.

There was nothing anyone could do—not even Milt Ebbins, who by now was constantly struggling to keep Peter Lawford's life on an even keel. Throughout 1969, Milt tried desperately to prevent the loss of another major part of Peter's life: the Santa Monica beach house.

The house had become a white elephant for Peter after the departure of Pat and the children. It was expensive to maintain, and Peter was having money woes. It was far too big for one person, even two. Peter hated to be alone, and he constantly urged friends to stay the night, if only in the guest house.

After Pat moved to New York, Layte Bowden, the stewardess Peter had visited the night before President Kennedy's funeral, moved into the house with him. "She was a very pretty girl," Milt Ebbins remembered. "As usual, after she moved in Peter got tired of her, and he asked me to tell her that it was over. I said, 'You gotta be kidding! I'm not gonna do it. There's no reason for me to do it.' But she knew what was happening, and she left pretty soon after that."

And then Peter felt crushingly lonely in this rambling house that had once been alive with children and parties and movie stars, had once served as the Western White

House. Now it was filled only with memories—"bad memories," Peter said. He wanted to be rid of it.

After the divorce from Pat, the Kennedys insisted that Peter immediately repay about a hundred thousand dollars that remained on a loan the family had extended to him with the house as collateral. Peter was desperate. Without Pat as part of his financial picture, he was a poor credit risk. Although he was still capable of making large sums of money, his work was sporadic, and his expenses were far beyond his means. There were the hotel lawsuits and a number of others on his credit record for nonpayment of debts. He doubted he could get a conventional mortgage.

Finally, Peter asked his old friend Henry Ford for a loan. Ford agreed to have his foundation pay off the Kennedys and hold the mortgage on the house. The original terms of the agreement were that Peter would make monthly payments and the balance would be paid back in one year. "Every year they came to us wanting their money," Milt Ebbins recalled, "and I'd tell them, 'No, we can't do it.' So they kept giving us one-year extensions."

All this time, Peter was trying to sell the house. He listed it for $250,000 and—incredible as it may sound to anyone familiar with Santa Monica beachfront real estate today—found no takers. The tremendous surge in Southern California's population had not yet begun, and the meteoric rise in real estate values in and around Los Angeles was still a number of years off. In 1969 beach houses in Santa Monica—as they had been in 1956, when Peter bought the L. B. Mayer house—were still a drag on the market.

Peter had rented out the house sporadically—to Warren Beatty and Leslie Caron for three thousand dollars a month at the height of their affair during the summer of 1966, and to Abby Mann, the director, for twenty-five hundred dollars in 1969—and Ebbins wanted to continue to do so. He suggested that Peter lease the house to a handyman, charge him just enough rent to pay the mortgage, and have him renovate the house—which was falling into disrepair—a little at a time. Its value as an investment would increase, Ebbins reasoned, and it would be not only maintained but improved. Peter said no, he wanted to sell—because, as he put it, the place held "too many memories."

Unless the house was being rented, Peter had trouble

making his monthly mortgage payment to the Ford Foundation. They were willing to be lenient largely because of Peter's friendship with Henry, but he soon alienated his
benefactor. For years, Ford had given the heads of studios
and production companies in Hollywood new cars every
year for one dollar. Because Peter and Ebbins had Chrislaw,
Ford had given them both gleaming new Lincoln Continen-
tals annually. When a new team of financial watchdogs was
installed at Ford, the policy was changed and the company
demanded that the cars be returned. Peter was furious. He
wrote Henry Ford a bitter letter, as he was wont to do.
"Peter was a great writer of vicious letters," Ebbins said.
"So that was the end of Peter with Henry Ford. The company threatened foreclosure unless we repaid the entire loan
immediately."

Peter still couldn't sell the house, and Ford twice instituted foreclosure proceedings that Ebbins was able to fore-
stall through litigation. But that only bought time; Peter was
sure to lose the house eventually if he couldn't pay Ford
off. Finally, Peter's real estate agent found a buyer, and
Peter agreed on a sale price of $207,500. It looked as though
a messy financial problem would have a neat ending. But
from that point on, matters just got messier and messier.

Peter entered into an escrow on December 12, 1969,
with a woman named Alma Mason, who put $40,500 down.
Later it was alleged that Mason was actually acting as an
"agent" for Lynn Wood, a neighbor of Peter's. Unconcerned about this, Peter allowed Wood to move into the
house before escrow closed.

But Wood was unable to come up with the additional
funds required to close escrow, and the deal fell through.
Later it was charged in court documents that Wood had
borrowed twenty thousand dollars of the down payment
from a woman named Gertrude Feldman with the promise
of a share in the equity of the house. When the escrow fell
through, the down payment was forfeited, and Gertrude
Feldman went to court to recoup her money. She charged
that Peter, Alma Mason, Lynn Wood, and her husband,
Ward Wood, had conspired to defraud her.

Peter knew nothing about any arrangements among
Wood, Mason, and Feldman, but the collapse of the sale
left him once again vulnerable to foreclosure. With no more

legal remedies available to Milt, the house was put up for auction at a trustee's sale on June 4, 1970, and was sold to another neighbor of Peter's, Louis Herson, for $142,961.

After payment was made to Henry Ford for the balance of the mortgage, a settlement of seventy-five hundred dollars was paid to Gertrude Feldman, and several liens attached to the house were satisfied, Peter's share of the sale amounted to forty thousand dollars.

There then ensued five years of lawsuits to determine the disbursement of that money. Finally, six thousand dollars of it was paid to Peter's attorney for handling these matters, sixty-six hundred dollars went to City National Bank in payment of a judgment against Peter for a defaulted loan (he hadn't made the monthly payments of one hundred fifty dollars), and fourteen thousand dollars was used to satisfy a variety of liens against him for unpaid state taxes in the years 1969 and 1970 and for unpaid federal taxes in 1970, 1971, and 1973.

Peter came away with less than fourteen thousand dollars to show for the sale of his showplace home, over which the presidential flag had flown. Milt Ebbins was heartbroken. "One hundred and forty-two thousand that house sold for! Do you know what that house is worth now [in 1989]? About *eight million dollars*. If Peter had taken my advice and rented it, he could have wound up a millionaire. And you know what—he blamed me for it later! He said, 'If it wasn't for you I wouldn't have lost my house.' That was Peter."

Bob Slatzer was a friend of Ward Wood's, and before the deal to buy Peter's house fell through, Slatzer and Wood took a tour through it. "It was in terrible, run-down condition," Slatzer recalled. "The carpeting was stained, the walls had scribbling on them—dirty sayings, like you'd find in a men's restroom. The rooms were cluttered and trashy—there were old bedspreads thrown into the corner. The pool was covered with algae, all green and scummy. Ward and I went into one of the bedrooms and he pulled out a drawer from the dresser and a huge swarm of termites flew out around us. It was like a horror movie. We got out of there fast."

BETWEEN LATE 1968 (when he left the beach house permanently) and 1971, Peter was something of a nomad.

He first rented a garden apartment in the flats of Beverly Hills, then a large, furnished, 1920s Hollywood house with a swimming pool on DeLongpre Avenue in West Hollywood. When he moved from the DeLongpre house in January 1970, its owner, Tom Douglas, threatened to sue him for $2,508 for damages to the premises and missing furniture, glassware, and objets d'art. Peter disputed seven hundred dollars of the claim, but agreed to pay the rest.

From DeLongpre, Peter moved into a penthouse apartment in the Sierra Towers, a modern high-rise at Doheny and Sunset on the border between Beverly Hills and West Hollywood. The apartment belonged to a friend of Peter's, Bob Beaumont, who leased it to Peter for a rent far below market value.

No matter how badly his life was going, Peter was always able to turn on the charm for a woman. He shared all of these residences with Geri Crane, a striking, rather androgynous-looking twenty-one-year-old model whom he had met in 1968. Crane thought of herself as a "sobering factor" on Peter, and indeed the period they were together was one of the better times in his life. He limited his alcohol consumption, and he used no drugs except for some occasional marijuana. It appears, in fact, that for once his life was close to conventional. "We had a very subdued, quiet life," Crane recalled.

At the beginning of their relationship, according to Crane, sex between them was "very normal," and she remembered no instances of impotence. Later, though, things began to change; although Crane said there was never any sadomasochism in their relationship, Peter did begin to require "different heights" in their sex life. "There would be one or two lesbian girlfriends or a hooker always hanging around," she recalled, "and it was a constant fight because he was always trying to convince me to go to bed with them."

Peter respected Crane's wishes most of the time, a fact to which she attributed their relative longevity together: "I tried to establish a normal one-on-one relationship with him. But having two women in bed with him was something he had been involved with for years. It didn't just start with me or a couple of years before me. I seem to recall that it might have been part of what broke up his marriage to Pat Lawford. And in the end it was the reason we broke up."

Crane tried to save the relationship, but she couldn't. In February 1970 she wrote him a note after their final rift, saying that she no longer wanted to "mess up" his head and apologizing for being "selfish" in her refusal to share him with other women. She concluded by telling him that he would always remain the love of her life.

It wasn't just Peter's sexual quirks that forced Geri into her unhappy decision to leave him, but also what she saw as the constant competition for his love and attention. "We couldn't go anywhere that women weren't slipping him their telephone numbers—on planes, in nightclubs. I became very jealous of these suspected relationships, which he claimed didn't exist. I think now my jealousy was unjustified. But it was just something I couldn't deal with—it was making me sick. I made the decision that it wasn't healthy for me and that we should separate. He didn't want to."

But he agreed, and he paid the rent for her to live in Marilyn Monroe's old apartment on Doheny Drive for several months. Early in 1971, Crane permanently severed her relationship with Peter and returned to New York.

PETER MAY NOT have indulged in anything heavier than marijuana during his years with Geri Crane, but even that cost him an important personal and professional relationship in 1970, the first of many he would lose because of his growing dependency on drugs.

Johnny Carson and Peter had become friendly in the latter half of the sixties, and Peter was a frequent guest—and occasionally a guest host—on Carson's *Tonight* show. Peter enjoyed subbing for Carson; it was not only lucrative but offered him a chance to display his wit and charm before a national audience of millions.

Things fell apart, however, at a party in Peter's thirtieth-floor penthouse. Peter and Geri Crane had invited Johnny and a few other friends for a late dinner, during which they drank a variety of liquors and smoked pot. At two in the morning, Milt Ebbins was awakened from his sleep by a phone call from Carson's producer, Rudy Telez.

"Jesus Christ, Milt," Telez began, very agitated. "I just got a call from Johnny. He was over at Peter's and he smoked something and got so fucked up he went out on the balcony and almost jumped off!"

"What?"

"He came *this close* to jumping, Milt, and he's furious now—he wants to know what Peter put in that cigarette. He says it had to be something other than marijuana. Like LSD or something."

Ebbins immediately called Peter. "Jesus Christ, what did you do to Johnny Carson?"

"What do you mean?" Peter replied. "I didn't do anything to him."

"C'mon, Peter, the guy was gonna jump off your goddamn terrace on the thirtieth floor. What did you do to him?"

"We had some grass, that's all."

"And what did you put *in* the grass?"

Peter hesitated. "Uh, nothing."

Milt didn't believe him. "Peter usually put *something* extra in his grass, so I think it's quite possible that's what happened."

Geri Crane denied it. "Nobody ever gave him anything. We only smoked grass. But if you smoke and drink at the same time you can get pretty stoned. Johnny got real high. And he wasn't accustomed to it. Johnny was a very odd bird. He would come to parties and just be very quiet and laid back. Everybody thought he was shy, but I think it was because he was always alone in a corner, drinking. That night, he was just really out of it and he freaked, that's all."

Carson could not be convinced that Peter or Geri hadn't laced the pot with something else. "So that finished Peter Lawford with Johnny Carson," Ebbins recalled. "Johnny never saw him again, never used him on his show. That was the end of him."

THIRTY-EIGHT

ROBERT D. FRANKS was not likely to forget Lady
Lawford. On April 1, 1967, the automobile salesman
sold the eighty-three-year-old woman a brand-new
convertible Ford Fairlane GT. Four days later, he heard the
news that May had backed the car out of her driveway at
forty miles per hour, shot across the street, run over a sap-
ling, and hit a car parked in another driveway. Her car
had then lurched forward, screeched across the street again,
missed a baby in a carriage by inches, and crashed into a
brick wall.

Her face a bloody mess, May was rushed to the Beverly
Hills Emergency Clinic. She refused treatment and tore up
her medical chart—"that awful clinic, nothing but niggers."
She saw her own doctor, who surgically removed nine of
May's teeth from the back of her throat and sewed her
nearly severed lower lip back on.·

Police sergeant C. O. Lewis wanted to file a hit-and-
run complaint against May, which incensed her. In response
to his questions she barked, "I'm not a Yank, and I don't
have to tell you a bloody thing. I'm a British subject and
immune." She told friends she would like to forget some of
the other things she said to Sergeant Lewis.

May claimed that the accelerator was faulty and had
stuck, and later hinted at a conspiracy designed to kill her
and make her death look like an accident. She convinced
the Ford dealership to replace the car, and on May 10,

441

salesman Franks delivered a replacement, a shiny new six-cylinder Mustang. The next day, he got a call from May. She'd lost the keys; could he bring over a new set?

Franks drove over and gave May the keys, but before he could get back to his own car she had started the Mustang. "I heard the car accelerate at a great rate of speed," Franks recalled. As he watched in horror, May roared backward out of her driveway and crashed into a house across the street, then roared forward toward Franks's car. "The Mustang hit my car," Franks said, "and continued accelerating. It pushed my car up on the parkway. Finally I reached her car and turned the ignition off."

May wasn't hurt this time, but the damage to the house and the two automobiles amounted to thirty-two hundred dollars. Sergeant Lewis conferred with the city attorney's office, but no charges were filed. The press made light of the incidents; a typical headline read, "Lady May Goes for Another Spin." *Sports Illustrated* told its readers, "Los Angeles residents who lack the time or money to make it out to the Indy 500 this month might just go and stand around Lady May Lawford's garage. . . ."

To Milt Ebbins, it wasn't a laughing matter. May had had other accidents, and when her license came up for renewal, Ebbins stepped in. He told the California Department of Motor Vehicles, "Don't give this woman a license. She can't drive. She's gonna kill somebody. She almost killed that baby—it was *inches*." May did no further driving.

By the end of the decade, when she was eighty-six years old, May's mental health had severely deteriorated. Just about everyone, she believed, was conspiring against her, everyone was a threat to her life. After a fall down a flight of stairs, which she blamed on a doctor overmedicating her for a cold, she was taken by ambulance to St. John's Hospital in Santa Monica. There she was X-rayed and sedated, and spent a quiet night. The next morning, the doctors told her they were studying her X-ray films and said she would have to remain in the hospital for a few days.

As soon as she was alone in her room, May put the wool dress she'd been wearing back on and walked, shoeless, out of the hospital. "She thought they were trying to kidnap her," her friend John Farquhar recalled. She commandeered a taxi that had come for someone else and had the driver—drunk, she claimed—take her home. There, she locked herself in.

His mother's erratic behavior left Peter at a loss. He tried to keep as much distance as possible between them, both physical and emotional, but her recurring crises made that very difficult to do. He was in St. John's Hospital, on his way to visit her, when she walked out. She had seen him and made sure he didn't see her, convinced as she was that he was part of the plots against her. More and more her inexplicable behavior weighed on him. "She's in bad shape," Peter said to Milt Ebbins. But what could be done?

During another of May's hospitalizations, Peter asked the doctors to perform psychiatric tests on her. May was typically pigheaded. She refused to cooperate and wrote to a friend, "I am incarcerated in UCLA psycho ward. Drs. have made sanity tests of me. This torture of a British subject cannot continue without active trouble."

The psychiatrists at UCLA told Peter that May was suffering from advancing senility and some paranoia, but they did not advise that she be institutionalized. When May was released from the hospital, she wrote her son a letter begging his forgiveness for the way she had treated him over the years: "Today for the first time I realize how very harsh and unkind I have been. My dear Peter I can't blame you for your past actions—Thank God I am a new woman."

But Peter found May's new attitude suspect, and in any event it was too late to mend fences. He continued to avoid her as much as possible and left it to Milt Ebbins to help her in day-to-day situations, pay her expenses, and send her flowers on Easter and Christmas.

May's isolation and loneliness were relieved only by the continual flow through her life of impressionable young men who were fascinated by her title, her regal bearing, her caustic wit, her stories of world travel and friendship with royalty, her connections to Hollywood and the Kennedys. Always, May made efforts to intrigue anyone who might come to her door. When a new boy from the local liquor market delivered her Southern Comfort, she would introduce herself grandly: "I'm Lady Lawford, Peter Lawford's mother. Would you like to come in?" If he did, she would regale the young man with stories of her husband's military exploits, of her friendships with kings and queens, of the young Duke of Windsor's drunkenness, of Joe Kennedy's chicanery, of her son's last telephone call to Marilyn Monroe.

But May was nothing if not contrary. Should a young man express admiration for Peter, May would snap, "He's a bastard! I haven't seen him in I don't know how long. He never calls me." Almost invariably, the reaction would be, "Oh, you poor dear," and the irrepressible Lady Lawford would have a new friend.

Too many of these "friends," however, were merely hucksters who saw a way to make a quick buck off a dotty old lady. She gave one young man she trusted a number of rings and silver pieces and asked him to have them appraised so that she could sell them and raise money—Peter was no longer paying her expenses at this point because he had so many debts of his own. Her friend returned a few days later, told her the items had been appraised for very little, and offered to sell them for her. He then gave May the pittance he had said the items were worth and pocketed the considerable difference. May lost all the diamonds she owned this way.

The one bright spot in Lady Lawford's declining years was her friendship with Buddy Galon, a twenty-five-year-old theater student at UCLA. May's friend Thelma Keaton, the widow of Buster Keaton, had met Galon when he was speaking on the subject of reincarnation at a symposium in Beverly Hills in the summer of 1966. May's interest in the occult had not waned; in 1968 her description of an encounter with a UFO appeared in newspapers across the country in a column of hard-to-explain occurrences. She had espied, she said, "a beautiful candelabra UFO with sparkling lights hanging all around it, which immediately sped away at terrific speed through a hole in the sky."

Thelma Keaton thought May might enjoy Galon, a boyishly handsome blond who had briefly been a "Mousketeer" on television's *Mickey Mouse Club* in the 1950s. She was right. Although there was a nearly sixty-year difference in their ages, May and Galon hit it off immediately. "Within fifteen minutes," he recalled, "there was that wonderful chemical reaction that happens between people. Having spoken an hour or so before on reincarnation, I believed I already knew this woman—that we had met in a previous life. And later on, we used it to explain our age difference, in that she arrived early on this Earth plane, whereas I arrived late."

Galon was amazed by Lady Lawford's interest in him. "She knew that trick of making someone you're with seem like the most important person in the world. Her whole concentration was on me, on the things that I was doing. And I thought, *This woman knew Queen Mary and Louis B. Mayer and the Kennedys, and she thinks I'm interesting.* That really attracted me to her."

The two of them saw each other almost daily for the next five years. As "the most exciting and fascinating woman I've ever met," May mesmerized the star-struck Galon with stories of royalty and movie stars. They discussed mysticism during a drive up the California coast. She helped him with his homework, and "she was," he noted, "no dummy when it came to Shakespeare." They had "vociferous" debates about international politics. They collapsed into helpless giggling at a Santa Barbara dinner party when an elderly German ambassador fell asleep facedown in his soup. In Palm Springs, they went skinny-dipping after midnight.

Nearly every day, they would have afternoon tea together at four o'clock. "It was a ritual," Galon recalled, "a carryover from her past. In the later years, it was just the two of us, but in the earlier years we had company—Patrick Mahoney came quite often. Patrick is the half brother of Sir Arthur Bliss, of the London Philharmonic. John Farquhar came, and so did Leo G. Carroll. Lady Victoria Stevenson, the queen's cousin, would come in from Claremont. I might have been bowled over by these people with titles and everything, but I learned that they go to the bathroom just like we do. They'd come in with wrinkled, dirty clothes, dandruff on their shoulders. And some of them are bores."

Galon has said that he and Lady Lawford were married on Easter Sunday, 1968, in Tijuana. Because he has no proof of this (according to him, the marriage certificate was destroyed) and because they never lived together, Galon's claim has aroused skepticism. But whether or not he and May were in fact married is irrelevant. What is clear is that the two were very important to each other. "I didn't want anything from the woman," he said. "I didn't make any claims on the estate. I had more than she had, really. But I had grown to love her. It wasn't a passionate love, but it was love nonetheless."

If their story is reminiscent of the Bud Cort and Ruth Gordon film *Harold and Maude,* it's because, according to Galon, the film's screenwriter, Colin Higgins, was told about his relationship with May. "That movie was based on us. Even the stuff about the young man being suicidal. I was fascinated by death when I first met May."

As the months went by, Galon began to see the less enchanting side of May Lawford. "I noticed the liquor around the house, I experienced the mood changes. She could be impossible, she was awful, she was insulting. It would be enough to make you cry. It would happen so quickly, I wouldn't be prepared for it. Sometimes a phone call would trigger these episodes, sometimes nothing at all. I called them her 'black moods.' I'd have to leave her place, and if I came back in an hour, she'd be fine.

"I'm not a psychiatrist, but it seemed to me she was manic-depressive. That makes some pieces of the puzzle fit into place. She could be so energetic, almost manic, when she was entertaining. She'd go into a frenzy. When you got her on a particular subject, she'd be like a motormouth.

"And then she'd turn. She showed me the *Sports Illustrated* piece about her accident and she sat there and roared about how humorous it was; then all of a sudden, she started to cry. It had been traumatic for her. And she worried, Will the same thing happen again?

"She would say, 'They really do want me dead. They are not going to let me stay alive.' In the beginning, I thought she was paranoid, that she was having delusions, hallucinations. But maybe because I was with her every day, I lost my objectivity. At the end, I came to believe her. Some of these things *were* real. I saw bruises on her that I don't believe she could have inflicted on herself in any way."

By March 1971, May, eighty-seven years old, seemed no longer able to function safely without constant attention. "She kept getting progressively worse," Milt Ebbins recalled. "She always thought people were coming to kill her." Peter and Milt conferred with May's doctor, and he told them that in his opinion May would be best off in a nursing home.

It was left to Ebbins to break the news to her. "Look,

May," he told her, "you don't feel well. You'll be much better taken care of there."

May had feared institutionalization. She often told friends, "They're going to put me away. I can't stand the thought of that." She asked Ebbins, "They'll be nice to me there, won't they?" He reassured her, describing the Monterey Park Convalescent Hospital as "palatial, a wonderful home, with a beautiful courtyard—very highly recommended." It was expensive, he added, and one of the best in Southern California. A private room in the facility cost thirty-four hundred dollars a month (equivalent to twice that in 1991 dollars). "And of course you'll have a private room, May. Don't worry about it."

"She trusted me," Ebbins recalled, "and she agreed." A few days later, he and Peter's maid, Erma Lee Riley, drove May to the home on Garfield Avenue in Monterey Park. "They put her in her room and she was a martinet. She drove them *crazy*. She complained about everything: 'Where's my soup?' she'd yell at them. 'The bacon's cold!' "

When Ebbins brought Peter to see May for the first time, they entered her room and Milt said, "May, look who's here." She stared at Peter and said, "Who are you?"

"May, it's Peter, your son," Ebbins said.

"No it isn't!" May insisted.

"Yes, May, it's Peter."

"No! That's Alan Mowbray."

Peter bolted out of the room, leaned against the corridor wall, and began to cry. Finally, Milt convinced May that Peter was indeed her son, not Mowbray, the elderly English character actor who had passed away in 1969. "Peter looked so much older than May remembered him looking," Ebbins said. "They hadn't seen each other in years. His hair was long and gray."

When Peter went back into the room, May looked at him closely and said, "Are you Peter?" He said, "Yes." She then adopted a regal attitude and said, "How are you?" Ebbins recalled that "she started to act like a queen talking to her son."

May remained in the Monterey Park Convalescent Hospital for almost a year. At first, the expenses of her hospitalization were paid from a conservancy account that Ebbins had set up with the nearly eighteen thousand dollars he had discovered in May's several savings accounts. Peter had joint access to the account, and Ebbins soon discovered that he was writing checks to prostitutes and drug dealers. "I told him, 'What are you, nuts? You could go to jail for that!' He said to me, 'Who's gonna know?' I told him a lot of people could find out and he was asking for trouble." When Peter didn't stop, Ebbins took access to the account away from him.

Buddy Galon, according to his account in his "as told to" autobiography of Lady Lawford, had gone out of town on family business, and when he returned he found May gone and her apartment bare. He did not know where she was and spent weeks trying to find out, telephoning a score of her friends without success. (He apparently never thought to ask Milt Ebbins where May was.) Six months later, he quite by accident discovered May's whereabouts and—pretending to be her grandson—went to see her.

He described her as "emaciated," her hair "hacked off" so closely that she looked like a concentration camp victim. She wore a thin muslin shift stained with urine and fecal matter. She was, Galon wrote, restrained at her ankles, waist, wrists, and mouth.

Milt Ebbins refuted the implications of Galon's description of May's condition. "She got excellent care. It was a very good hospital. I saw her from time to time. She wasn't shaven, she didn't have excrement on her. Now, toward the very end, she might have. But if you have somebody who can't take care of themselves, that happens. She might have been incontinent. And they might have shaved her hair very short to help keep her groomed."

He never saw May restrained in any way. "But it is possible that she had become violent. If the hospital felt that May might harm herself, they would have had to restrain her."

Ebbins paid May a visit toward the end. "She was lying down. I didn't notice if her hair was shaved because I couldn't see the back of her head. She didn't know anybody. She had grown quite feeble. She rambled. And then she went into a coma. They told me she probably wouldn't last very long. Peter wouldn't go to visit her. He didn't want to see her like that."

In his alarm over May's condition, Buddy Galon tried

to reach Peter in the hope that he could do something to help her. After a series of fruitless phone calls, he finally tracked Peter down in Puerto Vallarta, Mexico, on October 29. His emotions about to get the better of him, Galon pleaded with Peter to do something about the "horrors" he'd seen May subjected to. He expected Peter to be shocked and concerned about his mother and offer immediate help.

Instead, it was Galon who was shocked. He encountered a drunken, belligerent Peter on the telephone. When Galon said how concerned he was about May, Peter grunted. "Why don't you just shoot her in the goddamn leg and be done with it?" he spat. "Now leave me alone—I'm getting married!"

THIRTY-NINE

HE HAD VOWED not to do it. In July 1968 he
had told a journalist, "I won't marry again. . . . My
friends' marriages are all breaking up. Sammy's and
Frank's marriages both broke up in the same week." His
attitude changed, however, on the set of the television phenomenon *Rowan and Martin's Laugh-In,* the irreverent Monday night variety hour that starred comedians Dan Rowan
and Dick Martin and seemed to shoot up from nowhere to
become the number-one show in the country in 1968. Along
the way, it changed the face of TV comedy.

Helped along by a brilliant young cast of comics
headed by Lily Tomlin, Goldie Hawn, Henry Gibson, Judy
Carne, Alan Sues, JoAnne Worley, Ruth Buzzi, and Arte
Johnson, *Laugh-In* epitomized "hip" with its lightning-fast
blackouts, its devastating political commentary, and its frequent double entendres.

The cast and crew enjoyed nothing more than to keep
the NBC censors in a constant state of bewilderment while
they stretched the limits of what could be done—and said—
on television. As Dick Martin recalled, "Up until our show,
you'd send the standards and practices department a script
and they'd blue-pencil it—'you can't say this, you can't say
that.' With our show, they had to have someone come down
and sit on the set. And they would pick a real yo-yo. We
had, I think, seven pot jokes in the first show and they never
caught any of them. One was, 'My boyfriend is so dumb he

thinks a little pot is Tupperware for midgets.' The censor comes up to us and says, 'You can't say that!' We learned early on to feign ignorance. 'Why not?' we said. He said, 'Because it's a plug for Tupperware'!"

Another joke proved equally obscure to the censor: "For the first time in thirty years, everyone at the United Nations has agreed on everything. And they're still trying to figure out who put the grass in the air conditioner."

"The guy came down," Martin remembered, "and said to me, 'What's funny about grass in an air conditioner?' And we said, 'Well, you know, some guy mows the lawn and puts the grass in the air conditioner and people see all this green flying around and they don't think right.' He says, 'Oh. Well, that's not very *funny*.' And about eight weeks later he comes to me and says, 'You son of a bitch!' because by then he'd figured it out."

A staple of *Laugh-In* was the special guest star, and here again the show strived for the unusual. "We didn't want the ordinary names," Martin said. "Or, if we got Sonny and Cher, we'd put Sonny on one show and Cher on the other—we'd split 'em up. We'd get Sammy Davis but we wouldn't let him sing—we'd drop him through a trapdoor."

The first guest star was John Wayne—who did nothing during the taping but say, "Well, I don't think that's funny," a dozen times in front of the camera, without knowing what he was supposed to be reacting to. The comments were then interspersed throughout the finished show, usually after double entendres having to do with sex or drugs.

"John Wayne was the first big star who broke the barrier," Martin recalled. "Once Wayne did it, it was okay for Jack Lemmon and Kirk Douglas and all the other big stars to do it too. Peter Lawford was one of the unusual names we came up with who was adorable to be around but wasn't a big star. But we didn't need big stars for ratings. We already had the ratings."

Peter appeared on *Laugh-In* once or twice a season between 1968 and 1972. He would do brief song-and-dance routines, deliver one-liners in the "cocktail party" sequences, and do blackout sketches. Often the sketches were a parody of Peter's family background. As Martin recalled them, "He and I would be two British lords in India with the pith helmets and the queen's chairs. I don't remember what we said but it was probably 'How long have you been with William Morris?' "

Peter loved the atmosphere of *Laugh-In,* loved the camaraderie he established with the show's sharp young performers. Late in December 1970, while shooting a cocktail party sequence late one morning, he noticed a willowy dancer with long blond hair, about twenty-one.

"Who's that girl over there?" he asked Ian Bernard, the show's musical director. "She's beautiful."

"That's Mary Rowan, Dan's daughter," Bernard replied. "And Dan still thinks she's fifteen."

Peter laughed and left the set for lunch. When he returned, he became aware of Mary's constant stare—she had noticed Peter at the same time he noticed her. "I just stood there gasping," she recalled, "because this had to be the most gorgeous man I'd ever seen—all this thick hair with the gray at the temples, a great physique, groovy personality. I came back after lunch, although I wasn't needed, just to stick around and watch him. And it seemed to me he kept looking at *me.*"

When her father came back to the set from his lunch break, Mary asked him to introduce her to Peter. His response was curt: "He's too old for you."

"I don't care," she protested. "I just want to meet him."

Rowan pretended he hadn't heard her and walked away. But Ed Hookstratten, Rowan's attorney, couldn't help but notice that Peter and Mary barely took their eyes off each other for the rest of the day. At about seven-thirty, Hookstratten took Mary by the arm, guided her down a corridor, and deposited her amid a crowd of people in Peter's dressing room. "There was no introduction, nothing," Mary recalled. "I was so nervous, I couldn't talk. I didn't know anyone in the room. I was so scared and then Peter rescued me. He was charming. 'Please sit down,' he said, and handed me a glass of wine."

When Peter was called back to the set, he asked Mary to come along and watch the scene. When the day's shoot wrapped, about ten o'clock that night, he invited her to join him for a hamburger. They remained in the burger joint and talked until early morning. From that point on, they were inseparable.

Dick Martin recalled that "Mary and Peter were very cute together. Of course, when they started going together, we started making jokes. But Dan had less and less of a sense of humor about it as things went on."

"I'm sure that Dad thinks I fell in love with Peter because he is a movie star, the whole glamour bit," Mary said at the time. "But that was just the first two or three weeks. I was constantly nervous. I was always wondering, *What am I doing with Peter Lawford?* He was still, in my mind, a movie star, former brother-in-law of the former President, gorgeous, super. And all the girls kept calling him, his phone never stopped ringing, and all the while I'm wondering: *What am I doing here?*"

Dan Rowan's concern wasn't just that his daughter was falling in love with Peter because he was a glamorous celebrity, or even that at forty-seven Peter was too old for her. What worried him most was that Mary, immature for her age, saw in Peter a substitute for the father that Dan hadn't always been able to be. With that as its basis, he feared, the relationship was bound to fail.

According to Dick Martin, "The problem with Mary and Dan was the road. We were on the road for a long time before we hit it big, from the time Mary was about three. From that time on, over the next ten years, Dan was home very little. He used to take his son Tom on the road with him, and I'd take my son. But it was harder with a girl, so Mary didn't come along."

When Mary was in her midteens, Dan made up for his earlier absence in her life. "They became as close as I've ever seen a father and daughter," Martin observed. "In fact, she lived with him on a barge scouting around France for two years."

Although Mary had dated a number of young men her own age and had been involved with a drummer in a rock group for two years before meeting Peter, she found mature men appealing. "Older men are so much more understanding," she said. "They've been through it all. They can understand the things you are going through in your life where younger guys are on their own ego trips and just haven't got the understanding."

After a few months with Peter, Mary said, she had grown as a person. "He has taught me so much, gotten me interested in economics and sociology, what this country is all about, things I never really thought about before. This is an intellectual man and he's involved, tremendously involved with what's happening today. That's good for me."

Within weeks of their meeting, Mary moved into Peter's Sierra Towers apartment, but a short while later he decided to move—because of an earthquake on February 9, 1971, that killed sixty-five people in Southern California. Terrified by the way the Sierra Towers building had swayed in the temblor, Peter moved a few blocks away into a sprawling second-story apartment in a picturesque English-style complex on Cory Avenue near the Beverly Hills city line ("One block over and a thousand dollars less," Peter said). He loved the feel of the place, from the center court garden to his "veddy British" landlord, Bill Noad, who had known May and who treated him as a very special tenant indeed.

Shortly after the earthquake, Mary Rowan was called to Houston to take care of a sick friend. After a week's separation, Peter traveled to Texas and spent two weeks with her. After he returned to Los Angeles, she wrote to him that she wanted to come home—but couldn't. Once she did get home, she said, Peter wouldn't be able to get rid of her. In another letter, she told Peter how much she missed him: "I can't wait to make love to you—to see you—to kiss you."

At the beginning, Peter and Mary's life together was close to idyllic. "We're so in tune it's ridiculous," Peter said. "Finding someone I didn't think existed has helped me a lot. . . . She's an extraordinary, marvelous, endearing, kind human being. She's magnificent."

Mary was dazzled: there were limousines, trips to Hawaii, accounts at Bergdorf Goodman, custom-made clothes, helicopter jaunts, stays at the Waldorf-Astoria in New York, dinners at LA's finest restaurants. Even as Dan Rowan's daughter, Mary wasn't used to a way of life this sumptuous.

That summer, Peter went to Vancouver, British Columbia, to film one of the first made-for-television movies, *The Deadly Hunt,* for director John Newland. He brought Mary with him, along with his son, Christopher, now sixteen, who had flown to Los Angeles from New York in order to spend the summer with his father. Mary went to pick Chris up at the airport, but wasn't quite sure what he looked like; her only reference was a picture of him at twelve, as a close-cropped little boy.

At the airport she saw a thin, six-foot-two-inch young man with a backpack, hair down to his shoulders. "He had to be the cutest guy I'd ever seen," Mary recalled, "and of course it was Chris." In Vancouver, Mary and Chris visited Peter on the set, and the three of them smoked pot so much that John Newland became perturbed. "They did a lot of it, and Peter was always offering me some. Pot was kind of new then and I'd say 'No, no, no.' He'd never smoke during the shooting; it was always after work."

After they returned to Los Angeles in August, Peter nonchalantly said to Mary, "I want Chris to be my best man when we get married." She just laughed, thinking it was a joke, but a few nights later he gave her a delicately twisted band of gold and asked her to marry him. "Peter, do you honestly know what you're saying?" she asked him.

"I've been thinking about it for months," he replied—ever since that first late-night hamburger supper. Mary was surprised, first at him and then at herself for saying yes. "I guess when it happens, it happens."

When Mary told her father the news, she recalled, "he just kind of sat there looking at me stunned. He said, 'I thought you told me you'd never get married.' And I had to laugh because of course it was true. He was in a state of shock. All he did was try to talk me out of it. He thought it was a big mistake—that I shouldn't be marrying a man a year younger than my father. He wasn't exactly thrilled with Peter."

When the announcement of the October wedding plans made the newspapers in early September, reporters converged on Dan Rowan for his reaction. "I've known Peter Lawford for a number of years," Rowan said, measuring his words carefully, "and I've always found him to be a gentleman. He and Mary have been going steady for a year now and seem to know each other very well. I'd rather see her marry a man closer to her age than to mine. But they are in love." Told of Rowan's remark, Peter quipped, "Well, I was hoping for a younger father-in-law."

Peter and Mary were married in a small private ceremony in Puerto Vallarta on October 30, 1971, the day before her twenty-second birthday. Chris Lawford served as best man, and the entire wedding party—composed only of Peter's newer friends—wore jeans. Mary arrived at the ceremony aboard a yacht, wearing an antique lace blouse over her dungarees. Puerto Vallarta's municipal president, Luis Fabela Icaza, performed the ceremony, and everyone toasted the beaming couple after they were pronounced man and wife. There was now a new Mrs. Peter Lawford.

LESS THAN three months after her son's wedding, on January 23, 1972, at two-ten in the afternoon, May Lawford died. The death certificate lists the causes of death as cardiac failure, arteriosclerosis, and heart disease. Under "other significant condition" a doctor added by hand, "senility."

Within hours of her death, May was cremated and her ashes scattered at sea. According to Buddy Galon, when he learned that Peter planned no memorial service for his mother, he went ahead with plans for one on his own. He notified May's friends and family, and the media, that there would be a service at St. Alban's Episcopal Church. "Within twenty-four hours," Galon recalled, "a notice of the service came out of Milt Ebbins's office. They took over the arrangements from me. I didn't mind that as long as we got together."

In March, May's will was probated. The document, handwritten on October 26, 1961, named her friend Paul Simqu as executor and asked that her cat, Amber, be put to sleep "and not buried for twenty-four hours to prevent drugging for vivisection." May also stated that Paul Simqu "has my wishes regarding the disposal of my remains" and stated that "my body is to be kept the maximum time permitted by law." She had bequeathed all of her personal effects and any money left after her bills were paid to her sister Gretta, but since Gretta had died of arterial sclerosis in South Africa in the midsixties and May had not updated her will, she was without an heir except for Peter. She had expressly omitted him from the will and stipulated that anyone contesting its provisions should receive "the sum of $1—one dollar *only*."

The will, however, was ruled out of force because Paul Simqu was unable to provide the original or explain its absence. Peter, as May's closest living relative, was deemed executor and required to put up an eleven-thousand-dollar bond while the will was settled.

May's personal effects in 1961 (jewelry, furs, and objets d'art) had a total value of approximately twenty thousand dollars; by the time of her death so much of the best had been sold that when Milt Ebbins had thirty-seven pieces of furniture and artifacts that May had claimed were antiques appraised, their value was revealed to be just $1,097. There had also been several valuable oriental rugs and the eighteen thousand dollars in cash Ebbins had found in various bank accounts, but that had been consumed by the thirty-four-hundred-dollar monthly cost of May's care at Monterey Park Convalescent Hospital, her medical bills, and miscellaneous expenses.

After the bills were paid, Lady Lawford's estate totaled $221. The court awarded that amount to Peter to help offset his legal expenses as executor.

THE REALIZATION came gradually to Mary Rowan. There were apparently insignificant hints at first, then more and more clear signs that the effulgent life she was leading with Peter Lawford was little more than a house of cards. Nearly everything she admired about Peter, she had begun to see, had either been illusory from the start or was slowly disappearing. He was, she now realized, a man beset as no one she had ever known by problems and demons.

She was hit first by the fact that Peter was living far beyond his means. He worked fairly steadily; he made seven guest appearances on episodic television in 1971, played a small part in an MGM-reunion movie, *They Only Kill Their Masters* in the spring of 1972, and began a recurring role on *The Doris Day Show* in the summer.

But the pay for these jobs was often minimal, and Peter spent money as though he were still commanding seventy-five thousand dollars a picture and married to Pat Kennedy on top of it. Mary was forced to intercept dunning calls from an array of creditors, all of whom demanded immediate payment of long-outstanding bills. She was perplexed at first; surely Peter Lawford had the money to pay his bills. When she asked Peter about it, he blamed his business manager, as he was wont to do, but it was soon clear that no business manager in the world could have paid bills that his client didn't have the money to pay.

By 1971, Peter's financial situation was little short of disastrous. Between 1971 and 1973 alone, he was either threatened with legal action or taken to court by two dozen creditors for unpaid bills ranging from $203 to $18,000. Many of the lawsuits resulted in judgments against him.

Just a partial list of Peter's long-unpaid debts reveals a man living a life he could not afford. He owed $341 to the Surrey Cadillac Limousine Service; $241 to Steuben Glass; $4,348 to Grosvenor House, a London hotel; $2,183 to the Waldorf-Astoria in New York; $485 to Cartier of London; $203 to TWA; $545 to MacRane restaurant; and $455 to the interior decorator who had refurbished his Sierra Towers apartment.

Judgments against Peter included one that Clayton Plumbers won in 1970 for $8,974 in repairs to the beach house in 1969; by 1972 Peter still had not paid them, and Clayton was awarded another judgment, this one for $9,935 (the additional amount was interest). Peter finally settled with Clayton by paying them $7,000 in June 1977.

Other judgments, won in 1973 after all other attempts at collection had failed, were for $1,318 to the Credit Research Corp., a collection agency (which Peter settled for $400); $920 to Bergdorf Goodman; and $2,499 to Sy Devore, the most fashionable men's clothier in Los Angeles.

Mary might have been able to live with Peter's financial problems, might even have been able to help out, cut corners, live on a budget. But she knew now that Peter had a myriad of other problems that threatened to destroy their marriage. He had become increasingly dependent on marijuana, and he was now also using both Quaaludes and cocaine, which produced opposing effects. His oldest friends were drifting away from him because of the drug use; and a lot of strangers were suddenly on the scene, people from whom Peter could easily obtain drugs. They were people Mary didn't trust.

Drugs were a staple of the new "youth culture," and Peter felt using them was "hip," that it kept his image young, kept him from seeming twenty-six years older than his wife. "To Peter," Milt Ebbins recalled, "drugs were a badge of honor. He always wanted to be 'with it,' be in the vanguard, be a part of 'what's happening now.' And drugs were *it* in the early seventies. Plus, he convinced himself that drugs wouldn't harm his liver and thus weren't as bad for him as alcohol. Of course, after a while he started drinking *and* doing drugs, which was the worst thing he could do."

The combination caused his sexual performance to suffer once again. His impotence recurred, and he started to suggest sexual activities to Mary that she found distasteful and offensive. She was hurt, confused, crushingly disillusioned. She found herself thinking about calling it quits on the marriage and going home to her father.

In November 1972, however, the last thing on Mary's mind was leaving Peter Lawford—for he lay in a hospital close to death.

FORTY

E HAD NOTICED something was wrong that
August, when he started having twinges of pain in
his stomach. At first he tried to ignore them, attrib-
uting them to tension. But the spasms got worse. They began
first thing in the morning and continued throughout the day.
The stabbing pain would immobilize him, and he was unable
to sleep at night without sleeping pills. Finally, in mid-Sep-
tember, he saw a doctor. Immediately, he was admitted to
a Los Angeles hospital for diagnostic tests. The doctors determined that the problem wasn't Peter's liver, as they had
suspected at first. Although they were unable to come up
with a definite diagnosis, they told him that an ulcer was
the most likely culprit.

He remained in the hospital under observation for five
weeks, anesthetized with regular shots of morphine that
dulled the pain but couldn't disguise the fact that something
was still very wrong. "One day I realized my arms were like
a skeleton's," Peter later said. "I got up and looked in the
mirror. I was shocked to see my whole body was
emaciated."

His weight had dropped from 172 to 120 pounds.
Mary, alarmed, insisted that he consult other doctors and
enter a different hospital. He agreed, and on November 5
she drove him directly to the Scripps Clinic, one of the
country's top diagnostic centers, fifty miles south of Los
Angeles. Within minutes of his admission the doctors knew

what was wrong with him: he had a cyst on his pancreas, the organ that helps the body digest fat and also secretes insulin—and without which one cannot survive.

Peter didn't immediately realize the seriousness of the situation. "I was thinking of cysts from childhood," he said, "the tiny things you get on your eyelid. How bad could that be?" But the Scripps doctors told him that he required immediate surgery, and he found himself lying on a stretcher in an ambulance speeding back to Los Angeles and the UCLA Medical Center. "Why do I need an ambulance?" Peter remembered wondering. He was upset that the vehicle's curtains weren't drawn, because when the ambulance reached UCLA, it was surrounded, he said, by "gaping ghouls" craning their necks to get a glimpse of him.

Surgeons labored over Peter for six hours to remove the growth, which turned out to be the size of a grapefruit and perilously close to bursting. "I could have died on the operating table," he later said. "Or even in the ambulance on the way to the hospital. The doctors said that just the slightest bump could have been enough to burst the cyst."

If the mass hadn't been removed, the doctors told Peter, he would have died within two or three days. "I can truthfully say that Mary saved my life," Peter said. He remained in the hospital for two weeks and then returned home for another ten weeks of recuperation, most of it spent resting in bed. "Mary was incredible, the greatest of all nurses. She resolved to bring me back, and she accomplished it through patience, care, and deep love."

In mid-February 1973, Peter was well enough recovered to travel to Hawaii, where the Lawfords remained for six weeks as guests of Peter's friends Gordon and Sue Damon. It was there that the marriage finally fell apart as Mary came to realize that the problems that had been nagging at her had not been mitigated by Peter's illness, only postponed. In Hawaii, Peter—despite his fragile health—smoked pot, popped Quaaludes, took painkillers that he no longer needed, and drank at a time when his digestive system could least tolerate alcohol.

Mary shared many of the drugs with Peter because he wanted her to, but she didn't like doing it. She could see what was happening to him, and feared it might happen to her. "Peter was into drugs and he got me into them," she recalled. "It's a period of my life I'd rather forget. The marriage was a mistake. I don't have anything good to say about Peter Lawford."

She made the decision to leave him during a shopping trip to Hong Kong with Sue Damon while Peter returned to Los Angeles from Hawaii. "While I was away, I realized I wasn't happy with my life anymore. When I got back from Hong Kong, I wanted a separation." In early April, she moved out of Cory Avenue and back into her father's house in Holmby Hills. Peter wrote her a letter in which he apparently asked her to come back to him and promised that if she returned he would give up his drug use and his search for sexual variety.

She wrote him a reply on April 30, telling him that she did not believe his promise to give up "those two things." She closed the letter saying that she had loved him very much, and that he had given her a great deal—he had made her a woman. But, she concluded, she needed to have her own identity, not be a part of Peter Lawford's.

On June 16, the separation was made public. A few weeks later Peter gave an interview in which he said he would "fight like a tiger" to get Mary back. "I am not willing to accept the thought of a divorce," he said. "I will fight it. I need her and love her."

If there was any hope for a reconciliation, it was only on the condition that Peter change. Mary asked him to seek help for his addictions and get psychiatric counseling for his sexual problems—in other words, work toward removing what she saw as the obstacles to their marital happiness. When he wasn't willing to do that, she realized that there was no hope for the marriage, that he was too set in his ways to change. "I felt Peter could have done something to save the marriage," she said, "but he didn't. I was very bitter."

Peter didn't fight the divorce, and Mary won a final decree on January 2, 1975. She requested no alimony, but Peter was ordered by the court to make all future lease payments on Mary's 1970 Mercedes-Benz (license plate, "BUNDLE") and to purchase it for her at the end of the lease term. Two years later, Mary won a judgment against Peter in LA superior court for nonpayment of the car lease expenses ($1,426) and attorney's fees ($1,658). A garnishee of wages due Peter from Landsburg Productions netted $1,630, but none of the other companies Peter had worked for were able to provide more than a few dollars. The full judgment was never satisfied.

BY THIS TIME in his life, attachments of Peter's salary were an everyday occurrence, something Milt Ebbins had become expert at evading. "He was so besieged by creditors," Ebbins recalled, "that his salary was attached every time he turned around. They couldn't touch residuals, but every time he got a new job his salary was garnisheed. So I'd put his contracts in Chrislaw's name, and the creditors didn't know about Chrislaw—they were always wondering where the money went. To make sure they didn't have time to find out, I'd run down to the production companies the day before he finished the job and physically *get* the money." Aware as he was of Peter's financial troubles, Ebbins didn't take his commission from the earnings. "I had other clients, like Elizabeth Montgomery and Mort Sahl. Toward the end, for years, I never got a dime from Peter Lawford. I just never took it."

Peter's financial problems had taken on an extra dimension by 1973. He was still living as though he were a wealthy man, and still not paying many of his bills. Now, however, there was the added element of drug expenses. Peter's dependence on marijuana, cocaine, and Quaaludes—and his recent experimentation with PCP, MDA, and even heroin—drained his cash reserves and ate up whatever salary he received from the few television guest shots he was able to muster. (He did one TV movie in 1973, nothing else.)

Peter began to borrow money from friends, but he found that his new life-style had left him with few of his old cohorts. Now, drug users and drug dealers were the most important people in his life; they came and went at Cory Avenue at will, bringing with them hangers-on and groupies who were thrilled to meet Peter Lawford and more than happy to take advantage of his hospitality. In the process, almost all of Peter's closest longtime friends decided they no longer wanted to be part of his life.

This process of alienation had begun years before, prompted by his pot smoking. At first, he had tried to convert people. Barbara and Jackie Cooper remembered a weekend in Palm Springs in the late sixties when Peter, while he was staying with Anthony Newley and Joan Collins, threw a party for them. "In the middle of the party," Barbara Cooper recalled, "they all went into the other room. We were sitting there all by ourselves, like two idiots." The Coopers soon realized, as Jackie put it, that "they were smoking shit."

The next day, Peter went to the Coopers' house across the street in an exuberant mood. "Goddammit," he said. "Everybody stop drinking! This is what you have to do." He lit up a joint. "When you smoke this stuff, you're sharp, you feel good, you don't have hangovers. Look at me!"

"Like most people who started on pot in those days, he wanted to turn someone else on," Barbara Cooper recalled. "But in most cases he couldn't. Not with us, certainly. As time went on, we saw less and less of him because of that."

As Peter went from marijuana to harder drugs, more and more of his friends fell by the wayside, even those who had known and loved him for thirty years, people who remembered the sensitive, fun-loving athlete he had been. They found it very difficult to be around him now, and just as Judy Garland's friends had done with her, they "washed their hands" of him. "I never had much to do with Peter later," Roy Marcher said. "He'd make a date to come over to my house at seven, and at seven he'd call and be completely incoherent. Finally I just said, 'No more.'" Even Molly Dunne, who had introduced Peter to pot, withdrew from him when he started taking harder drugs.

Reporters, Peter discovered, were among his best friends at this point in his life. He gave lengthy interviews to several British newspapers for around ten thousand dollars each, providing just enough juicy tidbits so that no one quite realized he was giving away very few real secrets. There were many British journalists in Los Angeles, working for either the American tabloids or the Fleet Street papers, and they could be counted on to buy Peter meals and drinks in exchange for a few innocuous morsels about his past affiliations.

Milt Ebbins was one of the few friends who remained loyal, but even he began to distance himself. "Peter resented me being straight," Ebbins said. "Whenever they started doing drugs, I'd get up and walk out. Not marijuana, they could smoke that all they wanted, I didn't care. But when they started sniffing coke and doing PCP and all that shit, I got up and walked out. And druggies *hate* that."

Peter certainly did, and he grew nasty with friends who expressed disapproval of his drug taking. Jean MacDonald remembered a visit Peter made to Hawaii in the midseventies, when she went to his hotel room in the hope of talking him through his problems. "He was distressed over a lot of things, and I went there to try and be helpful to him. It was the most bizarre thing. He was like somebody I didn't know. He wanted me to turn on, and when I didn't want to he looked at me like *What's the matter with you?* And I'm looking at him like, What's the matter with *you*! He practically threw me out of the room."

Jean's reaction the next time she saw Peter, in Hawaii a few years later, was typical of many of his friends'. "I saw him coming out of a drugstore and my first impulse was to run over to him and say hello. But I thought, 'He's gonna put me down, he's gonna say something nasty. I don't need that.' So I just turned and went the other way. And I'll always remember that day with tremendous sadness."

PETER HAD plenty of company as a "druggie" in the early 1970s, particularly when cocaine became the drug of choice. Celebrities often had little trouble scoring drugs, often free of charge. At a party, Peter might meet someone who, when they shook hands, would slip him a packet of coke. The boast in Hollywood was no longer "I got his autograph," but rather "I dropped some stuff on him." That had become the ultimate in cool, and Hollywood had not had a similar rash of drug use since the twenties, when heroin, cocaine, and morphine ruined the lives and careers of a number of stars before the industry, fearing a public backlash against its product, instituted a morality code in 1930 and drug use became unfashionable. It remained so until the late sixties, when the pendulum swung back.

And it was now a pastime the children of celebrities were taking up as well. Christopher Lawford had turned eighteen in 1973, and like the children of Jack and Bobby Kennedy, he had grown up essentially fatherless. Peter had never been much of a paternal figure in his son's life, and

Chris had rarely seen him after Pat had moved him and his three sisters to New York when he was nine.

Bobby Kennedy had served as a surrogate father not only to John and Caroline but to Chris and his sisters as well, giving them strong guidance and a sense that they mattered as individuals. The thing all the Kennedy youngsters liked best about Uncle Bobby was that he never made them feel less worthy because they were kids. With Bobby's death, all that changed. The horror and disillusionment were bad enough, but suddenly the children had no rudder, no one who treated them as equals. Their uncle Ted tried to take up the slack, but, with his own personal problems, he was an inadequate replacement. Those who suffered the most were Bobby's oldest boys—Joe, Bobby Junior, and David—and Chris Lawford.

A canoe trip in 1969 was symbolic. Bobby had taken the older boys on the trip annually, working with them as part of a team to conquer the Green River in Colorado. Now, they were all looking forward to this first trip with Uncle Ted as a way to recapture their sense of Kennedy family cohesion.

The trip was a disaster. Ted and the other adults segregated themselves from the youngsters, left them to their own devices, and got angry when the boys tried to engage them in horseplay. As Chris put it to Peter Collier and David Horowitz, authors of a family biography *The Kennedys,* the adults "wanted to float along with their frozen daiquiris and not be bothered . . . we were all upset. We didn't want to have anything to do with them after that. For the rest of the trip we took our sleeping bags and found the hardest place to get to every night, places where they couldn't find us, and camped there. We'd sit in the darkness talking about what a drag the family was, what an incredible asshole Teddy was to let it happen, how it was never like this when Bobby was alive. We had the feeling that nobody cared enough about us anymore to make us part of the family."

Chris's closest relationships were with Bobby Junior and David Kennedy, both extremely troubled young men free-falling into drug dependency. There had first been pot, then LSD, then the amphetamine "black beauties." When Bobby was arrested with his cousin Bobby Shriver for marijuana possession, Ethel Kennedy threw him out of the house and he headed for San Francisco, riding freight cars with bums. "It was good," he said. "I could be one of them and not be a Kennedy." On Telegraph Hill, he panhandled for drug money.

Chris Lawford and David Kennedy, both fifteen, felt like orphans. David was estranged from his mother, who, friends say, treated him harshly. (She blamed him for just about everything that went wrong, David said. "Her idea was that it didn't really matter whether or not I had actually done anything. I would do it sooner or later, so she might as well get heavy with me in advance. I remember it all clearly. It was the point in my life when everything began to turn against me.")

In 1969, Pat Lawford put Christopher in a boarding school and left the United States for France with her daughters. "I don't want to have anything to do with this family for a while," Pat told Chris. "I'm going to France to get my own life together, away from the Kennedys."

David and Chris, both feeling abandoned, hitchhiked to New York during the summer; when they arrived they begged money from commuters in Grand Central Station. They made about forty dollars after an hour and then went to Central Park to buy drugs. They scored some heroin and snorted it, for the first time.

They met two girls and invited them to Pat's Fifth Avenue apartment for a party. Before long, the place was overrun with street people and hippies. David fell asleep; when he awoke in the early morning hours he found winos and motorcycle-gang types frying eggs in the kitchen. When the neighbors threatened to call the police, Chris and David persuaded everyone to clear out.

David's drug addiction ultimately killed him in a Palm Beach hotel room in 1984. Chris's was helped along by his father. Chris had been expelled from Middlesex for drug use, and when his mother discovered him behind a couch with a needle in his arm, she sent him out to his father for a while—and "that was a big mistake," Milt Ebbins recalled. David Kennedy said that when he came out to Peter's house to visit Christopher that summer of 1971, "I knocked on the door and there's Peter Lawford. I hadn't seen him for years. The first thing he does after saying hello is offer me a pipe full of hash."

Peter had no compunctions about sharing his drug supply with his son. Christopher came to stay with his father at Cory Avenue again in January 1973, and it seemed that drugs brought the two of them closer together. "Peter and I would stay up all night doing dope together and talking about family problems," Chris said. "We'd have what seemed a breakthrough—saying we loved each other and hugging and all that. But the next morning it would all be gone. He'd snap at me and absolutely cringe if I called him 'Dad' instead of 'Peter.'"

One night, when the drugs seemed to have created a special rapport between father and son, Chris let down his guard and told Peter how alienated he and his cousins felt, how badly they needed adult guidance and love. "I need you, Dad," Chris said finally, and started to cry. "I need you to be my father—at least for a little while. My life is a mess and if I go back East again it's going to get worse."

Peter grunted and told the boy, "You must be high on something. Get the hell out of here."

WHEN THERE was only fun to be had, Peter and Christopher got along beautifully. Not all of Peter's friends withdrew from him because of his drug use; some grew closer. One of these was Elizabeth Taylor, who hadn't seen Peter much during her years as Mrs. Richard Burton, when the volatile couple spent most of their time in Europe. In 1973, however, the Burtons separated and Liz returned to Los Angeles, where she renewed her closeness with Peter. "He and Elizabeth used to turn on together," Peter's companion Arthur Natoli remembered. "They were high on pot a lot. I don't know if he supplied her. When it came to him and drugs, I turned the other way."

Dominick Dunne, who had just produced Elizabeth's film *Ash Wednesday,* recalled an afternoon he and his daughter, Dominique, spent at Disneyland in 1973 with Liz and her daughters Liza Todd and Maria Burton, Peter, Christopher, George Cukor, and Roddy McDowall. "This huge helicopter picked us all up at the top of Coldwater Canyon and Mulholland Drive, and took us to Disneyland. It was the first helicopter ever allowed to land *inside* Disneyland."

Once the group started touring the park, a huge crowd

gathered and started to follow them—"because of Elizabeth," Dunne recalled. "It wasn't because of the rest of us, believe me." They were able to escape the prying eyes only inside rides like Pirates of the Caribbean, where the group tumbled into a gondola for a water trip through the buccaneers' nighttime world.

Once their boat was safely enveloped in darkness, the group got giddy. As Dunne remembered it, "Elizabeth had a bottle of Jack Daniel's, and Peter had something, and everybody got the bottles going. Then a bit of coke was going around and you'd hear sniffing. Everybody was just screaming with laughter. It was one of the maddest moments I ever saw in my life. And then the boat came out into the sunlight again. Everybody tried to compose themselves and Liz waved regally to the crowds as they cheered her."

A few years later, Dunne saw Peter at a party at the house of the literary agent Irving "Swifty" Lazar. "There was a woman at the party who shall remain nameless," Dunne recalled. "She said to Peter, 'You got anything? You got any stuff?' Now I used to be a drinker and I used to take the occasional drug, so we all went into the bathroom at this swell party we were at and did a couple of lines and all got screaming with laughter in the bathroom. While we were doing the lines, Peter asked us if we wanted to buy any. And then I felt this tremendous sadness to know that Peter Lawford was dealing drugs. The woman said to me later, 'Can you believe it? He's dealing! *Dealing!*' "

NO MATTER how badly things were going for Peter in his private life, when he worked he was the picture of professionalism. Doris Day enjoyed his sporadic appearances on her television sitcom in 1971 and 1972. "I was never aware of any problems Peter may have had with drinking," she recalled. "He did seem to be preoccupied, and he kept to himself a great deal. He wasn't a very open person. He was not one to shoot the breeze on the set. He would just do the scene and then go to his dressing room. But when we did our scenes together, we really had a good time. He was very warm, and I think he really enjoyed working with me. I think he was a very underrated actor. He enjoyed working the way I do, we both loved the spontaneity of the first take. He was great at improvising, and we'd throw things back and forth to each other. It was terrific. We really kept each other on our toes."

Peter's brief appearance in *They Only Kill Their Masters* in 1972 brought back bittersweet memories for him. A murder mystery, its gimmick was that in addition to its stars, James Garner and Katharine Ross, a great many cast members had been MGM contract players—Peter, June Allyson, and Ann Rutherford among them. The movie was the last filmed on the old Metro lot, which during the production was in the process of being dismantled and sold by the studio's new owners.

"It was a totally depressing scene," Peter said. "That old back lot, number two, hadn't been touched for years. We used the old Andy Hardy house in the film—it's completely overgrown with vines and bushes. . . . I get moments of melancholia. Middle-aged melancholia, if you will."

Peter, in fact, didn't have any scenes with the other MGM alumni. There was a minimum of interaction between him and June Allyson, limited mostly to the first day on the set, and the film's director James Goldstone recalled that it wasn't always pleasant. "There were jokes and light banter between them, and some of it got a little nasty. Peter found it rather amusing, in his way, which is a sort of fey, wan kind of sophisticated bemusement. Here he was back, burying the lot on which he was born."

The MGM reunion angle didn't help make *They Only Kill Their Masters* any more than a moderate success. As Goldstone put it, "I don't think 'Come see the stars of yesteryear' was a very good way to sell a sophisticated suspense mystery to contemporary audiences in 1972."

But the early seventies did see the advent of the nostalgia craze that hasn't waned to this day. Marilyn Monroe, James Dean, Clark Gable, W. C. Fields, Mae West—all became cultural icons again, for the young as well as the old. The sci-fi movies of the 1950s, trashy as they were, enjoyed a tremendous revival. So did the MGM musicals of the forties, as theaters across the country held revivals and invited such stars as Peter, Ann Miller, Van Johnson, and Cyd Charisse to attend. Invariably, they were mobbed by adoring fans of all ages.

Before long both MGM and the stars of its heyday were able to take lucrative advantage of the nostalgia boom. In

1973 the studio hired Peter, Gene Kelly, Elizabeth Taylor, Fred Astaire, Liza Minnelli, Donald O'Connor, Debbie Reynolds, Bing Crosby, James Stewart, Mickey Rooney, and Frank Sinatra to narrate *That's Entertainment,* a dazzling 132-minute compilation of the best MGM musical numbers.

As did the others, Peter narrated a single segment of the film, and he was shown in the "Varsity Drag" number from *Good News.* The clips were delightful, stirring pleasant memories in older audiences and allowing younger viewers to see what their parents had raved about for so long. The movie was a huge box-office hit.

The vogue for nostalgia persisted throughout the seventies, and it brought Peter other opportunities as well. He did a voice-over along with Liza Minnelli in the 1972 animated film *Return to the Land of Oz.* In 1976 he was paid handsomely to participate in "Peter Lawford Day," one of a series of "Sails with the Stars" offered by the Carras Cruise Lines. Passengers spent a few days at sea aboard the liner *Daphne,* saw a screening of *Good News,* and then heard Hollis Alpert, the movie critic for *Saturday Review,* interview Peter about his career.

In 1975, some news was made when *Oui* magazine offered Peter ten thousand dollars to pose nude along with one of his MGM costars, perhaps Esther Williams or Janet Leigh. Both of the actresses turned the offer down, and Peter told the press that the lady he posed with would probably have to be younger than he.

The Fleet Street papers reported that when Rose Kennedy heard about this, she "became quite livid" and ordered Senator Ted Kennedy to talk Peter out of the idea. Ted may well have done so, because Peter soon announced that he had declined to bare all, and explained his decision thus: "I wouldn't want to be guilty of disappointing the older generation or disillusioning the younger generation." (Peter was being overly modest; according to a number of sources, he was very well endowed.) The London *Daily Mirror* had the last word on the matter when they called the idea "the most ridiculous project he has embarked upon since the days when he walked around with his initials on his toe caps."

Another source of income for Peter was television game shows. Many of the shows hired the "stars of yesteryear" to appeal to their largely middle-aged viewers, and Peter's charm and his facility with word games had made him a particularly desirable guest star on such programs since the midsixties. (May boasted that Peter "holds the all-time record for winning *Password.*")

Marion Dixon, whom he dated for a year after his separation from Mary Rowan, was astonished by the professionalism Peter maintained despite whatever damage the excesses of the night before had done to him. "One morning he had to go to the studio to tape some game show—I think it was *Masquerade Party*," Dixon recalled. "Peter was so messed up he couldn't drive, so I had to take him over there. He wasn't even coherent in the car. I was sure he wouldn't be able to perform. When we got there he changed *dramatically*. It was like he was a completely different person. He seemed perfectly sober, he did a good job on the show, everything. I was astounded. Then, after the performance, he got back in the car and changed again. His head was lolling on the headrest, he was barely coherent."

Dixon broke off the relationship soon thereafter. "I couldn't take it. He had no control over the substance abuse. He wasn't strong enough to break away from it. He thought of himself as a victim. I could no longer handle baby-sitting him, which was what I was doing. Toward the end of our relationship, I told him how disappointed I was. When I was fourteen, I went to the opening of a big mall in my neighborhood, and Peter Lawford was one of the stars who made personal appearances at the ceremonies. I was so excited to see him I snuck under a police barricade and was able to run up to him and say hello. For all the intervening years I kept this glamorous image of him in my mind. And here I was with him and he was not the same person I had seen under those klieg lights. He wasn't nearly the person I had thought he would be.

"When I told him that, he didn't say a word. He just looked at me, and the look on his face was very sad."

IN FEBRUARY 1974, Christopher paid his father another visit. Chris and his cousins frequently stayed with Peter, and Bill Noad, Peter's landlord, wasn't always happy about it. "Chris and Bobby Junior used to come and stay in my cabana," Bill recalled. "I knew they were smoking pot and pot and doing drugs in there. Sometimes they'd stay a long time and Pat Kennedy would send me money to pay for them—she'd send one dollar a kid! I'd get a check for ten dollars from her!"

On this visit, Chris was alone at the Cory Avenue apartment with a friend; Peter was in Palm Springs. In the middle of the afternoon, Bill Noad heard screaming and rushed out of his apartment. He saw Chris's friend standing nude on Peter's balcony, "freaked out" on drugs and threatening to jump off.

Chris Lawford called Milt Ebbins and Noad called the police. When Ebbins got there, Chris was gone and the police were hauling out Peter's marijuana plants, seeds, glass pipes, and other drug paraphernalia. "Hold it!" Ebbins demanded. "Where are you going with that?"

"We're taking this stuff as evidence."

"Have you got a search warrant?" Ebbins asked.

"We don't need one."

"Oh yes you do," Ebbins said.

Finally one of the officers said, "Better do what he says." They left empty-handed, and Ebbins told Erma Lee Riley to throw out all the incriminating evidence. But Chris's friend had been arrested, and when word got to Peter about the incident he was frantic. Chris offered to take the rap for the marijuana plants, but Ebbins told him, "No, you keep your mouth shut. We'll take care of it." He called a lawyer who had worked in the Justice Department, and the matter was dropped. Peter was lucky: possession of marijuana was a felony in 1974, and he could well have ended up in jail.

Peter could hardly blame Christopher for the incident, because he had encouraged his son's drug use. On Chris's twenty-first birthday Peter had given him cocaine as a present. Chris sent him a thank-you note: "Dear Pedro: Thanks for making it cross-country for my birthday. You were a surprise and the most honored guest of the evening. You made the party and I thank you. Oh, thanks for the gift. Unfortunately it was not one I could hold on to for very long."

FORTY-ONE

ON A BALMY Los Angeles night early in June 1976, Peter Lawford was having a party. Men and women, most of them twenty-five to thirty years younger than he, drifted in and out of the rooms of the Cory Avenue apartment, drinking his vodka, smoking marijuana, snorting cocaine, and popping "soapers," large orange-colored Canadian-made methaqualone pills similar to Quaaludes. Many of the guests were people Peter didn't know. They were friends of his drug buddies, friends of friends of his drug buddies. Peter didn't care. They supplied him with dope and brought along pretty young girls who were thrilled to party with a movie star.

Tonight, though, Peter was restless. He was "with" one of the younger girls, but she bored him, and he asked another young woman if she had a friend who'd want to come over and join the party. Yes, she replied, adding that she thought Peter would like her.

It was eleven P.M. when her telephone rang, and Deborah Gould was getting ready for bed. "Debbie," she heard her friend say, "you've got to come to this party. There's someone here who wants to meet you."

"Who?"

"Peter Lawford!"

Deborah didn't know who that was at first. Then she recognized the name, but she couldn't put a face to it. She declined the invitation, saying she was going to bed. Her friend told her to wait and Peter came on the line. "I heard this British accent," she recalled, "and right away I was head over heels. We talked and he persuaded me to go over. He picked me up in a silver Seville."

Gould found her emotions pleasurably stirred by Peter's looks and his manner. "I had never met anyone quite like him before. It seemed to me that I had known him a long time. I was very comfortable with him. I felt right at home."

Peter liked her, too. She was twenty-five and pretty, with long brown hair and a sweet youthful vivacity. Back at Cory Avenue, they fell into a conversation. Peter asked questions and listened intently as Deborah told him about her upbringing in Miami as the daughter of a lawyer, about her car trip from Florida to Los Angeles in hopes of breaking into acting (just as he had done thirty-five years earlier, Peter told her), about her small parts on a few television shows. "He thought all that was very interesting, and he said that he thought he could be of help to me. He said he had a lot of connections, and he could get me a Screen Actors Guild card right away. He said he might be able to get me an agent."

The next time Deborah glanced at the clock, it was four in the morning. There were still a lot of people in the apartment, she noticed; there were all kinds of things going on in different rooms. She told Peter she had to be getting home. "No, I don't want you to leave," Peter protested. "You can stay in the guest bedroom. It's too late to leave now. I'll take you out to breakfast in the morning and then I'll take you home."

She agreed, and after all the guests had left she and Peter were still deep in conversation. "I sensed that something was going to happen. There was a strong physical as well as emotional attraction between us. I really was swept off my feet. He had a powerful, hypnotic way about him. He told me I wasn't like the normal girl he met in Hollywood, that I was different, special. I do think he meant that."

Deborah slept in the guest room. "There was no sex, no sexual advances, not even a kiss." As she prepared to leave the next day, Peter again asked her to stay. "But I need to get some clothes," she protested. "You don't need to get your clothes," Peter responded. "We'll send someone to get them. Or we'll buy new ones. Stay here."

She stayed, and began to notice Peter's surroundings. She had seen the photographs of Marilyn Monroe and the Kennedys on Peter's walls, but it still hadn't dawned on her just who he was. "Then he said he'd been married to Patricia Kennedy—and that's when everything clicked for me. My feelings for him didn't change, except maybe that I felt a little in awe."

After two days, Deborah insisted on picking up some clothes at her apartment. Peter drove her, and when she returned to his car Peter said, "I want to take you up to the mansion. We'll have lunch and go for a swim."

"The *mansion*?"

As Peter knew she would, Deborah wandered wide-eyed around Hugh Hefner's Playboy Mansion. "There was everything you wanted," she marvels. "Bathing suits, toothbrushes, makeup, anything. Peter had his own room there. He was very good friends with Hefner. We went up to Peter's room and I changed and we stayed there the whole afternoon, swimming and sunbathing; then we had dinner."

The guest room assigned permanently to Peter was decorated entirely in black and had mirrors on the ceiling and all four walls. The room was soundproof and had a stereo console built into the enormous round bed. All a guest's needs could be attended to just by dialing 33 on the bedside phone to summon the butler.

"I met Hefner that day," Deborah recalled. "He was very nice and we talked and he sat with his pipe. He and Peter were like brothers. They'd kid each other, they'd get loud and boisterous like kids."

Peter and Hefner had met at a party in the 1960s and had immediately liked each other. Hefner appreciated the cachet that Peter, resonant with history and culture as he was, lent to his somewhat checkered crowd, and Peter took full advantage of Hefner's hospitality and largesse. At the Playboy Mansion, he could always find beautiful girls to party with. Good food, sex, drugs, and alcohol were in abundant supply. Any hour of the day or night, Peter could drive up to the gate, be waved on by the guard, and have anything he wanted.

These and other aspects of Peter Lawford's life-style

much appealed to Deborah Gould. "It was exciting to meet people like Ringo Starr. I'll never forget it. We went to the club On The Rox above the Roxy on Sunset. It was midnight when we went—Peter wanted to get out of the house. Ringo was there, and Keith Moon, and they were all drinking heavily and using. It was one big party with lots of booze and drugs, anything you wanted. I got quite fascinated by all this. I didn't think about tomorrow, I thought about the moment I was in."

Deborah soon realized that her attraction to Peter was growing stronger. "He was a lot of fun. He was on the go all the time—let's do this, let's do that. He was a very up person. He was a very young fifty-two. I didn't even realize he was that old at the time."

Still, their relationship took on a father-daughter cast. He would say to her, "Come over here, Debber. Come here and sit by Daddy." Deborah would cuddle up next to him and put her head in his lap and he would gently stroke her hair. "That's what we had," she said. "He was Daddy and he liked that." So did she. It had seemed to her as a girl that her father was always working; he didn't spend much time at home with her and her five sisters. She had longed for a closer relationship with her father and fantasized about marrying someone like him.

Ten days after their first night together, Peter and Deborah were sunbathing at the Playboy Mansion. Peter turned to her and said, "We're gonna get married."

"He didn't say, 'Will you marry me?'" Deborah recalled. "He just said, 'When we get married, we'll do this and that. We'll go to Hawaii for our honeymoon, we'll fly on the Concorde.' He was always throwing things like that at me. Trying to dazzle me. I don't know why—I wasn't playing hard to get or anything." Still, she pooh-poohed the marriage idea.

The next day, she arose at eleven to find that Peter had never gone to bed. He said to her, "So what are we gonna do? Are we gonna get married?"

She was astonished. "Are you serious? Do you *really* want to get married now? What's the rush?"

"Don't you want to get married? Don't you love me?"

"Yes I love you and yes I want to marry you."

"So why don't we just do it?"

After a few more hems and haws, Deborah agreed.
"We were jumping around and happy—we were like two
little kids. And I was worried about what I was gonna wear
because he was talking about *now*—we were going to do
this in a few days. I didn't have time to prepare, I hadn't
told my family—they didn't even know I was *seeing* Peter
Lawford. Nobody knew anything."

They celebrated on the terrace with tall tumblers of
vodka and freshly squeezed orange juice, got a little tipsy,
and laughed and hugged and kissed. "I was on cloud nine,
and Peter was somewhere up there, too. We were sunbathing and he told me not to be modest, to take off my top,
so I did."

Peter called his friend Barry Marks in Arlington, Virginia, who agreed to host the wedding reception in his home
on June 25. Deborah called her parents, and her mother
was upset. "This is the biggest mistake you could ever
make," she told her daughter. "Peter Lawford is a horse's
ass." Her father, however, was surprisingly agreeable and
told her he would be at the wedding.

Then Peter called Pat. "He was looking for her approval," Deborah recalled. "She wished me luck and said,
'Take care, dear'—like a mother would say. I got the feeling
that she was trying to give me a warning."

Ringo Starr's reaction to the news was equally chilling.
"It's not gonna work out, take my word for it," he said.
There had been a number of warning signals for Deborah
Gould in the ten days she had known Peter, but she was
too naive—and too infatuated—to heed them. "We never
did have sexual relations before the wedding. I don't know
why. It wasn't that I was opposed to it. I know he found
me very attractive, but—I've never been able to figure out
why he didn't want to have sexual relations before the
marriage."

As much as she enjoyed Peter's hedonism, certain elements of it made Deborah uneasy. It seemed to her that
there were too many people around, using his place as a
crash pad. "We were never alone. People used to steal
things all the time. I'd tell him, 'These aren't your friends,
Peter,' but he didn't want to hear that. I started locking the
door when I went to bed, because when people get loaded
they get wild ideas. I didn't want anybody coming into my
bedroom in the middle of the night."

Although she admits she was "no stranger to drugs," she was distressed by the extent of Peter's use. "I only used drugs socially—'Okay, sure, I'll have some.' I wasn't obsessed with it, whereas Peter was. A couple of times I saw him so drunk or so stoned that he'd pass out, and then I'd be upset with him.

"But he said he was going to stop all of it. I thought I could change Peter, have a profound effect on him, get him away from all that. He promised he'd change. And he really seemed to mean it. He'd beg me to stay with him and help him. He said, 'Promise me you'll never leave me.' I had reason to think he'd change."

ON JUNE 24, Peter and Deborah took a limousine to Los Angeles Airport for the flight to Arlington, Virginia. While they waited to board their plane, Deborah went into a shop, and somehow she and Peter lost each other. They missed the plane.

Deborah was unfazed. "Big deal," she told him. "We'll stay in a hotel room for a few hours and then we'll get the next flight out." But Peter was furious. "He didn't speak to me for hours. That's what he used to do. The silent treatment. Punishment time. When he thought I'd had enough punishment, he'd talk to me again. It was like I was a child."

Peter, attracted to Deborah's youthful freshness, became annoyed that she didn't have the sophistication of an older woman. She was a young twenty-five, and Peter became upset with her a number of times when she asked him to explain something to her. "You don't know that?" he would snap. He corrected her grammar and syntax constantly, reminded her to say please and thank you. Deborah thought it was "very weird."

Matters didn't improve as the wedding hour approached. As they left the marriage license bureau in Arlington, the couple was accosted by a battery of newsmen who had been tipped off about the marriage. Deborah wore blue jeans and a T-shirt from a Carole King tour with "Thoroughbred" silk-screened across the front, and a reporter took the cue. "How does it feel to be marrying such a young filly, Peter?" he asked, and the other questions all carried the same sniggering implication. Deborah felt that Peter was jealous because "I was upstaging him. I was the new aspiring actress and he was the has-been. I didn't think of him that way, but all the reporters were latching onto the 'Aging Star Marries Young Starlet' angle."

At Barry Marks's house, Deborah's father and sisters joined Chris Lawford and a few of Peter's friends to prepare for the ceremony. Deborah's mother and Pat Lawford both refused to attend—and although Peter said that Ted Kennedy would be there, he wasn't. ("We did get a *call* from him," Deborah said.)

With the help of Barry Marks's girlfriend, the bride-to-be got ready, slipping into a floor-length off-white wedding gown that a friend of hers had never used. She was very excited. Peter came into her room and offered some Quaaludes. "You'd better take some of these," he told her. "You're going to give me a heart attack." She came downstairs looking wonderful in full wedding regalia and was shocked to find Peter wearing an open-necked shirt and a leisure suit. "Aren't you going to dress for the occasion?" she asked him.

"He didn't like that at all," Deborah recalled. "He didn't take criticism very well from anybody. He refused to change. Christopher Lawford was in a tuxedo and gave me two dozen yellow roses. And Peter was in a *leisure suit.*"

The ceremony took place in the chambers of Arlington special judge Francis Thomas. Peter, high on vodka and Quaaludes, forgot the marriage license and clowned around during the delay while it was retrieved, taking the yellow roses from Deborah's arms and putting them under his. Barry Marks joined in the buffoonery and hid the wedding ring while Peter frantically searched his pockets, thinking he'd misplaced it.

Finally, the vows were exchanged, but not until after Deborah asked Thomas to repeat a phrase, explaining, "It's my first time, Judge." The newlyweds, ogled by a small crowd of Arlington County employees who had gathered across the street, sped off in a limousine for the reception at Barry Marks's house.

There, what was supposed to have been a joyous wedding celebration quickly disintegrated into a debacle. Peter downed more vodka and popped more Quaaludes throughout the evening; by the time the wedding guests gathered to watch reports of the marriage on the eleven o'clock news, he was on the verge of a blackout.

The television accounts of his wedding upset Peter. He looked tired and haggard in the video footage, closer to sixty than fifty-two, especially next to his fresh-faced young bride. "Christopher was complimenting me," Deborah recalled. "We were very close, Chris and I. We were like buddies right off the bat. He looked so handsome in his tuxedo, like Prince Charming. Somebody made the stupid comment that I should have married Christopher instead of Peter. Peter did not like that *at all*."

His ego bruised, Peter began to flirt with one of the guests, a sexy girl about Deborah's age, and now it was the new Mrs. Lawford's turn to get upset. "Here it was my wedding night, I'm in love with this man, and he's flirting with another girl." Deborah pulled him aside. "What's wrong with you?" she hissed. "How dare you flirt with that girl. What are you, drunk? Stoned?"

"How dare *you*!" Peter spat back. "Who do you think you are?"

"I'm your *wife*, remember?"

"Oh yes. *Boy*, do I remember."

Deborah thought it could have been a bad movie. "I told him, 'Act appropriately in front of people, okay? I don't go for this.' He was furious because I was asserting myself for once. I was like his mother, criticizing his bad manners. Our roles had reversed."

Peter refused to apologize, and about an hour later, Deborah, herself now intoxicated, confronted him again. "I knew him well enough to know that he was coming on to this woman. He didn't even try to hide it. He kept saying, 'Isn't she sensuous?' And we had just gotten *married*. My pride was hurt. But it didn't register with him. I said, 'What did we get married for?' I was trying to talk sensibly to him but he couldn't comprehend. He was incoherent. I had never seen him that bad before. He was functioning, but he must have been in a blackout by this time."

Their argument escalated, and the bride became hysterical. "Oh, now you're gonna throw a temper tantrum, aren't you?" Peter taunted her. "You're not a very good actress." She took off her wedding ring and threw it across the room. "Don't do that!" Peter screamed. He fell to his hands and knees, scrambling across the floor to retrieve it, and became frantic when he couldn't find it. Deborah saw where it had gone, but she didn't tell him. "Never mind, Peter, it's over," she said, shaking with anger. "This isn't going to work out and you know it. This whole thing is ridiculous."

Peter stopped crawling and slumped into a sitting position on the floor. He looked up at Deborah, tears in his eyes. "Don't do this, Debber. Please don't do this." She looked at him, steely-eyed. "Well, you're gonna have to change. You can't keep on this way. We have to straighten things out somehow. We'll talk in the morning."

With that, the wedding reception was over. The mortified guests left, and Peter staggered downstairs to the basement. After she had had some time to cool off, Deborah followed him. She found her bridegroom spread across a mattress on the floor, an outside door wide open, fireflies whizzing in and out. She closed the door and lay down beside him. "I wanted to make love—we still had never done so—but there was no way he could have done it. I thought, *Well, there goes my wedding night.* I knew he hated to be alone, so I just held him in my arms until he passed out."

The next morning, Peter couldn't remember a thing about the previous day, including the fact that he'd gotten married. Assured that he had, he called Milt Ebbins. "I just got married," he told him. "How do I get out of it?"

Milt was dumbfounded. "Peter, I want you to tell me what went through your mind when you decided to marry a twenty-five-year-old girl you've known for three weeks. What could have possessed you?"

"She's a pusher," Peter replied. "She gets me drugs."

"You married her because she's a pusher?"

"Yeah, that's why I married her."*

THE MARRIAGE of Peter Lawford and Deborah Gould didn't end that day. Peter begged his bride's forgiveness, and their relationship was at last consummated. "We had a fairly normal sex life at first," Deborah recalled. "When it was possible, when he wasn't drinking or using.

---

*Deborah Gould denied this: "Peter Lawford didn't need me to get drugs for him. He had all the contacts in the world. How would I have had more contacts than he did? I'd been in Hollywood just about a year. He'd been there practically all his life."

"He kept telling me how much he loved me and that he wanted us to have a child. He was going to get away from the drug scene and the Hollywood scene. We were going to move to Hawaii and he was going to write a book about his life and I was gonna take it all down because I had secretarial skills."

But nothing changed, and the more Deborah got to know Peter, the more disquieted she became. "He was so strange. He had this phobia about being locked in a room. Once I locked our bedroom door and played around at hiding the key. He freaked out. He insisted that I give it to him and then he jammed the door trying to unlock it and we really were locked in. Well, talk about a panic attack! I said, 'What's wrong with being locked in your bedroom with your wife? Erma will let us out in the morning.' " Still, Peter struggled with the door until four in the morning, when he was finally able to open it.

Other fears gnawed at Peter, some concrete, some nameless and vague, shifting and replacing each other like shards of color in a kaleidoscope. He was afraid Deborah would come to feel he was too old for her. She woke up one morning while he was still in bed, and when she turned to put her arms around him, he pulled away from her, bolted out of bed, and ran into the bathroom. "He stayed in there for an hour, primping, getting himself ready for me to see him. He would do this every morning. He was afraid of me seeing him not looking his best."

Peter feared losing Deborah to a younger man. "If a young, good-looking guy paid attention to me, he'd be furious. His friends were always hitting on me. Nobody had any respect for anybody's wife or who anybody was with. One guy used to come over and I'd take a ride on his motorcycle with him. Peter would get very mad about that. I felt, at least he cares. I used to do things to get him jealous."

Peter's drug use magnified his terrors—and what Deborah had begun to suspect was a manic-depressive syndrome. She saw that he became very depressed when he came down from highs, would start to cry and shake. "He'd be terrified. He was afraid of death, but he toyed with it all the time because of the way he lived.

"He used to tell me that somebody was trying to kill him. He got paranoid. Nobody was trying to kill him. It was in his mind. But he wouldn't answer the phone, wouldn't go to the door. I had to take all the calls. He wouldn't talk to anyone." After a drug-and-alcohol-soaked night in which Peter had exposed his fears to his young wife, had cried his heart out in her lap, he was so embarrassed that she'd seen him so vulnerable that he wouldn't talk to her for most of the next day.

Impotence was another demon. Drunk, stoned, he was unable to get an erection. "He'd feel bad that he couldn't perform sexually," Deborah said, "and I'd try to reassure him that it wasn't that big a deal to me, but he didn't believe me. So it just put another wedge between us, because he thought he wasn't living up to the manly image I had of him."

Before long, Peter broached the subject of sadomasochistic sex to Deborah, and the idea disturbed her. "I was very turned off by it. He used to ask me to hurt him when we were making love. Either hit him as hard as I could on his face or tie him up, inflict pain on him any way I could.

"I couldn't do it. I said, 'Peter, this is not normal.' Then he'd get all upset. 'Who are you to say what's normal?' He'd get very angry whenever anybody suggested that anything he was doing was wrong."

When she further refused to engage in three-ways with Peter and another woman, he would taunt her about it, try to goad her into agreeing to do what he wanted. "You and I are cut from the same cloth, Charlie," he'd tell her.

"What do you mean by that?"

"You're just like me. You don't think you're bisexual, but you are. You love women."

"What are you saying? That you like men? That you're gay?"

"I like anybody who's beautiful," Peter replied.

But Deborah was adamant: "I will not have another woman in our bed!" A few weeks after the wedding, Peter began to seek sex outside the marriage. "He had to go with strangers, because people close to him like me wouldn't do what he wanted. He'd go up to the Playboy Mansion and stay there all day—he could get kinky sex over there, anything he wanted. I was bothered by all that mainly because I didn't want to get any diseases. I didn't know where he'd been."

After little more than a month of marriage, Deborah went back to sleeping in the guest room, and neither she nor Peter made any further attempts at sexual relations. In late July, Peter announced he was taking a trip to New York. Deborah wanted to accompany him, but he wouldn't let her. A few days later, Peter called her from his hotel room late at night. He sounded frightened. "He told me that there were some weird friends of his there, and he was scared because they were into necrophilia. I nearly died when I heard that. I said 'What?' and he said, 'Yes, I know, it's awful. I can't handle it.' That was too much, even for Peter."

Deborah begged him to come home immediately, and he said he would. "He fell asleep talking on the phone to me. He was afraid and I had to keep talking to him until he nodded off."

Close to the end of her rope, Deborah had become edgy, depressed, nearly suicidal. Her life with Peter had become a nightmare. "I was a mess. I was so disillusioned. Things were not at all as I had fantasized they'd be. And I thought it was my fault. He was always criticizing me for everything."

The marriage began to unravel precisely where Peter had first mentioned the idea to Deborah—at Hugh Hefner's. During a pool party, Deborah grew incensed at Peter when he got badly stoned, and she said loudly in front of others, "You'd better get it together, Peter, because I'm sick of being your nursemaid."

"Well, that set him off," she recalled. "He stormed out and got into his car. I yelled after him that he couldn't drive in that condition, but he drove away anyway." Deborah stayed at the mansion about an hour longer and then took a taxi back to Cory Avenue. When she fumbled through her purse for her house keys, she realized that Peter had taken them. She rang the bell and rapped on the door, but Peter wouldn't respond. She considered calling the police, but then decided to let him sleep it off and went to a girlfriend's for the night.

The next morning she returned, but Peter was still fuming. Deborah pounded on the door and "he just kept sending down this strange girl he had up there with him to say he wasn't going to let me in. But I told her to tell him that

I was going to stay there until he either let me in or someone came to get me. I just sat on the steps crying. I felt displaced, like the icing was melting off the cake and everything had turned bad. I wanted to go up there and strangle him. I really wanted to kill him. If I ever could have murdered somebody in my life, it would have been right then."

Peter telephoned Milt Ebbins, who went over to Cory Avenue immediately. "She was standing outside with a bag in her hand with a comb, a brush, and a hair dryer," Ebbins recalled. "She said, 'He threw me out. He told me to get lost.' "

Ebbins liked Deborah Gould. He thought she was "a nice little girl" and that Peter treated her terribly. "He could be vicious when he wanted to get rid of someone. He'd get really mean. No compassion at all. I think he *wanted* them to hate him." Milt went upstairs to talk to Peter, but he just screamed, "Ahh, for crissakes, let her get lost!" Ebbins recognized Peter's Mr. Hyde side again and tried to reason with him. "Listen to me, Peter," he said evenly. "She's still your wife. Her father's a *lawyer*. You keep this up and you're gonna pay through the nose."

Peter fell silent. Then he said, "Well, what do you want me to do?" Ebbins told him to take Deborah to the Hamburger Hamlet up the street on Sunset Boulevard. "Sit down, be nice to her, tell her you want to rethink the relationship, you might have gone into this too fast, you need some space." Peter grumbled a bit but finally agreed.

The "summit meeting" consisted of Peter asking Deborah, "Are you sorry for what you did?" and Deborah replying, "Yes. I was wrong and you were right." She was so agreeable only because she wanted to get back into the house and retrieve her belongings, but once she got there she remained a few more days in a shaky reconciliation—until Peter locked her out again after another spat.

When he let her back into the apartment this time, she grabbed her keys and went to Henry Wynberg's house. Wynberg, a used-car salesman and photographer who had romanced Elizabeth Taylor, had a coterie of young girls in residence at his Beverly Hills home most of the time and was one of the first of Peter's friends Deborah had met. "He seemed like a very nice guy," she recalled, "but I wasn't attracted to him. He said if I ever needed a place to stay I could use his. He had no designs on me; he had so many girlfriends—I mean, there were just too many of them around."

Still hopeful that she could patch things up with Peter, Deborah invited him to a large dinner party at Wynberg's a few days later. She knew she'd made a mistake when Peter got into an argument with Henry. "How *cozy,* you and Debbie cooking together, making *dinner,*" Peter sneered at his friend. "Maybe you two should be married."

Wynberg calmed Peter down, and he stayed at the party. But he paid less attention to Deborah during the evening than he did to Patty Seaton, one of Wynberg's occasional housemates, a plump-faced seventeen-year-old with, as Henry crudely put it, "great boobs and a great ass." Peter complimented her on the gold-plated Quaalude she was wearing around her neck and told her, "There's something about you that I like."

After a few minutes of conversation, Peter offered to drive Seaton home. Although she had a car of her own, she agreed, and he went off to tell Wynberg he was leaving. Patty sat down next to Deborah, who had been watching Peter's moves. "What are you doing?" Deborah asked her. "I'm leaving," she said. "I'm just waiting for someone."

When Peter returned, he coolly asked Patty if she was ready to go. Deborah stood up and glared at Seaton. "You're leaving with *my husband*?" Seaton said nothing, and neither did Peter. As Deborah watched, dumbfounded, they left.

He was taking her to the Playboy Mansion, Peter announced grandly to Patty as they got into his car. Along the way he leaned over to kiss her, and it was only then that he realized her jaw was wired shut. She had had recent surgery for a degenerative bone condition, and although the wiring allowed her to talk fairly normally, she could not open her mouth widely enough to take in solid food. "Oh, this is great," Peter said. "I find a girl and her jaw's wired shut."

Still, he took her to Hefner's, where they shared a Jacuzzi and spent the night in Peter's room, where he had wooed Deborah Gould just weeks before. He saw Patty the next three nights as well, but during the day his interest was elsewhere. A few days after Wynberg's party, Deborah drove up to her best girlfriend's apartment to pay her an unannounced visit. Peter's car was parked in front of the building. "I knocked on the door—I didn't have any pride left at this point—and said, 'It's Debbie.' My friend said, 'I can't come to the door right now.' I said, 'I can imagine why not. Just tell him that I'll be back at the house and I want him there in ten minutes!'"

When Deborah got to the apartment, she found that her key no longer worked—Peter had changed the locks. A few minutes later, he drove up with Deborah's friend and the three of them went upstairs. "He acted like nothing had happened and said, 'Hi, sweetheart.' I asked him why he'd changed the locks and he said it was to keep some crazy girl away from him. She'd stolen money from him and he was afraid she was going to kill him or something."

"I'm moving out of here," Deborah declared, and stalked around the room pulling pictures off the walls and stuffing wedding presents into shopping bags. The pronouncement elicited no response—Peter and the girl were making out on the couch. As Deborah went from room to room "getting my things together," Peter began to mock her. "I was badly hurt and I got very angry," Deborah recalled. "My heart was being broken and here these two were clowning around and thinking it was a joke."

Peter got up and started playing pool. Deborah grabbed the cue from him and cracked it in half across the tabletop, unintentionally smashing his finger. "I'm going to call the police!" he screamed at her.

"Go ahead, call the cops," Deborah yelled back. "The more the merrier!" But within a few minutes, her anger and defiance had turned to desolation, and she opened a bottle of Courvoisier cognac. "I hate the stuff, but I wanted to get to him. He was getting mad that I was drinking his best liquor. I drank the whole bottle; then I headed for the medicine cabinet. He tried to stop me but I was too fast for him and I locked myself in. He banged on the door and shouted that he was going to call the police."

Deborah popped into her mouth whatever drugs she could find—tranquilizers, Librium. "I was trying to get attention from him, or sympathy. I told him I was going to kill myself. I said, 'I love you, the marriage is gone, I'm gonna end it all.' What got me was how cool he was. He said, 'When are you gonna do this?' I said, 'Today, tonight sometime.' He said, 'Well, that's fine, but do me one favor—

don't leave any notes. I don't want to have to come over and clean up the note.' That hit me like a punch in the stomach. I thought to myself, *Marilyn Monroe*."

Sobbing, she left the town house and went to Henry Wynberg's, where she consumed more alcohol and more drugs. She wound up at a girlfriend's house, where she drank even more and dissolved into hysterics. Her friend gave her some tranquilizers to calm her down, and the next thing she can remember is lying in an emergency room after having had her stomach pumped.

"Peter didn't even come to see me in the hospital. That's when I realized that there was no possibility that we'd ever be able to make a go of it." She went home to Miami, and she and Peter continued their battles over the telephone. Peter refused to return clothes and some wedding presents she had left at his apartment. Moreover, he would not agree to a financial settlement with her. She asked for a modest monthly stipend—"I wasn't trying to take him to the cleaners or anything"—but Peter refused. He told her, "No, I'm not giving you a penny and I'm not sending your things back. If you want them you can bloody well come out here and get them. Tell your father where he can go, too!"

"What are you trying to do," Deborah shot back, "get me mad enough so that I'll come back out there, file for divorce, and take you to the cleaners? Because that's what I'll do."

"You do what you damn well please!" Peter shouted back.

"I wasn't in it for the money, although Peter thought I was," Deborah said. "He didn't have much money even though he always acted like he did."

For years, Peter refused to give Deborah a divorce. "He was living with Patty Seaton after I left, and as long as he was still married to me, he couldn't marry her. He didn't want to get into that trap again. Even when I wanted to marry somebody else, Peter kept putting me off. But I pushed it and finally we were divorced. I hated him for a long time. I called him one night and told him how much he had hurt me and how terrible he was to me and everything. He said, 'Well, you don't know how much you hurt me. How much I still hurt. I'm never gonna get over it.'

"I said to him, 'Peter, what did I do?' He just said,

'Think about it. Someday you'll realize.' I still don't know what it was. But apparently to him I was awful.

"I woke up one morning and I didn't hate him anymore. When I stopped blaming myself for everything, I just wasn't angry at him or myself any longer. I didn't want to be enemies with him. I wanted to be friends. But it never happened."

FORTY-TWO

WITHIN DAYS of Deborah Gould's departure,
Peter asked Patty Seaton to move in with him. She
was overwhelmed. A victim of childhood sexual
abuse, estranged from her family, she had been living with
a girlfriend. "I had a tremendous need to be wanted by a
man," she said, and to her it seemed incredible that someone handsome, famous, sophisticated, and apparently
wealthy wanted her to be a part of his life.

Afraid her roommate would be angry at her, Patty
moved out secretly while the girl was at work. She called
her parents, who were divorced, to tell them the news. Her
father threatened to kill Peter; her mother was delighted
and impressed. For the first time, Seaton later said, she felt
powerful, finally able to gain her parents' attention—even,
in her mother's case, some grudging respect. She was involved with a celebrity, and she was ecstatic about it.

Now that Patty was living with Peter Lawford, her
mother thought of her as "somebody," called her on the
telephone, took her to lunch. "My mother would wonder
what it was he saw in this ugly duckling daughter of hers
when she was more beautiful, more worldly, and quite successful. Being with Peter got me . . . both her envy and
approval."

The life Patty led with Peter Lawford thrilled her.
There were, as usual, the limousines, the Playboy Mansion,
the seemingly endless supply of drugs. It seemed to her that

she had fallen into the proverbial tub of butter. But a week after her arrival at Cory Avenue, the idyll was shattered. Milt Ebbins came to the door, and when she told him Peter was in the bedroom, he said he'd come to speak to *her*. Peter had called Ebbins and told him, "You've gotta get rid of her."

Ebbins did so very carefully. He told her that Peter's children were coming to visit with their mother and it would be inappropriate for her to be there. Patty looked at Ebbins in disbelief. Not only was her dream of life with a movie star shattered, but she had alienated her roommate and would be mortified to tell her parents what had happened. Peter avoided looking at her as she came into the bedroom to collect her things. Patty swallowed her pride, returned to her mother's house, and took to bed, where she remained for eight days, unsure if she wanted to live.

In the meantime, Peter took a flight to New York to celebrate his daughter Sydney's twentieth birthday. It was unusual for Peter to go to so much trouble for one of his children; often he would travel to New York and not let them know he was in town. When he did, it was usually Milt Ebbins who picked them up and brought them to a restaurant to see their father. According to Ebbins, "He never wanted to go upstairs into Pat's penthouse. One time he did, and when he walked into the kids' rooms he saw that they had his movie star pictures pinned up all over their walls. Sydney *adored* Peter. Her eyes would open up like balloons when she saw him. She looked at him like he was a god. He knew it, too."

At twenty, Sydney had developed into a tall, striking beauty with long luxuriant hair, chiseled features, and compelling dark eyes. She had remained out of the public eye for most of her life; the only press attention she had ever received was when she was seven and she and her cousin Maria Shriver set up a lemonade stand in Palm Beach that was closed down by the police because it was "dangerous" and "causing a traffic jam." She had been educated at the Foxcroft School in Virginia, at the University of Miami, and at Franklin College, in Lugano, Switzerland. At this point in her life she was interested in a fashion career and was about to begin study at the Tobé-Coburn School, in New York.

For Sydney's birthday on August 25, Peter took her and Christopher, who had turned twenty-one in March, to Trader Vic's for dinner. He gave Sydney a piece of jewelry from Van Cleef & Arpels. He also had a present for Christopher and a lapis lazuli choker for the other person at the dinner, Amy Rea, a model-actress in her early twenties.

Peter had met Amy a few days earlier when she had come to a dinner party he'd given in his Waldorf-Astoria suite, and he later told her it was love at first sight. "He sang 'Once in Love with Amy' for me," she recalled, "and he said that the song's range was one of the most difficult to achieve."

The two spent most of the evening discussing their mutual interest in sexual experimentation. "That was when he confessed to me that he had derived his greatest pleasure from having his nipples lacerated with razor blades, which one woman had done to him. He loved having his nipples pinched, squeezed, hurt. He could orgasm through the pain." That was a little beyond her tolerance, Amy told him, but she did enjoy some pain during sex, as well as bondage and "light S&M."

After the last guest had departed, Amy and Peter retired to the bedroom, which was lit only by candlelight. Peter took off his shirt and Amy removed her silk blouse and skirt, leaving on her black garter belt, red panties and hose, sheer bra, and gold-tipped high heels. "I shot onto the bed like a diver," she recalled. "We laughed and laughed and he showered me with compliments. He told me I was beautiful. His hands touched my waist and the curve of my hip bone so delicately that my skin became highly sensitized. I felt like a Persian cat, rolling over for my owner as he touched me. I assumed a posture like Marilyn Monroe's famous nude calendar shot on red velvet.

"I saw a look of recognition in Peter's eyes. 'My God,' he exclaimed, 'you remind me so much of Marilyn. The way you act, the way you move. You're like her reincarnation.' He showed me his goose bumps in the candlelight. Halfway naively, I asked him, 'You knew her?'"

Peter then went into a long dissertation about his relationships with Monroe and the Kennedys. As Amy recalled it, he didn't reveal anything he hadn't before, but he did subtly aggrandize himself as he spoke. After a good deal of this, she excused herself, saying she had to go to the bathroom.

"Can I watch?" Peter asked.

Amy laughed. "If you want."

Peter scrambled onto the floor and followed her on all fours into the bathroom. When she was finished, Amy saw that Peter had slumped against the wall. "Slap me," he begged her. "Please!"

"What?"

"Slap me. Slap me! Really hard. As hard as you can!"

"But you have glasses on," Amy protested.

Peter took off his glasses and began to hit his own face, as if to prepare himself for Amy's blows. She thought to herself, *If there was ever a time for me to experience this, this is it*. She raised her hand to hit Peter, but her arm felt like a heavy slab of stone.

She let her arm drop to her side. "I can't, Peter! I want to love you, not beat you. I could never hurt you like that! Please don't make me."

"But I enjoy it!"

"No, Peter, please. I can't—I just can't!"

She fell into his arms, sobbing, and he carried her back to the bed. "We lay there basking together in our newfound level of intimacy. We watched the candle and waited for daylight before speaking."

According to Amy Rea, Peter proposed marriage to her, but she declined. Despite what she saw as their "spiritual affinity," she insisted that Peter "scared the bejesus" out of her. "I could not fathom what a world of weirdness I would embrace by becoming his wife."

PATTY SEATON had no such misgivings when Peter called her on his return from New York and asked her to come back to him. He sent a limousine to pick her up and she moved once again into his apartment. But before long she realized just how much degradation she would have to accept in order to change her life.

She and Peter had not had any sexual relations beyond "extensive touching and intimate fondling" in the two interrupted weeks they'd been together, which Patty assumed was because of her wired jaws. When the wires were cut at the end of the second week, she expected that she and Peter would begin "a normal intimate relationship." It didn't happen. Three months passed, and Peter never made any overtures. All he was interested in was oral sex; he no longer even attempted traditional intercourse, and could reach orgasm only after several hours of fellatio. He had become primarily a voyeur, and he began to request things of Patty that she found "repugnant."

But unlike so many of the women who had passed through his life over the past decade, Patty Seaton was willing to do anything to please Peter Lawford, and she acceded to his every sexual demand—including, as she later wrote, that she have sex with another woman while he watched. She subjugated herself to him and got as involved with drugs as he was; she called herself "Captain Doper."

Excited by the private jet flights to Las Vegas, the limousines, Peter's famous friends, an occasional picture of herself and Peter in the newspaper, Patty was starry-eyed—and very likely terrified that Peter would tire of her. She didn't want to lose him, her glamorous new life, or the newfound respect of her mother and friends. As long as she did everything Peter wanted she could make sure that didn't happen.

The two continued an on-again, off-again relationship for the next eight years, interrupted by Patty's long sojourns in London and Hawaii. When she was gone, there was always a steady flow of women willing to have sex with other girls while Peter watched, willing to stay with him until he reached orgasm. But Peter told Patty that he loved her, left her affectionate notes every day, bought her little gifts—and that seemed to be enough for her.

JUST ABOUT everyone who had been close to Peter thoroughly disliked Patty Seaton, and his relationship with her drove another wedge between him and them. Fairly or not, they blamed her for his accelerating descent into drug abuse. "I had a genuine hatred for that woman," Bill Asher recalled. "She professed to help him. She'd tell me how she was going to straighten him out, but she was worse than he was. She was a doper, a major hitter when it comes to alcohol and pills, whatever it was they were doing."

Erma Lee Riley, who remained Peter's maid for twenty-five years, had a difficult time discussing this period of Peter's life without breaking down. "People didn't know the real Peter Lawford," she said. "In the later years, he wasn't himself. He was a gentle man. A shy man. A lot of people made him what he turned into. Some people in his life were out for themselves. He didn't have a chance with these people around and he knew it. They took such advantage of him. I was there one day and he sent Patty out of the house and when she left, he just put his head on my shoulder and cried—like a baby. He was someplace he didn't want to be."

Peter's friends are still astounded by the way Patty got Peter to finance her trip to London. According to them, she told him that her father had died and that he had left her millions of dollars. She had to take his body to England, she said, in order to claim the inheritance, and needed eight thousand dollars to make the trip.

Peter borrowed the money from several friends, including Bill Asher, and he promised to repay them as soon as she got her money. When she was ready to go, Peter later said, a hearse she claimed contained her father's body pulled up in front of their apartment and she drove off in it to the airport.

Patty told Peter she would wire him a hundred thousand dollars as soon as she could. According to Bill Asher, "Peter would call me up and say, 'She's going to the bank today.' Then he'd call up and say, 'She's going to the bank tomorrow.' I'd say, 'Peter, get real here—she's not telling you the truth.' He'd say, 'Oh yeah, she's gonna get the money.' The money never came. Peter wasn't in on this, he had just deluded himself into thinking it was true."

PETER AND Patty became more and more isolated as their behavior continued to drive away the few people in his life who still cared about him. Finally even loyal, stalwart Milt Ebbins couldn't take it anymore. Ebbins had put up with a great deal from Peter Lawford. He'd been called in the middle of the night to handle situations Peter should have handled himself. He'd been available at a moment's notice to step in and do Peter's dirty work, whether it was to get rid of a girl or put off a creditor. He again and again had gone far beyond the call of duty to help Peter, years after the glamour and excitement of Camelot had dimmed to a hazy memory.

In return, Peter had spent money he didn't have, and when the situation reached a point where Ebbins could no longer placate the creditors, Peter had blamed him for the ensuing problems. When Peter lost the beach house, he blamed Ebbins. When Peter lost his Tamarisk Country Club membership after falling a year behind in his dues, he blamed Ebbins.

The truth was that Peter rarely paid attention to Ebbins's often heroic efforts on his behalf; indeed, he sometimes actively prevented Milt from improving his affairs. The most vivid instance of this provided the coup de grace to their professional relationship.

During the last few months of 1976, Aaron Spelling, the TV producer, hired Peter to appear in the pilot for *Fantasy Island,* with the possibility of a recurring role on the show if it were picked up for a series. After Peter filmed his part, Ebbins grabbed the seventy-five hundred dollars for Peter's services in person, foiling yet another garnishee, and met with Peter at Cory Avenue to decide which of his many overdue bills would be paid with the funds.

"Listen, Milt," Peter told him, "I gotta have twenty-five hundred of that money right now."

"You gotta be kidding, Peter," Ebbins protested. "Look at these bills! You owe Bill Noad three thousand for back rent—"

"I don't give a damn! I owe a pusher twenty-five hundred bucks and I gotta have that fucking money!"

"I'm not gonna give you the money, Peter."

Peter's voice became guttural. "Whaddya mean you're not gonna give me the money?" He grabbed Milt and the two of them began to scuffle. Ebbins threw the money down and said, "Okay, Peter, it's your money. I can't hold it. Here it is."

As Ebbins started to leave, Peter continued to berate him. Milt got to the top of Peter's stairs and said to him, "You know, I feel sorry for you. You've gone down about as low as you can get." He walked down the stairs and Peter began to call him "every kind of dirty, vicious name you can imagine. I turned and looked up at him yelling down at me from the top of the stairs and I said to him, 'Peter, why don't you take a look at yourself in the mirror?' I walked out the door and he ran out on his balcony and screamed epithets at me like you wouldn't believe. I drove away."

Two hours later, Peter called Ebbins at home. "Do you know how badly you hurt me?" he asked quietly.

"What are you talking about?"

"Do you know how much you hurt me?"

"I never intentionally hurt you in my life, Peter."

"You told me to look at myself in the mirror. Don't you think I know what I look like?"

"I wasn't talking about your appearance, Peter," Milt told him. "I meant you should take a good look at yourself and see what you're doing to yourself."

With that, Peter reverted to form. "Aw, bullshit!" he spat, and hung up.

FORTY-THREE

Toward the end of the 1970s, Peter Lawford's acting career reached a virtual dead end. He appeared in only three movies between 1977 and 1984, all of them low budget, and made nine appearances in episodic television shows or TV movies. His total income for 1977 was fifty thousand dollars, a paltry sum compared to his past earning power.

Only a small fraction of this income derived from acting, but Peter was famous for being famous, and there were a number of other ways that he could make money. Peter's agent was now Gene Yusem, who got him twenty-seven jobs in 1977. They included game show appearances (*The Gong Show* four times, *Cross-Wits* twice); commercials (for the Captain Cook Hotel in Anchorage and the Brown Derby Restaurant in Cleveland); and paid talk-show guest spots. His fees ranged from eleven thousand dollars (plus five thousand for expenses) for a Tayside Scotch commercial shot in Australia to $267.50 for his appearance on the Peter Lupus talk show.

As the seventies ended and the eighties began, Peter's stock continued to decline. He did print ads for the New Jersey Dental Association and appeared on the cover of a promotional brochure for Rodeway Inns. In 1981, his photograph appeared, uncredited, on page 12 of the mail order catalogue for Norm Thompson, a Portland, Oregon, men's clothier. A company spokesman commented, "The nice thing is, he doesn't charge very much."

Peter signed up with an agency for radio voice-over commercials. Richard Stanley, who handled Peter, tried his best to get him an assignment. "I thought Peter had a terrific voice, perfect for things like wine spots where they'd want someone who sounded sophisticated and sexy. Whenever there was something I thought Peter was right for, I'd call him into my office, along with a number of other people. He'd sit in the waiting room, sometimes for hours, and then I'd have him come in and make a tape of the client's commercial copy. He was always polite and professional. I'd send out these tapes again and again, and do you know I never once had a client who would hire him!"

Part of the problem was Peter's new reputation for unreliability. In the past, no matter how badly out of it he was, he was able to pull himself together for a job. No longer. During one commercial spot that Gene Yusem arranged for him, taped at ten in the morning, Peter slurred his words and was incapable of reading the sixty seconds of copy straight through. There were so many retakes that it took ten hours of editing to turn out a usable commercial.

This kind of irresponsibility cost him; his burned bridges littered the Hollywood landscape. In December 1977 he went to Honolulu to appear on *Hawaii Five-0*, the Jack Lord series on CBS. As was the custom, the network paid for Peter's stay at the Kahala Hilton, but any incidentals (phone calls, room service, liquor, dry cleaning) were his responsibility.

During his nine-day stay at the hotel, Peter ran up an incidentals tab of $1,653—and never paid it. After the hotel dunned Peter for a year they revoked CBS's credit and threatened to sue the network unless *they* paid the bill. They did, and Peter agreed to repay CBS $1,819 (including interest) in payments of $150 a month. Not surprisingly, Peter never worked on a CBS series again.

When he wasn't able to make enough money working, Peter borrowed from the few friends he still had. Elizabeth Taylor, Jack Lemmon, Robert Wagner, and Bill Asher each lent him around ten thousand dollars. But, as Asher recalled, "Giving Peter money wasn't helping him. We thought we were helping him, but it just made it easier for him to buy drugs."

Because he did not share his interest in drugs with

them, Peter often avoided his daughters, embarrassed to have them learn about the life he was living. When they came to Los Angeles he pretended to be out of town, feigned illness, or—on a few occasions—simply didn't answer his door if he knew it was Sydney or Victoria.

In 1978, Peter received a letter from Victoria, then twenty, complaining that he hadn't responded to any of her letters. "Dear Daddy: I really don't know how to tell you this or how many times I've said this and meant it, but I love you. I don't know if you believe this but I hope to God you do. I've never really had a chance to sit down and talk to you as father to daughter, but I guess I feel just as close to you as if I had. I guess the circumstances leave it difficult to get to know one another, but I hope this changes in time, Daddy. . . . I didn't understand what's going on this year when you sent us all a typed letter trying to explain that you were happy, busy and in good health. All of that makes me happy, but I still don't understand it. I love you, Daddy, and I never want you to forget it."

One evening while Peter was in New York, he did the very unusual and invited Christopher, Sydney, and Victoria to an exclusive restaurant for dinner. At the end of the meal, he told Chris he didn't have the money to pay the check. When Chris said he didn't have either, Peter asked his son to put the tab on Pat Lawford's credit card. Reluctantly, Chris did so. As he dropped his children off at their apartment, Peter pulled his son aside and asked him if he could "score some cocaine" for him. Chris replied that he could, but that it would cost three hundred dollars. Peter pulled out his wallet and handed Chris three one-hundred-dollar bills. It was all Chris could do, he later related, to keep from decking his father.

When Peter was literally broke—and had borrowed from every friend he could—he scrounged up money wherever he could find it. He sold a box of his memorabilia to a cinema collector's shop on Hollywood Boulevard for one hundred dollars. He sent the *National Enquirer* a reminiscence of Judy Garland and was paid $62.50 for it. Photographer Don Pack, who had taken pictures of Peter with President Kennedy, ran into him at a supermarket near his apartment and lent him fifty dollars when Peter told him he didn't have enough money to pay for his groceries.

Matty Jordan, the owner of Matteo's, was the only one of Peter's restaurateur friends to remain loyal to him until the very end. As early as 1970, Jimmy Ullo, the owner of La Dolce Vita, had refused to send a plate of spaghetti and meatballs over to Peter's Sierra Towers apartment until he paid the fifteen-hundred-dollar tab he'd run up. Peter called Milt Ebbins, who suggested he go to the restaurant and talk to Ullo. Peter did and was refused in person: "You got a bill here, Lawford. Why don't you pay it?"

Peter again called Milt, who then went to La Dolce Vita himself. "How can you do that to him?" Ebbins asked Ullo. "Peter Lawford brought in so much business to you when you first opened. He made this place. So what if he owes you fifteen hundred dollars? Why don't you just wipe it off the books?"

But Ullo was intransigent, and Ebbins finally said, "Listen, I'm not gonna argue with you. Give *me* the spaghetti. I'll pay for it." He brought the dish up to Peter's apartment. "Some of the guys weren't loyal to Peter," Ebbins said. "He helped make those places. He got the biggest names in Hollywood to go into those restaurants, and he spent a fortune in them when he had money—he never got anything off the tabs, I'll tell you that."

Matty Jordan, on the other hand, allowed Peter to run up a five-thousand-dollar tab, which after several years he did pay. One night, Patty Seaton told Peter she wanted to go to Matteo's for dinner. They didn't have any money, but they went anyway and ate a big, expensive meal. When the check arrived, Peter told Matty he was embarrassed: he'd left his wallet at home and didn't have any money with him. Jordan told him it was no problem, he could sign for the tab. As he was leaving, he asked Matty for ten dollars to tip the parking attendant. Matty slipped him ten ten-dollar bills.

Jordan was happy to help Peter out. "I'll never forget Peter to the day I die," he said. "That's how much I liked him. He was a classy, beautiful man. Some people buy class, but Peter had it. And then all of a sudden he got fucked up and everybody turned their backs on him. I felt sorry for him. Who wants to be a bum?"

ANOTHER WAY Peter thought he could raise money was through lawsuits, and in the late seventies and early eighties he filed two major ones. The first was a $2.5-million action against Twentieth Century-Fox, Aaron Spelling, and Carol Lynley in 1977, following an injury he suffered while filming the *Fantasy Island* pilot in October 1976.

In the story, Carol Lynley was supposed to throw a five-inch crystal goblet at Dick Sargent in a moment of high emotion during a dinner party scene. Sargent and Peter sat in high-backed antique Spanish chairs with finials rising on both sides to about eye level. For the master shot, Lynley threw a "breakaway" sugar glass which hit Sargent's chair and harmlessly shattered. (Later, sound effects would be added to make it appear that a real glass had broken.) But according to a statement Peter gave in connection with the case, the prop man did not have another sugar glass for the next shot, a close-up of Lynley performing the same action. Peter said that the director, Dick Lang, then decided that since the schedule demanded the scene be completed that day, a real glass would have to be used.

Although they would not be on camera during Lynley's close-up, Peter and Dick Sargent remained in their chairs in order to speak the lines that Lynley was supposed to react to. For the close-up, Lynley planned to aim the glass midway between Peter and Sargent, and according to Peter, Lang positioned two prop men behind them to hold up a blanket with which to catch the glass. But when Lynley threw it, the heavy leaded crystal struck the chair finial to the left of Peter's head—and shattered.

Peter felt "a sharp pin prick" at the top of his left thigh just before director Lang yelled "Cut—that's a print!" He looked down and noticed a tear in his trousers about three inches long, "as if someone had taken a razor blade and made a small, clean incision in the cloth."

As blood began to gush out of the wound, Peter jumped up and pulled down his pants. Many of the cast and crew had no idea he'd been injured; one asked him, "What are you doing, trying to get laughs by taking your pants down?" But it soon became clear that Peter was bleeding badly, and the makeup man raced across the soundstage, pulled a cameraman's belt off, and wrapped it around Peter's leg, fearful that an artery had been cut.

Patty and Milt Ebbins took Peter to UCLA Medical Center, where doctors there found a 3½-inch long, 2½-inch deep laceration in his thigh. They closed the wound with twenty-two stitches through both muscle and skin and discharged Peter "with analgesic medication."

As he, Peter, and Patty were leaving, Ebbins asked the nurse to give Peter crutches. "What for?" Peter asked. "Peter, put the crutches on," Milt said. "And why don't you stay here for a couple of days? This is Twentieth Century-Fox you're talking about—and you've got one hell of a lawsuit." Peter took the crutches, but when he arrived home he discarded them. "Peter," Ebbins pleaded, "stay in the house a couple of days."

"Oh, c'mon, Milt," Peter replied. "You and the fucking crutches." The next day, he attended a Bob Hope charity benefit in Malibu, walking normally if carefully, signaling to everyone that his injury was not that serious.

A month later, Peter strained his back, aggravating a herniated disk, and experienced excruciating pain down his left leg. It was followed by numbness in his lower leg and foot. This time, he was admitted to UCLA, where he spent nine days. He told the doctors that he had been on crutches for three weeks following his leg injury and that he believed the use of the crutches and a limp he'd developed afterward had aggravated his back problem.

When Peter was discharged, his pain was "ninety-five percent improved"; he was able to walk and bear his own weight. He was given, according to his discharge summary, "a firm admonition in respect to the protocol of management at home" and a prescription for the painkiller Talwin.

On December 23, Peter filed the $2.5 million lawsuit against Twentieth Century-Fox, Spelling, and Lynley, charging that negligence, carelessness, and recklessness on their part caused his leg injury and that the injury led to his aggravated back problem. He claimed emotional and mental damage, loss of economic advantage, and loss of income.

Fox's lawyers petitioned the court to release Peter's medical and psychiatric records in an attempt to prove that other factors might have caused his back problem, but the judge refused.

The legal haggling dragged on for years, and it became clear that Peter didn't have much of a case; too many witnesses had seen him walking without crutches for him to claim that his leg injury caused his back problem. Eventu-

ally, Peter agreed to a twenty-five-thousand-dollar settlement, and the case was dismissed. "I was stupid, wasn't
I?" Peter said to Ebbins. "You're usually stupid," Ebbins
replied.

In 1981, Peter filed another lawsuit, this one prompted
by an incident aboard an airliner. On an American Airlines
flight from Los Angeles to Little Rock in April 1980, Peter
was asked to leave the plane during a stopover in Dallas
because of intoxication and obstreperous behavior.

An account Peter gave of the incident is disjointed and
disturbingly reminiscent of Lady Lawford's descriptions in
her later years of the many indignities and injustices visited
upon her. It affects a tone of righteous indignation over the
"completely unwarranted" treatment of him by a stewardess
he calls "Miss Charm." Nowhere in Peter's retelling does
he mention that he was anything but stone-cold sober during
the incidents he describes. Adding drunkenness to the equa-
tion puts an entirely different cast on his version of events.

According to Peter, his only infraction was to walk forward in the aircraft to get a copy of *Newsweek*. The stewardess told him, "You'll have to be seated, sir. We are
preparing for takeoff."

"Yes, miss, I know that," Peter replied. "I was just
getting a mag—"

The next thing he knew, Peter said, the stewardess was
"propelling" him back to his seat, all the time muttering
how embarrassing this was to her in front of the other passengers. After he sat down—"cogitating the rather brusque
occurrence which I had just experienced more with a reaction of amusement than anger"—the stewardess came back
up the aisle to him, leaned on his armrest, and said, "Sir, I
thought I'd better tell you that we will not be serving alcohol
on the flight today."

"Oh, that's okay," Peter replied. "I guess the booze
wagon must have blown up."

"No, sir, I think you misunderstood. I cannot serve *you*
any alcohol on this flight."

Peter asked her to "run that by me again." When she
did, he demanded to know why. "I don't have to tell you,"
the stewardess replied.

"At these prices I feel I am entitled to a logical reason
for your provocative and unqualified position," Peter an-

nounced loudly. "Did I vomit in the wing? Did I stumble coming aboard? Why wasn't I stopped at LAX for any irregularities in my personal behavior? Please explain *that* to me if you can!"

The woman repeated that she did not have to give a reason and asked Peter if he would like to deplane right then. He refused. He did not want, he said, to become involved in "some strange juvenile entrapment surrounding me" begun by a stewardess who was "in the advanced stages of paranoia as anyone could plainly see."

Throughout the flight, Peter repeatedly demanded a full written account from the stewardess and the captain of what had ensued, before the plane landed in Dallas. He didn't get it; instead, when the flight arrived, he was met by "a small bevy of men in dark suits looking suspiciously like security" and an agent from the airline. Peter was taken off the flight and took a private plane to Arkansas.

When the original flight arrived in Little Rock, Peter's host, who had come to meet him, was informed that he had been requested to deplane in Dallas because of "passenger misconduct." To him, Peter said, this represented "a most insidious, incriminating and damaging statement." He sued American Airlines, charging that the airline officials "did treat plaintiff in an outrageous manner" and falsely accused him of intoxication. "Said words and statements were made with reckless intent to injure plaintiff" and were overheard by Peter's fellow passengers, causing a defamation of his character. "Plaintiff has suffered general damages to his reputation in a sum in excess of $100,000," the complaint concluded.

Peter dropped the suit a year later without any monetary settlement from American. Proving that he had not been intoxicated and that the stewardess's actions were unwarranted and a result of "paranoia," of course, would have been difficult, especially with an airplane full of witnesses. Diplomatically, Peter's attorneys suggested to him that he drop the suit only because he would be unable to show any real damage. "The law requires an out-of-pocket loss in a case like this," they told him, "not just your natural feelings of frustration, anger and indignation."

OFTEN NOW, Peter tried to recapture his glory days. He had never let go of the memories, to the point where his

Cory Avenue apartment was a virtual shrine to them. "Every spare inch of wall space had pictures on it," Bill Asher remembered. "It was like wallpaper. I said to him, 'Take down those pictures, Peter. You can't live in the past. Who gives a fuck about Sinatra and those guys? And for that matter, Jack Kennedy? They're no longer a part of your life. The present is what matters, the future.' Peter said, 'Those are my memories.'"

He tried to make his memories his present again. In 1978, he wrote to Frank Sinatra complimenting him on the fact that he appeared to have "mellowed tremendously, grown about ten feet." He expressed the hope that should they ever see each other again, they could simply shake hands. That, Peter concluded, was something that would prove valuable to "the tranquillity of my being."

When Sinatra did not respond to the overture, Peter decided to go to Las Vegas with Patty and take in one of Sinatra's shows. He was sure that once Frank saw him in the audience, all would be well again. The reality could not have been worse. When Frank was told that Peter Lawford was in the room, he refused to take the stage until Peter and Patty were escorted out.

Some ghosts were stirred for Peter in 1980 when Ted Kennedy ran for president, challenging—as Bobby had—an incumbent president of his own party. Unlike earlier Kennedy efforts, however, Peter had to watch this one from afar. He admitted to a reporter that he "hadn't been asked" to participate in Ted's campaign, and added that the senator's election wouldn't restore Camelot because "too much has changed."

Peter was saddened by the news that Ted's wife, Joan, had been struggling against alcoholism. She had felt overwhelmed and alienated by the Kennedy family, inferior when confronted by their tremendous energy and intelligence, unable to rise to the demands of being a dutiful Senate wife. At least, Peter recalled thinking, he wasn't the only one who had found it difficult to be married to a Kennedy.

Ted's quest for the Democratic nomination failed by a few hundred votes. In the November election, Ronald Reagan defeated Jimmy Carter and became the thirty-ninth president of the United States. Peter was furious—Reagan was the antithesis of everything the Kennedys stood for. And

Peter's mood wasn't helped by the specter of Frank Sinatra performing at the Reagan inaugural. Frank had done a 180-degree political turnabout, working as hard for Reagan as he had for Jack Kennedy. Peter gleefully reminded reporters that when Reagan was governor of California, and Frank was still a Democrat, he used to sing a parody of "The Lady Is a Tramp" with the revised lyrics "Hate California, it's Reagan and damp."

Now, whenever he saw President Reagan on television, Peter would throw things at the screen.

THE LONGEST-lasting effect of Peter's back problem in 1976 was his addiction to the drug Talwin. At first, he needed it to ease the pain of his herniated disk. Once the pain had gone, however, he continued to use it for pleasure. He injected himself in the buttocks with the drug around the clock, carrying syringes with him whenever he left the house so that he could shoot up in the nearest available restroom.

Patty knew nothing about this until she discovered a bag under the bathroom sink filled with dozens of hypodermic needles. Later Peter suggested she take the drug for her menstrual pain. Before long, she too was addicted. "It gave us pleasure just to use it," she explained. "There was no need for us to have pain to be 'killed.' " Now, both of them carried syringes wherever they went.

Peter could never be without at least one drug to see him through the day, and this made international travel a problem for him. When he and Patty flew to Australia for the Tayside Scotch commercial job, they took several grams of cocaine along with them. Peter was worried that the coke might be discovered by customs, and the penalties for bringing drugs into Australia were harsh. He told Patty to hide the plastic packets inside her vagina. She protested, but he convinced her that there was no better way to assure that the drug wouldn't be discovered, and the prospect of being without it during their stay worried her as much as it did him: "I did not think we could function for a prolonged period without being able to get high."

After they landed, Patty joined him in greeting the executives of the whiskey company "with several grams of coke between my legs." It hadn't been necessary, though—their hosts had already cleared them through customs. By the time they reached their hotel, Patty was unable to remove the packets herself and Peter was forced to call a "sympathetic" doctor to do so—"an extremely painful and embarrassing procedure," Patty recalled.

ON MARCH 5, 1982, John Belushi, the comedian, was found dead in a bungalow of the Chateau Marmont Hotel above the Sunset Strip, a few miles from Peter's apartment. He had died of a combination of heroin and cocaine that he had asked a female companion to inject into his veins.

Belushi's death shocked his young fans and again turned the national spotlight on drug excesses in Hollywood. Two years earlier, the comedian Richard Pryor had nearly burned to death when a preparation of ether and cocaine he was concocting caught fire and blew up in his face.

Such news jarred many junkies out of their habits; some checked themselves into drug rehabilitation centers. No longer was cocaine seen as a harmless panacea. The rash of drug-related deaths, injuries, and arrests in the early 1980s resulted in a new wave of health consciousness, and although drugs were still a part of the Hollywood scene, they were no longer seen as a prerequisite for "hipness." The "fans" and sycophants who dropped five packets of cocaine into John Belushi's pockets at a single party no longer bragged about it. That was no longer "the LA way to send greetings," and drugs soon became a less destructive force in Hollywood.

This change in attitude, however, did not affect Peter Lawford, who was too far along in his addictions to be able to shake them off when they became unfashionable. Now nearly sixty, he spent most of the early eighties in a stupor, the only change in him being a new honesty about his problems. Although he had said in 1981 that it was "absolutely untrue" that he had a drinking problem, in 1983 he admitted to the British journalist Ian Brodie not only the problem, but its awful extent: "I can't stay away from the vodka bottle, and it's destroying me. Doctors say I've ruined seventy-five percent of my liver and that I won't live much longer if this nightmare of booze continues. I've reached a point where the days all merge into one long drunken haze. Things have got so bad I rarely leave my apartment."

His deteriorating condition led Peter to pretend not to

be home rather than let even his closest friends see him. While Elizabeth Taylor was in Los Angeles touring with the play *The Little Foxes* early in 1982, she and Tony Geary, the TV soap-opera star, came to visit Peter at Cory Avenue around one o'clock in the morning.

When Peter didn't answer their knocks, Liz and Tony went to the back courtyard of the complex and stood under his bedroom window yelling his name. "Suddenly there was this tremendous hullabaloo beside my garden," his downstairs neighbor Isabel Heyel recalled. "Screeching and running around. The two of them were absolutely snockered and Elizabeth was yelling, 'Peter! Peter!' I knew he was home, but he wouldn't let them in, because he never let anybody in at that point."

Part of the "tremendous hullabaloo" was caused when Elizabeth wandered into the toolshed. "She got all caught up in the rakes and hoes," Bill Noad remembered, "and started screaming and swearing. Then she was banging on the garbage cans, trying to get Peter to come to the window. But he never did."

Peter could no longer afford most drugs, so he concentrated on booze, drinking the cheapest available champagne most of the time. His daily routine consisted of watching game shows and soap operas, sleeping, and taking whatever drugs and alcohol he could afford that day. Sometimes, his behavior seemed insane.

When Patty returned to the apartment after a short while away following an argument, he came up behind her and put a loaded revolver against her head. He accused her of having had a sexual rendezvous and threatened to blow her brains out for leaving him. She was able to talk him into putting the gun down. "When his mind sufficiently cleared hours later," she said, "[he] was horrified by what had almost happened."

In the spring of 1982, Patty said, she was raped by her gynecologist. When Peter wondered whether she had encouraged the man, Patty left him again, this time for five months. She changed her name and went to live in Hawaii. When she came back to the mainland in October, she went to Las Vegas for a while. Then she returned to Los Angeles, where she found Peter in his most horrific condition yet. His hair and fingernails had grown so long that he resembled Howard Hughes toward the end of his life. He had been incontinent and had not bothered to change the sheets. Rotting food and cat feces were all over the apartment.

Patty tried to save his life. She cleaned him and the apartment; she threw out most of his booze and drugs; she made certain he ate properly. She attended meetings of Al-Anon, an Alcoholics Anonymous offshoot for people living with alcoholics. With Patty's new determination to help him, Peter took an interest in life again. He cut back on his drinking and regained many of the qualities that had made her fall in love with him—"he was his old charming self," she said.

He felt able to work again, and he reestablished his relationship with Milt Ebbins. Early in 1983, Ebbins got Peter an acting assignment in a European TV movie, *Where Is Parsifal?*, at an excellent salary of forty-five thousand dollars (from which Peter gladly paid Milt a commission). The picture, a zany comedy about a man who invents a sky-writing machine that can bring peace to the world, starred Tony Curtis and featured Orson Welles and Erik Estrada.

Peter and Patty traveled to England for the filming, which took place at Hamden House, an ancient mansion that had been used for a number of horror movies and that served as both set and housing for the cast and crew. The house was magnificent in its faded glory but uncomfortable. The toilet seats were wooden and prone to splinter; the bedrooms were cold and illuminated by bare light bulbs hanging from cords.

Orson Welles, his first day on the set, greeted Peter with his booming, resonant voice: "So there you are, Lawford, a man who knows no shame." He looked at Patty and asked what Peter was doing with such a young girl.

"I've been with her now for about seven years."

"Oh dear God help us!" Welles cried.

The filming proceeded smoothly. Peter was still taking drugs and drinking, but in manageable amounts. Victoria Burgoyne, a young British actress with a small part in the film, recalled that "Peter seemed completely together. His timing was good, he was alert. I wasn't aware that he was taking anything, and it certainly didn't affect his work. He had this wonderful charm and relaxed manner that relaxed everybody around him, and everyone liked him tremendously."

Peter had little to do in *Where Is Parsifal?* One funny

bit in which he enacted a faded matinee idol making a TV commercial pitch was intercut with other scenes and lost a lot of its effectiveness. During a dinner-party segment, he seemed slow and tired; there was very little spark left. The movie was shown on European television and occasionally turns up on cable TV in the United States. When Peter and Patty returned to Los Angeles, he resumed his heavy drinking and drug use. He went through the money from *Parsifal* quickly, and soon found himself once again desperate for cash, borrowing small sums from anyone who would help him.

ON SEPTEMBER 17, 1983, Sydney Lawford married Peter McKelvy, a television producer in Boston, and the wedding was followed by a reception at the Kennedy compound in Hyannis Port. The Kennedys did not want to invite Peter; Pat Lawford was prepared to have her brother Ted give Sydney away. But Sydney insisted that she wanted her father there, and so he was invited.

He told Milt Ebbins he didn't want to go. "You idiot!" Ebbins screamed at him. "What do you want to do, insult your daughter? You bet your ass you're going." Sydney paid for Peter's airfare, and his room at Dunfey's Hyannis Hotel was provided gratis. The night before the wedding, Peter, Christopher, "and several of Robert Kennedy's sons," according to the *Boston Herald,* "partied long and hard at the hotel."

The next day, Steve Connolly, a *Herald* reporter, corralled Peter in the hotel bar and reported that he was drinking triple vodkas to fortify himself for the wedding ceremony. Peter, who looked "pale and dissipated," told Connolly, "I wish I could dry out and kick this stuff. It's taking its toll, isn't it?"

Finally he told Connolly, "No one's sent a car for me," and when the reporter saw Bobby's twenty-five-year-old son Michael rushing out of the hotel he told him that Peter needed a lift to the church. As Michael directed Peter to a limousine waiting outside, Peter whispered to Connolly, "I need a drink."

As the Kennedys feared he would be, Peter once again was a public embarrassment to them. Tipsy at the rehearsal, he tripped and fell while walking Sydney down the aisle.

The wedding itself went off without a hitch, but at the reception Peter drank too much and was accompanied by a young black girl who wandered around with a champagne bottle in her hand.

The only member of the Kennedy family who didn't shun Peter was Jackie Onassis. Still fond of him, still feeling an outsider's kinship with him, Jackie went over to Peter as he sat alone and engaged him in conversation for over half an hour.

WHEN PETER returned to Los Angeles, Bill Noad began to pressure him for payment of almost three thousand dollars in back rent. Noad had been the picture of patience with Peter for years, and his request was polite. But Peter fired off a blistering letter to his landlord about everything that was wrong with the apartment and threatened to report what he called "building code violations." As he had many times before, he told Noad that he was going to move, and for the first time Noad didn't try to talk him out of it. Once Peter and Patty left, Noad said, he found that the apartment was a wreck: "The filth! And the stench! I don't blame Peter for that. I blame Pat Seaton. He was ill."

Isabel Heyel added, "I cannot imagine how they ever lived in that house. It was just so appalling. Disgusting. Nothing was maintained. The cat had peed on the sofa a million times. Everything smelled. Everything was trashed. I don't know how Pat Seaton could have lived there and not done something about it."

Peter and Patty moved into a tiny apartment in a complex on Havenhurst Drive in West Hollywood, and Peter was once again near rock bottom. He looked dreadful, a decade older than his sixty years. Despite what he had told the *Boston Herald* reporter about wanting to dry out, he refused to seek help—until December 1983, when he got a telephone call from Elizabeth Taylor. She had been waging her own battle against alcohol and prescription drugs and had decided to check herself into the Betty Ford Center in Rancho Mirage, an alcohol and drug rehabilitation clinic known for its tough detoxification and recovery program.

Elizabeth had finally admitted to herself—after a confrontation with her family—that she needed professional help. She told Peter that it was time he got help as well.

"You must follow my example," Taylor pleaded. "I'd hate to see anything happen to you. We've come to a crossroads in our lives. It's time to change before it's too late."

She convinced him that he had to follow her into the Betty Ford Center, and he did so on December 12. First, however, he made a telephone call. According to Milt Ebbins, Peter called up one of the supermarket tabloids and spilled the beans about Elizabeth's being in the Betty Ford Center. "He would have done anything for money at that point, and he knew they would pay very well for *that* story. And they did. He got something like fifteen thousand dollars."

FORTY-FOUR

PETER AND Patty flew from Los Angeles to Palm
Springs on December 12, then drove to the Betty Ford
Center in Rancho Mirage. On the flight, Peter downed
enough one-ounce bottles of vodka to get drunk. In the car,
he wasn't sure where they were going. When Patty told him,
"Betty Ford's," he seemed pleased. "I've always liked Betty
Ford," he replied—and Patty realized he thought they were
going to her house for dinner.

Once he arrived at the center, Peter understood where
he was and why, and he agreed to go through a program
designed to save his life. His first week there was a harrowing one of cold-turkey detoxification; his body sweated
and shook and burned for more drugs, more alcohol. Once
he got through it, he was far from a model patient. He
rebelled against the strictures of the center, refusing to make
his bed, vacuum his room, or do his laundry. (He had Patty
do it when she visited him.)

His days were spent in group and private therapy,
which he hated. He described his therapy sessions as "someone expressing an authoritarian spasm." He finally began
doing chores his second week there and played bridge during leisure hours with the other celebrities at what he called
"Stalag 17"—Elizabeth Taylor (who knew nothing of his
tip-off to the tabloid), Johnny Cash, and Desi Arnaz, Jr.

His therapy regimen included writing responses to
questions about his feelings and attitudes. He expressed re-

sentiment over having been forced to move from Cory Avenue "because of lack of funds. It makes one rather frustrated watching one's life going down instead of up—especially at my age." In response to the question, "Who do you think you may have hurt by your drinking or drug use?" Peter replied, "I only hurt myself, not others that I am aware of."

Another part of the therapy was to write letters to loved ones (dead or alive) that he may have hurt with his addictions and apologize for his behavior. Since he felt he hadn't hurt anyone, he wrote only to Jack Kennedy and Sir Sydney.

The letters, long and chatty, detail his activities and ask about theirs. He tells Jack he wouldn't like the Betty Ford Center because there was "not a pretty girl within miles." He asks him if he has been elected president of anything— "you must be running something, knowing you." He asks how Marilyn and Bobby are doing and asks Jack to give his best to Steve McQueen and Vic Morrow should he run into them.

Peter's letter to his father is extraordinary in its affectionate tone; he calls him "you marvelous rascal!" In his letter to Jack Kennedy, Peter admits that he is in the Betty Ford Center because of his drinking, but to his father he writes only that he has been having liver problems. He apologizes to Sir Sydney for not having been able to say goodbye to him when he went on his "trip" and tells him that they will talk soon. He closes the letter, "I adore you— Peter."

AN ALCOHOLIC or drug addict cannot be helped unless he truly wants to be, and Peter didn't—as Patty soon learned. "Peter has a death wish," she told one of the national tabloids. "There are days when I know he wants to destroy himself."

That Peter was slowly committing suicide became clear from his American Express bills, from which Patty learned to her shock that Peter had paid for a helicopter to fly cocaine into the vast desert area behind the Ford Center. He would take a long walk, meet the helicopter, do a few lines of coke, and return to the facility. Apparently, he was never found out.

Peter did remain alcohol free for the five weeks he spent at the clinic, and Patty described him as "looking wonderful" when he returned home. Three days later Peter went out on an errand, and a few hours later Patty got a phone call. It was the bartender at a nearby restaurant; Peter was so drunk she would have to come and help him home.

It was like this often during the last year of Peter's life; his deterioration proceeded with awful speed. Although he continued to try to work, no one would hire him. After Gene Yusem sent him to a producer for a possible role in a television pilot, the man called Yusem and asked him, "Have you *seen* Peter Lawford lately?"

Desperate, he took out a loan from the Motion Picture Relief Fund and sold the story of his treatment at the Betty Ford Center to a national tabloid for twelve thousand dollars. He set to work once again on his memoirs, this time on speculation. He worked with the freelance writer Wayne Warga, and Warga soon found himself frustrated by Peter's inability to concentrate and his unwillingness to be frank about the Kennedys. "Jack was a wonderful person and a wonderful President," Peter said later. "And I'm not going to blacken his name no matter how much I need the money." As before, the project never got off the ground.

In July 1984, Peter complained of stomach pains; before long his abdomen became distended and he coughed up blood. Patty took him to UCLA Medical Center, where he was diagnosed with a severely bleeding ulcer. He underwent emergency surgery, during which thirty-five percent of his stomach was removed.

While he was hospitalized, he wrote out a will in longhand, leaving "any and all belongings, possessions or assets owned and held by me" to "my common-law wife/companion Patricia Ann Seaton in the event of my demise." The next day, he and Patty were married in his hospital room by a justice of the peace in a ceremony witnessed by a nurse, Peter's lawyer, and the patient in the next bed, who vomited throughout the ceremony.

Patty wore white, and Peter insisted on standing next to her in his hospital gown despite the fact that he could barely stand and had IV tubes stuck into his arms.

Home again after the surgery, told never again to touch drugs or alcohol, Peter needed almost constant care. He had to be fed through a tube every ninety minutes around the clock, had to have his dressings changed every few hours and be helped with his bodily functions. There was no money to hire a nurse, and no one but Patty to take care of him. Finally, she spoke to Peter's children about putting him into a home where he could be cared for by professionals around the clock. According to Patty, they didn't feel that that was necessary.

Peter's condition worsened. When the doctors removed the gastric tube, he began to bleed uncontrollably; they discovered that his damaged liver had stopped secreting an enzyme necessary for optimal blood clotting. The bleeding was stemmed, but now he was suffering from coagulopathy, a potentially fatal blood clotting disorder. The next day, he bumped his arm and within minutes it swelled to twice its normal size. Three days later, blood came to the surface of the swollen arm as though it were perspiration; he spent another three weeks in the hospital.

Peter made a slow but steady recovery, and by November, he was again well enough to join Elizabeth Taylor at her house for dinner. She had used her influence to get him a small, two-day role in a television movie she was about to begin, *Malice in Wonderland,* in which she would play Louella Parsons, and Jane Alexander would play rival gossip columnist Hedda Hopper. Peter was to play an agent, and Taylor warned him that she had gone out on a limb for him and she didn't want him to "screw up." He laughed and teased her about her highly publicized new sobriety. "You used to have a personality," he told her. "You used to be interesting."

As the day approached for Peter to film his few scenes in the picture, he grew nervous. He didn't want to let Elizabeth down, and he wasn't at all certain that he wouldn't. He started to drink heavily again and reestablished some of his drug connections to obtain marijuana and cocaine.

Within a few days, he collapsed and was taken to Cedars-Sinai Medical Center. There, doctors used various treatments, including vitamin therapy, to cleanse his body of toxins and help his failing liver function. He rallied once again and was released from the hospital on the morning he was due to appear on the *Malice in Wonderland* set.

The night before, Milt Ebbins had paid him a visit. "I brought him some éclairs, which he liked, and I was with him for about two hours. Pat Seaton wasn't there. I sat with him and he said, 'You want to go over some lines with me?' I said, 'Sure.' He seemed to be in pretty good shape, pretty lucid."

Ebbins showed Peter his lines, and Peter said, "No, these are the wrong pages." He turned to the pages he wanted to read, and after Ebbins told him that his character wasn't even on them, he kept insisting they were the right sides. Finally Milt convinced him and they started reading, but Peter didn't know where he was on the page. Ebbins thought to himself, *He's never gonna make it.*

They stopped reading and sat silently for a few minutes. Then Peter said, "Milt, I want you to do me a favor. Please talk to Patricia." Ebbins hadn't spoken to Patty for months but he promised he would try to make it up with her. As Ebbins was leaving, Peter walked with him out to the elevator bank. When they got there he patted Milt on the cheek and said, "Milt, you're a good friend." Ebbins responded, "Hey, we've always been friends and we'll always be friends."

The next morning, Thursday, December 13, Patty went to the hospital to pick Peter up. When she got there she discovered that he had already been discharged. Worried, she began to look around the hospital grounds for him. Then she saw him walking down the street, "happy as could be." He had gone to a convenience store and bought several one-ounce bottles of vodka.

Milt Ebbins met Peter on the *Malice in Wonderland* set at eleven that morning. Next on the filming schedule was Peter's first scene in the picture, in which his character was to introduce himself to Hedda Hopper, and the two men waited in his dressing room. Ebbins was concerned that Peter appeared so lethargic. "It seemed to me like he had taken some kind of drug. At lunch he lay down and I thought, *This man is dying.* Peter looked at me and saw the concern in my face and said, 'I'll be okay.' "

Ebbins asked him if he wanted some lunch. "They've got lamb chops, roast beef," he said. "Let me get you a plate of roast beef and mashed potatoes and some of that ice cream that you like. And I'll get myself some, too." He got the plates, but when he returned to the dressing room Peter's eyes were closed, his face ashen. Ebbins didn't want to disturb him, so he ate his lunch on the set.

About one o'clock, an assistant director knocked on the dressing room door and called out, "Mr. Lawford, we're ready for you." Peter replied, "Okay," got up, and put on his blue suit jacket. He could barely walk. Milt helped him out to the set and he took his mark to begin the scene with Jane Alexander. The director yelled, "Action!" and the cameras began to roll. When the time came for Peter's first line, he mumbled the words inaudibly. "The whole set could tell what was happening," Ebbins recalled. "Jane was very concerned. She just looked at him." Finally the director called out loudly, "Peter, please speak up a little. We can't hear you."

He said his line again, but still no one could hear him. And again, the same thing. The director yelled, "Take five," and began to huddle with some of the crew members. Then the assistant director came over to him and said, "Peter, I want you to lie down. We'll do the scene later." But Peter never did do the scene. He left the soundstage in midafternoon and went home.

AROUND NOON on the following Sunday, Patty returned to the apartment after running an errand and found Peter on the kitchen floor, bleeding and nearly unconscious. She called 911, then decided to take Peter to the hospital herself to save time. As she was leaving, the telephone rang. It was the producer of *Malice in Wonderland*, Jay Benson, with the news that Peter would have to be discharged from the film.

Peter was admitted to Cedars-Sinai Medical Center in grave condition. His liver and kidneys were failing, and his coagulopathy made surgery extremely risky. The doctors put him on life support systems and once again tried to detoxify him, but it was clear that this time Peter's chances of surviving were slim.

As his kidneys failed, Peter's skin turned yellow from the buildup of uremic toxins. Friends and relatives were notified that he was close to death. His children flew in to visit him, then left for Jamaica and a planned Christmas holiday. Elizabeth Taylor spent two hours holding Peter's hand, then left to spend her Christmas in Switzerland. Some old friends came to visit; others, like Molly Dunne, couldn't bring themselves to. "I knew I wouldn't be able to handle seeing him like that," she said.

Patty remained at the hospital most of the time, sleeping in a room provided her. She read to Peter, tried to get some response from him. Jackie Gayle came in and did his stand-up comedy routine, trying to get Peter to laugh. Nothing worked to rally him. On December 19, he fell into a coma. He lingered in that condition for the next four days, and Arthur Natoli spent the night of December 23 with Patty at the hospital. She asked him to go out to a nearby store and bring back flowers and some champagne, which they drank together.

At eight-fifty the following morning, Peter stirred for the first time in days. His muscles contracted and his upper body rose jerkily, involuntarily. Suddenly, blood spurted from his mouth, his nose, his ears. Then he fell back onto the mattress. He was dead.

ON CHRISTMAS Day, the Los Angeles *Herald-Examiner* ran a banner front-page headline, "Peter Lawford Dead at 61." The secondary headline provided an epitaph that would have caused Peter, with his self-deprecating sense of humor, wry amusement: "Kennedy in-law was last to speak to Marilyn Monroe."

EPILOGUE

MANY PEOPLE found themselves surprised by how affected they were by the news that Peter Lawford was dead. Still another symbol of the seemingly simpler, happier times epitomized by the MGM musical was gone, and for many the world was a poorer place because of it. Patty was amazed by the deluge of telegrams, cards, and letters that poured in "from every corner of the world." Ronald Reagan sent condolences, as did other heads of state. Patty remembered thinking, "It was as though the world had lost a beloved friend . . . even though his time as a star had long since passed."

Senator Ted Kennedy issued a tribute: "The death of Peter Lawford is a special loss to all of us in the Kennedy family, and my heart goes out to his children, Christopher, Sydney, Victoria, and Robin. We take comfort from the fact that we know he will also be missed by all of the people who enjoyed his many roles in films and on television. He was a dedicated and creative actor as well as a loving father and loyal friend to all of us, especially in the challenging days of the New Frontier."

Peter was cremated on Christmas Day, and the following evening a small group of family and friends attended a closely guarded funeral at Westwood Village Mortuary. In a cold, driving rain, Patty, Milt, the four Lawford children, Caroline Kennedy, Bobby Kennedy, Jr., Bill Asher, and several more of Peter's longtime friends heard him eulogized by both a Catholic and an Episcopalian priest.

After the thirty-minute service, which included the playing of John Lennon's "Love," Peter's ashes were entombed in a double crypt fifty yards from Marilyn Monroe's.

EVEN IN DEATH there was little dignity for Peter Lawford. Newspapers reported that the probate of his estate revealed that he had died heavily in debt and without major assets. Claims against the estate, all of which went unpaid, included one from Hugh Hefner for ten thousand dollars that he had lent Peter in August 1982. It was to have been repaid with the proceeds from the sale of Peter's projected memoirs. Hefner was the only one of Peter's friends to make a claim on his estate for the repayment of a loan.

In 1988, much news was made when it came to light that Peter's funeral expenses had never been paid. Westwood Village Mortuary, under new management, had warned Patty that they might have to remove Peter's ashes from his crypt unless the account was settled. Patty told the press that she had never had the money to pay the bills (which amounted to around seven thousand dollars), and that even when she told Peter's children that their father's ashes might be evicted from the memorial park, they had refused to pay the bills.

Others tell a different story. As Patty's attorney, Marcus Wasson, recalled: "I was under the impression that Patty did have the money to pay the funeral expenses after Peter died." Indeed, within a few months of his death she had received a fifty-thousand-dollar lump-sum payment from his Screen Actors Guild pension. Still, the bills were not paid.

When the story became public, Patty painted the Kennedys—and specifically Peter's children—as the villains of the piece. She told reporters: "It's terrible. Their father was always good to them." The family issued a statement: "The children only recently learned of the existence of financial problems in connection with their father's funeral expenses and they have taken care of all such obligations. The children's primary concern has always been that their father's remains rest in peace, and they loved him."

The children didn't pay the expenses; before they would agree to do so they insisted that Patty relinquish control of the crypt. She decided that she "had had it with the Kennedy family," and—although the mortuary had not pressed the issue—she told Peter's children that she was proceeding with the removal of his ashes and planned to scatter them at sea. They assented to her wishes and agreed to pay the $430 fee for the disinterment (Victoria sent the mortuary a check).

On May 25, 1988, cemetery workers pried open the front of crypt C-3, swept away the dust and cobwebs, and handed Patty the urn containing Peter's ashes. She had made a deal with—as she put it—"my friends at the *National Enquirer*," giving the tabloid exclusive picture rights in exchange for a limousine to take her to Marina del Rey, and a boat from which to scatter Peter's ashes into the Pacific.

Newspapers around the country told the story of Peter Lawford's last great indignity—his eviction from his final resting place. "I think it's terrible," the stories quoted Patty as saying. "I never wanted him to be removed, but the children took a walk. I was tired of all the nonsense. I didn't care if the children cared or not. I was doing what had to be done—what was best for Peter and his memory."

The final paragraph of the report in the *Los Angeles Times* on the occasion reflected the assumption of many that the entire sorry episode was a publicity stunt: "Mrs. Lawford, 30, arrived at the cemetery in a black limousine, accompanied by a professional photographer. She said her book on Lawford will be out this summer."

INTENSELY PRIVATE, Peter Lawford's children have kept low profiles most of their lives. Only Christopher, thirty-five as of this writing, has embarked on a career that could put him in the public spotlight. Although he was arrested in 1980 for heroin possession, he was never prosecuted on the charge, and his battle with drugs was behind him two years after he graduated from Boston College Law School in 1983. He married his longtime girlfriend, Jeannie Olsson, a month before Peter's death and is now the father of two.

Interested initially in show-business law and producing, Christopher has appeared in several television commercials over the last several years; at one point in 1989 he could be seen on three separate ad spots in Los Angeles. "I'm my father's son," Chris has said, and he does seem to be following in Peter's acting footsteps—he has played small roles in several films, including *Run, The Doors,* and *Impulse.*

Sydney and Peter McKelvy now have two sons, Peter, born in 1985, and Christopher, born in 1987. Victoria is a television coordinator for Very Special Arts, a nonprofit affiliate of the John F. Kennedy Center for the Performing Arts in Washington that sponsors programs for the disabled. She was married in June 1987 to Robert Pender, an attorney with a Washington law firm. In 1988, the couple became parents to a girl, Alexandra Lawford Pender.

Robin Lawford, thirty, is unmarried as of this writing. She has worked as a stage manager for off-Broadway productions in New York and is now involved in the Kennedy family's efforts on behalf of retarded children.

PETER HAD sat with Jean MacDonald on a seawall in Hawaii and sobbed, afraid that he had nothing to offer his children, that the Kennedys would overshadow him in their estimation at every turn. In many ways, of course, he was right. But no matter how much the Kennedys achieved, and no matter how badly his own life and career foundered, Peter would never lose the adulation of his children.

In March 1980, twenty-four-year-old Sydney wrote Peter a letter from Palm Beach, where she was staying with her mother and sister Robin at the Kennedy compound. She told her father that although she was working in her uncle Ted Kennedy's presidential campaign, it wasn't her relationship to the senator that impressed people when she was introduced to them—it was the fact that she was Peter Lawford's daughter. When they hear that, she said, "people almost pass out!"

Sydney added that she was enclosing the address of a young man who was eager to receive an autographed picture of Peter and asked her father to oblige him. Then she concluded, "Don't be surprised if a million more [such requests] come in. You're really loved and admired by so many people, Daddy. It makes me feel so proud."

ACKNOWLEDGMENTS

I OWE HEARTFELT thanks to Milton Ebbins for sharing his memories of his thirty-two-year association with Peter Lawford so freely. They have enriched this book immeasurably, and I will always be grateful for his good humor and his patience with my endless questions during more than forty hours of interviews over the course of two years. He opened many other doors to me as well, and I thank him very much for that.

I enjoyed meeting and talking with Peter's other friends, acquaintances, and associates quoted in this book, all of whom impressed me with their openness and their affection for Peter. I am indebted to each and every one. I also greatly appreciated my conversations with those people who have not been quoted directly in the text, but whose observations and memories helped me weave the tapestry of Peter Lawford's life: Ross Acuna, Richard Anderson, Joe Bleeden, Malcolm Boyes, Richard Brian, George Campbell, Gordon Carroll, Sergeant Jack Clemmons, Fielder Cook, Carlyne Dick, Gordon Douglas, Lenny Dunne, Anne Francis, Ray Gosnell, Adolph Green, Clarence Greene, Robin Gregg, Herbert Hirschmoeller, Jean Howard, Ruth Jacobson, Ron Joy, Charles Lane, Bethel Leslie, George Maharis, Mickey McCardle, Doug McClure, Ann Miller, John Miner, Ricardo Montalban, Pauline Morton (Mrs. Laurence Harvey), Dorothy Neu, Larry Newman, John O'Grady, Leo Penn, Cesar Romero, Janice Rule, Vi Russell, Ann Rutherford, Mary Sanford, Don Short, Burt Solomon, Rick Somers, Bill Travilla, Hazel Washington, Watson Webb, Michael Winner, William Reed Woodfield, and Gene Yusem.

Thanks also to those who took the time to write to me with their memories and observations: Jules Dassin, Allan Davis, Irene Dunne, Greer Garson, Elizabeth Greenschpoon, Deborah Kerr, Pax Lohan, Arthur Schlesinger, Jr., and Fred Zinnemann.

For all of his help, advice, and enthusiasm, warm thanks to my able associate Christopher Nickens, whose thoughtful suggestions improved this book and whose sense of humor helped me through the tough stretches. I'm grateful as well to my agent, Kathy Robbins, who always pushes me to do the best work I can; to my insightful and keen-eyed editor, Charles Michener, who urged me to write a "big" book; to this project's original champion at Bantam, Steve Rubin; to my friend and former editor Laura Van Wormer, whose enthusiasms are infectious; to Lauren Field at Bantam, who good-naturedly answered all my legal questions; and to my British publisher, Mark Barty-King of Bantam U.K., who was very helpful in a number of ways.

For their assistance during my research and travels for this book, I'd like to thank the following good people:

In Los Angeles—Michael Szymanski, Cindy Jones, Tom Boghossian, Milo Speriglio, Gene Poe, Theresa Seeger, Tony Brenna, Karen Swenson, Randall Henderson, Jill Evans, Marci McKee, Diana Brown of Turner Entertainment, J. B. Annegan, Sabin Gray, Barry Dennen, Ben Platt, Garrett Glazer, and Rick Carl.

In London—Paul Easom, Tom Wordsworth, Tony Frost, Colin Dunne, Peter Evans, Mark Reid, Lieutenant Colonel P. Emerson of the Indian Army Officers' Association, T. R. Shaw, Patrick Davies of the Eastleigh Borough Council, Mrs. E. Smith of the Lord Chancellor's Department, the staffs of the Public Record Office and The India Office, Patricia Cowley, Mrs. C. Bourdillon, Mrs. Gladys M. Bain, Mrs. J. R. Boston, and N. Lawford.

In Palm Beach—Milton Green, Leslie Weinberg, Curtis Kelly, Bernard Shulman, and Thom Smith of the *Palm Beach Post*.

In Miami—Walter Finley and Kevin Van Horn.

In Honolulu—Frankie Anderson (Jean MacDonald) and the staff of the *Honolulu Star Bulletin.*

In Las Vegas—Bethel Van Tassel and Stephen Allen of the Las Vegas News Bureau.

In New York—Eddie Jaffe, Michel Parenteau, Allison Solow, Sharon Churcher, George Zeno, Lou Valentino, Loretta Barrett, Elizabeth Mackey, Nancy Stauffer, Loretta Weingel-Fidel, Lester Glassner, Edward Fay, F. Gilman Spencer, and Reed Sparling.

In Boston—Richard Branson, Bill Modlin, Eric MacLeish, and John R. Cronin of the *Herald.*

Many thanks for the courtesies extended to me by the following librarians: Marilyn Wurzburger, Carol Moore, Janette Emery, and Megan McShane, of the Special Collections Department of the Arizona State University Library in Tempe, Arizona, where Peter Lawford's papers are housed; Sam Gill and the staff of the Margaret Herrick Library of the Academy of Motion Picture Arts and Sciences; the staff of the Lincoln Center Library of the Performing Arts; the staff of the British Film Institute Library; Ned Comstock and the staff of the Department of Special Collections of the University of Southern California; Michael Desmond and the staff of the John F. Kennedy Library in Boston; the staffs of the Ronald Reagan, Jimmy Carter, Gerald Ford, Richard Nixon, Lyndon Johnson, Dwight Eisenhower, and Franklin D. Roosevelt presidential libraries.

Fellow authors who kindly provided me with assistance include Bart Andrews, Peter Collier and David Horowitz, Leo Damore, Lester David, Dominick Dunne, Barbara T. Gates, Fred Guiles, Neal Hitchens and Randall Reise, Cliff Jahr, J. Randy Tarraborelli, Anthony Summers, Robert Windeler, and Donald Zec.

I'd also like to thank my family and friends for their support, love, and encouragement throughout the nearly four years of work on this book, particularly my father, Joseph Spada, and my friends Glen DeFeo, Dan Conlon, Dennis Lowman, and Mark Meltzer.

NOTES ON SOURCES

PART ONE

I spent a resonant and rewarding month in London rummaging among the ghosts of Peter Lawford's ancestors, gathering the vital statistics of May Bunny and her husbands, and Sir Sydney Lawford and his wives, at the Public Record Office, the Lord Chancellor's Department, and The India Office.

I gleaned details of May's youth and early adulthood from an unpublished 1963 interview with Hedda Hopper, from various newspaper and magazine articles by and about her, and from *Bitch!—The Autobiography of Lady Lawford, as told to Buddy Galon* (Branden Press). Although *Bitch!* is a fascinating and entertaining book, I have made highly selective use of it because of Lady Lawford's penchant for exaggeration, obfuscation, and, sometimes, outright deceit about her past. I've used only those facts that jibe with independent research.

Many of the details of the courtship and marriage of May and Ernest Aylen were provided to me by his niece Katharine Eden during an interview conducted on March 9, 1989, and in her letters to me dated April 4 and June 19, 1989. May's descriptions of Indian railway travel were in a dispatch she wrote for the London *Evening News* in 1931. Additional details of May's background were provided by Buddy Galon in an interview conducted May 10, 1989.

Sir Sydney's cousin Valentine Lawford shared information on the Lawford family tree, of which he has made a study. Details of Sir Sydney's military career were provided by the Royal Regiment of Fusiliers, and by Sir Sydney's *Burke's Peerage* listing. Sir Jocelyn Lucas's reminiscences of Sir Sydney were published in the London *Times* on February 20, 1953.

I gathered the facts of Peter Lawford's early life and film career from a variety of magazine and newspaper interviews with him and Lady Lawford published during his rise to stardom in the 1940s. Principal among these was "Peter Lawford Life Story," a two-part biographical series by Kirtley Baskette published in *Modern Screen*, July and August, 1946, that is the most detailed and accurate account of Peter's early life ever published in a magazine format. Other sources were Lady Lawford's autobiography, her newspaper columns published in the early 1930s, and the April 26, 1931, profile of Peter in the London *Sunday Dispatch*, "Wise Little English Film Star."

I learned a great deal about Peter's childhood from my numerous interviews with Milt Ebbins between November 1988 and December 1990, as well as from my interview with Deborah Gould on August 23, 1989.

Lady Lawford's views on corporal punishment—and her use of the practice on Peter—were detailed in her article "I Favor the Hairbrush" in *The American Weekly*, July 9, 1950.

I used Patricia Seaton Lawford's memoir *The Peter Lawford Story* very selectively as a source; I have taken from it only information about Peter's life that I could independently verify.

Information about Peter's role in *Lord Jeff*, and details of his Screen Actors Guild day player and MGM contracts, are contained in the MGM legal files.

Louise Barker-Fred shared her reminiscences of Peter aboard ship in a letter to me dated December 17, 1989, and in an interview conducted on January 5, 1990.

Peter's life in Palm Beach and his earliest days at MGM were described for me during interviews with Lucille Ryman Carroll on June 28, 1989, Connie Savage Dalton on February 19, 1989, Dorothy Neu on May 5, 1989, Muriel O'Brien on May 6, 1989, Mary Sanford on May 5, 1989, and Lillian Burns Sydney on July 22, 1989. The files of the Palm Beach *Post* supplied several interviews with Peter over the years in which he discussed his life in Palm Beach.

Some of Peter Lawford's reminiscences about his career at MGM are contained in Aljean Harmetz's profile of the MGM players, "She Wanted to Be a Moooovie Star," in *The New York Times*, November 12, 1972.

PART TWO

The associates of Peter's with whom I spoke for Part Two, in addition to those already cited, include Mrs. Gary Cooper on April 27, 1989, Jackie and Barbara Cooper on December 8, 1989, Ken DuMain on March 2, 1988, Dominick Dunne on March 3, 1989, Molly Dunne on March 31, 1989, Richard Fielden on May 10, 1989, Leonard Gershe on June 4, 1989, Hurd Hatfield on March 23, 1990, Prince Franz Hohenlohe on April 10, 1989, Arthur Julian on November 16, 1988, Janet Leigh on June 8, 1989, Dick Livingston on March 23, 1989, Jean

MacDonald on April 3, 1989, and October 11, 1989, Roy Marcher on March 22, 1989, Joe Naar on August 31, 1988, Fred Otash on November 15, 1988, Peter Sabiston on June 6, 1989, Dick Sargent on January 24, 1990, Don Weis on November 21, 1989, and Paul Wurtzel on April 5, 1989.

Background on Lana Turner was provided by her autobiography and by Cheryl Crane and Cliff Jahr's *Detour*. Peter's quotes about Lana come from his 1940s interviews and from the interviews with him conducted by Jerry Le Blanc and published in the London *Sunday People* in November 1974.

Information on all of Peter's films and the details of his business relationship with MGM were culled from the MGM legal files and the files of the Margaret Herrick Library of the Academy of Motion Picture Arts and Sciences.

The information about Peter's visits to call girls was gathered from his voluminous FBI file, released to me by the Justice Department pursuant to the Freedom of Information Act.

Sal Mineo's revelation that he had an affair with Peter Lawford is contained in Boze Hadleigh's *Conversations with My Elders*. Lady Lawford's descriptions of Peter's homosexual liaisons are a part of her autobiography.

Peter's quotes about Elizabeth Taylor are from Jerry Le Blanc's series of interviews with him in the London *Sunday People*. Greer Garson's reminiscences of Peter's matchmaking are contained in a letter to me dated October 3, 1989.

Many of the details of Peter's romance with Sharman Douglas are contained in twelve letters she sent to Peter between July 19, 1949, and June 14, 1950.

Allan Davis's quotes about *Rogue's March* are contained in a letter to me dated August 6, 1989.

Some details of Sir Sydney's death were taken from *Bitch!*, as well as from contemporary Honolulu and Los Angeles newspaper accounts.

PART THREE

Interviews quoted in this section and not previously cited were with Bill Asher on June 1, 1989, Joey Bishop on February 16, 1989, Sammy Cahn on March 10, 1990, Jeanne Carmen on December 6, 1989, Rab and Alice Guild on October 11, 1989, Matty Jordan on March 28, 1989, Phyllis Kirk on April 20, 1989, Dick Martin on March 16, 1989, Dolores (Naar) Nemiro on January 5, 1989, Arthur Natoli on April 4, 1989, Bob Neal on June 28 and August 24, 1989, John Newland on November 21, 1989, Don Pack on November 9, 1988, Robert Slatzer on September 1, 1988, and Bonnie Williams on December 29, 1988.

Peter's quotes about his artistic free agency are contained in an interview published in the *Hollywood Citizen-News* on June 24, 1953. Many of the details of Peter's courtship of Pat Kennedy are contained in an interview with Peter by Maxine Arnold published in the June 1955 issue of *TV Radio Mirror*. Peter's description of his first encounters with Joseph P. Kennedy are contained in his London *Sunday People* interview. The quotes attributed to Lady Lawford in this section are from contemporary newspaper accounts.

May Lawford's meticulously kept scrapbook of her son's wedding, comprising hundreds of newspaper clippings, provided me with invaluable details from such publications as the New York *Daily News*, New York *Journal American*, Boston *Sunday Globe*, and the dispatches of the Associated Press, United Press International, and the International News Service. The *Honolulu Star Bulletin* provided some information about the honeymoon.

Alex Gottlieb's quotes are from the November 27, 1954, cover story on *Dear Phoebe* in *TV Guide*. Other articles supplying information about *Dear Phoebe* were "A He-Man Named Phoebe," by John Maynard, in the *Honolulu Advertiser*, April 24, 1955, and Maxine Arnold's *TV Radio Mirror* piece.

Dore Schary's memories of his part in John F. Kennedy's 1956 vice-presidential campaign are contained in his oral history at the John F. Kennedy Library in Boston.

These articles provided additional quotes and details on *The Thin Man*: *TV Guide*'s cover story of October 26, 1957; another *TV Guide* piece, "It's for Real," November 11, 1958; "Thin Man Lawford Fattening Up Career," by John L. Scott in the *Los Angeles Times*, October 11, 1959; "Chewing the Fat with the Thin Man," by Joe Hyams; "Rebellious Thin Man," *New York Herald Tribune*, April 12, 1959.

Sam Giancana's checkered history has been covered in a number of books. Judy Campbell's versions of her relationships with Giancana and Jack Kennedy have been published in her autobiography, *My Story*, in her *People* magazine interview with Kitty Kelley published on February 29, 1988, and in Gerri Hirshey's April 1990 *Vanity Fair* profile, "The Last Act of Judith Exner."

I culled some of the details of John F. Kennedy's presidential campaign from his numerous biographies, from *The Making of the President 1960*, by Theodore S. White, from the oral histories at the JFK Library, and from a scrapbook of campaign clippings Peter kept.

PART FOUR

Many of the aforementioned interviews contributed information for this section, as well as my conversations with Ken Annakin on July 3, 1989, Phil Ball on May 17, 1990, Bette Davis on October 5, 1988, Peter Dye on June 19, 1990, Daniel Greenson on June 3, 1990, James Hall on May 30, June 3, and June 5, 1990, Natalie Jacobs on June 9, 1990, Chuck Pick on January 9, 1989, Lee Remick on February 10, 1989, Mae Shoopman on March 2, 1990, Henry Silva on June 6, 1990, Scottie

Singer on May 9, 1989, Mickey Song on May 29, 1990, and Sam Yorty on March 3, 1990.

Stephen Birmingham's profile "The Peter Lawfords of Hollywood" appeared in *Cosmopolitan* in October 1961. Peter's extended interview with Vernon Scott, "The White House Is Still Wondering What To Do With Me," was published in *McCall's*, January 1963. *Good Housekeeping* published Helen Markel's portrait of Peter, "The Many Lives of Peter Lawford," in its February 1962 issue.

I found confirmation that Hedda Hopper's blind items early in 1962 concerned Peter and Lee Remick in her personal papers, which are maintained at the Margaret Herrick Library.

I drew many of the details of Marilyn Monroe's last few months from Anthony Summers's superb investigatory biography of Monroe, *Goddess*. There was additional information in the voluminous report of the Los Angeles district attorney's office of its 1982 re-investigation into Monroe's death, and in Robert Slatzer's book *The Curious Death of Marilyn Monroe*.

Peter's interview in Hyannis Port following Marilyn's death was with Marianne Means and syndicated by the Hearst Headline Service. The *New York Times* article on Susan Perry's evening at the White House was published on October 30, 1961.

PART FIVE

Interviews in this section not cited previously include Carroll Baker on May 11, 1990, Victoria Burgoyne on December 3, 1988, Doris Day on April 28, 1988, Marion Dixon on January 9, 1989, Richard Donner on July 19, 1990, John Farquhar on March 15, 1989, James Goldstone on September 6, 1989, Isabel Heyel on November 6, 1988, Erma Lee Riley on January 6, 1989, Mary Rowan on August 12, 1989, David Salven on September 6, 1989, Richard Stanley on January 19, 1990, and Graham Stark on April 3, 1990.

The separation agreement between Pat Lawford and Peter is part of the Peter Lawford collection of the Arizona State University Library.

Sally Marks's article about *Salt and Pepper*, "Hurricane Sammy Hits the Thames," was published in the *Los Angeles Times* on September 3, 1967.

Alma Cousteline gave me her version of what transpired the night Judy Garland cut her face with the razor blade for my 1983 book, *Judy and Liza*. Peter's quotes on the same subject are from a 1972 BBC documentary on Judy.

I reconstructed Lady Lawford's last years from her autobiography, contemporary newspaper accounts, her personal papers, court records, and a number of interviews with those who knew her toward the end of her life.

Many of the details of Peter's courtship of Mary Rowan are contained in an interview with both of them by Jane Ardmore, published in *Motion Picture* magazine, December 1972. The Lawford-Rowan divorce settlement is part of the public record in Los Angeles County, as are the numerous lawsuits filed by and against Peter. The letters Mary wrote Peter are in the Lawford collection at ASU.

Much of the information about the drug use of Christopher Lawford, Bobby Kennedy, Jr., and David Kennedy is based on interviews contained in the Collier and Horowitz book, *The Kennedys,* as well as on contemporary newspaper accounts.

In addition to my lengthy interview with Deborah Gould, details of her relationship with Peter came from contemporary accounts quoting Deborah, and *The Peter Lawford Story*.

Amy Rea's evening with Peter in New York is taken from an account of it she wrote on June 5, 1988, and kindly granted me permission to use.

My account of Peter's relationship with Patty Seaton is based on her own in *The Peter Lawford Story,* as well as on contemporary newspaper and magazine reports and interviews with many of Peter's friends and associates.

SELECTED
BIBLIOGRAPHY

Allyson, June, with Frances Spatz Leighton. *June Allyson*. New York: Putnam's, 1982.

Aronson, Theo. *The King in Love*. New York: Harper & Row, 1988.

Astor, Mary. *My Story*. New York: Doubleday, 1959.

Bergan, Ronald. *The United Artists Story*. New York: Crown, 1986.

Buck, Pearl S. *The Kennedy Women*. New York: Cowles, 1970.

Carey, Gary. *All the Stars in Heaven: Louis B. Mayer's MGM*. New York: Dutton, 1981.

Clarke, Gerald. *Capote*. New York: Simon & Schuster, 1988.

Collier, Peter, and David Horowitz. *The Kennedys: An American Drama*. New York: Summit, 1984.

Crane, Cheryl, with Cliff Jahr. *Detour*. New York: Avon, 1988.

David, Lester. *Joan—The Reluctant Kennedy*. New York: Funk & Wagnalls, 1974.

Davis, John H. *The Bouviers: Portrait of an American Family*. New York: Farrar, Straus & Giroux, 1969.

———. *The Kennedys: Dynasty and Disaster 1848–1983*. New York: McGraw-Hill, 1984.

Davis, Sammy, Jr., and Jane and Burt Boyar. *Yes I Can*. New York: Farrar, Straus & Giroux, 1967.

———. *Hollywood in a Suitcase*. New York: Morrow, 1980.

———. *Why Me?* New York: Farrar, Straus & Giroux, 1989.

Demaris, Ovid. *The Last Mafioso: The Treacherous World of Jimmy Fratianno*. New York: Times Books, 1981.

Dineen, Joseph. *The Kennedy Family*. Boston: Little, Brown, 1959.

Eames, John Douglas. *The MGM Story*. New York: Crown, 1982.

Exner, Judith, as told to Ovid Demaris. *My Story*. New York: Grove, 1977.

Finch, Christopher, and Linda Rosenkrantz. *Gone Hollywood.* New York: Doubleday, 1979.

Flamini, Roland. *Ava.* New York: Coward, McCann & Geoghegan, 1983.

Fordin, Hugh. *The World of Entertainment!* New York: Doubleday, 1975.

Frank, Gerold. *Judy.* New York: Harper & Row, 1975.

Gates, Barbara T. *Victorian Suicide.* Princeton, New Jersey: Princeton University Press, 1988.

Gehman, Richard. *Sinatra and His Rat Pack.* New York: Belmont, 1961.

Giancana, Antoinette, and Thomas C. Renner. *Mafia Princess: Growing Up in Sam Giancana's Family.* New York: Morrow, 1984.

Goodwin, Doris Kearns. *The Fitzgeralds and the Kennedys.* New York: Simon & Schuster, 1987.

Guiles, Fred Lawrence. *Legend: The Life and Death of Marilyn Monroe.* New York: Stein and Day, 1984.

Halliwell, Leslie. *Halliwell's Filmgoer's Companion, Ninth Edition.* New York: Scribners, 1988.

Heiman, Jim. *Out with the Stars.* New York: Abbeville, 1985.

Heymann, C. David. *A Woman Named Jackie.* New York: Lyle Stuart, 1989.

Hirschhorn, Clive. *The Warner Brothers Story.* New York: Crown, 1979.

———. *The Universal Story.* New York: Crown, 1983.

———. *The Columbia Story.* New York: Crown, 1990.

Holtzman, Will. *Judy Holliday.* New York: Putnam, 1982.

Jewell, Richard, with Vernon Harbin. *The RKO Story.* New York: Arlington House, 1982.

Kaiser, Charles. *1968 in America.* New York: Weidenfeld & Nicolson, 1988.

Kearns, Doris. *Lyndon Johnson and the American Dream.* New York: Harper & Row, 1976.

Kelley, Kitty. *Jackie Oh!* Secaucus, New Jersey: Lyle Stuart, 1979.

———. *Elizabeth Taylor: The Last Star.* New York: Simon & Schuster, 1981.

———. *His Way: The Unauthorized Biography of Frank Sinatra.* New York: Bantam, 1986.

Kennedy, Rose Fitzgerald. *Times to Remember.* New York: Doubleday, 1974.

Lawford, May, and Buddy Galon. *Bitch!—The Autobiography of Lady Lawford As Told to Buddy Galon.* Brookline, Mass.: Branden, 1986.

Lawford, Patricia Seaton, with Ted Schwarz. *The Peter Lawford Story.* New York: Carroll & Graf, 1988.

Leigh, Janet. *There Really Was a Hollywood.* New York: Doubleday, 1984.

Loke, Margarett. *The World As It Was 1865–1921.* New York: Summit, 1980.

Madsen, Axel. *Gloria and Joe*. New York: Arbor House/Morrow, 1988.

Manchester, William. *The Last Lion: Winston Spencer Churchill—Visions of Glory, 1874–1932*. Boston: Little, Brown, 1983.

———. *The Last Lion: Winston Spencer Churchill—Alone, 1932–1940*. Boston: Little, Brown, 1988.

McTaggert, Lynne. *Kathleen Kennedy: Her Life and Times*. New York: Dial Press, 1983.

Murray, Eunice, with Rose Shade. *Marilyn: The Last Months*. New York: Pyramid, 1975.

Nickens, Christopher. *Elizabeth Taylor: A Biography in Photographs*. New York: Doubleday, 1984.

Noguchi, Thomas T., with Joseph DiMona. *Coroner*. New York: Pocket Books, 1984.

Otash, Fred. *Investigation Hollywood!* Chicago: Regnery, 1976.

Pearsall, Ronald. *Edwardian Life and Leisure*. New York: St. Martin's, 1973.

Pepitone, Lena, and William Stadiem. *Marilyn Monroe Confidential*. New York: Pocket Books, 1979.

Powers, Richard Gid. *Secrecy and Power: The Life of J. Edgar Hoover*. New York: Macmillan, 1987.

Riese, Randall, and Neal Hitchens. *The Unabridged Marilyn: Her Life from A to Z*. New York: Congdon & Weed, 1987.

Salinger, Pierre. *With Kennedy*. New York: Doubleday, 1966.

Sampson, Anthony. *Anatomy of Britain*. London: Hodder and Stoughton, 1962.

Saunders, Frank, with James Southwood. *Torn Lace Curtain*. New York: Holt, 1982.

Schatz, Thomas. *The Genius of the System*. New York: Pantheon, 1988.

Schlesinger, Arthur M., Jr. *A Thousand Days: John F. Kennedy in the White House*. New York: Houghton Mifflin, 1965.

———. *Robert Kennedy and His Times*. Boston: Houghton Mifflin, 1978.

Sheppard, Dick. *Elizabeth: The Life and Career of Elizabeth Taylor*. New York: Doubleday, 1974.

Shulman, Arthur, and Roger Youman. *How Sweet It Was*. New York: Bonanza, 1966.

Shulman, Irving. *Harlow*. San Francisco: Mercury House, 1989.

Sinatra, Nancy. *Frank Sinatra, My Father*. New York: Doubleday, 1985.

Slatzer, Robert F. *The Life and Curious Death of Marilyn Monroe*. New York: Pinnacle, 1974.

Sorenson, Theodore C. *Kennedy*. New York: Harper & Row, 1965.

Spada, James, with George Zeno. *Monroe: Her Life in Pictures*. New York: Doubleday, 1982.

———, with Karen Swenson. *Judy and Liza*. New York: Doubleday, 1983.

Speriglio, Milo. *The Marilyn Conspiracy*. New York: Pocket Books, 1986.

————. *Marilyn Monroe: Murder Coverup*. Van Nuys, Calif.: Seville, 1982.

Stevenson, John. *British Society: 1914–1945*. Middlesex, England: Pelican, 1984.

Summers, Anthony. *Goddess: The Secret Lives of Marilyn Monroe*. New York: Macmillan, 1985; New American Library, 1986 (revised).

Swanson, Gloria. *Swanson on Swanson*. New York: Random House, 1980.

Taylor, Elizabeth. *Elizabeth Taylor*. New York: Harper & Row, 1965.

Teti, Frank. *Kennedy: The Next Generation*. New York: Delilah, 1983.

Thomas, Tony, and Aubrey Solomon. *The Films of 20th Century-Fox*. Secaucus, New Jersey: Citadel, 1985.

Todd, Richard. *In Camera*. London: Hutchinson, 1989.

Turner, Lana. *Lana*. New York: Dutton, 1982.

United Press International. *The Torch Is Passed*. New York, 1964.

White, Theodore. *The Making of the President, 1960*. New York: Atheneum, 1961.

————. *The Making of the President, 1968*. New York: Atheneum, 1969.

Wilde, Oscar. *The Picture of Dorian Gray*. New York: Bantam, 1982.

Winship, Michael. *Television*. New York: Random House, 1988.

Winters, Shelley. *Shelley*. New York: Morrow, 1980.

Woodward, Bob. *Wired*. New York: Simon & Schuster, 1984.

Zolotow, Maurice. *Marilyn Monroe*. New York: Harcourt Brace, 1960.

INDEX

Note: The abbreviation "PL" means "Peter Lawford." Names in subheadings appear first name first, but are alphabetized according to last name. "PL" is alphabetized as "Lawford, Peter." References to footnotes are indicated by an italic *n* next to the page number.

539

ABOUT THE AUTHOR

JAMES SPADA'S last book, *Grace: The Secret Lives of a Princess*, a biography of Grace Kelly, was a best-seller in twelve countries. His other best-sellers include *Streisand* and *Monroe: Her Life in Pictures*. He lives in Los Angeles and is at work on a biography of Bette Davis.

The *New York Times* bestseller
DOMINICK DUNNE

THE MANSIONS OF LIMBO

Fifteen provacative portraits of some of the most luminous figures of the decade: the movie legend who remains the only divorced wife of a U.S. president; the singing star who fell in love with a notorious mobster; the lavish wedding-that-never-was between an heiress and a counterfeit prince, and more. Filled with pathos and wit and the twenty-four-carat insight of a society insider, *The Mansions of Limbo* offers a peek into a rarified world where nothing is ever enough.

"A fascinating collection by *Vanity Fair's* most high-profile chronicler of the high-profile."—*The Washington Post*
❏ 29075-4 $5.99/$6.99 in Canada

FATAL CHARMS and Other Tales of Today

An unvarnished look at the gilded world of the real-life rich and famous. Here are the highly colorful and provocative close-up interviews Dominick Dunne has written for *Vanity Fair*. *Fatal Charms* is a startling exposé of charm—in all its guises—both fatal and benign.

"Powerful and personal...Dunne is at his brisk, acerbic best."—*Chicago Tribune*
❏ 26936-4 $4.95/$5.95 in Canada

And the steamy, fast-paced novels of Dominick Dunne

❏ **THE TWO MRS. GRENVILLES** 25891-5 $5.95/$6.95 in Canada
❏ **PEOPLE LIKE US** 27891-6 $5.99/$6.99 in Canada
❏ **AN INCONVENIENT WOMAN** 28906-3 $5.99/$6.99 in Canada

Available at your local bookstore or use this page to order.
Send to: Bantam Books, Dept. NFB 23
    2451 S. Wolf Road
    Des Plaines, IL 60018
Please send me the items I have checked above. I am enclosing
$_____ (please add $2.50 to cover postage and handling). Send check or money order, no cash or C.O.D.'s, please.

Mr./Ms._____

Address_____

City/State_____Zip_____
Please allow four to six weeks for delivery.
Prices and availability subject to change without notice.   NFB 23 8/92